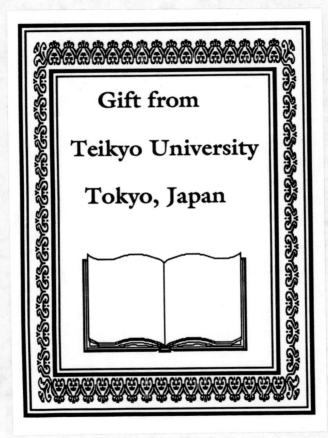

BEGINNING JAPANESE

PART I

by Eleanor Harz Jorden

with the assistance of Hamako Ito Chaplin

90-356

CHARLES E. TUTTLE COMPANY
Suido 1-chome, 2-6, Bunkyo-ku, Tokyo

Published by the Charles E. Tuttle Company, Inc.
of Rutland, Vermont and Tokyo, Japan
with editorial offices at
Suido 1-chome, 2-6, Bunkyo-ku, Tokyo, Japan
by special arrangement with
Yale University Press, New Haven, Connecticut

First Tuttle edition, 1974
Fourteenth printing, 1990

ISBN 0-8048-1574-7
PRINTED IN JAPAN

For

W. J. J.

Publisher's Foreword

Since the publication of *Beginning Japanese*, a quarter of a century ago, no other introductory text has served such a broad segment of students embarking on the study of Japanese. It has well proven its ability to guide the new student, from the uncertainties of one's first exposure to this fascinating language, through to the ease of everyday conversational fluency.

Beginning Japanese makes no attempt at promising that learning Japanese is easy, nor does it claim to offer shortcuts. Rather, in these two volumes, the "Jorden philosophy" is one that emphasizes the careful study of the fundamentals of the Japanese language—it is the author's firm conviction that thorough training at the beginning level will prove far more valuable than other less systematic methods. The original prospectus and objectives of *Beginning Japanese* have endured during a period of intense change in the techniques of teaching second languages, and this is eloquent testimony to the skill with which Dr. Eleanor Harz Jorden has structured her work: *Beginning Japanese* is just as valid and valuable a learning tool today as it was when first published.

The Charles E. Tuttle Company is pleased to be able to continue to keep this basic text in print, and believes that it will continue to serve well the needs of the many, serious beginning students of the Japanese language.

Tokyo
January, 1988

Acknowledgments

I am indebted to many people — in Japan and the United States — for their assistance in the preparation of this book:

to Hajime Aikawa, Shiro Sugata, Hiroshi Sakamoto, Mayako Matsuda, Kazu-hiko Mitsumoto, and Akira Kobayashi, who participated in the preparation of a short course, the expansion and revision of which was the basis for this text. I deeply appreciate their tireless efforts.

to Sayoko Kawamoto, Hiroshi Takano, Masayuki Minami, Yasukazu Tsuka-goshi, and Reiko Hummel — and to Gabriel Cordova, supervisor of recording — for assistance in the preparation of the tape recordings that accompany the text. Mrs. Kawamoto was particularly helpful in performing many of the tiresome chores that preceded and followed actual recording, as well as in assisting in the final revision of the text.

to Mrs. Tomoko Tanaka Campen for her excellent illustrations, drawn with such meticulous care.

to the Language Development Section of the Department of Health, Education, and Welfare, for a grant which expedited the completion of the book and made possible the preparation of the accompanying tapes.

to the Center for Applied Linguistics of the Modern Language Association, for a grant which expedited the publishing of the book.

to Samuel E. Martin, of Yale University, for discussions which suggested several useful revisions.

to Kyoko Edayoshi, for her careful typing of the manuscript and for several valuable suggestions pertaining to the text.

To my teacher, Bernard Bloch of Yale University, who directed my formal study of linguistics and introduced me to the Japanese language, I continue to owe an immeasurable debt.

To Hamako Ito Chaplin, of Yale University, who has been directly involved in the preparation of this text — and previous versions of it — during the past six years, I wish to express my deepest appreciation for her capable assist-ance and enthusiastic cooperation. Mrs. Chaplin has willingly and cheerfully performed innumerable tasks of writing, rewriting, checking, editing, and re-cording, always giving evidence of her outstanding ability and uncompromising standards of excellence. It is impossible to express adequately my gratitude to her.

To my husband, William J. Jorden, I wish to express my thanks for his encouragement, his advice, and his patience.

E. H. J.

Contents

Contents

Introduction

Beginning Japanese (Parts I and II) contains thirty-five lessons, all of which have the same basic pattern and involve the same procedures. Each lesson requires many hours of class work supplemented by outside study and, if possible, laboratory work.

The method underlying this text is guided imitation; the aim is automaticity. Ideally, there are two teachers: under the supervision of a scientific linguist, who talks ABOUT Japanese, the student learns to speak the language in direct imitation of a tutor who is a native speaker of Japanese. The tutor drills on the Japanese in the text, providing an authentic model for the student to imitate. Statements on how the language is manipulated are included in the explanatory notes in the text, which may be supplemented, if necessary, by further discussions on the part of the linguist.

Language learning is overlearning. Through memorization of whole utterances, and substitution within and manipulation of these utterances, a student achieves the fluency and automaticity that are necessary for control of a language. Language learning involves acquiring a new set of habits, and habits must be automatic. Just as the experienced driver performs the mechanics of driving—turning on the engine, shifting gears, applying the brakes, etc. — unconsciously, and concentrates on where he is going, so the fluent speaker of a language is concerned with what he is saying rather than the mechanics of how he is saying it.

This textbook is concerned only with spoken Japanese. Reading and writing involve a different set of habits and are best begun after acquiring some basic control of the spoken language. It is suggested that students interested in studying written Japanese begin using an introductory reading text only after completing at least ten or fifteen lessons of this volume. [1]

The student should note the following general suggestions and warnings: ALWAYS USE NORMAL SPEED. Do not permit yourself to speak more slowly than your tutor, and do not ask him to speak more slowly than is natural for him. The ability to understand slow, deliberate speech never heard outside of a classroom is of little practical value. The aim of the student should be to learn Japanese as it is spoken by the Japanese—not an artificial classroom dialect.

DRILL HOURS WITH A NATIVE TUTOR SHOULD BE CONDUCTED ENTIRELY IN JAPANESE FROM THE FIRST DAY. A class which fluctuates between Japanese and English, where valuable repetition and drill aimed at developing fluency are constantly interrupted by English questions and comments, never achieves the desired results. It is recommended that a specific time be designated as discussion period and that interruption of drill at

---

[1] For students who have completed Parts I and II, the forthcoming publication A Manual of Japanese Writing, by Chaplin and Martin, is suggested.

other times be avoided. A tutor who has not had technical linguistic training should not attempt technical explanations about Japanese. These are provided by the explanatory notes in the book and/or the scientific linguist.

REVIEW CONSTANTLY. DO NOT GO AHEAD TOO RAPIDLY. Remember that e a c h new lesson presupposes thorough mastery o f what has gone before.

Do not assume that the patterns of Japanese will resemble those of English, or that distinctions made in English will be present in Japanese. EXPECT DIFFERENCES AND BE SURPRISED AT SIMILARITIES.

Remember that USAGE—NOT LOGIC—DETERMINES WHAT IS ACCEPTED IN A LANGUAGE. A native speaker is the final judge of whether or not an utterance is acceptable in his dialect. Differences of dialect, of course, cause frequent disagreement among native speakers. Not all dialect differences are geographical; many are social and educational.

PROCEDURES

1. Basic Dialogues

Each of the thirty-five lessons begins with a group of Basic Dialogues which form the core of the lesson. A student controls a lesson to the extent to which he has learned the dialogues by heart. Thorough memorization of the dialogues means thorough mastery o f the text. Memorization is achieved by direct imitation of the native tutor in class, and by repeated use of tapes in the laboratory or at home.

Basic Dialogues are presented with their English equivalents. Numbered utterances in the dialogues are Basic Sentences. New words or phrases occurring in a Basic Sentence for the first time are listed separately, immediately before the s e n t e n c e, as breakdowns. They a r e indented and not numbered.

Some lessons contain Additional Vocabulary, at the end of the Basic Dialogues. The words in these sections are always to be drilled within an appropriate pattern sentence, never in isolation.

Following the Basic Dialogues are Notes on the Basic Dialogues, containing assorted information on specific sentences. The numbering of the notes corresponds to that of the sentences.

2. Grammatical Notes

Discussions of new patterns introduced in the Basic Dialogues are found in the Grammatical Notes. These are to be read outside of class after the Basic Dialogues have been introduced, but before proceeding to the drills.

In the Grammatical Notes, the procedure has been to introduce only material which will be o f immediate practical use to a beginning student. No attempt is made to present the full scientific analysis of Japanese on which the text is based; rather, explanations are provided which will be useful within the framework of the Japanese material being studied.

3. Drills

There are five basic kinds of drill in Beginning Japanese, each having a special purpose. However, the aim of all drills is the over-all aim of the course: to develop fluency and automaticity. Drills are to be performed in class with a tutor, and in the laboratory or at home with tapes. TEXTBOOKS SHOULD BE CLOSED DURING DRILL PRACTICE IN CLASS.

a. Substitution Drills

The tutor gives a pattern sentence which the student repeats. Immediately the tutor gives a word or phrase (called a <u>cue</u>) which the student substitutes appropriately in the original sentence. The tutor follows immediately with a new cue.

Example (English substitution drill):

Tutor:	Where did you put my book?
Student:	Where did you put my book?
Tutor:	pen
Student:	Where did you put my pen?
Tutor:	dictionary
Student:	Where did you put my dictionary?
	etc.

In more complicated substitution drills, there may be several substitution items (a <u>compound cue</u>) for each new sentence; or the successive cues may have to be substituted in different parts of the sentence; or the cue may require changes in the pattern sentence; or the cue may be given in its citation form (i.e. the basic form that regularly occurs in a dictionary) and have to be changed in order to occur within the pattern sentence.

Substitution drills whose cues occur in the same form in the pattern sentence are printed in two columns, with English equivalents on the left and drill sentences with cues underlined on the right. A drill that looks like this—

1. Please give me a cigarette.	Ta⌐bako o kudasa⌐i.
2. Please give me a match.	<u>Ma⌐tti</u> o kudasai.
3. Please give me a book.	<u>Ho⌐ñ</u> o kudasai.
etc.	

is to be drilled:

Tutor:	Ta⌐bako o kudasa⌐i.
Student:	Ta⌐bako o kudasa⌐i.
Tutor:	ma⌐tti
Student:	Ma⌐tti o kudasai.
Tutor:	ho⌐ñ
Student:	Ho⌐ñ o kudasai.
	etc.

When cues occur in their citation forms and must be changed by the student, they are given between virgules (//) immediately after the English equivalents on the left. A drill that looks like this—

1. Please wait here.	Ko⌐ko de ma⌐tte kudasai.
2. Please study here.	Ko⌐ko de beñkyoo-site kudasa⌐i.
/beñkyoo-suru/	

3. Please read here. Ko⌈ko de yo⌉n̄de kudasai.
/yo⌉mu/
etc.

is to be drilled:

Tutor: Ko⌈ko de ma⌉tte kudasai.
Student: Ko⌈ko de ma⌉tte kudasai.
Tutor: ben̄kyoo-suru
Student: Ko⌈ko de ben̄kyoo-site kudasa⌉i.
Tutor: yo⌉mu
Student: Ko⌈ko de yo⌉n̄de kudasai.

b. Grammar Drills

Here, on the basis of a model provided at the beginning of the drill, the student is required to perform parallel manipulation on a series of utterances by the tutor. For example, he may be required to change each of the tutor's utterances to the corresponding negative, or the past tense, etc.

Grammar Drills are printed in two columns, with the tutor's utterances on the left and the student's responses on the right.

c. Response Drill

On the basis of the model or directions occurring at the beginning of the drill, the student provides a parallel response to a series of questions or remarks by the tutor.

Like Grammar Drills, Response Drills are printed in two columns, with the tutor's utterances on the left and the student's responses on the right. In cases requiring a response clue from the tutor, this is given between virgules immediately following the tutor's utterance.

Example (English response drill):

Tutor	Student
What did you buy? /a book/	I bought a book.
What did you borrow? /a pencil/	I borrowed a pencil.
etc.	

d. Level Drill

Here, the student is asked to change the tutor's utterances to a different level of speech—to a more formal level, to the informal level, etc.

Again, this kind of drill is printed in two columns, with the tutor's utterance on the left and the student's equivalent on the right.

e. Expansion Drills

The usual kind of expansion drill in this text is a repetition drill which involves the buildup from short to long sentences. The tutor begins with a short sentence and gradually adds words and phrases to form a long, complex sentence. At each stage, the student repeats what the tutor has just said. These drills are printed in two columns, with the successively longer Japanese sentences on the right and English equivalents on the left.

In another kind of expansion drill, the student expands a pattern sentence with the cue provided by the tutor. A model is provided at the beginning of the drill. For such drills, the tutor's pattern sentence and cue (marked off with virgules) are in the left column, and the student's responses in the right column.

Drills are not meant to be grammatical puzzles for tricking the student; they are intended to develop fluency. The pace of all drills should be rapid. A student has mastered a drill only when he can provide the required oral responses promptly, fluently, and without reference to his textbook.

4. Supplementary Material

The supplementary material following the drills occurs in various forms: conversations of varying length (with English equivalents), narrative passages, and question drills.

When read aloud by the tutor, this material is a good test of comprehension—but it must be read at normal speed, and the students' books must be closed. It also provides a stimulus to conversation. The class can ask and answer questions pertaining to the material and make up similar material; and with conversations for which English equivalents are given, they may reconstruct the original conversations by referring only to the English.

5. Exercises

The final section of each lesson contains suggestions for additional practice appropriate to each lesson. These exercises should be performed orally. Only the student who is able to do them fluently and accurately is ready to proceed to the next lesson.

TAPES

The tape series which accompanies Beginning Japanese includes all Basic Dialogues, Drills, and Supplementary Material.

1. Basic Dialogues

Each dialogue is recorded four times:

(a) For listening

The dialogue (in its most contracted form) is spoken at normal speed just as you might overhear it.

LISTEN WITH YOUR BOOK CLOSED.

(b) For memorization

This phase includes breakdowns and Basic Sentences, followed by pauses[1] for students' repetition. Breakdowns are said once and Basic Sentences twice. When a contracted alternant occurs, it is said once, following the second repetition of the uncontracted equivalent.

REPEAT EVERYTHING ALOUD AND FOLLOW IN YOUR BOOK.

(c) For fluency

Each complete Basic Sentence is said once, with pause for repetition. For sentences which have a contracted equivalent, only the uncontract- alternant is included in this phase.

REPEAT ALOUD WITH YOUR BOOK CLOSED.

(d) For comprehension

This is a repetition of (a) above (the Dialogue for listening), but this time the student is expected to understand everything he hears.

LISTEN WITH YOUR BOOK CLOSED.

2. Drills

Students are expected to participate in the drills when working with tapes exactly as they do in the classroom, except that they may follow in their books as necessary.

For drills which require repetition — that is, most expansion drills — there are pauses on the tapes following each utterance to be repeated. For drills which require answering by the student — substitution, grammar, response, level, and some expansion drills — there is a pause on the tape permitting him to give his answer orally. This pause is <u>followed</u> by the correct re- sponse, which serves to reinforce — or correct — the student's response.

REPEAT OR ANSWER. FOLLOW IN YOUR BOOK AS NECESSARY.

3. Supplementary Material

During question drills, turn off the tape recorder after each question and take whatever time is necessary to answer. All other supplementary material is presented for comprehension practice.

LISTEN WITH YOUR BOOK CLOSED.

----

[1] All pauses on the tapes are timed to require the student to speak at a normal rate of speed. The student who cannot repeat within the allotted time is talking too slowly and needs more practice.

PRONUNCIATION

The so-called 'standard' dialect of Japanese (spoken by educated natives of Tokyo) can be described in terms of 113 distinct syllables, of the following kinds:

5	single vowel
67	consonant + vowel
36	consonant + y + vowel
5	single consonant

The student's first task is to learn (1) how the sounds of Japanese are pronounced and (2) how the Japanese sounds—which are different from the sounds of English—are represented in this text with the letters of our own alphabet. For (1), the student needs as a model a native speaker of Japanese and/or a recording made by a native speaker. For (2), he must study the chart and notes below, always bearing in mind that the letters are no more than arbitrary symbols which are meant to remind him of the actually occurring Japanese sounds. Although the symbols may seem unnecessarily arbitrary at the beginning, while the structure of Japanese is still unknown, the student becomes accustomed to them very quickly as he becomes familiar with the language.

Syllables of Japanese

1	2	3	4	5	6	7	8	9	10	11	12	13	14	15	16	17
a	ka	ga	ḡa	sa	za	ta	da	na	ha	pa	ba	ma	ya	ra	wa	k
i	ki	gi	ḡi	si	zi	ti	--	ni	hi	pi	bi	mi	--	ri	--	s
u	ku	gu	ḡu	su	zu	tu	--	nu	hu	pu	bu	mu	yu	ru	--	t
e	ke	ge	ḡe	se	ze	te	de	ne	he	pe	be	me	--	re	--	p
o	ko	go	ḡo	so	zo	to	do	no	ho	po	bo	mo	yo	ro	--	ñ
	kya	gya	ḡya	sya	zya	tya	--	nya	hya	pya	bya	mya	--	rya	--	
	kyu	gyu	ḡyu	syu	zyu	tyu	--	nyu	hyu	pyu	byu	myu	--	ryu	--	
	kyo	gyo	ḡyo	syo	zyo	tyo	--	nyo	hyo	pyo	byo	myo	--	ryo	--	

(In the following discussion, row numbers correspond to the numbers of the vertical rows in the chart above.   IN THIS SECTION ONLY, syllables within a word are separated by hyphens to show syllable division, and capital letters represent a pitch level higher than that represented by lower-case letters.)

Row 1	The symbol:	stands for a sound approximately like:	but the Japanese sound:
	a	'a' in 'father'	is short and clipped
	i	'i' in 'machine'	is short and clipped
	u	'u' in 'put'	is short, clipped, and without lip-rounding
	e	'e' in 'bet'	is short and clipped
	o	'o' in 'horse'	is short and clipped

When two or more Japanese vowels follow each other directly, each one retains its original quality and length, but the sequence is regularly pronounced as a continuum. The occurrence of the same vowel symbol twice indicates a long vowel: e.g. aa represents a + a pronounced without a break.

A word in Japanese has at least as many syllables as it has vowels.

Practice 1 [1]

a 'oh!'	A-o 'blue'	u-E 'top'	e 'picture'
A-a 'oh!'	I-i 'is good'	o-I 'nephew'	E-e 'yes'
A-i 'love'	i-E 'house'	o-O-i 'are many'	o-U 'owe'
A-u 'meet'	i-I-E 'no'	a-O-i 'is blue'	o-O-u 'conceal'

Row 2	The symbol:	stands for a sound approximately like:	but the Japanese sound:
	k before a, u, e, o	'c' in 'coot'	has less aspiration [2]
	ky, and k before i	'c' in 'cute'	has less aspiration [2]

The values of the vowel symbols remain the same as in Row 1 above.

Practice 2

ka-U 'buy'	a-KA-I 'is red'	ka-I-KE-E 'account'
ka-O 'face'	o-O-KI-i 'is big'	KYA-a 'eek!'
i-KE 'pond'	KE-e-ko 'practice'	KYO-o 'today'
ko-KO 'here'	ku-U-KO-O 'airport'	KYU-u 'grade'

[1] All the practice drills that follow are for pronunciation practice only.
[2] The corresponding English sound is followed by a strong puff of breath.

Row 3	The symbol:	stands for a sound approximately like:	but the Japanese sound:
	g before a, u, e, o	'g' in 'begone'	in initial position is more fully voiced than the corresponding English initial [1]
	gy, and g before i	'g' in 'regular'	in initial position is more fully voiced than the corresponding English initial [1]

Practice 3

GA-i 'injury'	gi-KO-O 'art'	GU-ke-e 'my elder brother'
GE-e 'craft'	GI-ka-i 'the Diet'	GYA-ku-i 'traitorous mind'
GO-i 'vocabulary'	go-KA-I 'misunderstanding'	gyo-O-KO-O 'good fortune'
gi-KE-E 'brother-in-law'	gu-U-I 'a moral'	GYU-u 'beef'

Row 4

The symbol $\bar{g}$ represents a sound like the 'ng' of 'singer' [2] — that is, it is a sound made with the tongue in position for a g but with the air escaping through the nasal passages. In Japanese, this sound never occurs at the beginning of an utterance.

Like gy and g before i, $\bar{g}y$ and $\bar{g}$ before i are pronounced with the tongue raised in a 'y' position, somewhat like the 'ngy' of 'bring you.'

The occurrence of $\bar{g}$ is a matter of dialect. While it is usually considered a feature of Tokyo Japanese, there are many Tokyo speakers who

---

[1] A voiced sound is one accompanied by vibration of the vocal cords. In English, a voiced consonant at the beginning of a word begins without voice (vibration); in Japanese, an initial voiced consonant is voiced throughout its articulation.

[2] This is a valid comparison only for those speakers of English who distinguish between the medial sounds of 'singer' and 'finger,' with the latter containing the medial sound of 'singer' + 'g.'

regularly use g̲ instead, and there are still others who alternate freely be-
between the two. The situation, as far as this text is concerned, is
as follows:

>Where g̲ is written, ḡ̲ is NOT to be substituted.
>Where ḡ̲ is written, g̲ can ALWAYS be substituted.

Example:

>GA̲-i̲: G̲ occurs in the speech of all speakers of Tokyo Japanese.

>KA̲-ḡ̲u: Some speakers say KA̲-ḡ̲u (with the nasal ḡ̲) consistently,
>others say KA̲-gu consistently, and still others alternate
>freely between the two pronunciations.

Whichever pronunciation a student uses, he must be able to understand both.[1] However, it s h o u l d be pointed out that the dialect which
includes ḡ̲ is considered the "prestige" dialect of Tokyo.

Practice 4

E-e-ḡ̲a	KA̲-ḡ̲e	ka-I-ḠI
'movie'	'shade'	'conference'
i-KA̲-ḡ̲a	GO̲-ḡ̲o	ka-I-ḠYA-KU [2]
'how?'	'afternoon'	'a jest'
KA̲-ḡ̲u	ko-O̲-ḠO	ka-I-ḠYU-U
'furniture'	'spoken language'	'sea-cow'
a-O̲-ḡ̲u	ku-ḠI	KO̲-o-ḡ̲yo-o
'look up'	'nail'	'industry'

Row 5	The symbol:	stands for a sound approximately like:	but the Japanese sound:
	s̲ before a̲, u̲, e̲, o̲	's' in 'see'	is pronounced further forward in the mouth
	sy̲, and s̲ before i̲	'sh' in 'she'	

---

[1] Accordingly, examples of g̲ substitution for ḡ̲ have been included on the
tapes that accompany this text.

[2] See the section on Whispered Syllables below.

Practice 5

A-sa 'morning'	o-SA-KE 'rice wine'	SYA-ka-i 'society'
a-SU 'tomorrow'	SU-g̃u 'right away'	HA-i-sya 'dentist'
A-se 'perspiration'	ko-O-SU-I 'perfume'	KYU-u-syu-u 'Kyushu'
a-SI 'leg'	o-I-SI-I 'is delicious'	sya-SYO-O 'conductor'
a-SO-KO 'there'	o-KA-SI-i 'is funny'	syu-U-SYO-O' 'grief'

Row 6	The symbol:	stands for a sound approximately like:	but the Japanese sound:
z before a, u, [1] e, o	'z' in 'bazaar'	is pronounced further forward in the mouth and is regularly fully voiced [2]
zy, and z before i	'j' in 'reject'	

Practice 6

za-I-KA 'inventory'	GO-zi 'five o'clock'	ZYU-u 'ten'
KA-zu 'number'	KA-zi 'a fire'	KA-zyu 'fruit tree'
ki-ZU 'a cut'	zi-E-E 'self-defense'	zyo-O 'feeling'
ZE-e 'a tax'	ZYA-a 'well then'	zyo-SE-E 'womanhood'
ZO-o 'elephant'	zya-KO-O 'musk'	ko-O-ZYO-o 'factory'

Row 7	The symbol:	stands for a sound approximately like:	but the Japanese sound:
t before a, e, o	't' in 'tip'	is pronounced with the tongue touching the teeth and with little aspiration
ty, and t before i	'ch' in 'cheap'	is pronounced further forward in the mouth
t before u	'ts' in 'tsetse fly'	is pronounced further forward in the mouth

---

[1] An alternate pronunciation of z before u is 'dz.'

[2] See footnote 1 on page xxiii.

Practice 7

ka-TA 'person'	TI-zu 'map'	o-SI-ḠO-TO-TYU-U 'in the middle of work'
ta-KA-i 'is high'	ti-I-SA-i 'is small'	ko-O-TYO-O 'director'
ki-I-TE 'listening'	o-TYA 'tea'	TYO-o-me-e 'long life'
to-O-KA 'ten days'	ko-O-TYA 'black tea'	TU-i-te 'concerning'
si-ḠO-TO 'work'	TYU-u-i 'warning'	tu-ZU-KI 'continuation'

Row 8	The symbol:	stands for a sound approximately like:	but the Japanese sound:
	d̲	'd' in 'redeem'	is pronounced with the tongue touching the teeth and is regularly fully voiced [1]

Practice 8

e-DA 'branch'	DE-te 'leaving'	KA-do 'street corner'
o-KA-DA (family name)	i-SO-i-de 'hurrying'	DO-ko 'where?'
ku-DA-SA-i 'give me'	de-KI-ḠO-to 'occurrence'	do-O-ḠU 'tool'

Row 9	The symbol:	stands for a sound approximately like:	but the Japanese sound:
	n̲ before a̲, u̲, e̲, o̲	'n' in 'deny'	is pronounced with the tongue touching the teeth and is regularly fully voiced [1]
	ny̲, and n̲ before i̲	'n' in 'menu,' 'avenue,'[2] etc.	

---

[1] See footnote 1 on page xxiii.

[2] Applicable only for those speakers who use a ' —nyu' pronunciation.

Practice 9

NA-ka 'inside'	o-KA-NE 'money'	NYA-o 'meow'
KI-nu 'silk'	so-NO 'that'	gyu-U-NYU-U 'milk'
te-NU-ḠU-I 'towel'	NA-ni 'what?'	nyu-U-ZYO-O 'entrance'
NE-ko 'cat'	ni-KA-I 'second floor'	NYO-o-ḡo 'court lady'

Row 10	The symbol:	stands for a sound approximately like:	but the Japanese sound:
	h before a, e, o	'h' in 'hot'	
	hy, and h before i	'h' in 'humid'	has more friction

H before u is made by bringing the upper and lower lips together and then puffing air out between them. Unlike English 'f,' which is the closest English sound, Japanese h before u does not involve the lower teeth in its production.

Practice 10

HA-i 'yes'	hi-ḠE 'beard'	HYO-o 'hail'
HA-ha 'mother'	ko-O-HI-i 'coffee'	HU-u 'manner'
he-E 'wall'	HYU-u-zu 'fuse'	HU-ne 'boat'
HO-o 'direction'	hya-KU-DO '100 times'	HU-zi 'Fuji'

Row 11	The symbol:	stands for a sound approximately like:	but the Japanese sound:
	p before a, u, e, o	'p' in 'poor'	has less aspiration
	py, and p before i	'p' in 'pure'	

Practice 11

PA-a-zi 'purge'	PU-u-pu-u (noise of a horn)	PO-o-zu 'a pause'
a-PA-a-to 'apartment'	pe-E-ZI 'page'	PYU-u-pyu-u (noise of a whistle)
de-PA-a-to 'department store'	PO-ka-po-ka 'repeatedly'	pi-A-NO 'piano'

Row 12	The symbol:	stands for a sound approximately like:	but the Japanese sound:
	b before a, u, e, o	'b' in 'rebel'	is regularly fully voiced [1]
	by, and b before i	'b' in 'rebuke'	

Practice 12

BA-ta 'butter'	ka-BE 'wall'	sa-BI-SI-i 'is lonely'
ta-BA-KO 'cigarette'	bo-O 'stick'	BYA-ku-e 'white robe'
a-SO-BU 'play'	o-BO-e-te 'remembering'	BYU-u-byu-u (noise of a whistle)
a-BU-NA-I 'is dangerous'	e-BI 'shrimp'	byo-O-BU 'screen'

Row 13	The symbol:	stands for a sound approximately like:	but the Japanese sound:
	m before a, u, e, o	'm' in 'remind'	is regularly fully voiced [1]
	my, and m before i	'm' in 'amuse'	

Practice 13

MA-e 'front'	mu-SU-ME 'daughter'	kyo-O-MI 'interest'
ma-TA 'again'	ME-e-zi 'Meiji'	mya-KU-DO-O 'pulse'
NO-mu 'drink'	I-tu mo 'always'	MYU-u-zu 'muse'
mu-KO-O 'over there'	MI-se-te 'showing'	ko-O-MYO-O 'great deed'

---

[1] See footnote 1 on page xxiii.

Row 14	The symbol:	stands for a sound approximately like:	but the Japanese sound:
y̲	'y' in 'year'	is regularly fully voiced [1]

Practice 14

ya-O-YA
  'vegetable store'
NA-ḡo-ya
  'Nagoya'
o-YA-SU-MI-NA-SA-i
  'good night'

o-YU
  'hot water'
yu-KI-yo
  'snowy night'
yu-U-ME-E
  'famous'

yo-SI-DA
  (family name)
sa-YO-O
  'that way'
o-HA-YO-O
  'good morning'

Row 15

The Japanese r̲ is a flap-r̲, made by flicking the tip of the tongue against the alveolar ridge (area behind the upper teeth). This sound closely resembles the 'r' in the British English pronunciation of 'very.' To speakers of American English, it often sounds like a d̲, but there are two main differences: (1) the Japanese r̲ is shorter than d̲; and (2) in the production of r̲, the tip of the tongue makes contact with the alveolar ridge, whereas in the production of d̲, it is the area of the tongue immediately behind the tip that makes contact against the upper teeth. When r̲ is immediately followed by i̲ or y̲, the r̲ articulation just described is accompanied by palatalization — that is, the back part of the tongue is in position to make a y̲ sound, while the tip makes the flap-r̲.

Practice 15

ra-KU
  'comfortable'
sa-YO-NA-RA
  'goodbye'
BI-ru
  'building'
RU-u-ru
  'rule'
KI-re-e
  'pretty'

o-HU-ro
  'bath'
o-MO-SI-RO-i
  'is interesting'
ri-KO-O
  'clever'
ko-O-RI
  'ice'
a-RI-ḡa-to-o
  'thank you'

rya-KU-ZI
  'simplified character'
ka-I-RYU-U
  'ocean current'
ryu-U-KO-O
  'fashion'
RYO-o-zi
  'consul'
ryo-O-RI-ya
  'restaurant'

---

[1] See footnote 1 on page xxiii.

Row 16	The symbol: _	stands for a sound approximately like:	but the Japanese sound:
	<u>w</u>	'w' in 'want'	is regularly fully voiced [1]

Practice 16

wa-KA-i	wa-KA-ru	wa-RE-WA-RE
'is young'	'understand'	'we'
he-E-WA	yu-BI-WA	wa-SU-RE-RU
'peace'	'ring'	'forget'

Row 17

K occurs as a syllable by itself immediately preceding a syllable having initial <u>k</u> (i.e. a syllable of Row 2). The back of the tongue is raised as in the production of a single (that is, short) <u>k</u> and is held in that position for a full syllable beat before being released (compare the somewhat similar long 'k' in English 'bookkeeper'). The following syllable, which has initial <u>k</u>, is pronounced without aspiration—that is, without a puff of breath after the <u>k</u>.

S occurs as a syllable by itself immediately preceding a syllable having initial <u>s</u> (i.e. a syllable of Row 5). Its articulation lasts for a full syllable beat and has the same quality as the <u>s</u> that follows (compare the somewhat similar long 's' in English 'less sleep' and the long 'sh' in 'horse-show').

T occurs as a syllable by itself immediately preceding a syllable having initial <u>t</u> (i.e. a syllable of Row 7). The front of the tongue is pushed against the back of the upper teeth as in the production of a single (that is, short) <u>t</u> and is held in that position for a full syllable beat before being released (compare the somewhat similar long 't' in English 'hot tip'). The following syllable, which has initial <u>t</u>, is pronounced without aspiration.

P occurs as a syllable by itself immediately preceding a syllable having initial <u>p</u> (i.e. a syllable of Row 11). The lips are brought together as in the production of a single (that is, short) <u>p</u> and are held in that position for a full syllable beat before being released (compare the somewhat similar long 'p' in English 'top part'). The following syllable, which has initial <u>p</u>, is pronounced without aspiration.

[1] See footnote 1 on page xxiii.

All double (that is, long) consonants in Japanese are characterized by tenseness.

Practice 17 a

mi-K-KA 'three days'	a-S-SA-ri 'briefly'
yu-K-KU-ri 'slowly'	ma-S-SU-g̅u 'straight'
NI-k-ko-o 'Nikko'	i-S-SO-O 'more'
ha-K-KI-ri 'clearly'	za-S-SI 'magazine'
se-K-KYO-o 'sermon'	ma-S-SI-RO 'all white'
ha-K-KYU-U 'small salary'	i-S-SYU-U 'one round'

ka-T-TA 'bought'	i-P-PA-I 'full'
i-T-TE 'going'	i-P-PU-U 'odd'
TYO-t-to 'a bit'	ri-P-PO-O 'legislation'
ma-T-TI-ba-ko 'matchbox'	ha-P-PI 'workman's coat'
ko-MA-t-tya-t-ta '[I]'m upset'	ha-P-PYA-KU-ME '800 momme'
yo-T-TU-ME 'fourth thing'	ha-P-PYO-O 'announcement'

Row 17 (continued)

N̄ represents a syllabic nasal: it is a sound which always has a full syllable beat of its own— that is, it constitutes a syllable— and is always pronounced with the nasal passage open; but its pronunciation varies depending on the sound that immediately follows in the same word or a following word.

1. Before a syllable beginning with p, b, or m (that is, a syllable of Row 11, 12, or 13), n̄ represents a syllabic m. [1]

2. Before a syllable beginning with z, t, d, n, or r (that is, a syllable of Row 6, 7, 8, 9, or 15), n̄ represents a syllabic n. [1]

3. Before a syllable beginning with k, g, or g̅ (that is, a syllable of Row 2, 3, or 4), n̄ represents a syllabic g̅. [1]

4. Elsewhere— that is, before a vowel (i.e. a syllable of Row 1) or a syllable beginning with s, h, y, or w (i.e. a syllable of Row 5, 10, 14, or 16) or at the end of an utterance— n̄ represents syllabic nasalization, articulated by raising the tongue toward the roof of the mouth but not making contact anywhere, and at the same time releasing the flow of air through the nasal passage and vibrating the vocal cords. When n̄ is followed by o, the o is anticipated and the combination sounds like n̄ + w + o. Similarly, n̄ followed by e sounds like n̄ + y + e.

---

[1] It constitutes a full syllable and is longer than the related sound which occurs as the initial part of a syllable.

Practice 17b

(1) sa-N̄-PO
    'a walk'
    SA-ñ-ba-i
    'three cupfuls'
    a-N̄-MA-RI
    'too much'

(2) be-N̄-ZYO
    'toilet'
    ke-N̄-TO-o
    'a guess'
    KO-ñ-do
    'this time'
    da-N̄-NA-SA-ma
    'master'
    BE-ñ-ri
    'convenient'

(3) be-N̄-KYO-O
    'study'
    ni-HO-N̄-GI-ñ-ko-o
    'Bank of Japan'
    ni-HO-N̄-ḠO
    'Japanese language'

(4) te-N̄-I-N̄ 'store clerk'
    ni-HO-ñ o 'Japan (as direct object)'
    ni-HO-ñ e 'to Japan'
    sa-N̄-SE-E 'approval'
    HA-ñ-ha-ñ 'half and half'
    HO-ñ-ya 'bookstore'
    de-N̄-WA 'telephone'
    a-RI-MA-SE-ñ 'there isn't any'

Whispered Syllables

The Tokyo dialect of Japanese is characterized by the frequent occurrence of whispered (that is, voiceless[1]) syllables. Whenever an i or u vowel[2] occurs between any two voiceless consonants (k, s, t, p, or h), the vowel automatically becomes voiceless or, in some cases, is lost. This happens whether the two consonants come in the same word or in consecutive words.

---

[1] A voiceless sound is one which is not accompanied by vibration of the vocal cords.

[2] Other vowels are only occasionally affected.

Practice 18

In the following practice drills, whispered (i.e. voiceless or lost) vowels are crossed by a virgule (/).

ki̸-SYA	su̸-SU-MU	hi̸-SYO
'train'	'advance'	'secretary'
ki̸-TE	su̸-TE-RU	hi̸-TO
'coming'	'throw away'	'person'
ki̸-T-TE	na-SU̸-t-te	hi̸-P-PA-ru
'stamp'	'doing'	'pull'
ku̸-SYA-mi	ti̸-KA-i	hu̸-KA-i
'sneeze'	'is close'	'is deep'
NA-ku̸-te	ti̸-T-TO-mo	hu̸-SI-ḠI
'not being any'	'[not] a bit'	'strange'
si̸-TE	tu̸-KI-MA-si̸-ta	hu̸-TO-i
'doing'	'[I] arrived'	'is big around'
si̸-T-TE	tu̸-TO-me-te	hu̸-T-TO-BO-o-ru
'knowing'	'being employed'	'football'
su̸-KI-i	hi̸-KI-MA-si̸-ta	hi̸-HA-N̄
'skiing'	'[I] pulled'	'criticism'

In the phrases in the left-hand column below, the final vowel of the first word is preceded AND followed by a voiceless consonant and accordingly is itself voiceless. In the phrases in the right-hand column, the final vowel of the first word is preceded but not followed by a voiceless consonant and accordingly has its full, voiced value—that is, it is accompanied by vibration of the vocal cords.

Practice 19

DO-t-ti̸ ka 'either one'   DO-t-ti ḡa 'which one (as subject)?'

DE-su̸ kara 'therefore'   DE-su ḡa 'however'

I-tu̸ kara 'since when?'   I-tu ma-de 'until when?'

hi̸-KO-o-ki̸ to 'airplane and'   hi̸-KO-o-ki no 'of an airplane'

When an i or u vowel preceded by a voiceless consonant comes at the end of an utterance, the vowel either has its full voiced value or is whispered. There is variation depending on the speaker, the occasion, and the word in question. Alternants like the following occur commonly:

Practice 20

hi̸-TO-tu̸   or   hi̸-TO-tu   'one unit'

SO-o de-su̸   or   SO-o de-su   'that's right'

o-HA-YO-O GO-ZA-I-MA-su̸   or   o-HA-YO-O GO-ZA-I-MA-su
   'good morning'

Accent

The rhythm of Japanese, unlike that of English, is regular and even: each syllable is given moderate, approximately equal stress, and has approximately equal length. However, some syllables seem more prominent than others. This prominence — or accent — is primarily a matter of pitch in Japanese, and only secondarily a matter of stress.

Any continuous Japanese sequence of one or more words is said to be accented if it contains at least one example of a single high-pitched syllable, or an uninterrupted series of high-pitched syllables, followed by an abrupt drop to a low-pitched syllable; and the accent is said to occur on the last (or only) high-pitched syllable, which is slightly stressed. Thus, an utterance that sounds like this:

$$a^{merikaryoozi}_{kan}\ \text{'American Consulate'}$$

is an accented utterance, and the accent occurs on the syllable zi, which is slightly stressed (i.e. louder).

For the purposes of this text, we recognize four significant pitch levels: two accented levels (high and medium-high) and two unaccented levels (neutral and low). These are not absolute pitch levels but are relative to each other within a given utterance.

Some Japanese utterances are accented and some are unaccented. The first syllable of an unaccented sequence of more than one syllable is automatically pronounced with low pitch, and the following syllables all have neutral pitch. An unaccented sequence which follows pause (that is, which occurs at the beginning of a sentence, or within a sentence after a pause) appears in this text without any special accent marks.

koko is pronounced ko^{ko} 'here'

asoko is pronounced a^{soko} 'there'

ano sakana is pronounced a$^{no\ sakana}$ 'that fish'

soko e iku is pronounced so$^{ko\ e\ iku}$ 'I'll go there'

moo iti-do itte is pronounced mo$^{o\ iti\text{-}do\ itte}$ 'saying it again'

However, when an unaccented word or phrase having the above pitch contour occurs in the middle of a sequence, the superscript symbol ꞈ appears over the single syllable which has low pitch: ꞈ indicates a rise in pitch from low level to neutral level. Thus:

kore wa zȧssi da   is pronounced   ko$^{re\ wa}$ za$^{ssi\ da}$

'this is a magazine'

An accented sequence contains one or more of the following superscript symbols: [1]

Symbol	Meaning
⌐	Rise from neutral to high pitch
˥	Drop from high to neutral or low pitch
⊦	Rise from neutral to medium-high pitch
˧	Drop from medium-high to neutral or low pitch

Thus:

do˥ozo <u>is pronounced</u> ^{do}ozo 'please'

a⌐na˥ta <u>is pronounced</u> a^{na}ta 'you'

a⌐o˥i <u>is pronounced</u> a^{o}i 'is blue'

wa⌐karimase˥ñ <u>is pronounced</u> wa^{karimase}ñ 'it isn't clear'

da⌐izyo˥obu <u>is pronounced</u> da^{izyo}obu 'safe'

mo⌐o iti-do itte kudasa˥i <u>is pronounced</u> mo^{o} iti-do itte kudasa$_{i}$ 'please say it again'

ki˥ree na o⊦zyo˧osañ <u>is pronounced</u> ^{ki}ree na o^{zyo}osañ 'a pretty girl'

na˥ḡaku ka⊦karima˧su kara <u>is pronounced</u> ^{na}ḡaku ka^{karima}su kara 'because it takes long'

o⌐oki˥i i⊦e˧ desu <u>is pronounced</u> o^{oki}i i^{e} desu 'it's a big house'

Note the following rules and conventions:

(1) Only a word which contains ˥ or ˧ is said to be accented, and the accent is said to occur on the syllable at whose end ˥ or ˧ occurs. [2]

(2) Any word containing ⌐ or ⊦, or the first word after a pause, or any word beginning with low plus neutral pitch, marks the start of a new accent phrase.

(3) Except in special circumstances, the first or only accented sequence of syllables of an utterance is said to be within the pitch

---

[1] A single accented word never has more than one high-pitched sequence and therefore cannot contain more than two of the accent superscripts—one rising and one falling.

[2] Actually the rise in pitch symbolized by ⌐ or ⊦ is automatic, given the

range designated as "high." Subsequent accented sequences in the same sentence which have the same[1] or higher pitch are also said to be within the high range; those which have significantly lower pitch (i.e. lower than high but higher than neutral) are said to be "medium-high."

Whispered syllables in Japanese cannot be distinguished by pitch. Their position within the pitch coutour is determined by other linguistic criteria.

Since accent in Japanese is a matter of high pitch relative to a following low pitch, it is impossible to hear accent without a following low syllable. The occurrence of ⌐ at the end of a single word in this text means that the word ordinarily has that accent when a following low syllable occurs. For example, hasi 'edge' and ha⌐si⌐ 'bridge' sound alike in isolation—in both, the first syllable is lower pitched than the second syllable—but when they are followed by a neutral or low syllable, they contrast with each other:

hasi wa (ha$^{si\ wa}$) 'as for the edge,' but

ha⌐si⌐ wa (ha^{si} wa) 'as for the bridge';

hasi da (ha$^{si\ da}$) 'it's the edge,' but

ha⌐si⌐ da (ha^{si} da) 'it's the bridge'; etc.

Similarly, ki 'spirit' and ki⌐ 'tree' are alike in isolation, but compare:

ki wa (ki ^{wa}) 'as for the spirit' and

ki⌐ wa (^{ki} wa) 'as for the tree.'

Accordingly we do speak of Japanese words that are accented on the final syllable, although we recognize that the accent can be heard in only some occurrences.

When a word is accented on its next-to-last syllable and the final syllable has a whispered alternant, the accent is regularly marked. For example, i⌐kima⌐su means either i$\underline{\underline{\qquad}}$^{kima}su[2] or i$\underline{\underline{\qquad}}$^{kima}su.

---

boundaries of the accent phrase. It always occurs on the second syllable of the accent phrase, unless the accent itself falls on the first syllable, in which case only the first syllable is high-pitched. Symbols for the rise are included here to simplify the reading of the transcription for the beginning student. It is possible to represent Japanese accent by using a traditional accent mark on the last high syllable (where this text has ⌐ or ¬), with no symbol to indicate the automatic rise—provided the boundaries of the accent phrase are identified. Thus: ho⌐ñ might be written hón, a⌐na⌐ta as anáta, i⌐kima⌐sita as ikimásita, mo⌐o iti-do itte kudasa⌐i as moo iti-do itte kudasái, and so on.

[1] 'Same' here refers to linguistic sameness, i.e. variation is within the bounds permitted by the native speaker for identification as the same. Usually, each successive occurrence of a given pitch level within a pause group represents a slightly lower alternant of that pitch.

[2] This is the more common alternant in Tokyo speech.

In animated or emphatic speech, the interval between pitch levels increases. In some cases, the interval between low and neutral pitch within one emphatic unaccented phrase may be as great as or greater than that between neutral and high pitch in a following unemphatic accented phrase. The symbol | (appearing only in Part II) marks the end of such an emphatic phrase. Thus:

oyoso kyo^romi na⁷i is pronounced o^{yoso kyo}^{omi na}i

'on the whole I have no interest'

but:

oyoso | kyo^romi na⁷i is pronounced o^{yoso} kyo^{omi na}i

'ON THE WHOLE I have no interest'

Accent presents difficulty for a foreign student of Japanese largely because of accent variation.[1] This variation is of three kinds:

(1) Variation in basic word accent

Many words have alternate accents within the Tokyo dialect. Thus, the accepted pronunciation of the word for 'policeman' is zyuñsa or zyu⁷ñsa; for 'streetcar,' deñsya or de⁷ñsya; for 'I,' boku or bo⁷ku.

(2) Gain and loss of accent in particular environments

Many basically unaccented· words sometimes acquire an accent, and many accented words sometimes lose their accent. For example, accented ku^rdasa⁷i loses its accent following an accented -te word:

i^rtte kudasa⁷i 'please say [it]'
ha^rna⁷site kudasai 'please talk'

An unaccented -te word acquires an accent before mo and kara:

itte 'saying [it]'

but:

i^rtte⁷ mo 'even if [I] say [it]'

and:

i^rtte⁷ kara 'after saying [it]'

(3) Variation in phrase accent

Many pairs of utterances, otherwise identical, are distinguished only by a difference in their phrase accent. Compare:

---

[1] The accents and intonations marked in this text follow those of the tapes that were recorded to accompany it, for all the material that was recorded.

(a) Kyo˥oto e i˦kima˧sita ka 'did you go to Kyoto (or did you go somewhere else)?'
(b) Kyo˥oto e i˥kima˥sita ka 'did you (or didn't you) go to Kyoto?'

(a) are wa ˥na˥ñ desu ka 'what is that?'
(b) a˥re wa na˥ñ desu ka 'what is THAT (in comparison with the other things)?'

(a) zu˥ibuñ ya˥su˥i desu ˥ne˥e 'it's very CHEAP, isn't it'
(b) zu˥ibuñ ya˦su˥i desu ˥ne˥e 'it's VERY cheap, isn't it'

(a) mo˥tto úsiro 'further BACK'
(b) mo˥tto usiro 'FURTHER back'

In general, it can be said that the occurrence of ˥ or ˨ on a word is a sign of primary interest in that word. Conversely, ˦ is never a sign of interest or emphasis.

Superimposed on these kinds of variation is dialectal variation. The accent of Tokyo Japanese is different from that of other parts of Japan. A student working with a tutor who is not a native of Tokyo will find that the pitch contours marked in this text often do not match those used by his tutor.

Doesn't this mean, then, that the student of Japanese might just as well ignore accent? Not at all! The fact that two different accents are sometimes acceptable does not mean that any accent at all is permitted. (Some native speakers of English say 'dry cléaning' and others say 'drý cleaning,' but no speaker says 'dry cleaníng.') Further indication of the importance of accent is the fact that many pairs of utterances with different meanings are distinguished only by their accent.

Intonation

The following intonation symbols are used in this text:

1. Period .

A period ending a sentence indicates that the final syllable and all immediately preceding unaccented syllables are pronounced with low pitch level, with the final syllable — if it is not whispered — lowest of all. In the event that the sentence, or its final accent phrase, contains no accent — that is, if the final or only pitch contour of the sentence is low + neutral — a final period indicates only the onset of silence.

Period intonation occurs most commonly at the end of statements, suggestions, rhetorical questions, and questions asked indirectly. At the end of direct questions, it often indicates abruptness, stiffness, aloofness, etc.

Examples:

Wa⌐karimase⌐ñ desita. 'I didn't understand.' <u>is pronounced</u>

wa^{karimase} ñ desi_{ta}

Asuko e iku. 'I'm going to go there.' <u>is pronounced</u>

^asuko e iku

2. Question mark <u>?</u>

A question mark ending a sentence indicates a rise in pitch on the final syllable,[1] usually with lengthening of that syllable. Question-mark intonation regularly changes a statement into a question, and is typical of familiar style.

Examples:

Wa⌐ka⌐ru? 'Is it clear?' <u>is pronounced</u> wa^{ka}ru^u

Kore? 'This one?' <u>is pronounced</u> ko^{re^e}

3. Rising hook <u>⌐</u>

A rising hook ending a sentence indicates a slight rise in pitch on the final syllable only, usually without lengthening of that syllable. The final syllable may start on a high or a low pitch.[2] This intonation occurs with certain sentence particles and implies friendliness and interest in the reaction of the person addressed. Wherever a rising hook occurs, it is possible to substitute a period as an alternate intonation without changing the meaning beyond making the sentence more abrupt. Examples:

Wa⌐karima⌐sita ka⌐ 'Did you understand?' <u>is pronounced</u>

wa^{karima}sita ka⌐ <u>or</u> wa^{karima}sita ^{ka⌐}

I⌐i desu yo⌐ 'It's all right!' <u>is pronounced</u>

ⁱi desu yo⌐ <u>or</u> ⁱi desu ^{yo⌐}

---

[1] With this intonation, the final syllable is never whispered.

[2] A high-pitched start is more common in women's speech.

4. Low bar _

A low bar ending a sentence indicates that the final syllable has neutral pitch. It usually is lengthened and there is a gradual fading into silence. This intonation denotes incompleteness.

Examples:

Ka⌐mawana⌐kereba_ 'If it doesn't matter...'   is pronounced

$ka^{mawana}kerebaa$_

So⌐o desu ḡa_ 'That's so but...'   is pronounced

$^{so}o\ desu\ \bar{g}aa$_

5. Exclamation point !

An exclamation point ending a sentence indicates that the final syllable starts high and has slightly falling pitch. Articulation ends abruptly and there is no significant lengthening of the final syllable.

Example:

Ano ne! 'Say there!'   is pronounced $a^{no^{ne}}$

6. Asterisk *

An asterisk at the beginning of a sequence indicates a special exclamatory intonation in which all pitch levels of the sequence become successively higher with each occurrence.

Examples:

* Yo⌐ku wa⌐karima⌐su ⌐ne⌐e.   'How well you understand!'

is pronounced $^{yo}ku\ wa^{karima}su^{ne}e$

* I⌐i o⌐te⌐ṅki desu ⌐ne⌐e.   'What nice weather!'   is pronounced

$i_i\ o\ ^{te}_ṅki\ de^{su}\ ^{ne}e$

7. Comma , and Semicolon ;

A comma within a sentence indicates a break within the utterance: X, Y means that there is a slight slowing down of articulation, with or without accompanying pause, at the end of X; that neutral syllables at the end of X have a low alternant of neutral pitch; and that Y starts a new accent phrase. [1]

---

[1] This means that if the first two syllables of Y have unaccented pitch, the first is low and the second neutral.

A semicolon marks the same general kind of division as a comma, but in sentences containing more than one such division, the semicolon is used to indicate a division of major rank.

Examples:

Su⌐peiñḡo o yamema⌐sita ḡa, ni⌐hoñḡo wa ma⌐da be⌐ñkyoo-site ima⌐su.
'I gave up Spanish, but Japanese I'm still studying.'

<u>is pronounced</u>

peiñḡo o yamema   hoñḡo wa ma

su   sita ḡa ni   da beñkyoo-site ima
                                                              su.

Zi⌐kañ ḡa na⌐i kara, su⌐peiñḡo o yamema⌐sita ḡa; ni⌐hoñḡo wa ma⌐da be⌐ñkyoo-site ima⌐su.
'I gave up Spanish because I have no time, but Japanese I'm still studying.'   <u>is pronounced</u>

kañ ḡa na   peiñḡo o yamema   hoñḡo wa ma

zi   ñkyoo-
          i kara su   sita ḡa ni   da be

     site ima

               su.

8. Dash —

A dash occurs within inverted sentences (cf. Lesson 11, Grammatical Note 5), indicating that what follows is to be pronounced without pause as if it were part of the preceding phrase. An accented sequence following the dash is medium-high.

Examples:

I⌐i desu ⌐ne⌐e — sore wa.   'Isn't it nice — that.'   <u>is pronounced</u>

i i desu ne e sore wa

I⌐kima⌐sita yo↵—[1] Kyo⌐oto e.   'I went — to Kyoto.'   <u>is pronounced</u>

i kima sita yo↵ kyo oto e

_____

[1] An intonation symbol which ordinarily occurs at the end of a sentence may occur in the middle of an inverted sentence.

Supplementary Pronunciation Drills

1. Vowel Combinations

a⌐raima⌐su 'wash (formal)'

arau 'wash (informal)'

a⌐rae⌐ 'wash!'

a⌐rao⌐o 'let's wash'

hiatari 'exposure to the sun'

iu (yuu) [1] 'say'

su⌐mi⌐e 'ink drawing'

ki⌐kio⌐ku 'hear (and keep in mind)'

huañ 'uneasiness'

huite 'wiping'

suehiro 'folding fan'

huoñ 'unrest'

deasi 'start'

deiri 'going in and out'

neuti 'value'

neoki 'lying down and getting up'

do⌐a 'door'

hi⌐ro⌐i 'is wide'

o⌐mo⌐u 'think'

ko⌐e 'voice'

2. Short and Long Vowels

obasañ 'aunt'

o⌐ba⌐asañ 'grandmother'

ha⌐ 'tooth'

ha⌐a 'yes'

ozisañ 'uncle'

o⌐zi⌐isañ 'grandfather'

ki⌐te⌐ 'coming'

kiite 'listening'

ku⌐roo 'trouble'

ku⌐uro 'air route'

husetu 'construction'

huuseetu 'rumor'

ki⌐re⌐ 'cloth'

ki⌐ree 'pretty'

seḡyoo 'management'

se⌐eḡyo 'control'

to⌐tte 'taking'

to⌐otte 'going through'

mu⌐ko 'bridegroom'

mukoo 'beyond'

tori 'bird'

to⌐ori⌐ 'avenue'

oki 'open sea'

o⌐oki⌐i 'is big'

---

[1] I + u is regularly pronounced yuu.

3. Short and Long Consonants

maki 'firewood'	ite 'being'
ma⌝kki 'the last years'	itte 'going'
Masao (proper name)	ko⌜na⌝ 'flour'
ma⌜ssa⌝o 'deep blue'	koñna 'this kind'
nisi 'west'	kono boosi 'this hat'
ni⌝ssi 'Japan and China'	ko⌝ñ no boosi 'navy blue hat'
ma⌜ti⌝ 'town'	Su⌜pe⌝iñ 'Spain'
ma⌝tti 'match'	su⌜ppa⌝i 'is sour'

4. su ~ tu Contrast

masu 'increase'	su⌝ri 'pickpocket'	su⌜ki⌝ 'liking'
ma⌝tu 'wait'	turi 'fishing'	tu⌜ki⌝ 'moon'
su⌝mi 'corner'	su⌜ḡi⌝ 'past'	susumu 'advance'
tu⌝mi 'crime'	tu⌜ḡi⌝ 'next'	tu⌜tu⌝mu 'wrap'

5. d ~ r Contrast

do⌝o 'how?'	hodo 'extent'	muda 'useless'
ro⌝o 'prison'	ho⌝ro 'hood'	mura 'village'
dañboo 'heating'	ma⌝de 'until'	sode 'sleeve'
rañboo 'rough'	ma⌜re⌝ 'rare'	sore 'that thing'

6. n ~ ḡ ~ ñ ~ ñḡ Contrast

kani 'crab'	kaneñ 'a combustible'	sa⌝ ni 'in what follows'
ka⌜ḡi⌝ 'key'	kaḡeñ 'moderation'	sa⌝ḡi 'fraud'
ka⌝ñi severe cold'	ka⌝ñeñ 'hepatitis'	sañi 'approval'
ka⌝ñḡi 'Korean singing girl'	kañḡeñ 'restoration'	sa⌝ñḡi 'participation in government'

7. Even Rhythm Practice

a 'oh!'
are 'that one'
asoko 'there'
to⌜kidoki⌝ 'sometimes'
ano sakana 'that fish'
ano tomodati 'that friend'
ano tomodati da 'it's that friend'
asoko no tomodati 'a friend from that place'
Amerika no tomodati 'an American friend'
Amerika no tomodati da 'it's an American friend'

8. Accent Contrasts

I⌐ma desu. 'It's now.'
I⌐ma⌐ desu. 'It's a living room.'

Ma⌐initi desu. 'It's every day.'
Ma⌐initi de⌐su. 'It's the Mainichi (a newspaper).'

Yo⌐ñde kudasai. 'Please read [it].'
Yo⌐ñde kudasa⌐i. 'Please call [him].'

Tu⌐yu de⌐su. 'It's the rainy season.'
Tu⌐yu desu. 'It's broth.'

A⌐tuku simasu. 'I'll make it hot.'
A⌐tuku sima⌐su. 'I'll make it thick.'

So⌐re o ki⌐ru kara_ 'Since I'm going to cut it . . .'
So⌐re o kiru⌐ kara_ 'Since I'm going to wear it . . .'

Ha⌐si desu. 'They're chopsticks.'
Ha⌐si de⌐su. 'It's the edge.'
Ha⌐si⌐ desu. 'It's a bridge.'

9. Intonation Contrasts

De⌐ki⌐ru. 'It's possible.'
De⌐ki⌐ru? 'Is it possible?'

So⌐o desyoo. 'That's probably so.'
So⌐o desyoo? 'That's so, isn't it?'

Sore. 'That one.'
Sore? 'That one?'

I⌐soḡasi⌐i. 'I'm busy.'
I⌐soḡasi⌐i? 'Are you busy?'

So⌐o desu ka. 'Oh.'
So⌐o desu ka⌐ 'Oh?'

Ti⌐ḡaima⌐su yo. 'They're different.'
Ti⌐ḡaima⌐su yo⌐ 'They're different.' [1]

_____

[1] Differences in the English equivalents are also differences of intonation.

O⌐warima⌐sita yo.   'I've finished.'
O⌐warima⌐sita yo⌐   'I've finished.' [1]

I⌐kima⌐su ka⌐   'Are you going?'
I⌐kima⌐su g̃a⌐   'I'm going but. . .'

O⌐nazi de⌐su yo.   'They're the same.'
O⌐nazi de⌐su g̃a⌐   'They're the same but. . .'

Zyo⌐ozu⌐ ni na⌐rima⌐sita ⌐ne⌐e.   'How proficient you've become!'
* Zyo⌐ozu⌐ ni na⌐rima⌐sita ⌐ne⌐e.   'How proficient you've become!' [1]

A⌐ñmari dekimase⌐ñ ⌐ne⌐e.   'He can't do very much, can he!'
* A⌐ñmari dekimase⌐ñ ⌐ne⌐e.   'He can't do very much, can he!' [1]

SPECIAL SYMBOLS AND CONVENTIONS

1. ( ), *[ ]*, [ ]

In a Japanese sequence, material enclosed in parentheses ( ) may be omitted. In every case, the shorter utterance is less formal and/or less polite. Thus, a(b) means that ab and a both occur with the same meaning except that a is less formal and/or less polite than ab.

Italicized brackets *[ ]*, on the other hand, enclose material that is optional without a difference of formality and/or politeness level: a*[b]* means that both ab and a occur in the given context without significant distinction.

Square brackets [ ] in the English equivalent of a Japanese sequence enclose material which is needed for natural English but does not correspond to anything in the Japanese sequence. Conversely, parentheses in the English equivalent enclose explanatory material or something literally translated from the Japanese which is not needed in the English. Compare:

I⌐kima⌐sita ka⌐   'Did [you] go?'

E⌐e, i⌐kima⌐sita.   'Yes, [I] did (go).'

---

[1] Differences in the English equivalents are also differences of intonation.

'You' and 'I' are needed for natural English but do not correspond to anything in the Japanese. 'Go' in the second sentence corresponds to something in the Japanese that is usually omitted in the English equivalent.

Square brackets and parentheses are used more frequently in the earlier lessons, as an aid to the beginning student.

2. ↑, ↓, +

A raised arrow pointing upward ↑ following a Japanese word or phrase indicates that the word or phrase is polite-honorific—that is, it exalts the person to whom it refers. Such a word is used only in reference to persons other than the speaker.

A raised arrow pointing downward ↓ following a Japanese word or phrase indicates that the word or phrase is polite-humble—that is, it humbles the person to whom it refers in deference to the person addressed. Such a word is used only in reference to the speaker, members of his family, or persons closely connected with him.

A raised plus sign + following a Japanese word or phrase indicates that the word or phrase is polite-neutral—that is, it is polite but does not exalt or humble the person to whom it refers or the person to whom it is addressed. Such a word is a neutral indication of politeness.

3. Miscellaneous

A radical √ enclosing the citation form of an inflected word indicates the given word in any or all of its derived inflected forms. Thus, √go (in English) is an abbreviation for go, goes, went, gone, etc.

Lit. is used throughout the text as an abbreviation for 'literally.'

In the Japanese material, only the first word in a sentence and names of persons and places are capitalized.

ROMANIZATION

Various systems of romanization—representation of the Japanese language by letters of the Roman alphabet—are in use in Japan today. The system used in this book is an adaptation of the Shin-kunrei-shiki 'New Official System' and will be designated as BJ Romanization. [1] Other common romanizations are

---

[1] However, Japanese words appearing throughout the book as non-quoted parts of English sentences (as in this explanatory paragraph) are spelled in Hepburn romanization.

Hepburn (also called Hyōjun-shiki 'Standard System') and Nippon-shiki 'Japanese System.' The differences among them are slight and can be learned with little difficulty. For example, the word for 'romanization' is variously represented as follows:

BJ:	roomazi
Shin-kunrei-shiki:	rômazi [1]
Hepburn:	rōmaji [1]
Nippon-shiki:	rōmadi [1]

Hepburn romanization is the system most familiar to Westerners; but there are three cogent reasons for not using it in a Japanese language textbook.

1. BJ, Shin-kunrei-shiki, and Nippon-shiki bear a direct relation to Japanese structure, whereas Hepburn has no such connection. Thus, in describing Japanese inflection, many statements become unnecessarily complicated and parallelism is obscured if Hepburn romanization is used. For example, compare the following:

In a text using BJ, Shin-kunrei-shiki, or Nippon-shiki:

To form the stem of -u-class verbals, change final -u to -i.

Corresponding statement in a text using Hepburn romanization:

To form the stem of -u-class verbals, change final -u to -i, but change final -tsu to -chi and final -su to -shi.

The complexity of the latter statement results not from "special cases" in Japanese verbal structure, but only from the fact that Hepburn romanization is based on languages of the West (its vowels have values roughly as in the Romance languages, its consonants as in English) rather than on the Japanese language.

2. For the student who plans to learn the native Japanese writing system, the transition from Hepburn is more difficult than from the other systems.

3. The Japanese themselves do not adhere consistently to any single system; in fact, they sometimes use a mixture of several within the same word! It therefore becomes necessary for the foreign student to familiarize himself with the symbols used in all the systems. BJ, Shin-kunrei-shiki, and Nippon-shiki romanizations take a little longer for the English-speaking student to master (though only in the initial stages); but once he has learned any one of them, he can switch to Hepburn with no trouble. The student who has used only Hepburn, however, finds the conversion to other systems a difficult one.

The minor differences between BJ on the one hand and Shin-kunrei-shiki and Nippon-shiki on the other result from an attempt to avoid certain inconsistencies and ambiguity in the latter systems. For example, in BJ, ee and ei consistently represent different and distinct sequences of sounds of Tokyo Japanese. The spelling of these sequences in all the other romanizations (including Hepburn) is inconsistent, so that it is often impossible for a student to be certain which value a given occurrence of ei represents.

---

[1] The long mark over the o is sometimes omitted.

CONVERSION TABLE OF ROMANIZATION[1]

Symbol in another romanization	Corresponding symbol in BJ
ā [2]	aa
ū [2]	uu
ē [2]	ee
ei	ee (or ei)
ye	e
ō [2]	oo
wo	o
-g-	-ḡ- (or -g-)
shi	si
sha	sya
shu	syu
sho	syo
ji	zi
ja	zya
ju	zyu
jo	zyo
di	zi
dz	z
chi	ti
cha	tya
chu	tyu
cho	tyo
tsu	tu
fu	hu
-n'-	-ñ-
-n (final)	-ñ
-n + consonant ōther than y-	-ñ-
-mp-	-ñp-
-mb-	-ñb-
-mm-	-ñm-

[1] The left-hand column includes symbols and combinations which either do not occur in BJ Romanization, or else they correspond to more than one BJ symbol so that their interpretation is ambiguous.

[2] A circumflex (ˆ) over a vowel has the same meaning as a macron (˜).

Classroom Instructions

1.	Please listen.	Ki⌐ite kudasa⌐i. or
		Ki⌐ite (i)te kudasa̅i.²
2.	Please say [it].	I⌐tte kudasa⌐i.
3.	Please say [it] again.	Mo⌐o iti-do itte kudasa⌐i.
4.	Please answer.	Ko⌐ta⌐ete kudasai.
5.	Please speak in Japanese.	Ni⌐hoñgo de hana⌐site kudasai.
6.	Please don't use English.	Eego (wa) tu⌐kawana⌐i de kudasai.
7.	Please open [your] book.	Hoñ (o) a⌐kete kudasa⌐i.
8.	Please look at [your] book.	Hoñ (o) ⌐mi⌐te kudasai.
9.	Please don't look at [your] book.	Hoñ (wa) ⌐mi⌐nai de kudasai.
10.	Please close [your] book.	Hoñ (o) ⌐to⌐zite kudasai.
11.	Please say [it] in chorus.	Mi⌐ñna⌐ de i⌐tte kudasa⌐i.
12.	Please say [it] one (person) at a time.	Hi⌐tori-zu⌐tu i⌐tte kudasa⌐i.
13.	Please speak more quickly.	Mo⌐tto ⌐ha⌐yaku ha⌐na⌐site kudasai.
14.	Please speak more clearly.	Mo⌐tto ha⌐kki⌐ri ha⌐na⌐site kudasai.
15.	Please speak in a louder voice.	Mo⌐tto ⌐o⌐oki na ⌐ko⌐e de ha⌐na⌐site kudasai.
16.	Please ask Mr. (or Mrs. or Miss) Tanaka.	Ta⌐naka-sañ ni kiite kudasa⌐i.

---

¹ These sentences are primarily for use by a Japanese instructor in giving classroom directions. It is suggested that introductory drill on them be conducted for the purpose of aural recognition.

² Accent of contracted alternant: Ki⌐ite⌐ te kudasai.

Introductory Lesson: Greetings and Useful Phrases

BASIC SENTENCES: FOR MEMORIZATION[1]

1. Oh, Mr. (or Mrs. or Miss) Tanaka! — A⌐a, Tanaka-san.
2. Good morning. — O⌐hayoo (gozaima⌐su).
3. Good afternoon. — Konniti wa.
4. Good evening. — Konban wa.
5. How are you? or Are you well? (Lit. Is it health?) — O⌐ge⌐nki desu ka
6. Yes. — Ha⌐i. or E⌐e.
7. [I'm fine,] thank you. And you? (Lit. As for you?) — Okaḡesama de. A⌐na⌐ta wa?
8. Goodnight. — O⌐yasumi-nasa⌐i.
9. Goodbye. — Sayo(o)nara.[2]
10. Excuse me (on leaving). — Si⌐tu⌐ree(-simasu).
11. Excuse me (for what I did). — Si⌐tu⌐ree-(simasita).
12. No. or Not at all. — Iie.
13. Don't mention it. or You're welcome. — Do⌐o itasimasite.
14. I'm sorry. or Thank you for your trouble. — Su⌐(m)imase⌐n.
15. I'm sorry (for what I did). or Thank you (for the trouble you took). — Su⌐(m)imase⌐n desita.
16. [Thanks] very much. — Do⌐o mo.
17. Thank you. — A⌐ri⌐ḡatoo (gozaimasu).
18. Thank you very much. — Do⌐o mo a⌐ri⌐ḡatoo (gozaimasu).
19. Thank you (for what you did). — A⌐ri⌐ḡatoo (gozaimasita).
20. Please (speaker requesting something). — O⌐neḡai-sima⌐su.
21. Please (speaker offering something). — Do⌐ozo.

NOTES ON THE BASIC SENTENCES[3]

1. -San is added to a family name (as in Tanaka-san), a given name (as in Ta⌐roo-san), or a family name plus a given name (as in Tanaka ⌐Ta⌐roo-san), but it is NOT added to one's own name or to that of members of one's

---

[1] Be sure to read the Introduction before beginning.

[2] Alternate accent: Sa⌐yo(o)na⌐ra.

[3] Numbers in this section correspond to Basic Sentence numbers.

own family or household when speaking to outsiders. Thus, Mr. Yamamoto calls Mr. Tanaka Tanaka-sañ, but Mr. Tanaka identifies himself simply as Tanaka.

2. Ohayoo is used when addressing a friend or colleague or inferior informally. O⌐hayoo gozaima⌐su is a formal greeting used in addressing a superior, or in any situation requiring formality.

5. O⌐ge⌐ñki is the honorific (†) equivalent of ge⌐ñki. Only the latter may be used in reference to oneself. In referring to others, ge⌐ñki is plain and o⌐ge⌐ñki is polite. (O)⌐ge⌐ñki desu ka⌐, may occur as the equivalent of 'How are you?' 'How is he?' 'How is she?' or 'How are they?,' provided the context makes the meaning clear.

6. In general, ha⌐i is a rather stiff word, whereas e⌐e is conversational. However, ha⌐i is the regular response to a knock at the door or the calling of one's name.

7. Okaḡesama de indicates the speaker's appreciation for interest in his personal affairs ('thanks for asking') and/or appreciation for assistance ('thanks to you'). It always accompanies, or itself implies, favorable or pleasant information.

9. Sayonara is the contracted, less formal equivalent of sayoonara.

10. Si⌐tu⌐ree-simasu means literally 'I [am about to] commit a rudeness.' It is a polite way of excusing oneself from someone's presence, sometimes in the sense 'Excuse me for a moment' and sometimes as 'Excuse me—goodbye.' Other uses will be introduced later.

11. Si⌐tu⌐ree-simasita is the past equivalent of the preceding and means literally 'I committed a rudeness.' It is an apology for something that has already been done.

12. Iie is used in negative replies to questions, in contradictions and denials, and as an informal reply to apologies, expressions of thanks, and compliments.

13. Do⌐o itasimasite is used alone, or with iie, as a formal reply to apologies, expressions of thanks, and compliments.

14. Su⌐imase⌐ñ is the contracted, less formal equivalent of su⌐mimase⌐ñ.

15. Su⌐(m)imase⌐ñ desita is the past equivalent of su⌐(m)imase⌐ñ and refers to an action already completed. It is commonly used to apologize or say thank you, by someone who is on the point of leaving. However, the non-past form is used in expressing thanks immediately upon receiving something.

16. Do⌐o mo, used alone as an expression of thanks, is informal. It means literally 'in every way.'

17, 18, 19. The forms with gozaimasu (or gozaimasita) are formal, and those without are informal. Compare 2, above.

19. A⌐ri⌐ḡatoo gozaimasita is the past equivalent of a⌐ri⌐ḡatoo gozaimasu and refers to an action already completed. See 15, above.

20. Among the more common English equivalents of o⌐neḡai-sima⌐su are such expressions as: 'Would you please do it?'; 'Please take care of things';

'Please do'; 'May I have it?'; 'I'd like to have it'; etc. The equivalent differs depending upon the context, but the basic meaning is always the same—'I make a request'—and the word is humble (↓).

21. Do⌐ozo, which occurs by itself as an expression of offering or invitation ('Please have some'; 'Go ahead'; 'Here you are'; etc.), also occurs within sentences of request, making the request softer and less abrupt. Thus, do⌐ozo o⌐negai-sima⌐su is a softer equivalent of o⌐negai-sima⌐su alone.

DRILLS

A. Response Drill

1.	Tanaka-sañ_	Ha⌐i.
2.	Ohayoo.	Ohayoo.
3.	O⌐hayoo gozaima⌐su.	O⌐hayoo gozaima⌐su.
4.	O⌐hayoo gozaima⌐su.	Ohayoo.
5.	Koñniti wa.	Koñniti wa.
6.	Koñbañ wa.	Koñbañ wa.
7.	O⌐ge⌐ñki desu ka_	Okaḡesama de.
8.	O⌐ge⌐ñki desu ka_	E⌐e, okaḡesama de. A⌐na⌐ta wa?
9.	O⌐ge⌐ñki desu ka_	E⌐e, a⌐ri⌐ḡatoo gozaimasu.
10.	O⌐yasumi-nasa⌐i.	O⌐yasumi-nasa⌐i.
11.	O⌐yasumi-nasa⌐i.	Sayonara.
12.	Sa⌐yoona⌐ra.	Sayoonara.
13.	Sayonara.	Sayonara.
14.	Sa⌐yoona⌐ra.	Sayonara.
15.	Sayonara.	O⌐yasumi-nasa⌐i.
16.	Si⌐tu⌐ree.	Do⌐ozo.
17.	Si⌐tu⌐ree-simasu.	Do⌐ozo.
18.	Si⌐tu⌐ree.	Sayonara.
19.	Si⌐tu⌐ree-simasu.	Sayoonara.
20.	Si⌐tu⌐ree.	Iie.
21.	Si⌐tu⌐ree-simasita.	Do⌐o itasimasite.
22.	Si⌐tu⌐ree-simasita.	Iie, do⌐o itasimasite.
23.	Su⌐mimase⌐ñ.	Iie.
24.	Su⌐mimase⌐ñ.	Iie, do⌐o itasimasite.
25.	Su⌐mimase⌐ñ desita.	Iie.
26.	Su⌐mimase⌐ñ desita.	Do⌐o itasimasite.
27.	A⌐ri⌐ḡatoo.	Iie.
28.	A⌐ri⌐ḡatoo gozaimasu.	Do⌐o itasimasite.
29.	A⌐ri⌐ḡatoo gozaimasita.	Iie, do⌐o itasimasite.
30.	Do⌐o mo a⌐ri⌐ḡatoo gozaimasita.	Iie, do⌐o itasimasite.
31.	Do⌐o mo.	Iie.
32.	Do⌐ozo.	Su⌐mimase⌐ñ.
33.	Do⌐ozo.	A⌐ri⌐ḡatoo gozaimasu.
34.	Do⌐ozo.	Do⌐o mo.
35.	O⌐negai-sima⌐su.	Do⌐ozo.
36.	O⌐negai-sima⌐su.	Ha⌐i ⌐do⌐ozo.
37.	Do⌐ozo o⌐negai-sima⌐su.	Do⌐ozo.

B. Level Drill [1]

1. Ohayoo.   O⌐hayoo ⌐gozaima⌐su.
2. Sayonara.   Sa⌐yoona⌐ra.
3. Si⌐tu⌐ree.   Si⌐tu⌐ree-simasu.   or
                                     Si⌐tu⌐ree-simasita.
4. Ge⌐ńki desu ka⌐   O⌐ge⌐ńki desu ka⌐
5. Su⌐imase⌐ń.   Su⌐mimase⌐ń.
6. Su⌐imase⌐ń desita.   Su⌐mimase⌐ń desita.
7. A⌐ri⌐gatoo.   A⌐ri⌐gatoo gozaimasu.   or
                                     A⌐ri⌐gatoo gozaimasita.
8. Do⌐o mo.   Do⌐o mo a⌐ri⌐gatoo gozaimasu.   or
                                     Do⌐o mo a⌐ri⌐gatoo gozaimasita.
9. Do⌐o mo a⌐ri⌐gatoo.   Do⌐o mo a⌐ri⌐gatoo gozaimasu.   or
                                     Do⌐o mo a⌐ri⌐gatoo gozaimasita.

EXERCISES

1. What would you say to Mr. Tanaka under the following circumstances?

    a. You have just met him in the morning.
    b. You have just met him in the afternoon.
    c. You have just met him in the evening.
    d. You offer him a cigarette.
    e. He has just given you something.
    f. He has just thanked you for something.
    g. You have just bumped into him.
    h. You are leaving.

2. Give Mr. Tanaka's reply to the preceding, wherever possible.

---

[1] The utterances in the right-hand column are more formal or polite equivalents of the utterances in the left-hand column.

Lesson 1. Getting Around

BASIC DIALOGUES: FOR MEMORIZATION

(a)

Smith

a bit or a little	tyo⌉tto
please wait	ma⌉tte kudasai
1. Just a minute!	Tyo⌉tto ˥ma⁴tte kudasai.

2. I don't understand.   Waᴦkarimase⌉ñ.

Tanaka

3. You don't understand?   Waᴦkarimase⌉ñ ka⌟

Smith

one time	iti-do
one time more	moo iti-do
please say	i⌐tte kudasa⌉i
4. No (i.e. that's right). Please say [it] once more.	E⌉e. Moˤo iti-do itte kudasa⌉i.

(b)

Smith

5. Do you understand?   Waᴦkarima⌉su ka⌟

Yamamoto

6. Yes, I do (understand).   E⌉e, waᴦkarima⌉su.

Smith

7. How about Mr. Tanaka? (Lit. As for Mr. Tanaka?)   Tanaka-sañ wa?

Yamamoto

8. Mr. Tanaka doesn't understand.   Taᴦnaka-sañ wa wakarimase⌉ñ.

(c)

Tanaka

9. Did you understand?   Waᴦkarima⌉sita ka⌟ ·

Smith

10. Yes, I did (understand).   E⌉e waᴴkarima⁴sita.

Tanaka

well or a good deal or often	yo⌉ku

11. You understand [very] well,   Yo⌐ku wakarimasu ⌐ne⌐e.
    don't you.

                          Smith

12. Oh, no!   Do⌐o itasimasite.

                          (d)

                          Smith

13. Did you do [it]?   Si⌐ma⌐sita ka⌐

                          Tanaka

    all or the whole thing   ze⌐ñbu
14. Yes, I did [it] all.   E⌐e, ze⌐ñbu si⌐ma⌐sita.

                          Smith

15. Thanks for your trouble.   Go⌐ku⌐roosama (desita).

                          Tanaka

16. Don't mention it.   Do⌐o itasimasite.

                          (e)

                          Smith

17. Did you go?   I⌐kima⌐sita ka⌐

                          Tanaka

18. No, I didn't (go).   Iie, i⌐kimase⌐ñ desita.

                  Smith (to Yamamoto)

19. How about you?   A⌐na⌐ta wa?

                          Yamamoto

    yesterday   ki⌐no⌐o
20. I went yesterday.   Ki⌐noo ikima⌐sita.

                          (f)

                          Smith

    tomorrow   a⌐sita⌐
21. Are you going to go to-   A⌐sita ikima⌐su ka⌐
    morrow?

                          Yamamoto

    today   kyo⌐o
22. No, I'm going to go today.   Iie, kyo⌐o ikimasu.

                          Smith

23. How about Mr. Tanaka?   Tanaka-sañ wa?

                          Yamamoto

24. He isn't going to go.   I⌐kimase⌐ñ.

NOTES ON THE BASIC DIALOGUES[1]

7. When addressing Mr. Tanaka, <u>Tanaka-sañ wa?</u> is equivalent to 'How about you, Mr. Tanaka?' It is less direct and more polite in Japanese to refer to the person by his name than by aˉnaˉta 'you.'

12. <u>Doˉo itasimasite</u>, in addition to its use as a reply to expressions of thanks and apology, occurs as a polite reply to compliments.

15. Goˉkuˉroosama desita — lit. 'it has been toil on your part' — is used especially commonly in addressing a subordinate. The alternant without <u>desita</u> is informal.

GRAMMATICAL NOTES

1. V e r b a l s

        waˉkarimaˉsu[2]   'understanding takes place'   <u>or</u>
                            'understanding will take place'

        waˉkarimaˉsita   'understanding took place'   <u>or</u>
                            'understanding has taken place'

        waˉkarimaseˉñ   'understanding does not take place'   <u>or</u>
                            'understanding will not take place'   <u>or</u>
                            'understanding has not taken place'

        waˉkarimaseˉñ desita   'understanding did not take place'

In Japanese there are words which are constant (i.e. have only one form) and those which are inflected (i.e. take particular sets of endings; compare English 'listen, listened, listening, listens'). Among the inflected words is a large group having forms similar to the four listed above (in addition to other forms). All such words are hereafter called VERBALS. [3]

The four forms listed above are named as follows:

(a) Form ending in -<u>maˉsu</u>: Formal non-past affirmative
      Meaning: 'something happens (or exists)'   <u>or</u>
                'something is going to or will happen (or exist)'

---

[1] Numbers in this section correspond to those of the sentences in the Basic Dialogues.

[2] For the accent, see Introduction, page xxxvi.

[3] Note that the term 'verbal' is being defined with particular respect to Japanese. It names the word-class to which all words inflected like waˉkarimaˉsu belong—namely, words having other forms ending in -maˉsita, -maseˉñ, etc.

(b) Form ending in -ma⌐sita: Formal past affirmative
   Meaning: 'something has happened (or existed)' <u>or</u>
        'something happened (or existed)'

(c) Form ending in -mase⌐ñ: Formal non-past negative
   Meaning: 'something does not happen (or exist)' <u>or</u>
        'something is not going to or will not happen (or exist)' <u>or</u>
        'something has not happened (or existed) up to the present
        time'

(d) Form ending in -mase⌐ñ desita: Formal past negative
   Meaning: 'something did not happen (or exist)'

The particular meaning of a given form is determined by context.

Verbals are impersonal and can occur by themselves as complete standard sentences. They can indicate the occurrence of an action or the existence of a state without grammatical reference to a subject. Contrast English 'I understand,' 'he understands,' 'they understand,' etc., with Japanese wa⌐karima⌐su 'understanding takes place,' 'there is understanding.' Most commonly, a verbal occurring alone refers to the speaker in a statement and to the person addressed in a question. For example:

     I⌐kima⌐sita ka ⌐ 'Did you go?' (Lit. 'Did going take place?')
     E⌐e i⌐kima⌐sita. 'Yes, I went.' (Lit. 'Yes, going took place.')

Different topics are indicated sometimes by the context, sometimes by the specific mention of a topic (which in some circumstances is followed by the particle <u>wa</u> 'as for,' about which more will be said later). For example, continuing the immediately preceding conversation:

     Tanaka-sañ wa? 'How about Mr. Tanaka?' (Lit. 'As for Mr. Tanaka?')
     I⌐kimase⌐ñ desita. 'He didn't go.' (Lit. 'Going didn't take place.')
     <u>or</u>
     Tanaka-sañ wa i⌐kimase⌐ñ desita. 'Mr. Tanaka didn't go.' (Lit. 'As for Mr. Tanaka, going didn't take place.')

In the lessons that follow, new verbals will be introduced first alone in their -ma⌐su form, with the dictionary form of the closest English equivalent, and then in a sentence (in the -ma⌐su form or another form) with an appropriate contextual equivalent. For example:

   write   ka⌐kima⌐su
  Are you going to write?   Ka⌐kima⌐su ka ⌐

  WARNING: Note that the -ma⌐su form of a verbal regularly refers to repeated action or future action, but not present action. Thus si⌐ma⌐su means '[I] do' or '[I] will do,' but never '[I] am doing.'

2. Question Particle <u>ka</u>

A Japanese sentence ending with the question particle[1] <u>ka</u> is a question. Any

---

[1] More will be said about particles in general later on.

statement can be made into a question by adding ka, provided the meaning makes sense. Compare:

(a) Waꞈkarimaseꞈn. ' [I] don't understand.' (Lit. 'There isn't understanding.')

(b) Waꞈkarimaseꞈn kaˑ '[You] don't understand?' or 'Don't [you] understand?' (Lit. 'There isn't understanding?')

Questions with ka end in rising intonation (represented in this text by the symbol ˑ) or in low intonation (represented by a period).

All sentences ending with the question particle ka are questions; but not all questions end with ka. For example, the phrase aꞈnaꞈta wa 'as for you' becomes a question when pronounced with question intonation (represented by a question mark).

3.   Answers to Yes-or-No Questions

Haꞈi[1] usually means ' what you just said is right.' In answer to affirmative questions, it corresponds to English 'yes,' but in answer to negative questions that anticipate a negative answer, it usually confirms the negative and corresponds to English 'no.'   Iie, the opposite of haꞈi, means 'what you just said is wrong' and behaves in a parallel way: in answer to affirmative questions it corresponds to English 'no,' but in answer to negative questions that anticipate a negative answer, it usually contradicts the negative and corresponds to English 'yes.'

	Literal English Equivalent	Normal English Equivalent
Iꞈkimaꞈsita kaˑ	'Going took place?'	'Did you go?'
Haꞈi. [Iꞈkimaꞈsita.] [2]	'That's right. [Going took place.]'	'Yes. [I did (go).]'
Iie. [Iꞈkimaseꞈn desita.]	'That's wrong. [Going didn't take place.]'	'No. [I didn't (go).]'
Iꞈkimaseꞈn desita kaˑ	'Going didn't take place?'	'Didn't you go?'
Haꞈi. [Iꞈkimaseꞈn desita.]	'That's right. [Going didn't take place.]'	'No. [I didn't (go).]'
Iie. [Iꞈkimaꞈsita.]	'That's wrong. [Going took place.]'	'Yes. [I did (go).]'

WARNING: English usage is as unexpected for a Japanese studying English as Japanese usage is for an American studying Japanese. Be wary of single-word answers given by a Japanese who is not yet fluent in English. In answer to 'Don't you have any bananas?' a 'Yes' from many Japanese means ' Yes. We have no bananas.'

---

[1] Throughout this note, whatever is said about haꞈi applies equally to eꞈe.

[2] Diagonal brackets ([---]) enclose optional portions of the answer.

To sum up: The meaning of <u>ha⌐i</u> and <u>iie</u> occurring in answer to a yes-or-no question usually depends on the inflected form of the preceding question: <u>Ha⌐i</u> means that the affirmative or negative of the question applies and <u>iie</u> means that it does not apply.

4. ne⌐e

<u>Ne⌐e</u> 'isn't it true!' at the end of a sentence indicates an exclamation. It sometimes indicates reflection or consideration, and it often implies agreement—actual or assumed—between speaker and person addressed, but it is not a question-word in its occurrences with statement intonation. Compare:

Tanaka-sañ wa ⌐yo⌐ku wakarimasu.	'Mr. Tanaka understands [very] well.'
Tanaka-sañ wa ⌐yo⌐ku wa⌐karima⌐su ka⌐	'Does Mr. Tanaka understand well?'
Tanaka-sañ wa ⌐yo⌐ku wakarimasu ⌐ne⌐e.	'Doesn't Mr. Tanaka understand well!' 'How well Mr. Tanaka understands!' 'Mr. Tanaka understands [very] well, doesn't he!' 'Come to think of it, Mr. Tanaka does understand well!' etc.

As always, unless the subject is explicitly stated, it is inferred from context. Thus, Wa⌐karimase⌐ñ ⌐ne⌐e. may mean 'You don't understand, do you!' or 'He doesn't understand, does he!' or 'They don't understand, do they!' or 'Come to think of it, I don't understand!' etc.

DRILLS

A. Substitution Drill

1.	I did [it] all.	Ze⌐ñbu si⌐ma⌐sita.
2.	I did a little.	Tyo⌐tto si⌐ma⌐sita.
3.	I did [it] once.	I⌐ti-do sima⌐sita.
4.	I did [it] yesterday.	Ki⌐noo sima⌐sita.
5.	I did [it] today.	Kyo⌐o si⌐ma⌐sita.
6.	I did [it] once more.	Mo⌐o iti-do sima⌐sita.

B. Substitution Drill

1.	I went yesterday.	Ki⌐noo ikima⌐sita.
2.	I went today.	Kyo⌐o i⌐kima⌐sita.
3.	I did [it] today.	Kyo⌐o si⌐ma⌐sita.
4.	I did [it] all.	Ze⌐ñbu si⌐ma⌐sita.
5.	I understood [it] all.	Ze⌐ñbu wa⌐karima⌐sita.
6.	I understood a little.	Tyo⌐tto wa⌐karima⌐sita.
7.	I'll do a little.	Tyo⌐tto simasu.
8.	I'll do [it] tomorrow.	A⌐sita sima⌐su.

C. Grammar Drill (based on Grammatical Note 1)

> Tutor: I⌐kima⌐su. (non-past verbal)
> Student: I⌐kima⌐sita. (past verbal)

1. Yo⌐ku wakarimasu.   Yo⌐ku wa⌐karima⌐sita.
2. A⌐ri⌐gatoo gozaimasu.   A⌐ri⌐gatoo gozaimasita.
3. Ze⌐ñbu simasu.   Ze⌐ñbu si⌐ma⌐sita.
4. Wa⌐karimase⌐ñ ka⌐   Wa⌐karimase⌐ñ desita ka⌐
5. Kyo⌐o ikimasu.   Kyo⌐o i⌐kima⌐sita.
6. Su⌐mimase⌐ñ.   Su⌐mimase⌐ñ desita.
7. Kyo⌐o si⌐ma⌐su ka⌐   Kyo⌐o si⌐ma⌐sita ka⌐
8. I⌐kima⌐su ka⌐   I⌐kima⌐sita ka⌐
9. Yo⌐ku wa⌐karimase⌐ñ.   Yo⌐ku wa⌐karimase⌐ñ desita.
10. Tanaka-sañ wa i⌐ki-   Tanaka-sañ wa i⌐kimase⌐ñ desita.
    mase⌐ñ.

D. Response Drill (based on Grammatical Note 3)

(What does the Ha⌐i. or Iie. answer to each of the following questions mean?)

1. I⌐kima⌐su ka⌐ /Ha⌐i./   Ha⌐i, i⌐kima⌐su.
2. Si⌐mase⌐ñ ka⌐ /Iie./   Iie, si⌐ma⌐su.
3. Wa⌐karima⌐sita ka⌐   Ha⌐i, wa⌐karima⌐sita.
    /Ha⌐i./
4. I⌐kima⌐sita ka⌐ /Iie./   Iie, i⌐kimase⌐ñ desita.
5. Si⌐ma⌐sita ka⌐ /Ha⌐i./   Ha⌐i, si⌐ma⌐sita.
6. Wa⌐karima⌐su ka⌐ /Iie./   Iie, wa⌐karimase⌐ñ.
7. I⌐kimase⌐ñ ka⌐ /Ha⌐i./   Ha⌐i, i⌐kimase⌐ñ.
8. Si⌐ma⌐su ka⌐ /Iie./   Iie, si⌐mase⌐ñ.
9. Wa⌐karimase⌐ñ ka⌐   Ha⌐i, wa⌐karimase⌐ñ.
    /Ha⌐i./
10. I⌐kimase⌐ñ desita ka⌐   Iie, i⌐kima⌐sita.
    /Iie./
11. Si⌐mase⌐ñ desita ka⌐   Ha⌐i, si⌐mase⌐ñ desita.
    /Ha⌐i./
12. Wa⌐karimase⌐ñ desita   Iie, wa⌐karima⌐sita.
    ka⌐ /Iie./

E. Expansion Drill

1. Please say [it].   I⌐tte kudasa⌐i.
    Please say [it] all.   Ze⌐ñbu i⌐tte kudasa⌐i.
    Please say [it] all once.   Iti-do ⌐ze⌐ñbu i⌐tte kudasa⌐i.
    Please say [it] all once   Moo iti-do ⌐ze⌐ñbu i⌐tte kudasa⌐i.
    more.
2. [He] understands.[1]   Wa⌐karima⌐su.

---

[1] Remember that the English equivalents given are not the only equivalents. Depending on context, there are various possibilities.

[He] understands, doesn't he!	Wa⌐karima⌐su ⌐ne⌐e.
How well [he] understands!	Yo⌐ku wakarimasu ⌐ne⌐e.
How well Mr. Tanaka understands!	Tanaka-sañ wa ⌐yo⌐ku wakarimasu ⌐ne⌐e.
3. [He]'s going to go.	I⌐kima⌐su.
Is [he] going to go?	I⌐kima⌐su ka⌐
Is [he] going to go tomorrow?	A⌐sita ikima⌐su ka⌐
Is Mr. Tanaka going to go tomorrow?	Tanaka - sañ wa a⌐sita ikima⌐su ka⌐
4. [He]'s not going to do [it].	Si⌐mase⌐ñ.
[He] didn't do [it].	Si⌐mase⌐ñ desita.
Didn't [he] do [it]?	Si⌐mase⌐ñ desita ka⌐
Didn't Mr. Tanaka do [it]?	Tanaka-sañ wa si⌐mase⌐ñ desita ka⌐

EXERCISES

1. Tell Tanaka-sañ:

   a. to wait a minute.
   b. to repeat.
   c. that you didn't understand.
   d. that you are going tomorrow.
   e. that you'll do the whole thing.
   f. that you appreciate his trouble.

2. Ask Tanaka-sañ:

   a. if he understood.
   b. if he is going today.
   c. if he did [it] yesterday.
   d. if he understood the whole thing.
   e. if he is well.

3. Exclaim (using ne⌐e) to Tanaka-sañ:

   a. how well Yamamoto-sañ understands.
   b. how well Yamamoto-sañ understood.
   c. how well Yamamoto-sañ is.
   d. that Yamamoto-sañ doesn't understand.

Lesson 2. Getting Around (cont.)

BASIC DIALOGUES: FOR MEMORIZATION

(a)

Tanaka (looking at a new kind of ball-point pen)

that thing	sore
as for that thing	sore wa
what?	na⌐ñ or
	na⌐ni
what is it?	na⌐ñ desu ka

1. What is that? (Lit. As for that thing, what is it?)   Sore wa ⌐na⌐ñ desu ka⌐

Smith

which thing (of 3 or more)   do⌐re

2. Which one is it? or Which one do you mean?   Do⌐re desu ka⌐

Tanaka (pointing)

3. It's that one. or I mean that one.   So⌐re de⌐su.

Smith

oh	a⌐a
pen	pe⌐ñ

4. Oh, that's a pen.   A⌐a, sore wa ⌐pe⌐ñ desu.

Tanaka

pencil	eñpitu
[it] isn't a pencil	e⌐ñpitu zya arimase⌐ñ

5. Isn't it a pencil?   E⌐ñpitu zya arimase⌐ñ ka⌐

Smith

is new	a⌐tarasi⌐i
new pen	a⌐tarasi⌐i ⌐pe⌐ñ

6. No (i.e. that's right). It's a new pen.   E⌐e. A⌐tarasi⌐i ⌐pe⌐ñ desu yo⌐

Tanaka

that way or thus or so   so⌐o

7. Oh, is that so? or Oh, really? or Oh?   A⌐a, so⌐o desu ka.

14

(b)

Smith

that thing over there	are
as for that thing over there	are wa
dictionary	ziˤbikiˈ or
	ziˈsyo

8. Is that (over there) a dictionary?   Are wa ziˤbikiˈ desu ka⌟

Tanaka

9. Yes, that's right (lit. it's that   Eˈe, soˈo desu.
way).

Smith

is small	tiˤisaˈi

10. Isn't it small!   Tiˤisaˈi desu ˈneˈe.

Tanaka

11. It is, isn't it!   Soˈo desu ˤneˈe.

Smith

is good or fine or all	iˈi
right	
good dictionary	iˈi zibiki

12. Is it a good dictionary?   Iˈi ziˈbikiˈ desu ka⌟

Tanaka

isn't good	yoˈku aˈrimaseˈñ

13. No, it isn't (good)!   Iie, yoˈku aˈrimaseˈñ yo⌟

Smith

14. Oh, really?   Aˈa, soˈo desu ka.

(c)

Smith (looking for something to read)

this thing	kore
as for this thing	kore wa
is interesting or unusual	oˤmosiroˈi
or fun	
book	hoˈñ
interesting book	oˤmosiroˈi ˈhoˈñ

15. Is this an interesting book?   Kore wa oˤmosiroˈi ˈhoˈñ desu ka⌟

Tanaka

16. No, it isn't (interesting).   Iie, oˤmosiˈroku aˈrimaseˈñ.

Smith

then or well then or	zyaˈa
in that case	

17. Well then, [how about] that?   Zyaˈa, sore wa?

Deze tekst

Tanaka

	magazine	zassi
18.	Do you mean the magazine?	Za⌐ssi de⌐su ka↵
19.	That's [very] good!	So⌐re wa i⌐i desu yo↵
20.	Here!	Do⌐ozo.

(d)

Smith (looking at some Japanese paperbacks)

21.	Is that a magazine?	Sore wa za⌐ssi de⌐su ka↵

Tanaka

22.	No, it isn't.	Iie, so⌐o zya a⌐rimase⌐ñ.
23.	It's a book.	Ho⌐ñ desu yo↵

Smith

24.	How about this one?	Kore wa?

Tanaka

	be different or be wrong	ti⌐gaima⌐su
25.	Oh, that's different.	A⌐a, so⌐re wa tigaima⌐su.
26.	That's a magazine.	So⌐re wa zassi de⌐su.

(e)

Tanaka (to Smith, who is about to buy a newspaper)

	newspaper	siñbuñ
	good newspaper	i⌐i siñbuñ
27.	That's not a [very] good news-paper, you know.	Sore wa ⌐i⌐i siñbuñ zya a⌐rimase⌐ñ yo↵

Smith

28.	Oh?	So⌐o desu ka.
	how?	do⌐o
29.	How is this one?	Ko⌐re wa do⌐o desu ka↵

Tanaka

	same	onazi
30.	It's the same.	O⌐nazi de⌐su.
	no good	da⌐me⌐
31.	It's no good!	Da⌐me⌐ desu yo.

ADDITIONAL VOCABULARY: OPPOSITES

A⌐tarasi⌐i desu. 'It's new or fresh.'

O⌐mosiro⌐i desu. 'It's interesting or fun or unusual.'

Hu⌐ru⌐i desu. 'It's old (i.e. not new) or stale.'

Tu⌐mara⌐nai desu. 'It's dull or boring or trifling.'

Ti⌐isa⌐i desu. 'It's small.'   O⌐oki⌐i desu. 'It's big.'
I⌐i desu. 'It's good.'   {Wa⌐ru⌐i desu. 'It's bad.'
  {Da⌐me⌐ desu. 'It's no good.'

NOTES ON THE BASIC DIALOGUES

1. Na⌐ñ occurs before d-, both na⌐ñ and na⌐ni before t- and n-, and na⌐ni elsewhere.

7, 9, 11, 14. So⌐o desu. 'That's right.' occurs in answer to questions. So⌐o
desu ⌐ne⌐e. 'That's right, isn't it.' follows statements (especially exclamations ending in ne⌐e.) containing known or recognized information, and
indicates agreement. So⌐o desu ka. 'Is that so?' follows statements containing information previously unknown or unrecognized, and indicates
attention and interest. Thus:

> O⌐mosiro⌐i ⌐ho⌐ñ desu ka⌐ 'Is it an interesting book?'
> So⌐o desu. 'That's right.'

> O⌐mosiro⌐i ⌐ho⌐ñ desu ⌐ne⌐e. 'It's an interesting book, isn't it.'
> So⌐o desu ⌐ne⌐e. 'It is, isn't it.' (i.e. I knew that, and I agree.)

> O⌐mosiro⌐i ⌐ho⌐ñ desu. 'It's an interesting book.'
> So⌐o desu ka. 'Is that so?' (i.e. I didn't know until you told me.)

12. Note these additional equivalents of i⌐i desu: 'it's fine,' 'it's nice,' 'it's
all set,' 'it's all right,' 'it's all right as it is,' 'never mind,' 'don't bother.'

20. In this context, do⌐ozo means 'take it,' or 'read it,' or 'look at it,' etc.—
i.e. Tanaka is offering it to Smith.

25. Ti⌐gaima⌐su is a verbal (cf. Lesson 1, Grammatical Note 1). However, the
non-past negative ti⌐gaimase⌐ñ is comparatively rare and should be avoided
by the beginning student.

31. Da⌐me⌐ desu may also refer to something that is broken or out of order or
spoiled.

GRAMMATICAL NOTES

1. Adjectivals

> o⌐mosiro⌐i desu 'it's interesting'
> o⌐mosi⌐roku a⌐rimase⌐ñ 'it isn't interesting'

The words o⌐mosiro⌐i 'it's interesting,' tu⌐mara⌐nai 'it's dull,' a⌐tarasi⌐i
'it's new,' hu⌐ru⌐i 'it's old,' ti⌐isa⌐i 'it's small,' o⌐oki⌐i 'it's big,' i⌐i 'it's good,'
and wa⌐ru⌐i 'it's bad' are all members of a class of inflected Japanese words
having the following characteristics: they have a form ending in -ai, -oi, -ui,
or -ii, and a form ending in -ku (in addition to others). All such words will
hereafter be called ADJECTIVALS. The form ending in -i will be called the
INFORMAL NON-PAST (it refers to present or future time) or the CITATION

FORM; it is the form under which an adjectival is regularly listed in a dictionary and the form by which it is cited. The form ending in -ku will be called the
ADVERBIAL.   The adverbial is regularly made from the -i form (i.e. the informal non-past) by dropping the -i and adding -ku.[1] Thus:

Informal Non-Past (Citation Form)	Adverbial
oꜛmosiroꜜi	oꜛmosiꜜroku
tuꜛmaraꜜnai	tuꜛmaraꜜnaku
aꜛtarasiꜜi	aꜛtaraꜜsiku
huꜛruꜜi	huꜛruku
tiꜛisaꜜi	tiꜛisaku
oꜛokiꜜi	oꜜokiku
waꜛruꜜi	waꜛruku

The only exception is iꜜi : yoꜜku. Iꜜi is a newer form of yoꜜi (which still occurs in present-day Japanese, alternating with iꜜi), but the -ku form of the
word is always based on the older root.

Adjectivals, like verbals, are impersonal and may refer to any subject.
Context or a stated topic (sometimes followed by particle wa 'as for') makes
clear what is described.

An adjectival may o c c u r in its -i form alone as a sentence in informal
speech; with a following desu,[2] it becomes formal. In other words, the only
difference between an -i form alone and an -i form plus desu is degree of formality. Thus:

	Informal	Formal
'It's interesting.'	Oꜛmosiroꜜi.	Oꜛmosiroꜜi desu.
'It's dull.'	Tuꜛmaraꜜnai.	Tuꜛmaraꜜnai desu.
'It's new.'	Aꜛtarasiꜜi.	Aꜛtarasiꜜi desu.
'It's old.'	Huꜛruꜜi.	Huꜛruꜜi desu.
'It's small.'	Tiꜛisaꜜi.	Tiꜛisaꜜi desu.
'It's big.'	Oꜛokiꜜi.	Oꜛokiꜜi desu.
'It's good.'	Iꜜi.	Iꜜi desu.
'It's bad.'	Waꜛruꜜi.	Waꜛruꜜi desu.

An adjectival which describes a verbal or any other inflected expression
occurs in its adverbial (-ku) form (cf. Yoꜜku wakarimasu ꜛneꜜe. 'You understand [very] well, don't you! '). When adjectivals occur before the negative
aꜛrimaseꜜn 'there isn't any,' we find:

---

[1] If the dictionary form is accented, the -ku form is also accented, but the
high-pitched sequence usually ends on an earlier syllable in the -ku form. However, many -ku forms occur with alternate accents.

[2] In this position, the adjectival is always accented, and the high-pitched
sequence normally ends on the next-to-last syllable. Deꜜsu after an accented
word loses its accent.

Oᴴmosiᴴroku aᴸrimaseᴴñ.	'It isn't interesting.'
Tuᴸmaraᴴnaku aᴸrimaseᴴñ.	'It isn't dull.'
Aᴸtaraᴴsiku aᴸrimaseᴴñ.	'It isn't new.'
Huᴴruku aᴸrimaseᴴñ.	'It isn't old.'
Tiᴴisaku aᴸrimaseᴴñ.	'It isn't small.'
Oᴴokiku aᴸrimaseᴴñ.	'It isn't big.'
Yoᴴku aᴸrimaseᴴñ.	'It isn't good.'
Waᴴruku aᴸrimaseᴴñ.	'It isn't bad.'

Since -mase⌐ñ forms are formal, non-past, and negative, the above combinations are also formal, non-past, and negative. They are further identified as the negative equivalents of adjectivals in their -i form plus desu. The formal adjectival pattern is outlined as follows:

Formal Non-Past Adjectival

Affirmative	Negative
-ai	-aku
-oi	-oku
-ui ⎬ + desu.	-uku ⎬ + aᴸrimaseᴴñ.
-ii	-iku

Note that in the negative combination, it is the aᴸrimaseᴴñ that is negative—not the -ku form. Tiᴴisaku aᴸrimaseᴴñ, for example, means literally something like 'being small, there isn't.'

WARNING: All adjectivals end in -ai, -oi, -ui, or -ii (in their informal non-past form); but not every word ending in one of these combinations is an adjectival. The word must also have a -ku form in order to be classified as an adjectival.

Hereafter, all new adjectivals will be introduced first in their citation form followed immediately by /-ku/ and defined without a subject, and then in a sentence with an appropriate contextual equivalent. For example:

is hot	aᴸtuᴴi /-ku/
Isn't it hot?	Aᴴtuku aᴸrimaseᴴñ ka⌐

2.   Nominals

The major word class of Japanese is a class of constants (i.e. uninflected words; those having only one form) which will hereafter be called NOMINALS. Any constant which in some of its uses occurs with de⌐su (meaning 'it is ——' or 'it will be ——') as a complete utterance is classed as a nominal.[1] The negative equivalent of nominal + de⌐su is nominal + zya + aᴸrimaseᴴñ 'it's not ——' or 'it won't be ——.' For example, so⌐o is a constant which may occur with desu as a complete utterance: So⌐o desu. 'It's that way' or 'That's right.'

---

[1] Not all words classed as nominals occur in this pattern. Other identifying characteristics of nominals will be introduced later.

So⌐o is therefore classed as a nominal. The negative of <u>So⌐o desu.</u> is <u>So⌐o zya a⌐rimase⌐ñ.</u> 'It's not that way' or 'That's n o t right.'   Other examples are:

ho⌐ñ 'book': Ho⌐ñ desu. 'It's a book.'
            Ho⌐ñ zya a⌐rimase⌐ñ. 'It's not a book.'

Tanaka-sañ 'Mr. Tanaka': Ta⌐naka-sañ de⌐su. 'It's Mr. Tanaka.'
                    Ta⌐naka-sañ zya arimase⌐ñ. 'It's not Mr. Tana-
                    ka.'
a⌐na⌐ta 'you': A⌐na⌐ta desu. 'It's you.'
              A⌐na⌐ta zya a⌐rimase⌐ñ. 'It's not you.'

kore 'this thing': Ko⌐re de⌐su. 'It's this (thing).'
               Ko⌐re zya arimase⌐ñ. 'It's not this (thing).'

The class of nominals includes—but is by no means limited to—all Japanese words which stand for tangible objects: chair, man, milk, book, etc.

<u>De⌐su</u> regularly loses its accent when it follows an accented nominal. Compare:

      Pe⌐ñ desu. 'It's a pen.'
      E⌐ñpitu de⌐su. 'It's a pencil.'

For the accent of zya + a⌐rimase⌐ñ following accented and unaccented nominals, note the examples above.

Nominals do not distinguish between singular and plural number. For example, ho⌐ñ may refer to one book or more than one; <u>kore</u> to this thing or these things; etc.

Nominal + <u>de⌐su</u> sequences, like verbals and adjectivals, are impersonal and may refer to any topic, stated explicitly or indicated only by the context. Thus, depending on context, <u>Ta⌐naka de⌐su</u> m a y be equivalent to 'I'm Tanaka,' 'he's Tanaka,' 'it's Tanaka,' etc.   <u>Kore wa ⌐ho⌐ñ desu,</u> with the topic indicated by <u>kore wa,</u> means either 'this is a book' or 'these are books,' since nominals do not distinguish between singular and plural.

An adjectival in its c i t a t i o n form may precede a nominal directly as a descriptive word:

       o⌐mosiro⌐i ⌐ho⌐ñ 'an interesting book'
       o⌐oki⌐i zibiki 'a big dictionary'

This form may also precede an adjectival + nominal sequence:

       ti⌐isa⌐i o⌐mosiro⌐i ⌐ho⌐ñ 'a small interesting book'
       a⌐tarasi⌐i o⌐oki⌐i zibiki 'a new big dictionary'

Compare now these three constantly recurring, basic patterns of Japanese:

F o r m a l   N o n - P a s t

	Affirmative	Negative
Verbal Pattern	Verbal ending in -ma⌐su (wa⌐karima⌐su)	Verbal ending in -mase⌐ñ (wa⌐karimase⌐ñ)
Adjectival Pattern	Adjectival ending in -i + desu (o⌐oki⌐i desu)	Adjectival ending in -ku + a⌐rimase⌐ñ (o⌐okiku a⌐rimase⌐ñ)
Nominal Pattern	Nominal + de⌐su (ho⌐ñ desu)	Nominal + zya + a⌐rimase⌐ñ (ho⌐ñ zya a⌐rimase⌐ñ)

So⌐o desu 'that's right' and so⌐o zya a⌐rimase⌐n̄ 'that's not right' are fre-quently used in answer to a question that ends with a nominal + de⌐su ka, but less commonly in answer to verbal or adjectival questions. Thus:

I⌐kima⌐su ka↲	E⌐e, i⌐kima⌐su.
	Iie, i⌐kimase⌐n̄.
O⌐oki⌐i desu ka↲	E⌐e, o⌐oki⌐i desu.
	Iie, o⌐okiku a⌐rimase⌐n̄.
Pe⌐n̄ desu ka↲	E⌐e, pe⌐n̄ desu. or E⌐e, so⌐o desu.
	Iie, pe⌐n̄ zya a⌐rimase⌐n̄. or Iie, so⌐o
	zya a⌐rimase⌐n̄.

In changing a sentence that ends with an adjectival + desu to its precise neg-ative equivalent, the adjectival pattern is used; but a sentence that ends with a nominal + de⌐su follows the nominal pattern in forming its exactly correspond-ing negative. Compare:

Ho⌐n̄ wa o⌐mosiro⌐i desu.   Ho⌐n̄ wa o⌐mosi⌐roku a⌐rimase⌐n̄.
  'The book is interesting.'   'The book isn't interesting.'

O⌐mosiro⌐i ⌐ho⌐n̄ desu.   O⌐mosiro⌐i ⌐ho⌐n̄ zya a⌐rimase⌐n̄.
  'It's an interesting book.'   'It's not an interesting book.'

In conversation, however, a reply to a question does not always follow the question pattern exactly. Thus, in answer to:

Sore wa a⌐tarasi⌐i ⌐pe⌐n̄ desu ka↲ 'Is that a new pen?'   (nominal pattern)

a common reply would be:

Iie, a⌐tara⌐siku a⌐rimase⌐n̄. 'No, it isn't new.' (adjectival pattern)

However, the exact negative equivalent would be:

Sore wa a⌐tarasi⌐i ⌐pe⌐n̄ zya a⌐rimase⌐n̄. 'That is not a new pen.'

Most new nominals can be recognized in the lessons that follow by a process of elimination: if a word is not a verbal (identified by a -ma⌐su ending) or an adjectival (identified by /-ku/) and is first introduced singly rather than in a phrase, it is a nominal. Other nominals, more difficult to recognize, can be identified on the basis of other criteria to be introduced later.

3.   k o r e,   s o r e,   a r e,   d o⌐r e

These four words are all nominals.

Kore refers to a thing or things[1] close to the speaker — i. e. 'near me.'

Sore refers to a thing or things (a) removed from the speaker but close to the person addressed — i. e. 'near you'; (b) within sight but slightly removed —

---

[1] These words are also used in reference to certain people: those who are inferiors, members of one's own family, etc.

i.e. neither 'here' nor 'over yonder'—from both speaker and person addressed;
or (c) already identified in what has gone before—i.e. 'that thing (or those
things) already under discussion.' In meaning (c), the English equivalent is
often 'it.'

Are refers to a thing or things 'over there' or 'over yonder,' removed from
both speaker and person addressed, either within sight or out of sight. Like
sore, it too may refer to something already identified in what has gone before,
but it always refers to something removed and usually indicates some particular concrete object(s) being pointed out and defined in terms of a particular
location. For example, 'medicine being manufactured today' would, after its
first mention, usually be referred to as sore, whereas Mount Fuji would most
often be referred to as are.

In a sequence containing both sore and are, are usually implies greater distance. But when sore—with meaning (b)—and are occur singly, it is impossible
to define the distance from the speaker at which sore ceases to be used and are
begins; the most that can be said is that sore means 'that-rather-near' and are
means 'that-over-there.'

Do⌐re is an interrogative nominal meaning 'which one (of a specified group,
usually containing at least three things)?'

4. Particle yo

Like question particle ka, yo occurs at the end of sentences. It is a particle
of emphasis: it means that the sentence is being stated with assurance. It is
often used in warnings, in contradictions, and in informative exclamations.
Sometimes it corresponds to conversational English 'you know,' 'I tell you,'
'say!' 'I'm sure,' etc.; but many times it corresponds to English exclamatory
intonation and therefore is difficult to indicate in a written equivalent. Like
sentences ending in ka, those ending in yo occur with rising or low intonation.

Compare:

> Da⌐me⌐ desu. 'It's no good.'
> Da⌐me⌐ desu ka⌣ 'Isn't it any good?'
> Da⌐me⌐ desu ⌐ne⌐e. 'It's no good, is it!' or 'Isn't it awful!' (i.e. I
> assume you know)
> Da⌐me⌐ desu yo. 'It's no good!' or 'It's no good, you know!' or
> 'Contrary to what you think, it's no good' or 'I'm telling you it's
> no good,' etc.

DRILLS

A. Substitution Drill

1. What is that?	Sore wa ⌐na⌐ñ desu ka⌣
2. Is that a book?	Sore wa ⌐ho⌐ñ desu ka⌣
3. Is that a magazine?	Sore wa za⌐ssi de⌐su ka⌣
4. Is that a newspaper?	Sore wa si⌐ñbuñ de⌐su ka⌣
5. Is that a dictionary?	Sore wa ⌐zi⌐syo desu ka⌣

6. Is that the same?   Sore wa oˉnazi deˉsu ka﹍
7. Is that out of order?   Sore wa daˉmeˉ desu ka﹍
8. Is that today?   Sore wa ˉkyoˉo desu ka﹍
9. Is that tomorrow?   Sore wa aˉsitaˉ desu ka﹍
10. How is that?   Sore wa ˉdoˉo desu ka﹍

B. Substitution Drill

1. This is an interesting   Kore wa oˉmosiroˉi ˉhoˉñ desu ˉneˉe.
   book, isn't it.

2. That is an interesting   Sore wa oˉmosiroˉi ˉhoˉñ desu ˉneˉe.
   book, isn't it.

3. That is a good book,   Sore wa ˉiˉi ˉhoˉñ desu ˉneˉe.
   isn't it.

4. That is a good diction-   Sore wa ˉiˉi ziˉbikiˉ desu ˉneˉe.
   ary, isn't it.

5. That (over there) is a   Are wa ˉiˉi ziˉbikiˉ desu ˉneˉe.
   good dictionary, isn't it.

6. That (over there) is a   Are wa oˉokiˉi ziˉbikiˉ desu ˉneˉe.
   big dictionary, isn't it.

7. That (over there) is a   Are wa oˉokiˉi zaˉssi deˉsu ˉneˉe.
   big magazine, isn't it.

8. That (over there) is a   Are wa tuˉmaraˉnai zaˉssi deˉsu
   dull magazine, isn't it.   ˉneˉe.

9. That (over there) is a   Are wa tuˉmaraˉnai siˉñbuñ deˉsu
   dull newspaper, isn't it.   ˉneˉe.

C. Response Drill (based on Grammatical Note 2)

(What does the Eˉe. or Iie. answer to each of the following questions
mean?)

1. Peˉñ desu ka﹍ /Eˉe./   Eˉe, peˉñ desu.
2. Eˉñpitu deˉsu ka﹍ /Iie./   Iie, eˉñpitu zya arimaseˉñ.
3. Soˉo desu ka﹍ /Eˉe./   Eˉe, soˉo desu.
4. Kyoˉo desu ka﹍ /Iie./   Iie, kyoˉo zya aˉrimaseˉñ.
5. Siˉñbuñ deˉsu ka﹍ /Eˉe./   Eˉe, siˉñbuñ deˉsu.
6. Oˉnazi deˉsu ka﹍ /Iie./   Iie, oˉnazi zya arimaseˉñ.
7. Zaˉssi deˉsu ka﹍ /Eˉe./   Eˉe, zaˉssi deˉsu.
8. Aˉsitaˉ desu ka﹍ /Iie./   Iie, aˉsitaˉ zya aˉrimaseˉñ.
9. Daˉmeˉ desu ka﹍ /Eˉe./   Eˉe, daˉmeˉ desu.
10. Taˉnaka-sañ deˉsu ka﹍   Iie, Taˉnaka-sañ zya arimaseˉñ.
   /Iie./

D. Response Drill (based on Grammatical Note 1)

(What does the Eˉe. or Iie. answer to each of the following questions
mean?)

1. Oˉokiˉi desu ka﹍ /Eˉe./   Eˉe, oˉokiˉi desu.
2. Aˉtarasiˉi desu ka﹍ /Iie./   Iie, aˉtaraˉsiku aˉrimaseˉñ.
3. Huˉruˉi desu ka﹍ /Eˉe./   Eˉe, huˉruˉi desu.
4. Iˉi desu ka﹍ /Iie./   Iie, yoˉku aˉrimaseˉñ.

5. Oˈmosiroˈi desu kaↄ /Eˈe./   Eˈe, oˈmosiroˈi desu.
6. Tiˈisaˈi desu kaↄ /Iie./   Iie, tiˈisaku aˈrimaseˈn̄.
7. Waˈruˈi desu kaↄ /Eˈe./   Eˈe, waˈruˈi desu.
8. Tuˈmaraˈnai desu kaↄ /Iie./   Iie, tuˈmaraˈnaku aˈrimaseˈn̄.
9. Iˈi desu kaↄ /Eˈe./   Eˈe, iˈi desu.
10. Oˈokiˈi desu kaↄ /Iie./   Iie, oˈokiku aˈrimaseˈn̄.

E. Response Drill

(What does the Iie. answer to each of the following questions mean?)

1. Iˈkimaˈsu kaↄ /Iie./   Iie, iˈkimaseˈn̄.
2. Huˈruˈi desu kaↄ /Iie./   Iie, huˈruku aˈrimaseˈn̄.
3. Oˈnazi deˈsu kaↄ /Iie./   Iie, oˈnazi zya arimaseˈn̄.
4. Waˈkarimaseˈn̄ desita kaↄ   Iie, waˈkarimaˈsita.
   /Iie./
5. Siˈn̄bun̄ zya arimaseˈn̄ kaↄ   Iie, siˈn̄bun̄ deˈsu.
   /Iie./
6. Oˈmosiˈroku aˈrimaseˈn̄   Iie, oˈmosiroˈi desu.
   kaↄ /Iie./
7. Siˈmaˈsu kaↄ /Iie./   Iie, siˈmaseˈn̄.
8. Ziˈsyo zya aˈrimaseˈn̄ kaↄ   Iie, ziˈsyo desu.
   /Iie./
9. Aˈtarasiˈi desu kaↄ /Iie./   Iie, aˈtaraˈsiku aˈrimaseˈn̄.
10. Koˈre deˈsu kaↄ /Iie./   Iie, koˈre zya arimaseˈn̄.

F. Response Drill

Answer with soˈo desu, soˈo desu ˈneˈe, or soˈo desu ka, whichever is appropriate. Assume that each statement not ending with ˈneˈe contains new information.

1. Waˈkarimaseˈn̄ desita.   Soˈo desu ka.
2. Oˈmosiroˈi desu ˈneˈe.   Soˈo desu ˈneˈe.
3. Zeˈn̄bu waˈkarimaˈsita.   Soˈo desu ka.
4. Peˈn̄ desu kaↄ   Soˈo desu.
5. Daˈmeˈ desu yoↄ   Soˈo desu ka.
6. Ziˈsyo desu kaↄ   Soˈo desu.
7. Iˈi desu ˈneˈe.   Soˈo desu ˈneˈe.
8. Tiˈḡaimaˈsu yoↄ   Soˈo desu ka.

G. Expansion Drill

1. [It] isn't a pen.   Peˈn̄ zya aˈrimaseˈn̄.
   [It] isn't a new pen.   Aˈtarasiˈi ˈpeˈn̄ zya aˈrimaseˈn̄.
   That isn't a new pen.   Sore wa aˈtarasiˈi ˈpeˈn̄ zya aˈri-
                                       maseˈn̄.
   Isn't that a new pen?   Sore wa aˈtarasiˈi ˈpeˈn̄ zya aˈri-
                                       maseˈn̄ kaↄ
2. [It]'s a book.   Hoˈn̄ desu.
   [It]'s an interesting book.   Oˈmosiroˈi ˈhoˈn̄ desu.
   This is an interesting book.   Kore wa oˈmosiroˈi ˈhoˈn̄ desu.
   Isn't this an interesting   Kore wa oˈmosiroˈi ˈhoˈn̄ desu ˈneˈe.
      book!

3. [It]'s dull.   Tu⌐mara⌐nai desu.
   That's dull.   Sore wa tu⌐mara⌐nai desu.
   You know, that's dull.   Sore wa tu⌐mara⌐nai desu yo⌟
   You know, Mr. Tanaka, that's   Tanaka-sañ, sore wa tu⌐mara⌐nai
   dull.   desu yo⌟
4. [It] isn't [any] good.   Yo⌐ku a⌐rimase⌐ñ.
   The dictionary isn't [any]   Zi⌐biki⌐ wa ⌐yo⌐ku a⌐rimase⌐ñ.
   good.
   The small dictionary isn't   Ti⌐isa⌐i zi⌐biki⌐ wa ⌐yo⌐ku a⌐rimase⌐ñ.
   [any] good.
   The small dictionary isn't   Ti⌐isa⌐i zi⌐biki⌐ wa ⌐yo⌐ku a⌐rimase⌐ñ
   [any] good, is it!   ⌐ne⌐e.

EXERCISES

1. Tanaka-sañ asks you what it is. You answer that:

   a. it's a book.
   b. it's a newspaper.
   c. it's a pencil.
   d. it's an old magazine.
   e. it's a new pen.

2. Tanaka-sañ asks: Your answer:

   a. if it's interesting.   Yes, it is (interesting).
   b. if it's small.   No, it's big.
   c. if it's new.   No, it isn't (new).
   d. if it's the same.   No, it's different.
   e. if it's an interesting book.   No, it isn't interesting.
   f. if it's a new magazine.   No, it's old.
   g. what it is.   Which one do you mean?

3. Following the Basic Dialogues of this lesson, make up new conversations by
   replacing the nominals and adjectivals with other words of the same word-
   class, wherever possible. Practice the new conversations using appropriate
   props. For example, using a newspaper and a magazine, you might practice Basic Dialogue (c) as follows:

   Smith: Kore wa a⌐tarasi⌐i za⌐ssi de⌐su ka⌟
   Tanaka: Iie, a⌐tara⌐siku a⌐rimase⌐ñ.
   Smith: Zya⌐a, sore wa?
   Tanaka: Si⌐ñbuñ de⌐su ka⌟
          So⌐re wa atarasi⌐i desu yo⌟ Do⌐ozo.

Lesson 3. Shopping

NUMERALS

1 i˹ti˺	10 zyu˹u	20 ni˹zyuu	30 sa˹ñzyuu
2 ni˺	11 zyu˹uiti˺	21 ni˹zyuu iti	31 sa˹ñzyuu iti
3 sañ	12 zyu˹uni˺	22 ni˹zyuu ni	32 sa˹ñzyuu ni
4 si˺ or yo˺ñ	13 zyu˹usañ	23 ni˹zyuu sañ	33 sa˹ñzyuu sañ
5 go˺	14 zyu˹usi˺	24 ni˹zyuu si	34 sa˹ñzyuu si
6 ro˹ku˺	15 zyu˹ugo	25 ni˹zyuu go	35 sa˹ñzyuu go
7 si˹ti˺ or na˺na	16 zyu˹uroku˺	26 ni˹zyuu roku	36 sa˹ñzyuu roku
8 ha˹ti˺	17 zyu˹usiti˺	27 ni˹zyuu siti	37 sa˹ñzyuu siti
9 ku˺ or kyu˺u	18 zyu˹uhati˺	28 ni˹zyuu hati	38 sa˹ñzyuu hati
	19 zyu˹uku	29 ni˹zyuu ku	39 sa˹ñzyuu ku

40 yo˹ñzyuu	50 go˹zyu˺u	60 ro˹kuzyu˺u	70 na˹na˺zyuu
41 yo˹ñzyuu iti	51 go˹zyuu iti˺	61 ro˹kuzyuu iti˺	71 na˹na˺zyuu iti
42 yo˹ñzyuu ni	52 go˹zyuu ni˺	62 ro˹kuzyuu ni˺	72 na˹na˺zyuu ni
43 yo˹ñzyuu sañ	53 gozyuu sañ	63 rokuzyuu sañ	73 na˹na˺zyuu sañ
44 yo˹ñzyuu si	54 go˹zyuu si˺	64 ro˹kuzyuu si˺	74 na˹na˺zyuu si
45 yo˹ñzyuu go	55 go˹zyuu go˺	65 ro˹kuzyuu go˺	75 na˹na˺zyuu go
46 yo˹ñzyuu roku	56 go˹zyuu roku˺	66 ro˹kuzyuu roku˺	76 na˹na˺zyuu roku
47 yo˹ñzyuu siti	57 go˹zyuu siti˺	67 ro˹kuzyuu siti˺	77 na˹na˺zyuu siti
48 yo˹ñzyuu hati	58 go˹zyuu hati˺	68 ro˹kuzyuu hati˺	78 na˹na˺zyuu hati
49 yo˹ñzyuu ku	59 go˹zyuu ku˺	69 ro˹kuzyuu ku˺	79 na˹na˺zyuu ku

80 ha˹tizyu˺u	90 kyu˹uzyuu
81 ha˹tizyuu iti˺	91 kyu˹uzyuu iti
82 ha˹tizyuu ni˺	92 kyu˹uzyuu ni
83 hatizyuu sañ	93 kyu˹uzyuu sañ
84 ha˹tizyuu si˺	94 kyu˹uzyuu si
85 ha˹tizyuu go˺	95 kyu˹uzyuu go
86 ha˹tizyuu roku˺	96 kyu˹uzyuu roku
87 ha˹tizyuu siti˺	97 kyu˹uzyuu siti
88 ha˹tizyuu hati˺	98 kyu˹uzyuu hati
89 ha˹tizyuu ku˺	99 kyu˹uzyuu kyuu

100 hya˹ku˺	1000 se˹ñ or i˹sse˺ñ	10,000 i˹tima˺ñ
200 ni˹hyaku˺	2000 ni˹se˺ñ	20,000 ni˹ma˺ñ
300 sa˹ñbyaku	3000 sa˹ñze˺ñ	30,000 sa˹ñma˺ñ
400 yo˹ñhyaku	4000 yo˹ñse˺ñ	40,000 yo˹ñma˺ñ
500 go˹hyaku˺	5000 go˹se˺ñ	50,000 go˹ma˺ñ
600 ro˹ppyaku˺	6000 ro˹kuse˺ñ	60,000 ro˹kuma˺ñ
700 na˹na˺hyaku	7000 na˹nase˺ñ	70,000 na˹nama˺ñ
800 ha˹ppyaku˺	8000 ha˹sse˺ñ	80,000 ha˹tima˺ñ
900 kyu˹uhyaku	9000 kyu˹use˺ñ	90,000 kyu˹uma˺ñ

BASIC DIALOGUES: FOR MEMORIZATION

(a)

Smith

cigarette(s) <u>or</u> tobacco	tabako
that cigarette <u>or</u> those cigarettes	sono tabako
how much?	i⌐i⌐kura <u>or</u> oikura[+]
1. How much are those cigarettes?	Sono tabako wa ⌐i⌐kura desu ka⌐

Clerk

which cigarette(s)?	do⌐no tabako
2. Which cigarettes are they? <u>or</u> Which cigarettes do you mean?	Do⌐no tabako desu ka⌐

Smith (picking up cigarettes)

this cigarette <u>or</u> these cigarettes	kono tabako
3. They're these cigarettes. <u>or</u> I mean these cigarettes.	Ko⌐no tabako de⌐su.

Clerk

1 yen	iti-eñ
2 yen	ni-eñ
3 yen	sañ-eñ
4 yen	yo⌐-eñ
4. They're ¥40.	Yo⌐ñzyu⌐u-eñ desu.

Smith

match(es)	ma⌐tti
this match <u>or</u> these matches	ko⌐no ma⌐tti
5. How about these matches?	Ko⌐no ma⌐tti wa?

Clerk

6. They're ¥2.	Ni-⌐eñ de⌐su.

Smith

here you are	ha⌐i
7. Here you are. ¥42.	Ha⌐i. Yo⌐ñzyuu ⌐ni⌐-eñ.

Clerk

8. Thank you.	A⌐ri⌐ḡatoo gozaimasu.

(b)

Tanaka (examining Smith's purchases on the counter)

ashtray(s)	ha⌐iza⌐ra
that little ashtray	sono ti⌐isa⌐i ha⌐iza⌐ra
pretty <u>or</u> clean	ki⌐ree
9. Isn't that little ashtray pretty!	Sono ti⌐isa⌐i ha⌐iza⌐ra wa ⌐ki⌐ree desu ⌐ne⌐e.

10.	Was it ¥ 400?	Yo⌐ñhyaku⌐-eñ desita ka⌟

Smith

11.	No, it wasn't (that way).	Iie. So⌐o zya a⌐rimase⌐ñ desita.
12.	It was ¥ 200.	Ni⌐hyaku⌐-eñ desita yo⌟

Tanaka

13.	(It was) ¥ 200?	Ni⌐hyaku⌐-eñ desita ka⌟
	is cheap or inexpensive	ya⌐su⌐i /-ku/
14.	How cheap! (Lit. It's cheap, isn't it.)	Ya⌐su⌐i desu ⌐ne⌐e.

(c)

Smith

	that big dictionary over there	ano o⌐oki⌐i zibiki
15.	How much was that big diction-ary over there?	Ano o⌐oki⌐i zi⌐biki⌐ wa ⌐i⌐kura desita ka⌟

Tanaka

16.	It was ¥ 1200.	Se⌐ñ nihyaku⌐-eñ desita.

Smith

	truth or true	hoñtoo
17.	Is that true? or Really? or Do you really mean it?	Ho⌐ñtoo de⌐su ka⌟
	extremely or to a con-siderable degree	zu⌐ibuñ
18.	How (very) cheap! (Lit. It's very cheap, isn't it.)	Zu⌐ibuñ ya⌐su⌐i desu ⌐ne⌐e.

(d)

Smith

19.	How much was that?	Sore wa ⌐i⌐kura desita ka⌟

Tanaka

	this book	ko⌐no ho⌐ñ
20.	Is it this book? or Do you mean this book?	Ko⌐no ho⌐ñ desu ka⌟
21.	It was ¥ 250.	Ni⌐hyaku gozyu⌐u-eñ desita.

Smith

	not very much or not so much or not too much	añmari + negative
	is expensive	ta⌐ka⌐i /-ku/
22.	It wasn't very expensive, was it.	A⌐ñmari ta⌐kaku a⌐rimase⌐ñ desita ⌐ne⌐e.

NOTES ON THE BASIC DIALOGUES

1. When 'cigarette' is being distinguished from other things to smoke—cigars, pipes, etc.—ma⌐kita⌐bako is used.

   Oikura, the polite (+) equivalent of i⌐kura, is used more commonly—but not exclusively—by women.

7. Ha⌐i is frequently used when handing something over to someone.

17. Ho⌐ntoo de⌐su ka⌐ 'Is that true?' indicates livelier interest and greater surprise than So⌐o desu ka⌐ 'Is that so?' or 'Oh?'

GRAMMATICAL NOTES

1. Numerals of Series I and Counter -eñ

The numerals listed on page 26 are Japanese numerals of Chinese origin; they will hereafter be designated as SERIES I NUMERALS. A second series, of native Japanese origin, will be introduced later.

Three numerals have alternate forms: '4' is yo⌐ñ or si⌐;[1] '7' is na⌐na or si⌐ti⌐; '9' is kyu⌐u or ku⌐. Depending on what follows, either the alternants are used interchangeably, or one alternant occurs much more commonly, or only one alternant occurs. Unfortunately, no general rules apply which will assist the student in choosing the correct alternant(s); he must learn each combination as it occurs.

Si⌐zyu⌐u occurs as a less common alternant of yo⌐ñzyuu, and si⌐tizyu⌐u as a less common alternant of na⌐na⌐zyuu.

Numerals from 1 to 100 are listed at the beginning of this lesson. Three-digit numerals are read in terms of the number of hundreds, the number of tens, and the single units. If a zero occurs within a written number, it is usually omitted in the spoken number. Thus:

    236: ni⌐hyaku sa⌐ñzyuu ro⌐ku⌐ (lit. '2 hundreds, 3 tens, 6')
    632: ro⌐ppyaku sa⌐ñzyuu ⌐ni⌐ (lit. '6 hundreds, 3 tens, 2')
    801: ha⌐ppyaku iti⌐ (lit. '8 hundreds, 1')

Four-digit numerals are read in terms of the number of thousands, the number of hundreds, the number of tens, and the single units. Thus:

    4578: yo⌐ñse⌐ñ gohyaku na⌐na⌐zyuu ha⌐ti⌐ (lit. '4 thousands, 5 hundreds, 7 tens, 8')
    8754: ha⌐sse⌐ñ na⌐na⌐hyaku go⌐zyuu si⌐ (lit. '8 thousands, 7 hundreds, 5 tens, 4')
    9023: kyu⌐use⌐ñ ⌐ni⌐zyuu sañ (lit. '9 thousands, 2 tens, 3')

---

[1] A third, less common alternant which occurs only in certain compounds is yo-.

Higher numerals often cause difficulties for English speakers and therefore require special attention. In reading numerals containing from five to eight digits,[1] the numeral is read in terms of how many ten-thousands (up to thousands of ten-thousands), how many thousands, how many hundreds, how many tens, and how many single units it contains. This can be simplified in the case of a written number by inserting a comma between the fourth and fifth digit counting from the right,[2] and reading what precedes the comma as an independent numeral + -ma⌐n 'ten-thousands.' Study the following examples:

  12,345 (rewritten 1,2345) is read: i⌐tima⌐n ni⌐se⌐n ⌐sa⌐ñbyaku ⌐yo⌐ñzyuu ⌐go⌐
    (lit. '1 ten-thousand, 2 thousands, 3 hundreds, 4 tens, 5')
  123,456 (rewritten 12,3456) is read: zyu⌐unima⌐n sa⌐ñze⌐n ⌐yo⌐ñhyaku go-
    ⌐zyuu roku⌐ (lit. '12 ten-thousands, 3 thousands, 4 hundreds, 5 tens, 6')
  1,234,567 (rewritten 123,4567) is read: hya⌐ku ni⌐zyuu sa⌐ñma⌐n yo⌐ñse⌐n
    gohyaku ro⌐kuzyuu siti⌐ (lit. '123 ten-thousands, 4 thousands, 5 hundreds,
    6 tens, 7')
  12,345,678 (rewritten 1234,5678) is read: se⌐n nihyaku ⌐sa⌐ñzyuu yo⌐ñma⌐n
    go⌐se⌐n roppyaku na⌐na⌐zyuu hati (lit. '1234 ten-thousands, 5 thousands, 6
    hundreds, 7 tens, 8')

Note that the Japanese equivalent of a million is hya⌐kuma⌐n (lit. '100 ten-thousands,' i. e. 100,0000).

The occurrence of -ma⌐n in a numeral is always a signal of four digits to come. The digits may be zero. Thus:

go⌐ma⌐n	'50,000'
go⌐ma⌐n i⌐sse⌐n	'51,000'
go⌐ma⌐n hya⌐ku⌐	'50,100'
go⌐ma⌐n ⌐zyu⌐u	'50,010'
go⌐ma⌐n i⌐ti⌐	'50,001'

The numerals of Series I regularly occur independently in mathematics, in counting cadence, and in serial counting.

The monetary unit of Japan is the yen. To count yen, -eñ is added to the numerals of Series I. Note, however, that before -eñ, '4' is yo⌐- instead of the more usual yo⌐ñ or si⌐. The forms from 1 to 10³ are:

iti-eñ	'1 yen'	roku-eñ	'6 yen'
ni-eñ	'2 yen'	na⌐na⌐-eñ or siti-eñ	'7 yen'
sañ-eñ	'3 yen'	hati-eñ	'8 yen'
yo⌐-eñ	'4 yen'	kyu⌐u-eñ	'9 yen'
go⌐-eñ	'5 yen'	zyuu-eñ	'10 yen'

The corresponding question word is na⌐ñ-eñ 'how many yen?'

---

[1] Numerals larger than this are not treated in this text.

[2] In English, numerals are divided into groups of threes; in Japanese, into groups of fours.

[3] In all such lists in this text, only commonly occurring alternants are included.

Forms like -eñ, which do not occur as independent words but are joined with numerals in compounds, will hereafter be called COUNTERS; and compounds that consist of numeral + counter will be called NUMBERS. All numerals and numbers are nominals.

2. Demonstratives: <u>kono</u>, <u>sono</u>, <u>ano</u>, <u>do˥no</u>

<u>Kono</u> 'this —,' <u>sono</u> 'that —,' <u>ano</u> 'that — over there,' and <u>do˥no</u> 'which — [of three or more]?' belong to a small class of Japanese constants (words having only one form) which occur only as a modifier of a following nominal.[1] Words of this class will be called DEMONSTRATIVES. Examples:

> ko˥no pe˥ñ 'this pen' (or, of course, 'these pens')
> sono eñpitu 'that pencil'
> a˥no ho˥ñ 'that book over there'
> kono o˥mosiro˥i ˥ho˦ñ 'this interesting book'
> do˥no tabako 'which cigarettes?'
> do˥no Tanaka-sañ 'which Mr. Tanaka?'

These four words must not be confused with <u>kore</u>, <u>sore</u>, <u>are</u>, and <u>do˥re</u>, which are nominals. Compare:

> Ko˥re de˥su. 'It's this.'
> Kore wa ˥ho˥ñ desu. 'This is a book.'
> Ko˥no ho˥ñ desu. 'It's this book.'
> So˥re zya arimase˥ñ. 'It's not that.'
> Sore wa ˥pe˥ñ zya a˥rimase˦ñ. 'That is not a pen.'
> So˥no pe˥ñ zya a˥rimase˦ñ. 'It's not that pen.'

The spatial and referential relationships of <u>kore</u>, <u>sore</u>, and <u>are</u> described above (pages 21–22) apply equally to the corresponding demonstratives <u>kono</u>, <u>sono</u>, and <u>ano</u>.

3. Copula

<u>De˥su</u> is a member of a certain set of inflected forms[2] which is neither a verbal (there are no forms ending in -ma˥su, -ma˥sita, etc.) nor an adjectival (there are no forms ending in -i or -ku). Actually, it is a unique set of forms; there are no other Japanese words with the same shapes or usage. Hereafter, <u>de˥su</u> and its derived forms—symbolized as √de˥su—[3] will be called the COPULA. The <u>de˥su</u> form itself is the formal non-past of the copula, corresponding to the -ma˥su form of a verbal.

------

[1] The nominal may have other modifiers as well. Note the fourth example.

[2] I.e. is one shape of a word having several shapes.

[3] The symbol √ indicates the enclosed word and its other forms. Thus √wa-˥karima˥su is a short-cut way of writing wa˥karima˥su, wa˥karima˥sita, etc.

It has already been pointed out that:

(a) de⌐su may follow an adjectival in its citation (-i) form, making the expression formal. The -i form alone is non-past informal; the -i form + de⌐su is non-past formal.

> o⌐oki⌐i desu 'it's big' (negative: o⌐okiku a⌐rimase⌐n̄ 'it's not big')

(b) de⌐su may follow a nominal, meaning 'it is ——' or 'it will be ——' (non-past formal).

> ho⌐ntoo de⌐su 'it's true' (negative: ho⌐ntoo zya arimase⌐n̄ 'it's not true')

In this lesson, the following new information is introduced:

(c) The past of de⌐su is de⌐sita[1] (also formal). It regularly occurs after a nominal, meaning 'it was ——.'

> kyo⌐o desu 'it's today'; kyo⌐o desita 'it was today.'

It sometimes follows an adjectival in its -i form, as the past equivalent of adjectival + de⌐su. However, this is only one of several formal past adjectival patterns,[2] and is not the most common pattern. An -i + desita pattern should not be used by a student without first checking with a native speaker of Japanese. If he hears it, however, he will have no trouble understanding it.

> (ya⌐su⌐i desu 'it's cheap'; ya⌐su⌐i desita 'it was cheap')

(d) Desita added to a formal non-past negative (ending in -mase⌐n̄) produces a formal past negative.

Formal Negatives

	Non-Past	Past
Verbal Pattern	wa⌐kariMASE⌐N̄ 'it isn't clear'	wa⌐kariMASE⌐N̄ DESITA 'it wasn't clear'
Adjectival Pattern	o⌐okiKU A⌐RIMASE⌐N̄ 'it isn't big'	o⌐okiKU A⌐RIMASE⌐N̄ DESITA 'it wasn't big'
Nominal Pattern	ho⌐ntoo ZYA ARIMASE⌐N̄ 'it isn't true'	ho⌐ntoo ZYA ARIMASE⌐N̄ DESITA 'it wasn't true'

---

[1] De⌐sita regularly loses its accent after an accented word.

[2] The others will be introduced later.

DRILLS

A. Substitution Drill

1.	Do you mean this dictionary?	Ko⌐no zibiki⌐ desu ka⌐
2.	Do you mean those cigarettes?	So⌐no tabako de⌐su ka⌐
3.	Do you mean those matches over there?	A⌐no ma⌐tti desu ka⌐
4.	Which book do you mean?	Do⌐no ⌐ho⌐ñ desu ka⌐
5.	Do you mean this magazine?	Ko⌐no zassi de⌐su ka⌐
6.	Do you mean that newspaper?	So⌐no siñbuñ de⌐su ka⌐
7.	Do you mean that ashtray over there?	A⌐no haiza⌐ra desu ka⌐
8.	Which Mr. Tanaka do you mean?	Do⌐no Ta⌐naka-sañ de⌐su ka⌐

B. Substitution Drill

1.	How much were those cigarettes?	Sono tabako wa ⌐i⌐kura desita ka⌐
2.	How much was that ashtray?	So⌐no haiza⌐ra wa ⌐i⌐kura desita ka⌐
3.	How much were those matches?	So⌐no ma⌐tti wa ⌐i⌐kura desita ka⌐
4.	How much was that newspaper?	Sono siñbuñ wa ⌐i⌐kura desita ka⌐
5.	How much was that magazine?	Sono zassi wa ⌐i⌐kura desita ka⌐
6.	How much was that book?	So⌐no ho⌐ñ wa ⌐i⌐kura desita ka⌐
7.	How much was that dictionary?	So⌐no zibiki⌐ wa ⌐i⌐kura desita ka⌐
8.	How much was that pencil?	Sono eñpitu wa ⌐i⌐kura desita ka⌐
9.	How much was that pen?	So⌐no pe⌐ñ wa ⌐i⌐kura desita ka⌐

C. Substitution Drill

1.	That big dictionary wasn't very expensive, was it!	Sono o⌐oki⌐i zi⌐biki⌐ wa a⌐ñmari ta⌐kaku a⌐rimase⌐ñ desita ⌐ne⌐e.
2.	That new dictionary wasn't very expensive, was it!	Sono a⌐tarasi⌐i zi⌐biki⌐ wa añmari ta⌐kaku a⌐rimase⌐ñ desita ⌐ne⌐e.
3.	That new dictionary wasn't very big, was it!	Sono a⌐tarasi⌐i zi⌐biki⌐ wa a⌐ñmari o⌐okiku a⌐rimase⌐ñ desita ⌐ne⌐e.
4.	That expensive dictionary wasn't very big, was it!	Sono ta⌐ka⌐i zi⌐biki⌐ wa a⌐ñmari o⌐okiku a⌐rimase⌐ñ desita ⌐ne⌐e.
5.	That expensive dictionary wasn't very good, was it!	Sono ta⌐ka⌐i zi⌐biki⌐ wa a⌐ñmari yo⌐ku a⌐rimase⌐ñ desita ⌐ne⌐e.
6.	That small dictionary wasn't very good, was it!	Sono ti⌐isa⌐i zi⌐biki⌐ wa a⌐ñmari yo⌐ku a⌐rimase⌐ñ desita ⌐ne⌐e.
7.	That small dictionary wasn't too bad, was it!	Sono ti⌐isa⌐i zi⌐biki⌐ wa a⌐ñmari wa⌐ruku a⌐rimase⌐ñ desita ⌐ne⌐e.
8.	That cheap dictionary wasn't too bad, was it!	Sono ya⌐su⌐i zi⌐biki⌐ wa a⌐ñmari wa⌐ruku a⌐rimase⌐ñ desita ⌐ne⌐e.

D. Response Drill (based on Grammatical Note 3)

(Give the _iie_ answer for each of the following.)

1. A⌐no tabako de┐sita ka⌐   Iie, a⌐no tabako zya arimase┐ñ desita.
2. Zi┐syo desita ka⌐   Iie, zi┐syo zya a┌rimase┐ñ desita.
3. Ki┐ree desita ka⌐   Iie, ki┐ree zya a┌rimase┐ñ desita.
4. Ho⌐ñtoo de┐sita ka⌐   Iie, ho⌐ñtoo zya arimase┐ñ d e s i t a.
5. Ta⌐naka-sañ de┐sita ka⌐   Iie, Ta⌐naka-sañ zya arimase┐ñ de-
                                  sita.
6. Hya⌐ku-eñ de┐sita ka⌐   Iie, hya⌐ku-eñ zya arimase┐ñ desita.
7. Ki⌐no┐o desita ka⌐   Iie, ki⌐no┐o zya a┌rimase┐ñ desita.
8. O⌐nazi de┐sita ka⌐   Iie, o⌐nazi zya arimase┐ñ desita.

E. Response Drill (based on Grammatical Note 3)

(Give the _iie_ answer for each of the following, using the adjectival pattern.)

1. O⌐mosiro┐i za┌ssi de┐sita   Iie, o⌐mosi┐roku a┌rimase┐ñ desita.
   ka⌐
2. Ya⌐su┐i ha┌iza┐ra desita ka⌐ Iie, ya┐suku a┌rimase┐ñ desita.
3. O⌐oki┐i zi┌biki┐ desita ka⌐ Iie, o┐okiku a┌rimase┐ñ desita.
4. I┐i ┌ho┐ñ desita ka⌐   Iie, yo┐ku a┌rimase┐ñ desita.
5. Tu⌐mara┐nai za┌ssi de┐sita   Iie, tu⌐mara┐naku a┌rimase┐ñ desita.
   ka⌐
6. Ta⌐ka┐i ta┌bako de┐sita ka⌐ Iie, ta┐kaku a┌rimase┐ñ desita.
7. A┌tarasi┐i si┌ñbuñ de┐sita ka⌐ Iie, a┌tara┐siku a┌rimase┐ñ desita.
8. Ti⌐isa┐i zi┌biki┐ desita ka⌐ Iie, ti┐isaku a┌rimase┐ñ desita.
9. Wa⌐ru┐i ┌ho┐ñ desita ka⌐   Iie, wa┐ruku a┌rimase┐ñ desita.
10. Hu⌐ru┐i si┌ñbuñ de┐sita ka⌐ Iie, hu┐ruku a┌rimase┐ñ desita.

F. Grammar Drill (based on Grammatical Note 2)

Tutor: Ko⌐no ho┐ñ wa ta⌐ka┐i desu ┌ne┐e. 'Isn't this book expensive!'
Student: Kore wa ta⌐ka┐i desu ┌ne┐e.   'Isn't this expensive!'

1. Ko⌐no pe┐ñ wa ya⌐su┐i desu   Kore wa ya⌐su┐i desu ┌ne┐e.
   ┌ne┐e.
2. So⌐no zibiki┐ wa ta⌐ka┐i desu Sore wa ta⌐ka┐i desu yo⌐
   yo⌐
3. A⌐no haiza┐ra wa ┌i┐kura   Are wa ┌i┐kura desita ka⌐
   desita ka⌐
4. Do┐no za┌ssi de┐su ka⌐   Do┐re desu ka⌐
5. Sono eñpitu wa da⌐me┐ desu   Sore wa da⌐me┐ desu ka⌐
   ka⌐
6. Ano siñbuñ wa hu⌐ru┐i desu   Are wa hu⌐ru┐i desu yo⌐
   yo⌐
7. Ko⌐no ho┐ñ wa o⌐mosiro┐i   Kore wa o⌐mosiro┐i desu ┌ne┐e.
   desu ┌ne┐e.

G. Expansion Drill

1. It's pretty.   Ki┐ree desu.
   Isn't it pretty!   Ki┐ree desu ┌ne┐e.
   Isn't the ashtray pretty! Ha⌐iza┐ra wa ┌ki┐ree desu ┌ne┐e.
   Isn't that ashtray pretty! So⌐no haiza┐ra wa ┌ki┐ree desu ┌ne┐e.

2. How much was it? Iˈkura desita ka⌐
How much was the dictionary? Ziˈbikiˈ wa ˈiˈkura desita ka⌐
How much was the big dictionary? Oˈokiˈi ziˈbikiˈ wa ˈiˈkura desita ka⌐
How much was this big dictionary? Kono oˈokiˈi ziˈbikiˈ wa ˈiˈkura desita ka⌐

3. It isn't expensive. Taˈkaku aˈrimaseˈñ.
It wasn't expensive. Taˈkaku aˈrimaseˈñ desita.
It wasn't very expensive. Aˈñmari taˈkaku aˈrimaseˈñ desita.
This book wasn't very expensive. Koˈno hoˈñ wa aˈñmari taˈkaku aˈrimaseˈñ desita.

4. It isn't true. Hoˈñtoo zya arimaseˈñ.
It wasn't true. Hoˈñtoo zya arimaseˈñ desita.
That wasn't true. Sore wa hoˈñtoo zya arimaseˈñ desita.
You know, that wasn't true! Sore wa hoˈñtoo zya arimaseˈñ desita yo⌐

SUPPLEMENTARY CONVERSATION

Smith: (Pointing) Oˈneḡai-simaˈsu.
Clerk: Koˈre deˈsu ka⌐
Smith: Eˈe.
Clerk: Doˈozo.
Smith: Iˈkura desu ka⌐
Clerk: Niˈseñ-eñ deˈsu.
Smith: Tyoˈtto taˈkaˈi desu ˈneˈe.
Clerk: (Showing another one) Koˈre wa yasuˈi desu. (Checking price tag) Seˈñ nihyakuˈ-eñ desu.
Smith: Aˈa, koˈre wa iˈi desu ˈneˈe. Oˈneḡai-simaˈsu. (Handing over money) Seˈñ nihyakuˈ-eñ. Haˈi.
Clerk: Aˈriˈḡatoo gozaimasu.

English Equivalent

Smith: May I see that, please? (Lit. I make a request.)
Clerk: (Do you mean) this one?
Smith: Yes.
Clerk: Here you are.
Smith: How much is it?
Clerk: (It's) ¥ 2000.
Smith: It's a little expensive, isn't it.
Clerk: This one is cheap. . . . It's ¥ 1200.
Smith: Oh, this one is fine! I'll take it. Here you are. ¥ 1200.
Clerk: Thank you.

EXERCISES

1. Read the following in Japanese:

a. 27   c. 604
b. 64   d. 358

e.	891	m.	3,456,789
f.	3,487	n.	7,250,000
g.	8,926	o.	10,500,000
h.	6,044	p.	¥360
i.	10,000	q.	¥1,800
j.	23,487	r.	¥36,000
k.	46,020	s.	¥650,000
l.	321,321	t.	¥1,000,000

2. The customer asks the price of the following objects and the clerk answers with the price indicated:

    a. those cigarettes.   (¥40)
    b. this ashtray.   (¥350)
    c. these matches.   (¥2)
    d. that pen over there.   (¥1000)
    e. that small dictionary.   (¥400)
    f. that big book.   (¥1800)

3. You ask: Tanaka-san answers:

    a. if this book is interesting.   No, it isn't very interesting.

    b. if that book was ¥350.   No, it was ¥450.

    c. if these cigarettes are ¥40.   Which cigarettes do you mean?

    d. if that thing over there is a pen.   No, it's a pencil.

    e. if these books are the same.   No, they're different.

    f. if this pen was ¥2500.   Yes, that's right.

    g. if that pencil is ¥10.   No, it's ¥15.

    h. if these pens are different.   Yes, they are.

    i. if that is a good pen.   No, it's not very good.

    j. if it was an expensive dictionary.   No, it wasn't very expensive.

4. Practice the Basic Dialogues with variations and appropriate props.

Lesson 4. Shopping (cont.)

BASIC DIALOGUES: FOR MEMORIZATION

(a)

Clerk

1. Welcome! I⌐rassya¹i. or
I⌐rassyaima¹se.

Smith

furoshiki (cloth square for wrapping)	hurosiki
furoshiki (as direct object)	hurosiki o
show or let [someone] see	mi⌐sema¹su
please show or please let [someone] see	mi¹sete kudasai

2. Please show [me] that furoshiki over there. A⌐no hurosiki (o) mi¹sete kudasai.

Clerk

is red	akai /-ku/[1]
red one(s)	a⌐ka¹i no

3. Do you mean the red one? Here you are. A⌐ka¹i no desu ka⌐ Do¹ozo.

Smith

is blue or green	a⌐o¹i /-ku/
blue one(s)	a⌐o¹i no
blue one(s) too	a⌐o¹i no mo

4. Please show me that blue one too. Sono a⌐o¹i no mo ᒷmi⌐sete kudasai.

(. . . looking them over)

a little or a few	su⌐ko¹si
a little more or a few more	mo⌐o suko¹si
big one(s)	o⌐oki¹i no
little bigger ones (as emphatic subject)	mo⌐o suko¹si o⌐oki¹i no ḡa
be necessary or need or want	i⌐rima¹su
[I] need but	i⌐rima¹su ḡa

5. I need a little bigger one but. . . Mo⌐o suko¹si o⌐oki¹i no ḡa i⌐rima¹su ḡa⌐

---

[1] This is the first example of an unaccented adjectival: akai, akaku, akai hurosiki, but a⌐ka¹i desu, a⌐ka¹i no.

37

Clerk (showing a third one)

is yellow	kiiroi /-ku/
yellow one(s)	ki⌈iro⌉i no
as for a yellow one	ki⌈iro⌉i no wa
how?	i⌈ka⌉ḡa +

6. How about this yellow one?   Kono ki⌈iro⌉i no (wa) i⌈ka⌉ḡa desu ka⌐
   or How is this yellow one?

Smith

7. Let me see. . . .   or   So⌉o desu ⌈ne⌉e.
   Hmmm. . . .

it's pretty but	ki⌉ree desu ḡa

8. It's pretty but I'm afraid it   Ki⌉ree desu ḡa, tyo⌉tto—
   won't do. . . (Lit. It's pretty
   but a bit. . .)

oh well or I guess	ma⌉a
this one (as direct object)	kore o
please give me	ku⌈dasa⌉i

9. Oh well, I'll take (lit. give me)   Ma⌉a, ko⌈re (o) kudasa⌉i.
   this one.

after that or and then or	sore kara
and	
red one(s) too	a⌈ka⌉i no mo

10. And give me this red one too.   Sore kara, kono a⌈ka⌉i no mo kudasai.

Clerk

in addition	hoka ni
something or anything	na⌉ni ka

11. Anything else?   Ho⌈ka ni na⌉ni ka?

Smith

just that	so⌈re dake⌉

12. That's all.   So⌈re dake⌉ desu.

13. Here you are — ¥1000.   Ha⌉i señ-eñ.

Clerk

a little	syo⌉osyoo +
please wait	o⌈mati-kudasa⌉i or
	o⌈mati-kudasaima⌉se

14. Just a moment, please.   Syo⌉osyoo o⌈mati-kudasa⌉i.   or
                                      Syo⌉osyoo o⌈mati-kudasaima⌉se.

(. . . returning with the wrapped package)

15. I'm sorry to have kept you   O⌈matase-itasima⌉sita. ↓
    waiting.

every time	maido

16. Thank you (again and again).   Ma⌈ido ari⌉ḡatoo gozaimasu.

	again	mata
17.	Please [come] again.	Maˤta doˈozo.

(b)

Smith

18.	Say there!	Tyoˈtto_
	ashtray (as emphatic subject)	ˈhaˤizaˈra ḡa
	be in a place (of inanimate objects) or have	aˤrimaˈsu or goˤzaimaˈsu +
19.	Are there any ashtrays? or Do you have any ashtrays?	Haˤizaˈra (ḡa) aˤrimaˈsu ka⌐

Clerk

	yes	haˈa+
20.	Yes, there are. or Yes, I have. Here you are.	Haˈa, goˤzaimaˈsu. Doˈozo.

Smith

	is black	kuˤroˈi /-ku/
	black one(s)	kuˤroˈi no
	black one(s) (as direct object)	kuˤroˈi no o
21.	Please show me that black one.	Sono kuˤroˈi no (o) ˥mi˩sete kudasai.
	is white	siˤroˈi /-ku/
	white one(s) too	siˤroˈi no mo
22.	And please show me that white one, too.	Sore kara, sono siˤroˈi no mo ˥mi˩sete kudasai.

. . .

23.	I'll take this black one.	Kono kuˤroˈi no (o) kudasai.

Clerk

	as for the white one	siˤroˈi no wa
24.	How about the white one?	Siˤroˈi no wa iˤka˩ḡa desu ka⌐

Smith

	as for that one	sore wa
25.	That one I don't want.	Soˤre wa irimaseˈn.

Clerk

26.	Certainly. (I.e. I have understood your request and will do as you ask.)	Kaˤsikomarimaˈsita. ↓

(c)

Smith

	what (as direct object)?	naˈni o
	buy	kaˤimaˈsu

27. What did you buy?   Na⌐ni (o) ka⌐ima⌐sita ka⌐

                          Tanaka

      book and magazine   ho⌐ñ to za͞ssi
      book and magazine (as   ho⌐ñ to za͞ssi o
        direct object)
28. I bought a book and a magazine.   Ho⌐ñ to za⌐ssi (o) kaima⌐sita.

                          Smith

29. What about a newspaper?   Siñbuñ wa?

                          Tanaka

      oh!   a
      forget   wa⌐surema⌐su
30. Oh, I forgot. I'm sorry.   A. Wa⌐surema⌐sita. Su⌐mimase⌐ñ.

      as for a newspaper   siñbuñ wa
31. I didn't buy a newspaper.   Siñbuñ wa ka⌐imase⌐ñ desita.

                          Smith

      later   a⌐to de
32. Well then, would you [get it]   Zya⌐a, a⌐to de onegai-simasu.
        later?

      match (as emphatic sub-   ma⌐tti g͞a
        ject)
33. Say, have you got a match?   Tyo⌐tto, ma⌐tti (g͞a) a⌐rima⌐su ka⌐

                          Tanaka

      as for a match   ma⌐tti wa
      there isn't but or I don't   a⌐rimase⌐ñ g͞a
        have but
      lighter   ra⌐itaa
      lighter (as emphatic sub-   ra⌐itaa g͞a
        ject)
34. A match I don't have but I have   Ma⌐tti wa a⌐rimase⌐ñ g͞a, ra⌐itaa g͞a
      a lighter. Here you are.   arimasu. Do⌐ozo.

NOTES ON THE BASIC DIALOGUES

1. I⌐rassya⌐i and i⌐rassyaima⌐se, imperatives of the honorific verbal i⌐ras-
    syaima⌐su 'come,' are regularly used for greeting a customer entering a
    store, restaurant, inn, etc., and also for welcoming a guest to one's home.
    The form with -ma⌐se, which is formal, is used by women and by male em-
    ployees of shops, restaurants, hotels, etc.

2. A furoshiki is a square of silk or cotton—or, more recently, plastic—used
    for wrapping packages which are to be hand-carried.

4. A⌐o⌐i covers that portion of the spectrum which includes both the 'blue' and
    'green' of English. Additional Japanese color words of more limited mean-
    ing will be introduced later.

5. With the meaning 'a little' or 'a few,' su⌐ko⌐si and tyo⌐tto are interchangeable, except that tyo⌐tto is less formal; but only tyo⌐tto is used as a means
of attracting attention (sentence 18) and as a polite refusal (sentence 8).

The affirmative forms of i⌐rima⌐su more often mean 'need' and the negative forms 'not want' (sentence 25).

6. I⌐ka⌐ga is a more polite equivalent of do⌐o which occurs in a more limited
number of constructions. Both are used in suggestions and in inquiring
how something or someone is. Thus, X (wa) $\left\{\begin{array}{l}\text{⌐do⌐o} \\ \text{i⌐ka⌐ga}\end{array}\right\}$ desu ka 'how about
X?' or 'how is X?'

7. Context, intonation, and/or rhythm make it possible to distinguish between
so⌐o desu ⌐ne⌐e 'that's right, isn't it,' 'isn't that true!' and so⌐o desu ⌐ne⌐e
'hmmm . . .' The latter is often pronounced so⌐oo desu ⌐ne⌐ee.

8. Tyo⌐tto is an indirect, hesitant—and polite—refusal of a suggestion, request, or invitation.

9. Ma⌐a indicates that what follows is said after some hesitation or with some
reluctance.

14. Syo⌐osyoo is a more polite equivalent of su⌐ko⌐si which occurs commonly
in this sentence. O⌐mati-kudasa⌐i is a more polite equivalent of ma⌐tte
kudasai. The formal -ma⌐se alternant is used most often by women.
(Compare the two alternants of sentence 1.)

15. O⌐matase-itasima⌐sita is a humble (↓) word meaning literally 'I have caused
you to wait.'

16. Ma⌐ido ari⌐gatoo gozaimasu is commonly used only by shopkeepers, clerks,
restaurant employees, etc.

18. Tyo⌐tto is an informal word used to attract attention.

20. Ha⌐a is a polite equivalent of ha⌐i which occurs in the same kinds of patterns.

26. Ka⌐sikomarima⌐sita means 'certainly—I have understood what you want me
to do' (never 'certainly—that's right'). It is addressed to a superior: for
example, an employer or a customer.

GRAMMATICAL NOTES

1. Particles: ga, o, wa, mo, to

There is a class of uninflected (i.e. non-changing) Japanese words which
occur within or at the end of a sentence, but never at the beginning. They are
never preceded by pause but rather they are regularly pronounced as though
they were part of the word before them. Within sentences, they relate what
precedes to what follows. At the end of sentences, they color the meaning of
the sentence as a whole, making it into a question, an exclamation, an emphatic
statement, etc. All such words are PARTICLES. Those that regularly occur
at the end of sentences—like question particle ka and emphatic particle yo—are
SENTENCE PARTICLES.

Japanese particles often correspond to English prepositions. Many times, however, they are reflected instead in a particular word order or stress-intonation pattern in English; and sometimes there is nothing that specifically corresponds to them in a natural English equivalent.

(a) g̱a

(1) When preceded by a non-past or past inflected word (i.e. verbal, or adjectival, or copula), g̱a marks a major division within a sentence: often it connects two sequences which are in contrast (corresponding to English 'but'); many times it separates a statement of fact from a related question or request (in which case, the most natural English equivalent is two inde-pendent sentences instead of two clauses with a connective).

Examples:

Ta⌐naka-sañ wa ikima⌐sita g̱a, Ya⌐mamoto-sañ wa ikimase⌐n̄ desita. 'Mr.Tanaka went but Mr. Yamamoto didn't go.'
Ya⌐su⌐i desu g̱a, ki⌐ree desu. 'It's cheap but it's pretty.'
Ko⌐re wa ki⌐ree desu g̱a, so⌐re wa ki⌐ree zya a⌐rimase⌐n̄. 'This is pretty but that isn't (pretty).'
O⌐mosiro⌐i ⌐ho⌐n̄ g̱a a⌐rima⌐su g̱a, i⌐ka⌐g̱a desu ka⌄ 'I have an inter-esting book. How about [reading] it?'

(2) G̱a preceded by a nominal singles out the nominal as the subject[1] of a following inflected expression. Observe the location of the emphasis in the English equivalents.

Examples:

Ta⌐naka-sañ g̱a sima⌐sita. 'MR. TANAKA did [it].' (tells who did it)
Ko⌐re g̱a atarasi⌐i desu. 'THIS is new.' (tells which one is new)
So⌐re g̱a dame⌐ desu. 'THAT's out of order.' (tells which one is out of order)

(b) o̱

The particle o̱ singles out the preceding nominal as the direct object[1] of a following inflected expression. Note the location of the emphasis in the English equivalents.

Examples:

So⌐re o kudasa⌐i. 'Give me THAT.' (tells which one I want)
Ra⌐itaa o ⌐mi⌐sete kudasai. 'Please show me some LIGHTERS.' (tells what I want to see)
Ta⌐bako o oneg̱ai-sima⌐su. 'I'd like a CIGARETTE.' (tells what I want to have)
Hu⌐rosiki o kaima⌐sita. 'I bought a FUROSHIKI.' (tells what I bought)

---

[1] The subject tells who or what does or is something, and the direct object tells who or what is directly acted upon. Thus, in 'Bill called John,' 'Bill' is the subject and 'John' the direct object; in 'John called Bill,' 'John' is the sub-ject and 'Bill' the direct object.

(c) <u>wa</u>

The particle <u>wa</u> 'as for,' 'in reference to' following a nominal occurs in two kinds of constructions:

(1) It follows the general topic (often one already under discussion) about which something new or significant is about to be stated or asked:[1] <u>X wa</u> 'I am talking about X—listen to what I am about to say'; 'as for X, the following is significant.'

Examples:

Tabako wa a⌐rimase⌐n. 'There AREN'T any cigarettes.' (in answer to the question 'Are there any cigarettes?'; i.e. 'I'm talking about cigarettes: what I want to say is that there AREN'T any.')

Sore wa ta⌐ka⌐i desu yo⌐ 'That one is EXPENSIVE, you know.' (i.e. 'I'm talking about that: what I want to say is that it's EXPENSIVE.')

Kore wa ⌐ra⌐itaa desu. 'This is a LIGHTER.' (i.e. 'I'm talking about this: what I want to say is that it's a LIGHTER.')

(2) <u>Wa</u> also occurs as the particle of comparison following a topic which is being compared:[2] <u>X wa</u> 'X in comparison with others' or 'insofar as we're talking about X.'

Examples:

Ta⌐bako wa arimase⌐n. ' Cigarettes I don't have.'

So⌐re wa taka⌐i desu yo⌐ 'That one (in comparison with others) is expensive, you know.'

Ko⌐re wa ra⌐itaa desu. 'This (in comparison with others) is a lighter.'

Note: <u>Wa</u> NEVER follows an interrogative word (i.e. a word that asks a question: 'what?' 'who?' 'when?' 'where?'etc.) and it NEVER follows the word or phrase that answers an interrogative word in a preceding question.

Now compare the following pairs:

Ma⌐tti ḡa a⌐rimase⌐n. 'There aren't any MATCHES.' (tells what is lacking)

Ma⌐tti wa a⌐rimase⌐n. 'There AREN'T any matches.' (answers the question 'Are there any matches?')

Ko⌐re ḡa aka⌐i desu. 'THIS is red.' (tells which one is red)

Kore wa a⌐ka⌐i desu. 'This is RED.' (tells what color this is)

---

[1] In this construction, the word after <u>wa</u> regularly begins a new accent phrase. (See Introduction, page xxxv.)

[2] In this construction, the word after <u>wa</u> often does not begin a new accent phrase. (See Introduction, page xxxv.)

Ta⌐bako o kaima⌐sita.   'I bought CIGARETTES.'   (tells what I bought)
Ta⌐bako wa kaima⌐sita.   'Cigarettes I bought.' (tells what happened to
cigarettes in comparison with other things)

Si⌐ñbuñ o wasurema⌐sita. 'I forgot the NEWSPAPER.' (tells what I forgot)
Si⌐ñbuñ wa wasurema⌐sita. 'The newspaper I forgot.' (tells what happened
to the newspaper in comparison with other things)

A phrase ending with <u>wa</u> usually occurs at, or near, the beginning of the
sentence. A phrase ending with subject particle <u>ḡa</u> usually precedes one ending
with <u>o</u>. However, a departure from the usual order changes only the emphasis.

Now study and compare the following examples.

Tanaka-sañ wa ⌐ho⌐ñ o ka⌐ima⌐sita. 'Mr. Tanaka bought a BOOK.' (tells
what Mr. Tanaka bought)
Tanaka-sañ ḡa ⌐ho⌐ñ o ka⌐ima⌐sita.   'MR. TANAKA bought a BOOK.'
(tells who bought what)
Ho⌐ñ wa Ta⌐naka-sañ ḡa kaima⌐sita.   'MR. TANAKA bought the book.'
(tells who bought the book being talked about)

There are some verbals which may occur with both a <u>wa</u> and a <u>ḡa</u> phrase but
never with an <u>o</u> phrase.   Three such verbals have already been introduced:
<u>wa⌐karima⌐su</u> 'understand' or 'be clear'; <u>a⌐rima⌐su</u> 'be in a place' or 'have';
<u>i⌐rima⌐su</u> 'need' or 'be necessary.' With all such verbals, both the person who
understands (has, needs, etc.) and the thing or person affected are followed by
<u>wa</u> or <u>ḡa</u>, depending on emphasis.   Note the following examples of some of the
possible combinations:

Ta⌐naka-sañ ḡa irima⌐su. 'MR. TANAKA needs [it].'
Pe⌐ñ ḡa irimasu. 'I need a PEN.'
Tanaka-sañ wa ⌐pe⌐ñ ḡa irimasu. 'Mr. Tanaka needs a PEN.'
Pe⌐ñ wa Ta⌐naka-sañ ḡa irima⌐su. 'The pen, MR. TANAKA needs.'
Ko⌐re ḡa wakarimase⌐ñ. 'I don't understand THIS.'
Ko⌐re wa Tanaka-sañ wa wakarima⌐su. 'This (in comparison with others)
Mr. Tanaka (in comparison with others) UNDERSTANDS.'
Tanaka-sañ wa zi⌐biki⌐ ḡa a⌐rimase⌐ñ. 'Mr. Tanaka doesn't have a DIC-
TIONARY.'

Ḡa, <u>wa</u>, and <u>o</u> are frequently omitted, [1] particularly in short
sentences; the result is a slightly less formal alternant. (Watch the parentheses
in the Basic Dialogues and note where these particles are optional.)

(d) <u>mo</u>

The particle <u>mo</u> following a nominal means 'also,' 'too,' or—with a negative —'/not/ either.' A phrase ending in <u>mo</u> occurs as the subject or object or
topic of a following inflected expression, without particles ga, o, wa.

_____

[1] But the <u>wa</u> of comparison is rarely omitted.

Examples:

Ta⌐naka-sañ mo ikima˥sita. 'Mr. Tanaka went too.'
Ta⌐naka-sañ mo wasurema˥sita. 'Mr. Tanaka forgot too.' or 'I forgot
Mr. Tanaka, too.'
Ko⌐re mo i˥i desu. 'This is good, too.'
So⌐re mo so˥o desu. 'That's right, too.'
Ko⌐re mo wakarimase˥ñ. 'I don't understand this either.'

(e) <u>to</u>

The particle <u>to</u> 'and' joins nominals (which may be preceded by descriptive
phrases. It does not regularly join verbals or adjectivals.

Examples:

ta⌐bako to ma˥tti 'cigarettes and matches'
kore to sore 'this and that'
a⌐na˥ta to Tānaka-sañ 'you and Mr. Tanaka'
ho˥ñ to zǎssi to siñbuñ 'a book and a magazine and a newspaper'
o⌐oki˥i zi⌐biki⌐ to ti⌐isa˥i ⌐ho˥ñ 'a big dictionary and a small book'

A series of two or more nominals joined by <u>to</u> occurs in the same kinds of
constructions as a nominal alone. Thus:

Ta⌐bako to ma˥tti o ku⌐dasa⌐i. 'Please give me a cigarette and match.'
Tanaka-sañ to Ya⌐mamoto-sañ de˥su. 'It's Mr. Tanaka and Mr. Yamamoto.'
Ho˥ñ to zǎssi to siñbuñ ḡa arima˥su. 'There's a book and a magazine
and a newspaper.'

2. a⌐rima˥su ~ go⌐zaima˥su

A⌐rima˥su and go⌐zaima˥su, meaning 'some THING is located in a place' or
'have,' are verbals of identical lexical meaning, but a⌐rima˥su is plain and
go⌐zaima˥su is polite-neutral.[1]

An utterance containing √a⌐rima˥su may be made more polite by substituting
√go⌐zaima˥su in its corresponding form. The reverse, however, is not always
true: some utterances containing √go⌐zaima˥su do not occur with a corresponding form of √a⌐rima˥su (for example, o⌐hayoo gozaima˥su).

In general, persons of equal status in the Japanese social structure use the
same politeness and formality level in conversing. Which level they use is determined by the formality of the situation and of the individuals involved as
well as by the closeness of their friendship. In conversations between persons
occupying different positions in the social scale (for example, employer and
employee, customer and salesgirl, etc.), the person of lower position usually

---

[1] Both are formal because of their -<u>ma˥su</u> endings.

uses a more polite and/or formal level of speech.[1] In general, women use polite speech more commonly than men; √go‾zaima‾su, for example, is much more typical of women's speech than of men's.

It is important to distinguish carefully between the use of nominal + √a‾rima‾su and nominal + √de‾su. Note the following contrasts:

Affirmative	Negative
Zi⌐biki⌐ (g̃a) arimasu.	Zi⌐biki⌐ (g̃a) a⌐rimase⌐ñ.
'There's a DICTIONARY.'	'There isn't a DICTIONARY.'
or 'I have a DICTIONARY.'	or 'I don't have a DICTIONARY.'
Zi⌐biki⌐ wa arimasu.	Zi⌐biki⌐ wa a⌐rimase⌐ñ.
'There is a dictionary (in	'There isn't a dictionary (in com-
comparison with other things).'	parison with other things).' or
or 'A dictionary I have.'	'A dictionary I don't have.'
Zi⌐biki⌐ desu.	Zi⌐biki⌐ zya a⌐rimase⌐ñ.
'It's a dictionary.'	'It isn't a dictionary.'

In each column the first two examples express existence or location in a place, or possession; the last example expresses equivalence or definition.

3. ku⌐dasa⌐i and Verbal Gerunds

Ku⌐dasa⌐i is the imperative of the verbal ku⌐dasaima⌐su⌐ '[someone] gives me.' Since it is a polite word, the imperative is often translated as 'please give me' and the -ma‾su form as '[someone] is kind enough to give me.'

In addition to the four inflected forms described in Lesson 1, verbals have a form ending in -te (or -de). This form will be called the GERUND or, more simply, the -TE FORM.

	Formal Non-Past	Gerund
'be (inanimate)' or 'have'	a⌐rima‾su	a‾tte
'say'	i⌐ima‾su	itte
'go'	i⌐kima‾su	itte
'need'	i⌐rima‾su	itte
'buy'	ka⌐ima‾su	katte
'wait'	ma⌐tima‾su	ma‾tte
'show'	mi⌐sema‾su	mi‾sete
'do'	si⌐ma‾su	site
'be different'	ti⌐g̃aima‾su	tig̃atte
'understand'	wa⌐karima‾su	wa⌐ka‾tte
'forget'	wa⌐surema‾su	wasurete

---

[1] This, of course, is not necessarily reflected in every part of the conversation but refers to the over-all level.

A verbal in its gerund form + ku⌐dasa¬i is a polite imperative expression. Ku⌐dasa¬i regularly loses its accent when the preceding word or phrase is accented. Examples:

mi⌐sema¬su '[I] show'	mi¬sete kudasai 'please show'
	[lit. 'please give me showing']
ka⌐ima¬su '[I] buy'	ka⌐tte kudasa¬i 'please buy'
ma⌐tima¬su '[I] wait'	ma¬tte kudasai 'please wait'
i⌐ima¬su '[I] say'	i⌐tte kudasa¬i 'please say'
i⌐kima¬su '[I] go'	i⌐tte kudasa¬i 'please go' [1]
si⌐ma¬su '[I] do'	si⌐te kudasa¬i 'please do'

The -te form has other uses which will be introduced later.

Ku⌐dasa¬i may also be preceded by a nominal (+ o):[2] E⌐ṅpitu (o) kudasa¬i. 'Please give me a pencil.'

O⌐mati-kudasa¬i, in Basic Sentence 14, is an example of another ku⌐dasa¬i pattern which will be discussed in a later lesson. It is equivalent to ma⌐tte ku-dasai except that it is more polite. Ku⌐dasaima¬se is a formal equivalent of ku⌐dasa¬i and is used most commonly by women.

4. no 'one(s)'

The no introduced in this lesson[3] is a nominal meaning 'one' or 'ones.' Like its English equivalents, it is used to refer to something or someone whose specific identity is known from the context. Thus, Japanese ya⌐su¬i no (o) ka⌐i-ma⁴sita and its English equivalents 'I bought a cheap one' or 'I bought cheap ones' are used when the objects referred to are known.

Unlike the nominals which have occurred previously, no is always preceded by a modifier. An adjectival preceding no is always accented, as it is before √de¬su: an unaccented adjectival acquires an accent on its pre-final syllable (cf. akai, but a⌐ka¬i no and a⌐ka¬i desu).

5. Fragments

All Japanese sentences which consist of, or end with, a past or non-past or imperative⁴ inflected form, with or without one or more sentence particles

---

[1] I⌐tte kudasa¬i 'please say' and i⌐tte kudasa¬i 'please go' are distinguished in the spoken language only by context.

[2] See Grammatical Note 1 above.

[3] See Basic Sentences 3, 4, 5, 6, 10, 21, 22, 23, 24.

[4] Or tentative (to be introduced later).

immediately following, are MAJOR SENTENCES.   All other sentences are
MINOR SENTENCES or FRAGMENTS.   Some of the fragments that have ap-
peared are: Koñbañ wa. Tyo˩tto. Ha˩i.

In conversational Japanese, a sentence may end in the middle of what would
be a major sentence if a portion of the preceding context were repeated and the
complete meaning is clear to the hearer; such utterances are also fragments.
Examples:

Na˩ni (o) ka˥ima⁻˩sita ka↲ 'What did you buy?'
    Siñbuñ (o). 'A newspaper.' (i.e. S˥iñbuñ (o) kaima˩sita. 'I bought a
    newspaper.')

Ta˥ka˩i desu ˥ne˩e. 'It's expensive, isn't it.'
    E˩e, zu˩ibuñ. 'Yes, very.' (i.e. E˩e, zu˩ibuñ ta˥ka⁻˩i desu. 'Yes, it's
    very expensive.')

Ta˥naka-sañ wa wakarima˩sita. A˥na˩ta wa? (i.e. A˥na˩ta wa wa˥karima⁻˩sita
    ka↲) 'Mr. Takana understood. How about you? (i.e. As for you, was
    there understanding?)'

Particularly common are fragments ending with ḡa 'but.' In some cases,
the ḡa implies a specific contrast to be supplied by the listener, as:

Si˥ñbuñ to zassi o kaima˩sita ka↲   'Did you buy a newspaper and a maga-
    zine?'
Si˥ñbuñ wa kaima˩sita ḡa– 'A newspaper I bought but [I didn't buy a maga-
    zine].'

Many times, however, X ḡa is simply a softer, more hesitant, less positive
way of saying X—indicating for example 'so-and-so is the case but. . . is that
all right? or should I do anything about it? or do you want to say something
different? or why do you ask? etc. In contrast with sentence-final yo, which
indicates finality and assurance on the part of the speaker, final ḡa is indirect
and polite. Often, the closest English equivalent of this ḡa is an intonation expressing hesitation.

Examples:

Ma˩tti o kudasai. 'Please give me a match.'
    A˥rimase˩ñ ḡa– 'I haven't any but [do you want me to get some?]'

Ko˥re wa irimase˩ñ. So˥re o kudasa˩i. 'I don't want this one. Give me that
    one.'
    O˥nazi de˩su ḡa– 'It's the same but [I'll give it to you if you want it].'

Ta˥naka-sañ de˩su ka↲ 'Are you Mr. Tanaka?'
    E˩e, Ta˥naka de˩su ḡa– 'Yes, I'm Tanaka but [what would you like? or
    why do you ask?]'

DRILLS

A. Substitution Drill

1.	Do you have a furoshiki?	Hu⌐rosiki (g̃a) arima⌐su ka⌐
2.	Do you have a lighter?	Ra⌐itaa (g̃a) a⌐rima⌐su ka⌐
3.	Do you have a match?	Ma⌐tti (g̃a) a⌐rima⌐su ka⌐
4.	Do you have a cigarette?	Ta⌐bako (g̃a) arima⌐su ka⌐
5.	Do you have an ashtray?	Ha⌐iza⌐ra (g̃a) a⌐rima⌐su ka⌐
6.	Do you have a pencil?	E⌐ñpitu (g̃a) arima⌐su ka⌐
7.	Do you have a pen?	Pe⌐ñ (g̃a) a⌐rima⌐su ka⌐
8.	Do you have a dictionary?	Zi⌐syo (g̃a) a⌐rima⌐su ka⌐

B. Substitution Drill

1.	Please give me that furoshiki over there.	A⌐no hurosiki (o) kudasa⌐i.
2.	Please give me that lighter.	So⌐no ra⌐itaa (o) kudasai.
3.	Please give me those matches over there.	A⌐no ma⌐tti (o) kudasai.
4.	Please give me those cigarettes.	So⌐no tabako (o) kudasa⌐i.
5.	Please give me that ashtray over there.	A⌐no haiza⌐ra (o) kudasai.
6.	Please give me that pencil.	So⌐no eñpitu (o) kudasa⌐i.
7.	Please give me that pen over there.	A⌐no pe⌐ñ (o) kudasai.
8.	Please give me that dictionary.	So⌐no zi⌐syo (o) kudasai.
9.	Please give me that book over there.	A⌐no ho⌐ñ (o) kudasai.
10.	Please give me that newspaper.	So⌐no siñbuñ (o) kudasa⌐i.

C. Substitution Drill

1.	Please let me see that blue furoshiki.	Sono a⌐o⌐i hurosiki (o) ⌐mi⌐sete kudasai.
2.	Please let me see that small dictionary over there.	Ano ti⌐isa⌐i zi⌐biki⌐ (o) ⌐mi⌐sete kudasai.
3.	Please let me see that big book.	Sono o⌐oki⌐i ⌐ho⌐ñ (o) ⌐mi⌐sete kudasai.
4.	Please let me see that white ashtray over there.	Ano si⌐ro⌐i ha⌐iza⌐ra (o) ⌐mi⌐sete kudasai.
5.	Please let me see that new magazine.	Sono a⌐tarasi⌐i zassi (o) ⌐mi⌐sete kudasai.
6.	Please let me see that black pen over there.	Ano ku⌐ro⌐i ⌐pe⌐ñ (o) ⌐mi⌐sete kudasai.

7. Please let me see that red   Sono aᴿkai eñpitu (o) miˀsete kudasai.
    pencil.
8. Please let me see that old   Ano huᴿruˀi siñbuñ (o) ᴴmiˀsete kuda-
    newspaper over there.   sai.

D. Substitution Drill

(Make whatever particle changes are necessary.)

1. What did you buy?   Naˀni (o) kaᴴimaˀsita ka⌐
2. What did you do?   Naˀni (o) siᴴmaˀsita ka⌐
3. What did you forget?   Naˀni (o) waᴿsuremaˀsita ka⌐
4. What do you need?   Naˀni (g̃a) iᴿrimaˀsu ka⌐
5. What do you have? or   Naˀni (g̃a) aᴿrimaˀsu ka⌐
    What is there?
6. What don't you understand?   Naˀni (g̃a) waᴴkarimaseˀñ ka⌐
7. Which one don't you under-   Doˀre (g̃a) waᴴkarimaseˀñ ka⌐
    stand?
8. Which one is the same?   Doˀre (g̃a) oᴴnazi deˀsu ka⌐
9. Which one is no good?   Doˀre (g̃a) daᴴmeˀ desu ka⌐
10. Which one is a dictionary?   Doˀre (g̃a) ziᴴbikiˀ desu ka⌐

E. Grammar Drill (based on Grammatical Notes 1 and 4)

       Tutor: Sono aᴿkai hoˀñ (o) kudasai. / aᶠoˀi/ 'Please give me that red
               book.'   book.'
       Student: Sono aᶠoˀi no mo kudasai.   'Please give me that blue one,
                 too.'   too.'

1. Oᶠokiˀi ziᴴbikiˀ (o) kaᴴimaˀsita.   Tiᶠisaˀi no mo kaᴴimaˀsita.
    /tiᶠisaˀi/
2. Aᴿkai eñpitu (o) oneg̃ai-simaˀsu.   Kuᴿroˀi no mo oneg̃ai-simasu.
    /kuᴿroˀi/
3. Kono huᴿruˀi ᴴmaˀtti (wa) daᴿmeˀ   Kono aᴿtarasiˀi no mo daᴴmeˀ
    desu. /aᴿtarasiˀi/   desu.
4. Yaᴿsuˀi hurosiki (o) kaᴴimaˀsita.   Taᴿkaˀi no mo kaᴴimaˀsita.
    /taᴿkaˀi/
5. Sono kuᴿroˀi ᴴhoˀñ (o) ᴴmiˀsete   Sono aᴿkaˀi no mo ᴴmiˀsete kuda-
    kudasai. /akai/   sai.
6. Kono siᴿroˀi hurosiki (wa) taᴿkaˀi Kono kuᴿroˀi no mo taᴿkaˀi desu.
    desu. /kuᴿroˀi/
7. Sono kiᶠiroi haizaˀra (o) kudasai. Sono aᶠoˀi no mo kudasai.
    / aᶠoˀi/
8. Tuᴿmaraˀnai ᴴhoˀñ (o) kaᴴi-   Oᶠmosiroˀi no mo kaᴴimaˀsita.
    maˀsita. /oᶠmosiroˀi/

F. Response Drill (based on Grammatical Note 1)[1]

1. Are wa ⌐na⌐n desu ka↲   [Are wa] hu⌐rosiki de⌐su.
    /hurosiki/

2. Na⌐ni ḡa iᵗrima⌐su ka↲   E⌐npitu ḡa irima⌐su.
    /eñpitu/

3. Na⌐ni o kaᵗima⌐sita ka↲   Ha⌐iza⌐ra o kaᵗima⌐sita.
    /ha⌐iza⌐ra/

4. A⌐tarasi⌐i zassi wa ⌐do⌐re   [A⌐tarasi⌐i zassi wa] a⌐re de⌐su.
    desu ka↲   /are/

5. Do⌐re ḡa daᵗme⌐ desu ka↲   Ko⌐re ḡa dame⌐ desu.
    /kore/

6. Kore wa i⌐ka⌐ḡa desu ka↲   [Kore wa] da⌐me⌐ desu.
    /da⌐me⌐/

7. Do⌐re o kaᵗima⌐sita ka↲   A⌐o⌐i no o kaᵗima⌐sita.
    /a⌐o⌐i no/

8. Do⌐no ⌐pe⌐ñ ḡa daᵗme⌐   A⌐no pe⌐ñ ḡa daᵗme⌐ desu.
    desu ka↲   /a⌐no pe⌐ñ/

9. A⌐no pe⌐ñ wa ⌐do⌐o desu ka↲   [A⌐no pe⌐ñ wa] da⌐me⌐ desu.
    /da⌐me⌐/

10. Do⌐no ziᵗbiki⌐ ḡa iᵗrima⌐su   So⌐no zibiki⌐ ḡa irimasu.
    ka↲   /so⌐no zibiki⌐/

G. Response Drill (based on Grammatical Notes 1 and 2)

1. Zi⌐biki⌐ (ḡa) aᵗrima⌐su ka↲   E⌐e, [zi⌐biki⌐ (ḡa)] arimasu.
    /E⌐e./

2. Zi⌐biki⌐ (ḡa) aᵗrima⌐su ka↲   Iie, [zi⌐biki⌐ (wa)] aᵗrimase⌐ñ.
    /Iie./

3. Zi⌐biki⌐ desu ka↲   /Iie./   Iie, zi⌐biki⌐ zya aᵗrimase⌐ñ.

4. Hu⌐rosiki (ḡa) gozaima⌐su   Ha⌐a, [hu⌐rosiki (ḡa)] gozaima⌐su.
    ka↲   /Ha⌐a./

5. Hu⌐rosiki (ḡa) gozaima⌐su   Iie, [hu⌐rosiki (wa)] gozaimase⌐ñ.
    ka↲   /Iie./

6. Hu⌐rosiki de⌐su ka↲   /Iie./   Iie, hu⌐rosiki zya arimase⌐ñ.

7. Ha⌐iza⌐ra (ḡa) aᵗrima⌐su   E⌐e, [ha⌐iza⌐ra (ḡa)] arimasu.
    ka↲   /E⌐e./

8. Ha⌐iza⌐ra (ḡa) aᵗrima⌐su   Iie, [ha⌐iza⌐ra (wa)] aᵗrimase⌐ñ.
    ka↲   /Iie./

9. Ha⌐iza⌐ra desu ka↲   /Iie./   Iie, ha⌐iza⌐ra zya aᵗrimase⌐ñ.

---

[1] Particles ordinarily designated as optional are not so marked in this exercise because drill on the particles is the purpose of the exercise.

H. Expansion Drill

1. Please show [it to me].   Mi˥sete kudasai.
    Please show [me] a furo-   Hu˩rosiki (o) mi˥sete kudasai.
    shiki.
    Please show [me] that furo-   A˩no hurosiki (o) mi˥sete kudasai.
    shiki.
    Say, please show [me] that   Tyo˥tto, a˩no hurosiki (o) mi˥sete ku-
    furoshiki.   dasai.

2. I need [it].   I˩rima˥su.
    I need a small one.   Ti˩isa˥i no (ḡa) irimasu.
    I need a little smaller one.   Mo˩o suko˥si ti˩isa˥i no (ḡa) iri-
                                        masu.
    I need a little smaller one   Mo˩o suko˥si ti˩isa˥i no (ḡa) i⊦ri-
    but [do you have one?]   ma˧su ḡa_

3. I'd like [it].   O˩neḡai-sima˥su.
    I'd like a red one too.   A˩ka˥i no mo oneḡai-simasu.
    I'd like this red one, too.   Kono a˩ka˥i no mo oneḡai-simasu.
    And I'd like this red one,   Sore kara, kono a˩ka˥i no mo oneḡai-
    too.   simasu.

4. [He] bought [it].   Ka˩ima˥sita.
    [He] bought a dictionary.   Zi˩biki˥ (o) ka⊦ima˧sita.
    [He] bought a magazine and   Za˩ssi to zibiki˥ (o) ka⊦ima˧sita.
    a dictionary.
    Mr. Tanaka bought a maga-   Tanaka-sañ (wa) za˩ssi to zibiki˥ (o)
    zine and a dictionary.   ka⊦ima˧sita.

5. Aren't there any?   A˩rimase˥ñ ka_
    Aren't there any ashtrays?   Ha˩iza˥ra (wa) a⊦rimase˧ñ ka_
    Aren't there any cheap ash-   Ya˩su˥i ha⊦iza˧ra (wa) a⊦rimase˧ñ
    trays?   ka_
    Aren't there any ashtrays   Mo˩o suko˥si ya˩su˥i ha⊦iza˧ra (wa)
    that are a little cheaper?   a⊦rimase˧ñ ka_

6. It's a dictionary.   Zi˩biki˥ desu.
    Is it a dictionary?   Zi˩biki˥ desu ka_
    Is it a new dictionary?   A˩tarasi˥i zi⊦biki˧ desu ka_
    Which one is a new dic-   Do˥re ḡa a⊦tarasi˧i zi⊦biki˧ desu ka_
    tionary?

SHORT DIALOGUE PRACTICE

1. Do you have a match?   Ma⊦tti (ḡa) a⊦rima˧su ka_
       No, I haven't.   Iie, a˩rimase˥ñ.
    How about a lighter?   Ra˥itaa wa?
       I don't have a lighter   Ra˥itaa mo a⊦rimase˧ñ.
       either.

2. Do you have magazines?   Za˩ssi (ḡa) arima˥su ka_
       No, we haven't.   Iie, a˩rimase˥ñ.

	How about papers?	Siñbuñ wa?
	Papers we have.	Si⌐ñbuñ wa arima⌐su.

3. Do you have a pencil? — E⌐ñpitu (ḡa) gozaima⌐su ka⌐

   Yes, I have. — Ha⌐a, go⌐zaima⌐su.

   How about a pen? — Pe⌐ñ wa?

   I have a pen, too. — Pe⌐ñ mo gozaimasu.

4. Do you have a cigarette? — Ta⌐bako (ḡa) arima⌐su ka⌐

   Yes, I have. — E⌐e, a⌐rima⌐su.

   How about a match? — Ma⌐tti wa?

   A match I don't have. — Ma⌐tti wa a⌐rimase⌐ñ.

5. Did you buy a book? — Ho⌐ñ (o) ka⌐ima⌐sita ka⌐

   Yes, I did (buy). — E⌐e, ka⌐ima⌐sita.

   How about a magazine? — Zassi wa?

   I bought a magazine, too. — Za⌐ssi mo kaima⌐sita.

6. Did you buy a pen? — Pe⌐ñ (o) ka⌐ima⌐sita ka⌐

   No, I didn't. — Iie, ka⌐imase⌐ñ desita.

   How about a pencil? — Eñpitu wa?

   I didn't buy a pencil either. — E⌐ñpitu mo kaimase⌐ñ desita.

7. Did you buy a paper? — Si⌐ñbuñ (o) kaima⌐sita ka⌐

   Yes, I did. — E⌐e, ka⌐ima⌐sita.

   How about a magazine? — Zassi wa?

   A magazine I didn't buy. — Za⌐ssi wa kaimase⌐ñ desita.

8. Did you buy a book? — Ho⌐ñ (o) ka⌐ima⌐sita ka⌐

   No, I didn't. — Iie, ka⌐imase⌐ñ desita.

   How about a dictionary? — Zi⌐biki⌐ wa?

   A dictionary I bought. — Zi⌐biki⌐ wa ka⌐ima⌐sita.

9. Did you buy cigarettes and matches? — Ta⌐bako to ma⌐tti (o) ka⌐ima⌐sita ka⌐

   Cigarettes I bought but matches I didn't buy. — Ta⌐bako wa kaima⌐sita ḡa, ma⌐tti wa ka⌐imase⌐ñ desita.

10. Did you buy a magazine? — Za⌐ssi (o) kaima⌐sita ka⌐

    A magazine I didn't buy but I bought a paper. — Za⌐ssi wa kaimase⌐ñ desita ḡa, siñ-buñ (o) kaima⌐sita.

11. Do you need a pen and pencil? — Pe⌐ñ to e⌐ñpitu (ḡa) irima⌐su ka⌐

    A pen I need but a pencil I don't need. — Pe⌐ñ wa i⌐rima⌐su ḡa, eñpitu wa irimase⌐ñ.

12. Do you need a pen? — Pe⌐ñ (ḡa) i⌐rima⌐su ka⌐

    A pen I don't need but I need a pencil. — Pe⌐ñ wa i⌐rimase⌐ñ ḡa, eñpitu (ḡa) irima⌐su.

SUPPLEMENTARY CONVERSATIONS

1. Smith (calling a clerk): O⌐negai-sima⌐su. So⌐no pe⌐ñ o ⌐mi⌐sete kudasai.
   Clerk: I⌐rassya⌐i.   Do⌐no ⌐pe⌐ñ desu ka⌐
   Smith: Sono ku⌐rd⌐i no desu.
   Clerk: Do⌐ozo.
   Smith: I⌐kura desu ka⌐
   Clerk: Ni⌐señ- eñ de⌐su.
   Smith: Tyo⌐tto ta⌐ka⌐i desu ⌐ne⌐e. Mo⌐o suko⌐si ya⌐su⌐i no wa a⌐rimase⌐ñ
           ka⌐
   Clerk: Kono a⌐ka⌐i no wa i⌐ka⌐ḡa desu ka. Se⌐ñ-eñ de⌐su ḡa⌐
   Smith: So⌐o desu ⌐ne⌐e. Sore mo ⌐tyo⌐tto⌐
   Clerk: A⌐a, ko⌐re wa ika⌐ḡa desu ka⌐ Se⌐ñ nihyaku⌐-eñ desu.
   Smith (trying it out): A⌐a, ko⌐re wa i⌐i ⌐pe⌐ñ desu ⌐ne⌐e. Ko⌐re o kudasa⌐i.
   Clerk: A⌐ri⌐ḡatoo gozaimasu. E⌐ñpitu mo ika⌐ḡa desu ka⌐
   Smith: E⌐ñpitu wa irimase⌐ñ. (Handing over money) Se⌐ñ gohyaku⌐- eñ.
           Ha⌐i.
   Clerk: Syo⌐osyoo o⌐mati-kudasa⌐i.

                              .   .   .
   Clerk (returning with package and change): O⌐matase-itasima⌐sita. Sa⌐ñ-
           byaku⌐-eñ desu. Ma⌐ido ari⌐ḡatoo gozaimasu. Ma⌐ta do⌐ozo.

2. Smith: Tyo⌐tto.
   Clerk: I⌐rassyaima⌐se.
   Smith: Are wa ⌐na⌐ñ desu ka⌐
   Clerk: A⌐re de⌐su ka⌐ Ha⌐iza⌐ra desu.
   Smith: So⌐o desu ka. Ki⌐ree desu ⌐ne⌐e. Tyo⌐tto ⌐mi⌐sete kudasai.
   Clerk: Ki⌐ird⌐i no desu ka⌐
   Smith: E⌐e.
   Clerk: Do⌐ozo.
   Smith: Ano a⌐ka⌐i no mo ⌐mi⌐sete kudasai.
   Clerk: Ka⌐sikomarima⌐sita.
   Smith: I⌐kura desu ka⌐
   Clerk: Ki⌐iro⌐i no wa sa⌐ñbyaku⌐-eñ desu. A⌐ka⌐i no wa ⌐sa⌐ñbyaku go⌐zyu⌐u-
           eñ desu.
   Smith: O⌐nazi zya arimase⌐ñ ⌐ne⌐e.
   Clerk: Ha⌐a. Ki⌐iro⌐i no wa ⌐tyo⌐tto ti⌐isa⌐i desu.
   Smith: A⌐a, so⌐o desu ka. A⌐ka⌐i no o ku⌐dasa⌐i.
   Clerk: A⌐ri⌐ḡatoo gozaimasu.
   Smith: Tyo⌐tto ⌐ma⌐tte kudasai. Ki⌐iro⌐i no mo onegai-simasu.
   Clerk: Ka⌐sikomarima⌐sita. Ho⌐ka ni na⌐ni ka?
   Smith: So⌐re dake⌐ desu.
   Clerk: Ro⌐ppyaku gozyu⌐u-eñ desu.
   Smith: Señ-eñ. Ha⌐i.
   Clerk: Syo⌐osyoo o⌐mati-kudasaima⌐se.

                              .   .   .
   Clerk: O⌐matase-itasima⌐sita. Sa⌐ñbyaku go⌐zyu⌐u- eñ d e s u .   Do⌐o mo
           a⌐ri⌐ḡatoo gozaimasita.

English Equivalents

1. Smith: Would you wait on me? Please show me that pen.
   Clerk: (Welcome.) Which pen do you mean?
   Smith: (It's) that black one.
   Clerk: Here you are.
   Smith: How much is it?
   Clerk: It's ¥2000.
   Smith: It's a little expensive, isn't it. Don't you have a little cheaper one?
   Clerk: How about this red one? It's ¥1000. . . .
   Smith: Hmmm. I'm afraid that one won't do either.
   Clerk: Oh, how about this one? It's ¥1200.
   Smith: Oh, this is a good pen, isn't it. I'll take this one.
   Clerk: Thank you. How about a pencil, too?
   Smith: I don't need any pencils. Here you are. ¥1500.
   Clerk: Just a moment, please.

   . . .

   Clerk: I'm sorry to have kept you waiting. [Your change] is ¥300. Thank you. Please come again.

2. Smith: Say there!
   Clerk: (Welcome.)
   Smith: What are those things?
   Clerk: Those? They're ashtrays.
   Smith: Oh? Aren't they pretty. Let me have a look.
   Clerk: Do you mean a yellow one?
   Smith: Yes.
   Clerk: Here you are.
   Smith: Let me see that red one, too.
   Clerk: Certainly.
   Smith: How much are they?
   Clerk: The yellow one is ¥300. The red one is ¥350.
   Smith: They're not the same, are they.
   Clerk: No (i.e. that's right). The yellow one is a little small[er].
   Smith: Oh? I'll take the red one.
   Clerk: Thank you.
   Smith: Just a minute. I'd like the yellow one, too.
   Clerk: Certainly. Anything else?
   Smith: That's all.
   Clerk: (It's) ¥650.
   Smith: Here you are. ¥1000.
   Clerk: Just a moment, please.

   . . .

   Clerk: I'm sorry to have kept you waiting. [Your change] is ¥350. Thank you very much.

EXERCISES

1. Mr. Smith asks the clerk: The clerk replies:

    a. to show him that big   Which one do you mean?
        book.
    b. if he has any small dic-   I do, but they aren't very good.
        tionaries.
    c. for that.   Here you are.
    d. for cigarettes and   Anything else?
        matches.
    e. how much that red   It's ¥ 350.
        furoshiki is.
    f. if that blue ashtray is   No, it's ¥ 500.
        ¥ 400.

2. Mr. Smith has just entered a stationery store.

    a. The clerk greets Mr. Smith.
    b. Mr. Smith asks if they have any pens.
    c. The clerk answers that they do.
    d. Mr. Smith asks the clerk to show him a black pen.
    e. The clerk shows him one and says that it is a fine pen.
    f. Mr. Smith asks the price.
    g. The clerk answers that it is ¥ 2500.
    h. Mr. Smith remarks that it is very expensive. He asks if they have
        any that are a little cheaper.
    i. The clerk answers that they have, but they aren't black. He suggests
        a blue one. It costs ¥ 1500.
    j. Mr. Smith thinks the blue pen is pretty. He remarks that it isn't very
        expensive. He decides to buy it.
    k. The clerk thanks Mr. Smith and asks if he wants anything else.
    l. Mr. Smith says that that's all he wants, and gives the clerk ¥ 2000.
    m. The clerk asks him to wait a moment. When he returns, he apolo-
        gizes for having kept Mr. Smith waiting and gives him ¥ 500 change.
        He thanks Mr. Smith and invites him to come again.
    n. Mr. Smith says goodbye.

3. Practice the Basic Dialogues with variations and appropriate props.

Lesson 5. Shopping (cont.)

BASIC DIALOGUES: FOR MEMORIZATION

(a)

Smith

more	mo˺tto

1. Do you have more of these?　　Kore (wa) ˹mo˺tto a˹rima˺su ka⌐
   (Lit. As for these, are
   there more?)

Clerk

much or many	ta˹kusa˺ñ

2. Yes, we have lots of those.　　Ha˺a, sore wa ta˹kusañ gozaima˺su.
   (Lit. As for those, there
   are many.)

Smith

one unit	hi˹to˺-tu
two units	hu˹ta-tu˺
three units	mi-˹ttu˺
four units	yo-˹ttu˺
five units	i˹tu˺-tu
six units	mu-˹ttu˺
seven units	na˹na˺-tu
eight units	ya-˹ttu˺
nine units	ko˹ko˺no-tu
ten units	to˺o
eleven units	zyu˹uiti˺
twelve units	zyu˹uni˺

3. I'd like five.　　I˹tu˺-tu onegai-simasu.

4. And then give me three of　　Sore kara, sono si˹ro˺i no mo mi-˹ttu
   those white ones, too.　　kudasa˺i.

Clerk

I'm sorry but	su˹mimase˺ñ ḡa

5. I'm sorry but that is all　　Su˹mimase˺ñ ḡa, si˹ro˺i no wa　so˹re
   we have of the white ones.　　dake˺ desu.
   (Lit. As for the white
   ones, it's just that.)

Smith

three units more	mo˹o mi-ttu˺

6. Then give me three more　　Zya˺a, kore (o) mo˹o mi-ttu kudasa˺i.
   of these.

(b)

Smith

	how many units?	i⌐kutu⌐ or
		oikutu+
7.	How many of these do you have? (Lit. As for these, how many are there?)	Kore (wa) ⌐i⌐kutu a⌐rima⌐su ka‿

Clerk

8.	We have five (but) . . .	I⌐tu⌐-tu go⌐zaima⌐su ḡa‿

Smith

	just three units	mi-⌐ttu dake⌐
9.	I'd like just three.	Mi-⌐ttu dake onegai-sima⌐su.
	one long, cylindrical unit	i⌐p-poñ
	two long, cylindrical units	ni⌐-hoñ
	three long, cylindrical units	sa⌐ñ-boñ
10.	And then give me three of those pencils, too.	Sore kara, sono eñpitu mo ⌐sa⌐ñ-boñ kudasai.

Clerk

	color	i⌐ro⌐
	what (kind of) color?	do⌐ñna iro
	is good or fine	yorosii /-ku/
11.	What color would you like? (Lit. What kind of color is good?)	Do⌐ñna i⌐ro⌐ ḡa yo⌐rosi⌐i desu ka‿

Smith

12.	I'd like one red one and two blue ones.	A⌐ka⌐i no (o) ⌐i⌐p-poñ to, a⌐o⌐i no (o) ⌐ni⌐-hoñ onegai-simasu.

(c)

Smith

	paper	ka⌐mi⌐
	this kind of paper	ko⌐ñna kami⌐
	one thin, flat unit	i⌐ti⌐-mai
	two thin, flat units	ni⌐-mai
	three thin, flat units	sa⌐ñ-mai
13.	How much is one sheet of this kind of paper?	Ko⌐ñna kami⌐ (wa) i⌐ti⌐-mai ⌐i⌐kura desu ka‿

Clerk

14.	It's ¥20.	Ni⌐zyuu-eñ desu.

Smith

15.	Give me two sheets of the red and three sheets of the white.	A⌐ka⌐i no (o) ⌐ni⌐-mai to, si⌐ro⌐i no (o) ⌐sa⌐ñ-mai kudasai.

one bound unit (as, a book, magazine, etc.)	i⌐s-satu⌐
two bound units	ni⌐-satu
three bound units	sa⌐ñ-satu

16. And then I'd like two of these small dictionaries, too. Sore kara, kono ti⌐isa⌐i zi⌐biki⌐ mo ⌐ni⌐-satu onegai-simasu.

(d)

Tanaka

17. What are you going to buy? Na⌐ni (o) ka⌐ima⌐su ka⌐

Smith

I or me	watakusi or bo⌐ku (man's word; has unaccented alternant)

18. (Do you mean) me? Wa⌐takusi de⌐su ka⌐ or Bo⌐ku desu ka⌐

map	ti⌐zu

19. I'm going to buy a map. Ti⌐zu (o) kaimasu.

(to the clerk)

Tokyo	Tookyoo
map of Tokyo	To⌐okyoo no ti⌐zu

20. Say! Do you have maps of Tokyo? Tyo⌐tto. To⌐okyoo no ti⌐zu (ga) a⌐rima⌐su ka⌐

Clerk

both big ones and small ones	o⌐oki⌐i no mo ti⌐isa⌐i no mo

21. Yes. We have (both) big ones and small ones (but)... Ha⌐a. O⌐oki⌐i no mo ti⌐isa⌐i no mo go⌐zaima⌐su ga⌐

Smith

just	tyo⌐tto

22. (Just) let me have a look. Tyo⌐tto ⌐mi⌐sete kudasai.

. . .

23. Oh, this one is fine. A⌐a, ko⌐re ga i⌐i desu.

24. Give me two. Ni⌐-mai kudasai.

(e)

Smith

today's newspaper	kyo⌐o no siñbuñ

25. Don't you have today's paper? Kyo⌐o no siñbuñ (wa) a⌐rimase⌐ñ ka⌐

Clerk

yesterday's newspaper	kinoo no siñbuñ

26. No (i.e. that's right). This is yesterday's paper. E⌐e, kore wa ki⌐noo no siñbuñ de⌐su.

as for today's (one) or
 today's (one), compara-
 tively speaking

kyo˥o no wa

soon or any minute or
 right away

su˥g̃u

come

ki˥ma˥su

27. Today's (one) will come any
 minute.

Kyo˥o no wa ⌈su˥g̃u ki⌈ma˥su yo˺

ADDITIONAL PLACE NAMES

Japan	Ni⌈ho˥ñ or Ni⌈ppo˥ñ	England	Ig̃irisu or Eekoku
Fukuoka	Hu⌈ku˥oka	London	Ro˥ñdoñ
Hokkaido	Ho⌈kka˥idoo	France	Huráñsu
Honshu	Ho˥ñsyuu	Paris	Pa˥rii
Kobe	Ko˥obe	Germany	Do˥itu
Kyushu	Kyu˥usyuu	Berlin	Beruriñ
Nara	Na˥ra	U.S.S.R.	So˥reñ or So⌈bie˥to
Nikko	Ni˥kkoo		
Osaka	Oosaka	Moscow	Mosukuwa
Sapporo	Sapporo	India	I˥ñdo
Shikoku	Si⌈ko˥ku	Korea	Tyo⌈ose˥ñ
Yokohama	Yokohama	China	Tyu˥ug̃oku
U.S.A.	Amerika or Beekoku	Formosa (Communist China)	Ta⌈iwa˥ñ Tyuukyoo)[1]
New York	Nyu⌈uyo˺oku		
San Fran- cisco	Sa⌈ñhuráñsi˥suko		
Washington	Wa⌈si˥ñtoñ		

NOTES ON THE BASIC DIALOGUES

8. 'We have five but—how many do you want? or is that enough? or did you
 want more than that? or I hope that is enough (etc.)'

11. Yorosii resembles i˥i in meaning and general usage, but is a more polite
 word. It occurs in the negative only under special circumstances.

18. Bo˥ku occurs in men's speech and is less polite than watakusi, which is
 used by both men and women. Watakusi is often contracted to watasi by
 men and women, and to atasi by women.

21. 'We have big ones and small ones but—which kind did you want?'

22. Tyo˥tto 'just' is not interchangeable with su⌈ko˥si.

27. The gerund of ki⌈ma˥su is ki⌈te˺.

---

[1] This name has become obsolete.

GRAMMATICAL NOTES

1. Numerals: Series II

The numerals of Series I (i⌐ti⌐, ni⌐, san̄, etc.) were introduced in Lesson 3. The second numeral series, of native Japanese origin, is introduced in this lesson:

hi⌐to⌐-	' 1 '	mu-	' 6 '
huta-	' 2 '	na⌐na⌐-	' 7 '
mi-	' 3 '	ya-	' 8 '
yo-	' 4 '	ko⌐ko⌐no⌐-	' 9 '
i⌐tu⌐-	' 5 '	to- or to⌐o-	' 10 '

This second series goes only as far as 10; beyond 10, Series I (zyu⌐uiti⌐, zyu⌐uni⌐, etc.) is used.

The numerals of Series I occur both as independent words (for example, in mathematics) and in number compounds (for example, combined with -en to count yen); but the numerals of Series II usually occur only in number compounds. Combined with -[t]tu 'unit,'[1] the numerals of Series II are used to count unit objects which are inanimate (see the list preceding Basic Sentence 3 in this lesson; note that in to⌐o ' 10 units.' the longer alternant for 10 occurs, without the -[t]tu which occurs in the equivalents of ' 1 unit' through ' 9 units'). To count the number of units beyond 10, the numerals of Series I are used independently.

Thus, ' 1 ' in reply to the question 'What is 3 minus 2?' is i⌐ti⌐, but ' 1 ' in reply to the question 'How many chairs do you need?' is hi⌐to⌐-tu; ' 11 ' in reply to both of the questions 'What is 21 minus 10?' and 'How many chairs do you need?' is zyu⌐uiti⌐.

The question word corresponding to the hi⌐to⌐-tu, hu⌐ta-tu⌐ series is i⌐kutu (polite, oikutu) 'how many units?' Oikutu is used more commonly, but not exclusively, by women.

Single units of some objects are always counted with the hi⌐to⌐-tu, hu⌐ta-tu⌐ series; some things are never counted with it (i. e. they use a specialized counter); and units of some objects are counted either with the hi⌐to⌐-tu, hu⌐ta-tu⌐ series or with a specialized counter (with some variation among individual speakers).[2]

---

[1] They also enter into other combinations, some of which will be introduced later. Examples: hi⌐to⌐-ban̄ ' 1 night'; hi⌐to⌐-kumi ' 1 set'; hi⌐to⌐-asi ' 1 pace.'

[2] In the last case there may be a difference of meaning, depending on whether the hi⌐to⌐-tu, hu⌐ta-tu⌐ series or a specialized counter is used. For example, in reference to tabako, i⌐p-pon̄, ni⌐-hon̄, etc. refer only to individual cigarettes, but hi⌐to⌐-tu, hu⌐ta-tu⌐ etc. may also be used to count packages of cigarettes.

2. C o u n t e r s :   -ho̅n, -mai, -satu

Single units of objects which are thin and flat in shape—sheets, blankets, furoshiki, handkerchiefs, plates, boards, rugs, leaves, etc.—are counted with the counter -mai, which combines with numerals of Series I. Numbers from 1 to 10 are:

iˈtiˈ-mai	' 1 thin, flat unit'	roˈkuˈ-mai	' 6 thin, flat units'
niˈ-mai	' 2 thin, flat units'	naˈnaˈ-mai or	
saˈn̄-mai	' 3 thin, flat units'	siˈtiˈ-mai	' 7 thin, flat units'
yoˈn̄-mai or		haˈtiˈ-mai	' 8 thin, flat units'
yo-mai	' 4 thin, flat units'	kyuˈu-mai	' 9 thin, flat units'
go-mai	' 5 thin, flat units'	zyuˈu-mai	' 10 thin, flat units'

Question word: naˈn̄-mai 'how many thin, flat units?'

Single units of objects which are long and cylindrical in shape — pens, pencils, cigarettes, bottles, arms, legs, trees, poles, cut flowers, etc.—are counted with the counter -ho̅n, which combines with numerals of Series I. Some combinations of numeral + counter in this series undergo assimilation: namely, ' 1,' ' 3,' ' 6,' ' 8,' ' 10.' The numbers from one to ten are:

iˈp-poñ	' 1 long, cylindrical unit'
niˈ-hoñ	' 2 long, cylindrical units'
saˈn̄-boñ	' 3 long, cylindrical units'
yoˈn̄-hoñ or siˈ-hoñ	' 4 long, cylindrical units'
go-hoñ	' 5 long, cylindrical units'
roˈp-poñ	' 6 long, cylindrical units'
naˈnaˈ-hoñ or siˈtiˈ-hoñ	' 7 long, cylindrical units'
haˈp-poñ or haˈtiˈ-hoñ	' 8 long, cylindrical units'
kyuˈu-hoñ	' 9 long, cylindrical units'
ziˈp-poñ or zyuˈp-poñ	' 10 long, cylindrical units'

Question word: naˈn̄-boñ 'how many long, cylindrical units?'

Single units of bound objects—books, magazines, albums, etc.—are counted with the counter -satu, which combines with numerals of Series I. Some combinations of numeral + counter in this series undergo assimilation: namely, ' 1,' ' 8,' ' 10.' The numbers from one to ten are:

iˈs-satuˈ	' 1 bound unit'	roˈku-satuˈ	' 6 bound units'
niˈ-satu	' 2 bound units'	naˈnaˈ-satu or	
saˈn̄-satu	' 3 bound units'	siˈti-satuˈ	' 7 bound units'
yoˈn̄-satu	' 4 bound units'	haˈs-satuˈ	' 8 bound units'
go-ˈsatuˈ	' 5 bound units'	kyuˈu-satu	' 9 bound units'
		ziˈs-satuˈ or	
		zyuˈs-satuˈ	' 10 bound units'

Question word: naˈn̄-satu 'how many bound units?'

Numbers are nominals and accordingly occur in the same kinds of patterns as nominals. They occur frequently in the nominal pattern described in the following note.

3. Extent

A Japanese word or phrase which asks or answers the question 'how many?' 'how much?' 'how far?' or 'how long?' with reference to an inflected expression, regularly occurs without a following particle.[1] Compare:

Pe˥ñ o kudasai. 'Please give me a pen.' (tells WHAT I want)

Su˥ko˥si kudasai. 'Please give me a little (or a few).' (tells HOW MUCH or HOW MANY I want)

Hu˥rosiki ḡa arima˥su. 'I have a furoshiki.' (tells WHAT I have)

I˥ti˥-mai arimasu. 'I have one (thin, flat object).' (tells HOW MANY I have)

Hurosiki (ḡa) i˥ti˥-mai arimasu. 'I have one furoshiki.' (lit. 'There are furoshiki to the extent of one thin, flat unit.') contains the information of the last two sentences. In Japanese, the WHAT occurs as the subject or object or topic followed by particle ḡa, o, or wa, and the HOW MANY or HOW MUCH occurs as an extent expression, without a following particle.

When the WHAT is apparent from the context, it is regularly omitted. For example, in Zyu˥u-eñ kudasa˥i. 'Please give me ¥ 10.' zyuu-eñ tells HOW MUCH I want; the WHAT (i.e. money) is apparent from the counter and is not explicitly stated.

Examples:

Kore (o) ˥mo˥tto oneḡai-simasu. 'I'd like more of this.' (Lit. 'I'd like this to a greater extent.')

Sore (o) ˥ze˥ñbu si˥ma˥sita. 'I did all of that.' (Lit. 'I did that to the extent of the whole thing.')

Ha˥iza˥ra (ḡa) ta˥kusañ irima˥su. 'I need lots of ashtrays.' (Lit. 'Ashtrays are needed to the extent of many.')

Eñpitu (ḡa) ˥na˥ñ-boñ a˥rima˥su ka‿ 'How many pencils are there?' (Lit. 'There are pencils to the extent of how many long, cylindrical units?')

Ha˥iza˥ra (o) mi-˥ttu kaima˥sita. 'I bought three ashtrays.' (Lit. 'I bought ashtrays to the extent of three units.')

The hi˥to˥-tu, hu˥ta-tu˥ series is regularly used to count all the many inanimate unit objects for which there are no specialized counters. It is also frequently used alternatively with specialized counters for counting inanimate unit objects which do have specialized counters. This series, then, is safer for the beginning student to use until his stock of specialized counters is enlarged. For example, if a student didn't know the counter -satu and said Ho˥ñ o hu˥ta-tu kaima˥sita 'I bought two books,' a Japanese would have no difficulty understanding him, whereas if he substituted the mathematical ni˥ without a counter, most Japanese listeners would be baffled.

---

[1] Irrespective of formality. This is different from the optional omission of ḡa, wa, and o in conversation.

The order of the WHAT preceding the quantity expression in the above examples is the usual one.   The reverse order also exists, however, with no
difference in basic structure but only in emphasis.   Thus: Ta⌐kusa⌐ñ ha⌐i-
za⌐ra ḡa irimasu.   'I need LOTS of ashtrays.'

The particle to 'and' may occur with extent patterns. A common pattern
consists of—

  nominal being counted or measured (+ particle wa, ḡa, or o)
    + extent expression
    + to,
    + nominal being counted or measured (+ particle wa, ḡa, or o)
    + extent expression

Thus:

  Ka⌐mi⌐ (o) ⌐ni⌐- mai to, eñpitu (o) ⌐sa⌐ñ-boñ ka⌐ima⌐sita.   'I bought two
  sheets of paper and three pencils.'

See also Basic Sentences 12 and 15.

4.   Particle no

The particle no occurs between nominals with the meaning 'the preceding
nominal describes the following nominal'—that is to say, A no B is an A kind
of B. For example:

To⌐okyoo no ti⌐zu	'Tokyo map(s)' or 'map(s) of Tokyo'
Amerika no tabako	'American cigarettes' or ' cigarettes in Amer- ica'
asita no siñbuñ	'tomorrow's newspaper(s)' or 'newspaper(s) to- morrow'
Tookyoo no siñbuñ	'Tokyo newspaper(s)' or 'Tokyo's newspaper(s)' or 'newspapers in Tokyo'
Tookyoo no Tanaka-sañ	'Mr. Tanaka from Tokyo' or 'Mr. Tanaka in To- kyo'
a⌐na⌐ta no zibiki	'your dictionary'
wa⌐takusi no ho⌐ñ	'my book'

There is no single word in English which is exactly equivalent to no. Sometimes (by no means always) it corresponds to English 'of.' A nominal + no
sequence may indicate possession, location, origin, or other things; but in every
instance, it is descriptive.

An adjectival or demonstrative describing a nominal has no connecting particle; but a nominal describing a nominal is regularly followed by no. Compare:

  a⌐tarasi⌐i zassi 'new magazine'
  kono zassi 'this magazine'
  Nihoñ no zassi 'Japanese magazine'

When a nominal has more than one describing word or phrase, a nominal + <u>no</u> sequence may be separated from the nominal it describes by another descriptive word or phrase.[1] Thus:

Tookyoo no oꜛokiꜜi ꜛtiꜜzu 'a big map of Tokyo'
  (tiꜜzu described by <u>Tookyoo</u> and <u>oꜛokiꜜi</u>)

Tanaka-sañ no soꜛno hoꜜñ 'that book of Mr. Tanaka's'
  (hoꜜñ described by <u>Tanaka-sañ</u> and <u>sono</u>)

Tanaka-sañ no Toꜛokyoo no tiꜜzu 'Mr. Tanaka's map of Tokyo'
  (tiꜜzu described by <u>Tanaka-sañ</u> and <u>Tookyoo</u>)

It is also possible for the nominal of a nominal + <u>no</u> sequence to be described:[2]

aꜛtarasiꜜi zaꜜssi no kami   'the paper in new magazines'
                                    (kaꜛmiꜜ described by <u>zassi</u>,
                                     which is described by <u>aꜛtarasiꜜi</u>)

soꜛno zibikiꜜ no kami   'the paper in that dictionary'
                                    (kaꜛmiꜜ described by <u>ziꜛbikiꜜ</u>,
                                     which is described by <u>sono</u>)

Niꜛhoñ no hoꜜñ no kami[3]   'the paper in Japanese books'
                                    (kaꜛmiꜜ described by <u>hoꜜñ</u>,
                                     which is described by <u>Niꜛhoꜜñ</u>)

In some special cases, a nominal describes another nominal directly without an intervening <u>no</u> (for example: moꜛo sukoꜜsi 'a little more'). Such combinations should be memorized as they occur.

When particle <u>no</u> immediately precedes the nominal <u>no</u> 'one(s),' the two <u>no</u> are contracted to a single <u>no</u>: that is, <u>x no no</u> is contracted to <u>x no</u> [4] (with <u>no</u> accented if <u>x</u> is unaccented). The contraction occurs in the same kinds of patterns as nominals. Compare:

---

[1] In such cases, the two descriptive words or phrases are usually not in the same accent phrase.

[2] In such cases, the descriptive words or phrases are usually in the same accent phrase.

[3] With different intonation, these three phrases could mean 'new paper in (or for) magazines,' 'that paper in (or for) dictionaries,' 'Japanese paper in (or for) books.' With these meanings, the final nominal in each case has two modifiers (cf. the examples in the preceding group above).

[4] <u>x no</u> (in which <u>no</u> = particle) and <u>x no</u> (the contraction of <u>x no no</u>) are distinguished by context: the former must be followed by a nominal which it describes.

Ta⌐naka-sañ de⌐su. 'It's Mr. Tanaka.'
Ta⌐naka-sañ no ho⌐ñ desu. 'It's Mr. Tanaka's book.'
Ta⌐naka-sañ no⌐ desu. 'It's Mr. Tanaka's (one).'
  (Tanaka-sañ no 'Mr. Tanaka's' + no 'one' = Ta⌐naka-sañ no⌐   ' one
belonging to Mr. Tanaka')

Tookyoo wa o⌐oki⌐i desu. 'Tokyo is big.'
To⌐okyoo no ti⌐zu wa o⌐oki⌐i desu. 'The map of Tokyo is big.'
To⌐okyoo no⌐ wa o⌐oki⌐i desu. 'The one of Tokyo is big.'
  (Tookyoo no 'of Tokyo' + no 'one' = To⌐okyoo no⌐ 'the one of Tokyo')

A⌐tarasi⌐i To⌐okyoo no ti⌐zu wa o⌐oki⌐i desu. 'The new map of Tokyo
  is big.'
A⌐tarasi⌐i To⌐okyoo no⌐ wa o⌐oki⌐i desu. 'The new one of Tokyo is
  big.' (No 'one' modified by a⌐tarasi⌐i and by Tookyoo no, with no +
  no contracted to a single no)

5. koñna, soñna, añna, do⌐ñna

Koñna 'this kind (of),' soñna and añna 'that kind (of),' and do⌐ñna 'what kind
(of)?' modify nominals directly, without an intervening particle. The nominals
may or may not be preceded by other descriptive words or phrases. The spatial and relational meanings of this series are parallel to those of the kore and
kono series.

Examples:

    koñna eñpitu 'this kind of pencil'
    so⌐ñna ti⌐zu 'that kind of map'
    a⌐ñna waru⌐i ⌐ho⌐ñ 'a bad book like that'
    do⌐ñna a⌐tarasi⌐i ⌐pe⌐ñ 'what kind of new pen?'

The Japanese equivalent of 'what color?' is do⌐ñna iro (lit. 'what kind of
color?') or the compound word naniiro.

6. moo ~ mo⌐tto

Mo⌐tto means ' more.' It occurs as an extent expression with verbals
(mo⌐tto ka⌐ima⌐sita 'I bought more'), adjectivals (mo⌐tto ⌐i⌐i 'it's better'), and
a nominal + √de⌐su (mo⌐tto ⌐ki⌐ree desu 'it's prettier').

Moo means 'more' IF FOLLOWED IMMEDIATELY WITHIN THE SAME
ACCENT PHRASE BY A NUMBER OR INDEFINITE QUANTITY EXPRESSION.[1]

---

[1] Ta⌐kusa⌐ñ 'many' or 'much' does not occur in this pattern.

Examples:

> moo iti-do 'one time more'
> mo⌐o⌐ iti⌐¹-mai 'one thin, flat unit more'
> mo⌐o⌐ hyaku⌐¹-eñ '¥100 more'
> mo⌐o⌐ suko⌐¹si 'a little more'

7. dake

A nominal followed by dake 'just,' 'only,' 'no more than' may occur as an extent expression without a following particle.

Examples:

> Ta⌐naka-sañ dake ikima⌐¹sita. 'Just Mr. Tanaka went.'
> Su⌐ko⌐¹si dake onegai-simasu. 'I'd like just a little.'
> O⌐mosiro⌐¹i zassi wa ko⌐re dake⌐¹ desu.[1] 'This is the only interesting magazine.' (Lit. 'As for interesting magazines, it's just this.')

8. —— mo —— mo

x mo y mo, in which x and y are subject or object nominals (with or without preceding descriptive expressions), means 'both x and y' or 'x AND y.' With a negative, it means 'neither x nor y,' 'not x OR y.'

Examples:

> Pe⌐¹ñ mo e⌐ñpitu mo arima⌐¹su. 'There are pens AND pencils.'
> Ti⌐isa⌐¹i ⌐ti⌐zu mo o⌐oki⌐¹i ⌐ti⌐zu mo ku⌐dasa⌐i. 'Give me the small map AND the big map.'
> A⌐na⌐ta no mo Ta⌐naka-sañ no⌐¹ mo onegai-simasu. 'I'd like both yours (lit. your one) and Mr. Tanaka's (one).'
> Pe⌐¹ñ mo e⌐ñpitu mo arimase⌐¹ñ. 'I don't have a pen OR a pencil.'

DRILLS

A. Substitution Drill

1. I'd like one of those.	Sore (o) hi⌐to⌐¹-tu onegai-simasu.
2. I'd like two of those (thin, flat objects).	Sore (o) <u>⌐ni⌐¹-mai</u> onegai-simasu.
3. I'd like three of those (bound objects).	Sore (o) <u>⌐sa⌐¹ñ-satu</u> onegai-simasu.
4. I'd like four of those (long, cylindrical objects).	Sore (o) <u>⌐yo⌐¹ñ-hoñ</u> onegai-simasu.

---

[1]
Dake is regularly accented (da⌐ke⌐¹) in its occurrences before √desu.

5. I'd like more of that.   Sore (o) ⌐motto oneḡai-simasu.
6. I'd like a little more of that.   Sore (o) mo⌐o sukȯsi oneḡai-simasu.
7. I'd like one more of those.   Sore (o) mo⌐o hito⌐-tu oneḡai-simasu.
8. I'd like all of that.   Sore (o) ⌐ze⌐ñbu oneḡai-simasu.
9. I'd like just a little of that.   Sore (o) su⌐ko⌐si dake oneḡai-simasu.
10. I'd like ten of those.   Sore (o) to⌐o oneḡai-sima⌐su.

B. Substitution Drill

1. I bought lots of cigarettes.   Tabako (o) ta⌐kusañ kaima⌐sita.
2. I bought one ashtray.   Ha⌐iza⌐ra (o) hi⌐to⌐-tu ka⌐ima⌐sita.
3. I bought three maps.   Ti⌐zu (o) ⌐sa⌐n-mai ka⌐ima⌐sita.
4. I bought a little paper.   Ka⌐mi⌐ (o) su⌐ko⌐si ka⌐ima⌐sita.
5. I bought ten pencils.   Eñpitu (o) ⌐zyu⌐p-poñ ka⌐ima⌐sita.
6. I bought two dictionaries.   Zi⌐biki⌐ (o) ⌐ni⌐-satu ka⌐ima⌐sita.
7. I bought three furoshiki.   Hurosiki (o) ⌐sa⌐ñ-mai ka⌐ima⌐sita.
8. I bought one pen.   Pe⌐ñ (o) ⌐i⌐p-poñ ka⌐ima⌐sita.
9. I bought one book.   Ho⌐ñ (o) i⌐s-satu kaima⌐sita.
10. I bought five sheets of paper.   Ka⌐mi⌐ (o) go-⌐mai kaima⌐sita.

C. Substitution Drill

1. I have both a newspaper and   Si⌐ñbuñ mo zassi mo arima⌐su.
   a magazine. [1]
2. I have neither a newspaper   Si⌐ñbuñ mo zassi mo arimase⌐ñ.
   nor a magazine.
3. I bought both a newspaper   Si⌐ñbuñ mo zassi mo kaima⌐sita.
   and a magazine.
4. I forgot both the newspaper   Si⌐ñbuñ mo zassi mo wasurema⌐sita.
   and the magazine.
5. I have both a newspaper and   Si⌐ñbuñ mo zassi mo gozaima⌐su.
   a magazine.
6. I have neither a newspaper   Si⌐ñbuñ mo zassi mo gozaimase⌐ñ.
   nor a magazine.
7. I'd like both a newspaper   Si⌐ñbuñ mo zassi mo oneḡai-sima⌐su.
   and a magazine.
8. Please give me both a news-   Si⌐ñbuñ mo zassi mo kudasa⌐i.
   paper and a magazine.
9. Please show me both the   Si⌐ñbuñ mo zassi mo mi⌐sete kudasai.
   newspaper and the magazine.

D. Substitution Drill

1. That's all there are of ash-   Ha⌐iza⌐ra wa so⌐re dake⌐ desu.
   trays.

_____

[1] In any given situation, the use of 'a' or 'the' in the English equivalents
would be determined by the context in which the Japanese sentence occurred.

2. That's all there are of dic-   Zi⌐biki⌐ wa so⌐re dake⌐ desu.
   tionaries.

3. That's all there are of this   Ko⌐nna no⌐ wa so⌐re dake⌐ desu.
   kind (of one).

4. That's all there are of new ones. A⌐tarasi⌐i no wa so⌐re dake⌐ desu.

5. That's all there are of good   I⌐i no wa so⌐re dake⌐ desu.
   ones.

6. That's all there are of red   A⌐ka⌐i no wa so⌐re dake⌐ desu.
   ones.

7. That's all there are of maps   A⌐merika no ti⌐zu wa so⌐re dake⌐
   of America.   desu.

8. That's all there are of to-   Kyo⌐o no sinbun wa so⌐re dake⌐ desu.
   day's papers.

9. That's all there are of yes-   Ki⌐no⌐o no wa so⌐re dake⌐ desu.
   terday's (ones).

10. That's all there are of Eng-   I⌐girisu no⌐ wa so⌐re dake⌐ desu.
    lish ones.

E. Substitution Drill

1. What (kind of) color would   Do⌐nna i⌐ro⌐ ga yo⌐rosi⌐i desu ka⌐
   you like? (Lit. What kind
   of color is good?)

2. Which one would you like?   Do⌐re ga yo⌐rosi⌐i desu ka⌐

3. What would you like?   Na⌐ni ga yo⌐rosi⌐i desu ka⌐

4. Which map would you like?   Do⌐no ⌐ti⌐zu ga yo⌐rosi⌐i desu ka⌐

5. What kind of map would you   Do⌐nna ⌐ti⌐zu ga yo⌐rosi⌐i desu ka⌐
   like?

6. Would you like this kind of   Ko⌐nna kami⌐ ga yo⌐rosi⌐i desu ka⌐
   paper?

7. Would you like that kind of   So⌐nna zassi ga yorosi⌐i desu ka⌐
   magazine?

8. Would you like that map?   A⌐no ti⌐zu ga yo⌐rosi⌐i desu ka⌐

F. Substitution Drill (based on Grammatical Note 4)

(Insert the substitution item in the model sentence as a modifier of pe⌐n
with or without a following particle as required.)

1. Please show me that pen.   So⌐no pe⌐n (o) ⌐mi⌐sete kudasai.

2. Please show me your pen.   A⌐na⌐ta no ⌐pe⌐n (o) ⌐mi⌐sete kudasai.

3. Please show me a good pen.   I⌐i ⌐pe⌐n (o) ⌐mi⌐sete kudasai.

4. Please show me this kind of   Ko⌐nna pe⌐n (o) ⌐mi⌐sete kudasai.
   pen.

5. Please show me a black pen.   Ku⌐ro⌐i ⌐pe⌐n (o) ⌐mi⌐sete kudasai.

6. Please show me an American   A⌐merika no pe⌐n (o) ⌐mi⌐sete kuda-
   pen.   sai.

7. Please show me Mr. Tana-   Ta⌐naka-san no pe⌐n (o) ⌐mi⌐sete ku-
   ka's pen.   dasai.

8. Please show me that pen   A⌐no pe⌐n (o) ⌐mi⌐sete kudasai.
   over there.

9. Please show me a blue pen.   Aˈoˈi ˈpeˈñ (o) ˈmiˈsete kudasai.
10. Please show me a Japanese   Niˈhoñ no peˈñ (o) ˈmiˈsete kudasai.
    pen.

G. Grammar Drill (based on Grammatical Note 4)

Tutor: Toˈokyoo no tiˈzu desu. 'It's a map of Tokyo.'
Student: Toˈokyoo noˈ desu. 'It's one of Tokyo.'

1. Siˈñbuñ no kamiˈ desu kaˌ   Siˈñbuñ noˈ desu kaˌ
2. Oˈokiˈi ˈtiˈzu (o) kaˈimaˈsi-   Oˈokiˈi no (o) kaˈimaˈsita.
   ta.
3. Taˈnaka-sañ no raˈitaa desu   Taˈnaka-sañ noˈ desu kaˌ
   kaˌ
4. Aˈnaˈta no ˈhoˈñ desu kaˌ   Aˈnaˈta no desu kaˌ
5. Kyoˈo no siñbuñ (wa) ˈsuˈḡu   Kyoˈo no (wa) ˈsuˈḡu kimasu.
   kimasu.
6. Aˈmerika no peˈñ (o) ˈmiˈ-   Aˈmerika noˈ (o) ˈmiˈsete kudasai.
   sete kudasai.
7. Waˈtakusi no siñbuñ deˈsu   Waˈtakusi noˈ desu yoˌ
   yoˌ
8. Aˈkai eñpitu (o) onegai-   Aˈkaˈi no (o) onegai-simasu.
   simaˈsu.

H. Expansion Drill

1. I'd like [it].   Oˈnegai-simaˈsu.
   I'd like three.   Mi-ˈttu onegai-simaˈsu.
   I'd like three white ones,   Siˈroˈi no mo mi-ˈttu onegai-simaˈsu.
   too.
   I'd like three of those white   Sono siˈroˈi no mo mi-ˈttu onegai-si-
   ones, too.   maˈsu.

2. I bought [it].   Kaˈimaˈsita.
   I bought two (long cylin-   Niˈ-hoñ kaˈimaˈsita.
   drical units).
   I bought two pencils.   Eñpitu (o) ˈniˈ-hoñ kaˈimaˈsita.
   I bought one pen and two   Peˈñ (o) ˈiˈp-poñ to, eñpitu (o) ˈniˈ-
   pencils.   hoñ kaˈimaˈsita.

3. How much is [it]?   Iˈkura desu kaˌ
   How much is one (thin, flat   Iˈtiˈ-mai ˈiˈkura desu kaˌ
   unit)?
   How much is one sheet of   Kaˈmiˈ (wa) iˈtiˈ-mai ˈiˈkura desu kaˌ
   paper?
   How much is one sheet of   Koˈñna kamiˈ (wa) iˈtiˈ-mai ˈiˈkura
   this kind of paper?   desu kaˌ

4. Do you have [any]?   Goˈzaimaˈsu kaˌ
   Do you have maps too?   Tiˈzu mo goˈzaimaˈsu kaˌ

Do you have maps of America too?	A⌐merika no ti˥zu mo go˥zaima˧su ka⌐
Do you have maps of England AND maps of America?	I⌐ḡirisu no ti˥zu mo A⌐merika no ti˥zu mo go˥zaima˧su ka⌐

5.   It's a dictionary.   Zi⌐biki˥ desu.

      It's a new dictionary.   A⌐tarasi˥i zi⌐biki˧ desu.

      It's my new dictionary.   Bo˥ku no a⌐tarasi˥i zi⌐biki˧ desu.

      This is my new dictionary. Kore wa ⌐bo˥ku no a⌐tarasi˥i zi⌐biki˧ desu.

6.   I don't want [it]!   I⌐rimase˥ñ yo⌐

      I don't want any books!   Ho˥ñ wa i⌐rimase˥ñ yo⌐

      I don't want any dull books! Tu⌐mara˥nai ⌐ho˧ñ wa i⌐rimase˥ñ yo⌐

      I don't want any dull books like that! So⌐ñna tumara˥nai ⌐ho˧ñ wa i⌐rimase˥ñ yo⌐

SUPPLEMENTARY CONVERSATIONS

1. Smith: Sore o to⌐o kudasa˥i.
   Clerk: To˥o desu ka⌐ Ha˥i.
   Smith: A˥a, tyo˥tto ⌐ma˧tte kudasai. Zyu⌐uni onegai-sima˥su.
   Clerk: Mo⌐o huta-tu˥ desu ka⌐
   Smith: E˥e, so˥o desu.
   Clerk: Ka⌐sikomarima˥sita. A⌐riḡatoo gozaimasu.

2. Smith: Sono a⌐o˥i ha⌐iza˧ra o mu-⌐ttu kudasa˥i.
   Clerk: Su⌐mimase˥ñ ḡa, kore wa i⌐tu˥-tu da⌐ke˥ desu ḡa_
   Smith: So˥o desu ka_ Ano ki⌐iro˥i no wa?
   Clerk: A⌐re mo itu˥-tu da⌐ke˧ desu. Do˥o mo su⌐mimase˧ñ.

English Equivalents

1. Smith: Give me ten of those.
   Clerk: Ten? All right.
   Smith: Oh, wait a minute. I'd like twelve.
   Clerk: Two more?
   Smith: Yes, that's right.
   Clerk: Certainly. Thank you.

2. Smith: Give me six of those blue ashtrays.
   Clerk: I'm sorry but there are only five of these (lit. as for these, it's just five). . .
   Smith: Oh? How about those yellow ones?
   Clerk: There are (lit. It is) just five of those, too. I'm very sorry.

EXERCISES

1. Ask for each of the following:

    a. one cigarette
    b. two of those dictionaries
    c. three red pencils
    d. ten sheets of this kind of white paper
    e. five of those small ashtrays
    f. one of those magazines
    g. two of these blue furoshiki
    h. a few of these
    i. all of that
    j. more of those
    k. a little more of that
    l. one more of those (i.e. ashtrays)
    m. one more of those (i.e. pens)
    n. one more of those (i.e. furoshiki)
    o. one more of those (i.e. books)
    p. one sheet of white paper and two sheets of blue paper
    q. two red pencils and three black ones

2. Practice the Basic Dialogues with variations and appropriate props.

Lesson 6. Locating People and Things

BASIC DIALOGUES: FOR MEMORIZATION

(a)

Tanaka

that place or there	soko
embassy	ta⌐isi⌐kañ
American Embassy	A⌐merika-taisi⌐kañ

1. Is that (place) the American Embassy? — Soko (wa) A⌐merika-taisi⌐kañ desu ka⌐

Smith

consulate	ryo⌐ozi⌐kañ

2. No, it's the consulate. — Iie, ryo⌐ozi⌐kañ desu yo⌐

Tanaka

what place? or where?	do⌐ko

3. Where's the embassy? — Ta⌐isi⌐kañ wa ⌐do⌐ko desu ka⌐

Smith

in Tokyo	Tookyoo ni

4. It's in Tokyo. — To⌐okyoo ni arima⌐su.

this place or here	koko
as for in this place or in this place, comparatively speaking	ko⌐ko ni⌐ wa

5. There isn't [one] here. — Ko⌐ko ni⌐ wa a⌐rimase⌐ñ.

(b)

Smith (pointing)

station	e⌐ki
Tokyo Station	To⌐okyo͡o-eki
this one (of two) or this way or hereabouts or here	kotira
side or direction or alternative	ho⌐o
this side or this direction	ko⌐tira no ho͡o

6. Is Tokyo Station this way? — To⌐okyo⌐o-eki (wa) ko⌐tira de⌐su ka⌐
   or Is Tokyo Station in this direction or on this side? — To⌐okyo⌐o-eki (wa) ko⌐tira no ho⌐o desu ka⌐

73

Stranger

building (Western style)	bi⌐ru
beyond _or_ over there _or_ the far side	mukoo
beyond the building	bi⌐ru no mūkoo

7. Yes. It's beyond that big build-ing.   E⌐e. Ano o⌐oki⌐i ⌐bi⌐ru no mu⌐koo de⌐su.

Smith

8. I see. Thank you.   Wa⌐karima⌐sita. A⌐ri⌐gatoo gozaima-sita.

(c)

Smith

that place over there _or_	asoko _or_
over there	asuko
hotel (Western style)	ho⌐teru
it's probably a hotel	ho⌐teru desyoo

9. Do you suppose that (place) is a hotel?   Asoko (wa) ⌐ho⌐teru desyoo ka.

Yamamoto

hmm	sa⌐a

10. I wonder. . . .   Sa⌐a. Do⌐o desyoo ka ⌐ne⌐e.

Tanaka

11. Oh, that IS a hotel.   A⌐a, ho⌐teru desu yo⌐

Smith

12. It's probably expensive, isn't it. _or_ It must be expensive!   Ta⌐ka⌐i desyoo ⌐ne⌐e.

Yamamoto

13. It must be (that way)!   So⌐o desyoo ⌐ne⌐e.

(d)

Smith

be in a place (of animate beings)	i⌐ma⌐su _or_ o⌐rima⌐su ↑ _or_ i⌐rassyaima⌐su ↑

14. Is Mr. Tanaka [in]?   Tanaka-sañ (wa) i⌐ma⌐su ka⌐   _or_ Tanaka-sañ (wa) i⌐rassyaima⌐su ka⌐

Yamamoto

15. No, he isn't.   Iie, i⌐mase⌐ñ. _or_ Iie, o⌐rimase⌐ñ. _or_ Iie, i⌐rassyaimase⌐ñ.

Smith

which one (of two)? or	do⌐tira
which way? or	
whereabouts? or where?	
in what place? or where?	do⌐ko ni or
	do⌐tira ni
16. Where is he?	Do⌐ko ni iᴸma⌐su ka⌟ or
	Do⌐tira ni iᴸrassyaima⌐su ka⌟

Yamamoto

in Kyoto	Kyo⌐oto ni
17. He's in Kyoto.	Kyo⌐oto ni imasu. or
	Kyo⌐oto ni orimasu. or
	Kyo⌐oto ni irassyaimasu.

(e)

Smith

in this area or around here	kono heñ ni
telephone	deñwa or
	o⌐de⌐ñwa +
18. Is(n't) there a telephone around here?	Kono heñ ni deñwa (wa) arimase⌐ñ ka⌟

Tanaka

front	ma⌐e
front of the station	e⌐ki no ⌐ma⌐e
side	yoⱱko
both in front and at the side	ma⌐e ni mo yoⱱko ni⌐ mo
19. There is (indeed). There's [one] in front of the station AND at the side.	Aⱱrima⌐su yo⌟ E⌐ki no ⌐ma⌐e ni mo yoⱱko ni⌐ mo arimasu.
department store	deⱱpa⌐ato
in the department store too	deⱱpa⌐ato ni mo
20. And then there's [one] in that department store, too.	Sore kara, sono deⱱpa⌐ato ni mo arimasu.

Smith

building	taⱱtemo⌐no
21. Which building is the department store?	Deⱱpa⌐ato (wa) ⌐do⌐no taᴸtemo⌐no desu ka⌟ or
	Do⌐no taᴲtemo⌐no ḡa deᴸpa⌐ato desu ka⌟

Tanaka

next door or adjoining	tonari
next door to the station	e⌐ki no to⌐nari
22. It's next door to the station.	E⌐ki no toⱱnari de⌐su.

(f)

Smith

post office	yu⌐ubi⌐ŋkyoku
the post office here <u>or</u>	ko⌐ko no yuubi⌐ŋkyoku
the post office in this place	

23. Where's the post office in this place? Ko⌐ko no yuubi⌐ŋkyoku (wa) ⌐do⌐ko ni a⌐rima⌐su ka⌐

Tanaka

vicinity	so⌐ba
immediate vicinity	su⌐ḡu ⌐so⌐ba
right near the station	e⌐ki no ⌐su⌐ḡu ⌐so⌐ba

24. The post office? It's right near the station. Yu⌐ubi⌐ŋkyoku desu ka⌐ E⌐ki no ⌐su⌐ḡu ⌐so⌐ba ni arimasu.

bank	giñkoo
next door to the bank	giñkoo no to̅nari
the building next door to the bank	giñkoo no to⌐nari no bi⌐ru

25. It's [the building] next door to the big bank. O⌐oki⌐i giñkoo no to⌐nari [no bi⌐ru] desu. [1]

(g)

Smith

inquire	u⌐kaḡaima⌐su ↓
I'm just going to ask [you something] (but)	tyo⌐tto u⌐kaḡaima⌐su ḡa
Imperial Hotel	Te⌐ekoku-ho⌐teru

26. Excuse me but where is the Imperial Hotel? Tyo⌐tto u⌐kaḡaima⌐su ḡa, Te⌐ekoku-ho⌐teru (wa) ⌐do⌐ko desyoo ka.

Stranger

ahead	saki
a little further ahead	mo⌐o suko⌐si saki

27. The Imperial Hotel? It's a little further ahead. Te⌐ekoku-ho⌐teru desu ka⌐ Mo⌐o suko⌐si saki desu.

Smith

left	hidari
the left side <u>or</u> toward the left	hi⌐dari no ho⌐o

28. Is it [on] the left side? Hi⌐dari no ho⌐o desu ka⌐

---

[1] Accent of short alternant: de⌐su.

Stranger

right	miği
the right side or	miği no hoŏo
toward the right	

29. No, it's [on] the right side.　　Iie, miği no hoŏo desu.

Smith

Nikkatsu Building	Niᴿkkatuᴸ-biru[1]
beyond the Nikkatsu	Niᴿkkatuᴸ-biru no muŏkoo
Building	

30. Is it beyond the Nikkatsu Build-　　Niᴿkkatuᴸ-biru no muᴿkoo deᴸsu ka⌐
ing?

Stranger

this side	temae

31. No, it's this side [of it].　　Iie, teᴿmae deᴸsu.

ADDITIONAL VOCABULARY [2]

bookstore	hoᴸñya
cigar store	tabakoya
drugstore	kusuriya
fish market	sakanaya
flower shop	haᴿnaᴸya
inn (Japanese style)	ryokañ
meat market	niᴿkuᴸya
park	kooeñ
school	gakkoo
store or shop (small)	miᴿseᴸ
theater	gekizyoo
toilet	beñzyoᴸ [3] or
	teᴿaᴸrai or
	oᴿteaᴸrai + [4] or
	toᴸiretto
vegetable store	yaoya

NOTES ON THE BASIC DIALOGUES

1. Words like Aᴿmerika-taisiᴸkañ, Toᴿokyoᴸo-eki (sentence 6), Teᴿekoku-hoᴸte-
ru (sentence 26), and Nikkatu - biru (sentence 30) are single, compound

---

[1] Has unaccented alternant.

[2] Practice these words as substitutes for deñwa in Basic Sentence 18 (cf.
Drill G, page 86.

[3] Man's word.

[4] Woman's word.

nominals, which name specific buildings or organizations. Compare
Tóokyóo-eki 'Tokyo Station' and Tóokyoo no eki 'station(s) in Tokyo' —
i.e. any one(s) at all.

7. Remember that an A no B combination (in which A and B are nominals)
    refers to a kind of B. Thus, biʼru no mukoo is a kind of mukoo, i.e. 'the
    far side described by the building' or 'beyond the building.' Muʼkoo no
    biʼru, on the other hand, is a kind of biʼru, i.e. 'the building described by
    the far side' or 'the building over there.'

8. Waʼkarimaʼsita often means 'I have understood what you just said (i.e. the
    information you just gave me, or what you just told me to do).'

18. The negative here occurs as a less direct—and slightly more polite—
     alternative. It does not mean that the speaker expects a negative reply.

21. Taʼtemoʼno is the general word for 'building,' but biʼru is commonly used
     only in reference to large, Western-style buildings. The first alterna-
     tive of sentence 21 means literally ' As for the department store, which
     building is it? '

23. Koko here refers to 'this place' meaning 'this town' or 'this village' or
     'this particular section.' Koʼko no yuubiʼnkyoku is another example of the
     particle no between nominals the first of which describes the second.

24. Suʼguʼ soʼba is an example of one nominal describing another without the
     intervening particle no. Only certain nominals occur in this pattern.

26. √Uʼkagaimaʼsu (gerund ukagatte) is a humble polite verbal. Tyoʼtto uʼka-
     gaimaʼsu ga and suʼmimaseʼn ga are both common Japanese equivalents
     of English 'excuse me but': the former is used when the speaker is about
     to request information, and the latter is an apology for interrupting,
     bothering, etc. Thus, in stopping a stranger on the street to ask for di-
     rections, either one may be used; in asking someone to do something,
     however, the former does not occur.

27. Saki usually means ' ahead—on the same street or route,' whereas mukoo
     'beyond,' 'over there' is a word of more general meaning.

GRAMMATICAL NOTES

1. Copula: Tentative

De'syoʼo is the less positive, less direct equivalent of deʼsu. It will hereafter be called the TENTATIVE of deʼsu. Compare:

> Hoʼn desu. 'It's a book.'
> Hoʼn desyoo. 'It's probably a book,' 'I think it's a book,' 'It must be
> a book,' etc.

Both deʼsu and deʼsyoʼo are formal.

Like deʼsu, deʼsyoʼo may refer to present or future time, and it follows
nominals and adjectivals. (Other uses will be introduced later.) It is unaccented
when the preceding word or phrase is accented.

Examples:

Ta⌐naka-sañ desyo⌐o. 'It probably is (or will be) Mr. Tanaka.'
I⌐i desyoo. 'I guess it's all right.'
So⌐o desyoo. 'I guess that's right.'
O⌐mosiro⌐i desyoo. 'It's probably interesting.'

In questions, the less direct de⌐syo⌐o is slightly more polite than de⌐su. Compare:

Do⌐ko desu ka‿ 'Where is it?'
Do⌐ko desyoo ka. 'Where would it be?' 'Where do you suppose it is?'
etc.—or simply 'Where is it?'

The indicated difference in intonation is common.

Both de⌐syo⌐o statements and de⌐syo⌐o ka questions are often followed by exclamatory ne⌐e (Lesson 1, Grammatical Note 4). Thus:

Da⌐me⌐ desyoo ⌐ne⌐e. 'It must be out of order!' 'I guess it is out of order, isn't it.'
Ya⌐su⌐i desyoo ⌐ne⌐e. 'It must be cheap!' 'I guess it is cheap, isn't it.'
Na⌐ñ desyoo ka ⌐ne⌐e. 'What DO you suppose it is!' 'I'm wondering what it is,' 'What is it indeed!'
Do⌐o desyoo ka ⌐ne⌐e. 'I wonder [about what you said],' 'I wonder how [what you said] would be,' 'How WOULD it be!'

WARNING: Be sure to distinguish between the pronunciation of de⌐syo⌐o (de-⌐syo⌐-o) and de⌐su yo (de⌐-su-yo). The former indicates doubt, probability, indefiniteness, indirectness, etc., whereas the latter indicates certainty, assurance, emphasis, etc.

2. do⌐ko desu ka ~ do⌐ko ni a⌐rima⌐su ka

X de⌐su (in which X is a nominal) has two basic meanings: '[it] is X' or '[it] is described by X.' Accordingly, depending on context, To⌐okyoo de⌐su means either '[it] is Tokyo' or '[it] is described by—i.e. has something to do with—Tokyo.' Compare:

Koko wa To⌐okyoo de⌐su. 'This (place) is Tokyo.'

and:

Ta⌐isi⌐kañ wa To⌐okyoo de⌐su. 'The embassy is described by Tokyo' —i.e. 'The embassy is in Tokyo.'

In other words, if √de⌐su is preceded by a place word (or phrase), the combination may signify equivalence or it may describe the location of something or someone. Accordingly, do⌐ko desu ka, depending on context, means either 'what place is it?' or 'what place describes it?'—i.e. 'where is it?'

Examples:

Koko wa ⌐do⌐ko desu ka‿ 'What place is this (place)?'
Tanaka-sañ wa ⌐do⌐ko desu ka‿ 'Mr. Tanaka is described by what place?'—i.e. 'Where is Mr. Tanaka?'

Koko wa Oˊosaka deˋsu. 'This (place) is Osaka.'
Aˊno hoˋteru wa Oˊosaka deˋsu. 'That hotel is described by Osaka'—
i.e. 'That hotel is in Osaka.'

There is a second construction, used only in describing location:

$$\text{Place expression} + \underline{ni} + \begin{cases} \sqrt{a^\lceil rima^\rceil su} \\ \sqrt{i^\lceil ma^\rceil su} \end{cases}$$

Aˊrimaˋsu in its location meaning refers to inanimate objects and iˊmaˋsu refers to the location of animate beings. The particle ni follows the place expression which tells where something or someone is.

Examples:

Taˊisiˋkañ wa Toˊokyoo ni arimaˋsu. 'The embassy is located in
Tokyo.'
Tanaka-sañ wa ˊdoˋko ni iˊmaˋsu ka⌣ 'Where (i.e. in what place) is
Mr. Tanaka located?'
Aˊno hoˋteru wa Oˊosaka ni arimaˋsu. 'That hotel is located in
Osaka.'

To sum up: Place expression + deˋsu means either '[it] is the place' or
'[it] is described by the place.' In the latter meaning, it is used more or less
interchangeably with a pattern consisting of place expression + ni + aˊrimaˋsu
~ iˊmaˋsu. '[something or somebody] is located in the place.' Thus, the
equivalent of 'it is the front' is maˋe desu; the equivalent of 'it is in front' is
maˋe desu or maˋe ni arimasu.

3. iˊmaˋsu ~ oˊrimaˋsu ~ iˊrassyaimaˋsu

These three verbals all occur with the same lexical meaning: 'an animate
object is located in a place.' They differ only in politeness.

Iˊmaˋsu belongs to the plain level—the level of aˊrimaˋsu, waˊkarimaˋsu,
kaˊrimaˋsu, etc.

Like goˏzaimaˋsu, oˊrimaˋsu and iˊrassyaimaˋsu are polite words, but
goˏzaimaˋsu is neutrally polite (+), whereas oˊrimaˋsu is humble (↓) and iˊrassyaimaˋsu is honorific (↑).

Oˊrimaˋsu is used most commonly in reference to oneself, members of one's
own family, and one's own close friends, or in any situation where the speaker
wishes to talk politely without exalting the position of the subject to which the
verbal refers. Iˊrassyaimaˋsu, on the other hand, exalts the position of its
subject and, accordingly, is NEVER USED IN REFERENCE TO ONESELF.
Compare:

{ Employee: Taˊnaka-sañ irassyaimaˋsu ka⌣ 'Is Mr. Tanaka (i.e. the boss)
in?'
Tanaka's Secretary: Haˋa, iˊrassyaimaˋsu. 'Yes, he is.'

{ Visitor: Taˊnaka-sañ irassyaimaˋsu ka⌣ 'Is Mr. Tanaka in?'
Tanaka's co-worker: Haˋa, oˊrimaˋsu. 'Yes, he is.'

Oꜝrimaꜞsu and iꜝrassyaimaꜞsu, like many other polite words introduced previously, are used more commonly—though by no means exclusively—by women.

4. Particle _ni_ of Location

The particle _ni_ 'in,' 'on,' 'at' follows a nominal of place which indicates the location of something animate or inanimate, and is followed by √aꜝrimaꜞsu or √iꜝmaꜞsu or a more polite equivalent (cf. Note 2 above).

Examples:

>Aꜝsoko ni arimaꜞsu. 'It's over there (lit. in that place).'
>Asoko ni koꜝoeñ ḡa arimaꜞsu. 'Over there there's a park.'
>Gaꜝkkoo no maꜝe ni imasu. '[He] is in front of the school.'
>Teꜝekoku-hoꜞteru ni orimasu. 'I'm at the Imperial Hotel.'

Note that particle _ni_ is not ordinarily used in _desu_ sentences. Compare:

>Tonari wa giꜝñkoo deꜞsu. 'Next door is a bank.'

but:

>Tonari ni giꜝñkoo ḡa arimaꜞsu. '(In the place) next door there's a bank.'

5. Multiple Particles

In Japanese there are many occurrences of multiple particles—sequences of more than one consecutive particle. That is to say, a particle may follow a sequence that ends with a particle. Study the following examples:

>waꜝtakusi no hoꜞñ ni 'in my book'
>waꜝtakusi no hoꜞñ ni mo 'in my book too,' as in—

Taꜝnaka-sañ no hoꜞñ ni arimasu. . . . Waꜝtakusi no hoꜞñ ni mo arimasu. 'It's in Mr. Tanaka's book. . . . It's in my book, too.'

>koko ni 'in this place'
>koꜝko niꜞ wa[1] 'in this place, comparatively speaking,' as in—

Doꜝko ni aꜟrimaꜞsu ka⌣ . . . Toꜝokyoo ni arimaꜞsu. Koꜝko niꜞ wa aꜝrimaseꜞñ. 'Where is it? . . . It's in Tokyo. It isn't here.'

Particles _wa_ and _mo_ may follow _ni_ and various other particles which will be introduced later; but they replace, rather than follow, _ḡa_ and _o_. Compare the following groups:

>{ Koꜝko ni arimaꜞsu. 'It's here.'
> Soꜝko niꜞ wa aꜝrimaseꜞñ. 'It isn't there.'
> Aꜝsoko niꜞ mo aꜟrimaseꜞñ. 'It isn't over there either.'

---

[1] Particle _ni_ acquires an accent when it follows an unaccented word and is followed by an unaccented particle.

⎰ Ta⌐bako g̃a arima⌐su. 'There are cigarettes.'
⎱ Ma⌐tti mo arimasu. 'There are matches, too.'
  Ra⌐itaa wa a⌐rimase⌐n̄. 'There isn't a lighter.'

⎰ Ho⌐n̄ o ka⌐ima⌐sita. 'I bought a book.'
⎱ Za⌐ssi mo kaima⌐sita. 'I bought a magazine, too.'
  Sin̄buñ wa ka⌐mase⌐n̄ desita. 'A paper I didn't buy.'

6. Place-Word Series

koko	kotira	ko⌐tti⌐
soko	sotira	so⌐tti⌐
asoko	atira	a⌐tti⌐
do⌐ko	do⌐tira	do⌐tti

The above words—all nominals—bear an obvious resemblance to the <u>kore</u>, <u>kono</u>, and <u>koñna</u> series.

The first group (<u>koko</u>, <u>soko</u>, etc.) refer specifically to place:

    koko 'this place' or 'here'
    soko 'that place' or 'there'
    asoko[1] 'that place over there' or 'over there'
    do⌐ko 'what place?' or 'where?'

The words of the second group (<u>kotira</u>, <u>sotira</u>, etc.) have several meanings:

(1) they refer to one alternative out of two possibilities.[2]

    Compare: Do⌐re desu ka⌐ . . . Ko⌐re de⌐su. 'Which one (of three or
    more) is it? . . . It's this one.'

    and: Do⌐tira desu ka⌐ . . . Ko⌐tira de⌐su. 'Which one (of two) is
    it? . . . It's this one.'

(2) they have a directional meaning. In a different context—for example,
pointing to a fork in the road—the last example above would have a different meaning:

    Do⌐tira desu ka⌐ . . . Ko⌐tira de⌐su. 'Which way is it? . . .
    It's this way.'

(3) they have an indefinite locational meaning: 'hereabouts,' 'thereabouts,'
'whereabouts.' The indirect and vague, as mentioned before, is more
polite in Japanese than the direct and specific; accordingly, the <u>kotira</u>
series with meaning (3) often occurs as a polite equivalent of the <u>koko</u>

---

[1] <u>Asuko</u> is an alternant of <u>asoko</u>. It is particularly common in rapid speech.

[2] The <u>kore</u> series more commonly refers to inanimate objects, but the <u>kotira</u> series in meaning (1) refers equally to animate beings and to objects.

series. Thus, in asking a stranger for the location of something, do˥tira desyoo ka [lit.] 'whereabouts would it be?' is simply a more indirect—and therefore m o r e polite—way of saying 'where is it?' Similarly, with polite √go⌐zaima˥su and √i⌐rassyaima˥su, the kotira series is more common than the koko series. Do˥tira ni i⌐rassyaima˥su ka is a more polite way of saying do˥ko ni i⌐ma˥su ka 'where is he?'

One further use of the kotira series will be introduced later.

Summary: kotira 'this one (of two),' 'this way,' 'hereabouts,' 'here'

   sotira and atira[1] 'that way (of two),' 'that way,' 'thereabouts,' 'there'

   do˥tira 'which one (of two)?' 'which way?' 'whereabouts?' 'where?'

The ko⌐tti˥ series in an informal, contracted equivalent of the kotira series. Its members have the same meanings but they are used in less formal speech.

7. -ya

Product name + -ya means 'place where the product is sold' or 'dealer in the product.' Thus:

tabako 'cigarette' or 'tobacco'	tabakoya 'cigar store' or 'tobacco dealer'
ho˥ñ 'book'	ho˥ñya 'bookstore' or 'book dealer'
ha⌐na˥ 'flower'	ha⌐na˥ya 'flower shop' or 'florist'
kusuri 'medicine'	kusuriya 'drugstore' or 'druggist'
ni⌐ku˥ 'meat'	ni⌐ku˥ya 'meat market' or 'butcher'
sakana 'fish'	sakanaya 'fish market' or 'fish man'

The dealer is often addressed with the appropriate -ya word + -sañ. For example:

   Ku⌐suriyasañ de˥su ka⌐ 'Are you the druggist?'

DRILLS

A. Substitution Drill

1. Where is that?	Sore (wa) ⌐do˥ko desu ka⌐
2. Which one (of three or more) is that?	Sore (wa) ⌐do˥re desu ka⌐
3. How is that? or How about that?	Sore (wa) ⌐do˥o desu ka⌐

1
   The differences between the two words are parallel to the differences between sore and are (cf. Lesson 2, Grammatical Note 3).

    4. What is that?   Sore (wa) ⌈na⌉n̄ desu ka↲

    5. Which way (or which of   Sore (wa) ⌈do⌉tira desu ka↲
        two, or whereabouts) is
        that?

    6. Which building is that?   Sore (wa) ⌈do⌉no ⌐bi⌐ru desu ka↲

    7. How is that? or   Sore (wa) i⌈ka⌉ḡa desu ka↲
        How about that?

    8. How much is that?   Sore (wa) ⌈i⌉kura desu ka↲

    9. How many yen is that?   Sore (wa) ⌈na⌉n̄-en̄ desu ka↲

  10. Which way (or which of   Sore (wa) ⌈do⌉tti desu ka↲
        two, or whereabouts) is
        that?

B. Substitution Drill

    1. It's beyond the embassy.   Ta⌈isi⌉kan̄ no mu⌈koo de⌉su.

    2. It's in front of the embassy. Ta⌈isi⌉kan̄ no ⌈ma⌉e desu.

    3. It's at the side of the em- Ta⌈isi⌉kan̄ no yo⌈ko de⌉su.
        bassy.

    4. It's next door to the em- Ta⌈isi⌉kan̄ no to⌈nari de⌉su.
        bassy.

    5. It's near the embassy.   Ta⌈isi⌉kan̄ no ⌈so⌉ba desu.

    6. It's right near the embassy. Ta⌈isi⌉kan̄ no ⌈su⌉ḡu ⌐so⌐ba desu.

    7. It's up ahead, past the em- Ta⌈isi⌉kan̄ no sa⌈ki de⌉su.
        bassy.

    8. It's this side of the em- Ta⌈isi⌉kan̄ no te⌈mae de⌉su.
        bassy.

    9. It's to the right of the em- Ta⌈isi⌉kan̄ no mi⌈ḡi de⌉su.
        bassy.

  10. It's to the left of the em- Ta⌈isi⌉kan̄ no hi⌈dari de⌉su.
        bassy.

C. Substitution Drill

    1. It's the store over there. Mu⌈koo no mise⌉ desu.

    2. It's the store in front.   Ma⌈e no mi⌐se⌐ desu.

    3. It's the store at the side. Yo⌈ko no mise⌉ desu.

    4. It's the store next door.   To⌈nari no mise⌉ desu.

    5. It's the store right near. Su⌈ḡu ⌐so⌐ba no mi⌐se⌐ desu.

    5. It's the store up ahead.   Sa⌈ki no mise⌉ desu.

    7. It's the store on the right. Mi⌈ḡi no mise⌉ desu.

    8. It's the store on the left. Hi⌈dari no mise⌉ desu.

    9. It's a store in Tokyo.   To⌈okyoo no mise⌉ desu.

  10. It's a store in America.   A⌈merika no mise⌉ desu.

D. Substitution Drill

(The Japanese sentences with the intonations as marked correspond to English sentences having the emphasis on the final word or words.)

    1. It's the school next door   Ko⌈oen̄ no tonari no gakkoo de⌉su.
        to the park.

2. It's the park next (door) to   Ga⌐kkoo no tonari no <u>kooeñ</u> de⌐su.
   the school.

3. It's the vegetable store next   Ha⌐na⌐ya no to⌐nari no <u>yaoya</u> de⌐su.
   door to the florist.

4. It's the florist next door to   Ya⌐oya no tonari no <u>hana⌐ya</u> desu.
   the vegetable store.

5. It's the cigar store next   Ho⌐ñya no to⌐nari no <u>tabakoya</u> de⌐su.
   door to the bookstore.

6. It's the bookstore next door   Ta⌐bakoya no tonari no <u>ho⌐ñya</u> desu.
   to the cigar store.

7. It's the drugstore next door   Ni⌐ku⌐ya no to⌐nari no <u>kusuriya</u> de⌐su.
   to the meat market.

8. It's the meat market next   Ku⌐suriya no tonari no <u>niku⌐ya</u> desu.
   door to the drugstore.

9. It's the post office next   Gi⌐ñkoo no tonari no <u>yuubi⌐ñkyoku</u>
   door to the bank.   desu.

10. It's the bank next door to   Yu⌐ubi⌐ñkyoku no to⌐nari no <u>giñkoo</u>
    the post office.   de⌐su.

E. Substitution Drill

1. The park is next (door) to   Kooeñ wa ga⌐kkoo no tonari de⌐su.
   the school. [1]

2. The school is next door to   Gakkoo wa <u>ko⌐oeñ</u> no tonari de⌐su.
   the park.

3. The florist is next door to   Ha⌐na⌐ya wa <u>ya⌐oya</u> no tonari de⌐su.
   the vegetable store.

4. The vegetable store is next   Yaoya wa <u>ha⌐na⌐ya</u> no to⌐nari de⌐su.
   door to the florist.

5. The bookstore is next door   Ho⌐ñya wa <u>ta⌐bakoya</u> no tonari de⌐su.
   to the cigar store.

6. The cigar store is next   Tabakoya wa <u>⌐ho⌐ñya</u> no to⌐nari de⌐su.
   door to the bookstore.

7. The meat market is next   Ni⌐ku⌐ya wa <u>ku⌐suriya</u> no tonari de⌐su.
   door to the drugstore.

8. The drugstore is next door   Kusuriya wa <u>ni⌐ku⌐ya</u> no to⌐nari de⌐su.
   to the meat market.

9. The bank is next door to   Giñkoo wa <u>yu⌐ubi⌐ñkyoku</u> no to⌐nari
   the post office.   de⌐su.

10. The post office is next door   <u>Yu⌐ubi⌐ñkyoku</u> wa <u>gi⌐ñkoo</u> no tonari
    to the bank.   de⌐su.

---

[1] In order to correspond to the Japanese sentences, the emphasis of the English sentences in this drill must fall on the second half of the sentence. After mastering the drill in its present form, go through it again replacing every <u>wa</u> with <u>ga</u>; now the emphasis in the English shifts to the first half of the sentence.

F. Substitution Drill

1. Next (door) to the school is a park.[1]   Gakkoo no tonari wa ko⌐oeñ de⌐su.

2. Next door to the park is a school.   Kooeñ no tonari wa ga⌐kkoo de⌐su.

3. Next door to the vegetable store is a florist.   Yaoya no tonari wa ha⌐na⌐ya desu.

4. Next door to the florist is a vegetable store.   Ha⌐na⌐ya no tonari wa ya⌐oya de⌐su.

5. Next door to the cigar store is a bookstore.   Tabakoya no tonari wa ⌐ho⌐ñya desu.

6. Next door to the bookstore is a cigar store.   Ho⌐ñya no tonari wa ta⌐bakoya de⌐su.

7. Next door to the drugstore is a meat market.   Kusuriya no tonari wa ni⌐ku⌐ya desu.

8. Next door to the meat market is a drugstore.   Ni⌐ku⌐ya no tonari wa ku⌐suriya de⌐su.

9. Next door to the post office is a bank.   Yu⌐ubi⌐ñkyoku no tonari wa gi⌐ñkoo de⌐su.

10. Next door to the bank is a post office.   Giñkoo no tonari wa yu⌐ubi⌐ñkyoku desu.

G. Substitution Drill

1. Is(n't) there a telephone around here?   Kono heñ ni de⌐ñwa (wa) arimase⌐ñ ka⌐

2. Is(n't) there a station around here?   Kono heñ ni ⌐e⌐ki (wa) a⌐rimase⌐ñ ka⌐

3. Is(n't) there a hotel around here?   Kono heñ ni ⌐ho⌐teru (wa) a⌐rimase⌐ñ ka⌐

4. Is(n't) there a department store around here?   Kono heñ ni de⌐pa⌐ato (wa) a⌐rimase⌐ñ ka⌐

5. Is(n't) there a bank around here?   Kono heñ ni gi⌐ñkoo (wa) arimase⌐ñ ka⌐

6. Is(n't) there a consulate around here?   Kono heñ ni ryo⌐ozi⌐kañ (wa) a⌐rimase⌐ñ ka⌐

7. Is(n't) there an embassy around here?   Kono heñ ni ta⌐isi⌐kañ (wa) a⌐rimase⌐ñ ka⌐

8. Is(n't) there a post office around here?   Kono heñ ni yu⌐ubi⌐ñkyoku (wa) a⌐rimase⌐ñ ka⌐

---

[1] In order to correspond to the Japanese sentences, the emphasis of the English sentences in this drill must fall on the second half of the sentence. After mastering the drill in its present form, go through it again replacing every wa with ga; now the emphasis in the English shifts to the first half of the sentence.

H. Substitution Drill

1. Excuse me, but where is the American Embassy?	Tyoᐟtto uᒷkaḡaimaᐟsu ḡa, Aᒷmerika-taisiᐟkañ (wa) ᒷdoᐟko desyoo ka.
2. Excuse me, but where is Tokyo Station?	Tyoᐟtto uᒷkaḡaimaᐟsu ḡa, Toᒷokyoᒷo-eki (wa) ᒷdoᐟko desyoo ka.
3. Excuse me, but where is the Imperial Hotel?	Tyoᐟtto uᒷkaḡaimaᐟsu ḡa, Teᒷekoku-hoᐟteru (wa) ᒷdoᐟko desyoo ka.
4. Excuse me, but where is the Nikkatsu Building?	Tyoᐟtto uᒷkaḡaimaᐟsu ḡa, Nikkatu-biru (wa) ᒷdoᐟko desyoo ka.
5. Excuse me, but where is the Bank of Japan?	Tyoᐟtto uᒷkaḡaimaᐟsu ḡa, Niᒷhoñ-giᐟñkoo (wa) ᒷdoᐟko desyoo ka.
6. Excuse me, but where is the British Embassy?	Tyoᐟtto uᒷkaḡaimaᐟsu ḡa, Eᒷekoku-taisiᐟkañ (wa) ᒷdoᐟko desyoo ka.
7. Excuse me, but where is the Tokyo Hotel?	Tyoᐟtto uᒷkaḡaimaᐟsu ḡa, Toᒷokyoo-hoᐟteru (wa) ᒷdoᐟko desyoo ka.
8. Excuse me, but where is the Bank of America?	Tyoᐟtto uᒷkaḡaimaᐟsu ḡa, Aᒷmerika-giᐟñkoo (wa) ᒷdoᐟko desyoo ka.

I. Grammar Drill (based on Grammatical Note 5)

Tutor: Koᒷko ni arimaᐟsu. /soko/ 'It's here.' /'there'/
Student: Soᒷko niᐟ mo arimasu. 'It's there, too.'

1. Eᐟki no ᒷmaᐟe ni arimasu. /yoko/	Eᐟki no yoᒷko niᐟ mo arimasu.
2. Tanaka-sañ (wa) Toᒷokyoo ni imaᐟsu. /Yamamoto-sañ/	Yaᒷmamoto-sañ mo Tookyoo ni imaᐟsu.
3. Tookyoo ni ryoᒷoziᐟkañ (ḡa) arimasu. /Koᐟobe/	Koᐟobe ni mo ryoᒷoziᐟkañ (ḡa) arima-su.
4. Koko (wa) oᒷteaᐟrai desu. /asuko/	Aᒷsuko mo oteaᐟrai desu.
5. Koko ni oᒷteaᐟrai (ḡa) arimasu. /asuko/	Aᒷsuko niᐟ mo oᒷteaᐟrai (ḡa) arima-su.
6. Ziᐟsyo (o) kaᒷimaᐟsita. /siñbuñ/	Siᒷñbuñ mo kaimaᐟsita.
7. Taᒷbako (o) oneḡai-simaᐟsu. /raᐟitaa/	Raᐟitaa mo oneḡai-simasu.
8. Kono heñ ni niᒷkuᐟya (wa) aᒷrimaseᐟñ. /sakanaya/	Kono heñ ni saᒷkanaya mo arimaseᐟñ.

J. Grammar Drill (based on Grammatical Note 1)

Tutor   Peᐟñ desu. 'It's a pen.'
Student: Peᐟñ desyoo. 'It's probably a pen.'

1. Huᒷruᐟi desu.	Huᒷruᐟi desyoo.
2. Gaᒷkkoo deᐟsu.	Gaᒷkkoo desyoᐟo.
3. Soᐟo desu.	Soᐟo desyoo.
4. Naᐟñ desu ka⌐	Naᐟñ desyoo ka.
5. Taᒷnaka-sañ noᐟ desu.	Taᒷnaka-sañ noᐟ desyoo.
6. Soᐟo desu ᒷneᐟe.	Soᐟo desyoo ᒷneᐟe.

7. Ta⌐ka⌐i desu ˥ne˩e.   Ta⌐ka⌐i desyoo ˥ne˩e.
8. Do⌐ko desu ka˩   Do⌐ko desyoo ka.

K. Response Drill (based on Grammatical Note 2)

(Give the answer in the same basic form as the question.)

1. Koko (wa) ⌐do⌐ko desu ka˩   Ko⌐obe desu.
    /Ko⌐obe/
2. A⌐merika-taisi⌐kañ (wa)   To⌐okyoo ni arima⌐su.
    ⌐do⌐ko ni arimasu ka˩
    /Tookyoo/
3. Asoko ni ⌐na⌐ni (g̃a) arimasu   Ko⌐oeñ (g̃a) arima⌐su.
    ka˩   /kooeñ/
4. Kooeñ (wa) ⌐do⌐ko ni arima-   A⌐soko ni arima⌐su.
    su ka˩   /asoko/
5. Kooeñ (wa) ⌐do⌐ko desu ka˩   A⌐soko de⌐su.
    /asoko/
6. Tanaka-sañ (wa) ⌐do⌐ko ni   A⌐soko ni ima⌐su.
    imasu ka˩   /asoko/
7. Te⌐ekoku-ho⌐teru no ˥ma˩e   Ko⌐oeñ de⌐su.
    (wa) ⌐na⌐ñ desu ka˩
    /kooeñ/
8. Te⌐ekoku-ho⌐teru no ˥ma˩e   Ko⌐oeñ (g̃a) arima⌐su.
    ni ⌐na⌐ni (g̃a) arimasu
    ka˩   /kooeñ/
9. Kooeñ (wa) ⌐do⌐ko desu ka˩   Te⌐ekoku-ho⌐teru no ˥ma˩e desu.
    /Te⌐ekoku-ho⌐teru no
    ˥ma˩e/
10. Kooeñ (wa) ⌐do⌐ko ni ari-   Te⌐ekoku-ho⌐teru no ˥ma˩e ni ari-
    masu ka˩   /Te⌐ekoku-   masu.
    ho⌐teru no ˥ma˩e/

L. Level Drill[1]

1. Ta⌐naka-sañ ima⌐su ka˩   Ta⌐naka-sañ irassyaima⌐su ka˩
2. Ta⌐bako arima⌐su ka˩   Ta⌐bako gozaima⌐su ka˩
3. Tyo⌐tto ˥ma˩tte kudasai.   Syo⌐osyoo o˥mati-kudasa˩i.
4. Tanaka-sañ (wa) ⌐do⌐ko ni   Tanaka-sañ (wa) ⌐do⌐tira ni i˥rassyai-
    i˥ma˩su ka˩   ma˩su ka˩
5. I⌐kura desu ka˩   O⌐ikura de⌐su ka˩
6. I⌐kutu a˥rima˩sita ka˩   O⌐ikutu gozaima⌐sita ka˩
7. Ge⌐ñki desu ka˩   O⌐ge⌐ñki desu ka˩

_____

[1] The sentences on the right are more polite equivalents of the sentences on
the left.

   8. Ta⌐naka ima⌐su ka˩ [1]   Ta⌐naka orima⌐su ka˩
   9. Kono heñ ni yu⌐ubi⌐ñkyoku   Kono heñ ni yu⌐ubi⌐ñkyoku (wa) go˩za-
      (wa) a˩rimase˩ñ ka˩   imase˩ñ ka˩
  10. Tanaka-sañ (wa) i⌐mase⌐ñ   Tanaka-sañ (wa) i⌐rassyaimase⌐ñ de-
      desita ka˩   sita ka˩

M. Expansion Drill

   1. [It]'s beyond.   Mu⌐koo de⌐su.
      [It]'s beyond the post office.   Yu⌐ubi⌐ñkyoku no mu⌐koo de⌐su.
      [It]'s beyond the big post of-   O⌐oki⌐i yu˩ubi˩ñkyoku no mu⌐koo
      fice.   de⌐su.
      [It]'s beyond that big post   Ano o⌐oki⌐i yu˩ubi˩ñkyoku no mu⌐koo
      office.   de⌐su.
      Tokyo Station is beyond that   To⌐okyo⌐o - eki (wa) ano o⌐oki⌐i yu˩u-
      big post office.   bi˩ñkyoku no mu⌐koo de⌐su.

   2. [It]'s probably expensive.   Ta⌐ka⌐i desyoo.
      [It] must be expensive!   Ta⌐ka⌐i desyoo ˩ne˩e.
      The inn must be expensive!   Ryokañ (wa) ta⌐ka⌐i desyoo ˩ne˩e.
      The new inn must be expen-   A⌐tarasi⌐i ryokañ (wa) ta⌐ka⌐i desyoo
      sive!   ˩ne˩e.
      A new inn like that must be   So⌐ñna atarasi⌐i ryokañ (wa) ta⌐ka⌐i
      expensive!   desyoo ˩ne˩e.

   3. There is.   A⌐rima⌐su.
      There's a toilet.   To⌐iretto (g̃a) arimasu.
      There's a toilet over there,   A⌐soko ni⌐ mo ˩to˩iretto (g̃a) arima-
      too.   su.
      There's a toilet here AND   Ko⌐ko ni⌐ mo a⌐soko ni⌐ mo ˩to˩iret-
      over there.   to (g̃a) arimasu.

   4. There is.   A⌐rima⌐su.
      Where is [it]?   Do⌐ko ni a˩rima˩su ka˩
      Where is the hotel?   Ho⌐teru (wa) ⌐do⌐ko ni a˩rima˩su ka˩
      Where is the new hotel?   A⌐tarasi⌐i ˩ho˩teru (wa) ⌐do⌐ko ni a˩ri-
                                                   ma˩su ka˩
      Where is the new hotel in   Oosaka no a⌐tarasi⌐i ˩ho˩teru (wa)
      Osaka?   ⌐do⌐ko ni a˩rima˩su ka˩

   5. There isn't [any].   A⌐rimase⌐ñ.
      Isn't there [any]?   A⌐rimase⌐ñ ka˩
      Is(n't) there an inn?   Ryo⌐kañ (wa) arimase⌐ñ ka˩
      Is(n't) there a good inn?   I⌐i ryo˩kañ (wa) arimase˩ñ ka˩
      Is(n't) there a good inn   Kono heñ ni ⌐i⌐i ryo˩kañ (wa) arima-
      around here?   se˩ñ ka˩

---

[1] Spoken for example by a relative of Mr. Tanaka's.

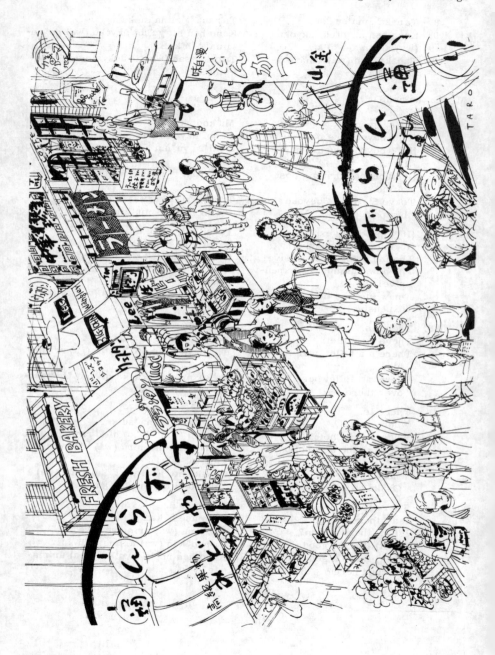

6. What is [it]?   Na⌐a⌐ñ desyoo ka.
   What is the big building?   O⌐oki⌐i ⌐bi⌐ru (wa) ⌐na⌐ñ desyoo ka.
   What is the big building on   Miḡi no o⌐oki⌐i ⌐bi⌐ru (wa) ⌐na⌐ñ de-
     the right?   syoo ka.
   What is the big building to   E⌐ki no miḡi no o⌐oki⌐i ⌐bi⌐ru (wa)
     the right of the station?   ⌐na⌐ñ desyoo ka.

7. [It]'s a florist.   Ha⌐na⌐ya desu.
   Is [it] a florist?   Ha⌐na⌐ya desu ka⌐.
   Is [it] a new florist?   A⌐tarasi⌐i ha⌐na⌐ya desu ka⌐.
   Is [it] that new florist?   Sono a⌐tarasi⌐i ha⌐na⌐ya desu ka⌐.
   Which shop is that new   Do⌐no mi⌐se⌐ ḡa sono a⌐tarasi⌐i
     florist?   ha⌐na⌐ya desu ka⌐.

8. There's a drugstore.   Ku⌐suriya (ḡa) arima⌐su.
   There's a big drugstore.   O⌐oki⌐i ku⌐suriya (ḡa) arima⌐su.
   [Up] ahead there's a big   Saki ni o⌐oki⌐i ku⌐suriya (ḡa) arima⌐-
     drugstore.   su.
   A little ahead there's a big   Su⌐ko⌐si saki ni o⌐oki⌐i ku⌐suriya (ḡa)
     drugstore.   arima⌐su.
   A little further ahead there's   Mo⌐o suko⌐si saki ni o⌐oki⌐i ku⌐suri-
     a big drugstore.   ya (ḡa) arima⌐su.

SHORT SUPPLEMENTARY DIALOGUES

1. A: Wa⌐takusi no zi⌐syo ⌐do⌐ko desu ka⌐
   B: Ko⌐ko de⌐su yo⌐

2. A: Kyo⌐o no siñbuñ ko⌐ko de⌐su yo⌐
   B: Wa⌐karima⌐sita.   Do⌐o mo.

3. A: Ta⌐naka-sañ to Yamamoto-sañ ima⌐su ka⌐
   B: Ta⌐naka-sañ wa ima⌐su ḡa, Ya⌐mamoto-sañ wa imase⌐ñ.

4. Visitor: Ta⌐naka-sañ irassyaima⌐su ka⌐
   Secretary: Ha⌐a, i⌐rassyaima⌐su. Syo⌐osyoo o⌐mati-kudasa⌐i.

5. Mrs. Tanaka (calling her husband's office): Ta⌐naka orima⌐su ka⌐
   Secretary: Ha⌐a, i⌐rassyaima⌐su. Syo⌐osyoo o⌐mati-kudasaima⌐se.

6. A: Be⌐ñzyo⌐ ko⌐tti⌐ desu ka⌐
   B: Iie, so⌐tti⌐ desu yo.

7. A: So⌐ñna ho⌐ñ (wa) ta⌐ka⌐i desyoo ⌐ne⌐e.
   B: So⌐o desyoo ⌐ne⌐e.

8. A: Sore wa ⌐na⌐ñ desyoo ka.
   B: Na⌐ñ desyoo ka ⌐ne⌐e.

9. A: Soko wa ga⌐kkoo desyo⌐o ka.
   B: Sa⌐a. Do⌐o desyoo ka ⌐ne⌐e.

10. A: I⌐i desu ka⌐
    B: Ma⌐a ⌐i⌐i desyoo.

English Equivalents

1.   A: Where's my dictionary?
     B: Here it is!

2.   A: Today's paper is [over] here!
     B: I see.   Thanks.

3.   A: Are Mr. Tanaka and Mr. Yamamoto in?
     B: Mr. Tanaka is (in) but Mr. Yamamoto isn't (in).

4.   Visitor: Is Mr. Tanaka in?
     Secretary: Yes, he is (in).   Just a moment, please.

5.   Mrs. Tanaka: Is [Mr.] Tanaka in?
     Secretary: Yes, he is (in).   Just a moment, please.

6.   A: Is the toilet this way?
     B: No, it's that way.

7.   A: A book like that must be expensive!
     B: It must be!

8.   A: What do you suppose that is?
     B: What DO you suppose it is!   (or   What is it, indeed!)

9.   A: Would that (place) be a school?
     B: I wonder . . .

10. A: Is it all right?
     B (reluctantly): I guess it probably is (all right).

—oOo—

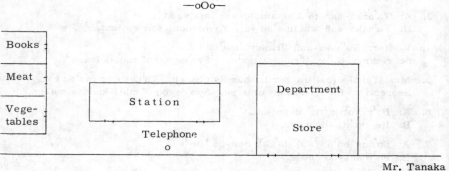

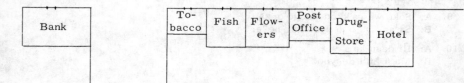

EXERCISES

1. Answer the following on the basis of the diagram on page 92.

   a. True – False

      (1) E⌐ki no ⌐ma⌐e ni de⌐ñwa ḡa arima⌐su.
      (2) E⌐ki no tonari wa de⌐pa⌐ato desu.
      (3) Ga⌐kkoo wa arima⌐su ḡa, gi⌐ñkoo wa arimase⌐ñ.
      (4) Yu⌐ubi⌐ñkyoku no tonari ni sa⌐kanaya ḡa arima⌐su.
      (5) E⌐ki no yoko ni mi⌐se⌐ ḡa arimasu.

   b. Answer the following questions for Mr. Tanaka, who is facing in the di-
      rection of the arrow.

      (1) Giñkoo wa sa⌐ki de⌐su ka⌐
      (2) E⌐ki wa ⌐do⌐tira desyoo ka⌐
      (3) Kono heñ ni ⌐ho⌐ñya wa a⌐rimase⌐ñ ka⌐
      (4) Do⌐ñna mi⌐se⌐ ḡa ⌐e⌐ki no yo⌐ko ni arima⌐su ka⌐
      (5) Yaoya wa ⌐e⌐ki no te⌐mae de⌐su ka⌐

2. Using the diagram on page 92, other similar diagrams, photographs, or
   models, take turns asking and answering questions about the identity and
   location of the buildings.   Always use 'left' and 'right' relative to a position facing the front of a building.

3. You ask a stranger: The stranger replies:

   a. where the American Em-   It's that way.
      bassy is.
   b. where the Imperial Hotel   It's near the Nikkatsu Building.
      is.
   c. where Tokyo Station is.   It's beyond that big building.
   d. where the British Consulate   It's this side of that white building.
      is.
   e. if there is(n't) a telephone   There's [one] in front of the station.
      around here.
   f. if that is the Nikkatsu Ho-   No, it's the Imperial Hotel.
      tel.
   g. if Tokyo is in this direction.   No, it's that way.
   h. if there is(n't) a post office   There is. It's next to that big bank.
      around here.
   i. if the Imperial Theater is on   No, it's on the right.
      the left.

4. Practice the Basic Dialogues with variations and appropriate props.

Lesson 7. Around Town

BASIC DIALOGUES: FOR MEMORIZATION

(a)

Smith

now	i⌐ma
to what place?	do⌐ko e <u>or</u>
	do⌐ko ni <u>or</u>
	do⌐tira e <u>or</u>
	do⌐tira ni
go	i⌐kima⌐su <u>or</u>
	ma⌐irima⌐su ↑ <u>or</u>
	i⌐rassyaima⌐su ↑

1. Where are you going to go now?

   I⌐ma ⌐do⌐ko │e / ni│ i⌐kima⌐su ka⌐ <u>or</u>

   I⌐ma ⌐do⌐tira │e / ni│ i⌐rassyaima⌐su ka⌐

Tanaka

movie theater	e⌐eḡa⌐kañ
to a movie theater	e⌐eḡa⌐kañ e <u>or</u>
	e⌐eḡa⌐kañ ni

2. I'm going to go to a movie (theater).

   E⌐eḡa⌐kañ │e / ni│ ikimasu. <u>or</u>

   E⌐eḡa⌐kañ │e / ni│ mairimasu.

3. Won't you go too? <u>or</u>
   Wouldn't you [like to] go too?

   A⌐na⌐ta mo i⌐kimase⌐ñ ka⌐ <u>or</u>
   A⌐na⌐ta mo i⌐rassyaimase⌐ñ ka⌐

Smith

4. Thank you but I'm afraid I can't [just] now.

   A⌐ri⌐ḡatoo gozaimasu ḡa, i⌐ma wa ⌐tyo⌐tto⌐

(b)

Smith

Marunouchi Building (in Tokyo)	Maru-biru
to the Maru-biru	Maru-biru e <u>or</u>
	Maru-biru ni
want to go <u>or</u> would like to go	ikitai /-ku/
street <u>or</u> road <u>or</u> way	miti

5. I want to go to the Maru-biru   Ma⌐ru - biru │ e │ ikita⌐i n̄ desu ḡa,
    but I don't know the way (lit.   │ ni│
    the road isn't clear).   mi⌐ti ḡa wakarimase⌐n̄.

     write or draw   ka⌐kima⌐su
     would you write (or draw)   ka⌐ite ku⌐dasaimase⌐n̄ ka
       for me
6. Would you (just) draw a map   Tyo⌐tto, ti⌐zu (o) ⌐ka⌐ite ku⌐dasai-
    for me?   mase⌐n̄ ka⌐

              Tanaka

     avenue or wide street   to⌐ori⌐
7. A map? The Maru-biru is a   Ti⌐zu desu ka⌐ Maru-biru (wa) ko⌐no
    little further along this street   toori⌐ no mo⌐o suko⌐si sa⌐ki de⌐su
    (but)...   ḡa⌐

              Smith

8. Then I don't need a map, do I.   Zya⌐a, ti⌐zu wa i⌐rimase⌐n̄ ⌐ne⌐e.

                 (c)

              Smith

     (a section between Tokyo   Kawasaki
       and Yokohama)
     to Kawasaki   Kawasaki e   or
                    Kawasaki ni
     teach or inform   o⌐siema⌐su
     would you teach (or in-   o⌐siete kudasaimase⌐n̄ ka
       form) me?
9. I want to go to Kawasaki. Would   Ka⌐wasaki │ e │ ikita⌐i n̄ desu ḡa,
    you show me the way?   │ ni│
                                       mi⌐ti (o) osiete kudasaimase⌐n̄ ka⌐

              Tanaka

     space between   aida
     between Tokyo and Yoko-   Tookyoo to Yokohama no aida
       hama
10. Kawasaki? Why, it's between   Ka⌐wasaki de⌐su ka⌐ To⌐okyoo to
    Tokyo and Yokohama.   Yokohama no aida de⌐su yo⌐

              Smith

11. Oh? Then, it's that road,   So⌐o desu ka. Zya⌐a, so⌐no miti de⌐su
    isn't it.   ⌐ne⌐e.

              Tanaka

12. That's right.   So⌐o desu yo⌐

                 (d)

              Smith

     policeman   zyun̄sa[1]

---

[1] Alternate accent: zyu⌐n̄sa.

13. Is(n't) there a policeman around   Kono heñ ni zyuᶜñsa (wa) imaseˀñ ka⌐
     here?

Tanaka

     police box   koobañ
14. There's a police box over there.   Asoko ni koᶜobañ g̃a arimaˀsu yo⌐

Smith (to policeman)

     hospital   byooiñ
     St. Luke's Hospital   Seᶜeroka-byoˀoiñ
15. Say! Where (or which way) is   Tyoˀtto.   Seᶜeroka-byoˀoiñ (wa) ᶜdoˀ-
     St. Luke's Hospital?   tira desu ka⌐

Policeman

     up ahead from here   kono saki
16. St. Luke's Hospital? Why, it's   Seᶜeroka-byoˀoiñ desu ka⌐ Kono saki
     the big building on the left side   no hiᶜdari no hoˀo no oᶜokiˀi taᵗte-
     up ahead (from here).   moᵗno desu yo⌐

Smith

17. I see.   Thank you very much.   Waᶜkarimaˀsita.   Doˀo mo aᵗriᵗg̃a-
                                           too gozaimasita.

(e)
Tanaka

     by means of what?   naˀñ de
     let's go   iᶜkimasyoˀo   or
                                           maᶜirimasyoˀo ↓
     shall we go?   iᶜkimasyoˀo ka   or
                                           maᶜirimasyoˀo ka
18. How shall we go?   Naˀñ de iᵗkimasyoᵗo ka.   or
                                           Naˀñ de maᵗirimasyoᵗo ka.

Smith

     taxi   taˀkusii
     by taxi   taˀkusii de
19. Let's go by taxi.   Taˀkusii de iᵗkimasyoᵗo.   or
                                           Taˀkusii de maᵗirimasyoᵗo.

· · ·

Driver

20. Where to?   Doˀtira |e / ni| ?

Tanaka

     as far as Tokyo Station   Toᶜokyoˀo-eki made
     please go   iᵗte kudasaˀi
21. (Go as far as) Tokyo Station,   Toᶜokyoˀo-eki made (iᵗte kudasaᵗi).
     please.

· · ·

Smith

be in a hurry	i⌐soḡima⌐su
please don't hurry	i⌐soḡa⌐nai de kudasai

22. Please don't go so fast. Añmari i⌐soḡa⌐nai de kudasai.

. . .

Driver

23. [This] is Tokyo Station (but) . . . To⌐okyo⌐o-eki desu ḡa＿

Tanaka

automobile	zi⌐do⌐osya
car or cart	kuruma
back or rear	usiro
at the back	usiro de
bring to a halt	to⌐mema⌐su
please bring to a halt	to⌐mete kudasa⌐i

24. Please stop in back of that black car. Ano ku⌐ro⌐i kuruma no u⌐siro de to-mete kudasa⌐i.

(f)

Passenger

(section of Tokyo)	Giñza
1-chome	i⌐t-tyoome⌐
2-chome	ni-⌐tyoome⌐
as far as 4-chome	yo⌐ñ-tyoome⌐ made

25. (Go as far as) Ginza 4-chome, please. . . . Giñza yoñ-tyoome⌐ made (i⌐tte kudasa⌐i). . . .

is dangerous	abunai /-ku/

26. Oh! Look out! A. Abunai.

Driver

safe or all right	da⌐izyo⌐obu

27. It's all right! . . . Da⌐izyo⌐obu desu yo. . . .

28. [This] is 4-chome (but) . . . Yo⌐ñ-tyoome⌐ desu ḡa＿

Passenger

next	tu⌐gi⌐
street corner	ka⌐do
next corner	tu⌐gi⌐ no ⌐ka⌐do
make a turn	ma⌐ḡarima⌐su
turn a corner	ka⌐do o ma⌐ḡarima⌐su
turn to the right	mi⌐ḡi e maḡarima⌐su or mi⌐ḡi ni maḡarima⌐su
please turn	ma⌐ḡatte kudasa⌐i

29. Please turn right at the next corner. (Lit. Please turn the next corner to the right.) . . . Tu⌐gi⌐ no ⌐ka⌐do (o) mi⌐ḡi | e / ni | ma-ḡatte kudasa⌐i. . . .

straight	ma⌐ssu⌐ğu
going straight along this street	kono miti o ma⌐ssu⌐ğu itte
end of a street or corridor	tukiatari
turn at the end of the street	tu⌐kiatari o mağarima⌐su

30. Please go straight along this street, and turn (to the) left at the end. . . .

Kono miti (o) ma⌐ssu⌐ğu itte, tuki-atari (o) hi⌐dari |e ni| mağatte kuda-sa⌐i. . . .

at that place over there	asoko de

31. Please stop over there.   . . .

A⌐soko de tomete kudasa⌐i.   . . .

go back	mo⌐dorima⌐su
please go back	mo⌐do⌐tte kudasai

32. Please back up a little.   . . .

Tyo⌐tto mo⌐do⌐tte kudasai.   . . .

33. Here we are! Thanks (for your trouble).

Ko⌐ko de⌐su yo⌐   Go⌐ku⌐roosama.

NOTES ON THE BASIC DIALOGUES

1. I⌐ma 'now' is a nominal (i⌐ma desu 'it's now'; i⌐ma zya a⌐rimase⌐ñ 'it isn't now'). I⌐ma with a non-past verbal refers to immediate future, and with a past verbal to immediate past: I⌐ma simasu 'I'll do [it] now'; i⌐ma si⌐ma⌐sita 'I just did [it].'

5. Remember that √wa⌐karima⌐su is never preceded by particle o. Both the person who understands and the thing which is clear are followed by ğa or wa, depending upon emphasis.

7. 'It's a little further along this street but—if you want a map, I'll draw one.' To⌐ori⌐ usually refers to a broad avenue, whereas miti is any street or road. As the second part of a compound, to⌐ori⌐ becomes -doori: thus, Ya⌐esu-do⌐ori 'Yaesu Avenue,' Na⌐miki-do⌐ori 'Namiki Avenue.'

9. Mi⌐sema⌐su means 'show—i.e. let someone see'; o⌐siema⌐su means 'show —i.e. explain.' Note particle ğa connecting a statement of fact with a re-lated question or request.

14. Koobañ 'police boxes' are booths located at frequent intervals throughout Japanese cities where one or more policemen are on duty at all times.

16. Ta⌐temo⌐no has three modifiers in this sentence: kono saki, hi⌐dari no ho⌐o, and o⌐oki⌐i. The first two are nominal modifiers, each followed by particle no. O⌐oki⌐i, an adjectival modifier, takes no connecting par-ticle.

21. Itte here is the gerund of i⌐kima⌐su 'go.' This itte is not to be confused with the itte of mo⌐o iti-do itte kudasa⌐i 'please say it once more,' the gerund of i⌐ima⌐su 'say.' The two gerunds sound alike; they are distin-guished only by context in the spoken language.

22. The gerund of i⌐soğima⌐su is i⌐so⌐ide. This is the first example of a

gerund ending in -<u>de</u> instead of the more common -<u>te.</u>

23. 'This is Tokyo Station but—where shall I go from here? <u>or</u> where do you want to get out?'

24. 'Stop' here means 'stop the taxi,' 'bring the taxi to a halt.'

26. Note the use of the informal adjectival. The formal equivalent would be a͡buna͡i desu.

27. Da͡izyo͡obu, a nominal, has many English equivalents: 'safe,' 'all right,' 'O.K.,' 'don't worry,' 'I can manage,' etc. The underlying meaning is one of safety or security or lack of concern.

28. See 23 above.

GRAMMATICAL NOTES

1.   Adjectivals Ending in -<u>tai</u> 'want to —'

Take a verbal in its -<u>ma͡su</u> form: replace -<u>ma͡su</u> with -<u>tai,</u> and the result is an ADJECTIVAL meaning 'want to (<u>or</u> would like to) do so-and-so.'[1] For example:

ka͡kima͡su	'[I] write'	ka͡kita͡i	'[I] want to write'
i͡kima͡su	'[I] go'	ikitai	'[I] want to go'
ka͡ima͡su	'[I] buy'	kaitai	'[I] want to buy'
si͡ma͡su	'[I] do'	sitai	'[I] want to do'

Like all other adjectivals, a -<u>tai</u> form alone is informal. The formal equivalent is the informal + <u>de͡su</u>—in this case, yielding -<u>ta͡i desu</u>—and the formal negative is the derived -<u>ku</u> form + a͡rimase͡n. Compare:

ti͡isa͡i desu '[it] is small' : ti͡isaku a͡rimase͡n '[it] is not small'
i͡kita͡i desu '[I] want to go' : i͡kitaku arimase͡n '[I] don't want to go'

A common formal pattern, frequently followed by g͡a 'but,' is -ta͡i ñ desu— an example of the pattern adjectival + nominal + <u>de͡su</u> (cf. ti͡isa͡i ͡ho͡ñ desu 'it is a small book'). Ñ[2] is a nominal meaning something like 'matter,' 'fact,' 'case,' and i͡kita͡i ñ desu means literally 'it is a wanting-to-go matter.'

The adjectival + ñ desu pattern is not limited to -<u>tai</u> adjectivals; any other adjectival may occur in the same construction. Thus:

---

[1] Whether or not a -<u>tai</u> word is accented depends on the verbal root from which it is derived. But all adjectivals—and therefore all -<u>tai</u> words—are accented in their occurrences before √de͡su.

[2] Ñ is the contraction of a nominal <u>no</u>, which occurs in more formal, precise speech.

⌐a┐buna┐i ñ desu 'it is dangerous' (lit. 'it is a matter of being dangerous')

i┐i ñ desu 'it's fine' (lit. 'it is a matter of being fine')

The alternative with ñ is considered softer and less abrupt than the alternative without ñ.   More will be said about this pattern later.

The particle g̃a 'but' frequently follows a -tai pattern. In final position it serves to qualify and/or soften the preceding: 'I'd like to do so-and-so but—do you mind?' or 'is it all right?' or 'I don't know how to proceed' or 'I can't,' etc. (Cf. Lesson 4, Grammatical Note 5.)

In statements, -tai patterns usually refer to the speaker, and in questions, to the person addressed.

-Tai words have one special characteristic: the direct object (followed by particle o) of a verbal often becomes the subject (followed by particle g̃a) of the adjectival -tai derivative. Thus:

Si⌐ñbuñ o kaima┐su. 'I am going to buy a newspaper.'

but:

Si⌐ñbuñ g̃a kaita┐i ñ desu g̃a— 'I want to buy a newspaper but . . .'

Siñbuñ o kaitai also occurs and has the same meaning. With many -tai words the g̃a alternant is more common, but with some o is more usual. Observe individual examples as they occur.

WARNING: A -tai question means 'do you WANT to do so-and-so?' 'is so-and-so what you want to do?' in a literal sense.   It does not carry the same connotation as English questions beginning 'would you like to do so-and-so?'; these are invitations, and the usual Japanese equivalent is a negative question. Example:

A⌐sita kimase┐ñ ka— 'Won't you come tomorrow?' 'Would(n't) you like to come tomorrow?' etc.

Compare also Basic Sentence 3 in this lesson.

2.   Verbal Tentative

The tentative of a formal verbal is made by changing the -ma┐su ending to -masyo┐o (compare de┐su and de⌐syo┐o).   One English equivalent is 'let's do so-and-so' or, in a question, 'shall we do so-and-so?'; another will be introduced in a later lesson.

Examples:

So⌐o simasyo┐o. 'Let's do that.' or 'Let's do [it] that way.'

I⌐sog̃imasyo┐o. 'Let's hurry.'

I⌐kimasyo┐o ka. 'Shall we go?'

In polite speech, the humble form—not the honorific—is used:

Ma⌐irimasyo┐o ka. 'Shall we go?'

Ma⌐irimasyo┐o. 'Let's go.'

Note: The use of the assertive sentence particle yo following the formal tentative—for example, i⌐kimasyo⌐o yo 'let's go!'—is typical of women's speech.

3. Particles e 'to,' ni 'to,' ma⌐de 'as far as,' de 'at,' de 'by means of,' o 'through'

    a. e and ni

    A nominal of place followed by particle e 'to' modifies an inflected expression directly or is followed by another particle; it indicates a goal. When a phrase ending in e modifies a nominal, it is regularly followed by no. Examples:

> Do⌐ko e i⌐kimasyo⌐o ka.   'Where (lit. to what place) shall we go?'
> Tanaka-san wa To⌐okyoo e kima⌐su ka⌐   'Is Mr. Tanaka coming to Tokyo?'
> Ko⌐oen e⌐ mo i⌐kima⌐sita. 'I went to the park, too.'
> Kyo⌐oto e wa i⌐kimase⌐n desita. 'I didn't go to Kyoto (in comparison with other places).'
> To⌐okyoo e no miti de⌐su ka⌐ 'Is it the road to Tokyo?'

In this pattern, ni 'to' may usually be used instead of e. For example, the first two sentences cited just above could be changed to Do⌐ko ni i⌐kimasyo⌐o ka. and Tanaka-san wa To⌐okyoo ni kima⌐su ka⌐ with no significant difference in meaning. This ni must not be confused with ni meaning 'in'; the two particles are distinguished by the immediate context, particularly the accompanying verbal. Compare:

> Kyo⌐oto ni arimasu. 'It's in Kyoto.'
> Kyo⌐oto ni ikimasu. 'I'm going to Kyoto.'
> Ga⌐kkoo ni imase⌐n desita. '[He] wasn't in school.'
> Ga⌐kkoo ni kimase⌐n desita. '[He] didn't come to school.'

Sometimes a larger context is required. For example, i⌐rassyaima⌐su has been introduced as the honorific equivalent of both i⌐ma⌐su and i⌐kima⌐su. Therefore, depending on context, ga⌐kkoo ni irassyaima⌐su might mean 'he is in school' or 'he is going to go to school.'

    b. ma⌐de

    A nominal of place followed by ma⌐de 'as far as,' 'up to and including but not beyond' occurs as a modifier of inflected expressions directly or followed by another particle, and indicates how far something proceeds. When a phrase ending in ma⌐de modifies a nominal, it is regularly followed by no. Ma⌐de normally loses its accent when it follows an accented word.

    Examples:

> Do⌐ko made i⌐kima⌐sita ka⌐ 'How far (lit. as far as what place) did you go?'
> Ko⌐ko ma⌐de si⌐ma⌐sita. 'I did [it] as far as this point' (indicating a place in the lesson, for example).

A⌐merika e⌐ wa[1] i⌐kima⌐sita ḡa, Nyu⌐uyo⌐oku made wa[1] i⌐kimase⌐ñ
desita.   'I did go to America, but I didn't go as far as New York.'
To⌐okyoo ma⌐de no mi⌐ti de⌐su ka⌐   'Is it the road [that goes] as
far as Tokyo?'

c. <u>de</u> 'at,' 'in'

A nominal of place followed by particle <u>de</u> occurs as a modifier of inflected expressions directly or followed by another particle, and indicates the
place where something happens. This is in contrast with the pattern consisting
of a place word + <u>ni</u> + √ a⌐rima⌐su or √ i⌐ma⌐su meaning 'something <u>or</u> someone
is statically located in a place.' Examples:

A⌐soko de tomete kudasa⌐i. 'Please stop [the car] over there.'
De⌐pa⌐ato de ka⌐ima⌐sita. 'I bought [it] at a department store.'
Ho⌐ñya de wa[1] ka⌐imase⌐ñ desita. 'I didn't buy [it] at a bookstore.'
Ga⌐kkoo de kakima⌐sita. 'I wrote [it] at school.'
Do⌐ko de si⌐masyo⌐o ka. 'Where shall we do [it]?'

d. <u>de</u> 'by means of'

A nominal + <u>de</u> 'by means of' occurs as a modifier of an inflected expression directly or followed by another particle and indicates the means by
which an action is accomplished. Examples:

Ta⌐kusii de ki⌐ma⌐sita. 'I came by taxi.'
E⌐ñpitu de kakima⌐sita. 'I wrote with a pencil.'
Pe⌐ñ de wa[1] ka⌐kimase⌐ñ desita. 'I didn't write with a pen.'
Ma⌐tti de si⌐ma⌐sita. 'I did [it] with a match.'

e. <u>o</u> 'through,' 'along'

A nominal of place + <u>o</u> followed by a word of motion indicates the place
through which the motion takes place. Examples:

A⌐no miti o ikimasyo⌐o. 'Let's go along that street.'
Tu⌐ḡi⌐ no ⌐ka⌐do o ma⌐ḡatte kudasa⌐i. 'Please turn the next corner.'
(Lit. 'Please make a turn through the next corner.')

Like particle <u>o</u> which follows a direct object (for example, ho⌐ñ o ka⌐ima⌐sita
'I bought a book'), this <u>o</u> is often omitted in conversation.

4.   Verbal Gerund + <u>ku⌐dasaimase⌐ñ ka</u>

Reread Grammatical Note 3 of Lesson 4.

The gerund (i. e. the -te or -de form) of a verbal + <u>ku⌐dasaimase⌐ñ ka</u>—lit.
'won't you [be kind enough to] give me?'—is a very polite request, softer and

---

[1] <u>Wa</u> = the <u>wa</u> of comparison.

less direct than one consisting of a gerund + the imperative ku⌐dasa⌐i.   Examples:

> Ma⌐tte ku⌐dasaimase⌐n̄ ka˩ 'Would you be kind enough to wait for me?' (Lit. 'Won't you [be kind enough to] give me waiting?')
>
> Mi⌐sete ku⌐dasaimase⌐n̄ ka˩ 'Would you be kind enough to show me?' (Lit. 'Won't you [be kind enough to] give me showing?')
>
> O⌐siete kudasaimase⌐n̄ ka˩ 'Would you be kind enough to instruct me?' (Lit. 'Won't you [be kind enough to] give me instructing?')

5. . . . ma⌐ssu⌐ḡu itte   . . . ma⌐ḡatte kudasa⌐i

Observe the following four pairs of independent sentences:

1. (a) Kono miti (o) ma⌐ssu⌐ḡu i⌐tte kudasa⌐i. 'Please go straight along this street.'
   (b) Tukiatari (o) hi⌐dari e maḡatte kudasa⌐i. 'Please turn left at the end.'

2. (a) Kono miti (o) ma⌐ssu⌐ḡu ikimasu. '[I] go (or will go) straight along this street.'
   (b) Tukiatari (o) hi⌐dari e maḡarima⌐su. '[I] turn (or will turn) left at the end.'

3. (a) Kono miti (o) ma⌐ssu⌐ḡu i⌐kima⌐sita. '[I] went straight along this street.'
   (b) Tukiatari (o) hi⌐dari e maḡarima⌐sita. '[I] turned left at the end.'

4. (a) Kono miti (o) ma⌐ssu⌐ḡu i⌐kimasyo⌐o. 'Let's go straight along this street.'
   (b) Tukiatari (o) hi⌐dari e maḡarimasyo⌐o. 'Let's turn left at the end.'

Each pair can be combined into a single, complex sentence, meaning 'A and [then] B,' simply by replacing the inflected word or phrase at the end of the first sentence with its corresponding gerund.[1] The gerund regularly ends with comma intonation, and the next word begins a new accent phrase. Thus:

1. Kono miti (o) ma⌐ssu⌐ḡu itte, tukiatari (o) hi⌐dari e maḡatte kudasa⌐i. 'Please go straight along this street, and turn left at the end.'

2. Kono miti (o) ma⌐ssu⌐ḡu itte, tukiatari (o) hi⌐dari e maḡarima⌐su. '[I] go (or will go) straight along this street, and turn left at the end.'

3. Kono miti (o) ma⌐ssu⌐ḡu itte, tukiatari (o) hi⌐dari e maḡarima⌐sita. '[I] went straight along this street and turned left at the end.'

4. Kono miti (o) ma⌐ssu⌐ḡu itte, tukiatari (o) hi⌐dari e maḡarimasyo⌐o. 'Let's go straight along this street, and turn left at the end.'

---

[1] When three or more sentences are combined in this way, the inflected word or phrase at the end of every sentence except the last is replaced by the corresponding gerund.

Note that regardless of whether the sentence final is past, non-past, tentative, imperative, etc., the gerund is used in the middle. In other words, the time and mode of complex sentences like these are determined only by the time and mode of the inflected forms at the end of the sentence and by context—unless, of course, a time word like 'today,' 'tomorrow,' etc. furnishes additional time evidence.

6. i⌐kima¬su ~ ma⌐irima¬su ~ i⌐rassyaima¬su

I⌐kima¬su 'go' is a plain formal verbal, and ma⌐irima¬su and i⌐rassyaima¬su are polite formal verbals with the same meaning. Ma⌐irima¬su, a humble verbal, is used in polite speech in reference to oneself or members of one's own family, while i⌐rassyaima¬su, an honorific, is used in reference to persons other than the speaker, in an exalting sense.

The following is a chart of the verbals introduced thus far that have polite equivalents:

Meaning	Plain Formal	Polite Formal		
		Neutral [+]	Humble [↓]	Honorific [↑]
'be located (inanimate) or have'	a⌐rima¬su	go⌐zaima¬su		
'be located (animate)'	i⌐ma¬su		o⌐rima¬su	i⌐rassyaima¬su
'go'	i⌐kima¬su		ma⌐irima¬su	i⌐rassyaima¬su

7. kono saki

Kono saki means 'up ahead, from here,' and sono saki means 'up ahead, from there,' 'further (along the road) than that.' Words of the kono series plus other nominals of place have parallel meanings. For example:

> ko⌐no ma¬e 'in front of this'
> sono usiro 'in back of that'
> ano mukoo 'beyond that'
> kono tonari 'next door to this [place]'
> so⌐no so¬ba 'near that'

8. -tyoome 'chome'

With the exception of the names of a few main arteries, street names are rarely used in Japan. Addresses are usually given in terms of location within particular sections, and directions are regularly given in terms of landmarks —hence the common use of maps and diagrams and the frequent stops at police boxes for instructions.

One of the divisions into which some sections of a city are divided is the -tyoome. While it is one of the smallest divisions, its size is not fixed, and there may be considerable variation among the -tyoome of a given section. The numerals of Series I (i⌐ti¬, ni¬, sañ, etc.) combine with -tyoome to name (not count!) the -tyoome. Study the following list, noting particularly the forms for '1,' '8,' and '10':

i⌐t-tyoome¬	'1-chome'[1]	ro⌐ku-tyoome¬	'6-chome'
ni-⌐tyoome¬	'2-chome'	na⌐na-tyoome¬	'7-chome'
sa⌐ñ-tyoome¬	'3-chome'	ha⌐t-tyoome¬	'8-chome'
yo⌐ñ-tyoome¬	'4-chome'	kyu⌐u-tyoome¬	'9-chome'
go-⌐tyoome¬	'5-chome'	zi⌐t-tyoome¬ or	
		zyu⌐t-tyoome¬	'10-chome'

na⌐ñ-tyoome¬ 'what number chome?'

The lower numbers occur more frequently.

DRILLS

A. Substitution Drill

(Insert no whenever appropriate.)

1.	Please turn the next corner.	Tu⌐gi¬ no ⌐ka⌐do (o) ma⌐gatte kuda-sa¬i.
2.	Please turn that corner.	A⌐no ka⌐do (o) ma⌐gatte kudasa¬i.
3.	Please turn the corner where the school is.	Ga⌐kkoo no ka⌐do (o) ma⌐gatte kuda-sa¬i.
4.	Please turn the corner where the department store is.	De⌐pa⌐ato no ⌐ka⌐do (o) ma⌐gatte ku-dasa¬i.
5.	Please turn the corner where the police box is.	Ko⌐obañ no ka⌐do (o) ma⌐gatte kuda-sa¬i.
6.	Please turn the corner where the hospital is.	Byo⌐oiñ no ka⌐do (o) ma⌐gatte kuda-sa¬i.
7.	Please turn the corner where the drugstore is.	Ku⌐suriya no ka⌐do (o) ma⌐gatte ku-dasa¬i.
8.	Please turn the corner where the cigar store is.	Ta⌐bakoya no ka⌐do (o) ma⌐gatte ku-dasa¬i.

---

[1] This is the usual English equivalent, although 'chome 1' or '1st chome' would be more accurate.

B. Substitution Drill

1.	It's between Tokyo and Yo-kohama.	Tookyoo to Yoᶜkohama no aida deˀsu.
2.	It's between Japan and America.	Niˀhoˀn̄ to Aᶜmerika no aida deˀsu.
3.	It's between a bank and a department store.	Giñkoo to deᶜpaˀato no aᵗida deˀsu.
4.	It's between a bookstore and a flower shop.	Hoˀñya to haˀnaˀya no aᵗida deˀsu.
5.	It's between the embassy and the consulate.	Taˀisiˀkañ to ryoᶜoziˀkañ no aᵗida deˀsu.
6.	It's between the books and the magazines.	Hoˀn̄ to zaᶜssi no aida deˀsu.
7.	It's between Mr. Tanaka and Mr. Yamamoto.	Tanaka-sañ to Yaᶜmamoto-sañ no ai-da deˀsu.
8.	It's between the car and the taxi.	Kuruma to ᶜtaˀkusii no aᵗida deˀsu.

C. Substitution Drill

1.	MR. TANAKA went.	Taᶜnaka-sañ ḡa ikimaˀsita.
2.	Mr. Tanaka (compared with the others) went.	Taᶜnaka-sañ wa ikimaˀsita.
3.	Mr. Tanaka went, too.	Taᶜnaka-sañ mo ikimaˀsita.
4.	He went by cab.	Taˀkusii de iᵗkimaˀsita.
5.	He went along that street.	Soᶜno miti (o) ikimaˀsita.
6.	He went to the bank.	Giᶜñkoo e ikimaˀsita.
7.	He went to the bank.	Giᶜñkoo ni ikimaˀsita.
8.	He went as far as the bank.	Giᶜñkoo maˀde iᵗkimaˀsita.

D. Substitution Drill

1.	Please stop here.	Koᶜko de tomete kudasaˀi.
2.	Please wait here.	Koᶜko de maˀtte kudasai.
3.	Please write here.	Koᶜko de kaˀite kudasai.
4.	Please do [it] here.	Koᶜko de site kudasaˀi.
5.	Please buy [it] here.	Koᶜko de katte kudasaˀi.
6.	Please say [it] here.	Koᶜko de itte kudasaˀi.

E. Grammar Drill (based on Grammatical Note 2)

Tutor: Aᶜsoko e ikimaˀsu. 'I'm going to go there.'
Student: Aᶜsoko e ikimasyoˀo. 'Let's go there.'

1.	Eᶜeḡaˀkañ e maᵗirimaˀsu.	Eᶜeḡaˀkañ e maᵗirimasyoˀo.
2.	Tiˀzu (o) kaᵗkimaˀsu.	Tiˀzu (o) kaᵗkimasyoˀo.
3.	Iᶜsoḡimaˀsu.	Iᶜsoḡimasyoˀo.
4.	Gaᶜkkoo no maˀe de toᵗme-maˀsu.	Gaᶜkkoo no maˀe de toᵗmemasyoˀo.
5.	Tuᶜḡiˀ no ᵗkaˀdo (o) maᵗḡa-rimaˀsu.	Tuᶜḡiˀ no ᵗkaˀdo (o) maᵗḡarimasyoˀo.

6. Ka⌐do made mo˥dorima˧su.   Ka⌐do made mo˥dorimasyo˧o.
7. Kyo⌐o no si˥ñbuñ (o) kai-   Kyo⌐o no si˥ñbuñ (o) kaimasyo˧o.
   ma˧su.
8. So⌐o sima⌐su.   So⌐o simasyo⌐o.

F. Grammar Drill (based on Grammatical Note 1)

    Tutor: Ma⌐ru-biru e ikima⌐su. 'I'm going to go to the Maru-biru.'
    Student: Maru-biru e i⌐kita⌐i ñ desu ḡa_ 'I'd like to go to the Maru-
             biru (but) . . .'

1. A⌐sita⌐ mo i˥kima˧su.   A⌐sita⌐ mo i⌐kita⌐i ñ desu ḡa_
2. E⌐ñpitu de kakima⌐su.   Eñpitu de ka⌐kita⌐i ñ desu ḡa_
3. E⌐eḡa⌐kañ no ˥ka˧do (o)   E⌐eḡa⌐kañ no ˥ka˧do (o) ma⌐ḡarita⌐i
   ma˥ḡarima˧su.   ñ desu ḡa_
4. Ze⌐ñbu si˥ma˧su.   Ze⌐ñbu si⌐ta⌐i ñ desu ḡa_
5. Yu⌐ubi⌐ñkyoku e i˥kima˧su.   Yu⌐ubi⌐ñkyoku e i⌐kita⌐i ñ desu ḡa_
6. A⌐tarasi⌐i ku˥ruma (o) kai-   A⌐tarasi⌐i kuruma (o) ka⌐ita⌐i ñ desu
   ma˧su.   ḡa_
7. Tyo⌐tto u˥kaḡaima˧su ḡa_   Tyo⌐tto u⌐kaḡaita⌐i ñ desu ḡa_
8. A⌐soko de tomema⌐su.   Asoko de to⌐meta⌐i ñ desu ḡa_

G. Grammar Drill (based on Grammatical Note 4)

    Tutor: A⌐na⌐ta no siñbuñ (o) ⌐mi⌐sete kudasai. 'Please show me your
             paper.'
    Student: A⌐na⌐ta no siñbuñ (o) ⌐mi⌐sete ku˥dasaimase˧ñ ka_ 'Would
             you be kind enough to show me your paper?'

1. Pe⌐ñ de ˥ka˧ite kudasai.   Pe⌐ñ de ˥ka˧ite ku˥dasaimase˧ñ ka_
2. Ko⌐ko de tomete kudasa⌐i.   Ko⌐ko de tomete kudasaimase⌐ñ ka_
3. Ka⌐do made mo⌐do⌐tte kuda-   Ka⌐do made mo⌐do⌐tte ku˥dasaima-
   sai.   se˧ñ ka_
4. A⌐sita⌐ mo i˥tte kudasa⌐i.   A⌐sita⌐ mo i˥tte kudasaimase⌐ñ ka_
5. Mi⌐ti (o) osiete kudasa⌐i.   Mi⌐ti (o) osiete kudasaimase⌐ñ ka_
6. Mo⌐o iti-do itte kudasa⌐i.   Mo⌐o iti-do itte kudasaimase⌐ñ ka_
7. Tu⌐ḡi⌐ no ˥ka˧do (o) ma-   Tu⌐ḡi⌐ no ˥ka˧do (o) ma⌐ḡatte kudasa-
   ⌐ḡatte kudasa⌐i.   imase⌐ñ ka_
8. Koko de ⌐ma⌐tte kudasai.   Koko de ⌐ma⌐tte ku˥dasaimase˧ñ ka_

H. Grammar Drill (based on Grammatical Note 5)

    Tutor: Ko⌐no miti (o) itte kudasa⌐i. Tu⌐ḡi⌐ no ˥ka˧do (o) ma⌐ḡatte
             kudasa⌐i. 'Please go along this street. Please turn at the
             next corner.' (2 sentences)
    Student: Kono miti (o) itte, tu⌐ḡi⌐ no ˥ka˧do (o) ma⌐ḡatte kudasa⌐i.
             'Please go along this street and turn at the next corner.'
             (1 complex sentence)

1. Ka⌐do made mo˥dorima˧sita.   Ka⌐do made mo˥do˧tte, so⌐ko de to-
   So⌐ko de tomema⌐sita.   mema⌐sita.
2. To⌐okyo⌐o-eki no ˥ma˧e de   To⌐okyo⌐o-eki no ˥ma˧e de tŏmete,
   to⌐mete kudasa⌐i.   soko de ⌐ma⌐tte kudasai.
   Soko de ⌐ma⌐tte kudasa⌐i.

3. Tu⌐g̅i⌐ no ⌐ka⁴do (o) mi⌐g̅i   Tu⌐g̅i⌐ no ⌐ka⁴do (o) mig̅i e ma-
   e mag̅arima⌐su.   g̅atte, ano miti (o) tu⌐kiatari ma⌐de
   Ano miti (o) tu⌐kiatari ma⌐de   ikimasu.
   ikimasu.
4. Ho⌐ñya e i⌐kimasyo⁴o.   Ho⌐ñya e itte, a⌐tarasi⌐i zi⌐biki⁴ (o)
   A⌐tarasi⌐i zi⌐biki⁴ (o) ka⌐i-   ka⌐imasyo⁴o.
   masyo⁴o.

I. Grammar Drill

Tutor: Wa⌐karima⌐su.   'It's clear.' (affirmative)
Student: Wa⌐karimase⌐ñ. 'It isn't clear.' (negative)

1. A⌐buna⌐i desu.   A⌐bunaku arimase⌐ñ.
2. Gi⌐ñkoo no ma⌐e desu.   Gi⌐ñkoo no ma⌐e zya a⌐rimase⌐ñ.
3. Ma⌐g̅arima⌐sita.   Ma⌐g̅arimase⌐ñ desita.
4. Ma⌐ssu⌐g̅u desu.   Ma⌐ssu⌐g̅u zya a⌐rimase⌐ñ.
5. I⌐kita⌐i desu.   I⌐kitaku arimase⌐ñ.
6. To⌐mema⌐su.   To⌐memase⌐ñ.
7. E⌐eg̅a⌐kañ desita.   E⌐eg̅a⌐kañ zya a⌐rimase⌐ñ desita.
8. A⌐o⌐i desu.   A⌐oku a⌐rimase⌐ñ.

J. Level Drill[1]

1. Ta⌐bako (g̅a) arima⌐su ka⌐   Ta⌐bako (g̅a) gozaima⌐su ka⌐
2. I⌐ma i⌐kimasyo⁴o.   I⌐ma ma⌐irimasyo⁴o.
3. Ta⌐naka ima⌐su ka⌐   Ta⌐naka orima⌐su ka⌐
4. Tanaka-sañ (wa) ⌐do⌐ko ni   Tanaka-sañ (wa) ⌐do⌐tira ni i⌐rassya-
   i⌐kima⁴su ka⌐   ima⁴su ka⌐
5. Tanaka-sañ (wa) ⌐do⌐ko ni   Tanaka-sañ (wa) ⌐do⌐tira ni i⌐rassya-
   i⌐ma⁴su ka⌐   ima⁴su ka⌐
6. Tyo⌐tto ⌐ma⁴tte kudasai.   Syo⌐osyoo o⌐mati-kudasa⁴i.
7. I⌐kutu a⌐rima⁴sita ka⌐   O⌐ikutu gozaima⌐sita ka⌐
8. Watakusi (wa) i⌐kimase⌐ñ   Watakusi (wa) ma⌐irimase⌐ñ desita.
   desita.

K. Expansion Drill

1. I'm not going to go.   I⌐kimase⌐ñ.
   Wouldn't you [like to] go?   I⌐kimase⌐ñ ka⌐
   Wouldn't you [like to] go   E⌐eg̅a⌐kañ e i⌐kimase⌐ñ ka⌐
   to a movie (theater)?
   Wouldn't you [like to] go   A⌐na⌐ta mo e⌐eg̅a⌐kañ e i⌐kimase⌐ñ
   to a movie (theater), too?   ka⌐

---

[1] In each case, the sentence on the right is the polite equivalent of the sentence on the left.

2. I don't understand.   Wa⌐karimase⌐ñ.
    I don't know the way.   Mi⌐ti ḡa wakarimase⌐ñ.
    I want to go, but I don't   I⌐kita⌐i ñ desu ḡa, mi⌐ti ḡa wakari-
        know the way.   mase⌐ñ.
    I want to go to Yokohama,   Yo⌐kohama e ikita⌐i ñ desu ḡa, mi⌐ti
        but I don't know the way.   ḡa wakarimase⌐ñ.

3. Would(n't) you give [it] to   Ku⌐dasaimase⌐ñ ka⌐
        me?
    Would you be kind enough   O⌐siete kudasaimase⌐ñ ka⌐
        to teach me?
    Would you be kind enough   Mi⌐ti (o) osiete kudasaimase⌐ñ ka⌐
        to show me the way?
    I'd like to go. Would you   I⌐kita⌐i ñ desu ḡa, mi⌐ti (o) osiete
        be kind enough to show   kudasaimase⌐ñ ka⌐
        me the way?
    I'd like to go to the Imperi-   Te⌐ekoku-ge⌐kizyoo e i⌐kita⌐i ñ desu
        al Theater. Would you   ḡa, mi⌐ti (o) osiete kudasaimase⌐ñ
        be kind enough to show   ka⌐
        me the way?

4. It's a building.   Ta⌐temo⌐no desu.
    It's a big building.   O⌐oki⌐i ta⌐temo⌐no desu.
    It's a big building on the   Mi⌐ḡi no ho⌐o no o⌐oki⌐i ta⌐temo⌐no
        right.   desu.
    It's a big building on the   Saki no mi⌐ḡi no ho⌐o no o⌐oki⌐i ta-
        right up ahead.   temo⌐no desu.
    It's a big building on the   Sono byooiñ no saki no mi⌐ḡi no ho⌐o
        right up ahead of that   no o⌐oki⌐i ta⌐temo⌐no desu.
        hospital.

5. Let's go.   I⌐kimasyo⌐o.
    Shall we go?   I⌐kimasyo⌐o ka.
    Shall we go by cab?   Ta⌐kusii de i⌐kimasyo⌐o ka.
    Shall we go to the station   E⌐ki e ⌐ta⌐kusii de i⌐kimasyo⌐o ka.
        by cab?

6. I brought [it] to a halt.   To⌐mema⌐sita.
    I brought the car to a halt.   Ku⌐ruma (o) tomema⌐sita.
    I stopped the car in front.   Ma⌐e de ku⌐ruma (o) tomema⌐sita.
    I stopped the car in front of   Ga⌐kkoo no ma⌐e de ku⌐ruma (o) to-
        the school.   mema⌐sita.

7. Please make a turn.   Ma⌐ḡatte kudasa⌐i.
    Please make a turn to the   Mi⌐ḡi e maḡatte kudasa⌐i.
        right.
    Please go as far as the end   Tu⌐kiatari ma⌐de itte, mi⌐ḡi e ma-
        of the street and turn to   ḡatte kudasa⌐i.
        the right.
    Please go along this street   Kono miti (o) tu⌐kiatari ma⌐de itte,
        as far as the end, and   mi⌐ḡi e maḡatte kudasa⌐i.
        turn to the right.

8. Please stop. [1]	To⌐mete kudasa⌐i.
Please stop there.	So⌐ko de tomete kudasa⌐i.
Please back up and stop there.	Mo⌐do⌐tte, so⌐ko de tomete kudasa⌐i.
Please back up as far as the corner and stop there.	Ka⌐do made mo⌐do⌐tte, so⌐ko de to-mete kudasa⌐i.

SUPPLEMENTARY CONVERSATIONS

1. Cab driver: Do⌐tira made?
    Smith: Go⌐tañda⌐[2]-eki made.
    Cab driver: Ha⌐i wa⌐karima⌐sita.
    Smith: Añmari i⌐soḡa⌐nai de kudasai↲
    Cab driver: Da⌐izyo⌐obu desu yo. . . .   Ko⌐ko ḡa Gotañda⌐-eki desu ḡa_
    Smith: Ko⌐no e⌐ki no ⌐so⌐ba no byo⌐oiñ e ikita⌐i ñ desu ḡa, kono heñ
                  ni ko⌐obañ wa arimase⌐ñ ka↲   Byo⌐oiñ wa koobañ no usiro
                  de⌐su ḡa_
    Cab driver: A⌐soko ni koobañ ḡa arima⌐su yo↲   Ho⌐ñya no mi⌐ḡi no ho⌐o
                  desu.
    Smith: A⌐a, so⌐o desu ⌐ne⌐e. So⌐no koobañ no ka⌐do o hi⌐dari e ma-
                  ḡatte kudasa⌐i.
    Cab driver: Ha⌐i.
    Smith: Mo⌐o suko⌐si sa⌐ki ma⌐de i⌐tte kudasa⌐i. A.   Ko⌐ko de⌐su yo↲
                  Go⌐ku⌐roosama. I⌐kura desu ka↲
    Cab driver: Ni⌐hyaku⌐-eñ desu. A⌐ri⌐ḡatoo gozaimasu.

2. Smith: Tyo⌐tto u⌐kaḡaima⌐su ḡa, To⌐okyoo-gi⌐ñkoo ko⌐no heñ   de⌐su
                  ka↲
    Stranger: To⌐okyoo-gi⌐ñkoo desu ka↲   Ni⌐hoñ-gi⌐ñkoo zya a⌐rimase⌐ñ
                  ka↲   Ni⌐hoñ-gi⌐ñkoo wa so⌐no depa⌐ato no to⌐nari de⌐su ḡa_
    Smith: To⌐okyoo-gi⌐ñkoo desu ḡa_
    Stranger: So⌐o desu ka. Ko⌐no heñ ni⌐ wa a⌐rimase⌐ñ yo↲

English Equivalents

1. Cab driver: Where to? (lit. How far?)
    Smith: (As far as) Gotanda Station.
    Cab driver: All right.
    Smith: Don't go so fast.
    Cab driver: Don't worry! . . . Here's Gotanda Station (but) . . .
    Smith: I want to go to a hospital near this station.   Is(n't) there a po-

---

[1] Lit. 'bring something to a halt.'

[2] Section of Tokyo.

lice box around here? The hospital is behind the police box (but)... [1]

Cab driver: There's a police box over there! It's to the right of the bookstore.

Smith: Oh, that's right. Turn left at the corner where that police box is.

Cab driver: All right.

Smith: Go a little further ahead. Oh, this is the place! Thanks (for your trouble). How much is it?

Cab driver: (It's) ¥200. Thank you.

2. Smith: Excuse me but is the Bank of Tokyo around here?

Stranger: The Bank of Tokyo? Don't you mean the Bank of Japan? The Bank of Japan is next door to that department store (but)...

Smith: It's the Bank of Tokyo [I'm looking for] (but)... [2]

Stranger: Oh? It's not around here.

EXERCISES

1. Give the following instructions to the taxi driver:

   a. Imperial Hotel, please.
   b. American Embassy, please.
   c. St. Luke's Hospital, please.
   d. Please hurry.
   e. Please don't go so fast.
   f. Turn right.
   g. Turn left.
   h. Go straight.
   i. Turn right at the next corner.
   j. Turn left at the corner where the bank is.
   k. Stop here.
   l. Stop in front of the department store.
   m. Stop in back of that taxi.
   n. Back up a little.
   o. Back up to the corner.
   p. Look out!

2. Using a detailed street map of any area—real or imaginary—practice conversations between a taxi driver and his customer by choosing particular destinations and giving explicit directions.

---

[1] 'but—where is the police box?'

[2] 'but—maybe it isn't around here.'

3. Practice conversations between Mr. Smith and a Japanese stranger, asking
    how to reach particular destinations.

4. Practice the Basic Dialogues with appropriate variations and props.

Lesson 8. Time

BASIC DIALOGUES: FOR MEMORIZATION

(a)

Tanaka

what time?	na⌐n⌐-zi
1. What time is it (now)?	I⌐ma ⌐na⌐n-zi desu ka⌐ or I⌐ma ⌐na⌐n-zi?

Yamamoto

one o'clock	i⌐ti⌐-zi
2. It's one o'clock.	I⌐ti⌐-zi (desu).

Tanaka

exactly	tyoodo
3. Is it exactly one o'clock?	Tyo⌐odo iti⌐-zi desu ka⌐ or Tyo⌐odo iti⌐-zi?

Yamamoto

two minutes or minute two[1]	ni⌐-huñ
minute two past or after	ni-⌐hu⌐ñ-suḡi
4. No. It's ⌐1:02. or No. It's two minutes after one.	Iie. I⌐ti⌐-zi ⌐ni⌐-huñ (desu). or Iie. I⌐ti⌐-zi ni-⌐hu⌐ñ-suḡi (desu).

Tanaka

clock or watch	tokee
5. This watch is out of order.	Kono tokee (wa) da⌐me⌐ (desu).

ten minutes or minute ten	zi⌐p-puñ or zyu⌐p-puñ
minute ten before the hour	zi⌐p-pu⌐ñ-mae
6. It says (lit. is) ten minutes before.	Zi⌐p-pu⌐ñ-mae (desu).

(b)

Tanaka

first day of the month	tu⌐itati⌐
7. Is today the first?	Kyo⌐o (wa) tu⌐itati⌐ desu ka⌐

---

[1] I.e. 'minute two of a sixty-minute hour.'

113

Smith

second day of the month or two days	hutu-ka

8. Why no, it's the second.   Iie. Hu⌐tu-ka de⌐su yo⌟

Tanaka

Monday	getuyoo[1] or ge⌐tuyo⌐obi

9. It isn't Monday?   Ge⌐tuyoo zya arimase⌐ñ ka⌟

Smith

Tuesday	ka⌐yo⌐o (bi)[2]
Wednesday	su⌐iyo⌐o (bi)[2]
Thursday	mo⌐kuyo⌐o (bi)[2]
Friday	ki⌐ñyo⌐o (bi)[2]
Saturday	do⌐yo⌐o (bi)[2]
Sunday	nitiyoo or ni⌐tiyo⌐obi

10. No (i.e. that's right). It's
Tuesday.   E⌐e, ka⌐yo⌐o desu yo⌟

Tanaka

11. Oh, that's right!   A⌐a, so⌐o desu ⌐ne⌐e.

(c)

Tanaka

when	i⌐tu
come	ki⌐ma⌐su or ma⌐irima⌐su † or i⌐rassyaima⌐su †

12. When did you come here?   I⌐tu ko⌐ko e kima⌐sita ka⌟   or
                              I⌐tu ko⌐tira e irassyaima⌐sita ka⌟

Smith

three years or the year three	sañ-neñ
three years before or ago	sa⌐ñ-neñ ma⌐e
at a time three years ago	sa⌐ñ-neñ ma⌐e ni

13. I came three years ago.   Sa⌐ñ-neñ ma⌐e ni ki⌐ma⌐sita.   or
                                 Sa⌐ñ-neñ ma⌐e ni ma⌐irima⌐sita.

Meiji Era (1868–1912)	me⌐ezi
Taisho Era (1912–1926)	taisyoo
Showa Era (1926–)	syoowa

---

[1] Alternate accented form: ge⌐tuyo⌐o.

[2] Short form has unaccented alternant.

	32 years or the year 32	sa⌐nzyuu ⌐ni⌐-neñ
14.	That was Showa 32.	Sore wa syōowa ⌐sa⌐nzyuu ⌐ni⌐-neñ desita.

Tanaka

	airplane	hi⌐ko⌐oki
15.	Did you come by plane?	Hi⌐ko⌐oki de ki⌐ma⌐sita ka⌐ or Hi⌐ko⌐oki de i⌐rassyaima⌐sita ka⌐

Smith

	ship	hu⌐ne
16.	No. I came by ship.	Iie, hu⌐ne de ki⌐ma⌐sita. or Iie, hu⌐ne de ma⌐irima⌐sita.

Tanaka

	about how long?	dono-ḡurai
	be required or take	ka⌐karima⌐su
17.	About how long did it take?	Do⌐no-ḡurai kakarima⌐sita ka⌐

Smith

	two weeks	ni-⌐syu⌐ukañ
	about two weeks	ni-⌐syuukañ-ḡu⌐rai
18.	It took about two weeks.	Ni-⌐syuukañ-ḡu⌐rai ka⌐karima⌐sita.

(d)

Tanaka

	day before yesterday	o⌐toto⌐i
19.	Say, I went to Nikko the day before yesterday.	Ototoi ⌐Ni⌐kkoo e i⌐kima⌐sita yo⌐

Smith

20.	Oh? How was it?	So⌐o desu ka. Do⌐o desita ka⌐

Tanaka

	exceedingly or very	totemo or
		tottemo
21.	It was very pretty. Wouldn't you [like to] go too?	To⌐ttemo ki⌐ree desita. A⌐na⌐ta mo i⌐kimase⌐ñ ka⌐

Smith

	from here	koko kara
22.	I'd like to go some (lit. one) time. About how long does it take from here to Nikko?	Iti-do i⌐kita⌐i ñ desu ḡa, ko⌐ko kara Ni⌐kkoo made do⌐no-ḡurai kakarima⌐su ka⌐

Tanaka

	electric train or street car	de⌐ñsya[1]

---

[1]
Has unaccented alternant.

(steam) train	ki⌐sya⌐
bus	ba⌐su
three hours	sa⌐ñ-zi⌐kañ
three hours and a half	sa⌐ñ-zikañ-ha⌐ñ
about three hours and a	sa⌐ñ-zikañ-hañ-g̃u⌐rai
half	

23. I went by electric train. It took about three hours and a half.

Watakusi wa ⌐de⌐ñsya de i⌐kima⌐sita g̃a, sa⌐ñ- zikañ- hañ- g̃u⌐rai ka⌐karima⌐sita.

(e)
Smith

vacation or holiday or	ya⌐sumi⌐ or
time off	oyasumi ⌐

24. When is your vacation? Oyasumi (wa) ⌐i⌐tu desu ka⌐

Tanaka

this year	kotosi
August	ha⌐ti-g̃atu⌐
about August	ha⌐ti-g̃atu-g̃o⌐ro

25. This year it will be about August (but) . . .

Kotosi wa ha⌐ti-g̃atu-g̃o⌐ro desu g̃a⌐

Smith

one month	i⌐k-ka⌐g̃etu

26. Will it be a month? I⌐k-ka⌐g̃etu desu ka⌐

Tanaka

27. Heavens no! To⌐nde mo arimase⌐ñ.

ten days or tenth of	too-ka
the month	

28. It will be ten days. To⌐o-ka de⌐su yo⌐

NOTES ON THE BASIC DIALOGUES

1. The Japanese equivalent WITH i⌐ma and the English equivalent WITHOUT 'now' are more usual.

5. Tokee is the general term for 'timepiece,' covering all kinds of clocks and watches.   There are more specific terms which can be used when it is necessary to distinguish among different kinds of timepieces.

9, 10.   The shorter forms of the days of the week, without -bi, are less formal, and common in conversation.

12. Particle e may be replaced here by particle ni (cf. Lesson 7, Grammatical Note 3 a).

14. The Japanese regularly count years according to eras, which in recent times have coincided with the reigns of their emperors. Each era, or reign, has its own name. When a new emperor takes the throne, a new

era begins; the remainder of the current calendar year is the year 1 (ga⌐nneñ) of that era, the next calendar year is the year 2, and so on. Thus 1926—the end of the Taisho Era—began as Taisho 15 (the 15th year of Taisho) but, with the accession of a new emperor, became Showa 1; 1927 was Showa 2. To distinguish the Western system, seereki is used to designate the Christian Era: syoowa 35, for example, corresponds to seereki 1960.

17. Ka⌐karima⌐su (gerund ka⌐ka⌐tte) means 'take' or 'require,' as in 'take time,' 'take money.' Like wa⌐karima⌐su, i⌐rima⌐su, and a⌐rima⌐su, ka⌐karima⌐su may occur with particles ḡa and/or wa, but never with particle o. Ka⌐karima⌐su frequently occurs with extent constructions, as in the present instance, with no particle.

19. See Note 12 above.

21. Tottemo is the more emphatic alternant of totemo. Intensifying words like totemo and zu⌐ibuñ have a complicated distribution, and students can learn where they occur only by observing how native speakers use them. For example, before ta⌐ka⌐i, both totemo and zu⌐ibuñ occur frequently, but before i⌐i, only totemo is common. Distinguishing among the meanings of these intensifying words is something like trying to distinguish among degrees of intensity of English 'it is very difficult,' 'it is extremely difficult,' 'it is terribly difficult,' 'it is exceedingly difficult,' 'it is awfully difficult,' etc.
Note the use of negative + ka as an invitation.

22. Note the use of particle ḡa connecting a statement with a related question.

23. Here the particle ḡa connects a qualification with the direct answer to a question. The answer to the question 'how long does it take?' is 'it took about three hours and a half,' but this answer is subject to the immediately preceding qualification—'I went by electric train.'

25. 'but—why do you ask?'

27. To⌐ñde mo arimase⌐ñ is an emphatic rejection of what has been said and, accordingly, must be used with caution. Common English equivalents are 'Ridiculous!' 'Far from it!' 'Nothing of the kind!' 'Don't be silly!' 'Never happen!'

28. The same sentence in a different context could mean 'It is (or will be) the tenth (of the month).'

GRAMMATICAL NOTES

1. Time Counters: -huñ, -zi, -zikañ, -ka/-niti, -syuukañ, -ḡatu, -kaḡetu, -neñ

The above counters can be divided into three groups:

A. those that combine with numerals to NAME:
    (1) -zi—to name the o'clocks
    (2) -ḡatu—to name the calendar months

B. those that combine with numerals to COUNT:
  (1) -zikañ—to count the number of hours
  (2) -syuukañ—to count the number of weeks
  (3) -kaḡetu—to count the number of months

C. those that combine with numerals to NAME AND COUNT:
  (1) -huñ—to name the minute of a sixty-minute hour and count the number of minutes
  (2) -ka/-niti—to name the days of the month[1] and count the number of days
  (3) -neñ—to name the years[2] and count the number of years

With the exception of -ka/-niti, all the above counters combine with numerals of Series I (i⌐ti⌐, ni⌐, sañ, etc.). -Ka/-niti combines with some numerals of Series I and some of Series II (the hi⌐to⌐, huta, mi series), and there are some irregular forms.

Study the following lists, noting particularly the assimilated forms (for example, ro⌐ku⌐ + -huñ = ro⌐p-puñ) and the irregular forms (for example, hutu-ka, nano-ka, etc.).

-huñ		-zi		-zikañ	
i⌐p-puñ	'1 minute' or 'minute 1'	i⌐ti⌐-zi	'1 o'clock'	i⌐ti-zi⌐kañ	'1 hour'
ni⌐-huñ	'2 minutes' or 'minute 2'	ni⌐-zi	'2 o'clock'	ni-⌐zi⌐kañ	'2 hours'
sa⌐ñ-puñ	'3 minutes' or 'minute 3'	sa⌐ñ-zi	'3 o'clock'	sa⌐ñ-zi⌐kañ	'3 hours'
yo⌐ñ-puñ	'4 minutes' or 'minute 4'	yo⌐-zi	'4 o'clock'	yo-⌐zi⌐kañ	'4 hours'
go⌐-huñ	'5 minutes' or 'minute 5'	go⌐-zi	'5 o'clock'	go-⌐zi⌐kañ	'5 hours'
ro⌐p-puñ	'6 minutes' or 'minute 6'	ro⌐ku⌐-zi	'6 o'clock'	ro⌐ku-zi⌐kañ	'6 hours'
na⌐na⌐-huñ or si⌐ti⌐-huñ	'7 minutes' or 'minute 7'	si⌐ti⌐-zi	'7 o'clock'	na⌐na-zi⌐kañ or si⌐ti-zi⌐kañ	'7 hours'
ha⌐ti⌐-huñ or ha⌐p-puñ	'8 minutes' or 'minute 8'	ha⌐ti⌐-zi	'8 o'clock'	ha⌐ti-zi⌐kañ	'8 hours'
kyu⌐u-huñ	'9 minutes' or 'minute 9'	ku⌐-zi	'9 o'clock'	ku-⌐zi⌐kañ	'9 hours'
zi⌐p-puñ or zyu⌐p-puñ	'10 minutes' or 'minute 10'	zyu⌐u-zi	'10 o'clock'	zyu⌐u-zi⌐kañ	'10 hours'
na⌐ñ-puñ	'how many minutes?' or 'what minute?'	na⌐ñ-zi	'what time?'	na⌐ñ-zi⌐kañ	'how many hours?'

---

[1] Except the first day of the month, for which there is the special word tu⌐itati⌐.

[2] Except the year 1. See the note on sentence 14 above. There are also counters -neñkañ and -kaneñkañ, which combine with numerals to count (but not name) years and hence belong in Group B above.

-ka/-niti

(tuˈitatiˈ	'the first day of the month')		
iˈti-nitiˈ	'one day'		
hutu-ka	'the second'	or	'2 days'
mi-kka	'the third'	or	'3 days'
yo-kka	'the fourth'	or	'4 days'
itu-ka	'the fifth'	or	'5 days'
mu-ika	'the sixth'	or	'6 days'
nano-ka	'the seventh'	or	'7 days'
yoo-ka	'the eighth'	or	'8 days'
koˈkono-kaˈ	'the ninth'	or	'9 days'
too-ka	'the tenth'	or	'10 days'
zyuˈuiti-nitiˈ	'the eleventh'	or	'11 days'
zyuˈuni-nitiˈ	'the twelfth'	or	'12 days'
zyuˈusañ-niti	'the thirteenth'	or	'13 days'
zyuˈuyo-kka	'the fourteenth'	or	'14 days'
zyuˈugo-niti	'the fifteenth'	or	'15 days'
zyuˈuroku-nitiˈ	'the sixteenth'	or	'16 days'
zyuˈusiti-nitiˈ	'the seventeenth'	or	'17 days'
zyuˈuhati-nitiˈ	'the eighteenth'	or	'18 days'
zyuˈuku-niti	'the nineteenth'	or	'19 days'
hatu-ka	'the twentieth'	or	'20 days'
niˈzyuu iˈti-nitiˈ	'the twenty-first'	or	'21 days'
niˈzyuu ni-ˈnitiˈ	'the twenty-second'	or	'22 days'
niˈzyuu ˈsaˈñ-niti	'the twenty-third'	or	'23 days'
niˈzyuu yō-kka	'the twenty-fourth'	or	'24 days'
niˈzyuu ˈgoˈ-niti	'the twenty-fifth'	or	'25 days'
niˈzyuu roˈku-nitiˈ	'the twenty-sixth'	or	'26 days'
niˈzyuu siˈti-nitiˈ	'the twenty-seventh'	or	'27 days'
niˈzyuu haˈti-nitiˈ	'the twenty-eighth'	or	'28 days'
niˈzyuu ˈkuˈ-niti	'the twenty-ninth'	or	'29 days'
saˈñzyuˈu-niti	'the thirtieth'	or	'30 days'
saˈñzyuu iˈti-nitiˈ	'the thirty-first'	or	'31 days'
naˈñ-niti	'what date?'	or	'how many days?'

-syuukañ

iˈs-syuˈukañ	'1 week'
ni-ˈsyuˈukañ	'2 weeks'
saˈñ-syuˈukañ	'3 weeks'
yoˈñ-syuˈukañ	'4 weeks'
go-ˈsyuˈukañ	'5 weeks'
roˈku-syuˈukañ	'6 weeks'
naˈna-syuˈukañ or	
siˈti-syuˈukañ	'7 weeks'
haˈs-syuˈukañ	'8 weeks'
kyuˈu-syuˈukañ	'9 weeks'
ziˈs-syuˈukañ or	
zyuˈs-syuˈukañ	'10 weeks'
naˈñ-syuˈukañ	'how many weeks?'

-g̃atu		-kag̃etu	
i⌐ti-g̃atu⌐	'January'	i⌐k-ka⌐g̃etu	'1 month'
ni-⌐g̃atu⌐	'February'	ni-⌐ka⌐g̃etu	'2 months'
sa⌐ñ-g̃atu	'March'	sa⌐ñ-ka⌐g̃etu	'3 months'
si-⌐g̃atu⌐	'April'	yo⌐ñ-ka⌐g̃etu	'4 months'
go⌐-g̃atu⌐	'May'	go-⌐ka⌐g̃etu	'5 months'
ro⌐ku-g̃atu⌐	'June'	ro⌐k-ka⌐g̃etu	'6 months'
si⌐ti-g̃atu⌐	'July'	si⌐ti-ka⌐g̃etu or	
ha⌐ti-g̃atu⌐	'August'	na⌐na-ka⌐g̃etu	'7 months'
ku⌐-g̃atu	'September'	ha⌐ti-ka⌐g̃etu or	
zyu⌐u-g̃atu⌐	'October'	ha⌐k-ka⌐g̃etu	'8 months'
zyu⌐uiti-g̃atu⌐	'November'	ku-⌐ka⌐g̃etu or	
zyu⌐uni-g̃atu⌐	'December'	kyu⌐u-ka⌐g̃etu	'9 months'
na⌐ñ-g̃atu	'what month?'	zi⌐k-ka⌐g̃etu or	
		zyu⌐k-ka⌐g̃etu	'10 months'
		na⌐ñ-ka⌐g̃etu	'how many months?'

-neñ	
i⌐ti⌐-neñ	'1 year'
(ga⌐ñneñ	'the year 1')
ni⌐-neñ	'2 years' or 'the year 2'
sañ-neñ	'3 years' or 'the year 3'
yo-neñ	'4 years' or 'the year 4'
go-neñ	'5 years' or 'the year 5'
ro⌐ku⌐-neñ	'6 years' or 'the year 6'
si⌐ti⌐-neñ or	
na⌐na⌐-neñ	'7 years' or 'the year 7'
ha⌐ti⌐-neñ	'8 years' or 'the year 8'
ku-neñ or	
kyu⌐u-neñ	'9 years' or 'the year 9'
zyu⌐u-neñ	'10 years' or 'the year 10'
na⌐ñ-neñ	'how many years?' or 'what year?'

The regular order of Japanese dates is year—month—day, with the smaller unit always following the larger. The units are usually joined without intervening particles.[1] Examples:

---

[1] But they can be joined by particle no. Ni-g̃atu kŏkono-ka might be compared to 'February 9th,' and ni-⌐g̃atu no kokono-ka⌐ to 'the 9th of February [rather than of another month].'

[syoowa] ⌐zyu¹uku-neñ ⌐sa¹ñ-g̈atu mi-kka 'March 3, 19 [Showa]
    (= A. D. 1944)'
[seereki] ⌐se¹ñ ⌐kyu⁴uhyaku go⌐zyu¹u-neñ hati-g̈atu mu-ika
    'August 6, 1950 [Christian era]'

-Ha¹ñ added to a number means 'a half added to the preceding':

    i⌐ti-zi-ha¹ñ '1:30'
    i⌐ti-zikañ-ha¹ñ 'one hour and a half'
    ni-⌐neñ-ha¹ñ 'two years and a half'

But hañ- + counter means 'a half of one counter unit' (not all counters occur in this combination):

    ha⌐ñ-zi¹kañ 'a half hour'
    ha⌐ñ-niti¹ 'a half day'

2.   Telling Time

    For telling time in terms of the hour only, a numeral + counter -zi is used.
Thus:

    Yo¹-zi desu.   'It's 4 o'clock.'

To indicate time before the hour, ma¹e is added, and to indicate time after the hour, su⌐g̈i¹ is added. Thus:

    Si⌐ti-zi ma¹e desu. 'It's before 7.'
    Ku-⌐zi sug̈i¹ desu. 'It's after 9.'

    To tell time in terms of hours and minutes, two patterns are used. The simpler pattern consists of the o'clock + the minute. This corresponds to the English pattern of '2:10,' '8:15,' '10:45,' etc. Thus:

    Ni¹-zi ⌐zyu¹p-puñ desu. 'It's 2:10.' (Lit. 'It's 2 o'clock minute 10.')
    Ha⌐ti¹-zi ⌐zyu¹ugo-huñ desu. 'It's 8:15.'
    Zyu¹u-zi ⌐yo¹ñzyuu ⌐go⁴-huñ desu.   'It's 10:45.'

The alternate pattern consists of (a) the o'clock + the minute before + -mae 'before' (when the minute hand is in the left half of the clock; compare English '5 of 2,' '20 minutes to 3,' 'a quarter of 8,' etc.); and (b) the o'clock + the minute after + -sug̈i 'beyond' (when the minute hand is in the right half of the clock; compare English ' 10 after 2,' 'a quarter past 3,' etc.). The accent of the minute expression shifts to the first syllable of the counter. Thus:

    Ni¹-zi go-⌐hu¹ñ-mae desu. 'It's 5 of 2.' (Lit. 'It's 2 o'clock minute 5 before.')
    Ha⌐ti¹-zi zyu⌐ugo-hu¹ñ-mae desu.   'It's a quarter of 8.'
    Ni¹-zi zi⌐p-pu¹ñ-sug̈i desu. 'It's 10 after 2.'
    Sa¹ñ-zi zyu⌐ugo-hu¹ñ-sug̈i desu. 'It's a quarter after 3.'

    In all the above examples, -huñ occurs as a naming counter (cf. Group C of the preceding grammatical note), telling WHICH minute of the hour. -Huñ also occurs as an enumerating counter, telling HOW MANY minutes, before ma¹e 'ago,' 'before' and also in various other expressions. Compare the following:

Zi⌐p-pu⌐ñ-mae desita.   'It was 10 of.' (i. e. it was 10 minutes before
the hour)

Zi⌐p-puñ ⌐ma⌐e desita.
 or   } 'It was 10 minutes ago.'
Zi⌐p-puñ ma⌐e desita.

Sentences like those in the groups above are differentiated by accent. Elsewhere, context determines whether -huñ is naming or counting.

3. Informal Speech

The subject of speech levels has already been introduced in connection with
the occurrence of parallel pairs such as a⌐rima⌐su and go⌐zaima⌐su, i⌐kima⌐su
and i⌐rassyaima⌐su, ge⌐ñki and o⌐ge⌐ñki, i⌐kura and oikura. In general, we
can speak of two major levels: the POLITE and the PLAIN. The polite includes NEUTRAL POLITE (like go⌐zaima⌐su+), HUMBLE (like ma⌐irima⌐su+),
and HONORIFIC (like i⌐rassyaima⌐su+). In addition to politeness levels, there
are formality levels — the FORMAL and the INFORMAL. A given verbal may
be formal polite, informal polite, formal plain, or informal plain. Verbals
ending in -ma⌐su and all of its derived forms (-ma⌐sita, -mase⌐ñ, -mase⌐ñ desita, and -masyo⌐o) and copula forms de⌐su, de⌐sita, and de⌐syo⌐o are all
formal forms. Thus, a⌐rima⌐su is formal plain style, whereas go⌐zaima⌐su
is formal polite; i⌐kima⌐su is formal plain, but ma⌐irima⌐su and i⌐rassyaima⌐su
are formal polite. [1]

In general, a sentence is assigned to the level of its final (or only) inflected
word—provided, of course, that it has an inflected word. Other features of the
sentence may make it a more or less formal and/or polite degree of that major
level. A speech sequence is said to belong to the level which characterizes
most of its sentences.

The ability to choose the appropriate level for any given situation requires
a thorough knowledge of Japanese social structure. In general, the informal
style of speech is used most commonly in addressing friends and in speaking to
social inferiors in informal situations; formal speech is used in addressing
strangers, casual acquaintances, and superiors, and in speaking to social inferiors in formal situations; polite words are usually used in reference to persons of equal or superior social standing; the plain level is usually used in
reference to persons of equal or inferior social standing; women use polite and
formal speech more commonly than men. This is at best an oversimplification;
one of the most complicated phases of the problem for a foreigner is to determine the bases for social inferiority and superiority in the Japanese system,
and to know when a formal, comparatively stiff style of speech is appropriate
and when it is fitting to be informal.

---

[1] Informal equivalents will be introduced later.

The following are two patterns typical of the informal style of speech:[1]

a. Adjectivals and nominals occur at the end of statements without the deꜜsu which follows them in formal speech.

Examples:

Formal	Informal
Oꜛokiꜜi desu. 'It's big.'	Oꜛokiꜜi. 'It's big.'
Peꜜñ desu. 'It's a pen.'	Peꜜñ. 'A pen.'

Note that the only difference between an adjectival + desu and an adjectival alone is in the formality; an adjectival in its -i form has tense and is a complete, major—but informal—sentence when it occurs alone. A nominal, on the other hand, has no tense and occurs as a sentence by itself only in fragments (cf. Lesson 4, Grammatical Note 5) similar to English sentences like these: ' A book.' 'Some bread.' 'That ashtray.' etc.

b. Adjectivals and nominals occur with question-mark intonation in questions, without the deꜜsu + ka which occurs in formal speech.

Examples:

Formal	Informal
Oꜛokiꜜi desu ka⌐ 'Is it big?'	Oꜛokiꜜi? 'Is it big?'
Peꜜñ desu ka⌐ 'Is it a pen?'	Peꜜñ? 'A pen?'

But note the following:

Formal	Informal[2]
Soꜜo desu ka⌐ 'Is that right?'	Soꜜo? 'Really?'
Soꜜo desu ka. 'Is that right.'	Aꜛaꜛsoꜜo. 'Oh.' or 'Oh?'
Soꜜo desu ⌐neꜛe. 'That's right, isn't it.'	Soꜜo. 'Right.'
Soꜜo desu. 'That's right.'	Soꜜo. 'Right.'

The first form in each column is more animated than the second and shows livelier interest. The difference between Soꜜo. occurring as the informal equivalent of Soꜜo desu. and of Soꜜo desu ⌐neꜛe. is determined by context.

Additional informal patterns and forms will be introduced later.

---

[1] But these are by no means the only informal equivalents of the given formal patterns.

[2] Again, each informal expression mentioned here is only one of several possibilities; others will be described later.

4. Particles: <u>kara</u> 'from,' <u>ni</u> (time when)

a. <u>kara</u> 'from'

The particle <u>kara</u> following a nominal means 'from.' A phrase ending with <u>kara</u> may modify an inflected expression directly, or it may be followed by another particle.   When a <u>kara</u> phrase describes a nominal it is followed by <u>no</u>. Examples:

Kyoˈoto kara kiˈ┌maˈ┐sita. 'I came from Kyoto.'
Asita ⌈kuˈ┐-zi kara koˈko ni imaˈsu.   'I'll be here from 9 o'clock [on] tomorrow.'
Taˈnaka-sañ kara wa kimaseˈñ desita. 'It didn't come from Tanaka [but where it did come from I don't know].'
Are wa ⌈Niˈkkoo kara no ┌baˈsu desu ka⌟ 'Is that the bus from Nikko?'

Compare also <u>sore kara</u> 'from that' (i.e. 'after that' or 'next').

b. <u>ni</u> 'in,' 'on,' 'at'

Time expressions modifying an inflected expression, and indicating the time at which something happens, a r e divided into two main groups: those which occur without a following particle, and those which are followed by <u>ni</u>. (Compare the English use of 'on' with days of the week, 'in' with months and years, 'at' with hours of the day, and no preposition with 'today,' 'tomorrow,' 'yesterday,' etc.) In general, time words whose meaning is relative to the time of usage—for example, <u>iˈma</u> 'now,' <u>kyoˈo</u> 'today,' <u>aˈsitaˈ</u> 'tomorrow,' and <u>kiˈnoˈo</u> 'yesterday'—occur without a following particle, while other time expressions are more apt to take <u>ni</u>, but the rule is not hard and fast.

Some time expressions—for example, those ending with -ḡoˈro (cf. the following note)—occur both with or without <u>ni</u> in this kind of construction.

Examples:

Iˈtu iˈ┌kimaˈ┐su ka⌟ 'When are you going to go?'
Aˈsita simaˈsu. 'I'll do [it] tomorrow.'
Iˈma kaˈ┌kimaˈ┐sita. 'I just wrote [it].'
Kuˈ-zi ⌈zyuˈugohuñ ni kiˈ┌maˈ┐sita. 'I came at 9:15.'
Siˈti-ḡatuˈ ni iˈ┌kimasyoˈ┐o. 'Let's go in July.'
Toˈo-ka ni kaimaˈsita. 'I bought [it] on the tenth.'

Such time expressions, both those with <u>ni</u> and those without <u>ni</u>, may be followed by particles <u>wa</u> or <u>mo</u>:

Kyoˈo wa iˈ┌kimaˈ┐su ḡa⌿ 'Today (in comparison with other times) I'll go but...'
Siˈti-ḡatuˈ ni wa iˈ┌kimaˈ┐su ḡa⌿ 'In July (in comparison with other times) I'll go but...'
Aˈsitaˈ mo kimasu. 'I'll come tomorrow, too.'
Toˈo-ka niˈ mo kimasu. 'I'll come on the tenth, too.'

All the preceding applies only when the time expression tells when

something occurs. Time expressions also occur in other nominal constructions. Compare the following pairs of examples:

1. (a) Sore (wa) ⌐na⌐n desu ka⌐   'What is that?'
   (b) Kyo⌐o (wa) na⌐ñyo⌐obi desu ka⌐   'What day is today?'

2. (a) Na⌐ni g̃a ˥i˦i desyoo ka.   'What would be good?'
   (b) Na⌐ñyo⌐obi g̃a ˥i˦i desyoo ka.   'What day would be good?'

3. (a) A⌐merika no zido⌐osya desu.   'It's an American car.'
   (b) Ro⌐kuzyu⌐u-neñ no zi˥do˦osya desu.   'It's a '60 car.'

5. -g̃o⌐ro ~ -g̃u⌐rai 'about'

-G̃o⌐ro is added to time expressions which ask or answer the question
'when?'; it means 'approximate point of time.'

-G̃u⌐rai 'approximate quantity' is added to quantity expressions which ask
or answer the questions 'how much?' 'how many?' 'how far?' or 'how long?'
and to kono, sono, ano, and do⌐no.

An expression ending with -g̃o⌐ro is always a nominal time expression but
one ending with -g̃u⌐rai may be any kind of nominal quantity expression.

Speaking in terms of the time counter groups introduced in Grammatical
Note 1 above, those in Group A (-zi and -g̃atu) may be followed by -g̃o⌐ro; those
in Group B (-zikañ, -syuukañ, and -kag̃etu) may be followed by -g̃u⌐rai; and
those in Group C (-huñ, -ka/-niti, and -neñ) may be followed by -g̃o⌐ro when
naming a time and by -g̃u⌐rai when counting time.

Before -g̃o⌐ro and -g̃u⌐rai, an accented word regularly loses its accent; and
in some combinations, -g̃o⌐ro and -g̃u⌐rai also lose their accents (note examples
below).

Examples:

itu-g̃oro 'about when?'
sa⌐ñ-zi-g̃o⌐ro 'about 3 o'clock'
sa⌐ñ-zi zi˥p-puñ-g̃o˦ro 'about 3:10'
go-⌐huñ-mae-g̃o⌐ro 'about five minutes of [the hour]'
go-⌐huñ-sug̃i-g̃o⌐ro 'about 5 minutes after [the hour]'
do⌐yoobi-g̃o⌐ro 'about Saturday'
to⌐o-ka-g̃o⌐ro 'about the 10th of the month'
se⌐ñ ˥kyu˦uhyaku go˥zyuu-neñ-g̃o˦ro 'about 1950'
dono-g̃urai 'about how much?'
kono-g̃urai 'about this much'
zi⌐p-puñ-g̃u⌐rai 'about 10 minutes'
sa⌐ñ-zikañ-g̃u⌐rai 'about 3 hours'
to⌐o-ka-g̃u⌐rai 'about 10 days'
yo⌐ñ-kag̃etu-g̃u⌐rai 'about 4 months'
zyu⌐u-neñ-g̃u⌐rai 'about 10 years'
to⌐o-g̃u⌐rai 'about 10 (units)'
hya⌐ku-eñ-g̃u⌐rai 'about ¥100'

When a phrase ending in -g̃o⌐ro tells the approximate time at which something happens, it may occur with particle ni, but more commonly occurs without it (cf. Grammatical Note 4b above). Compare English 'I'm going [at] about 4 o'clock.'

Examples:

Sa⌐ñ-zi-ḡo⌐ro [ni] i⌐kimasyo⌐o. 'Let's go [at] about 3 o'clock.'
Sa⌐ñ-ḡatu-ḡo⌐ro [ni] ki⌐ma⌐sita. 'He came [in] about March.'
So⌐no ho⌐ñ wa syoowa zyu⌐u-neñ-ḡo⌐ro [ni] ka⌐kima⌐sita.   'That book he wrote [in] about Showa 10.'

6. ki⌐ma⌐su ~ ma⌐irima⌐su ~ i⌐rassyaima⌐su

Ki⌐ma⌐su 'come' is a plain formal verbal; ma⌐irima⌐su and i⌐rassyaima⌐su are polite formal verbals with the same meaning. Ma⌐irima⌐su, a humble verbal, refers to the actions of the speaker (or members of his own family), in polite speech. I⌐rassyaima⌐su, an honorific verbal, refers to the actions of persons other than the speaker, whose position is being elevated or exalted, in polite speech.

Three meanings for i⌐rassyaima⌐su and two for ma⌐irima⌐su have now been introduced. Study the following chart:

	Plain Formal	Polite Formal	
		Humble [+]	Honorific [+]
'be located (animate)'	i⌐ma⌐su	o⌐rima⌐su	i⌐rassyaima⌐su
'go'	i⌐kima⌐su	ma⌐irima⌐su	i⌐rassyaima⌐su
'come'	ki⌐ma⌐su	ma⌐irima⌐su	i⌐rassyaima⌐su

Ki⌐ma⌐su regularly means motion toward—and i⌐kima⌐su motion away from—the speaker's position. Thus, the Japanese equivalent of 'I'm not coming to school tomorrow' said, for example, during a telephone conversation from outside, with someone at the school, would be A⌐sita⌐ wa ga⌐kkoo e ikimase⌐ñ lit. 'I'm not going to school tomorrow.' A⌐sita⌐ wa ga⌐kkoo e kimase⌐ñ would be said only by someone actually at the school.

DRILLS

A. Substitution Drill

1. It took 2 hours.   Ni-⌐zi⌐kañ ka⌐karima⌐sita.
2. It took 2 minutes.   Ni⌐-huñ ka⌐karima⌐sita.
3. It took 2 days.   Hu⌐tu-ka kakarima⌐sita.
4. It took 2 years.   Ni⌐-neñ ka⌐karima⌐sita.
5. It took 2 months.   Ni-⌐ka⌐ḡetu ka⌐karima⌐sita.
6. It took 2 weeks.   Ni-⌐syu⌐ukañ ka⌐karima⌐sita.
7. It took 2½ years.   Ni-⌐neñ-ha⌐ñ ka⌐karima⌐sita.

8. It took 2½ hours.   Ni-⌐zikañ-ha⌉ñ ka┌karima┘sita.
9. It took a half day.   Ha⌐ñ-niti kakarima⌉sita.
10. It took a half hour.   Ha⌐ñ-zi⌉kañ ka┌karima┘sita.

B. Substitution Drill

1. I did [it] at 2 o'clock.   Ni⌉-zi ni si┌ma┘sita.
2. I did [it] 2 days ago.   Hu⌐tu-ka ma⌉e ni si┌ma┘sita.
3. I did [it] in Showa 2.   Syoowa ⌐ni⌉-neñ ni si┌ma┘sita.
4. I did [it] in February.   Ni-⌐gatu⌉ ni si┌ma┘sita.
5. I did [it] at 2:30.   Ni-⌐zi-ha⌉ñ ni si┌ma┘sita.
6. I did [it] on Tuesday.   Ka⌐yo⌉obi ni si┌ma┘sita.
7. I did [it] 2 hours ago.   Ni-⌐zikañ ma⌉e ni si┌ma┘sita.
8. I did [it] on the second. Hu⌐tu-ka ni sima⌉sita.

C. Substitution Drill

1. I went to the station by bus today.
   Kyo⌉o ⌐e⌉ki e ⌐ba⌉su de i┌kima┘sita.
2. I went to the station by bus yesterday.
   Kinoo ⌐e⌉ki e ⌐ba⌉su de i┌kima┘sita.
3. I went to the hospital by bus yesterday.
   Kinoo byooiñ e ⌐ba⌉su de i┌kima┘sita.
4. I went to the hospital by taxi yesterday.
   Kinoo byooiñ e ⌐ta⌉kusii de i┌kima┘si-ta.
5. I came to the hospital by taxi yesterday.
   Kinoo byooin e ⌐ta⌉kusii de ki┌ma┘sita.
6. I came to the hospital by taxi the day before yesterday.
   Ototoi byooiñ e ⌐ta⌉kusii de ki┌ma┘si-ta.
7. I came to school by taxi the day before yesterday.
   Ototoi gakkoo e ⌐ta⌉kusii de ki┌ma┘si-ta.
8. I came to school by electric train the day before yesterday.
   Ototoi gakkoo e ⌐de⌉ñsya de ki┌ma┘si-ta.
9. I came here by electric train the day before yesterday.
   Ototoi koko e ⌐de⌉ñsya de ki┌ma┘sita.
10. I came here by plane the day before yesterday.
   Ototoi koko e hi⌐ko⌉oki de ki┌ma┘si-ta.
11. I came here by plane this year.
   Kotosi koko e hi⌐ko⌉oki de ki┌ma┘si-ta.
12. I came here by ship this year.
   Kotosi koko e ⌐hu⌉ne de ki┌ma┘sita.

D. Substitution Drill

1. I came 10 years ago.   Zyu⌐u-neñ ma⌉e ni ki┌ma┘sita.
2. I came 5 minutes ago.   Go-⌐huñ ma⌉e ni ki┌ma┘sita.
3. I came 1 hour ago.   I⌐ti-zikañ ma⌉e ni ki┌ma┘sita.
4. I came 10 days ago.   To⌐o-ka ma⌉e ni ki┌ma┘sita.

5. I came 6 months ago.   Ro⌐k-kaḡetu ma⌐e ni ki⊦ma⌐sita.
6. I came 3 weeks ago.   Sa⌐n-syuukañ ma⌐e ni ki⊦ma⌐sita.
7. I came a little (while) ago.   Su⌐ko⌐si ⊦ma⌐e ni ki⊦ma⌐sita.
8. I came a little (while) ago.   Tyo⌐tto ⊦ma⌐e ni ki⊦ma⌐sita.

E. Substitution Drill

1. When is that?   Sore (wa) ⌐i⌐tu desu ka⌐
2. What is that?   Sore (wa) ⌐na⌐ñ desu ka⌐
3. Which one is that?   Sore (wa) ⌐do⌐re desu ka⌐
4. Where is that?   Sore (wa) ⌐do⌐ko desu ka⌐
5. How is that?   Sore (wa) ⌐do⌐o desu ka⌐
6. What month is that?   Sore (wa) ⌐na⌐ñ-ḡatu desu ka⌐
7. What time is that?   Sore (wa) ⌐na⌐ñ-zi desu ka⌐
8. What day is that?   Sore (wa) na⌐ñyo⌐obi desu ka⌐
9. How much is that?   Sore (wa) ⌐i⌐kura desu ka⌐
10. How many yen is that?   Sore (wa) ⌐na⌐ñ-eñ desu ka⌐

F. Substitution Drill

1. I went from the hotel.   Ho⌐teru kara i⊦kima⌐sita.
2. I went by train.   Ki⌐sya⌐ de i⊦kima⌐sita.
3. I went as far as the station. E⌐ki made i⊦kima⌐sita.
4. I went on the third.   Mi-⌐kka ni ikima⌐sita.
5. I went along that road.   So⌐no miti (o) ikima⌐sita.
6. I went.   Wa⌐takusï ḡa ikima⌐sita.
7. I (in comparison with oth-   Wa⌐takusi wa ikima⌐sita.
    ers) went.
8. I went the day before yes-   O⌐totoi ikima⌐sita.
    terday.
9. I went about 9 o'clock.   Ku-⌐zi-ḡo⌐ro i⊦kima⌐sita.
10. I went to the consulate.   Ryo⌐ozi⌐kañ e i⊦kima⌐sita.

G. Grammar Drill (based on Grammatical Note 5)

     Tutor: Yo⌐-zi desu. 'It's 4 o'clock.'
     Student: Yo-⌐zi-ḡo⌐ro desu. 'It's about 4 o'clock.'

1. To⌐o-ka ima⌐sita.   To⌐o-ka-ḡu⌐rai i⊦ma⌐sita.
2. To⌐o-ka ni ima⌐sita.   To⌐o-ka-ḡo⌐ro i⊦ma⌐sita.
3. Ku⌐-ḡatu desu.   Ku-⌐ḡatu-ḡo⌐ro desu.
4. Mo⌐kuyo⌐o ni i⊦kimasyo⌐o.   Mo⌐kuyoo-ḡo⌐ro i⊦kimasyo⌐o.
5. Go-⌐neñ ima⌐sita.   Go-⌐neñ-ḡu⌐rai i⊦ma⌐sita.
6. Go-⌐neñ ni ima⌐sita.   Go-⌐neñ-ḡo⌐ro i⊦ma⌐sita.
7. Zyu⌐s-syu⌐ukañ desita.   Zyu⌐s-syuukañ-ḡu⌐rai desita.
8. Zi⌐p-puñ ka⊦karima⌐sita.   Zi⌐p-puñ-ḡu⌐rai ka⊦karima⌐sita.

H. Level Drill (The sentences on the right are the plain equivalents of the po-
    lite sentences on the left.)

1. I⌐tu ko⊦tira e irassyaima⌐si-   I⌐tu ko⊦ko e kima⌐sita ka⌐
    ta ka⌐

2. Ya⌐mamoto orima˥su ka˩   Ya⌐mamoto ima˥su ka˩
3. I˥ma ma⌐irimasyo˥o ka.   I˥ma i⌐kimasyo˥o ka.

4. Ta⌐naka-sañ irassyaima˥su
   ka˩

	ima˥su	
Ta⌐naka-sañ	kima˥su	ka˩
	ikima˥su	

5. Ra˥itaa go├zaima˩su ka˩   Ra˥itaa a├rima˩su ka˩
6. Ni˥-neñ ┌ma˩e ni ko├tira   Ni˥-neñ ┌ma˩e ni ko├ko e kima˩sita.
   e mairima˩sita.
7. Do˥tira e i├rassyaima˩su   Do˥ko e i├kima˩su ka˩
   ka˩
8. To⌐ñde mo gozaimase˥ñ.   To⌐ñde mo arimase˥ñ.

I. **Level Drill** (The sentences on the right are informal equivalents of the sentences on the left.)

1. Kyo˥o tu⌐itati˥ desu ka˩   Kyo˥o tu˥itati?
2. Tyo⌐odo yo˥-zi desu.   Tyo⌐odo yo˥-zi.
3. A˥a, so˥o desu ka.   A˥a, so˥o.
4. To⌐ttemo i˥i desu.   To⌐ttemo i˥i.
5. Yo⌐rosi˥i desu ka˩   Yorosii?
6. Sore ⌐na˥ñ desu ka˩   Sore ⌐na˥ni?

J. **Expansion Drill**

1. [He] went.   I⌐kima˥sita.
   [He] went to France.   Hu⌐rañsu e ikima˥sita.
   [He] went to France six   Ro⌐k-kaḡetu ma˥e ni Hu⌐rañsu e iki-
   months ago.   ma˥sita.
   Mr. Tanaka went to France   Tanaka-sañ (wa) ro⌐k-kaḡetu ma˥e ni
   six months ago.   Hu⌐rañsu e ikima˥sita.

2. I came.   Ki⌐ma˥sita.
   I came on the 24th.   Ni˥zyuu yo-⌐kka ni kima˥sita.
   I came on August 24th.   Hati-ḡatu ⌐ni˥zyuu yo-⌐kka ni kima˥si-
                                                  ta.
   I came on August 24, 35 (i.e.   Sa˥ñzyuu go-neñ hati-ḡatu ⌐ni˥zyuu yo-
   of the Showa Era).   ⌐kka ni kima˥sita.

3. About how many days does it   Na˥ñ-niti-ḡu˥rai ka├karima˩su ka˩
   take?
   About how many days does it   Hu˥ne de na⌐ñ-niti-ḡu˥rai ka├karima˩-
   take by ship?   su ka˩
   About how many days does it   A⌐merika ma˥de ⌐hu˥ne de na⌐ñ-niti-ḡu˥-
   take by ship, as far as   rai ka├karima˩su ka˩
   America?
   About how many days does it   Ni⌐ho˥ñ kara A⌐merika ma˥de ⌐hu˥ne de
   take from Japan as far as   na⌐ñ-niti-ḡu˥rai ka├karima˩su ka˩
   America by ship?

4. I'd like to go . . .	I⌈kita⌉i ñ desu ḡa_
I'd like to go by car . . .	Zi⌈do⌉osya de i⊢kita⊣i ñ desu ḡa_
I'd like to go to Nikko by car . . .	Ni⌉kkoo e zi⌈do⌉osya de i⊢kita⊣i ñ desu ḡa_
I'd like to go to Nikko by car some (lit. one) time . . .	Iti-do ⌈Ni⌉kkoo e zi⌈do⌉osya de i⊢kita⊣i ñ desu ḡa_
5. It will probably be about July.	Si⌈ti-ḡatu-ḡo⌉ro desyoo.
[His] vacation will probably be about July.	Oyasumi (wa) si⌈ti-ḡatu-ḡo⌉ro desyoo.
[His] vacation this year will probably be about July.	Kotosi no oyasumi (wa) si⌈ti-ḡatu-ḡo⌉ro desyoo.
Mr. Tanaka's vacation this year will probably be about July.	Tanaka-sañ no ko⌉tosi no oyasumi (wa) si⌈ti-ḡatu-ḡo⌉ro desyoo.
6. [They]'re good!	I⌉i desu yo⌋
[They]'re very good!	To⌈ttemo i⌉i desu yo⌋
The new hotels are very good!	A⌈tarasi⌉i ⊢ho⊣teru (wa) to⌈ttemo i⌉i desu yo⌋
The new hotels in Tokyo are very good!	Tookyoo no a⌈tarasi⌉i ⊢ho⊣teru (wa) to⌈ttemo i⌉i desu yo⌋

QUESTION SUPPLEMENT

Answer the following questions, using a calendar when necessary:

1. I⌈ti-zi⌉kañ wa ⌈na⌉ñ-puñ desu ka⌋
2. I⌈ti-niti⌉ wa na⌈ñ-zi⌉kañ desu ka⌋
3. I⌈s-syu⌉ukañ wa ⌈na⌉ñ-niti desu ka⌋
4. I⌈k-ka⌉ḡetu wa na⌈ñ-niti-ḡu⌉rai desu ka⌋
5. I⌈k-ka⌉ḡetu wa na⌈ñ-syuukañ-ḡu⌉rai desu ka⌋
6. I⌈ti⌉-neñ wa ⌈na⌉ñ-niti desu ka⌋
7. I⌈ti⌉-neñ wa na⌈ñ-syu⌉ukañ desu ka⌋
8. I⌈ti⌉-neñ wa na⌈ñ-ka⌉ḡetu desu ka⌋
9. Kyo⌉o wa na⌈ñyo⌉obi desu ka⌋
10. A⌈sita⌉ wa ⌈na⌉ñ-niti desu ka⌋
11. Ki⌈no⌉o wa ⌈na⌉ñ-niti na⌈ñyo⌉obi desita ka⌋
12. O⌈toto⌉i wa ni⌈tiyoo de⌉sita ka⌋
13. Kotosi no i⌉ti-ḡatu ha⌉tu-ka wa na⌈ñyo⌉obi desu ka⌋
14. Kotosi no ⌈go⌉-ḡatu mi⌉-kka wa na⌈ñyo⌉obi desu ka⌋
15. Kotosi no si⌉ti-ḡatu ⌈ni⌉zyuu si⊢ti-niti⊣ wa na⌈ñyo⌉obi desu ka⌋
16. Kotosi no ha⌉ti-ḡatu hu⌉tu-ka wa na⌈ñyo⌉obi desu ka⌋
17. Ko⌈tosi no Kurisu⌉masu ['Christmas'] wa na⌈ñyo⌉obi desu ka⌋
18. Watakusi wa ha⌈ñ-zikañ ma⌉e ni ki⊢ma⊣sita. Na⌉ñ-zi ni ki⊢ma⊣sita ka⌋
19. Watakusi wa tyo⌉odo sa⌈ñ-kaḡetu ma⌉e ni ⌈Ni⌉kkoo e i⊢kima⊣sita. Na⌉ñ-ḡatu ⌈na⌉ñ-niti ni i⊢kima⊣sita ka⌋

20. Watakusi wa tyóodo i⌐s-syuukañ ma⌉e ni ko⌐no kuruma o kaima⌉sita.
    Na⌉ñ-niti ni ka├ima⌉sita ka⌐

21. Syoowa ⌐zyu⌉u-neñ wa séereki ⌐na⌉ñ-neñ desita ka⌐

22. Me⌉ezi ⌐ga⌉ñneñ wa séereki ⌐na⌉ñ-neñ desita ka⌐

23. Kotosi wa ⌐na⌉ñ-neñ desu ka⌐

EXERCISES

1. Mr. Tanaka has asked what time it is. Give the following answers:

   a. It's 4 o'clock.
   b. It's just 7:30.
   c. It's 10 after 6.
   d. It's 10:45.
   e. It's 5:15.
   f. It's about 7 o'clock.
   g. It's about a quarter to eight.
   h. It's 2:28.
   i. It's one minute after 1.
   j. It's 10 to 12.
   k. It's 20 to 11.
   l. It's probably about 9.

2. Mr. Tanaka has just asked you when you came here. Tell him that you
   came:

   a. In 1955.
   b. In January.
   c. In March, 1953.
   d. On April 14th.
   e. In Showa 29.
   f. About six months ago.
   g. About two years ago.
   h. About ten weeks ago.

3. Using a calendar, practice asking and answering questions pertaining to
   dates and days of the week.

4. Practice asking and answering questions on how long it takes from one
   given geographical point to another by a given mode of transportation. The
   geographical points may include everything f r o m countries to buildings
   within a c i t y.   Timetables are useful as the basis for some questions.

5. Practice the Basic Dialogues with appropriate variations.

Lesson 9. Time (cont.)

(a)

Tanaka

every day	ma˥initi
return home	ka⌐erima˥su or
	o⌐kaeri ni narima˥su †

1. What time do you go home every day?

   Ma˥initi ⌐na˥ñ-zi ni ka⌐erima˩su ka⌐

   or

   Ma˥initi ⌐na˥ñ-zi ni o⌐kaeri ni narima˩su ka⌐

Smith

usually	taitee
sometimes	to⌐kidoki˥

2. I usually go home at 5:30, but sometimes I go home about 6.

   Taitee go-⌐zi-ha˥ñ ni ka⌐erima˩su ḡa, tokidoki ro⌐ku-zi-ḡo˥ro kaerimasu.

Tanaka

morning	a˥sa
home	uti or
	otaku †
go out or leave	de⌐ma˥su or
	o⌐de ni narima˥su †

3. What time do you leave home in the morning?

   A˥sa ⌐na˥ñ-zi ni u⌐ti (o) dema˩su ka⌐

   or

   A˥sa ⌐na˥ñ-zi ni o⌐taku (o) ode ni narima˩su ka⌐

Smith

always	i˥tu mo
a little after 8	ha⌐ti˥-zi tyo⌐tto suḡi˥

4. I always leave at a little after 8.

   I˥tu mo ha⌐ti˥-zi tyo⌐tto suḡi˥ ni demasu.

going out or leaving	de˥te
business office	zi⌐mu˥syo
arrive	tu⌐kima˥su

5. I leave the house about 8, and arrive at the office about 9.

   Ha⌐ti-zi-ḡo˥ro u⌐ti (o) de˥te, ku-⌐zi-ḡo˥ro zi⌐mu˥syo ni tukimasu.

132

(b)

Tanaka

6. (About) when are you going back to America?	I⌜tu-ḡoro Amerika ni kaerima⌝su ka⌴ or I⌜tu-ḡoro Amerika ni okaeri ni narima⌝su ka⌴

Smith

by October	zyu⌜u-ḡatu⌝ made ni
7. I'd LIKE to go back by October (but) . . .	Zyu⌜u-ḡatu⌝ made ni ka⌜erita⌝i ñ desu ḡa_

Tanaka

be possible or can do	de⌜kima⌝su or o⌜deki ni narima⌝su↑
8. Can't you?	De⌜kimase⌝ñ ka⌴ or O⌜deki ni narimase⌝ñ ka⌴

Smith

9. Hmm. I wonder.	Sa⌝a. Do⌝o desyoo ka ⁺ne⁻e.

(c)

At a government office

Employee

tomorrow morning	a⌜sita no a⌝sa
please come	ki⌜te⌝ kudasai or i⌜rassya⌝tte↑ kudasai or i⌜ra⌝site↑ kudasai
10. Please come again tomorrow morning.	A⌜sita no a⌝sa ma⌜ta kite⌝ kudasai. or A⌜sita no a⌝sa ma⌜ta irassya⌝tte kudasai. or A⌜sita no a⌝sa ma⌜ta ira⌝site kudasai.

Tanaka

I guess I'll come	ki⌜masyo⌝o or ma⌜irimasyo⌝o↓
shall I come?	ki⌜masyo⌝o ka or ma⌜irimasyo⌝o ka↓
11. What time shall I come?	Na⌝ñ-zi ni ki⁺masyo⁻o ka. or Na⌝ñ-zi ni ma⁺irimasyo⁻o ka.

Employee

by 9 o'clock	ku⌝-zi made ni

12. Please come by 9 o'clock.

Ku⌝-zi made ni ki⌐te⌐ kudasai.
or
Ku⌝-zi made ni i⌐rassya⌐tte kudasai.
or
Ku⌝-zi made ni i⌐ra⌐site kudasai.

Tanaka

    is fast or early — ha⌐ya⌝i /-ku/

13. That's early! — Ha⌐ya⌝i desu ⌐ne⌝e.

    be(come) distressing or troublesome or annoying or inconvenient or perplexing — ko⌐marima⌝su

14. I'm afraid that will be a bit inconvenient. . . — Tyo⌝tto ko⌐marima⌝su ḡa_

Employee

15. Well then, how about 10 o'clock? — Zya⌝a, zyu⌝u-zi wa ⌐do⌐o desu ka.
or
Zya⌝a, zyu⌝u-zi wa i⌐ka⌐ḡa desu ka.

Tanaka

    fine — ke⌝kkoo+
    by 10 o'clock — zyu⌝u-zi made ni

16. That's fine. I'll come by 10. — I⌝i desu yo_ Zyu⌝u-zi made ni kimasu.
or
Ke⌝kkoo desu. Zyu⌝u-zi made ni mairimasu.

(d)

Secretary

    until what time? — na⌝ñ-zi made
    how long? (i.e. from what time until what time?) — na⌝ñ-zi kara ⌐na⌝ñ-zi made
    I guess I'll be or stay — i⌐masyo⌝o or o⌐rimasyo⌝o +
    shall I be or stay? — i⌐masyo⌝o ka or o⌐rimasyo⌝o ka +

17. How long shall I stay here tomorrow? — Asita ⌐na⌝ñ-zi kara ⌐na⌝ñ-zi made ko⌐ko ni orimasyo⌐o ka_

Smith

    afternoon or p.m. — go⌝ḡo
    until 3 o'clock — sa⌝ñ-zi made
    please be or stay — i⌐te kudasa⌝i or i⌐rassya⌝tte + kudasai or i⌐ra⌝site + kudasai

18. Please be [here] from 9 in the morning until 3 in the afternoon.

A⌐sa ⌐ku˩-zi kara ⌐go⌐go ⌐sa⌐n̄-zi made i⌐te kudasa⌐i.

Secretary

19. Certainly. I'll be here (lit. come) by 9.

Ka⌐sikomarima⌐sita. Ku⌐-zi made ni mairimasu.

(e)

Smith

this morning

ke⌐sa

20. Did you go to the bank this morning?

Ke⌐sa gin̄koo e ikima⌐sita ka⌐

Tanaka

make no difference or
be all right

ka⌐maimase⌐n̄

21. No, I'm going later. Is that all right?

Iie, a⌐to de i⌐kima⌐su ḡa, ka⌐maimase⌐n̄ ka⌐

Smith

until 3 o'clock

sa⌐n̄-zi made

22. The bank closes at (lit. is until) 3, you know.

Gin̄koo (wa) ⌐sa⌐n̄-zi made desu yo⌐

Tanaka

well then or then
I guess I'll go

zya
i⌐kimasyo⌐o or
ma⌐irimasyo⌐o

23. Oh, of course! Then I guess I'll go now.

A. ⌐So⌐o ⌐so⌐o. Zya, i⌐ma i⌐kimasyo⌐o.

NOTES ON THE BASIC DIALOGUES

1. Ma⌐initi: compare also ma⌐iasa 'every morning,' maisyuu 'every week,' maituki or maiḡetu 'every month,' and maitosi or mainen̄ 'every year.' All are time nominals and all occur without particle ni indicating time when something happens.

   Ka⌐erima⌐su means 'return to a place where one habitually spends time— one's own home, office, native land, etc.' The gerund (-te form) of ka⌐erima⌐su is ka⌐ette.

2. Remember that after -ḡo⌐ro, time particle ni is optional but more often omitted. Ni does not occur after taitee and to⌐kidoki⌐.

3. A⌐sa is another time word which indicates time when something happens, without a following particle.

   Note these expressions: Place word + o + de⌐ma⌐su 'leave a place'; place word + kara + de⌐ma⌐su 'leave from a place.'

5. De⌐te is the gerund (-te form) of de⌐ma⌐su. The gerund of tu⌐kima⌐su is tu⌐ite. Zi⌐mu⌐syo ni tukimasu may be replaced by zi⌐mu⌐syo e tukimasu without significant difference in meaning.

6. Amerika e or Amerika ni. Compare the preceding note.

7. 'I'd like to, but—I don't know whether I can or not.'

8. Like √wa⌐karima⌐su, √a⌐rima⌐su, √i⌐rima⌐su, and √ka⌐karima⌐su, √de⌐kima⌐su does not occur with particle o. Both the person who can and the thing which is possible are followed by particles wa or ğa, depending on emphasis. The gerund (-te form) of de⌐kima⌐su is de⌐kite.

10. Note the difference between a⌐sita no a⌐sa ki⌐te⌐ kudasai (in which a⌐sita⌐ describes a⌐sa) 'please come tomorrow morning' and asita ⌐a⌐sa ki⌐te⌐ kudasai (in which both a⌐sita⌐ and a⌐sa tell 'time when' and modify ki⌐te⌐ kudasai) 'please come tomorrow, in the morning.'

Ki⌐te⌐ is the gerund (-te form) of ki⌐ma⌐su. I⌐rassya⌐tte and i⌐ra⌐site are alternate gerunds of the honorific i⌐rassyaima⌐su 'come,' 'go,' or 'be,' with i⌐ra⌐site the less stiff and more conversational of the two.

13. Like all adjectivals, ha⌐ya⌐i occurs in its adverbial (-ku) form when it modifies an inflected expression. Thus: ha⌐yaku a⌐rimase⌐ñ 'it isn't fast or early,' ha⌐yaku si⌐te kudasa⌐i 'do [it] quickly or early,' ha⌐yaku ki⌐ma⌐sita 'I came early or quickly,' etc. Compare: Ha⌐ya⌐i ⌐ta⌐kusii de ki⌐ma⌐sita 'I came in a fast taxi' and ha⌐yaku ⌐ta⌐kusii de ki⌐ma⌐sita 'I came quickly by taxi.'

14. Ko⌐marima⌐su and ko⌐marima⌐sita have many varied English equivalents: 'Oh, dear!' 'What am I going to do?' 'What a mess I'm in!' 'This is a bad situation'; etc. The -ma⌐su form usually refers to a general or future situation, while the -ma⌐sita form indicates either that the difficult situation has taken place (i. e. I'm affected now) or did take place. Both what is troublesome and the person affected are followed by particles wa or ğa depending on emphasis. The gerund of ko⌐marima⌐su is ko⌐ma⌐tte.

The final ğa qualifies the statement politely: 'It will be a bit inconvenient but—I don't like to insist on your making a change' or 'I don't like to mention it,' etc. Basic Sentence 14 is a close equivalent of English 'I'm afraid it will be a bit inconvenient . . .'

16. The nominal ke⌐kkoo is a polite word which usually occurs in affirmative statements. Like adjectivals i⌐i and yorosii, it refers to situations which are 'fine,' 'good,' 'all right,' and also to those which are 'fine as they are—nothing more needed.' Accordingly, in some contexts the closest English equivalent is 'never mind.'

18. Go⌐ğo is used both as a conversational term for 'afternoon' and as a technical term corresponding to English p.m. In the latter meaning, its opposite is go⌐zeñ 'a.m.,' while the conversational word for morning is a⌐sa. Go⌐ğo occurs both with and without following particle ni in indicating time when something happens.

Ite is the gerund (-te form) of i⌐ma⌐su.

20. Ke⌐sa occurs without a following particle in indicating time when something happens.

21. Ka⌐maimase˥n̄, a verbal negative whose corresponding affirmative is comparatively rare, has many English equivalents: 'It makes no difference'; 'It doesn't matter'; 'I don't care'; 'I don't mind'; 'It doesn't bother me'; 'It's all right'; etc. Ko⌐marima˥su usually occurs as its opposite. Thus: Ko⌐marima˥su ka⌐ 'Will it be inconvenient?' . . . 'Iie, ka⌐maimase˥n̄. 'No, it doesn't matter.'

23. Repeated so˥o is emphatic. So˥o here is the informal equivalent of so˥o desu ⌐ne˥e. Zya is a more clipped, terse alternant of zya˥a.

GRAMMATICAL NOTES

1. Verbals: More About the Tentative

In Lesson 7, Grammatical Note 2, the tentative of verbals was introduced, meaning 'let's do so-and-so' in statements, and 'shall we do so-and-so?' in questions. Thus:

I⌐kimasyo˥o ka. 'Shall we go?'
E˥e, i⌐kimasyo˥o. 'Yes, let's go.'

The verbal tentative has a second use, distinguished from the first only by context. It may indicate a suggestion by the speaker directed to himself alone: 'I guess I'll do so-and-so'; and in its more common use — in questions — this second kind of tentative is an offer: 'Shall I do so-and-so?' In such cases, the affirmative reply is an appropriate imperative, or o⌐neḡai-sima˥su, or another request expression. Possible negative replies include i˥i desu and the more polite ke˥kkoo desu meaning 'never mind.'

Examples:

Ti˥zu (o) ka⌐kimasyo˥o ka. 'Shall I draw a map?'
E˥e, ka˥ite kudasai. 'Yes, please (draw).'   or
E˥e, o⌐neḡai-sima˥su. 'Yes, please do.'

Ta⌐bako (o) kaimasyo˥o ka. 'Shall I buy some cigarettes?'
Iie, i˥i desu yo.   or ⎫
Iie, ke˥kkoo desu.   ⎬ 'No, never mind.'
                               ⎭

2. Verbals: Honorific Equivalents Ending in √na⌐rima˥su

The polite verbals previously introduced (√go⌐zaima˥su, √i⌐rassyaima˥su, etc.) were words which had to be memorized along with their plain equivalents because structurally they were unrelated. Such polite verbals are limited in number. Far more common are those having the same root as their plain equivalents.

One of the most common types of honorific (†) consists of the polite o- prefixed to the stem of a plain verbal (the stem is the -ma˥su form minus -ma˥su) + particle ni + √na⌐rima˥su. (√Na⌐rima˥su as an independent verbal means 'become,' 'come to be'; it will occur in later lessons.) The form of √na⌐rima˥su shows whether the combination is non-past or past, affirmative or negative, etc. The accent of the combination occurs on √na⌐rima˥su. The combination is the honorific equivalent of the corresponding plain verbal.

Examples:

Plain	(Stem)	Honorific (†) Equivalent
ka⌐erima⌐su	(ka⌐eri)	o⌐kaeri ni narima⌐su '[he] returns (or will return) home'
de⌐ma⌐sita	(de⌐)	o⌐de ni narima⌐sita '[he] went out'
tu⌐kimase⌐ñ	(tu⌐ki)	o⌐tuki ni narimase⌐ñ '[he] doesn't (or won't) arrive or hasn't arrived'
de⌐kimase⌐ñ desita	(de⌐ki)	o⌐deki ni narimase⌐ñ desita '[he] couldn't do it'

The gerund of the honorific is o- + verbal stem + ni + na⌐tte.

The corresponding form for √i⌐ma⌐su, √i⌐kima⌐su, and √ki⌐ma⌐su is irregular: o⌐ide ni √narima⌐su.   Like √i⌐rassyaima⌐su, it occurs as the honorific equivalent of all three plain verbals.

Like all honorifics, these are used only in reference to persons other than the speaker, in polite speech. The plain equivalent is used as a corresponding non-honorific form. Thus:

> A: Tanaka-sañ (wa) o⌐wakari ni narima⌐su ka⌐
> 'Does Mr. Tanaka understand?'
>
> B: Ha⌐a, o⌐wakari ni narima⌐su.
> 'Yes, he understands.'
>
> A: A⌐na⌐ta mo o⌐wakari ni narima⌐su ka⌐
> 'Do you understand too?'
>
> B: Ha⌐a, wa⌐takusi mo wakarima⌐su.
> 'Yes, I understand too.'

WARNING: Don't try to make up o-⌐(stem) ni √narima⌐su honorific equivalents for all plain verbals. As always, let the usage of native speakers be your guide.

3. **P a r t i c l e s : ma⌐de** 'until,' **ma⌐de ni** 'by'

a. **ma⌐de** 'until'

Reread Lesson 7, Grammatical Note 3b.

The particle ma⌐de after a time expression means 'until'—i.e. 'up to and including part or all of.'

Examples:

> a⌐sita⌐ made 'until tomorrow'
> i⌐tu made 'until when?'

  iˤti-g̃atu maˡde[1] 'until January'
  iˤma maˡde[1] 'until now'

b. maˡde ni 'by'

The particle sequence maˡde ni preceded by a time expression means
'at a point in the time until,' i.e. 'by' the given time. It regularly occurs with
an inflected expression which indicates action.

Examples:

  Aˤsitaˡ made ni kimasu. 'He'll come by tomorrow.'
  Iˤti-g̃atu maˡde ni tukimasu. 'He'll arrive by January.'
  Iˤma maˡde ni deˤmaˡsita. 'It has left by now.'
  Kuˤ-zi maˤde niˤ wa kaerimasu. 'By 9 (comparatively speaking) I'll
    be home (lit. return home).'

4. √deˡsu Following a Particle

Besides occurring after adjectivals and nominals, √deˡsu also occurs immediately after phrases which end in some particles—for example, it may
follow kara and maˡde but it rarely follows wa, g̃a, or o directly. √Deˡsu is
accented if the preceding phrase is unaccented.

Examples:

  Saˡñ-zi made desu. 'It is until 3'—i.e. 'it lasts until 3' or 'it ends at
    3' or 'it closes at 3' or 'it is open until 3.'

  Saˡñ-zi kara desu. 'It is from 3'—i.e. 'it begins at 3' or 'it opens at
    3.'

The negative equivalent of a sequence ending in particle + √deˡsu ends in
particle + zya aˤrimaseˡñ:

  Saˡñ-zi kara zya aˤrimaseˤñ. 'It isn't from 3 o'clock'—i.e. 'it does-
    n't begin at 3' or 'it doesn't open at 3.'

DRILLS

A. Substitution Drill

  1. I usually come by bus.   Taitee ˤbaˡsu de kimasu.
  2. I sometimes come by bus.   Tokidoki ˤbaˡsu de kimasu.
  3. I always come by bus.   Iˡtu mo ˤbaˡsu de kimasu.
  4. I come by bus a good deal.   Yoˡku ˤbaˡsu de kimasu.
  5. I come by bus every day.   Maˡiniti ˤbaˡsu de kimasu.

---

[1] Note the irregular accent of this phrase.

6. I come by bus in the afternoon.

   Go˥ḡo ˩ba˩su de kimasu.

7. I come by bus in the morning.

   A˩sa ˩ba˩su de kimasu.

8. I come by bus every morning.

   Ma˩iasa ˩ba˩su de kimasu.

B. Substitution Drill

1. Mr. Tanaka HAS LEFT.

   Tanaka-sañ (wa) de˩ma˩sita.

2. MR. TANAKA left.

   Ta˩naka-sañ ḡa dema˩sita.

3. He left the office.

   Zi˩mu˩syo (o) de˩ma˥sita.

4. He left from the office.

   Zi˩mu˩syo kara de˩ma˥sita.

5. He left today.

   Kyo˩o de˩ma˥sita.

6. He left in the afternoon.

   Go˩ḡo ⌐ni⌐ de˩ma˥sita.

7. He left at 8 o'clock.

   Ha˩ti˩-zi ni de˩ma˥sita.

8. He left by 8 o'clock.

   Ha˩ti˩-zi made ni de˩ma˥sita.

9. I left, too.

   Wa˩takusi mo dema˩sita.

C. Substitution Drill

1. Please come again to-
   morrow.

   Asita ma˩ta kite˩ kudasai.

2. Please come again in the
   afternoon.

   Go˩ḡo ma˩ta kite˩ kudasai.

3. Please come again on
   Monday.

   Ge˩tuyo˩obi ni ma˩ta kite˩ kudasai.

4. Please come again in
   April.

   Si-˩ḡatu˩ ni ma˩ta kite˩ kudasai.

5. Please come again about
   4.

   Yo-˩zi-ḡo˩ro ma˩ta kite˩ kudasai.

6. Please come again at 7:30.

   Si˩ti-zi-ha˩ñ ni ma˩ta kite˩ kudasai.

7. Please come again tomorrow morning.

   A˩sita no a˩sa ma˩ta kite˩ kudasai.

8. Please come again tomorrow about 10.

   Asita zyu˩u-zi-ḡo˩ro ma˩ta kite˩ kudasai.

D. Substitution Drill

1. I'm going later. Is that
   all right?

   A˩to de i˩kima˥su ḡa, ka˩maimase˩ñ
   ka⌐

2. I'm not coming tomorrow.
   Is that all right?

   A˩sita kimase˩ñ ḡa, ka˩maimase˩ñ ka⌐

3. I'd like to go home early.
   Is that all right?

   Ha˩yaku ka˩erita˥i ñ desu ḡa, ka˩mai-
   mase˩ñ ka⌐

4. I'm going to leave from the
   office. Is that all right?

   Zi˩mu˩syo kara de˩ma˥su ḡa, ka˩mai-
   mase˩ñ ka⌐

5. I'll arrive about 10. Is
   that all right?

   Zyu˩u-zi-ḡo˩ro tu˩kima˥su ḡa, ka˩mai-
   mase˩ñ ka⌐

6. I'll be [here] until afternoon. Is that all right?

   Go˩ḡo made i˩ma˥su ḡa, ka˩maimase˩ñ
   ka⌐

7. I bought a cheap furoshiki. Is that all right?   Ya⌐su⌐i hu⌐rosiki (o) kaima⌐sita ḡa, ka⌐maimase⌐ñ ka⌐

8. There aren't any cigarettes. Is that all right?   Ta⌐bako (wa) arimase⌐ñ ḡa, ka⌐maimase⌐ñ ka⌐

9. This one is a little different. Is that all right?   Kore (wa) su⌐ko⌐si ti⌐ḡaima⌐su ḡa, ka⌐maimase⌐ñ ka⌐

10. It's a little expensive. Is that all right?   Su⌐ko⌐si ta⌐ka⌐i desu ḡa, ka⌐maimase⌐ñ ka⌐

E. Substitution Drill

1. I was here from morning until afternoon.   A⌐sa kara ⌐go⌐ḡo made ko⌐ko ni ima⌐sita.

2. I was in the office from 9 until 5.   Ku⌐-zi kara ⌐go⌐-zi made zi⌐mu⌐syo ni i⌐ma⌐sita.

3. I was at home from Friday until Sunday.   Ki⌐ñyo⌐o kara ni⌐tiyoo ma⌐de u⌐ti ni ima⌐sita.

4. I was at the hospital from April until August.   Si-⌐ḡatu⌐ kara ha⌐ti-ḡatu⌐ made byo⌐oiñ ni ima⌐sita.

5. I was in school from the year 30 until this year.   Sa⌐ñzyu⌐u-neñ kara ko⌐tosi ma⌐de ga⌐k-koo ni ima⌐sita.

6. I was in the park from about 10 until about 11:30.   Zyu⌐u-zi-ḡo⌐ro kara zyu⌐uiti-zi-hañ-ḡo⌐ro made ko⌐oeñ ni ima⌐sita.

7. I was at that hotel from the first until the tenth.   Tu⌐itati⌐ kara to⌐o-ka ma⌐de a⌐no ho⌐-teru ni i⌐ma⌐sita.

8. I was at an inn in Kyoto from the day before yesterday until yesterday.   O⌐toto⌐i kara ki⌐no⌐o made ⌐Kyo⌐oto no ryo⌐kañ ni ima⌐sita.

9. I was in the post office from 10 to 10 until 5 after.   Zyu⌐u-zi zyu⌐p-pu⌐ñ-mae kara go-hu⌐ñ-suḡi made yu⌐ubi⌐ñkyoku ni i⌐ma⌐sita.

10. I was at Mr. Tanaka's house from yesterday morning until this morning.   Ki⌐noo no a⌐sa kara ⌐ke⌐sa made Ta⌐naka-sañ no otaku ni ima⌐sita.

F. Substitution Drill

1. I am always at home about 8.   I⌐tu mo ha⌐ti-zi-ḡo⌐ro u⌐ti ni ima⌐su.

2. I usually am at home about 8.   Taitee ha⌐ti-zi-ḡo⌐ro u⌐ti ni ima⌐su.

3. I usually am at home at exactly 9.   Taitee tyo⌐odo ku⌐-zi ni u⌐ti ni ima⌐su.

4. I usually am in the office at exactly 9.   Taitee tyo⌐odo ku⌐-zi ni zi⌐mu⌐syo ni imasu.

5. I usually arrive at the office at exactly 9.   Taitee tyo⌐odo ku⌐-zi ni zi⌐mu⌐syo ni tukimasu.

6. Every day I arrive at the office at exactly 9.   Ma⌐initi tyo⌐odo ku⌐-zi ni zi⌐mu⌐syo ni tukimasu.

142 Lesson 9. Time (cont.)

7. Every day I arrive at the office at a little before 9.

Ma˥initi ⌐ku˥-zi ⌐tyo˥tto ˥ma˥e ni zi-⌐mu˥syo ni tukimasu.

8. Every day I arrive at school at a little before 9.

Ma˥initi ⌐ku˥-zi ⌐tyo˥tto ˥ma˥e ni ga⌐kkoo ni tukima˥su.

9. Every day I go to school at a little before 9.

Ma˥initi ⌐ku˥-zi ⌐tyo˥tto ˥ma˥e ni ga⌐kkoo ni ikima˥su.

G. Grammar Drill

Tutor: I˥ma desu ka⌐ 'Is it now?' (affirmative)
Student: I˥ma zya a˥rimase˥ñ ka⌐ 'Isn't it now?' (negative)

1. Ma˥initi desu ka⌐
Ma˥initi zya a˥rimase˥ñ ka⌐

2. O⌐wakari ni narima˥su ka⌐
O⌐wakari ni narimase˥ñ ka⌐

3. Ke˥sa desita yo⌐
Ke˥sa zya a˥rimase˥ñ desita yo⌐

4. Sa˥ñ-zi kara desu ka⌐
Sa˥ñ-zi kara zya a˥rimase˥ñ ka⌐

5. Kinoo o⌐kaeri ni narima˥si-ta ka⌐
Kinoo o⌐kaeri ni narimase˥ñ desita ka⌐

6. Ha⌐ya˥i desu ka⌐
Ha˥yaku a˥rimase˥ñ ka⌐

7. Yo˥-zi made desu ka⌐
Yo˥-zi made zya a˥rimase˥ñ ka⌐

8. De⌐kima˥sita ka⌐
De⌐kimase˥ñ desita ka⌐

9. A˥na˥ta mo o˥de ni narima˥su ka⌐
A˥na˥ta mo o˥de ni narimase˥ñ ka⌐

10. Ta⌐naka-sañ no˥ desu yo⌐
Ta⌐naka-sañ no˥ zya a˥rimase˥ñ yo⌐

H. Response Drill[1]

Tutor: I⌐kimasyo˥o ka. 'Shall I go?' (an offer)
Student: E˥e, i⌐tte kudasa˥i. 'Yes, please (go).' (affirmative answer)

1. Ti˥zu (o) ka˥kimasyo˥o ka.
E˥e, ka˥ite kudasai.

2. Ma⌐timasyo˥o ka.
E˥e, ma˥tte kudasai.

3. Wa⌐takusi mo mairimasyo˥o ka.
Ha˥a, i⌐ra˥site kudasai.

4. A⌐sita˥ mo ki˥masyo˥o ka.
E˥e, ki˥te˥ kudasai.

5. Ko⌐re (o) simasyo˥o ka.
E˥e, si⌐te kudasa˥i.

6. Mo˥o iti-do iimasyo˥o ka.
E˥e, i⌐tte kudasa˥i.

7. Ro⌐ku˥-zi made i˥masyo˥o ka.
E˥e, i˥te kudasa˥i.

8. Si⌐ñbuñ mo kaimasyo˥o ka.
E˥e, ka⌐tte kudasa˥i.

---

[1] Based on Grammatical Note 1. After practicing the drill in its given form, practice it with o⌐negai-sima˥su as an alternate affirmative reply, and with i˥i desu and ke˥kkoo desu as negative replies.

I. Level Drill[1]

1. I⌐tu-g̃oro kaerima¬su ka⌐⌐   I⌐tu-g̃oro okaeri ni narima¬su ka⌐⌐
2. Wa⌐surema¬sita ka⌐⌐   O⌐wasure ni narima¬sita ka⌐⌐
3. To⌐kee (g̃a) arima¬su ka⌐⌐   To⌐kee (g̃a) gozaima¬su ka⌐⌐
4. Na¬ñ-zi ni u⌐ti (o) dema⁴su   Na¬ñ-zi ni o⌐taku (o) ode ni narima⁴su
   ka⌐⌐   ka⌐⌐

5. Go¬g̃o made i⌐ma⁴su ka⌐⌐   Go¬g̃o made │ i⌐rassyaima⁴su   │ ka⌐⌐
                                                  │ o⌐ide ni narima⁴su   │

6. I¬tu ko⌐ko ni kima⁴sita ka⌐⌐   I¬tu ko⌐tira ni │ irassyaima⁴sita   │ ka⌐⌐
                                                     │ oide ni narima⁴sita   │

7. Wa⌐karima¬sita ka⌐⌐   O⌐wakari ni narima¬sita ka⌐⌐
8. Na¬ñ-niti-g̃o¬ro tu⌐kima⁴su   Na¬ñ-niti-g̃o¬ro o⌐tuki ni narima⁴su ka⌐⌐
   ka⌐⌐

J. Expansion Drill

1. I guess I'll come.   Ki⌐masyo¬o.
   Shall I come?   Ki⌐masyo¬o ka.
   Shall I come again?   Ma⌐ta kimasyo¬o ka.
   Shall I come again tomor-   A⌐sita mata kimasyo¬o ka.
   row?

2. I go back.   Ka⌐erima¬su.
   I go back to Kyoto.   Kyo¬oto ni kaerimasu.
   I go back to Kyoto in June.   Ro⌐ku-g̃atu¬ ni ⌐Kyo¬oto ni kaerimasu.
   I usually go back to Kyoto   Taite ro⌐ku-g̃atu¬ ni ⌐Kyo¬oto ni kae-
   in June.   rimasu.

3. I'm [here].   I⌐ma¬su.
   I'm in the office.   Zi⌐mu¬syo ni imasu.
   I'm in the office until 5:30.   Go-⌐zi-ha¬ñ made zi⌐mu¬syo ni imasu.
   I'm in the office from 9   Ku¬-zi kara go-⌐zi-ha¬ñ made zi⌐mu¬-
   until 5:30.   syo ni imasu.
   I'm in the office every day   Ma¬initi ⌐ku¬-zi kara go-⌐zi-ha¬ñ made
   from 9 to 5:30.   zi⌐mu¬syo ni imasu.

4. [He] arrived.   Tu⌐kima¬sita.
   [He] arrived in America.   A⌐merika ni tukima¬sita.
   [He] arrived in America   Ni-⌐syuukañ-g̃u¬rai ⌐ma⁴e ni A⌐meri-
   about 2 weeks ago.   ka ni tukima¬sita.
   Mr. Tanaka arrived in   Tanaka-sañ (wa) ni-⌐syuukañ-g̃u¬rai
   America about 2 weeks   ⌐ma⁴e ni A⌐merika ni tukima¬sita.
   ago.

---

[1] In each case the sentence on the right is the polite equivalent of the sentence on the left.

5. Is it all right?   Ka⌐maimase⌉ñ ka⌣
    I'd like to leave. Is it   De⌐ta⌉i ñ desu ḡa, ka⌐maimase⌉ñ ka⌣
    all right?
    I'd like to leave here. Is   Ko⌐ko (o) deta⌉i ñ desu ḡa, ka⌐maima-
    it all right?   se⌉ñ ka⌣
    I'd like to leave here by 3   Sa⌉ñ-zi made ni ko⌐ko (o) deta⌉i ñ de-
    o'clock. Is it all right?   su ḡa, ka⌐maimase⌉ñ ka⌣

6. I arrived.   Tu⌐kima⌉sita.
    I arrived in Japan.   Ni⌐ho⌉ñ ni tu⌐kima⌐sita.
    I arrived in Japan on the   Zyu⌐ugo-niti ni Ni⌐ho⌉ñ ni tu⌐kima⌐si-
    15th.   ta.
    I left America on the 1st   Tu⌐itati⌉ ni A⌐merika (o) de⌉te, zyu⌐u-
    and arrived in Japan on   go-niti ni Ni⌐ho⌉ñ ni tu⌐kima⌐sita.
    the 15th.

7. I can't do [it].   De⌐kimase⌉ñ.
    I can't do [it] (I tell you).   De⌐kimase⌉ñ yo⌣
    All of it, I can't do (I tell   Ze⌉ñbu wa de⌐kimase⌐ñ yo⌣
    you).
    I can do a little but I can't   Su⌐ko⌉si wa de⌐kima⌐su ḡa, ze⌉ñbu wa
    do all of it (I tell you).   de⌐kimase⌐ñ yo.

8. It's troublesome.   Ko⌐marima⌉su.
    It's troublesome (I tell you).   Ko⌐marima⌉su yo⌣
    It's a little troublesome (I   Tyo⌉tto ko⌐marima⌐su yo⌣
    tell you).
    This is a little troublesome   Kore wa ⌐tyo⌉tto ko⌐marima⌐su yo⌣
    (I tell you).
    That doesn't matter, but   So⌐re wa kamaimase⌉ñ ḡa, kore wa
    this is a little troublesome   ⌐tyo⌉tto ko⌐marima⌐su yo⌣
    (I tell you).

SUPPLEMENTARY CONVERSATIONS

(with questions)

1. Yamamoto (a visitor): Ta⌐naka-sañ irassyaima⌉su ka⌣
   Secretary: Ta⌐naka-sañ de⌉su ka⌣ Yo⌐kohama e irassyaima⌉sita ḡa_
   Yamamoto: So⌉o desu ka. Na⌐ñ-zi-ḡo⌉ro o⌐kaeri ni narima⌐su ka⌣
   Secretary: Yo⌐ku wa⌐karimase⌐ñ ḡa, ni-⌐zi-ḡo⌉ro desyoo.
   Yamamoto: So⌉o desu ka. Zya⌉a, ma⌐ta a⌉to de ma⌐irimasyo⌐o. Do⌉o mo
              a⌐ri⌐ḡatoo gozaimasita.
   Secretary: Do⌉o itasimasite.

Questions (Answer in Japanese on the basis of the above conversation.)

        1. Tanaka-sañ wa i⌐ma⌉su ka⌣
        2. Tanaka-sañ wa ⌐do⌉ko ni i⌐ma⌐su ka⌣
        3. Tanaka-sañ wa ⌐i⌉tu ka⌐erima⌐su ka⌣

4. Yamamoto-sañ wa ⌐do⌐o si⌐ma⌐su ka⌐[1]

2. Mr. Smith: A⌐sita⌐ kara[2] Ka⌐makura[3] e ikima⌐su ḡa, a⌐na⌐ta mo ĩti-do i⌐ki-
mase⌐ñ ka⌐
Tanaka: A⌐ri⌐ḡatoo gozaimasu ḡa⌐
Smith: Tu⌐ḡi⌐ no ni⌐tiyo⌐obi wa ⌐do⌐o desu ka.
Tanaka: A⌐ri⌐ḡatoo gozaimasu. Tu⌐ḡi⌐ no ni⌐tiyo⌐obi ⌐na⌐ñ-niti desyoo
ka.
Smith: Ha⌐tu-ka de⌐su ḡa⌐ Do⌐o desu ka. I⌐kimase⌐ñ ka⌐
Tanaka: A⌐ri⌐ḡatoo gozaimasu. Ka⌐maimase⌐ñ ka⌐
Smith: E⌐e, do⌐ozo ⌐do⌐ozo. Na⌐ñ de i⌐kima⌐su ka⌐
Tanaka: So⌐o desu ⌐ne⌐e. De⌐ñsya de i⌐kima⌐su ḡa⌐
Smith: Na⌐ñ-zi-ḡo⌐ro tu⌐kima⌐su ka⌐ Tookyoo kara tyóodo i⌐ti-zi⌐kañ
ka⌐karima⌐su ḡa⌐
Tanaka: Zya⌐a, zyu⌐u-zi-ḡo⌐ro Ka⌐makura-e⌐ki e tu⌐kimasyo⌐o ka.
Smith: I⌐i desu yo⌐ Bo⌐ku wa ⌐zyu⌐u-zi made ni ⌐e⌐ki e itte, e⌐ki no
⌐ma⌐e ni imasu.
Tanaka: A⌐ri⌐ḡatoo gozaimasu. Do⌐ozo o⌐negai-sima⌐su.
Smith: Zya⌐a mata.
Tanaka: Sayonara.
Smith: Sayonara.

Questions:

1. Su⌐misu-sañ wa a⌐sita⌐ kara ⌐do⌐ko e i⌐kima⌐su ka⌐
2. Ta⌐naka-sañ mo asita ikima⌐su ka⌐
3. Tanaka-sañ wa na⌐ñyo⌐obi ni i⌐kima⌐su ka⌐
4. Tanaka-sañ wa ⌐na⌐ñ-niti ni i⌐kima⌐su ka⌐
5. Tanaka-sañ wa ⌐na⌐ñ de i⌐kima⌐su ka⌐
6. Tanaka-sañ wa ⌐na⌐ñ-zi ni Ka⌐makura e tukima⌐su ka⌐
7. To⌐okyoo kara Kamakura ma⌐de ⌐de⌐ñsya de do⌐no-ḡurai kakarima⌐su
ka⌐
8. Su⌐misu-sañ wa tu⌐ḡi⌐ no ni⌐tiyo⌐obi no ⌐na⌐ñ-zi ni Ka⌐makura-e⌐ki
e i⌐kima⌐su ka⌐
9. Kamakura wa ⌐do⌐ko desu ka.

---

[1] 'What (lit. how) will Mr. Yamamoto do?'

[2] Lit. 'I go from tomorrow' —i.e. 'I go tomorrow and stay on.'

[3] A resort city near Yokohama.

English Equivalents of Conversations

1. Yamamoto: Is Mr. Tanaka in?
   Secretary: Mr. Tanaka? He went to Yokohama but [is there anything I can do for you?]
   Yamamoto: Oh. (About) what time will he be back?
   Secretary: I'm not sure but it will probably be about 2 o'clock.
   Yamamoto: Oh. Then I guess I'll come again later. Thank you very much.
   Secretary: Not at all.

2. Mr. Smith: I'm going to Kamakura tomorrow to stay for a while. Won't you come (lit. go[1]) too some (lit. one) time?
   Tanaka: Thank you but . . .
   Smith: How about next Sunday?
   Tanaka: Thank you. What date is next Sunday?
   Smith: It's the 20th. . . . How about it? Won't you come?
   Tanaka: Thank you. (Hesitantly) Will it be all right?
   Smith: Yes. Please [come]! How will you come?
   Tanaka: Let's see. I'll come by electric train but [will that be convenient?]
   Smith: About what time will you arrive? It takes just an hour from Tokyo . . .
   Tanaka: Well then, shall I arrive at Kamakura Station about 10?
   Smith: That will be fine. I'll go to the station by 10, and I'll be in front (of the station).
   Tanaka: Thank you. Would you do that [i.e. meet me]?
   Smith: Well then, [I'll see you] again.
   Tanaka: Goodbye.
   Smith: Goodbye.

EXERCISES

1. You ask Mr. Tanaka: Mr. Tanaka replies:

   a. to come again tomorrow   Certainly.
      afternoon.
   b. if you should come again   Please do.
      tomorrow afternoon.
   c. how long (i.e. until what   Until 5:30.
      time) he will be here.
   d. what time he goes home.   Usually at 5:00.
   e. if he always goes home at   No. Sometimes I go home at
      about 5:00.   about 6:00.

---

[1] Reread Lesson 8, Grammatical Note 6, last paragraph.

f.	what time you should come on Saturday.	By 10:30.
g.	what time he is coming on Saturday.	At 10:30.
h.	how late the post office is open.	I think it's until about 5:30.
i.	to wait until 4:30.	I'm sorry but I can't.
j.	to stay here from 12:00 to 1:00.	All right.
k.	if Mr. Yamamoto has gone home.	Yes, he went home at 5:00.
l.	when he is returning to Tokyo.	I'd like to go back tomorrow.
m.	to come here by 6:30.	I'm afraid that's a bit inconvenient.
n.	if you should draw a map.	No, never mind.
o.	if he is coming here again tomorrow morning.	Yes, at 8:45.
p.	if he is coming here again on the 19th.	No, on the 20th.
q.	if he will be here until 6:00.	No, I'm going home at 5:00.
r.	if he will be in Tokyo until March.	No, I'm returning to Osaka in February.
s.	if you should turn this corner to the left.	No, to the right.
t.	if you should back up a little.	It doesn't matter.
u.	what time he leaves home in the morning.	Usually, at 7:45.
v.	when he arrived in Kyoto.	I came here in March of this year.

2. Using a timetable, real or made up, practice asking and answering questions like the following:

(Time) ni (place) o de⌐ma⌐sita. ⌐Na⌐ñ-zi ni (another place) ni tu⌐kima⌐sita ka?

(Time) ni (place) ni tu⌐kima⌐sita. Na⌐ñ-zi ni (another place) o de⌐ma⌐sita ka?

3. Practice asking and answering questions like the following:

Ge⌐tuyo⌐o kara ki⌐ñyo⌐o made ⌐na⌐ñ-niti a⌐rima⌐su ka⌐
Sa⌐ñ-zi kara ku-⌐zi-ha⌐ñ made na⌐ñ-zi⌐kañ a⌐rima⌐su ka⌐
Si-ḡatu tu⌐itati⌐ kara, ⌐go⌐-ḡatu ⌐sa⌐ñzyuu i⌐ti-niti⌐ made, na⌐ñ-ka⌐ḡetu a⌐rima⌐su ka⌐

4. Practice the Basic Dialogues with appropriate variations.

Lesson 10. Meeting People

BASIC DIALOGUES: FOR MEMORIZATION

(a)

Smith

female	o⌐ñna⌐
person	hi⌐to⌐ or ka⌐ta⌐ †
woman	o⌐ñna no hito⌐ or o⌐ñna no kata⌐ †
who?	da⌐re or do⌐nata †

1. Who is that woman?　　Ano o⌐ñna no hito⌐ (wa) ⌐da⌐re desu ka⌐
or
Ano o⌐ñna no kata⌐ (wa) ⌐do⌐nata desu ka⌐
or
Ano o⌐ñna no kata⌐ (wa) ⌐do⌐nata de (i)rassyaimasu ka⌐

Tanaka

an American　　a⌐merika⌐ziñ
2. Do you mean the American?　　A⌐merika⌐ziñ desu ka⌐

Smith

a Japanese　　ni⌐hoñzi⌐ñ
3. No, I mean the Japanese.　　Iie, ni⌐hoñzi⌐ñ desu.

Tanaka

4. Oh, that (person) is Miss (or Mrs.) Yamada.　　A⌐a, a⌐no⌐ hito wa Ya⌐mada-sañ de⌐su.
or
A⌐a, a⌐no kata⌐ wa Ya⌐mada-sañ de⌐su.
or
A⌐a, a⌐no kata⌐ wa Ya⌐mada-sañ de (i)rassyaima⌐su.

Smith

friend　　tomodati or
otomodati †
5. Is she a friend?　　To⌐modati de⌐su ka⌐
or
O⌐tomodati de⌐su ka⌐
or
O⌐tomodati de (i)rassyaima⌐su ka⌐

148

Tanaka

name	namae or onamae ꜛ
know	si⌐tte˥ (i)ma˥su or si⌐tte˥ orima˥su ꜛ or si⌐tte˥ (i)rassyaima˥su ꜛ

6. No, she isn't a friend, but I know her name.

Iie, to⌐modati zya arimase˥n̄ ḡa, na⌐mae wa sitte (i)ma˥su.

or

Iie, to⌐modati de˥ wa go⌐zaimase˥n̄ ḡa, o⌐namae wa sitte orima˥su.

(b)

Smith

rudeness or rude	si⌐tu˥ree
it is rude [of me] but	si⌐tu˥ree desu ḡa or si⌐tu˥ree de gozaimasu ḡa

7. Excuse me [for asking] but [what is] your name?

Si⌐tu˥ree desu ḡa, onamae wa?

or

Si⌐tu˥ree de gozaimasu ḡa,   onamae wa?

Sato

8. I'm Yukio Sato.

Sa˥too Yu⌐kio de˥su.

or

Sa˥too Yu⌐kio de gozaima˥su.

Smith

work	siḡoto or o⌐si˥ḡoto ꜛ

9. What do you do? (Lit. As for your work?)

O⌐si˥ḡoto wa?

Sato

for the American Embassy	A⌐merika-taisi˥kan̄ ni
become employed	tu⌐tomema˥su
be employed	tu⌐to˥mete (i)masu or tu⌐to˥mete orimasu ꜛ or tu⌐to˥mete (i)rassyaimasu ꜛ

10. I'm working for the American Embassy.

A⌐merika-taisi˥kan̄ ni tu⌐to˥mete (i)masu.

or

A⌐merika-taisi˥kan̄ ni tu⌐to˥mete orimasu.

(c)

Smith

marry	ke⌐kkon̄-sima˥su

be married

ke⌐kkoñ-site (i)ma⌐su <u>or</u>
ke⌐kkoñ-site orima⌐su † <u>or</u>
ke⌐kkoñ-site (i)rassyaima⌐su †

11. Excuse me [for asking] but
    are you married?

Si⌐tu⌐ree desu ḡa, ke⌐kkoñ-site (i)ma⌐-
su ka⌐
     <u>or</u>
Si⌐tu⌐ree de gozaimasu ḡa, ke⌐kkoñ-
site (i)rassyaima⌐su ka⌐

                                   Tanaka

single

hi⌐to⌐ri <u>or</u>
ohitori †

12. No, I'm single. How about
    you?

Iie, hi⌐to⌐ri desu. A⌐na⌐ta wa?
     <u>or</u>
Iie, hi⌐to⌐ri de gozaimasu. A⌐na⌐ta wa?

                                   Smith

13. I'm married.

Ke⌐kkoñ-site (i)ma⌐su.
     <u>or</u>
Ke⌐kkoñ-site orima⌐su.

                                   Tanaka

child

kodomo <u>or</u>
okosañ †

14. (a) Do you have any
        children?

    <u>or</u>

    (b) Are there any children
        [in your family]?

Ko⌐domo (ḡa) arima⌐su ka⌐
     <u>or</u>
O⌐kosañ (ḡa) gozaima⌐su ka⌐

Ko⌐domo (ḡa) ima⌐su ka⌐
     <u>or</u>
O⌐kosañ (ḡa) irassyaima⌐su ka⌐

                                   Smith

1 person
2 people
3 people

hi⌐to⌐-ri
hu⌐ta-ri⌐
sa⌐ñ-ni⌐ñ

15. (a) Yes, I have two.

    <u>or</u>

    (b) Yes, there are two.

E⌐e, hu⌐tari arima⌐su.
     <u>or</u>
E⌐e, hu⌐tari gozaima⌐su.

E⌐e, hu⌐tari ima⌐su.
     <u>or</u>
E⌐e, hu⌐tari orima⌐su.

                                   Tanaka

how old?

i⌐kutu <u>or</u>
oikutu †

16. How old are they?

I⌐kutu desu ka⌐
     <u>or</u>
O⌐ikutu de⌐su ka⌐
     <u>or</u>
O⌐ikutu de (i)rassyaima⌐su ka⌐

Smith

1 year old	hi⌐to¬-tu
2 years old	hu⌐ta-tu¬
being 12 years old	zyu⌐uni¬ de
this month	koñḡetu
become	na⌐rima¬su
become 8 years old	ya-⌐ttu¬ ni narimasu

17. One is 12 and the other (lit.   Hi⌐to¬-ri wa zyu⌐uni¬ de, mo⌐o hito¬-ri
one more person) will be 8   wa kŏñḡetu ya-⌐ttu¬ ni narimasu.
this month.

Tanaka

both	do¬tira mo[1]
male	o⌐toko¬
boy	o⌐toko¬ no ko or
	o⌐toko¬ no okosañ †

18. Are both boys?   Dotira mo o⌐toko¬ no ko desu ka⌐

                  or

                  Dotira mo o⌐toko¬ no o⌐kosañ de (i)ra-
                  ssyaima⌐su ka⌐

Smith

over or top or topmost or oldest	ue
under or below or bottom or youngest	sita
being a boy	o⌐toko¬ no ko de
girl	o⌐ñna¬ no ko or
	o⌐ñna¬ no okosañ †

19. No. The older is a boy and   Iie. U⌐e wa otoko¬ no ko de, sita wa
the younger is a girl.   o⌐ñna¬ no ko desu.

                  or

                  Iie. U⌐e wa otoko¬ no ko de, sita wa
                  o⌐ñna¬ no ko de gozaimasu.

(d)

Smith

that child	a⌐no¬ ko or
	ano okosañ †
child of what place (i.e. what household)?	do¬ko no ko or
	do¬tira no okosañ †

---

[1] Has unaccented alternant (cf. sentence following).

20. Whose child is that? (Lit.   A⌐no⌐ ko (wa) ⌐do⌐ko no ko ⌐de⌐su ka⌐
That child is the child of   or
what place?)   Ano okosañ (wa) ⌐do⌐tira no o⌐kosañ
de gozaima⌐su ka⌐

Tanaka

belonging or pertaining   uti no   or
to one's household   otaku no ⌐
21. Why, that's our Taro.   Uti no ⌐Ta⌐roo desu yo⌐
or
Uti no ⌐Ta⌐roo de gozaimasu yo⌐

Smith

Master Taro   Ta⌐roo-tyañ
22. (Is he) your Taro?   Otaku no ⌐Ta⌐roo-tyañ desu ka.
or
Otaku no ⌐Ta⌐roo-tyañ de (i)rassyai-
masu ka.

become big   o⌐okiku narimasu or
o⌐okiku o⌐nari ni narima⌐su ⌐
23. Hasn't he grown!   ⁎ O⌐okiku na⌐rima⌐sita ⌐ne⌐e.
or
⁎ O⌐okiku o⌐nari ni narima⌐sita ⌐ne⌐e.

ADDITIONAL NATIONALITIES

(All the following words refer to people only.[1])

Japanese   ni⌐hoñzi⌐ñ or
ni⌐ppoñzi⌐ñ

American   a⌐merika⌐ziñ or
be⌐ekoku⌐ziñ

Korean   tyo⌐oseñzi⌐ñ
(or ka⌐ñkoku⌐ziñ[2])

Chinese   tyu⌐ugoku⌐ziñ
(or si⌐na⌐ziñ[3])

Englishman   i⌐girisu⌐ziñ or
e⌐ekoku⌐ziñ

---

[1] Compare:
Ni⌐hoñzi⌐ñ desu. 'He's Japanese.'
Ni⌐hoñ no⌐ desu. 'It's Japanese.'

[2] Refers to South Koreans only. Preferred by them to preceding older term, which refers to all Koreans.

[3] Formerly a commonly used word, now considered insulting by many Chinese.

Frenchman	hu⌐rañsu⌐zin
German	do⌐itu⌐zin
Russian	ro⌐sia⌐zin
Indian (from India)	i⌐ndo⌐zin
what nationality?	na⌐ni⌐zin

NOTES ON THE BASIC DIALOGUES

Sentences for which alternate forms are given are in the order of increasing politeness. Polite alternants are used more commonly, but not exclusively, by women.

5. The polite otomodati usually refers to someone else's friend(s), but some women use it in reference to their own friends as well—i.e. as a polite neutral (+) word.

6. Si⌐tte ima⌐su 'know' implies knowledge, whereas wa⌐karima⌐su 'understand,' 'can tell,' 'be clear' implies understanding or recognition by the senses. For example, I know (si⌐tte ima⌐su) Mr. Tanaka—perhaps because I have been introduced to him—but I can tell (wa⌐karima⌐su) who Mr. Tanaka is— perhaps because he is the only Japanese in the room.

The wa following namae is the wa of comparison: i.e. 'even if I don't know her well, her name I know.'

7. The nominal si⌐tu⌐ree + desu (or de go⌐zaima⌐su) ga is common before questions of a personal nature. It is also used to introduce an interruption.

8. Remember that -sañ is not used with one's own name.

The family name precedes the given name in Japanese. When -sañ is used with the full name, it comes last, after the given name (for example, Sa⌐too Yukio-sañ). -Sañ may also be used with the given name alone.

Additional examples of family names:

Aoyama	Ikeda	Ueda
Gotoo	Kimura	Watanabe
Hasimoto	Oota	Yamada
Hatoyama	Ta⌐mura	Yosida

Additional examples of given names:

Men's		Women's	
Haruo	Siĝeru	Ha⌐nako	Ma⌐sako
Hi⌐rosi	Syo⌐ozi	Ha⌐ru	Mi⌐dori
Masao	Ta⌐roo	Harue	Si⌐ĝe
Masaru	Yosio	Ha⌐ruko	Yo⌐siko
Sa⌐buro⌐o	Zi⌐roo	Haruyo	Yu⌐kiko

11. Ke⌐kkoñ-sima⌐su is one of a vast number of verbals consisting of a nominal compounded with the verbal √si⌐ma⌐su 'make' or 'do.' Kekkoñ is a nominal meaning 'marriage.'

14. √A⌐rima⌐su occurs with both animate and inanimate subjects (corresponding to objects in English) when it means 'have'; thus, ko⌐domo ḡa √arima⌐su (polite √go⌐zaima⌐su) 'have children.' In the given context, 14 (a) and (b) and 15 (a) and (b) are used almost interchangeably, except for differences of politeness.

18. Do⌐tira mo is used in reference to inanimate objects as well as living beings.

19. Compare: u⌐e no ho⌐ñ 'top book' and ho⌐ñ no ue 'top of the book'; si⌐ta no ho⌐ñ 'bottom book' and ho⌐ñ no sita 'under the book.'

22. -Tyañ is added to boys' and girls' given names. It is polite, but less formal than -sañ. While it is used in talking TO one's own children, it is not ordinarily used in talking ABOUT them to those outside the family or circle of very close friends.

GRAMMATICAL NOTES

1. √de⌐su: Polite Equivalents

√de⌐su ～ √de go⌐zaima⌐su ～ √de (i)⌐rassyaima⌐su

The polite neutral (+) equivalent of de⌐su following a nominal or a particle is de go⌐zaima⌐su (de = the gerund of de⌐su). The past is de go⌐zaima⌐sita, and the tentative de go⌐zaimasyo⌐o.

Examples:

	Plain	Polite +
'It's a book.'	Ho⌐ñ desu.	Ho⌐ñ de gozaimasu.
'It's that one.'	So⌐re de⌐su.	So⌐re de gozaima⌐su.
'It was pretty.'	Ki⌐ree desita.	Ki⌐ree de gozaimasita.
'It's probably the same.'	O⌐nazi desyo⌐o.	O⌐nazi de gozaimasyo⌐o.
'It's until tomorrow.'	A⌐sita⌐ made desu.	A⌐sita⌐ made de gozaimasu.

WARNING: Do not confuse the above with:

'There's a book.' or		
'I have a book.'	Ho⌐ñ(ḡa) arimasu.	Ho⌐ñ (ḡa) gozaimasu.

The negative equivalent of de go⌐zaima⌐su following a nominal or a particle is de⌐[1] wa go⌐zaimase⌐ñ (past, de⌐ wa go⌐zaimase⌐ñ desita).

---

[1] De is accented before wa, unless an accented word or phrase precedes.

Examples:

	Plain	Polite [+]
'It isn't a book.'	Ho⌐n zya a⌐rima- se⌐ñ.	Ho⌐ñ de wa go⌐zaima- se⌐ñ.
'It isn't that.'	So⌐re zya arima- se⌐ñ.	So⌐re de⌐ wa go⌐zaima- se⌐ñ.
'It wasn't a taxi.'	Ta⌐kusii zya a⌐ri- mase⌐ñ desita.	Ta⌐kusii de wa go⌐zai- mase⌐ñ desita.
'It doesn't start at 3 o'clock.'	Sa⌐ñ-zi kara zya a⌐rimase⌐ñ.	Sa⌐ñ-zi kara de wa go- ⌐zaimase⌐ñ.

Actually, zya is the contracted equivalent of de⌐ wa, and the two can be used interchangeably anywhere, with only a difference of formality.

If a nominal (with or without following particle) + de⌐su refers to a PERSON other than the speaker, it has a second polite equivalent which is honorific (†) —namely, nominal + de (i)⌐rassyaima⌐su[1] (past, de (i)⌐rassyaima⌐sita; tentative, de (i)⌐rassyaimasyo⌐o; negative, de⌐ wa i⌐rassyaimase⌐ñ; past negative, de⌐ wa i⌐rassyaimase⌐ñ desita).

Thus:

	Plain	Polite
'He is Mr. Sato.'	Sa⌐too-sañ desu.	(Neutral) Sa⌐too-sañ de go- zaimasu. or (Honorific) Sa⌐too-sañ de (i)rassyaimasu.

But:

	Plain	Polite
'I am Mr. Sato.'	Sa⌐too desu.	Sa⌐too de gozaimasu.

The de go⌐zaima⌐su alternative represents simply a polite style of speech, whereas the de (i)⌐rassyaima⌐su alternative exalts the person under discussion besides being a polite style of speech. Of the two, the latter is more common— unless, of course, the speaker is talking politely about himself, a member of his own family, or someone of inferior social status.

WARNING: De⌐su following an adjectival (for example, ta⌐ka⌐i) is NOT re- placed by de go⌐zaima⌐su or de (i)⌐rassyaima⌐su in the polite style.

---

[1] The form without i- is a contracted form, very common in conversation. Compare the end of Note 2 following.

2. Verbal Gerund + $\sqrt{\text{i}^\ulcorner\text{ma}^\urcorner\text{su}}$

The non-past of a verbal usually refers to repeated or future punctual[1] occurrence.

A present or future durative[1] action or state is regularly indicated by a verbal gerund + i⌐ma⌐su. This pattern means either (a) 'an action is now or will be taking place over a period of time' or (b) 'the state resulting from an action now exists, or will exist, over a period of time.' Meaning (b) is more common among verbals which never take a direct object — particularly among verbals indicating motion from one place to another and among those which basically mean 'become so-and-so.' Depending on the individual verbal, the subject may be animate or inanimate.

Examples:

| Non-Past | Gerund + i⌐ma⌐su |

Meaning (a)

si⌐ma⌐su '[someone] does' or '[someone] will do'
— si⌐te ima⌐su '[someone] is doing' or '[someone] will be doing'

ka⌐kima⌐su '[someone] writes' or '[someone] will write'
— ka⌐ite imasu '[someone] is writing' or '[someone] will be writing'

ka⌐ima⌐su '[someone] buys' or '[someone] will buy'
— ka⌐tte ima⌐su '[someone] is buying' or '[someone] will be buying'

Meaning (b)

ke⌐kkoñ-sima⌐su '[someone] gets married' or '[someone] will get married'
— ke⌐kkoñ-site ima⌐su '[someone] is married' or '[someone] will be married (i.e. in a married state)'

tu⌐tomema⌐su '[someone] becomes employed' or '[someone] will become employed'
— tu⌐to⌐mete imasu '[someone] is employed' or '[someone] will be employed (i.e. in an employed state)'

i⌐kima⌐su '[someone] goes' or '[someone] will go'
— i⌐tte ima⌐su[2] '[someone] is gone' or '[someone] will be gone'

---

[1] PUNCTUAL indicates simple occurrence without any reference to duration of time, whereas DURATIVE indicates occurrence over a period of time, during which something else may happen. Compare: 'I wrote a letter' (punctual) and 'I was writing a letter' (durative).

[2] Also occurs with meaning (a): '[Someone] is going (i.e. repeatedly, over a period of time)' as in 'He is going to that school.'

Gerund + i⌈ma⌉su may also indicate an action or state which began in the past and is still continuing. A time expression + particle <u>kara</u> tells when the action or state began and a time expression without following particle tells how long the action or state has been continuing. Thus:

Kyo⌉neñ kara ⌐ma⌐tte imasu. 'I have been waiting since last year.' (Lit. 'I am waiting from last year.')

Ni⌉-neñ ⌐ma⌐e kara tu⌐to⌐mete imasu. 'I have been employed for the last two years.' (Lit. 'I am employed from two years ago.')

Sa⌈ñ-neñ-g̃u⌉rai o⌐siete ima⌐su. 'I have been teaching for about three years.'

<u>Si⌈tte ima⌉su</u>, meaning literally '[someone] is in a state of having come to know'—i. e. '[someone] knows'—is another example of the gerund + i⌈ma⌉su pattern. The opposite is si⌈rimase⌉ñ '[someone] doesn't know' (lit. '[someone] has not come to know').[1]

Following a gerund, √i⌈ma⌉su and its more polite equivalents √o⌈rima⌉su and √i⌈rassyaima⌉su may occur in the affirmative or negative, non-past or past, etc., with corresponding equivalents. Thus:

ma⌉tte orimasu 'I'm waiting'
ke⌈kkoñ-site irassyaimase⌉ñ '[he] is not married'
ka⌉ite i⌐ma⌐sita '[I] was writing'
ka⌉ette i⌐mase⌐ñ desita '[I] wasn't back (home)'

In rapid speech, the initial <u>i-</u> of √i⌈ma⌉su and √i⌈rassyaima⌉su is regularly dropped after a gerund. Thus:

ke⌈kkoñ-site rassyaimase⌉ñ
ka⌉ite masita
ka⌉ette ma⌐se⌐ñ desita

3. √de⌉su: Gerund

The gerund of √<u>de⌉su</u> is <u>de</u>. Preceded by a nominal or particle, it occurs in the middle of sentences, coordinate with what follows (cf. Lesson 7, Grammatical Note 5). Thus:

2 sentences: A⌈merika⌉ziñ desu. 'I'm an American.'
A⌈merika-taisi⌉kañ ni tu⌐to⌐mete imasu. 'I work for the American Embassy.'

1 sentence: A⌈merika⌉ziñ de, A⌈merika-taisi⌉kañ ni tu⌐to⌐mete imasu. 'I'm an American and I work for the American Embassy.'

---

[1] WARNING: Do not attempt to use the corresponding negative of si⌈tte ima⌉su (i.e. ~ i⌈mase⌉ñ) or the corresponding -ma⌉su affirmative of si⌈rimase⌉ñ.

Additional examples:

Ue wa zyu⌐uni⌐ de, sita wa ya-⌐ttu⌐ desu.   'The older one is 12 and the younger one is 8.'

Dotira mo ōnazi de, dotira mo da⌐me⌐ desu.   'They're both the same and they're both no good.'

Sono kuruma wa I⌐girisu no⌐ de, to⌐ttemo taka⌐i desu yo.   'That car is a British one and it's very expensive.'

4. Adjectival + √na⌐rima⌐su ～ Nominal + <u>ni</u> + √na⌐rima⌐su

An adjectival modifying an inflected expression is regularly in its adverbial (-<u>ku</u>) form:

Yo⌐ku na⌐rima⌐sita.   '[It] has become good.' or '[It] has improved.'

Ta⌐kaku narimasu.   '[It] gets (<u>or</u> is going to get) expensive.'

O⌐okiku na⌐rimase⌐ñ.   '[It] doesn't (<u>or</u> won't) get big.' or '[It] hasn't grown big.'

Ya⌐suku na⌐rimase⌐ñ desita.   '[It] didn't get cheap.'

I⌐kitaku narima⌐sita.   'I've reached the point where I want to go.' (Lit. 'I've become wanting to go.')

When the goal of √na⌐rima⌐su is a nominal, the nominal is followed by the goal particle <u>ni</u>: X ni √na⌐rima⌐su 'become X,' 'get to be X.'

De⌐pa⌐ato ni na⌐rima⌐sita.   '[It] has become a department store.'

Da⌐me⌐ ni narimasu.   '[It] gets (<u>or</u> will get) bad.'

To⌐modati ni⌐ wa[1] na⌐rita⌐ku a⌐rimase⌐ñ.   'I don't want to become a friend.'

O⌐nazi ni⌐ wa[1] na⌐rimase⌐ñ desita.   '[It] didn't become the same.'

Note the regular difference in usage between:

I⌐kura desu ka⌐ 'How much is it?' (i.e. one item)

and:

I⌐kura ni na⌐rima⌐su ka⌐ 'How much does it (<u>or</u> will it) come to?' (i.e. several items purchased)

<u>Na⌐rima⌐su</u> frequently corresponds to an English future, provided a change in situation is involved. Compare:

'It will be cheap tomorrow' (i.e. it isn't today): A⌐sita⌐ wa ⌐ya⌐suku narimasu.

'It will be cheap tomorrow, too' (i.e. as it is today; no change): A⌐sita⌐ mo ya⌐su⌐i desu.

---

[1] The <u>wa</u> of comparison.

5. Counting People and Their Ages

The counter for people has two shapes, -ri for ' 1' and ' 2' and -niñ for higher numerals. -Ri combines with the numerals of Series II and -niñ with the numerals of Series I. Thus:

hi⌐to⌐-ri ' 1 person'	ro⌐ku⌐-niñ ' 6 people'
hu⌐ta-ri⌐ ' 2 people'	si⌐ti⌐-niñ '7 people'
sa⌐ñ-ni⌐ñ ' 3 people'	ha⌐ti⌐-niñ ' 8 people'
yo-⌐ni⌐ñ ' 4 people'	ku-⌐ni⌐ñ ' 9 people'
go-⌐ni⌐ñ ' 5 people'	zyu⌐u-niñ ' 10 people'

na⌐ñ-niñ ' how many people?'

The numbers used in counting people's ages are identical with those used in counting unit objects (hi⌐to⌐-tu, hu⌐ta-tu⌐, mi-⌐ttu⌐, etc.; see Lesson 5, Grammatical Note 1), except for the special word ha⌐tati ' 20 years old.' ' 20 units' is ni⌐zyuu.

Compare the following examples:

Hi⌐to⌐ri no kodomo wa o⌐ñna⌐ no ko desu.   'One child is a girl.'
Hi⌐to⌐tu no kodomo wa o⌐ñna⌐ no ko desu.   'The one-year-old child is a girl.'

DRILLS

A. Substitution Drill

1. Who is your friend?   Otomodati (wa) ⌐do⌐nata desu ka⌣
2. Where is your friend?   Otomodati (wa) ⌐do⌐ko desu ka⌣
3. How is your friend?   Otomodati (wa) i⌐ka⌐ḡa desu ka⌣
4. How old is your friend?   Otomodati (wa) o⌐ikutu de⌐su ka⌣
5. Is your friend English?   Otomodati (wa) i⌐ḡirisu⌐ziñ desu ka⌣
6. Is your friend single?   Otomodati (wa) o⌐hitori de⌐su ka⌣
7. Which one (lit. person) is   Otomodati (wa) ⌐do⌐no ka├ta┤ desu ka⌣
    your friend?
8. What kind of person is your   Otomodati (wa) ⌐do⌐ñna ka├ta┤ desu
    friend?   ka⌣

B. Substitution Drill

1. A woman has come.   O⌐ñna no hito⌐ (ḡa) ki├ma┤sita.
2. A man has come.   O⌐toko no hito⌐ (ḡa) ki├ma┤sita.
3. A little girl has come.   O⌐ñna⌐ no ko (ḡa) ki├ma┤sita.
4. A little boy has come.   O⌐toko⌐ no ko (ḡa) ki├ma┤sita.
5. A friend (i.e. a lady) has   O⌐ñna no tomodati (ḡa) kima⌐sita.
    come.
6. A friend (i.e. a man) has   O⌐toko no tomodati (ḡa) kima⌐sita.
    come.

C. Substitution Drill

1. I'm working for the American Embassy.
A⌐merika-taisi⌐kañ ni tu⌐to⌐mete (i)-masu.

2. I'm working for the British Consulate.
E⌐ekoku-ryoozi⌐kañ ni tu⌐to⌐mete (i)-masu.

3. I'm working for the Bank of Japan.
Ni⌐hoñ-gi⌐ñkoo ni tu⌐to⌐mete (i)masu.

4. I'm working for the Yokohama Post Office.
Yo⌐kohama-yuubi⌐ñkyoku ni tu⌐to⌐me-te (i)masu.

5. I'm working for a Tokyo department store.
To⌐okyoo no depa⌐ato ni tu⌐to⌐mete (i)masu.

6. I'm working for a Kyoto hotel.
Kyo⌐oto no ⌐ho⌐teru ni tu⌐to⌐mete (i)-masu.

7. I'm working for St. Luke's Hospital.
Se⌐eroka-byo⌐oiñ ni tu⌐to⌐mete (i)ma-su.

8. I'm working for an American school.
A⌐merika no gakkoo ni tuto⌐mete (i)-masu.

D. Substitution Drill

1. Who did [it]?
Da⌐re ḡa si⌐ma⌐sita ka ⌐

2. Who doesn't understand?
Da⌐re ḡa wa⌐karimase⌐ñ ka ⌐

3. Who wants to go?
Da⌐re ḡa i⌐kita⌐i ñ desu ka ⌐

4. Who is here?
Da⌐re ḡa i⌐ma⌐su ka ⌐

5. Who wrote [it]?
Da⌐re ḡa ka⌐kima⌐sita ka ⌐

6. Who bought [it]?
Da⌐re ḡa ka⌐ima⌐sita ka ⌐

7. Who needs [it]?
Da⌐re ḡa i⌐rima⌐su ka ⌐

8. Who is waiting?
Da⌐re ḡa ⌐ma⌐tte (i)masu ka ⌐

9. Who isn't here?
Da⌐re ḡa i⌐mase⌐ñ ka ⌐

10. Who didn't come?
Da⌐re ḡa ki⌐mase⌐ñ desita ka ⌐

E. Substitution Drill

1. One (person) is 12 and the other is 10.
Hi⌐to⌐-ri wa zyu⌐uni⌐ de, mo⌐o hito⌐-ri wa ⌐to⌐o desu.

2. One (person) is 8 and the other is 4.
Hi⌐to⌐-ri wa ya-⌐ttu⌐ de, mo⌐o hito⌐-ri wa yo-⌐ttu⌐ desu.

3. One (person) is 20 and the other is 21.
Hi⌐to⌐-ri wa ⌐ha⌐tati de, mo⌐o hito⌐-ri wa ⌐ni⌐zyuu i⌐ti⌐ desu.

4. One (person) is French and the other is German.
Hi⌐to⌐ri wa hu⌐rañsu⌐ziñ de, mo⌐o hito⌐-ri wa do⌐itu⌐ziñ desu.

5. One (person) is a boy and the other is a girl.
Hi⌐to⌐-ri wa o⌐toko⌐ no ko de, mo⌐o hi-to⌐-ri wa o⌐ñna⌐ no ko desu.

6. One (person) is a man and the other is a woman.
Hi⌐to⌐-ri wa o⌐toko no hito⌐ de, mo⌐o hito⌐-ri wa o⌐ñna no hito⌐ desu.

7. One (person) is a policeman and the other is a druggist.
Hi⌐to⌐-ri wa zyu⌐ñsa de, mo⌐o hito⌐-ri wa ku⌐suriya de⌐su.

8. One (person) is a book dealer and the other is a florist.
Hi⌐to⌐-ri wa ⌐ho⌐ñya de, mo⌐o hito⌐-ri wa ha⌐na⌐ya desu.

F. Substitution Drill

1. One woman came.   O⌐ñna no hito⌐ (ḡa) hi⌐to⌐-ri ki⌐ma⁻si-
                                ta.
2. Two friends came.   Tomodati (ḡa) hu⌐ta̠-ri kima⌐sita.
3. Three children came.   Kodomo (ḡa) sa⌐ñ-niñ kima⌐sita.
4. Four policemen came.   Zyuñsa (ḡa) yo-⌐niñ kima⌐sita.
5. Five Koreans came.   Tyo⌐oseñzi⌐ñ (ḡa) go-⌐niñ kima⌐sita.
6. Six Russians came.   Ro⌐sia⌐ziñ (ḡa) ro⌐ku⌐-niñ ki⌐ma⁻sita.
7. Seven Indians came.   I⌐ndo⌐ziñ (ḡa) si⌐ti⌐-niñ ki⌐ma⁻sita.
8. Eight Chinese came.   Tyu⌐uḡoku⌐ziñ (ḡa) ha⌐ti⌐-niñ ki⌐ma⁻-
                                sita.

G. Substitution Drill

1. I'm doing [it] now.   I⌐ma si⌐te (i)ma⁻su.
2. I've been doing [it] for the Zi⌐p-puñ ⌐ma⁻e kara si⌐te (i)ma⁻su.
    last 10 minutes.
3. I've been waiting for the   Zi⌐p-puñ ⌐ma⁻e kara ⌐ma⁻tte (i)ma-
    last 10 minutes.   su.
4. I've been waiting since last Kyo⌐neñ[1] kara ⌐ma⁻tte (i)masu.
    year.
5. I've been teaching since last Kyo⌐neñ kara o⌐siete (i)ma⁻su.
    year.
6. I've been teaching for about Zyu⌐u-neñ-ḡu⌐rai o⌐siete (i)ma⁻su.
    10 years.
7. I've been employed for about Zyu⌐u-neñ-ḡu⌐rai tu⌐to⁻mete (i)masu.
    10 years.
8. I'm employed now.   I⌐ma tu⌐to⁻mete (i)masu.

H. Grammar Drill (based on Grammatical Note 4)

        Tutor: O⌐oki⌐i desu. '[It] is big.'
        Student: O⌐okiku na⌐rima⁻sita. '[It] has become big.'

1. A⌐ka⌐i desu.   A⌐kaku narima⌐sita.
2. Ge⌐ñki desu.   Ge⌐ñki ni na⌐rima⁻sita.
3. Tu⌐mara⌐nai desu.   Tu⌐mara⌐naku na⌐rima⁻sita.
4. I⌐i desu.   Yo⌐ku na⌐rima⁻sita.
5. Ha⌐tati desu.   Ha⌐tati ni na⌐rima⁻sita.
6. O⌐mosiro⌐i desu.   O⌐mosiro⌐ku na⌐rima⁻sita.
7. To⌐modati de⌐su.   To⌐modati ni narima⌐sita.
8. Wa⌐ru⌐i desu.   Wa⌐ruku na⌐rima⁻sita.
9. Da⌐me⌐ desu.   Da⌐me⌐ ni na⌐rima⁻sita.
10. A⌐buna⌐i desu.   A⌐bunaku narima⌐sita.

I. Grammar Drill (based on Grammatical Note 3)

        Tutor: Ue wa o⌐toko⌐ no ko desu. Sita wa o⌐ñna⌐ no ko desu. 'The
                  oldest is a boy. The youngest is a girl.'   (2 sentences)
        Student: Ue wa o⌐toko⌐ no ko de, sita wa o⌐ñna⌐ no ko desu. 'The old-
                  est is a boy and the youngest is a girl.' (1 sentence)

---

[1] Kyo⌐neñ 'last year'

1. Tomodati wa ni⌐hoñzi⌐ñ
   desu.
   A⌐merika-gi⌐ñkoo ni tu˩to˥-
   mete (i)masu.

   Tomodati wa ni⌐hoñzi⌐ñ de, A⌐merika-
   gi⌐ñkoo ni tu˩to˥mete (i)masu.

2. Ta⌐roo-tyañ wa ko⌐ko⌐no-tu
   desu.
   Ha⌐ruko-tyañ wa na⌐na⌐-tu
   desu.

   Ta⌐roo-tyañ wa ko⌐ko⌐no-tu de, Ha⌐ru-
   ko-tyañ wa na⌐na⌐-tu desu.

3. Ni⌐ho⌐ñ de ke˩kkoñ-sima˥-
   sita.
   A⌐merika e kaerima⌐sita.

   Ni⌐ho⌐ñ de kekkoñ-site, A⌐merika e
   kaerima⌐sita.

4. Kore wa wa⌐takusi no⌐ desu.
   Sore wa ⌐tomodai no⌐ desu.

   Kore wa wa⌐takusi no⌐ de, sore wa to-
   ⌐modati no⌐ desu.

5. A⌐no ka⌐do ni mo˩do˥tte
   kudasai.
   Mi⌐ḡi e maḡatte kudasa⌐i.

   A⌐no ka⌐do ni mo˩do˥tte, mi⌐ḡi e maḡatte kudasa⌐i.

6. Kono hurosiki wa ni⌐hya-
   ku⌐-eñ desu.
   Sore wa sa⌐ñbyaku⌐-eñ
   desu.

   Kono hurosiki wa ni⌐hyaku⌐-eñ de, sore wa sa⌐ñbyaku⌐-eñ desu.

7. Tu⌐itati⌐ wa ge⌐tuyo⌐o desu.
   Nano-ka wa ni⌐tiyoo de⌐su.

   Tu⌐itati⌐ wa ge⌐tuyo⌐o de, nano-ka wa
   ni⌐tiyoo de⌐su.

8. Ha⌐ti⌐-zi ni u˩ti (o) dema˥-
   sita.
   Ro⌐ku-zi-ḡo⌐ro ka˩erima˥-
   sita.

   Ha⌐ti⌐-zi ni u˩ti (o) de˥te, ro⌐ku-zi-
   ḡo⌐ro ka˩erima˥sita.

J. Response Drill

(Give the corresponding negative reply—same politeness level—to each
question.)

1. To⌐modati de⌐su ka↲   To⌐modati zya arimase⌐ñ.
2. Si⌐ma⌐su ka↲   Si⌐mase⌐ñ.
3. Si⌐te (i)ma⌐su ka↲   Si⌐te (i)mase⌐ñ.
4. Ga⌐kkoo de gozaima⌐su ka↲   Ga⌐kkoo de⌐ wa go˩zaimase˥ñ.
5. O⌐toto⌐i de go˩zaima˥sita   O⌐toto⌐i de wa go˩zaimase˥ñ desita.
   ka↲
6. So⌐no kata⌐ (wa) a⌐merika⌐ziñ   So⌐no kata⌐ (wa) a⌐merika⌐ziñ de wa
   de (i)rassyaimasu ka↲   i˩rassyaimase˥ñ.
7. Tanaka-sañ (wa) tu⌐to⌐mete   Tanaka-sañ (wa) tu⌐to⌐mete (i)˩ras-
   (i)rassyaimasu ka↲   syaimase˥ñ.
8. Si⌐tu⌐ree desu ka↲   Si⌐tu⌐ree zya a˩rimase˥ñ.
9. Si⌐tte (i)ma⌐su ka↲   Si⌐rimase⌐ñ.
10. A⌐buna⌐i desu ka↲   A⌐bunaku arimase⌐ñ.

K. Level Drill (The sentences on the right are the polite equivalents of those
on the left.)

1. Do⌐ko desu ka↲   Do⌐tira de gozaimasu ka↲
2. I⌐tu desu ka↲   I⌐tu de gozaimasu ka↲
3. A⌐sita⌐ desu.   A⌐sita⌐ de gozaimasu.

4. Ko⌐re de⌐su.   Ko⌐re de gozaima⌐su.
5. U⌐siro de⌐su.   U⌐siro de gozaima⌐su.
6. Ya⌐sumi⌐ desu ka⌐   O⌐yasumi de gozaima⌐su ka⌐
7. Ra⌐itaa desu.   Ra⌐itaa de gozaimasu.
8. Ga⌐kkoo de⌐su.   Ga⌐kkoo de gozaima⌐su.

L. Level Drill (The sentences on the right are the polite equivalents of those
    on the left.)

1. Na⌐ñ desu ka⌐   Na⌐ñ de gozaimasu ka⌐
2. A⌐na⌐ta (wa) Ta⌐naka-sañ   A⌐na⌐ta (wa) Ta⌐naka-sañ de (i)ras-
   de⌐su ka⌐   syaima⌐su ka⌐
3. Wa⌐surema⌐sita ka⌐   O⌐wasure ni narima⌐sita ka⌐
4. Ko⌐domo (ḡa) ima⌐su ka⌐   O⌐kosañ (ḡa) │irassyaima⌐su │ka⌐
                                                      │oide ni narima⌐su│
5. Na⌐ñ-zi ni ki⌐ma⌐sita   Na⌐ñ-zi ni │i⌐rassyaima⌐sita   │ka⌐
   ka⌐   │o⌐ide ni narima⌐sita│
6. O⌐tomodati de⌐su ka⌐   O⌐tomodati de (i)rassyaima⌐su ka⌐
7. Ko⌐domo (ḡa) arima⌐su   O⌐kosañ (ḡa) gozaima⌐su ka⌐
   ka⌐
8. Do⌐ko ni tu⌐to⌐mete (i)ma-   Do⌐tira ni tu⌐to⌐mete (i)rassyaimasu
   su ka⌐   ka⌐
9. Na⌐ni (ḡa) i⌐rima⌐su ka⌐   Na⌐ni (ḡa) o⌐iri ni narima⌐su ka⌐
10. Watakusi wa ke⌐kkoñ-site   Watakusi wa ke⌐kkoñ-site orimase⌐ñ.
    imase⌐ñ.

M. Expansion Drill

1. I don't know.   Si⌐rimase⌐ñ.
   The name I don't know.   Na⌐mae wa sirimase⌐ñ.
   He's employed but I don't   Tu⌐to⌐mete (i)masu ḡa, na⌐mae wa si-
     know his name.   rimase⌐ñ.
   He's employed here (lit. for   Ko⌐ko ni tuto⌐mete (i)masu ḡa, na⌐mae
     this place) but I don't know   wa sirimase⌐ñ.
     his name.

2. Are you working (lit. doing   Si⌐goto (o) site (i)ma⌐su ka⌐
     work)?
   What kind of work are you   Do⌐ñna si⌐goto (o) site (i)ma⌐su ka⌐
     doing?
   What kind of work are you   I⌐ma ⌐do⌐ñna si⌐goto (o) site (i)ma⌐su
     doing now?   ka⌐
   Excuse me [for asking],   Si⌐tu⌐ree desu ḡa, i⌐ma ⌐do⌐ñna si⌐go-
     but what kind of work are   to (o) site (i)ma⌐su ka⌐
     you doing now?

3. [They]'re in America.   A⌐merika ni ima⌐su.
   Both are in America.   Do⌐tira mo A⌐merika ni ima⌐su.
   I have two (people) but both   Hu⌐ta-ri arima⌐su ḡa, do⌐tira mo A⌐me-
     are in America.   rika ni ima⌐su.
   I have two children but both   Kodomo ḡa hu⌐ta-ri arima⌐su ḡa, do⌐ti-
     are in America.   ra mo A⌐merika ni ima⌐su.

4. It's become expensive.   Ta⌐kaku na⌐rima⌐sita.
   It's become awfully expen-   Zu⌐ibuñ ⌐ta⌐kaku na⌐rima⌐sita.
   sive.
   It's become awfully expen-   Kotosi ⌐zu⌐ibuñ ⌐ta⌐kaku na⌐rima⌐sita.
   sive this year.
   Meat has become awfully   Ni⌐ku⌐ wa kŏtosi ⌐zu⌐ibuñ ⌐ta⌐kaku na-
   expensive this year.   ⌐rima⌐sita.
   Meat has become awfully   Ni⌐ku⌐ wa kŏtosi ⌐zu⌐ibuñ ⌐ta⌐kaku na-
   expensive this year,   ⌐rima⌐sita ⌐ne⌐e.
   hasn't it!

5. Would you be kind enough   Ka⌐ite ku⌐dasaimase⌐ñ ka◡
   to write [it]?
   Would you be kind enough   Pe⌐ñ de ⌐ka⌐ite ku⌐dasaimase⌐ñ ka◡
   to write [it] with a pen?
   Would you be kind enough   Onamae o ⌐pe⌐ñ de ⌐ka⌐ite ku⌐dasa-
   to write your name with   imase⌐ñ ka◡
   a pen?
   I'm sorry but would you   Su⌐mimase⌐ñ ḡa, onamae o ⌐pe⌐ñ de
   be kind enough to write   ⌐ka⌐ite ku⌐dasaimase⌐ñ ka◡
   your name with a pen?

6. How old is [he]?   O⌐ikutu de (i)rassyaima⌐su ka◡
   How old is Taro?   Ta⌐roo-tyañ (wa) o⌐ikutu de (i)rassya-
                                         ima⌐su ka◡
   How old is your Taro?   O⌐taku no Ta⌐roo-tyañ (wa) o⌐ikutu de
                                         (i)rassyaima⌐su ka◡
   Excuse me [for asking],   Si⌐tu⌐ree desu ḡa, o⌐taku no Ta⌐roo-
   but how old is your   tyañ (wa) o⌐ikutu de (i)rassyaima⌐-
   Taro?   su ka◡

SUPPLEMENTARY SELECTIONS

(with questions)

(Give precise answers for each group of questions according to the information contained in the statements that precede them.)

1. Ko⌐domo ḡa sañ-niñ ima⌐su. Ha⌐ruko ḡa ŭe no ko de, ⌐to⌐o desu. Tu⌐ḡi⌐ wa
   ⌐Ta⌐roo de, na⌐na⌐-tu desu. Zi⌐roo ḡa sĭta no ko de, si-⌐ḡatu⌐ ni yo-⌐ttu⌐ ni
   narimasu.

       Kodomo ḡa ⌐na⌐ñ-niñ i⌐ma⌐su ka◡
       Ue no ko no namae wa ⌐na⌐ñ desu ka◡
       Ue wa o⌐toko⌐ no ko desu ka◡
       Da⌐re ḡa ⌐to⌐o desu ka◡
       Ta⌐roo-tyañ wa ⌐i⌐kutu desu ka◡
       Sita wa o⌐nna⌐ no ko desu ka◡
       Zi⌐roo-tyañ wa ⌐i⌐ma ⌐i⌐kutu desu ka◡
       Ue no ko ḡa si-⌐ḡatu⌐ ni yo-⌐ttu⌐ ni na⌐rima⌐su ka◡

2. Keˈsa aˈmerikaˈziñ to iˈgirisuˈziñ ḡa waˈtakusi no zimuˈsyo e kiˈmaˈsita.
Aˈmerikaˈziñ wa oˈtoko no hitoˈ de, Aˈmerika-giˈñkoo ni tuˈtoˈmete imasu.
Iˈgirisuˈziñ wa oˈñna no hitoˈ de, Eˈekoku-taisiˈkañ ni tuˈtoˈmete imasu.
Aˈmerikaˈziñ no namae wa ˈSuˈmisu de, iˈgirisuˈziñ no namae wa ˈZyoˈoñzu
desu.

       Naˈñ-niñ waˈtakusi no zimuˈsyo e kiˈmaˈsita kaᴗ
       Doˈtira mo aˈmerikaˈziñ desu kaᴗ
       Doˈtira ḡa oˈñna no hitoˈ desu kaᴗ
       Doˈtira ḡa taˈisiˈkañ ni tuˈtoˈmete imasu kaᴗ
       Doˈtira ḡa ˈSuˈmisu-sañ desu kaᴗ

3. Yamamoto-sañ wa go-ˈneñ maˈe ni keˈkkoñ-simaˈsita.   Tanaka-sañ wa
kōtosi zyuˈuni-ḡatuˈ ni keˈkkoñ-simaˈsu.

       Doˈtira ḡa ˈiˈma keˈkkoñ-site imaˈsu kaᴗ
       Soˈnoˈ hito wa ˈnaˈñ-neñ ni keˈkkoñ-simaˈsita kaᴗ
       Soˈnoˈ hito wa ˈnaˈñ-neñ kara keˈkkoñ-site imaˈsu kaᴗ
       Soˈnoˈ hito wa ˈnaˈñ-neñ ˈmaˈe kara keˈkkoñ-site imaˈsu kaᴗ
       Soˈnoˈ hito wa ˈnaˈñ-neñ keˈkkoñ-site imaˈsu kaᴗ
       Doˈtira ḡa koˈtosi kekkoñ-simaˈsu kaᴗ

EXERCISES

1. Using pictures of familiar people, practice asking and answering questions
about their names, nationalities, marital status, and age.

2. You ask Mr. Tanaka: Mr. Tanaka replies:

   a. what his name is.   I'm Taro Tanaka.
   b. to write his name.   I'm sorry but I don't have a pencil.
   c. how old he is.   I'm 52.
   d. what kind of work he does.   I work for the Bank of Japan.
   e. if he is married.   Yes, I am.
   f. if he has any children.   Yes, I have three.
   g. who that is.   That's Yukio Sato.
   h. who that Japanese is.   He's a friend.
   i. who that woman is.   I don't know her name but she works
                                 for the embassy.
   j. if Mr. Jones is American.   No, he's English.

3. Practice the Basic Dialogues with appropriate variations.

Lesson 11. Meeting People (cont.)

BASIC DIALOGUES: FOR MEMORIZATION

(a)

(Mr. and Mrs. Tanaka meet Mr. Smith)

Mr. Tanaka

a while (long or short)   si⌐ba⌐raku

1. Mr. Smith! It's been a long time [since I last saw you].   Su⌐misu-sañ. Si⌐ba⌐raku desita.

Mr. Smith

2. Oh, Mr. Tanaka! It <u>has</u> been a long time.   A⌐a, Tanaka-sañ. Si⌐ba⌐raku desita ⌐ne⌐e.

Mr. Tanaka

everyone <u>or</u> everything   miñna
everyone   mi⌐na⌐sañ ⁺

3. Is everyone well?   Mi⌐na⌐sañ o⌐ge⌐ñki desu ka⌐

Mr. Smith

4. Yes, thank you. Is everyone at your house [well], too?   E⌐e, okaḡesama de. O⌐taku no mina⌐sañ mo?

Mr. Tanaka

5. Yes, thank you.   E⌐e, a⌐ri⌐ḡatoo gozaimasu.

wife   ka⌐nai <u>or</u>
o⌐kusañ ⁺

6. Mr. Smith, this is my wife.   Su⌐misu-sañ. Kore (wa) ⌐ka⌐nai desu.

(addressing his wife)

this person   kotira

7. This is Mr. Smith from the American Embassy.   Kotira (wa) A⌐merika-taisi⌐kañ no ⌐Su⌐misu-sañ desu.

Mr. Smith

the first time   ha⌐zi⌐mete
meet <u>or</u> see (a person)   o⌐me ni kakarima⌐su ⁺
how do you do   ha⌐zimema⌐site <u>or</u>
how do you do (lit. I meet you for the first time)   ha⌐zi⌐mete ome ni kakarimasu ⁺

8. Are you Mrs. [Tanaka]? I'm [Mr.] Smith. How do you do.   O⌐kusañ desu ka⌐ Su⌐misu desu. Ha⌐zimema⌐site.

Mrs. Tanaka

9. I'm [Mrs.] Tanaka. How do
you do. I'm glad to meet
you.

Ta⌐naka de gozaima⌐su. Ha⌐zi⌐mete
ome ni kakarimasu. Do⌐ozo yᴏ̄rosi-
ku.

    Japanese language

    nihoñgo or
    nippoñgo

10. You can [speak] Japanese very
well, can't you!

Nihoñgo (ḡa) ⌐yo⌐ku o⌐deki ni nari-
ma⌐su ⌐ne⌐e.

Mr. Smith

    study
    be studying

    beñkyoo-sima⌐su
    beñkyoo-site (i)ru (informal) or
    be⌐ñkyoo-site (i)ma⌐su

    because [I] am studying
    or [I] am studying, so

    be⌐ñkyoo-site (i)ru⌐ kara or
    be⌐ñkyoo-site (i)ma⌐su kara

11. Oh, no! I am studying so I can
[speak it] a little but . . .

Do⌐o itasimasite. Be⌐ñkyoo-site (i)ru⌐
kara, su⌐ko⌐si wa de⌐kima⌐su ḡa‿
          or
Do⌐o itasimasite. Be⌐ñkyoo-site (i)-
ma⌐su kara, su⌐ko⌐si wa de⌐kima⌐su
ḡa‿

    considerably or more
      than expected
    is difficult

    nakanaka

    muzukasii /-ku/

12. It's quite difficult, isn't it—
Japanese.

Na⌐kanaka muzukasi⌐i desu ⌐ne⌐e—nihoñgo wa.

Mrs. Tanaka

    foreign language
    is easy

    gaikokuḡo
    yasasii /-ku/

13. Foreign languages aren't easy,
are they!

Ga⌐ikokuḡo wa yasasiku gozaimase⌐ñ
⌐ne⌐e.

(b)

Smith

14. Whose is this?

Kore (wa) ⌐da⌐re no desu ka‿

Tanaka

15. It's Mr. Kobayashi's, isn't
it?

Ko⌐bayasi-sañ no⌐ desyoo?

Smith

16. It isn't yours?

A⌐na⌐ta no zya a⌐rimase⌐ñ ka‿

Tanaka

17. No (i.e. that's right). It's
his.

E⌐e, a⌐no⌐ hito no desu.

Smith

18. What about yours?

A⌐na⌐ta no wa?

Tanaka

19. Hmm. I wonder where it is.   Sa⌐a. Do⌐ko desyoo ka ⌐ne⌐e. Ko⌐rko
    It <u>was</u> here but. . . .   ni arima⌐sita g̃a_

(c)

Smith

is late <u>or</u> slow   osoi /-ku/
become late   o⌐soku na⌐ru (informal) <u>or</u>
                                         o⌐soku narima⌐su

because it becomes late   o⌐soku na⌐ru kara <u>or</u>
    <u>or</u> it becomes late so   o⌐soku narima⌐su kara
20. Well, it's getting late so if   Zya⌐a, o⌐soku na⌐ru kara, si⌐tu⌐ree.
    you'll excuse me. . .   <u>or</u>
                                         Zya⌐a, o⌐soku narima⌐su kara, si⌐tu⌐-
                                         ree-simasu.

Tanaka

meet <u>or</u> see a person   a⌐ima⌐su
21. Well, I'll see you again. Goodbye.   Zya⌐a, ma⌐ta (aimasyo⌐o). Sayonara_

Smith

to everyone   mi⌐na⌐sañ ni ⌐
22. Give my regards to everyone.   Mi⌐na⌐sañ ni yo⌐rosiku. Sayonara_
    Goodbye.

(d)

Smith

why?   na⌐ze
why? <u>or</u> how?   do⌐o site
23. Why aren't you going to go?   Na⌐ze i⌐kimase⌐ñ ka_ <u>or</u>
                                         Do⌐o site i⌐kimase⌐ñ ka_

Tanaka

father   ti⌐ti⌐ <u>or</u> o⌐to⌐osañ ⌐
sickness <u>or</u> sick   byooki <u>or</u> gobyooki ⌐
is sick   byooki da (informal) <u>or</u>
                                         byo⌐oki de⌐su

because [he] is sick <u>or</u>   byo⌐oki da⌐ kara <u>or</u>
    [he] is sick so   byo⌐oki de⌐su kara
24. Because my father is sick.   Ti⌐ti⌐ g̃a byo⌐oki da⌐ kara.
                                            <u>or</u>
                                         Ti⌐ti⌐ g̃a byo⌐oki de⌐su kara.

Smith

25. He's sick?   Go⌐byooki de⌐su ka.

26. That's too bad.   I⌐kemase⌐ñ ⌐ne⌐e.

27. Take care.   Odaizi ni.

Tanaka

28. Thank you.   A⌐ri⌐g̃atoo gozaimasu.

(e)

Smith

last night	yu⌐ube⌐
Foreign Office	ga⌐imu⌐syoo
meet or see Mr. Yamada	Ya⌐mada-sañ ni aima⌐su

29. You know, I saw Mr. Yamada
from the Foreign Office last
night.

Yuube ga⌐imu⌐syoo no Ya⌐mada-sañ ni aima⌐sita yo⌐

Tanaka

30. You did? Was it the first
time?

So⌐o desu ka.   Ha⌐zi⌐mete desita ka⌐

Smith

31. Yes, that's right.

E⌐e, so⌐o desu.

Tanaka

32. He's a fine man, isn't he?

I⌐i ka⌐ta⌐ desyoo?

Smith

33. Yes, very.

E⌐e, tottemo.

FAMILY TERMS [1]

	Plain or Humble[‡] Word	Polite Honorific [†] Word
family	ka⌐zoku	go⌐ka⌐zoku
grandfather	so⌐hu	o⌐zi⌐isañ [2]
grandmother	so⌐bo	o⌐ba⌐asañ [3]
parent	o⌐ya⌐	oyaḡosañ
both parents	ryo⌐osiñ	go⌐ryo⌐osiñ
father	ti⌐ti⌐	o⌐to⌐osañ
mother	ha⌐ha	o⌐ka⌐asañ
son	musuko	musukosañ or bo⌐ttyañ
daughter	mu⌐sume⌐	musumesañ or o⌐zyo⌐osañ
husband	syu⌐ziñ	go⌐syu⌐ziñ
wife	ka⌐nai	o⌐kusañ

---

[1] Practice these words according to the pattern of Drill I. page 185.

[2] Also means 'old man.'

[3] Also means 'old woman.'

	Plain or Humble [†] Word	Polite Honorific [†] Word
uncle	ozi	ozisañ [1]
aunt	oba	obasañ [2]
brothers and/or sisters [3]	kyo⌐odai	go⌐kyo⌐odai
older brother	a⌐ni	ni⌐isañ or o⌐ni⌐isañ
older sister	ane	ne⌐esañ or o⌐ne⌐esañ
younger brother	o⌐tooto⌐	otootosañ
younger sister	i⌐mooto⌐	imootosañ or oimotosañ
cousin	i⌐to⌐ko	oitokosañ
nephew	oi	oiḡosañ
niece	me⌐e	meeḡosañ
grandchild	ma⌐ḡo⌐	omaḡosañ

ADDITIONAL LANGUAGE NAMES [4]

(All the following words refer to languages only)

English	eeḡo
French	hurañsuḡo
German	doituḡo
Russian	rosiaḡo
Korean	tyooseñḡo
Chinese	tyuuḡokuḡo (or sinaḡo [5])
Spanish	supeiñḡo

NOTES ON THE BASIC DIALOGUES

3. For Americans from the South, mi⌐na⌐sañ is the most common equivalent
of 'you-all.'

---

[1] Also an informal word for 'man' used especially commonly by children
and in talking to children; often used in reference to a close friend of the family.

[2] Also means 'woman'; its usage parallels that of ozisañ.

[3] I.e. 'siblings.'

[4] Practice these words as substitutes for nihoñḡo in Basic Sentence 10 (cf.
Drill A, page 181.

[5] Formerly a commonly used word, now considered insulting by many
Chinese.

7. The <u>kotira</u> series is frequently used in reference to people. In this usage, it is polite (+). <u>Kotira</u>, depending on context, means either 'this person — close to me' or 'this person — i.e. myself.' Similarly, <u>sotira</u> means 'that person — not far away' or 'the person I'm addressing — i.e. you.'

8, 9. In Japanese, it is customary to repeat one's own name according to the patterns of Basic Sentences 8 and 9, immediately upon being introduced.

Ha⌐zi¬mete is a nominal: <u>ha⌐zi¬mete desu</u> 'it's the first time'; <u>ha⌐zi¬mete zya a⌐rimase⌐ñ</u> 'it's not the first time.' Its formal equivalent <u>ha⌐zimema¬site</u> is used only in introductions as a shorter equivalent of humble-polite <u>ha⌐zi¬mete ome ni kakarimasu</u>.

<u>Yorosiku</u> is the adverbial (-<u>ku</u> form) of the adjectival <u>yorosii</u>. <u>Do¬ozo yōrosiku</u> means 'please [treat our acquaintance] favorably.' A person who is being introduced regularly says <u>ha⌐zimema¬site</u> OR <u>ha⌐zi¬mete ome ni kakarimasu</u> AND/OR <u>do¬ozo yorosiku</u>.

Note the use of polite speech by Mrs. Tanaka in addressing Mr. Smith— typical in the given situation. Mr. Smith may use plain or polite speech, depending on circumstances of position, age, etc.

10. In reference to a language, √de⌐kima¬su 'be possible' or 'can do' means 'know' or 'can speak.' Remember that both the thing that is possible and the person to whom it is possible are followed by particles g̱a and/or <u>wa</u>.

11. √Be⌐ñkyoo-sima¬su is a compound verbal (like √ke⌐kkoñ-sima¬su) made up of the nominal <u>beñkyoo</u> 'study (noun)' + √si⌐ma¬su 'do.'

The <u>wa</u> here is the <u>wa</u> of comparison: 'A little I can speak it but—not very well.'

13. <u>Gaikoku</u> means 'foreign country' and <u>gaikoku̱go</u> is the language of a foreign country. <u>Gaikokuziñ</u> means 'foreigner'; this word frequently occurs in the abbreviated form <u>gaiziñ</u>, which now usually refers to Westerners.

<u>Ya⌐sasiku gozaimase¬ñ</u> is the polite (+) equivalent of <u>ya⌐sasiku arimase¬ñ</u>. Remember that √a⌐rima¬su can regularly be replaced by the appropriate form of √go⌐zaima¬su to form a polite equivalent.

14-18. Note the contraction of particle <u>no</u> + nominal <u>no</u> into a single <u>no</u>.

19. 'It was here but—I don't know where it is now.'

20. O⌐soku narima¬sita 'it has become late' is often used as an apology for being late.

21. A⌐ima¬su is a formal plain verbal, and <u>o⌐me ni kakarima¬su</u> (sentence 9 above) is its humble (↓) equivalent. The honorific (↑) equivalent is <u>o⌐ai ni narima¬su</u>. These verbals usually mean 'meet' or 'see' in the sense 'meet up with and talk to,' not 'catch sight of' or 'look at.' The person seen or met is followed by particle <u>ni</u> (sentence 29 below).

Ma⌐ta aimasyo¬o means '(I guess) I'll see you again' or 'let's meet again.'

23. As an equivalent of 'why?' <u>do¬o site</u> (literally 'doing how?') is softer and less direct than <u>na¬ze</u>.

26. I⌐kemase¬ñ is a verbal negative which has taken on a specialized meaning

(compare su⌐mimase⌐ñ). It is used to prohibit ('it won't do,' 'you mustn't do that'), and with ne⌐e, it occurs as an expression of sympathy in regard to a matter of not too serious a nature.

27. **Odaizi ni** is an admonition to 'treat yourself — or someone close to you — carefully.' Daizi (polite odaizi⌐) is a nominal meaning 'important,' 'valuable.'

Family terms:

The plain words in the list of family terms, besides being used as general terms without reference to any particular individuals, are used in talking about members of one's own family, whereas the polite words are used in polite reference to members of the families of others. O⌐zi⌐isañ, o⌐ba⌐asañ, o⌐to⌐osañ, o⌐ka⌐asañ, ozisañ, obasañ, ni⌐isañ, and ne⌐esañ are also used in addressing one's own relatives. Thus:

> ti⌐ti⌐ 'my father,' 'a father'
> o⌐to⌐osañ 'your father,' 'his father,' etc., and 'Father!'

In reference to someone else's young son and daughter, bo⌐ttyañ and o⌐zyo⌐osañ are more polite than musukosañ and musumesañ; but the latter terms are regularly used in reference to someone else's adult son and daughter. Bo⌐ttyañ may also be used in addressing boys and o⌐zyo⌐osañ in addressing girls and young ladies, not related to the speaker.

O⌐kusañ is the regular polite way to address married women — including strangers. It is the Japanese equivalent of 'madam' and 'Mrs. ———.'

To distinguish among different members of a given family, kinship terms are regularly used preceded by the family name + no. Thus:

> Ta⌐naka-sañ no gosyu⌐ziñ 'Mr. Tanaka'
> Ta⌐naka-sañ no o⌐kusañ 'Mrs. Tanaka'
> Ta⌐naka-sañ no ozyo⌐osañ 'Miss Tanaka'
> Ta⌐naka-sañ no bo⌐ttyañ 'Master Tanaka'

GRAMMATICAL NOTES

1. Verbals: Informal Non-past, Stem, and Gerund

A verbal ending in -ma⌐su is formal, non-past, and affirmative. Its informal equivalent — i.e. informal, non-past, affirmative — introduced in this lesson for the first time, is the form regularly listed in dictionaries and will hereafter be referred to as the CITATION FORM. A verbal stem (the -ma⌐su form minus -ma⌐su) and gerund (the -te form) are related to the citation form according to regular patterning.

Toward the end of this note is a chart listing the informal non-past affirmative (i.e. the citation form; other informal forms will be introduced later), stem, gerund, and English equivalent of verbals introduced thus far. Study the chart carefully while noting the following points:

(1) Informal Non-past Affirmative (Citation Form)

Henceforth, all new verbals will be cited in this form when they first occur.

THIS FORM IS IDENTICAL IN MEANING WITH THE -MA⁷SU FORM EXCEPT THAT IT IS LESS FORMAL. Don't make the very common mistake of equating it with the English infinitive and then translating it 'to do so-and-so.' Just as Waʳkarima⁷su. may occur as a complete sentence meaning 'It's clear.' 'I understand.' so Waʳka⁷ru. occurs with the same meanings, as its informal equivalent.

Verbals may be divided into 4 groups:

(a) The -RU GROUP includes verbals which have -ru in the informal (citation form) corresponding to -ma⁷su in the formal. In all such verbals, the vowel preceding -ru is e or i.

Example: de⁷ru/deʳma⁷su 'go out'

(b) The -U GROUP includes verbals which have -u in the informal (citation form) corresponding to -ima⁷su in the formal. In all such verbals, the -u is preceded by one of 8 consonants—t, r, s, k, ḡ, b, m, or n—or by a vowel other than e.

Example: ka⁷eru/kaʳerima⁷su 'return (home)'

(c) The -ARU GROUP includes verbals which have -aru in the informal (citation form) corresponding to -aima⁷su in the formal. This group includes only 5 verbals, all of which are polite.

Example: kuʳdasa⁷ru/kuʳdasaima⁷su 'give me'

(d) The IRREGULAR GROUP includes only 2 verbals:

suru/siʳma⁷su 'do'
ku⁷ru/kiʳma⁷su 'come'

In subsequent lessons, a new verbal will be identified at its first appearance according to its group. For example:

kaʳke⁷ru /-ru/

(2) Stem

The stem is the -ma⁷su form minus -ma⁷su.[1] It is the form to which the

---

[1] The stem is accented if the citation form is accented. The accent of the citation form must be learned for each verbal. A -ma⁷su form is regularly accented on the ma syllable except in environments where the accent is lost.

adjectival -tai ending, meaning 'want to do so-and-so,' is added (for example, KAItai 'want to buy,' IKItai 'want to go,' etc.).[1] The polite nominals which are derived from verbals and which occur in polite patterns consist of the polite prefix o- plus the stem[2] (for example, o⌐DEKI ni narima¬su ka 'can you do it?'; o⌐KAERI ni narima¬su ka 'are you going to go home?'). Other uses of the stem will be introduced later.

To determine the stem, given the citation form:

(a) for verbals of the -ru group, drop the -ru ending.

     Example: wasureru 'forget,' stem wasure

(b) for verbals of the -u group, change final -u to -i.

     Example: kau 'buy,' stem kai

(c) for verbals of the -aru group, change final -aru to -ai.

     Example: go⌐za¬ru 'be,' 'have,' stem go⌐za¬i

(d) irregular:

     suru 'do,' stem si
     ku¬ru 'come,' stem ki¬

(3) Gerund (the -te form)

The gerund has been introduced in the following patterns:

     O⌐namae o KA¬ITE kudasai. 'Please write your name.'
     O⌐namae o KA¬ITE ku⌐dasaimase¬ñ ka↲ 'Would you be kind enough to write your name?'
     So⌐re o KA¬ITE, ka⌐erima¬sita. 'I wrote it and went home.'
     Na⌐mae o KA¬ITE (i)masu. 'I'm writing my name.'

Other uses will be introduced later.

To determine the gerund, given the citation form:

(a) for -ru verbals, change the final -ru to -te.

     Example: wasureru 'forget' : wasurete

---

[1] When -tai is added to an accented stem, the combination is accented on syllable ta; when it is added to an unaccented stem, the combination is also unaccented.

[2] The combination is an unaccented word.

(b) for -u verbals: change final—

-tu to -tte	Example:	ma꜒tu 'wait' : ma꜒tte
-ru to -tte		ka꜒eru 'return' : ka꜒ette
vowel + -u to vowel + -tte		kau 'buy' : katte
-su to -site		ha⌐na꜒su 'speak' : ha⌐na꜒site
-ku to -ite		ka꜒ku 'write' : ka꜒ite
-ḡu to -ide		i⌐so꜒ḡu 'hurry' : i⌐so꜒ide
-bu to -ñde		yobu[1] 'call' : yo⌐ñde
-mu to -ñde		yo꜒mu[1] 'read' : yo꜒ñde
-nu to -ñde		sinu[1] 'die' : siñde (unique example)

(c) for -aru verbals, change the final -aru to -atte, but note also the alternate forms in the chart below.

    Example: i⌐rassya꜒ru 'go,' 'come,' 'be' : i⌐rassya꜒tte
                                       (and i⌐ra꜒site)

(d) irregular:

    suru 'do' : site
    ku꜒ru 'come' : ki⌐te꜒

A stem and gerund are accented only if the informal non-past (citation) form from which they are derived is accented. In the -ru group, the accent of the stem and gerund occurs one syllable nearer the beginning of the word than the accent of the citation form, unless that accent is on the first syllable (example: non-past mi⌐se꜒ru, stem mi⌐se, gerund mi⌐sete); elsewhere, the accent of the stem and gerund regularly occurs on the same syllable as the accent of the citation form (example: non-past ka꜒ku, stem ka꜒ki, gerund ka꜒ite). [2]

Once you have learned the five -aru and two irregular verbals, any other verbal not ending in -eru or -iru must belong to the -u group. A verbal ending in -eru or -iru may belong to the -ru group or the -u group; this cannot be determined unless other inflected forms of the word are known or unless the word is specifically identified as to group. Compare:

    iru (-ru) 'be in a place (animate)':

        stem i
        formal i⌐ma꜒su
        gerund ite

    iru (-u) 'be needed':

        stem iri
        formal i⌐rima꜒su
        gerund itte

---

[1] These verbals and others ending in -bu and -mu will occur in later lessons. They are mentioned here only for the sake of completeness.

[2] The accent of ki⌐te꜒, gerund of ku꜒ru, is irregular.

VERBALS

Informal Non-past (Citation Form)	Stem	Gerund	English Equivalent
-RU Group:			
de'ki'ru	de'ki	de'kite	'be possible'
de'ru	de'	de'te	'go out'
iru[1]	i	ite	'be in a place (animate)'
mi'se'ru	mi'se	mi'sete	'show'
osieru	osie	osiete	'teach,' 'inform'
tomeru	tome	tomete	'bring to a halt'
tu'tome'ru	tu'to'me	tu'to'mete	'become employed'
wasureru	wasure	wasurete	'forget'
-U Group:			
-tu			
ma'tu	ma'ti	ma'tte	'wait'
-ru			
a'ru	a'ri	a'tte	'be in a place (inanimate),' 'have'
iru	iri	itte	'be needed'
ka'eru	ka'eri	ka'ette	'return home'
ka'ka'ru	ka'ka'ri	ka'ka'tte	'be required' (ome ni ～ + 'meet')
ko'ma'ru	ko'ma'ri	ko'ma'tte	'be upsetting'
maḡaru	maḡari	maḡatte	'make a turn'
ma'iru ↓	ma'iri	ma'itte	'come,' 'go'
mo'do'ru	mo'do'ri	mo'do'tte	'go back,' 'back up'
na'ru	na'ri	na'tte	'become' (o- + stem ni ～ = honorific)
o'ru ↓	o'ri	o'tte	'be in a place (animate)'
siru	siri	sitte	'come to know'
wa'ka'ru	wa'ka'ri	wa'ka'tte	'be comprehensible'
-Vowel + u			
a'u	a'i	a'tte	'meet,' 'see (a person)'

---

[1] (i)ru, (i), (i)te following a gerund.

	iu[1]	ii	itte	'say'
	kau	kai	katte	'buy'
	tiḡau	tiḡai	tiḡatte	'be different'
	ukaḡau ↓	ukaḡai	ukaḡatte	'inquire'
-su	ha⌐na⌐su	ha⌐na⌐si	ha⌐na⌐site	'talk'
-ku	ka⌐ku	ka⌐ki	ka⌐ite	'write,' 'draw'
	tu⌐ku	tu⌐ki	tu⌐ite	'arrive'
	iku	iki	itte[2]	'go'
-ḡu	i⌐so⌐ḡu	i⌐so⌐ḡi	i⌐so⌐ide	'be in a hurry'

-ARU Group:	go⌐za⌐ru ↓ [3]	go⌐za⌐i	——	'be in a place (inanimate),' 'have'
	i⌐rassya⌐ru ↓	i⌐rassya⌐i	i⌐rassya⌐tte or i⌐ra⌐site	'go,' 'come,' 'be in a place (animate)'
	ku⌐dasa⌐ru ↓	ku⌐dasa⌐i	ku⌐dasa⌐tte or ku⌐dasu⌐tte	'give to me'

Irregular Group:	ku⌐ru	ki⌐	ki⌐te⌐	'come'
	suru	si	site	'make,' 'do' (beñkyoo-∼ 'study,' kekkoñ-∼ 'marry,' etc.)

In informal speech, used most commonly in addressing close friends, relatives, or inferiors, the majority of inflected forms that occur are informal. They occur at the end of sentences as well as within longer sentences, in the informal speech of both men and women—but with specific differences. Remember that it is possible to be polite and informal at the same time, for example with forms like i⌐rassya⌐ru ↓. Informal speech will be discussed in greater detail in later lessons.

Even in formal speech, informal inflected forms frequently occur as non-final inflected forms, in some patterns. (There is no difference here between the speech of men and women except that men use informal forms more frequently.) For one such pattern, see Note 3 below.

---

[1] The combination i + u is regularly pronounced yuu. The spelling iu is preferred here because it helps the student determine the other inflected forms.

[2] Itte, the gerund of iku, is an irregular form, but since it is the only irregular form, iku is not listed among the irregular verbs.

[3] This form is rare in conversational Japanese.

2 .   C o p u l a :   I n f o r m a l   N o n - p a s t da

The informal equivalent of de⌐su is da, which will hereafter be designated as the citation form of the copula. It occurs after nominals and particles.

Examples:

> so⌐o da 'that's right'
> sa⌐ñ-zi made da 'it's until 3 o'clock'

De, the gerund of the copula, has already been introduced. The copula has no form corresponding to a verbal stem.

WARNING: Remember that the informal equivalent of an adjectival + de⌐su is the adjectival alone. Thus: ta⌐ka⌐i desu 'it's expensive' (formal); ta⌐ka⌐i 'it's expensive' (informal).

Study the following chart:

Affirmative Non-past Inflectional Patterns

	Formal	Informal
Verbal Pattern	Verbal ending in -ma⌐su (wa⌐karima⌐su)	Verbal ending in -[r]u (wa⌐ka⌐ru)
Adjectival Pattern	Adjectival ending in -i + de⌐su (o⌐oki⌐i desu)	Adjectival ending in -i (o⌐oki⌐i)
Nominal[1] Pattern	Nominal[1] + de⌐su (ho⌐ñ desu)	Nominal[1] + da (ho⌐ñ da)

3 .   P a r t i c l e kara ' s o '

The particle kara following a nominal and meaning 'from' was described in Lesson 8, Grammatical Note 4.

Following an inflected expression (verbal, adjectival, or copula) in the non-past or past or tentative, affirmative or negative, kara means 'so,' 'therefore,' or 'because,' with the following differences in word order: x kara y 'x so y,' 'x therefore y,' or 'because x y.' In this pattern, kara usually ends with comma intonation.

Examples:

> A⌐sita ikima⌐su kara, kyo⌐o wa i⌐kimase⌐ñ.
> 'I'm going tomorrow, so today I'm not going to go.'

---

[1] With or without following particle.

Wa⌐karimase¬ñ desita kara, mo⌐o iti-do itte kudasa¬i.
'I didn't understand so please say it again.'
Ta⌐ka¬i desyoo kara, ka⌐imase¬ñ.
'It's probably expensive so I'm not going to buy it.'
Ta¬kaku a┌rimase┐ñ kara, mo⌐o hito┐-tu ka┌imasyo┐o.
'They're not expensive so let's buy one more.'
Tanaka-sañ wa byo⌐oki de¬su kara, ki⌐mase¬ñ.
'Mr. Tanaka isn't going to come because he's sick.'

An informal inflected expression before <u>kara</u> has the same meaning (except for formality) as its formal equivalent in the same position. Before <u>kara</u>, a normally unaccented verbal or nominal-plus-<u>da</u> expression acquires an accent on its final syllable, and a non-past adjectival on its next-to-last syllable.

A⌐sita iku¬ kara, kyo¬o wa i⌐kimase¬ñ. [1]
Ta⌐ka¬i kara, ka⌐imase¬ñ. 'It's expensive so I'm not going to buy it.'
Tanaka-sañ wa byo⌐oki da¬ kara, ki⌐mase¬ñ. [1]

A major sentence as a whole is assigned to the level of its final inflected form. That form is as formal as, or more formal than, inflected forms occurring earlier in the sentence. [2]

Compare:

(a) Be⌐ñkyoo-site (i)ru¬ kara, su⌐ko¬si wa┌ka┐ru.
(b) Be⌐ñkyoo-site (i)ru¬ kara, su⌐ko¬si wakarimasu.
(c) Be⌐ñkyoo-site (i)ma¬su kara, su⌐ko¬si wakarimasu.

All three sentences mean 'I am studying so I understand a little.' Sentence (a) is said to be informal because final wa⌐ka¬ru is informal, and sentences (b) and (c) are both said to be formal because of final wa⌐karima¬su, which is formal. Within the formal style, sentence (c) is more formal than (b) because its non-final inflected form (i)⌐ma¬su is also formal.

A sentence (i.e. a fragment) may consist of a sequence ending with <u>kara</u> if the over-all meaning is clear from the context. For example:

(To a taxi driver) I⌐sogima¬su kara_ 'I'm in a hurry so [please go fast].'
Ta¬kusii de i┌kima┐su ka⌐ . . . Iie. Ku⌐ruma ḡa arima¬su kara_ 'Are you going by taxi? . . . No. I have a car so [I don't need a cab].'

---

[1] The English equivalent is the same as for the corresponding sentence just above.

[2] G̱a 'but' is one of the few particles which is usually preceded only by an inflected form of the same level as the final one in the sentence. An informal inflected form before g̱a occurs only in men's informal speech.

Do⌐o site i⌐kimase⌐ñ ka⌐ . . . Ki⌐noo ikima⌐sita kara. 'Why aren't
you going to go? . . . Because I went yesterday [I'm not going to
go].'
Na⌐ze ka⌐imase⌐ñ ka⌐ . . . Ta⌐ka⌐i kara. 'Why aren't you going to
buy it? . . . Because it's expensive [I'm not going to buy it].'

A minor sentence like the last, ending with an informal form + <u>kara</u>, may
occur in both informal and formal speech (determined by the formality of final
inflected forms in surrounding sentences), but one ending with a formal form +
<u>kara</u> occurs only in formal speech.

4.   <u>desyoo?</u>

Sentence-final <u>desyoo</u> with question-mark intonation indicates a question
which anticipates agreement from the person addressed. Thus:

Koñna tokee wa ta⌐ka⌐i desyoo? 'Watches like these a r e   expensive,
aren't they?'
Kore to are wa ōnazi desyoo? 'This one and that one are the same,
aren't they?'
Koko no giñkoo wa ⌐sa⌐ñ-zi made desyoo? 'The banks here are [open]
until 3, aren't they?'

<u>Desyoo?</u> in sentence-final position is always unaccented. It often occurs
with shortening of the final vowel (<u>desyo?</u>).

5.   I n v e r t e d   S e n t e n c e s

Na⌐kanaka muzukasi⌐i desu ⌐ne⌐e — nihoñgo wa

The above is an example of a Japanese INVERTED SENTENCE. If the
order of the first part (<u>na⌐kanaka muzukasi⌐i desu ⌐ne⌐e</u>) and the second part
(<u>nihoñgo wa</u>) is reversed, the result is a standard Japanese sentence of identical meaning except that it is more formal. Inverted sentences are common in
conversation.

Examples:

Standard	Inverted
Sore wa ⌐na⌐ñ desu ka.	Na⌐ñ desu ka — sore wa. [1]
'What is that?'	'What is [it] — that thing?'
So⌐ko e ikima⌐sita yo.	I⌐kima⌐sita yo — soko e.
'You know, I went there.'	'You know, I went — to that place.'

---

[1] For the dash, see Introduction, page xli.

Standard	Inverted

Si⌐nbuñ o kaima⌐sita ⌐ne⌐e.
'You bought the news-
paper, didn't you.'
So⌐re wa i⌐i desu yo⌟
'Why, that's fine.'

Ka⌐imasita ⌐ne⌐e — siñbuñ o.
'You bought [it], didn't you — the
newspaper.'
I⌐i desu yo⌟ — sore wa.
'It's fine — that.'

What normally occurs as a kind of sentence-final intonation occurs within an inverted sentence at the end of the first part, with the initial word of the second part pronounced as if it were part of the same accent phrase. An intonation other than period intonation is indicated by its regular symbol, preceding the dash (cf. the last example above).

DRILLS

A. Substitution Drill

1. You can [speak] Japanese
   very well, can't you!

   Nihoñgo (ḡa) ⌐yo⌐ku de⌐kima⌐su ⌐ne⌐e.

2. You can [speak] English
   very well, can't you!

   Eeḡo (ḡa) ⌐yo⌐ku de⌐kima⌐su ⌐ne⌐e.

3. You can [speak] French
   very well, can't you!

   Hurañsuḡo (ḡa) ⌐yo⌐ku de⌐kima⌐su ⌐ne⌐e.

4. You can [speak] Chinese
   very well, can't you!

   Tyuuḡokuḡo (ḡa) ⌐yo⌐ku de⌐kima⌐su ⌐ne⌐e.

5. You can [speak] Spanish
   very well, can't you!

   Supeiñḡo (ḡa) ⌐yo⌐ku de⌐kima⌐su ⌐ne⌐e.

6. You can [speak] German
   very well, can't you!

   Doituḡo (ḡa) ⌐yo⌐ku de⌐kima⌐su ⌐ne⌐e.

7. You can [speak] Russian
   very well, can't you!

   Rosiaḡo (ḡa) ⌐yo⌐ku de⌐kima⌐su ⌐ne⌐e.

8. You can [speak] foreign
   languages very well,
   can't you!

   Gaikokuḡo (ḡa) ⌐yo⌐ku de⌐kima⌐su ⌐ne⌐e.

B. Substitution Drill

1. You know, I met Mr. Yamada
   from the Foreign Office last
   night.

   Yuube ga⌐imu⌐syoo no Ya⌐mada-sañ ni aima⌐sita yo⌟

2. You know, I met Mr. Yamada
   from the Foreign Office for
   the first time.

   Ha⌐zi⌐mete ga⌐imu⌐syoo no Ya⌐mada-sañ ni aima⌐sita yo⌟

3. You know, I met Mr. Yamada
   from the Bank of Japan for
   the first time.

   Ha⌐zi⌐mete Ni⌐hoñ-gi⌐ñkoo no Ya⌐ma-da-sañ ni aima⌐sita yo⌟

4. You know, I met your (older) brother from the Bank of
   Japan for the first time.

   Ha⌐zi⌐mete Ni⌐hoñ-gi⌐ñkoo no o⌐ni⌐isañ ni a⌐ima⌐sita yo⌟

5. You know, I met your (older) brother from the Bank of Japan for the first time.

Ha⌐zi⌐mete Ni⌐hoñ-gi⌐ñkoo no o⌐ni⌐isañ ni o⌐me ni kakarima⌐sita yo⌐

6. You know, I met your (older) brother from the Bank of Japan the day before yesterday.

Ototoi Ni⌐hoñ-gi⌐ñkoo no o⌐ni⌐isañ ni o⌐me ni kakarima⌐sita yo⌐

C. Grammar Drill (based on Grammatical Note 4)

Tutor: Ta⌐ka⌐i desu. 'It's expensive.'
Student: Ta⌐ka⌐i desyoo? 'It's expensive, isn't it?'

1. Mi⌐ñna onazi de⌐su.   Miñna onazi desyoo?
2. Koñna siḡoto (wa) mu⌐zukasi⌐i desu.   Koñna siḡoto (wa) mu⌐zukasi⌐i desyoo?
3. Gakkoo (wa) ⌐ku⌐-zi kara desu.   Gakkoo (wa) ⌐ku⌐-zi kara desyoo?
4. Gekizyoo no tonari (wa) ku⌐suriya de⌐su.   Gekizyoo no tonari (wa) kŭsuriya desyoo?
5. A⌐no ba⌐su (wa) Yo⌐kohama ma⌐de desu.   A⌐no ba⌐su (wa) Yo⌐kohama ma⌐de desyoo?
6. Ko⌐ñna huru⌐i kuruma (wa) o⌐so⌐i desu.   Ko⌐ñna huru⌐i kuruma (wa) o⌐so⌐i desyoo?
7. A⌐no zibiki⌐ (wa) Tãnaka-sañ no ⌐bo⌐ttyañ no desu.   A⌐no zibiki⌐ (wa) Tãnaka-sañ no ⌐bo⌐ttyañ no desyoo?
8. Yokohama (wa) a⌐no toori⌐ desu.   Yokohama (wa) a⌐no toori⌐ desyoo?

D. Grammar Drill (based on Grammatical Note 5)

Tutor: I⌐i desu ⌐ne⌐e— sore wa. 'Isn't it nice— that!' (inverted order)
Student: Sore wa ⌐i⌐i desu ⌐ne⌐e. 'That's nice, isn't it!' (standard order)

1. Yo⌐ku wa⌐karima⌐su ⌐ne⌐e— nihoñḡo ḡa.   Nihoñḡo ḡa ⌐yo⌐ku wa⌐karima⌐su ⌐ne⌐e.
2. Mu⌐zukasi⌐i desu yo⌐ — koñna siḡoto wa.   Koñna siḡoto wa mu⌐zukasi⌐i desu yo⌐
3. Ya⌐sasi⌐i desu ⌐ne⌐e— kore wa.   Kore wa ya⌐sasi⌐i desu ⌐ne⌐e.
4. Ka⌐ima⌐sita yo⌐ — a⌐tarasi⌐i kuruma o.   A⌐tarasi⌐i kuruma o ka⌐ima⌐sita yo⌐
5. Yu⌐ube ikima⌐sita ⌐ne⌐e— Te⌐ekoku-ge⌐kizyoo ni.   Te⌐ekoku-ge⌐kizyoo ni yu⌐ube ikima⌐sita ⌐ne⌐e.
6. O⌐kaeri ni narima⌐su ka⌐ — i⌐ma.   I⌐ma o⌐kaeri ni narima⌐su ka⌐
7. O⌐okiku na⌐rima⌐sita ⌐ne⌐e— bo⌐ttyañ wa.   Bo⌐ttyañ wa ⌐o⌐okiku na⌐rima⌐sita ⌐ne⌐e.
8. A⌐rimase⌐ñ yo⌐ — tabako ḡa.   Tabako ḡa a⌐rimase⌐ñ yo⌐

E. Grammar Drill (based on Grammatical Note 3)

    (Retain the formal level before <u>kara</u>)

        Tutor: Be⌐ŋkyoo-site (i)ma⌐su. Wa⌐karima⌐su. 'I'm studying. I understand.'
        Student: Be⌐ŋkyoo-site (i)ma⌐su kara, wa⌐karima⌐su. 'I'm studying so I understand.'

1.	I⌐ma be⌐ŋkyoo-site (i)mase⌐ñ. Mi⌐ñna wasurema⌐sita.	I⌐ma be⌐ŋkyoo-site (i)mase⌐ñ k a r a , mi⌐ñna wasurema⌐sita.
2.	Tyo⌐oseŋgo (ga) dekimase⌐ñ. Wa⌐karimase⌐ñ desita.	Tyo⌐oseŋgo (ga) dekimase⌐ñ kara, wa-⌐karimase⌐ñ desita.
3.	Sa⌐ñ-zi sugi⌐ desu. U⌐ti e kaerimasyo⌐o.	Sa⌐ñ-zi sugi⌐ desu kara, u⌐ti e kaerimasyo⌐o.
4.	Ha⌐zi⌐mete desu. A⌐ñmari wakarimase⌐ñ.	Ha⌐zi⌐mete desu kara, a⌐ñmari wakarimase⌐ñ.
5.	Ta⌐kusii wa ta⌐ka⌐i desu. De⌐ñsya de i⌐kimasyo⌐o.	Ta⌐kusii wa ta⌐ka⌐i desu kara, de⌐ñsya de i⌐kimasyo⌐o.
6.	I⌐sogima⌐su. Ha⌐yaku site kudasai.	I⌐sogima⌐su kara, ha⌐yaku site kudasai.
7.	A⌐ñmari ki⌐ree zya a⌐rimase⌐ñ desita. Ka⌐imase⌐ñ desita.	A⌐ñmari ki⌐ree zya a⌐rimase⌐ñ desita kara, ka⌐imase⌐ñ desita.
8.	Hu⌐ne wa o⌐so⌐i desu. Hi⌐ko⌐oki de i⌐kima⌐sita.	Hu⌐ne wa o⌐so⌐i desu kara, hi⌐ko⌐oki de i⌐kima⌐sita.
9.	Hu⌐ruku na⌐rima⌐sita. A⌐tarasi⌐i no (ga) ka⌐i-ta⌐i ñ desu ga_	Hu⌐ruku na⌐rima⌐sita kara, a⌐tarasi⌐i no (ga) ka⌐ita⌐i ñ desu ga_
10.	Byo⌐oki ni narima⌐sita. Kyo⌐o wa de⌐kimase⌐ñ.	Byo⌐oki ni narima⌐sita kara, kyo⌐o wa de⌐kimase⌐ñ.

F. Level Drill[1]

        Tutor: A⌐sita ikima⌐su kara. (formal verbal)   } 'Because I'm going
        Student: A⌐sita iku⌐ kara. (informal verbal) } to go tomorrow.'

1.	Tanaka-sañ (ga) ⌐yo⌐ku de⌐kima⌐su kara.	Tanaka-sañ (ga) ⌐yo⌐ku de⌐ki⌐ru kara.
2.	Sa⌐ñ-gatu ni Too̅kyoo de ke⌐kkoñ-sima⌐su kara.	Sa⌐ñ-gatu ni Too̅kyoo de ke⌐kkoñ-suru⌐ kara.

---

[1] This drill is based on Grammatical Notes 1 and 3. After practicing it in its given form, reverse the procedure, with the tutor giving the sentence on the right and the student the sentence on the left.

3. I˥tu mo tu⌐itati˥ ni ko┌ko   I˥tu mo tu⌐itati˥ ni ko┌ko ni tu˩ku ka-
   ni tukima˩su kara.   ra.

4. Ka⌐mi˥ ḡa ta⌐kusañ iri-   Ka⌐mi˥ ḡa ta⌐kusañ iru˥ kara.
   ma˥su kara.

5. Zyu˥u-neñ ˥ma˩e kara   Zyu˥u-neñ ˥ma˩e k a r a tu⌐to˥mete
   tu⌐to˥mete (i)˥ma˩su   (i)˥ru˩ kara.
   kara.

6. A˥sa ha⌐ti˥-zi wa ⌐tyo˥tto   A˥sa ha⌐ti˥-zi wa ⌐tyo˥tto ko⌐ma˥ru ka-
   ko⌐marima˥su kara.   ra.

7. Tu⌐ḡi˥ no ˥ka˩do (o)   Tu⌐ḡi˥ no ˥ka˩do (o) ma⌐ḡaru˥ kara.
   ma⌐ḡarima˥su kara.

8. Ma˥initi ro⌐ku-zi-ḡo˥ro   Ma˥initi ro⌐ku-zi-ḡo˥ro zi˥mu˩syo (o)
   zi˥mu˩syo (o) de˥ma˩su   ˥de˩ru kara.
   kara.

9. Koñ̄ḡetu A⌐merika e oka-   Koñ̄ḡetu A⌐merika e okaeri ni na˥ru
   eri ni narima˥su kara.   kara.

10. Tookyoo (o) ⌐yo˥ku si˥tte   Tookyoo (o) ⌐yo˥ku si˥tte (i)ru˩ kara.
    (i)ma˩su kara.

11. Koko kara yo-⌐zikañ-ḡu˥-   Koko kara yo-⌐zikañ-ḡu˥rai ka˥ka˩ru
    rai ka˥karima˩su kara.   kara.

12. Tanaka-sañ mo ⌐Ni˥kkoo   Tanaka-sañ mo ⌐Ni˥kkoo e i˥rassya˩-
    e i˥rassyaima˩su kara.   ru kara.

G. Level Drill[1]

    Tutor: Byo⌐oki de˥su kara. (formal inflected word) ⎫ 'Because I'm
    Student: Byo⌐oki da˥ kara.   (informal inflected word) ⎭   sick.'

1. Dotira mo da⌐me˥ desu kara.   Dotira mo da⌐me˥ da kara.

2. A⌐tarasi˥i kuruma (wa) ta-   A⌐tarasi˥i kuruma (wa) ta⌐ka˥i kara.
   ⌐ka˥i desu kara.

3. Koñna miti (wa) a⌐buna˥i   Koñna miti (wa) a⌐buna˥i kara.
   desu kara.

4. A⌐no˥ hito (wa) zyu⌐ñsa   A⌐no˥ hito (wa) zyu⌐ñsa da˥ kara.
   de˥su kara.

5. A⌐no mise˥ (wa) ha⌐na˥ya   A⌐no mise˥ (wa) ha⌐na˥ya da kara.
   desu kara.

6. Ko⌐ñna ho˥ñ (wa) o⌐mosi-   Ko⌐ñna ho˥ñ (wa) o⌐mosiro˥i kara.
   ro˥i desu kara.

7. Kyo˥o go-⌐zi ma˩e ni   Kyo˥o go-⌐zi ma˩e ni ka˥erita˩i kara.
   ka˥erita˩i desu kara.

8. Tanaka-sañ (wa) ⌐i˥i to-   Tanaka-sañ (wa) ⌐i˥i to˥modati da˩
   ˥modati de˩su kara.   kara.

H. Level Drill[1]

1. Na⌐n̄-zi-ḡo⌐ro ka⌐erima⌐su
   ka↲

   Na⌐n̄-zi-ḡo⌐ro o⌐kaeri ni narima⌐su
   ka↲

2. O⌐kusañ desu ka↲

   O⌐kusañ de (i)⌐rassyaima⌐su ka↲

3. A⌐sita⌐ mo ki⌐te⌐ kudasai.

   A⌐sita⌐ mo |i⌐rassya⌐tte | kudasai.
             |o⌐ide ni na⌐tte|

4. Mi⌐na⌐sañ o⌐ge⌐ñki desu
   ka↲

   Mi⌐na⌐sañ o⌐ge⌐ñki de (i)⌐rassyaima⌐su
   ka↲

5. Ha⌐zi⌐mete desyoo?

   Ha⌐zi⌐mete de gozaimasyoo?

6. Si⌐ba⌐raku desita.

   Si⌐ba⌐raku de gozaimasita.

7. Kore (wa) ⌐da⌐re no desu
   ka↲

   Kore (wa) ⌐do⌐nata no de go⌐zaima⌐su
   ka↲

8. Ni⌐hoñḡo (o) beñkyoo-site
   (i)ma⌐su ka↲

   Ni⌐hoñḡo (o) beñkyoo-site (i)rassyai-
   ma⌐su ka↲

I. Response Drill

Tutor: O⌐kusañ desu ka↲ 'Is it your wife?'
Student: E⌐e, ka⌐nai desu. 'Yes, it's my wife.'

1. Ni⌐isañ desu ka↲   E⌐e, a⌐ni desu.
2. O⌐zyo⌐osañ desu ka↲   E⌐e, mu⌐sume⌐ desu.
3. O⌐ka⌐asañ desu ka↲   E⌐e, ha⌐ha desu.
4. Bo⌐ttyañ desu ka↲   E⌐e, mu⌐suko de⌐su.
5. Ne⌐esañ desu ka↲   E⌐e, a⌐ne de⌐su.
6. O⌐to⌐osañ desu ka↲   E⌐e, ti⌐ti⌐ desu.
7. O⌐iḡosañ de⌐su ka↲   E⌐e, o⌐i de⌐su.
8. Go⌐syu⌐ziñ desu ka↲   E⌐e, syu⌐ziñ desu.

J. Expansion Drill

1. [He] can do it, can't he!

   O⌐deki ni narima⌐su ⌐ne⌐e.

   [He] can do it very well,
   can't he!

   Yo⌐ku o⌐deki ni narima⌐su ⌐ne⌐e.

   [He] can [speak] English
   very well, can't he!

   Eeḡo (ḡa) ⌐yo⌐ku o⌐deki ni narima⌐su
   ⌐ne⌐e.

   Mr. Tanaka can [speak]
   English very well, can't
   he!

   Tanaka-sañ (wa) eeḡo (ḡa) ⌐yo⌐ku o-
   ⌐deki ni narima⌐su ⌐ne⌐e.

   Mr. Tanaka at the Foreign
   Office can [speak] Eng-
   lish very well, can't he!

   Ga⌐imu⌐syoo no Tanaka-sañ (wa) eeḡo
   (ḡa) ⌐yo⌐ku o⌐deki ni narima⌐su ⌐ne⌐e.

---

[1] In each case, the sentence on the right is a more polite equivalent of the
sentence on the left.

2. [They]'re good, aren't they!
   [They]'re quite good, aren't
   they!
   They're quite good, aren't
   they—American pens!
   They're quite good, aren't
   they—American pens like
   this!

   Iˈi desu ˈneˈe.
   Naˈkanaka iˈi desu ˈneˈe.

   Naˈkanaka iˈi desu ˈneˈe—Aˈmerika
   no peˈñ wa.
   Naˈkanaka iˈi desu ˈneˈe—koˈñna Amerika no peˈñ wa.

3. It's interesting, isn't it?
   It's quite interesting, isn't
   it?
   The work is quite interesting, isn't it?
   This kind of work is quite
   interesting, isn't it?

   Oˈmosiroˈi desyoo?
   Naˈkanaka omosiroˈi desyoo?

   Sigoto (wa) naˈkanaka omosiroˈi desyoo?
   Koñna sigoto (wa) naˈkanaka omosiroˈi
   desyoo?

4. I'm not going to go.
   Today I'm not going to go.
   [She]'s sick so today I'm
   not going to go.
   My wife is sick too, so
   today I'm not going to go.
   My mother AND my wife
   are sick so today I'm not
   going to go.

   Iˈkimaseˈñ.
   Kyoˈo wa iˈkimaseˈñ.
   Byoˈoki daˈ kara, kyoˈo wa iˈkimaseˈñ.

   Kaˈnai mo byoˈoki daˈ kara, kyoˈo wa
   iˈkimaseˈñ.
   Haˈha mo ˈkaˈnai mo byoˈoki daˈ kara,
   kyoˈo wa iˈkimaseˈñ.

5. Please study.
   Please study some more.
   It will get interesting so
   please study some more.
   From this point [on] it will
   get interesting so please
   study some more.
   Japanese will get interesting from this point [on] so
   please study some more.

   Beˈñkyoo-site kudasaˈi.
   Moˈtto beˈñkyoo-site kudasaˈi.
   Oˈmosiˈroku ˈnaˈru kara, moˈtto be-
   ˈñkyoo-site kudasaˈi.
   Kore kara oˈmosiˈroku ˈnaˈru kara,
   moˈtto beˈñkyoo-site kudasaˈi.

   Nihoñgo wa kóre kara oˈmosiˈroku
   ˈnaˈru kara, moˈtto beˈñkyoo-site
   kudasaˈi.

6. You know, I met [her].
   You know, I met [his]
   wife.
   You know, I met Mrs. Kobayashi.
   You know, I met Mrs. Kobayashi for the first
   time.
   You know, I met Mrs. Kobayashi for the first
   time, at the Imperial
   Theater.
   You know, I met Mrs. Ko-

   Aˈimaˈsita yo⌣
   Oˈkusañ ni aˈimaˈsita yo⌣

   Koˈbayasi-sañ no oˈkusañ ni aˈimaˈ-
   sita yo⌣
   Haˈziˈmete Koˈbayasi-sañ no oˈkusañ
   ni aˈimaˈsita yo⌣

   Teˈekoku-geˈkizyoo de haˈziˈmete Ko-
   ˈbayasi-sañ no oˈkusañ ni aˈimaˈsita yo⌣

   Yuube Teˈekoku-geˈkizyoo de haˈziˈ-

bayashi for the first   mete Ko⌐bayasi-sañ no o⌐kusañ ni
time, at the Imperial   aᴴima⌐sita yo⌐
Theater last night.

SHORT SUPPLEMENTARY DIALOGUES

(The following are commonly occurring exchanges at meeting or parting.)

1. Guest: De⌐ wa, si⌐tu⌐ree-simasu.
   Host[ess]:   Sayoonara. Ma⌐ta do⌐ozo. O⌐kusañ ni yŏrosiku.
   Guest: A⌐ri⌐gatoo gozaimasu. Sayoonara.

2. Tanaka: O⌐soku na⌐ru kara, si⌐tu⌐ree.
   Yamamoto: Zya⌐a, mata.
   Tanaka: Sayonara.

3. Watanabe: Kore wa ti⌐ti⌐ desu. Ko⌐no kata⌐ wa A⌐merika - ryoozi⌐kañ no
                   ⌐Su⌐misu-sañ desu.
   Father: Wa⌐tanabe de⌐su. Do⌐ozo yŏrosiku.
   Smith: Su⌐misu desu. Ha⌐zimema⌐site.

4. Tanaka: Kore wa ⌐ha⌐ha de gozaimasu.   Kotira wa Nyu⌐uyo⌐oku no
                   ⌐Zyo⌐oñzu-sañ de irassyaimasu.
   Mother: Ta⌐naka de gozaima⌐su. Ha⌐zi⌐mete ome ni kakarimasu.
   Jones: Zyo⌐oñzu de gozaimasu. Ha⌐zimema⌐site. Do⌐ozo yŏrosiku.

5. Tanaka: A⌐a, Kobayasi-sañ. Si⌐ba⌐raku.
   Kobayashi: Si⌐ba⌐raku. Mi⌐na⌐sañ o⌐ge⌐ñki?
   Tanaka: E⌐e, okagesama de. Otaku mo?
   Kobayashi: E⌐e. A⌐ri⌐gatoo.

6. Employee: Zya⌐a, si⌐tu⌐ree-simasu.
   Employer: Go⌐ku⌐roosama. Sayonara.

7. Yamamoto: Ka⌐nai ga byo⌐oki de⌐su kara, kyo⌐o wa ⌐ha⌐yaku kaᴴerita⌐i ñ
                   desu ga⌐
   Watanabe: Go⌐byooki de⌐su ka⌐ I⌐kemase⌐ñ ⌐ne⌐e. Odaizi ni.
   Yamamoto: A⌐ri⌐gatoo gozaimasu.

8. Visitor: Ta⌐naka-sañ irassyaima⌐su ka⌐
   Secretary: Ha⌐a irassyaimasu. Syo⌐osyoo oᴴmati-kudasa⌐i.

English Equivalents

1. Guest: Well, I must be leaving.
   Host[ess]:   Goodbye. Please come again. Regards to your wife.
   Guest: Thank you. Goodbye.

2. Tanaka: It's getting late so if you'll excuse me . . .
   Yamamoto: Well, [I'll see you] again.
   Tanaka: Goodbye.

3. Watanabe: This is my father. This is Mr./Mrs./Miss Smith from the
                 American Consulate.
    Father: (I'm Watanabe.) I'm glad to meet you.
    Smith: (I'm Smith.) How do you do.

4. Tanaka: This is my mother. This is Mr./Mrs./Miss Jones from New
                 York.
    Mother: (I'm Tanaka.) How do you do?
    Jones: (I'm Jones.) How do you do? I'm glad to meet you.

5. Tanaka: Oh, Mr./Mrs./Miss Kobayashi! I haven't seen you for
                 ages.
    Kobayashi: It has been a long time. Is everyone well?
    Tanaka: Yes, thank you. [Everyone at] your house too?
    Kobayashi: Yes, thanks.

6. Employee: Well, I'll be leaving.
    Employer: (Thanks for your trouble.) Goodbye.

7. Yamamoto: My wife is sick so today I'd like to go home early...
    Watanabe: She's sick? That's too bad. Take care.
    Yamamoto: Thank you.

8. Visitor: Is Mr. Tanaka in?
    Secretary: Yes, he is. Just a moment, please.

EXERCISES

1. On the basis of the following family tree, answer the questions below.

        (M = Male; F = Female; Number = Age)

                          Yukio════════Tosie
                          M-46   F-41

Ta⌐roo   Ha⌐ruko   A⌐kiko   Zi⌐roo   Sa⌐buro⌐o   To⌐meko
M-20   F-17   F-15   M-11   M-8   F-4

    a. Fill in the blanks:

        1. Yu⌐kio-san no o⌐kusan no namae wa _____ de⌐su.
        2. Yu⌐kio-san to Tosie-san no ozyo⌐osan no namae wa _____ to _____
            to _____ desu.
        3. Yukio-san wa ⌐Ta⌐roo-san no _____ desu.
        4. Ta⌐roo-san no o⌐ka⌐asan no namae wa _____ de⌐su.
        5. Yukio-san wa To⌐sie-san no _____ desu.
        6. Yu⌐kio-san to Tosie-san no _____ wa ⌐Ta⌐roo-san to ⌐Zi⌐roo-san to
            Sa⌐buro⌐o-san desu.

7. _____ to _____ to _____ wa o⌐toko⌐ de, _____ to _____ to _____
   wa o⌐ñna⌐ desu.

8. _____ wa ⌐ha⌐tati desu.

b. Answer the following questions:

1. Yukio-sañ to Tosie-sañ wa ŏkosañ ḡa ⌐na⌐ñ-niñ imasu ka↲
2. Bo⌐ttyañ ḡa ⌐na⌐ñ-niñ imasu ka↲
3. Ta⌐roo-sañ to ⌐Zi⌐roo-sañ to Sa⌐buro⌐o-sañ wa o⌐ikutu de⌐su ka↲
4. Tosie-sañ wa o⌐toko⌐ desu ka↲
5. To⌐meko-sañ wa ya-⌐ttu⌐ desu ka↲
6. Yu⌐kio-sañ no o⌐kusañ wa o⌐ikutu de⌐su ka↲
7. Ko⌐no ka⌐zoku wa ⌐na⌐ñ-niñ desu ka↲

c. Determine whether the following statements are true or false:

1. A⌐kiko-sañ wa ⌐Ha⌐ruko-sañ no mu˩sumesañ de˩su.
2. Yukio-sañ wa ⌐To⌐meko-sañ no o˩to⌐osañ desu.
3. Ta⌐roo-sañ wa hu⌐ta-tu⌐ desu.
4. To⌐meko-sañ wa Yŭkio-sañ to Tosie-sañ no u⌐e no ozyo⌐osañ desu.
5. Ha⌐ruko-sañ wa zyu⌐usiti⌐ de, A⌐kiko-sañ wa ⌐zyu⌐ugo de, do⌐tira mo
   otoko⌐ no ko desu.
6. Yukio-sañ to Tosie-sañ wa o⌐zyo⌐osañ ḡa go-⌐niñ arima⌐su.

2. Within the framework of the vocabulary and sentence patterns you have
   learned, practice asking and answering questions concerning families, and
   on the basis of the information acquired, draw family trees similar to the
   above.

3. Practice introductions. Take turns performing introductions and being introduced.

4. (a) Give the single Japanese word which is the equivalent of each of the
       following:

   (Example: kodomo no kodomo   Answer: ma⌐go⌐)

   1. ti⌐ti⌐ to ⌐ha⌐ha
   2. o⌐ya no ha⌐ha
   3. oya no o⌐toko no kyo⌐odai
   4. oñna no kodomo
   5. kyo⌐odai no o⌐ñna⌐ no ko

   (b) For each of the following words, give a defining phrase:

   (Example: musuko   Answer: otoko no kodomo)

   1. so⌐hu
   2. oba
   3. ha⌐ha
   4. oi
   5. i⌐to⌐ko

5. Practice the Basic Dialogues with appropriate variations.

Lesson 12. Telephoning

BASIC DIALOGUES: FOR MEMORIZATION

(a)

Smith

to Mr. Hashimoto	Hasimoto-sañ ni
telephone (verb)	de⌐ñwa o kake⌐ru /-ru/
number	ba⌐ñg̃o⌐o
telephone number	de⌐ñwaba⌐ñg̃oo
what number?	na⌐ñ-bañ

1. I'd like to telephone Mr. Hashimoto. What (number) is
his telephone number?

Ha⌐simoto-sañ ni deñwa (o) kaketa⌐i
ñ desu g̃a, de⌐ñwaba⌐ñg̃oo(wa) ⌐na⌐ñ-
bañ desyoo ka.

Tanaka

business company <u>or</u> company office	kaisya

2. Do you mean his home('s), or
his office('s)?

O⌐taku no⌐ desu ka, ka⌐isya no⌐ desu
ka⌐

Smith

3. I mean his office('s).

Ka⌐isya no⌐ desu.

Tanaka

4. I don't know either. . . .

Wa⌐takusi mo sirimase⌐ñ g̃a⌐

Smith

telephone book	deñwatyoo
see <u>or</u> look at	mi⌐ru /-ru/

5. Then would you look it up in
(lit. look at) the phone book?

Zya⌐a, de⌐ñwatyoo (o) mi⌐te ku⌐da-
saimase⌐ñ ka⌐

Yamamoto

6. Are you talking about Mr.
Hashimoto's telephone [num-
ber]?

Ha⌐simoto-sañ no deñwa de⌐su ka⌐

number 21	ni⌐zyuu i⌐ti⌐-bañ <u>or</u> hu⌐ta⌐zyuu i⌐ti⌐-bañ

7. It's 481-7921.

Yo⌐ñhyaku ha⌐ti⌐zyuu i⌐ti⌐ no, na-
⌐na⌐señ ⌐kyu⌐uhyaku hu⌐ta⌐zyuu i⌐ti⌐-
bañ desu.

Smith

extension	naiseñ

8. How about the extension?

Naiseñ wa?

Yamamoto

9. The extension I don't know. . . .   Na⌐iseñ wa sirimase⌐ñ ḡa_

Smith

telephone operator (i.e.   ko⌐oka⌐ñsyu
   central or switchboard)
ask a question or listen   kiku /-u/
   or hear
ask the operator   ko⌐oka⌐ñsyu ni kiku
10. Then would you ask the oper-   Zya⌐a, ko⌐oka⌐ñsyu ni ki⌐ite kudasa-
    ator?   imase⌐ñ ka_

(b)

(On the telephone)

Smith

11. Hello (on the telephone) or   Mo⌐simosi.
    Say there!

Operator

12. Hello. (This is the) Bank   Mo⌐simosi. Ni⌐hoñ-gi⌐ñkoo de go-
    of Japan.   zaimasu.

Smith

number 10   zyu⌐u-bañ or
                                      to⌐o-bañ

13. Extension 210, please.   Naiseñ nïhyaku ⌐to⌐o-bañ |e | oneḡai-
                                                               |ni |
                                      simasu.
                                      or
                                      Naiseñ nïhyaku ⌐to⌐o-bañ (o) oneḡai-
                                      simasu.

14. Hello. Is Yoshio Hashi-   Mo⌐simosi. Ha⌐simoto Yosio - sañ
    moto there?   ima⌐su ka_

Secretary

the person addressed   sotira
who?   do⌐tirasama †
15. Who is calling, please?   Sotira (wa) ⌐do⌐tirasama de (i)⌐ras-
    (Lit. Who are you?)   syaima⌐su ka_

Smith

16. This is [Mr.] Smith of the   A⌐merika-taisi⌐kañ no ⌐Su⌐misu desu
    American Embassy. . . .   ḡa_

Secretary

seat or assigned place   se⌐ki or
                                      o⌐se⌐ki †
be at one's place   se⌐ki ni iru
17. Mr. Hashimoto isn't at his   Hasimoto - sañ (wa) ⌐i⌐ma o⌐se⌐ki ni
    desk (lit. place) [just] now. . . .   i⌐rassyaimase⌐ñ ḡa_

Smith

later	notihodo
make a telephone call	deñwa-suru <u>or</u>
	o⌐de⌐ñwa-suru⁺

18. Well then, I'll call again later (so). . .   Zya⌐a, ma⌐ta notihodo ode⌐ñwa-si-masu kara⌐

Secretary

19. Thank you very much.   Do⌐o mo su⌐mimase⌐ñ.

(c)

(On the telephone)

Smith

the Yoshida residence   Yosida-sañ no otaku ⁺

20. Is this the Yoshida residence?   Sotira (wa) Yo⌐sida-sañ no otaku de (i)rassyaima⌐su ka⌐

Maid

that way <u>or</u> thus <u>or</u> so   sayoo

21. Yes, that's right.   Ha⌐a, sa⌐yoo de gozaima⌐su.

Smith

master	da⌐ñnasa⌐ma ⁺
mistress	o⌐kusañ ⁺ <u>or</u>
	o⌐kusama ⁺

22. Is Mr. Yoshida (lit. the master) in?   Da⌐ñnasa⌐ma i⌐rassyaima⌐su ka⌐

Maid

away from home   ru⌐su <u>or</u>
                   o⌐ru⌐su ⁺

23. He's out [just] now. . . .   I⌐ma o⌐ru⌐su de gozaimasu ḡa⌐

Smith

24. About what time will he be back?   Na⌐ñ-zi-ḡo⌐ro o⌐kaeri ni narima⌐su ka⌐

Maid

he probably returns (<u>or</u> will return) home   ka⌐eru desyoo <u>or</u>
                                                     o⌐kaeri ni na⌐ru desyoo ⁺

25. He will probably be back by about 6 o'clock. . . .   Ro⌐ku-zi-ḡo⌐ro ma⌐de ni⌐ wa o⌐kaeri ni na⌐ru desyoo ḡa⌐

Smith

excuse me (i.e. for breaking away or interrupting)   go⌐meñ-kudasa⌐i or
                                                        go⌐meñ-kudasaima⌐se

26. I see. Goodbye.   Wa⌐karima⌐sita. Go⌐meñ-kudasa⌐i.

Maid

27. Goodbye.   Go⌐meñ-kudasaima⌐se.

(d)

(On the telephone)

Yamamoto

	zero	re゛e or
		ze゛ro
	number 4	yo゛ñ-bañ

28. Hello. Is this 080-0704?   Mo゛simosi. Sotira (wa) ⌐re゛e ha⌐ti-zyu⌐u no, re゛e na⌐na゛hyaku ⌐yo゛ñ-bañ desu ka⌐

Secretary

29. Yes, that's right. . . .   Ha゛a, sa⌐yoo de gozaima゛su ḡa＿

Yamamoto

30. Is Mr. Yamada in?   Ya⌐mada-sañ ima゛su ka⌐

Secretary

in the middle of work   siḡoto-tyuu or
                         osiḡoto-tyuu †

31. He's busy [just] now. . . .   I゛ma o⌐siḡoto-tyuu de (i)rassyaima゛su ḡa＿

Yamamoto

the person speaking   kotira
Japan Travel Bureau   ko⌐otuuko゛osya
free time or leisure   hima or
                        ohima †
time or occasion   to⌐ki゛
at a free time   hi゛ma na toki゛ /ni/

32. This is [Mr.] Yamamoto of the Japan Travel Bureau. Please give me a call when he is free.   Kotira (wa) ko⌐otuuko゛osya no Ya-⌐mamoto de゛su ḡa, o゛hima na toki゛ /ni/ o⌐de゛ñwa (o) kudasai.

Secretary

33. Certainly.   Ka⌐sikomarima゛sita.

Yamamoto

34. Goodbye.   Sayonara.

Secretary

35. Goodbye.   Go⌐meñ-kudasaima゛se.

NOTES ON THE BASIC DIALOGUES

1. The ni following Hasimoto-sañ is the ni of goal: 'I want to make a telephone call TO Mr. Hashimoto.' Compare Yo⌐kohama ni ikima゛sita 'I went to Yokohama.' Following a place expression, both goal particles—ni and

e — occur, but following a person, only ni is used.

Ba⌐ngo⌐o means 'number' in the sense of 'assigned number' or 'serial number' — not 'mathematical numeral.' Similarly, na⌐ñ-bañ means 'what assigned number?' or 'what serial number?'

2. Kaisya 'private company' is also commonly used in reference to the office of such a company. While zi⌐mu⌐syo 'business office' has a broader meaning (it includes a private individual's office, an embassy, etc.), it is used less commonly than kaisya in situations where kaisya applies. As the second part of a compound, kaisya often becomes -ḡaisya (for example, ga⌐suḡa⌐isya 'gas company').

4. 'I don't know either but—is there any way I can help you?'

5. Mi⌐ru more commonly refers to seeing or looking at things. When used with a personal object, it means 'look at': for example, it is used in reference to a doctor's looking at a patient. When 'see a person' corresponds to 'meet and talk to,' the Japanese equivalent is a⌐u.

9. 'The extension I don't know but — is there any way I can help you?'

10. Note the following particles which occur with kiku: the person who asks, listens, or hears is followed by particle ḡa (or wa); the thing asked, listened to, or heard is followed by particle o (or wa); the person asked or listened to is followed by particle ni; the person from whom something is heard is followed by particle kara or ni.

11. Mo⌐simosi is the most common way of saying hello on the telephone. It is also a polite way of attracting attention (in this usage it is similar to, but more polite than, tyo⌐tto)—particularly when addressing strangers.

When making a telephone call in Japan, it is the person who places the call who usually says mo⌐simosi first; he speaks when he hears a click at the other end of the line.

13. The first alternant means 'I'd like [to be connected] to extension 210.' The second alternant means 'I'd like extension 210.'

15. Do⌐tirasama and do⌐natasama are honorific words, more polite than do⌐nata alone. Do⌐tirasama is especially common in telephone conversations.

16. 'This is Mr. Smith but— may I speak to Mr. Hashimoto?'

17. 'Mr. Hashimoto isn't at his desk but—is there anything I can do?'

18. 'I'll call later so—you won't have to do anything.'

Notihodo is a formal equivalent of a⌐to de.

21. Sa⌐yoo de gozaima⌐su is the polite equivalent of so⌐o desu.

22. Da⌐ñnasa⌐ma is used commonly by servants and in conversations with servants. It is also sometimes used as a synonym for go⌐syu⌐ziñ.

O⌐kusama is a more polite equivalent of o⌐kusañ. Compare also the very polite words o⌐to⌐osama 'father,' o⌐ka⌐asama 'mother,' go⌐syu⌐ziñsama 'husband,' o⌐zyo⌐osama 'daughter,' etc.; the comparable form for bo⌐ttyañ

'son' is o꜖bo꜒ttyama.   Note also that -sama is added to proper names as a
more polite equivalent of -san (for example, Tanaka-sama).

25.   'He'll probably be back . . . but—I can't be sure.'

The wa is the wa of comparison.

26.   Go꜖men-kudasa꜒i is also used when entering a house or a shop, to attract
attention.   Compare English 'Hello there!' and 'Is anybody home?'

Go꜖men-kudasaima꜒se is the formal equivalent of gomen-kudasai, used
most commonly by women, and by men who are employees of shops, res-
taurants, hotels, etc.

29.   'That's right but—what can I do for you?'

32.   Koosya (as in ko꜖otuuko꜒osya) refers to a public corporation, whereas kaisya is a private company.

GRAMMATICAL NOTES

A Japanese telephone number consisting of two numerical parts—for example, 481-5021—is regularly read in one of the following ways:

1) The first number (i.e. the exchange number) is read in terms of individual digits and is followed by particle no; the second number is also read as
individual digits.   In this system '4' is regularly yo꜒n (not si꜒), '7' is na꜒na (not
si꜖ti꜒), '9' is kyu꜒u (not ku꜒); '2' has a special alternant ni꜒i, and '5' go꜒o; '0' is
ze꜒ro or re꜒e and is regularly included in reading.   Thus:

  yo꜒n hati i꜔ti꜕ no, go꜒o ꜖ze꜕ro ꜖ni꜒i iti
  '(lit.) five zero two one of four eight one'

    or

2) The exchange number is read as an independent number (in terms of
hundreds, tens, and units, if it consists of three digits) and is followed by particle no; the following four-digit number is read in terms of thousands, hundreds, tens, and digits, plus counter -ban 'number.'   An initial zero in the
exchange number is read re꜒e or ze꜒ro; otherwise it is often omitted in this
style of reading.   Thus:

  yo꜒nhyaku ha꜔tizyu꜕u i꜔ti꜕ no, go꜖se꜒n [꜖re꜕e] ni꜒zyuu i꜔ti꜕-ban
  '(lit.) number five thousand twenty-one of four hundred eighty-one'

In this system, '4', '7', and '9' have the same alternants as above; '2' is ni꜒
or hu꜖ta꜒, and '10' is zyu꜒u or to꜒o.
Formerly, the second type of reading described above (i.e. the style used
in Dialogue A of this lesson) was more common, but recently the first type has
become more prevalent.
The numerals of Series I (with alternants for '2' and '10' from Series II)

combine with the counter -bañ to name telephone numbers, seat numbers, license numbers, etc. The numbers from 1 to 10 are:

i⌐ti⌐-bañ	'number 1'	ro⌐ku⌐-bañ	'number 6'
ni⌐-bañ or		na⌐na⌐-bañ	'number 7'
hu⌐ta⌐-bañ	'number 2'	ha⌐ti⌐-bañ	'number 8'
sañ-bañ	'number 3'	kyu⌐u-bañ	'number 9'
yo⌐ñ-bañ	'number 4'	zyu⌐u-bañ or	
go-bañ	'number 5'	to⌐o-bañ	'number 10'

na⌐ñ-bañ   'what number?'

2. desyoo Following a Non-past Verbal

Desyoo, the formal tentative of da indicating probability or uncertainty, has been introduced previously as occurring after an adjectival ending in -i, a nominal, or a phrase ending with a particle:

> Ta⌐ka⌐i desyoo. 'It's probably expensive.'
> Da⌐me⌐ desyoo. 'It's probably no good.'
> Tanaka-sañ kara desyoo? 'It's from Mr. Tanaka, isn't it?'

Desyoo also occurs after non-past[1] verbals, informal or formal. Since desyoo is formal, the combination is always classified as formal; but a formal verbal + desyoo is more formal than an informal verbal + desyoo.

When it follows an accented verbal, desyoo is unaccented:

> Ku⌐ru desyoo.

A normally unaccented verbal + desyoo is accented according to one of two possible patterns, depending upon the speaker; either the verbal acquires an accent on its final syllable, or desyoo is accented on its next-to-last syllable:

> I⌐ku⌐ desyoo.
>   or
> I⌐ku desyo⌐o.

Desyoo following a verbal indicates probability or uncertainty or indirectness, just as it does after words of other classes:

> I⌐ku desyo⌐o. 'He probably goes (or probably will go).'
> Be⌐ñkyoo-site (i)ru desyo⌐o. 'He's probably studying (or probably will be studying).'
> Wa⌐karima⌐su desyoo? 'It's clear, isn't it?'
> A⌐ni ni ⌐a⌐u desyoo ka. 'Do you suppose you'll see my older brother?'

---

[1] Desyoo occurs after past forms also. These patterns, as well as all informal negatives, will be taken up later.

Ta⌐roo-tyañ wa ⌐na⌐ni o si⌐te (i)ru desyo⌐o ka. 'What do you suppose
Taro is doing?'
Si⌐te (i)ru desyo⌐o ka ⌐ne⌐e. 'I wonder if he does know!'
Ka⌐maimase⌐ñ desyoo? 'It doesn't matter, does it?'

Do not confuse a verbal + <u>desyoo</u> with a tentative verbal, which indicates a
suggestion: [1]

Ka⌐u desyo⌐o. '[Someone] probably buys (<u>or</u> will probably buy) [it].'
Ka⌐imasyo⌐o. 'Let's buy [it].' <u>or</u> 'I guess I'll buy [it].'

3.   Alternate Questions

Two questions occurring within a sentence with the pattern <u>A ka B ka</u> are
alternate questions—'is it A, or is it B?'

Examples:

Ko⌐marima⌐su ka, ka⌐maimase⌐ñ ka. 'Is it inconvenient, or doesn't it
matter?'
O⌐mosiro⌐i desu ka, tu⌐mara⌐nai desu ka. 'Is it interesting, or is it
dull?'
O⌐nazi de⌐su ka, ti⌐gaima⌐su ka. 'Is it the same or is it different?'
Ma⌐e desu ka, u⌐siro de⌐su ka. 'Is it in front, or is it in back?'

4.   na

Prior to this lesson, words or phrases used as descriptions of nominals
have been of four kinds:

1. An adjectival (or a sequence ending with an adjectival)

Examples: ta⌐ka⌐i zi⌐do⌐osya 'expensive car'
to⌐temo i⌐i hito 'a very nice person'

2. A demonstrative

Example: kono tokee 'this watch'

3. A nominal + <u>no</u> or a nominal phrase (consisting of a nominal preceded
by descriptive words and/or followed by particles) + <u>no</u>

Examples: a⌐na⌐ta no ⌐ho⌐ñ 'your book'
o⌐mosiro⌐i ⌐ho⌐ñ no namae 'the name of an interesting
book'
A⌐merika kara no hu⌐ne 'a ship from America'

---

[1] In the standard spoken language, a verbal + <u>desyoo</u> may refer to first,
second, or third person, but a tentative verbal regularly refers to the first
person.

4. A nominal alone (in special combinations only)

  Examples: su⌐g̃u ⌐so⌐ba 'immediate vicinity'
      tyo⌐tto ⌐ma⌐e 'a little before'

Within the class of nominals, there is a subclass having the following special characteristic: when they describe another nominal, they are followed by
na.

Examples:

   hi⌐ma na toki⌐ 'time of leisure'
   ki⌐ree na uti 'a pretty house'
   si⌐tu⌐ree na hito 'a rude person'

All na-nominals describe qualities; but since not all quality nominals take
na, they must be memorized as they occur. Ge⌐ñki 'healthy,' 'peppy,' for
example, is a na-nominal, but byooki 'sick' is not:

   ge⌐ñki na kodomo 'a healthy child'
   byooki no kodomo 'a sick child'

Among the n o m i n a l s introduced up to this point, the following are na-
nominals:

   (o)⌐ge⌐ñki 'healthy,' 'peppy'
   da⌐me⌐ 'no good'
   ki⌐ree 'pretty,' 'clean'
   da⌐izyo⌐obu 'safe'
   ke⌐kkoo 'fine'
   si⌐tu⌐ree 'rude'
   (o)hima 'free (of time)'
   da⌐izi 'important,' 'valuable'

In the lessons that follow, all na-nominals will be so designated when they
are first introduced.

Besides being followed by na when describing another nominal, na-nominals
regularly occur before various forms of √da, and before particle ni (as in
da⌐me⌐ ni na⌐rima⌐sita 'it went bad' [lit. 'it became no good']).

DRILLS

A. Substitution Drill

1.	When you are free, please give me a call.	O⌐hima na toki⌐ ni o⌐de⌐ñwa (o) kuda-sai.
2.	When you are free, please come again.	O⌐hima na toki⌐ ni ma⌐ta kite⌐ kuda-sai.
3.	When you are free, please look at this.	O⌐hima na toki⌐ ni ko⌐re (o) mi⌐te ku-dasai.
4.	When you are free, please let me see that.	O⌐hima na toki⌐ ni a⌐re (o) mi⌐sete kudasai.
5.	When you are free, please show me the way.	O⌐hima na toki⌐ ni mi⌐ti (o) osiete kudasa⌐i.

6. When you are free, please draw a map.

O⌐hima na toki⌐ ni ⌐ti⌐zu (o) ⌐ka⌐ite kudasai.

7. When you are free, please come to see me (lit. come to my house).

O⌐hima na toki⌐ ni u⌐ti e ira⌐site kudasai.

8. When you are free, please telephone Mr. Tanaka.

O⌐hima na toki⌐ ni Ta⌐naka-sañ ni deñwa (o) ka⌐kete kudasai.

B. Substitution Drill

1. I saw [it] at that school.
A⌐no gakkoo de mima⌐sita.
2. I asked at that school.
A⌐no gakkoo de kikima⌐sita.
3. I telephoned at that school.
A⌐no gakkoo de deñwa-sima⌐sita.
4. I saw [him] at that school.
A⌐no gakkoo de aima⌐sita.
5. I studied at that school.
A⌐no gakkoo de beñkyoo-sima⌐sita.
6. I wrote [it] at that school.
A⌐no gakkoo de kakima⌐sita.
7. I bought [it] at that school.
A⌐no gakkoo de kaima⌐sita.
8. I did [it] at that school.
A⌐no gakkoo de sima⌐sita.

C. Substitution Drill

1. I asked (or heard [it] or listened).
Wa⌐takusi ḡa kikima⌐sita.
2. I (comparatively speaking) asked (or heard [it] or listened).
Wa⌐takusi wa kikima⌐sita.
3. I too asked (or heard [it] or listened).
Wa⌐takusi mo kikima⌐sita.
4. I asked (or heard [it] from) a friend.
To⌐modati ni kikima⌐sita.
5. I heard [it] from a friend.
To⌐modati kara kikima⌐sita.
6. I asked (or heard or listened to) that.
So⌐re o kikima⌐sita.
7. That I asked (or heard or listened to).
So⌐re wa kikima⌐sita.
8. I asked (or heard or listened to) that, too.
So⌐re mo kikima⌐sita.
9. I asked (or heard [it] or listened) at the Japan Travel Bureau.
Ko⌐otuuko⌐osya de ki⌐kima⌐sita.
10. I asked (or heard [it] or listened) at 3 o'clock.
Sa⌐ñ-zi ni ki⌐kima⌐sita.

D. Substitution Drill

1. I'd like to telephone a friend. . . .
To⌐modati ni deñwa (o) kaketa⌐i ñ desu ḡa_

2. I'd like to telephone my home. . . .
U⌐ti | ni / e | deñwa (o) kaketa⌐i ñ desu ḡa_

3. I'd like to telephone a cousin in Osaka. . . .

O͞osaka no ito⌉ko ni de͞ñwa (o) ka-
keta⌐i ñ desu g̃a_

4. I'd like to telephone my uncle in Kyoto. . . .

Kyo⌉oto no o͞zi ni deñwa (o) kake-
ta⌐i ñ desu g̃a_

5. I'd like to telephone Mrs.
Hashimoto. . . .

Ha͞simoto-sañ no o⌉kusañ ni de͞ñwa
(o) kaketa⌐i ñ desu g̃a_

6. I'd like to telephone Miss
Kobayashi. . . .

Ko͞bayasi-sañ no ozyo⌉osañ ni de͞ñ-
wa (o) kaketa⌐i ñ desu g̃a_

7. I'd like to telephone my
child's school. . . .

Ko͞domo no gakkoo | ni | deñwa (o)
                   | e |
kaketa⌉i ñ desu g̃a_

8. I'd like to telephone the
Japan Travel Bureau. . . .

Ko͞otuuko⌉osya | ni | de͞ñwa (o) ka-
              | e |
keta⌐i ñ desu g̃a_

9. I'd like to telephone (our)
Jiro. . . .

U͞ti no Zi⌉roo ni de͞ñwa (o) kake-
ta⌐i ñ desu g̃a_

10. I'd like to telephone Mr.
Tanaka at the Foreign
Office. . . .

Ga͞imu⌉syoo no Ta͞naka-sañ ni deñwa (o) kaketa⌐i ñ desu g̃a_

E. Substitution Drill

1. He'll probably return home
by about 6 o'clock.

Ro͞ku-zi-g̃o⌉ro made ni wa o͞kaeri
ni na⌐ru desyoo.

2. He'll probably return home
by tomorrow.

A͞sita ma⌉de ni wa o͞kaeri ni na⌐ru
desyoo.

3. He'll probably come (or go)
by tomorrow.

A͞sita ma⌉de ni wa i͞rassya⌐ru desyoo.

4. He'll probably come (or go)
by Wednesday.

Su͞iyo⌉o made ni wa i͞rassya⌐ru desyoo.

5. He'll probably arrive by
Wednesday.

Su͞iyo⌉o made ni wa o͞tuki ni na⌐ru
desyoo.

6. He'll probably arrive by
April.

Si-͞g̃atu⌉ made ni wa o͞tuki ni na⌐ru
desyoo.

7. He'll probably be able to
do [it] by April.

Si-͞g̃atu⌉ made ni wa o͞deki ni na⌐ru
desyoo.

8. He'll probably be able to
do [it] by the first.

Tu͞itati⌉ made ni wa o͞deki ni na⌐ru
desyoo.

9. He'll probably leave by the
first.

Tu͞itati⌉ made ni wa o͞de ni na⌐ru
desyoo.

10. He'll probably leave by a
quarter after.

Zyu͞ugo-hu⌉ñ-sug̃i made ni wa o͞de
ni na⌐ru desyoo.

F. Grammar Drill (based on Grammatical Note 2)

(Use the informal verbal before desyoo.)

Tutor: Asita ͞Ni⌉kkoo ni ikimasu. '[He] is going to go to Nikkoo to-
          morrow.'
Student: Asita ͞Ni⌉kkoo ni i͞ku desyo⌐o. '[He] is probably going to
          go to Nikkoo tomorrow.'

1. Ma⌐ta asita aima¬su.
2. So⌐re wa komarima¬su.
3. U⌐ti no usiro de tomema¬su.
4. Ko⌐ñna siḡoto wa dekima¬su.
5. Ni⌐hoñḡo to eeḡo wa wakarima¬su.
6. Ko⌐re to sore wa tiḡaima¬su.
7. Hi⌐ma na toki¬ ni mi⌐ma¬su.
8. Asoko ni tabako (ḡa) ⌐mo¬tto arimasu.
9. Go¬ḡo made u⌐ti ni ima¬su.
10. A⌐sita Yokohama ni tukima¬su.

Ma⌐ta asita a¬u desyoo.
So⌐re wa koma¬ru desyoo.
U⌐ti no usiro de tomeru desyo¬o.
Ko⌐ñna siḡoto wa deki¬ru desyoo.
Ni⌐hoñḡo to eeḡo wa waka¬ru desyoo.
Ko⌐re to sore wa tiḡau desyo¬o.
Hi⌐ma na toki¬ ni ⌐mi⌐ru desyoo.
Asoko ni tabako (ḡa) ⌐mo¬tto ⌐a⌐ru desyoo.
Go¬ḡo made u⌐ti ni iru desyo⌐o.
A⌐sita Yokohama ni tu¬ku desyoo.

G. Grammar Drill (based on Grammatical Note 3)

Tutor: I⌐kima¬su. I⌐kimase¬ñ. 'I'll go. I won't go.' (2 statements)
Student: I⌐kima¬su ka, i⌐kimase¬ñ ka⌐ 'Are you going, or aren't you going?' (alternate questions)

1. Ryo⌐kañ de¬su. Ho¬teru desu.
2. Si⌐tte (i)ma¬su. Si⌐rimase¬ñ.
3. Mu⌐zukasi¬i desu. Ya⌐sasi¬i desu.
4. Bo¬ttyañ no desu. O⌐zyo¬osañ no desu.
5. Ki⌐no¬o desita. O⌐toto¬i desita.
6. Ke⌐kkoñ-site ima¬su. O⌐hitori de¬su.
7. De⌐kima¬sita. De⌐kimase¬ñ desita.
8. Sa¬ñ-zi made desu. Yo¬-zi made desu.

Ryo⌐kañ de¬su ka, ho¬teru desu ka⌐
Si⌐tte (i)ma¬su ka, si⌐rimase¬ñ ka⌐
Mu⌐zukasi¬i desu ka, ya⌐sasi¬i desu ka⌐
Bo¬ttyañ no desu ka, o⌐zyo¬osañ no desu ka⌐
Ki⌐no¬o desita ka, o⌐toto¬i desita ka⌐
Ke⌐kkoñ-site (i)ma¬su ka, o⌐hitori de¬su ka⌐
De⌐kima¬sita ka, de⌐kimase¬ñ desita ka⌐
Sa¬ñ-zi made desu ka, yo¬-zi made desu ka⌐

H. Grammar Drill (based on Grammatical Note 4)

Tutor: Ko⌐no ho¬ñ (wa) ta⌐ka¬i desu ⌐ne¬e. 'This book is expensive, isn't it.'
Student: Kore (wa) ta⌐ka¬i ⌐ho⌐ñ desu ⌐ne¬e. 'This is an expensive book, isn't it.'

1. Ano kodomo (wa) ⌐ge¬ñki desu ⌐ne¬e.
2. Ko⌐no ba¬su (wa) o⌐so¬i desu ⌐ne¬e.
3. So⌐no mise¬ (wa) sa̅ki desyoo?

Are (wa) ⌐ge¬ñki na ko⌐domo de⌐su ⌐ne¬e.
Kore (wa) o⌐soi ba¬su desu ⌐ne¬e.
Sore (wa) sa⌐ki no mise¬ desyoo?

4. Kono siḡoto (wa) ⌐ma⌐initi desyoo?

Kore (wa) ⌐ma⌐initi no siḡoto de-syoo?

5. O⌐zyo⌐osañ (wa) ⌐ki⌐ree desu ⌐ne⌐e.

Ki⌐ree na o⌐zyo⌐osañ desu ⌐ne⌐e.

6. So⌐no ka⌐do (wa) tu⌐ḡi⌐ de-syoo?

Sore (wa) tu⌐ḡi⌐ no ⌐ka⌐do desyoo?

7. A⌐no zido⌐osya (wa) hu⌐ru⌐i desu ⌐ne⌐e.

Are (wa) hu⌐ru⌐i zi⌐do⌐osya desu ⌐ne⌐e.

8. Ano zyuñsa (wa) si⌐tu⌐ree desita ⌐ne⌐e.

Are (wa) si⌐tu⌐ree na zyu⌐ñsa de⌐si-ta ⌐ne⌐e.

9. Kono miti (wa) a⌐buna⌐i desu ⌐ne⌐e.

Kore (wa) a⌐bunai miti de⌐su ⌐ne⌐e.

I. Expansion Drill

1. [He] didn't know.

Si⌐rimase⌐ñ desita.

I asked, but [he] didn't know.

Ki⌐kima⌐sita ḡa, si⌐rimase⌐ñ desita.

I asked the telephone num-ber, but [he] didn't know.

De⌐ñwaba⌐ñḡoo (o) ki⌐kima⌐sita ḡa, si⌐rimase⌐ñ desita.

I asked the telephone num-ber of the Foreign Office, but [he] didn't know.

Ga⌐imu⌐syoo no de⌐ñwaba⌐ñḡoo (o) ki⌐kima⌐sita ḡa, si⌐rimase⌐ñ de-sita.

I asked my friend the tele-phone number of the For-eign Office, but [he] didn't know.

Tomodati ni ga⌐imu⌐syoo no de⌐ñwaba⌐ñḡoo (o) ki⌐kima⌐sita ga, si⌐ri-mase⌐ñ desita.

2. I'll probably see [him].

A⌐u desyoo.

I'll probably see your friend.

O⌐tomodati ni a⌐u desyoo.

I'm going to go, so I'll probably see your friend.

I⌐kima⌐su kara, o⌐tomodati ni a⌐u desyoo.

I'm going to go to the Ja-pan Travel Bureau, so I'll probably see your friend.

Ko⌐otuuko⌐osya e i⌐kima⌐su kara, o⌐tomodati ni a⌐u desyoo.

I'm going to go to the Ja-pan Travel Bureau now, so I'll probably see your friend.

I⌐ma ko⌐otuuko⌐osya e i⌐kima⌐su ka-ra, o⌐tomodati ni a⌐u desyoo.

3. You know, I saw [it].

Mi⌐ma⌐sita yo⌐

You know, I saw [it] for the first time.

Ha⌐zi⌐mete mi⌐ma⌐sita yo⌐

You know, I saw the house for the first time.

Uti (o) ha⌐zi⌐mete mi⌐ma⌐sita yo⌐

You know, I saw a pretty house for the first time.

Ki⌐ree na uti (o) ha⌐zi⌐mete mi⌐ma⌐-sita yo⌐

<table>
<tr><td>You know, I saw your son's pretty house for the first time.</td><td>Musukosañ no ⌐ki⌐ree na uti (o) ha-⌐zi⌐mete mi⌐ma⌐sita yo⌐</td></tr>
</table>

You know, I saw your son's pretty house for the first time.	Musukosañ no ⌐ki⌐ree na uti (o) ha-⌐zi⌐mete mi⌐ma⌐sita yo⌐
You know, I saw your son's pretty house for the first time last night.	Yuube mūsukosañ no ⌐ki⌐ree na uti (o) ha⌐zi⌐mete mi⌐ma⌐sita yo⌐

4.
Did you ask?	Ki⌐kima⌐sita ĸa⌐
Did you ask the operator?	Ko⌐oka⌐ñsyu ni ki⌐kima⌐sita ka⌐
Did you see [it] or did you ask the operator?	Mi⌐ma⌐sita ka, ko⌐oka⌐ñsyu ni ki⌐kima⌐sita ka⌐
Did you look at the phone book or did you ask the operator?	De⌐ñwatyoo (o) mima⌐sita ka, ko⌐oka⌐ñsyu ni ki⌐kima⌐sita ka⌐

5.
Is it number 2?	Hu⌐ta⌐-bañ desu ka⌐
Is it number 22?	Hu⌐ta⌐zyuu hu⌐ta⌐-bañ desu ka⌐
Is it number 422?	Yo⌐ñhyaku hu⌐ta⌐zyuu hu⌐ta⌐-bañ desu ka⌐
Is it number 0422?	Re⌐e ⌐yo⌐ñhyaku hu⌐ta⌐zyuu hu⌐ta⌐-bañ desu ka⌐
Is it (number) 081-0422?	Re⌐e ha⌐tizyu⌐u i⌐ti⌐ no, re⌐e ⌐yo⌐ñhyaku hu⌐ta⌐zyuu hu⌐ta⌐-bañ desu ka⌐
Is this (i.e. the person I'm addressing) (number) 081-0422?	Sotira (wa) ⌐re⌐e ha⌐tizyu⌐u i⌐ti⌐ no, re⌐e ⌐yo⌐ñhyaku hu⌐ta⌐zyuu hu⌐ta⌐-bañ desu ka⌐

SUPPLEMENTARY CONVERSATIONS

1. Smith: Ki⌐mura-sañ no deñwaba⌐ñḡoo o si⌐tte ma⌐su ka⌐

   Tanaka: Tyo⌐tto ⌐ma⌐tte kudasai⌐ . . . Go⌐hyaku nana⌐zyuu i⌐ti⌐ no, sa⌐ñze⌐ñ ⌐yo⌐ñzyuu i⌐ti⌐-bañ desu yo⌐

   Smith: Ma⌐e wa so⌐no bañḡo⌐o desita ḡa, i⌐ma wa ⌐so⌐o zya a⌐rimase⌐ñ yo.

   Tanaka: A⌐a, so⌐o desu ka⌐ Zya⌐a, kinoo Ha⌐simoto-sañ ḡa Kimura-sañ ni deñwa-sima⌐sita kara, Ha⌐simoto-sañ wa sitte ru⌐ de-syoo.

   Smith: Zya⌐a, Ha⌐simoto-sañ ni kikimasyo⌐o. Do⌐o mo su⌐mimase⌐ñ.

   Tanaka: Iie.

2. Mr. Tanaka: Mo⌐simosi⌐

   Maid: Mo⌐simosi⌐

   Mr. Tanaka: Ya⌐mada-sañ no otaku de⌐su ka⌐

   Maid: Ha⌐a, sa⌐yoo de gozaima⌐su.

   Mr. Tanaka: Yu⌐kio-sañ ima⌐su ka⌐

   Maid: Bo⌐ttyañ wa ⌐i⌐ma ga⌐kkoo de gozaima⌐su ḡa, do⌐tira-sama de i⌐rassyaima⌐su ka⌐

Mr. Tanaka: Azabu[1] no Ta⌐naka de⌐su ḡa, na⌐ñ-zi-ḡo⌐ro ka⌐erima⌐su ka⌐

Maid: Kyo⌐o wa do⌐yo⌐o desu kara i⌐ti-zi-ḡo⌐ro o⌐kaeri ni narima⌐su ḡa, notihodo ko⌐tira kara ode⌐ñwa si⌐masyo⌐o ka.

Mr. Tanaka: Iie. Ma⌐ta a⌐to de ⌐bo⌐ku ḡa de⌐ñwa suru⌐ kara.

Maid: Sa⌐yoo de gozaima⌐su ka⌐

Mr. Tanaka: Zya⌐a, sayonara.

Maid: Go⌐meñ-kudasaima⌐se.

3. Smith: Tyo⌐tto de⌐ñwa (o) kaketa⌐i ñ desu ḡa⌐

Tanaka: Ko⌐no deñwa do⌐ozo.

Smith: A⌐ri⌐ḡatoo. De⌐ñwaba⌐ñḡoo si⌐rimase⌐ñ ḡa⌐

Tanaka: De⌐ñwatyoo arima⌐su yo⌐ Do⌐nata ni ka⌐keta⌐i ñ desu ka⌐

Smith: Ki⌐mura Yosio de⌐su.

Tanaka: Ki⌐mura Yosio de⌐su ka⌐ Tyo⌐tto ⌐ma⌐tte kudasai⌐ A⌐a, A⌐o⌐-yama[1] ro⌐ku-tyoome⌐ no Ki⌐mura-sañ de⌐su ka⌐

Smith: E⌐e, so⌐o desu.

Tanaka: Yo⌐ñhyaku ha⌐tizyu⌐u i⌐ti⌐ no, yo⌐ñse⌐ñ happyaku ⌐to⌐o-bañ de-su yo.

Smith: Tyo⌐tto ⌐ma⌐tte kudasai—ka⌐kima⌐su kara.

Tanaka: Do⌐ozo. E⌐ñpitu arima⌐su ka⌐

Smith: E⌐e, a⌐rima⌐su. Su⌐mimase⌐ñ ḡa, mo⌐o iti-do itte kudasaima-se⌐ñ ka⌐

Tanaka: Yo⌐ñhyaku ha⌐tizyu⌐u i⌐ti⌐ no, yo⌐ñse⌐ñ happyaku ⌐to⌐o-bañ de-su yo.

Smith: Do⌐o mo su⌐mimase⌐ñ desita.

Tanaka: Do⌐o itasimasite.

English Equivalents

1. Smith: Do you know Mr. Kimura's telephone number?

Tanaka: Just a minute. It's 571-3041.

Smith: It was that number before, but it isn't that now.

Tanaka: Oh? Well then, Mr. Hashimoto telephoned Mr. Kimura yesterday so Mr. Hashimoto probably knows.

Smith: Well then, I'll ask Mr. Hashimoto. Thanks very much.

Tanaka: Not at all.

2. Mr. Tanaka: Hello.

Maid: Hello.

Mr. Tanaka: Is this the Yamada residence?

Maid: Yes, it is.

Mr. Tanaka: Is Yukio there?

1
  A section of Tokyo.

Maid: He (lit. the young master) is [at] school now.   Who is calling, please?

Mr. Tanaka: This is Mr. Tanaka in Azabu.   About what time will he be home?

Maid: Today is Saturday so he'll be home about 1.   Do you want him to call you later? (Lit. Shall we call later from this side?)

Mr. Tanaka: No.   (Because) I'll call again later.

Maid: Oh.

Mr. Tanaka: Well, goodbye.

Maid: Goodbye.

3. Smith: I'd (just) like to make a telephone call. . . .

Tanaka: Here, [use] this telephone.

Smith: Thanks.   I don't know the telephone number. . . .

Tanaka: I have a telephone book.   Who is it you want to call?

Smith: It's Yoshio Kimura.

Tanaka: Yoshio Kimura?   Just a minute. . . .   Oh, is it Mr. Kimura in Aoyama 6-chome?

Smith: Yes, that's right.

Tanaka: It's 481-4810.

Smith: Just a minute—because I'm going to write it [down].

Tanaka: Certainly.   Do you have a pencil?

Smith: Yes, I have.   I'm sorry but would you say it again?

Tanaka: It's 481-4810.

Smith: Thanks very much.

Tanaka: You're welcome.

EXERCISES

1.   Read the following telephone numbers aloud in Japanese:

   a.   371-3923   f.   251-0360
   b.   481-1333   g.   622-2011
   c.   047-3092   h.   996-0520
   d.   891-1510   i.   291-5272, extension 607
   e.   611-6161   j.   631-0044, extension 941

2.   Mr. Tanaka has just telephoned and asked for Mr. Yamamoto.   Give the following answers, practicing different levels, if appropriate:

   a.   Just a moment, please.
   b.   Mr. Yamamoto isn't at his desk just now. . . .
   c.   Mr. Yamamoto is busy just now.   Would you like him to call later? (Lit. Shall we call later from this side?)
   d.   Mr. Yamamoto is in Osaka.   He'll be back tomorrow.
   e.   Who is calling, please?
   f.   Mr. Yamamoto is in Mr. Sato's office just now.   It's extension 243.
   g.   Mr. Yamamoto is away from home just now.   He'll be back on the first of the month. (Mrs. Yamamoto speaking)

    h. Mr. Yamamoto is at the office. He'll be back at about 6:00. (Mrs. Yamamoto speaking)

    i. Mr. Yamamoto will be away from home until Saturday. (Maid speaking)

    j. Do you mean Yosio Yamamoto, or Yukio Yamamoto?

3. Practice the Basic Dialogues with appropriate variations.

Lesson 13. Telephoning (cont.)

BASIC DIALOGUES: FOR MEMORIZATION

(a)

Sakamoto

1. Hello. Is Mr. Smith there? — Mo⌉simosi_ Su⌉misu - sañ i⌈ras-syaima⌉su ka⌣

Secretary

set out or go out — dekakeru /-ru/

2. No. He stepped out for a minute. . . . — Iie, tyo⌉tto de⌈kakema⌉sita ĝa_

Sakamoto

message or the giving of a message — kotozuke or okotozuke+

make or do — itasu↓ /-u/

request — ne⌈ĝa⌉u↓/-u/ or o⌈neĝai-itasima⌉su↓

3. Well then, I'd like to leave a message for Mr. Smith. — Zya⌉a, Su⌉misu - sañ ni o⌈kotozuke (o) oneĝai-itasima⌉su.

Secretary

4. Certainly. — Do⌉ozo.

Sakamoto

university — daiĝaku

Tokyo University — To⌈okyoo-da⌉iĝaku or Toodai

5. This is [Mr.] Sakamoto at Tokyo University. . . . — Kotira (wa) Tōodai no Sa⌈kamoto de gozaima⌉su ĝa_

Secretary

6. Yes. — Ha⌉a.

Sakamoto

this evening or tonight — ko⌉ñbañ

say — o⌈ssya⌉ru↑ /-aru/

say that or say [it] that way — so⌈o ossya⌉ru

7. Please tell him that I will be waiting in front of the Maru-biru at 7 o'clock this evening. (Lit. I'll be waiting in front of the Maru-biru at 7 o'clock this evening so please say [it] that way.) — Ko⌉ñbañ si⌈ti⌉ - zi ni Ma⌈ru-biru no ma⌉e de ⌈ma⌉tte orimasu kara, so⌈o ossya⌉tte kudasai.

Secretary

report <u>or</u> communicate <u>or</u> convey a message	tutaeru /-ru/ <u>or</u> o⌐tutae-itasima⌐su ‡

8. I understand. I'll give him your message.

Wa⌐karima⌐sita. O⌐tutae-itasima⌐-su.

(b)

Tanaka

9. Hello.

Mo⌐simosi.

Yamamoto

10. Hello. . . . Hello.

Mo⌐simosi_ . . . Mo⌐simosi.

Tanaka (in a louder voice)

is far	tooi /-ku/
have trouble hearing (on the phone)	deñwa ḡa tooi
voice	ko⌐e
with a loud voice	o⌐oki⌐i ⌐ko⌐e de <u>or</u> o⌐oki na ⌐ko⌐e de
speak <u>or</u> talk	ha⌐na⌐su /-u/

11. Hello. Say, I can't hear so please talk in a little louder voice.

Mo⌐simosi⌐ Tyo⌐tto, deñwa ga to-⌐oi⌐ desu kara ne? Mo⌐o suko⌐si ⌐o⌐o-ki na ⌐ko⌐e de ha⌐na⌐site kudasai.

Yamamoto (still louder)

be audible <u>or</u> can hear	kikoeru /-ru/

12. Hello. Hello. Can you hear [me]?

Mo⌐simosi_ Mo⌐simosi_ Ki⌐koe-ma⌐su ka⌐

Tanaka (shouting)

cut <u>or</u> cut off <u>or</u> hang up (the telephone)	ki⌐ru /-u/

13. It's no good so I'll hang up now and call again later.

Da⌐me⌐ desu kara ne? I⌐ma ⌐ki⌐tte ne? Ma⌐ta a⌐to de de⌐ñwa-sima⌐su yo.

(c)

Smith

know	go⌐zo⌐ñzi desu ‡

14. Do you know Mr. Ito's telephone [number]?

Itoo-sañ no deñwa (o) go⌐zo⌐ñzi desu ka⌐

Tanaka

don't know	zo⌐ñzimase⌐ñ ‡

15. No, I don't know [it]. . . .

Iie, zo⌐ñzimase⌐ñ ḡa_

Yoshida

know	zo⌐ñzite orimasu ‡

name card <u>or</u> calling
card
                     meesi

16. I know—because I have Mr.
Ito's card.
       Wa⌐takusi wa zo⌐ñzite o r i m a s u _
I⌐too-sañ no meesi ḡa gozaima⌐su
kara.

Smith

read
                   yo⌐mu /-u/
17. Would you read it for me?
       Yo⌐ñde ku⌐dasaimase⌐ñ ka↲

slowly
               yu⌐kku⌐ri
18. I'm going to write it [down]
so [read it] slowly, please.
       Ka⌐kima⌐su kara yu⌐kku⌐ri oneḡai-
simasu.

(d)

Secretary

make <u>or</u> do
                na⌐sa⌐ru ↑ /-aru/
make a telephone call
                o⌐de⌐ñwa-nasaru ↑
19. Did you telephone the school?
       Gakkoo $\left|\begin{array}{c} ni \\ e \end{array}\right|$ o⌐de⌐ñwa-nasaimasita
ka↲

Smith

talking <u>or</u> a talk <u>or</u>
a story
                hanasi <u>or</u>
ohanasi ↑
in the middle of talking
                hanasi-tyuu <u>or</u>
ohanasi-tyuu ↑
nobody
                dare mo /+ negative/
answer (the telephone)
                de⌐ru /-ru/
20. Five minutes ago the line was
busy but now no one answers. . . .
       Go - ⌐huñ ma⌐e ni wa ha⌐nasi-tyuu
de⌐sita ḡa, i⌐ma wa da⌐re mo demase⌐ñ ḡa_

Secretary

strange
                he⌐ñ /na/
21. Isn't that strange!
       He⌐ñ desu ⌐ne⌐e.

(e)

Tanaka

22. Hello. Is this Tokyo University?
       Mo⌐simosi_ To⌐odai de⌐su ka↲

Stranger

23. Wrong number.
       Ti⌐ḡaima⌐su.

Tanaka

24. Oh, I'm sorry. (Lit. I
committed a rudeness.)
       A. Si⌐tu⌐ree-simasita.

(f)

Husband

out of order	kosyoo
25. This telephone is out of order.	Kono deñwa kōsyoo da yo⌐

Wife (testing phone)

do what? or act how?	do⌐o suru
26. It is, isn't it. What are you going to do?	Hoñtoo ⌐ne⌐e. Do⌐o suru?

Husband

borrow or rent	kariru /-ru/
say to the operator or tell the operator	ko⌐oka⌐ñsyu ni iu
27. I'm going to borrow the telephone next door and tell the operator.	Tonari no deñwa karite, ko⌐oka⌐ñsyu ni i⌐u⌐ yo.

(On the telephone)

say! or hey there!	ano ne
fix or repair	na⌐o⌐su /-u/
28. Say! 401-5602 is out of order so please fix it.	Ano ne? Yo⌐ñhyaku i⌐ti⌐ no ne? Go-⌐se⌐ñ rŏppyaku ⌐ni⌐-bañ wa ne? Ko-⌐syoo da⌐ kara ne? Na⌐o⌐site kudasai.

(g)

Mr. Tanaka

(Mr.) Sato	Sa⌐too-kuñ
is busy	i⌐sog̃asi⌐i /-ku/ or o⌐isog̃asi⌐i † /-ku/
29. Sato, are you busy?	Sa⌐too-kuñ, i⌐sog̃asi⌐i?

Mr. Sato

30. No, not especially.	Iie, betu ni⌐ [1]

Mr. Tanaka

call or summon	yobu /-u/

---

[1] Regularly followed by the negative in longer sentences.

31. Call Okada—because he has   Okada-kuñ yoñde— de⌐ñwa da⌐ kara.
    (lit. it is) a phone call.

                              Mr. Sato

32. Where is Okada now?   Okada-kuñ ⌐i⌐ma ⌐do⌐ko?

                             Mr. Tanaka

    room   he⌐ya⌐ or
                                        oheya ↑
33. He's in the next room.   To⌐nari no heya⌐ ni iru yo⌐」

NOTES ON THE BASIC DIALOGUES

Dialogue (a): Sakamoto uses polite speech in talking to Smith's secretary
as a sign of respect for Smith.

2. 'He stepped out but— is there anything I can do?'

Dekakeru means 'go out' or 'set out' or 'start out,' whereas de⌐ru means
'go out' or 'leave' or 'emerge.'

3. Itasu is the polite humble (↓) equivalent of suru, both as an independent
word and as part of compounds like beñkyoo - suru (humble, beñkyoo-
itasu).

7. O⌐ssya⌐ru is the polite honorific equivalent of iu, used as an exalting
form in reference to people other than the speaker, in polite speech. It
belongs to the same subclass of verbals as i⌐rassya⌐ru, ku⌐dasa⌐ru, and
go⌐za⌐ru: its stem is o⌐ssya⌐i and its -ma⌐su form o⌐ssyaima⌐su.

11. The opposite of o⌐oki⌐i (or o⌐oki na) ⌐ko⌐e is ti⌐isa⌐i (or ti⌐isa na) ⌐ko⌐e
'low voice.'

Remember that verbals ending in -su in their citation form have gerunds
ending in -site.

12. Kikoeru is another verbal which does not occur with particle o. Both the
thing which is audible and the person who can hear are followed by particle
wa or ḡa.

13. Ki⌐ru, like iru 'be necessary,' is a verbal ending in -iru but belonging to
the -u class of verbals: stem, ki⌐ri; -ma⌐su form, ki⌐rima⌐su; gerund,
ki⌐tte.

14, 15, 16. The verbal zo⌐ñzi⌐ru ↓ (-ru) 'come to know' is not included in the
lists of this book. It will occur only in the following forms:

   zo⌐ñzite (i)masu and zo⌐ñzite orimasu 'I know (humble equivalents of
   si⌐tte (i)ma⌐su and si⌐tte orima⌐su)

   zo⌐ñzimase⌐ñ 'I don't know' (humble equivalent of si⌐rimase⌐ñ)

   go⌐zo⌐ñzi desu (desita, desyoo, etc.) '[you] know (knew, probably know,
   etc.)' (honorific equivalent of si⌐tte [i]ma⌐su [(i)ma⌐sita, etc.])

15. 'No, I don't know it but— is there anything I can do?'

16. Meesi are used in Japan in professional circles to a much greater extent than calling cards are used in America. They are regularly exchanged by new acquaintances. They usually include name, title, business affiliation, address, and telephone number.

17. Verbals ending in -mu in their citation form have gerunds ending in -ñde.

18. Yu⌜kku⌝ri means 'slowly,' 'without hurrying,' 'in a relaxed way.' Unlike the adjectival osoi, it has no connotation of lateness.

19. Na⌜sa⌝ru is the polite honorific equivalent of suru, both as an independent word and as part of compounds like beñkyoo-suru (honorific, be⌜ñkyoo-na-sa⌝ru). Compare:

	'Did you study?'	'Yes, I studied.'
Plain:	Be⌜ñkyoo-sima⌝sita ka⌣	E⌝e, be⌜ñkyoo-sima⌝sita.
Polite:	Be⌜ñkyoo-nasaima⌝sita ka⌣	Ha⌝a, be⌜ñkyoo-itasima⌝sita.

Na⌜sa⌝ru, like o⌜ssya⌝ru above (sentence 7), belongs to the same subclass of verbals as i⌜rassya⌝ru, ku⌜dasa⌝ru, and go⌜za⌝ru: its stem is na⌜sa⌝i and its gerund na⌜sa⌝tte (alternant: na⌜su⌝tte). These five verbals are the only members of the -aru subclass.

20. 'Now no one answers but—I wonder why.' The two wa's in this sentence are wa of comparison.

25. Note also: kosyoo-suru 'break down.'

28. Ano ne is a less polite equivalent of tyo⌝tto 'say there!' It does not ordinarily occur in polite conversation, but is used most commonly in addressing close friends and inferiors. It is usually wise to avoid it when speaking to strangers whose position is not known.

29. -Kuñ, like -sañ, is added to the family or given names of persons other than the speaker. However, it is a man's word, and is usually used by men in reference to men. It is an informal word and implies familiarity. It may be compared to the English use of a last name without 'Mr.' as a term of address.

30. When betu ni occurs alone, it implies an appropriate negative. Here, it means betu ni i⌜soga⌝siku a⊢rimase⌝ñ 'I'm not especially busy.'

31. Verbals ending in -bu in their citation form have gerunds ending in -ñde. Note the difference in accent between yo⌝ñde 'reading' and yoñde 'calling.'

GRAMMATICAL NOTES

1. ne? and the Explicit Style

Ne? occurs at the end of sentences and means 'are you following me?' or 'do you understand me?' or 'do you agree with me?' It must not be confused with confirming or exclamatory ne⌝e. Ne? is an actual question, inviting agreement or acknowledgment. Compare:

Ta⌐ka⌐i desu ⌐ne⌐e. 'Isn't it expensive!' 'It's expensive, isn't it.'
Ta⌐ka⌐i desu ne? 'It's expensive, don't you think so?'

The latter is similar to: Ta⌐ka⌐i desyoo?

When speaking explicitly, or when speaking in a situation where there is some question of the comprehension of the listener (for example, when talking on the telephone, or when giving complicated instructions or explanations, or when talking to an inferior, etc.), it is common to break up a long sentence into a series of shorter sentences ending in ne? The shorter the sentences, the more explicit they are. The listener usually replies to each of these sentences with ha⌐i, e⌐e, ha⌐a, so⌐o, etc.—or with a nod—indicating that he is following the conversation.

However, the frequent occurrence of ne in ordinary, non-explicit conversation is usually a sign of informality and familiarity; to use it appropriately and naturally is very difficult for a foreigner. Beginning students of Japanese should use it sparingly except in the situations described above.

Compare:

Ordinary style:

Asita tyo⌐odo ku⌐-zi ni ko⌐ko e kite⌐ kudasai.
'Please come here tomorrow at 9 sharp.'

Explicit style:

Asita ne? 'Tomorrow—understand?'
Ha⌐i. 'Yes.'
Tyo⌐odo ku⌐-zi ni ne? 'At 9 sharp—understand?'
Ha⌐i. 'Yes.'
Ko⌐ko e kite⌐ kudasai. 'Come here.'
Ha⌐i. Ka⌐sikomarima⌐sita. 'Yes. Certainly.'

Compare also sentences 11, 13, and 28 in the Basic Dialogues.

2. More About Informal Speech

In informal speech, informal inflected forms occur in sentence-final position and before sentence particles as well as within longer sentences. The following are a few of the common patterns:

(a) Informal verbals and adjectivals occur in sentence-final position in statements and questions, in the speech of men and women. [1]

---

[1] But informal honorific verbals in this position are typical of women's speech. Example: I⌐rassya⌐ru? 'Are you going (or coming)?' or 'Will you be here?'

	Formal	Informal
'It's clear.'	Wa⌐karima⌐su.	Wa⌐ka⌐ru.
'Is it clear?'	Wa⌐karima⌐su ka‿	Wa⌐ka⌐ru?
'It's expensive.'	Ta⌐ka⌐i desu.	Ta⌐ka⌐i.
'Is it expensive?'	Ta⌐ka⌐i desu ka‿	Ta⌐ka⌐i?

(b) Both men and women use nominals in sentence-final position in statements and questions as the informal equivalents of nominal + de⌐su or de⌐su ka (cf. Lesson 8, Grammatical Note 3); but the occurrence of a nominal + informal da in statement-final position is typical only of men's speech.

	Formal	Informal	
		Men	Women
'It's true.'	Hõntoo de⌐su.	Hõntoo.	Hõntoo.
		or	
		Hõntoo da.	
'Is it true?'	Hõntoo de⌐su ka‿	Hõntoo?	Hõntoo?

(c) Informal verbals and adjectivals occur before sentence particle yo and before ne⌐[e] predominantly in informal men's speech.

	Formal	Informal— Men
'It is clear (I tell you).'	Wa⌐karima⌐su yo‿	Wa⌐ka⌐ru yo‿
'It is expensive (I tell you).'	Ta⌐ka⌐i desu yo‿	Ta⌐ka⌐i yo‿
'It's clear, isn't it?'	Wa⌐karima⌐su ne?	Wa⌐ka⌐ru ne?
'It's expensive, isn't it!'	Ta⌐ka⌐i desu ⌐ne⌐e.	Ta⌐ka⌐i ⌐ne⌐e.

(d) As the informal equivalent of a nominal + de⌐su + yo or ne⌐[e], men regularly use nominal + da + yo or ne⌐[e], while women use nominal + yo or ne⌐[e].

	Formal	Informal	
		Men	Women
'It is true (I tell you).'	Hõntoo de⌐su yo‿	Hõntoo da yo‿	Hõntoo yo‿
'It's true, isn't it!'	Hõntoo de⌐su ⌐ne⌐e.	Hõntoo da ⌐ne⌐e.	Hõntoo ⌐ne⌐e.

Basic Dialogues (f) and (g) in this lesson are informal. Sentences 25, 27, and 33 are typical of men's informal speech, and Hõntoo ⌐ne⌐e. in 26 is typical of women's informal speech. The remaining sentences of these two dialogues occur in the speech of both men and women, except that -kuñ of sentences 29, 31, and 32 would ordinarily be replaced by -sañ in women's speech.

3. Gerunds As Informal Requests

The gerund of a verbal may occur in sentence-final position, or pre-final before a particle, as an informal request. It is normally used in addressing an equal who is well known to the speaker, or an inferior.

Examples:

So⌈re o mi⌉sete. 'Show me that.'
Tyo⌉tto ⊢ma⊣tte yo. 'Wait a minute!'
Yu⌈kku⌉ri ha⊢na⊣site ne? 'Speak slowly, would you?'

The gerund of an honorific is also often used in this way by women, in informal but polite requests.

Examples:

Ko⌈tti⌉ e i⊢ra⊣site. 'Come here.'
Tyo⌉tto o⊢mati ni na⊣tte. 'Wait a minute.'
Yu⌈kku⌉ri o⊢hanasi ni na⊣tte ne? 'Speak slowly, would you?'

4. Verbals: Humble Equivalents in √-suru and √-itasu

A compound verbal consisting of the polite prefix o- + a verbal stem + √suru (or its humble equivalent √itasu) is a humble equivalent of the verbal, used in reference to oneself, members of one's own family, etc. The form with √itasu is more humble than the corresponding form with √suru. Study the following chart:

Plain (Citation Form)	Polite (Citation Form)	
	Humble ↓	Honorific ↑
yobu 'call'	oyobi-suru or oyobi-itasu	o⌈yobi ni na⌉ru
ha⌈na⌉su 'speak'	ohanasi-suru or ohanasi-itasu	o⌈hanasi ni na⌉ru
tutaeru 'report'	otutae-suru or otutae-itasu	o⌈tutae ni na⌉ru

A corresponding humble form does NOT exist for all verbals. Some verbals have only special humble equivalents with unrelated roots (for example, iku and ku⌉ru have the humble equivalent ma⌉iru; iru has o⌉ru; etc.), and some have no commonly occurring humble equivalents.

In general, honorific (↑) verbals are more common than humble (↓) verbals.

Humbling oneself represents a greater degree of politeness in Japanese than exalting others. Accordingly, it is not unusual to use a plain verbal in reply to an honorific question (cf. Lesson 9, Grammatical Note 2):

> Oʳyobi ni narimaˈsita ka﹍ 'Did you call?'
> Eˈe, yoʳbimaˈsita. 'Yes, I did (call).'

The use of oʳyobi-simaˈsita (or oʳyobi-itasimaˈsita) in the above reply would be an indication of considerable deference.

However, some humble polite verbals are extremely common. Oʳneḡai-simaˈsu and oʳneḡai-itasimaˈsu are humble polite equivalents of neʳḡaimaˈsu (informal, neʳḡaˈu[1]). In this case, the humble polite forms probably occur more commonly than the plain form.

Another commonly occurring example of a polite humble verbal is oʳmatase-itasimaˈsita, based on the plain verbal maˈtaseˈru /-ru/ 'make [someone] wait.'

5. oʳokiˈi ～ oˈoki na

A few adjectivals—for example, oʳokiˈi and tiʳisaˈi—have a derived nominal which is a na-nominal (see Lesson 12, Grammatical Note 4). It is formed by dropping the final -i of the adjectival and moving the accent toward the beginning of the word (oʳokiˈi ～ oˈoki, tiʳisaˈi ～ tiˈisa). These nominals are used in combination with na to describe a following nominal: oˈoki na ˻hoˈn̄ 'big book,' tiˈisa na zibiki 'small dictionary,' etc.

Thus, oʳokiˈi MODIFYING A FOLLOWING NOMINAL is interchangeable with oˈoki na, and tiʳisaˈi with tiˈisa na.

DRILLS

A. Substitution Drill

1.	Who is reading [it]?	Daˈre ḡa ˻yoˉnde (i)masu ka﹍
2.	Who is calling?	Daˈre ḡa yoˈnde (i)maˉsu ka﹍
3.	Who is fixing [it]?	Daˈre ḡa naˈoˉsite (i)masu ka﹍
4.	Who is speaking?	Daˈre ḡa haˈnaˉsite (i)masu ka﹍
5.	Who is saying [it]?	Daˈre ḡa iˈtte (i)maˉsu ka﹍
6.	Who is renting (or borrowing) [it]?	Daˈre ḡa kaˈrite (i)maˉsu ka﹍
7.	Who is listening (or asking)?	Daˈre ḡa kiˈite (i)maˉsu ka﹍

---

[1] This verbal, in all its forms, is usually used only in reference to the speaker.

8.	Who is cutting [it]?	Da⌐re g̈a ⌐ki⌐tte (i)masu ka⌐
9.	Who is looking at [it]?	Da⌐re g̈a ⌐mi⌐te (i)masu ka⌐
10.	Who is waiting?	Da⌐re g̈a ⌐ma⌐tte (i)masu ka⌐

B. Substitution Drill

1.	Whom are you calling?	Da⌐re o yo⌐ñde (i)ma⌐su ka⌐
2.	Whom are you waiting for?	Da⌐re o ⌐ma⌐tte (i)masu ka⌐ [1]
3.	Whom are you looking at?	Da⌐re o ⌐mi⌐te (i)masu ka⌐
4.	What are you looking at?	Na⌐ni o ⌐mi⌐te (i)masu ka⌐
5.	What are you reading?	Na⌐ni o ⌐yo⌐ñde (i)masu ka⌐
6.	What are you fixing?	Na⌐ni o na⌐o⌐site (i)masu ka⌐
7.	What are you saying?	Na⌐ni o i⌐tte (i)ma⌐su ka⌐
8.	What are you listening to?	Na⌐ni o ki⌐ite (i)ma⌐su ka⌐
9.	What are you cutting?	Na⌐ni o ⌐ki⌐tte (i)masu ka⌐
10.	What are you writing?	Na⌐ni o ⌐ka⌐ite (i)masu ka⌐

C. Substitution Drill

1.	I'm going to read this paper this morning.	Ke⌐sa ko⌐no siñbuñ (o) yomima⌐su.
2.	I'm reading this paper this morning.	Ke⌐sa ko⌐no siñbuñ (o) yo⌐ñde (i)ma-su.
3.	I was reading this paper this morning.	Ke⌐sa ko⌐no siñbuñ (o) yo⌐ñde (i)ma-sita.
4.	I read this paper this morning.	Ke⌐sa ko⌐no siñbuñ (o) yomima⌐sita.
5.	Let's read this paper this morning.	Ke⌐sa ko⌐no siñbuñ (o) yomimasyo⌐o.
6.	He's probably going to read this paper this morning.	Ke⌐sa ko⌐no siñbuñ (o) yo⌐mu desyoo.
7.	He's probably reading this paper this morning.	Ke⌐sa ko⌐no siñbuñ (o) yo⌐ñde (i)⌐ru desyo⌐o.
8.	Do you suppose he's reading this paper this morning?	Ke⌐sa ko⌐no siñbuñ (o) yo⌐ñde (i)⌐ru desyo⌐o ka.
9.	Shall we (or I) read this paper this morning?	Ke⌐sa ko⌐no siñbuñ (o) yomimasyo⌐o ka.
10.	Please read this paper this morning.	Ke⌐sa ko⌐no siñbuñ (o) yo⌐ñde kuda-sai.

---

[1] Note: X o ⌐ma⌐tu 'wait for X,' 'await X.'

D. Substitution Drill

1. I'm not especially busy.
2. I don't especially want to go.
3. It doesn't especially matter.
4. I'm not in any special hurry.
5. It isn't especially strange.
6. It isn't especially far.
7. It isn't especially difficult.
8. It isn't especially rude.

Betu ni i⌐soḡa⌐siku a⌐rimase⌐n.
Betu ni i⌐kitaku arimase⌐n.

Betu ni ka⌐maimase⌐n.

Betu ni i⌐soḡimase⌐n.

Betu ni ⌐he⌐n zya a⌐rimase⌐n.
Betu ni to⌐oku arimase⌐n.
Betu ni mu⌐zukasiku arimase⌐n.
Betu ni si⌐tu⌐ree zya a⌐rimase⌐n.

E. Substitution Drill

1. Nobody answers.
2. Nobody knows. or I don't know anybody.
3. Nobody understands.
4. Nobody can.
5. Nobody is here.
6. Nobody wants to do [it].
7. Nobody is busy.
8. Nobody is sick.
9. Nobody is out (of the house).
10. Nobody has free time.

Da⌐re mo demase⌐n.
Da⌐re mo sirimase⌐n.

Da⌐re mo wakarimase⌐n.
Da⌐re mo dekimase⌐n.
Da⌐re mo imase⌐n.
Da⌐re mo sitaku arimase⌐n.
Da⌐re mo isoḡa⌐siku a⌐rimase⌐n.
Da⌐re mo byooki zya arimase⌐n.
Da⌐re mo ru⌐su zya a⌐rimase⌐n.

Da⌐re mo hima ḡa arimase⌐n.

F. Substitution Drill

1. I know—because I have Mr. Ito's card.

2. I know—because I read the paper.
3. I know—because I looked at the phone book.
4. I know—because I heard [it] from a friend.
5. I know—because I studied hard.
6. I know—because I asked a policeman.
7. I know—because I go there a good deal.

8. I know—because I telephone him every day.

Wa⌐takusi wa zo⌐nzite orimasu—I⌐too-san no meesi (ḡa) gozaima⌐su kara.
Wa⌐takusi wa zo⌐nzite orimasu—si⌐nbun (o) yomima⌐sita kara.
Wa⌐takusi wa zo⌐nzite orimasu—de⌐nwatyoo (o) mima⌐sita kara.
Wa⌐takusi wa zo⌐nzite orimasu—to⌐modati kara kikima⌐sita kara.
Wa⌐takusi wa zo⌐nzite orimasu—⌐yo⌐ku be⌐nkyoo-sima⌐sita kara.
Wa⌐takusi wa zo⌐nzite orimasu—zyu⌐nsa ni kikima⌐sita kara.
Wa⌐takusi wa zo⌐nzite orimasu—⌐yo⌐ku a⌐soko e mairima⌐su kara.
Wa⌐takusi wa zo⌐nzite orimasu—a⌐no⌐ hito ni ⌐ma⌐initi de⌐nwa (o) kakema⌐su kara.

9. I know—because I come
   (or go) by car.

Wa⌐takusi wa zo⌐ñzite orimasu—<u>ku-</u>
⌐ruma de mairima⌐su kara.

10. I know—because I was able
    to hear well.

Wa⌐takusi wa zo⌐ñzite orimasu—
⌐yo⌐ku ki⌐koema⌐sita kara.

G. Substitution Drill

1. Call Mr. Okada—because
   he has a phone call.

Okada-kuñ (o) yoñde—de⌐ñwa da⌐
kara.

2. Call Mr. Okada—because
   this won't do.

Okada-kuñ (o) yoñde—ko⌐ma⌐ru
kara.

3. Call Mr. Okada—because
   I want to see [him].

Okada-kuñ (o) yoñde—a⌐ita⌐i kara.

4. Call Mr. Okada—because
   I'm in a hurry.

Okada-kuñ (o) yoñde—i⌐so⌐g̅u kara.

5. Call Mr. Okada—because
   I want to talk [to him].

Okada-kuñ (o) yoñde—ha⌐nasita⌐i
kara.

6. Call Mr. Okada—because
   it's out of order.

Okada-kuñ (o) yoñde—ko⌐syoo da⌐
kara.

7. Call Mr. Okada—because
   I'm going out for a minute.

Okada-kuñ (o) yoñde— tyo⌐tto de-
⌐kakeru⌐ kara.

8. Call Mr. Okada—because
   it's no good.

Okada-kuñ (o) yoñde—da⌐me⌐ da
kara.

H. Substitution Drill

1. Please tell him that I'll be
   waiting in front of the Maru-biru. [1]

Ma⌐ru-biru no ma⌐e de ⌐ma⌐tte (i)ru
kara, so⌐o itte kudasa⌐i.

2. Please tell him that I want
   to talk [to him] at (lit.
   from) about 3:30.

<u>Sa⌐ñ-zi-hañ-g̅o⌐ro kara ha⌐nasita⌐i</u> ka-
ra, so⌐o itte kudasa⌐i.

3. Please tell him that I want
   to go home early today.

<u>Kyo⌐o ⌐ha⌐yaku ka⌐erita⌐i</u> kara, so⌐o
itte kudasa⌐i.

4. Please tell him that I'll telephone again later.

<u>Ma⌐ta a⌐to de de⌐ñwa-suru⌐</u> kara,
so⌐o itte kudasa⌐i.

5. Please tell him that I'm going to the office by bus today.

<u>Kyo⌐o ka̅isya e ⌐ba⌐su de i⌐ku⌐</u> kara,
so⌐o itte kudasa⌐i.

6. Please tell him that I'll be
   studying at home tonight.

<u>Ko⌐ñbañ u⌐ti de beñkyoo-site (i)ru⌐</u> ka-
ra, so⌐o itte kudasa⌐i.

7. Please tell him that our
   car is out of order.

<u>Uti no kuruma (wa) ko⌐syoo da⌐</u> kara,
so⌐o itte kudasa⌐i.

---

[1] Lit. 'I'll be waiting in front of the Maru-biru so please say [it] that way.'

8. Please tell him that I'll   A⌐sita⌐ made i⌐soḡasi⌐i kara, so⌐o it-
    be busy through tomorrow.   te kudasa⌐i.

9. Please tell him that school   Ga⌐kkoo (wa) yo⌐-zi made da kara,
    lasts (lit. is) until 4.   so⌐o itte kudasa⌐i.

10. Please tell him that Mr. Ta-   Ta⌐naka-sañ (wa) koñḡetu yasumi⌐ da
    naka is on vacation this   kara, so⌐o itte kudasa⌐i.
    month.

I.   Response Drill

1. To⌐oi⌐ desu ka   Iie, to⌐oku arimase⌐ñ.
2. He⌐ñ desu ka   Iie, he⌐ñ zya a⌐rimase⌐ñ.
3. I⌐soḡasi⌐i desu ka   Iie, i⌐soḡa⌐siku a⌐rimase⌐ñ.
4. A⌐na⌐ta (wa) ko̅re (o) go⌐zo̅-   Iie, zo⌐ñzimase⌐ñ.
    ñzi desu ka
5. A⌐no ka⌐ta (wa) ko̅re (o) go-   Iie, go⌐zo⌐ñzi zya a⌐rimase⌐ñ. [1]
    ⌐zo⌐ñzi desu ka
6. Ko⌐syoo de⌐su ka   Iie, ko⌐syoo zya arimase⌐ñ.

J.   Level Drill [2]

1. Yu⌐kku⌐ri neḡaimasu.   Yu⌐kku⌐ri oneḡai- { simasu.
                                                      { itasimasu.

2. Yo⌐bimasyo⌐o ka.   O⌐yobi- { simasyo⌐o } ka.
                                          { itasimasyo⌐o }

3. Si⌐rimase⌐ñ.   Zo⌐ñzimase⌐ñ.
4. Ke⌐sa da⌐iḡaku e ikima⌐sita. Ke⌐sa da⌐iḡaku e mairima⌐sita.
5. Si⌐tu⌐ree-simasita.   Si⌐tu⌐ree-itasimasita.
6. Ta⌐naka-sañ ni aima⌐sita.   Ta⌐naka-sañ ni ome ni kakarima⌐si-
                                   ta.

7. O⌐de⌐ñwa si⌐masyo⌐o ka.   O⌐de⌐ñwa i⌐tasimasyo⌐o ka.

8. So⌐o tutaema⌐su.   So⌐o otutae- { sima⌐su.
                                               { itasima⌐su.

K.   Level Drill [3]

1. Kosyoo da ne?   (M)   Ko⌐syoo de⌐su ne?

---

[1] Compare the preceding humble answer (referring to the speaker) with this honorific answer (referring to someone else).

[2] In each case, sentences on the right are humble equivalents of the sentences on the left.

[3] Based on Grammatical Note 2.   In each case, the sentence on the right is a formal equivalent of the sentence on the left. Informal sentences marked (M) occur predominantly in men's speech and those marked (W) predominantly in women's speech.

2. I⌐soḡasi⌐i?   I⌐soḡasi⌐i desu ka⌐

3. He⌐ñ ⌐ne⌐e.   (W)   He⌐ñ desu ⌐ne⌐e.

4. I⌐ma ⌐tyo⌐tto dekakeru   (M)   I⌐ma ⌐tyo⌐tto de⌐kakema⌐su yo⌐
   yo⌐

5. Kikoeru?   Ki⌐koema⌐su ka⌐

6. Wa⌐ru⌐i yo⌐   (M)   Wa⌐ru⌐i desu yo⌐

7. Do⌐re (o) ⌐yo⌐mu?   Do⌐re (o) yo⌐mima⌐su ka⌐

8. So⌐o yo⌐   (W)   So⌐o desu yo⌐

9. Na⌐ñ de ⌐ki⌐ru?   Na⌐ñ de ki⌐rima⌐su ka⌐

10. Zu⌐ibuñ tooi yo⌐   (M)   Zu⌐ibuñ to⌐oi⌐ desu yo⌐

L. Expansion Drill

1. Telephone. [1]   Deñwa-site.
    YOU telephone.   A⌐na⌐ta ḡa deñwa-site.
    [I] am busy so YOU tele-   I⌐soḡasi⌐i kara, a⌐na⌐ta ḡa deñwa-si-
    phone.   te.
    [I] am very busy so YOU   To⌐ttemo isoḡasi⌐i kara, a⌐na⌐ta ḡa
    telephone.   deñwa-site.
    I am very busy so YOU   Bo⌐ku wa to⌐ttemo isoḡasi⌐i kara,
    telephone.   a⌐na⌐ta ḡa deñwa site.

2. Would you speak?   Ha⌐na⌐site ku⌐dasaimase⌐ñ ka⌐
    Would you speak in a loud   O⌐oki na ⌐ko⌐e de ha⌐na⌐site ku⌐da-
    voice?   saimase⌐ñ ka⌐
    Would you speak in a louder   Mo⌐tto ⌐o⌐oki na ⌐ko⌐e de ha⌐na⌐site
    voice?   ku⌐dasaimase⌐ñ ka⌐
    I can't hear so would you   Ki⌐koemase⌐ñ kara, mo⌐tto ⌐o⌐oki na
    speak in a louder voice?   ⌐ko⌐e de ha⌐na⌐site ku⌐dasaima-
                                              se⌐ñ ka⌐
    I can't hear very well so   Yo⌐ku ki⌐koemase⌐ñ kara, mo⌐tto
    would you speak in a   ⌐o⌐oki na ⌐ko⌐e de ha⌐na⌐site ku-
    louder voice?   ⌐dasaimase⌐ñ ka⌐

3. It's all right (I tell you).   Da⌐izyo⌐obu desu yo⌐
    Now it's all right (I tell   I⌐ma wa da⌐izyo⌐obu desu yo⌐
    you).
    It was out of order but   Ko⌐syoo de⌐sita ḡa, i⌐ma wa da⌐i-
    now it's all right (I   zyo⌐obu desu yo⌐
    tell you).
    Yesterday it was out of   Ki⌐no⌐o wa ko⌐syoo de⌐sita ḡa, i⌐ma
    order but now it's all   wa da⌐izyo⌐obu desu yo⌐
    right (I tell you).

---

[1] This English sentence and its Japanese equivalent are equally abrupt.

4. It can't be heard, can it!

Ki⌐koemase˥ñ ⌐ne˥e.

[He] speaks in a low voice, so you can't hear [him] (isn't that so)!

Ti˥isa na ⌐ko˥e de ha⌐na˥su kara, ki⌐koemase˥ñ ⌐ne˥e.

[He] always speaks in a low voice so you can't hear [him] (isn't that so)!

I˥tu mo ⌐ti˥isa na ⌐ko˥e de ha⌐na˥su kara, ki⌐koemase˥ñ ⌐ne˥e.

He always speaks in a low voice so you can't hear [him] (isn't that so)!

A⌐no˥ hito (wa) i˥tu mo ⌐ti˥isa na ⌐ko˥e de ha⌐na˥su kara, ki⌐koemase˥ñ ⌐ne˥e.

5. I'll convey [the message].

O⌐tutae-sima˥su.

I'll convey [it] all.

Ze˥ñbu otutae-simasu.

I'll convey all of that.

Sore (o) ⌐ze˥ñbu otutae-simasu.

I'll convey all of that by telephone.

Deñwa de so̅re (o) ⌐ze˥ñbu otutae-simasu.

I'll convey all of that by telephone now.

I˥ma deñwa de sore (o) ⌐ze˥ñbu otutae-simasu.

6. Would you say [it]?

O⌐ssya˥tte ku⌐dasaimase˥ñ ka˩

Would you say [it] once more?

Mo⌐o iti-do ossya˥tte ku⌐dasaimase˥ñ ka˩

I didn't understand so would you say [it] once more?

Wa⌐karimase˥ñ desita kara, mo⌐o iti-do ossya˥tte ku⌐dasaimase˥ñ ka˩

I didn't understand your name so would you say [it] once more?

O⌐namae (g̃a) wakarimase˥ñ desita kara, mo⌐o iti-do ossya˥tte ku⌐dasaimase˥ñ ka˩

I'm sorry but I didn't understand your name so would you say it once more?

Su⌐mimase˥ñ g̃a; o⌐namae (g̃a) waka-rimase˥ñ desita kara, mo⌐o iti-do ossya˥tte ku⌐dasaimase˥ñ ka˩

SHORT INFORMAL DIALOGUES

(M = man; W = woman; X = either)

1. X(1): Iku?
   X(2): Iku.

2. X: I˥i?
   M: Da⌐me˥ da yo.

3. W: Ki˥ree ⌐ne˥e.
   M: So˥o da ⌐ne˥e.

4. X: Wa⌐ka˥ru?
   M: Wa⌐ka˥ru yo˩

5. X: Kosyoo?
   W: So˥o yo˩

6. M: He⌐ñ da ⌐ne⌐e.
   W: So⌐o ⌐ne⌐e.

7. X: Sore ⌐do⌐o?
   M: O⌐mosiro⌐i yo⌐

8. M(1): Sore ⌐na⌐ni?
   M(2): A⌐tarasi⌐i deñwatyoo.
   M(1): Tyo⌐tto ⌐mi⌐sete. . . . O⌐oki⌐i ⌐ne⌐e.
   M(2): So⌐o da ⌐ne⌐e.

9. M(1): Tyo⌐tto, ta⌐kusii yo⌐bu⌐ kara, koko de ⌐ma⌐tte te.[1]
   M(2): Bo⌐ku ḡa deñwa-suru⌐ kara.
   M(1): I⌐i yo. Boku ḡa suru yo.

10. X: Su⌐misu-sañ si̇tte ru?
    M: E⌐e, yo⌐ku.
    X: A⌐no⌐ hito ni̇hoñḡo de⌐ki⌐ru?
    M: Na⌐kanaka yo⌐ku de⌐ki⌐ru yo⌐ Yo-⌐neñ-ḡu⌐rai ⌐ma⌐e kara be⌐ñkyoo
       site ru⌐ kara.

SUPPLEMENTARY TELEPHONE CONVERSATIONS

1. Jones: Mo⌐simosi⌐
   Secretary: Ni⌐hoñḡo-ga⌐kkoo de gozaimasu.
   Jones: Ta⌐isi⌐kañ no ⌐Zyo⌐oñzu desu ḡa; kyo⌐o wa ga⌐kkoo e iki-
          mase⌐ñ[2] kara, Sa⌐too-sañ ni so⌐o itte kudasa⌐i.
   Secretary: Wa⌐karima⌐sita. Do⌐o mo a⌐ri⌐ḡatoo gozaimasita.
   Jones: O⌐neḡai-sima⌐su. Sayonara.

2. Mr. Matsumoto: Mo⌐simosi⌐ Ta⌐mura-sañ no o⌐taku de⌐su ka⌐
   Mrs. Tamura: Ha⌐i. Sa⌐yoo de gozaima⌐su.
   Mr. Matsumoto: Kotira wa Ma⌐tumoto de⌐su ḡa; su⌐mimase⌐ñ ḡa, otonari
                  no ⌐U⌐eno ⌐Ha⌐ruko- sañ o yo⌐ñde kudasaimase⌐ñ ka⌐
   Mrs. Tamura: Ha⌐i. Syo⌐osyoo o⌐mati-kudasaima⌐se.

              . . . . .

   Miss Ueno: Mo⌐simosi. O⌐matase-itasima⌐sita.
   Mr. Matsumoto: Aa, Ha⌐ruko-sañ? Bo⌐ku desu. O⌐ge⌐ñki?
   Miss Ueno: E⌐e. A⌐na⌐ta mo?

---

[1] Ma̱tte (i)te 'be waiting,' 'stay here and wait.'

[2] Compare Japanese gakkoo e IKIMASEÑ (lit. 'I'm not going to school') and
English 'I'm not COMING to school (where you are).

Mr. Matsumoto: Ko⌐ñbañ ōhima?
Miss Ueno: E⌐e. Hi⌐ma de⌐su ḡa—
Mr. Matsumoto: Ni⌐tiḡeki[1] e ikimase⌐ñ ka⌐
Miss Ueno: A⌐ri⌐ḡatoo. Na⌐ñ-zi kara?
Mr. Matsumoto: Go-⌐zi-ha⌐ñ kara. Go⌐-zi ni o⌐taku e ikima⌐su yo.
Miss Ueno: Zya⌐a, ma⌐tte masu kara, o⌐neḡai-sima⌐su.
Mr. Matsumoto: Zya⌐a, ma⌐ta a⌐to de.
Miss Ueno: E⌐e. Notihodo ne? Do⌐o mo a⌐ri⌐ḡatoo.
Mr. Matsumoto: Sayonara.
Miss Ueno: Sayonara.

3. Mr. Yamada: Mo⌐simosi—
    Maid: Mo⌐simosi— Ya⌐mada de gozaima⌐su. [2]
    Mr. Yamada: Yo⌐si-sañ?
    Maid: Ha⌐a, sa⌐yoo de gozaima⌐su. Da⌐ñnasa⌐ma de irassyai-
                  masu ka—
    Mr. Yamada: E⌐e, bo⌐ku. O⌐kusañ iru?
    Maid: Iie, tyo⌐tto o⌐dekake ni narima⌐sita ḡa—
    Mr. Yamada: A⌐a, so⌐o. Ano ne? Ko⌐ñbañ ne?
    Maid: Ha⌐a.
    Mr. Yamada: A⌐merika-taisi⌐kañ no ⌐Su⌐misu-sañ no o⌐taku e iku⌐ ka-
                  ra ne?
    Maid: Ha⌐a.
    Mr. Yamada: O⌐kusañ ni so⌐o itte⌐ yo.
    Maid: Ha⌐a, o⌐tutae-itasima⌐su. Na⌐ñ-zi-ḡo⌐ro o⌐kaeri ni narima⌐su ka—
    Mr. Yamada: Zyu⌐uiti-zi suḡi⌐ ni ⌐na⌐ru yo.
    Maid: Ha⌐a, wa⌐karima⌐sita.
    Mr. Yamada: Zya⌐a.
    Maid: Go⌐meñ-kudasaima⌐se.

English Equivalents

1. Jones: Hello.
    Secretary: This is the Japanese Language School.
    Jones: This is [Mr.] Jones from the Embassy. Please tell Mr.
                 Sato that I'm not coming to school today.
    Secretary: Certainly. Thank you very much [for calling].
    Jones: Please take care of this for me. Goodbye.

---

[1] Abbreviated name of Nihoñ-gekizyoo, a theater in Tokyo.

[2] A maid usually answers the telephone with the name of her employer.

2. Mr. Matsumoto: Hello. Is this the Tamura residence?
    Mrs. Tamura: Yes, it is.
    Mr. Matsumoto: This is [Mr.] Matsumoto. I'm sorry to bother you but
                    would you call Miss Haruko Ueno (who lives) next door?
    Mrs. Tamura: Yes. Just a moment, please.

                                  . . . . .

    Miss Ueno: Hello. (I'm sorry to have kept you waiting.)
    Mr. Matsumoto: Oh, Haruko? It's me. How are you?
    Miss Ueno: Fine. And you?
    Mr. Matsumoto: Are you free tonight?
    Miss Ueno: Yes, I'm free but [why do you ask?]
    Mr. Matsumoto: Would you like to go to the Nichigeki?
    Miss Ueno: Thanks. (From) what time?
    Mr. Matsumoto: (From) 5:30. I'll come to your house at 5.
    Miss Ueno: Well, I'll be waiting so do [come].
    Mr. Matsumoto: Well, [I'll talk to you] again later.
    Miss Ueno: Yes, later (right?). Thanks very much.
    Mr. Matsumoto: Goodbye.
    Miss Ueno: Goodbye.

3. Mr. Yamada: Hello.
    Maid: Hello. This is the Yamada residence.
    Mr. Yamada: Yoshi?
    Maid: Yes. Is this Mr. [Yamada]?
    Mr. Yamada: Yes, it's me. Is Mrs. [Yamada] in?
    Maid: No. She went out for a while but [is there anything I can
                    do?]
    Mr. Yamada: Oh. Say! Tonight—
    Maid: Yes.
    Mr. Yamada: I'm going to the home of Mr. Smith from the American
                    Embassy so—
    Maid: Yes.
    Mr. Yamada: Tell Mrs. [Yamada] (that).
    Maid: Yes. I'll give her the message. About what time will
                    you be home?
    Mr. Yamada: It will be after 11.
    Maid: I understand.
    Mr. Yamada: Well then. . . .
    Maid: Goodbye.

EXERCISES

1. Make the following telephone calls:

    a. Call the Tanaka home and ask if Mrs. Tanaka is in.
    b. Call the American Embassy and leave a message for Mr. Smith
        that you are not coming today.
    c. Call your home and tell the maid that you are going to the Satos'
        house and will be home about 11:30.

    d. Call a friend and ask her to go to the Nichigeki with you. Tell her you'll come to her house at 2:30.

    e. Call Mr. Sato's house and ask Mr. Sato to call (i.e. summon) Mr. Yoshio Ito who lives next door. [1]

    f. Call Mr. Yamamoto's house and ask when Mr. Yamamoto is returning to Tokyo.

    g. Report that Extension 636 is out of order and request that it be fixed.

2.   Leave the following telephone messages for Mr. Yoshida:

    a. You'll be waiting in front of the Nichigeki at 6 this evening.

    b. You want to see him before 3 o'clock today.

    c. You are leaving the office early today because your wife is sick.

    d. You'll telephone him from Osaka tomorrow morning at about 10:30.

    e. You'll be at Tokyo University today until 5:30.

    f. Your new office telephone number is 481-7600.

    g. Mr. Smith arrived at Yokohama last night and is now at the Imperial Hotel.

3.   Practice the conversations preceding the Exercises, using other politeness and/or formality levels.

4.   Practice the Basic Dialogues with appropriate variations.

---

[1] This is normal procedure when someone does not have a telephone.

Lesson 14. Eating and Drinking

BASIC DIALOGUES: FOR MEMORIZATION

(a)

(Tanaka has taken Smith to a restaurant)

Waitress

already or yet or now   mo⌐o /+ affirmative/
already or soon now
place an order   tyuumoñ-suru   or
        tyuumoñ-itasu ⁺   or
        go⌐tyuumoñ-nasa⌐ru⁺

1. Have you ordered yet?   Mo⌐o go⌐tyuumoñ-nasaima⌐sita ka⌐

Tanaka

it is yet [to happen]   ma⌐da da
not yet   ma⌐da /+ negative/

2. No, not yet.   Iie, ma⌐da desu.
        or
No, I haven't (ordered yet).   Iie, ma⌐da tyu⌐umoñ-simase⌐ñ.

Waitress

into what?   na⌐ñ ni   or
        na⌐ni ni

3. What would you like?   Na⌐ñ ni i⌐tasimasyo⌐o ka.
(Lit. Into what shall I make
[it]?)

Tanaka (to Smith)

thing   mo⌐no⌐
eat   ta⌐be⌐ru /-ru/   or
        itadaku ⁺ /-u/   or
        mesiaḡaru⁺ /-u/

4. What (kind of things) shall   Do⌐ñna mo⌐no⌐ (o) ta⌐bemasyo⌐o
we eat?   ka.

Smith

5. What WOULD be good?   Na⌐ni ḡa yo⌐rosi⌐i desyoo ka ⌐ne⌐e.

Waitress

tempura (kind of Japa-   teñpura
nese food)
6. How about tempura?   Teñpura (wa) i⌐ka⌐ḡa de go⌐zaima-
     syo⌐o ka.

Tanaka (to Smith)

into tempura	teñpura ni
make it tempura <u>or</u>	teñpura ni suru
decide on tempura	

7. Shall we decide on tempura?   Te⌐ñpura ni simasyo⌐o ka.

Smith

8. That will be fine!   Ke⌐kkoo desu ⌐ne⌐e.

Tanaka (to waitress)

9. Then let's make [it] that   Zya, so⌐o simasyo⌐o.
    (way).

Japanese rice wine	sake <u>or</u>
	osake⁺
bring (of things)	mo⌐tte ku⌐ru

10. And please bring some sake   Sore kara, sa⌐ke mo motte⌐ kite
    too.   kudasai.

(to Smith)

is cold (of weather)	sa⌐mu⌐i /-ku/
is hot	a⌐tu⌐i /-ku/
is delicious	oisii /-ku/

11. It's cold so hot sake will   Sa⌐mu⌐i kara, a⌐tu⌐i sake (wa) o⌐i-
    probably taste good, won't   si⌐i desyoo ne?
    it?

(b)

(Tanaka has invited Smith to have something to drink with him)

Tanaka

beer	bi⌐iru
drink	no⌐mu /-u/ <u>or</u>
	itadaku⁺/-u/ <u>or</u>
	mesiaḡaru⁺/-u/

12. Will you have some beer?   Bi⌐iru (o) me⌐siaḡarima⌐su ka⌐

Smith

13. Thank you. I will (drink).   A⌐ri⌐ḡatoo gozaimasu. I⌐tadakima⌐-
                                       su.

Tanaka (to waitress)

14. Two bottles of beer, please.   Bi⌐iru (o) ⌐ni⌐-hoñ oneḡai-simasu.
    (Lit. I'd like beer to the ex-
    tent of two long, cylindrical
    units.)

. . .

Tanaka (when beer is brought)

15. Here you are.   Do⌐ozo.

Smith

16. (I'll have some.)   I⌐tadakima⌐su.

    is cold   tumetai /-ku/
17. Isn't it delicious— cold   O⌐isi⌐i desu ⌐ne⌐e— tu⌐metai bi⌐iru
    beer!   wa.

. . .

Tanaka

    one glassful or cupful   i⌐p-pai
18. How about another glass?   Mo⌐o i⌐p-pai i⌐ka⌐ḡa desu ka⌐

Smith

    half   ha⌐ñbu⌐ñ
19. Well, just half, please.   Zya⌐a, ha⌐ñbuñ dake oneḡai-sima⌐su.

. . .

Tanaka

20. Won't you have a little   Mo⌐o suko⌐si me⌐siaḡarimase⌐ñ
    more?   ka⌐

Smith

21. No, thank you. (Lit. No,   Iie, mo⌐o ta⌐kusa⌐ñ desu.
    already it's a lot or fine.)   or
                                       Iie, mo⌐o ⌐ke⌐kkoo desu.

    a feast or delicious   gotisoo   or
    food and/or drink   gotisoosama +
22. It was delicious.   Go⌐tisoosama de⌐sita.

(c)

(Smith and Yamamoto meet on the street)
Yamamoto

    is pale   a⌐o⌐i /-ku/
    face or expression   kao
    be pale   a⌐o⌐i kao o suru
23. Mr. Smith. You're pale!   Su⌐misu-sañ. A⌐o⌐i ka⌐o (o) site
                                       (i)ma⌐su yo⌐

24. What happened?   Do⌐o simasita ka.

Smith

    shrimp or prawn   ebi
    shrimp tempura   ebi no teñpura
    become spoiled   i⌐ta⌐mu /-u/
    became spoiled (informal)   i⌐ta⌐ñda
    spoiled shrimp   i⌐ta⌐ñda ebi
    it was shrimp (informal)   e⌐bi da⌐tta
25. Last night I ate shrimp tem-   Yuube Gíñza de e⌐bi no teñpura (o)
    pura in the Ginza (but) I got   tabema⌐sita ḡa, i⌐ta⌐ñda e⌐bi da⌐tta
    sick because it was bad   kara, byo⌐oki ni narima⌐sita yo.
    shrimp.

Yamamoto

26. That's too bad.   I⌐kemase⌐ñ ⌐ne⌐e.

Smith

medicine   kusuri
take (of medicine)   no⌐mu /-u/
get well or recover   na⌐o⌐ru /-u/

27. I took some medicine but   Ku⌐suri (o) nomima⌐sita ḡa, ma⌐da
     I'm not better (lit. I have-   na⌐orimase⌐ñ.
     n't recovered) yet.

Yamamoto

28. Take care of yourself.   Odaizi ni.

(d)

(Tanaka and Smith are in a tea shop)

Smith

make a request or   ta⌐no⌐mu /-u/
   place an order
requested or ordered   ta⌐no⌐ñda
   (informal)
probably requested or or-   ta⌐no⌐ñda desyoo
   dered

29. You ordered a long time ago,   Zu⌐ibuñ ⌐ma⌐e ni ta⌐no⌐ñda desyoo?
     didn't you?

Tanaka

30. Yes. I ordered about ten   E⌐e. Mo⌐o zyu⌐p-puñ-ḡu⌐rai ⌐ma⌐e
     minutes ago (already) but   ni ta⌐nomima⌐sita ḡa, ma⌐da mo⌐tte
     they haven't brought [it]   kimase⌐ñ ⌐ne⌐e.
     yet, have they!

Smith

31. They'll probably bring it   Mo⌐o mo⌐tte ku⌐ru desyoo ḡa, o⌐so⌐i
     soon now but they are   desu ⌐ne⌐e.
     slow, aren't they!

(e)

(Two friends are talking)

Tanaka

ate (informal)   ta⌐beta
32. Did you eat that?   A⌐re ta⌐beta?

Yamamoto

too much or so much   añmari / + affirmative/
is spicy or salty   ka⌐ra⌐i /-ku/
was spicy or salty (in-   ka⌐rakatta
   formal)
33. No, because it was too spicy.   Iie, añmari ⌐ka⌐rakatta kara.

Tanaka

34. It was spicy?   Ka⌐rakatta?

Yamamoto

    yeah   ñ [1]
    is bad-tasting   ma⌐zu⌐i /-ku/
    was bad-tasting (in-   ma⌐zukatta
    formal)
35. Yeah. It tasted awful!   N̄. To⌐ttemo ma⌐zukatta yo.

(f)

Tanaka

36. How about a cigarette?   Ta⌐bako do⌐o desu ka↲

Smith

    smoke   no⌐mu /-u/ or
                                                   suu /-u/
37. No, I don't smoke.   Iie, no⌐mimase⌐ñ.

Tanaka

38. You don't smoke? Since   No⌐mimase⌐ñ ka↲ I⌐tu kara desu
when?   ka↲

Smith

    last month   se⌐ñǵetu
    quit or give up   yameru /-ru/
39. Why, I quit last month.   Se⌐ñǵetu ya⌐mema⌐sita yo.

ADDITIONAL EATING AND DRINKING VOCABULARY [2]

1. Shall we eat at a Ginza   Gi⌐ñza no <u>teñpuraya</u> de tabemasyo⌐o
tempura shop?   ka.

    dining room   syokudoo
    noodle shop   so⌐ba⌐ya or osobaya+
    restaurant (Japanese style)   ryo⌐ori⌐ya
    restaurant (Western style)   re⌐sutorañ

---

[1] Man's word, informal.

[2] Drill on the new words by substituting them for the underlined word in the
pattern sentence.

| sushi shop | su⌐si˥ya or osusiya + |
| tearoom | kissateñ [1] |

2. I'd like a little more <u>shrimp</u>.   Ebi (o) mo⌐o suko˥si oneḡai-simasu.

fish	sakana or osakana +
meat	ni⌐ku˥ or o⌐ni˥ku +
fowl or chicken	tori
egg	ta⌐ma˥ḡo
vegetable	yasai or o⌐ya˥sai +
fruit	ku⌐da˥mono
cooked rice or food	go˥hañ
uncooked rice	ko⌐me˥ or okome +
bread and butter	pa˥ñ to ⌐ba˥ta
toast	to˥osuto
cake or sweets	o⌐ka˥si +
noodles	so˥ba or o⌐so˥ba +
sashimi (raw fish)	sa⌐simi˥ or osasimi +
sushi (rice with fish, sea-weed, egg, etc.)	su˥si or o⌐su˥si +
sukiyaki (stew of vegetables with meat or chicken or fish)	sukiyaki
tempura (batter-fried fish and vegetables)	teñpura
sugar	sa⌐to˥o or osatoo +
salt	si⌐o˥ or o⌐si˥o +
pepper	ko⌐syo˥o
soy sauce	syooyu or osyooyu +

3. Please bring some <u>sake</u>.   Sa⌐ke (o) motte˥ kite kudasai.

cold water	mizu or omizu +
hot water	oyu +
coffee	ko⌐ohi˥i
tea	otya +
black tea	kootya
milk	mi˥ruku or gyuunyuu
ice	koori

4. Don't you want a <u>knife</u>?   Na˥ihu wa i˥rimase˥ñ ka↲

| fork | ho˥oku |
| spoon | su⌐pu˥uñ |

---

[1] With <u>kissateñ</u>, substitute no⌐mimasyo˥o for ta⌐bemasyo˥o in the pattern sentence. Alternate accent: ki⌐ssa˥teñ.

chopsticks	ha⌐si or o⌐ha⌐si +
dish	sara or osara +
bowl	wañ or owañ +
napkin	na⌐pukiñ
tray	oboñ +
glass for drinking	koppu
cup or small bowl (Japanese style)	tyawañ or o⌐tya⌐wañ +
cup (with handles)	ko⌐ohiizya⌐wañ

5. It's so <u>spicy</u> that it doesn't taste good. — A⌐ñmari <u>kara⌐i</u> kara, o⌐isiku arimase⌐ñ.

is weak or thin (of liquids) or is light (of colors)	usui /-ku/
is strong or thick (of liquids) or is dark (of colors)	ko⌐i /-ku/
is sweet or sugary or insufficiently salted	amai /-ku/
is bitter	ni⌐ga⌐i /-ku/
is acid or sour	su⌐ppa⌐i /-ku/

NOTES ON THE BASIC DIALOGUES

1. Tyuumoñ (honorific, <u>gotyuumoñ</u>†) is a c o m m o n l y occurring nominal. Example: <u>Gotyuumoñ wa?</u> 'Your order?'

4. <u>Mo⌐no⌐</u> refers to things that are tangible.

Ta⌐be⌐ru 'eat' has a second honorific equivalent, o⌐tabe ni na⌐ru, which is less common than— and not quite as polite as— <u>mesiaḡaru</u>. Both honorific equivalents are, of course, used only in polite speech, in reference to the action of someone other than the speaker. Conversely, the humble equivalent refers to the action of the speaker, in polite speech.

10. <u>Mo⌐tte ku⌐ru</u> means literally 'come holding' or 'come carrying.' <u>Mo⌐tte</u> is the gerund of the verbal <u>mo⌐tu</u> 'hold,' 'have,' 'own.' Note also <u>motte iku</u> 'take (something somewhere)' (lit. 'go holding'). The polite equivalents of these words are: humble (†), <u>mo⌐tte ma⌐iru</u> honorific (†), <u>mo⌐tte irassya⌐ru</u> and <u>mo⌐tte oide ni na⌐ru</u>.

12. <u>No⌐mu</u> 'drink' has a second honorific equivalent, <u>o⌐nomi ni na⌐ru</u>, which is not quite as polite as <u>mesiaḡaru</u>. See the note on Sentence 4 above.

16. A guest always says i⌐tadakima⌐su (or an equivalent) just before beginning to eat or drink.

17. <u>Tumetai</u> is the general term meaning 'is cold,' but it is rarely used in reference to weather or atmosphere. <u>Sa⌐mu⌐i</u>, on the other hand, refers only to weather and a t m o s p h e r e . <u>A⌐tu⌐i</u> is the opposite of b o t h words.

21. The second alternative is more polite. Both are refusals of second or later helpings. Ke˺kkoo desu (without mo˺o) is a commonly occurring polite refusal of a first offering. I˼i and yorosii are also used as refusals in the same kinds of patterns.

22. Go˼tisoosama (de˺sita) is regularly said, upon finishing eating or drinking, by a guest to his host, or by a person served to the person who prepared or served the food and/or drink. It is also said by a guest at the conclusion of a visit during which refreshments were served.

29. Ta˼no˺mu 'make a request' is a verbal of more general meaning than tyuumoñ-suru 'place an order for something.' The thing requested is followed by particle o (or wa); the person of whom the request is made is followed by particle ni (i.e. the request is made TO someone). Compare:

    I asked Mr. Tanaka (= I asked him a question):
        Ta˼naka-sañ ni kikima˼sita.
    and
    I asked Mr. Tanaka (= I asked him to do something):
        Ta˼naka-sañ ni tanomima˼sita.

Ta˼no˺mu [yo] is used by men as a plain informal equivalent of o˼neḡai-sima˼su.

Eating and Drinking Vocabulary:

    In general, where alternate forms are given, women almost invariably use the polite alternant, whereas men use either, depending on the level of politeness being used. In a few cases—for example, otya 'tea' (the drink) and oyu 'hot water'—the polite form is regularly used by both men and women.

GRAMMATICAL NOTES

1. Verbals: Informal Past

The informal past of a verbal is made by changing the final -e of the gerund to -a. Thus, the informal past always ends in -ta or -da. It is the exact equivalent of the -ma˼sita form except that it is informal. The informal past and the gerund regularly have the same accent. Examples:

Informal Non-past (Citation Form)	Gerund	Informal Past	Formal Past
(-ru): ta˼be˺ru 'eat'	ta˼bete	ta˼beta	ta˼bema˼sita
mi˼ru 'see'	mi˼te	mi˼ta	mi˼ma˼sita
(-u): ma˼tu 'wait'	ma˼tte	ma˼tta	ma˼tima˼sita
ka˼eru 'return'	ka˼ette	ka˼etta	ka˼erima˼sita
kau 'buy'	katte	katta	ka˼ima˼sita
ha˼na˼su 'talk'	ha˼na˼site	ha˼na˼sita	ha˼nasima˼sita
ka˼ku 'write'	ka˼ite	ka˼ita	ka˼kima˼sita
iku 'go'	itte (irreg.)	itta	i˼kima˼sita

iˢoˉgu 'be in a hurry'	iˢoⁱide	iˢoⁱida	iˢoḡimaˢita
yobu 'call'	yoñde	yoñda	yoˢbimaˢsita
yoˢmu 'read'	yoˢñde	yoˢñda	yoˢmimaˢsita
(-aru): oˢssyaˢru ‡ 'say'	oˢssyaˢtte	oˢssyaˢtta	oˢssyaimaˢsita
(Ir-reg.): kuˢru 'come'	kiˢteˢ	kiˢta [1]	kiˢmaˢsita
suru 'do'	site	sita	siˢmaˢsita

2. Adjectivals: Informal and Formal Past

The informal past of an adjectival is made by dropping the final -i of the non-past and adding -katta. If the non-past is unaccented, the past is regularly accented on the syllable immediately preceding the -katta; if the non-past is accented, the past is also accented but usually on an earlier syllable. [2]

Examples:

Informal Non-past (Citation Form)	Informal Past
amai 'is sweet'	aˢmaˢkatta 'was sweet'
aˢtuˢi 'is hot'	aˢtukatta 'was hot'
huˢruˢi 'is old'	huˢrukatta 'was old'
muzukasii 'is difficult'	muˢzukasiˢkatta 'was difficult'
tiˢisaˢi 'is small'	tiˢisakatta 'was small'
ikitai 'wants to go'	iˢkitaˢkatta 'wanted to go'

The comparatively r a r e formal past consisting of an adjectival in its -i form + formal desita (for example, taˢkaˢi desita 'it was expensive') has already been mentioned in Lesson 3, Grammatical Note 3(c). Another formal past adjectival pattern consists of an informal past adjectival ending in -katta + formal desu.

Examples:

	Informal Past	Formal Past
'was sweet'	aˢmaˢkatta	aˢmaˢkatta desu
'was hot'	aˢtukatta	aˢtukatta desu
'was old'	huˢrukatta	huˢrukatta desu
'was difficult'	muˢzukasiˢkatta	muˢzukasiˢkatta desu

---

[1] Note the difference in accent between this form and the gerund.

[2] However, an accented -tai word is accented on the -ta- syllable in both the non-past and the past: taˢbetaˢi 'want to eat,' taˢbetaˢkatta 'wanted to eat.'

3. Copula: Informal Past

The past of da is da┐tta. It is the informal equivalent of de┐sita, but like da, it follows nominals and particles but does NOT occur immediately after verbals or adjectivals. It regularly loses its accent following an accented word or phrase.

Examples:

Informal Non-past	Informal Past	Formal Past
tomodati da 'it's a friend'	to┌modati da┐tta 'it was a friend'	to┌modati de┐sita
tomodati kara da 'it's from a friend'	to┌modati kara da┐tta 'it was from a friend'	to┌modati kara de┐sita

Now study the following chart:

	Affirmative Past Inflectional Patterns	
	Formal	Informal
Verbal Pattern	Verbal ending in -ma┐sita (wa┌karima┐sita)	Verbal ending in -ta (wa┌ka┐tta)
Adjectival Pattern	Adjectival ending in: -katta + desu (o┐okikatta desu) or -i + desita (o┌oki┐i desita)	Adjectival ending in: -katta (o┐okikatta)
Nominal[1] Pattern	Nominal + de┐sita (ho┐n desita)	Nominal + da┐tta (ho┐n datta)

4. Uses of the Informal Past

In informal speech, the uses of verbal and adjectival informal past forms parallel the uses of corresponding non-past forms, but there are some differences between the uses of non-past da and past da┐tta.

The following are past equivalents of the non-past examples in Lesson 13, Grammatical Note 2. Compare and study them carefully.

---

[1] With or without following particle.

	Formal	Informal— Men and Women
'It was clear.'	Wa⌐karima⌐sita.	Wa⌐ka⌐tta.
'Was it clear?'	Wa⌐karima⌐sita ka⌐	Wa⌐ka⌐tta?
'It was expensive.'	Ta⌐kakatta desu.	Ta⌐kakatta.
	(or Ta⌐ka⌐i desita.)	
'Was it expensive?'	Ta⌐kakatta desu ka⌐	Ta⌐kakatta?
	(or Ta⌐ka⌐i desita ka⌐)	
'It was true.'	Ho⌐ntoo de⌐sita.	Ho⌐ntoo da⌐tta.
'Was it true?'	Ho⌐ntoo de⌐sita ka⌐	Ho⌐ntoo da⌐tta?

		Informal — Men
'It was clear (I tell you).'	Wa⌐karima⌐sita yo⌐	Wa⌐ka⌐tta yo⌐
'It was clear, wasn't it?'	Wa⌐karima⌐sita ne?	Wa⌐ka⌐tta ne?
'It was expensive (I tell you).'	Ta⌐kakatta desu yo⌐	Ta⌐kakatta yo⌐
	(or Ta⌐ka⌐i desita yo⌐)	
'It was expensive, wasn't it!'	Ta⌐kakatta desu ⌐ne⌐e.	Ta⌐kakatta ⌐ne⌐e.
	(or Ta⌐ka⌐i desita ⌐ne⌐e.)	
'It was true (I tell you).'	Ho⌐ntoo de⌐sita yo⌐	Ho⌐ntoo da⌐tta yo⌐
'It was true, wasn't it!'	Ho⌐ntoo de⌐sita ⌐ne⌐e.	Ho⌐ntoo da⌐tta ⌐ne⌐e.

In formal speech, the use of verbal and adjectival informal past forms before de⌐syo⌐o, and of verbal, adjectival, and copula informal past forms before particle kara 'so' is parallel to that of corresponding non-past forms.   The accentuation is also parallel.   Thus:

> Informal (or formal[1]) past + formal tentative de⌐syo⌐o = 'it probably happened or was true' or 'it probably has happened or has been true' (formal)

Examples:

> I⌐tta desyo⌐o. 'He probably went.'
> Yo⌐nde (i)ta desyoo. 'He was probably reading.'
> Wa⌐karima⌐sita desyoo? 'You understood, didn't you?'
> Ta⌐kakatta desyoo? 'It was expensive, wasn't it?'
> Mi⌐ta⌐katta desyoo. 'He probably wanted to see [it].'
> Wa⌐ka⌐tta desyoo ka. 'Do you suppose he understood?' or 'Did you understand?' (indirect)

---

[1] A formal verbal may also occur before formal de⌐syo⌐o. The combination is more formal than an informal verbal + de⌐syo⌐o. See the third example following.

Informal (or formal[1]) past + <u>kara</u> 'so' = 'so-and-so happened (<u>or was</u> true) so' or 'so-and-so has happened (<u>or</u> has been true) so'

Examples:

Kinoo ⌐yo˥ku be˩ŋkyoo-sita˥ kara, kyo˥o wa ⌐yo˥ku wakarimasu. 'I studied hard yesterday so today I understand well.'

Ta˥kakatta kara, ka⌐imase˥ñ desita. 'It was expensive so I didn't buy [it].'

Ma⌐zu˥i ku˩da˥mono datta kara, a⌐ñmari tabemase˥ñ desita. 'It was awful fruit so I didn't eat very much.'

In addition, the informal past <u>da˥tta</u> (or, less commonly, formal <u>de˥sita</u>) following a nominal or particle may occur before the formal tentative <u>de⌐syo˥o</u> with the meaning 'it probably was <u>or</u> has been so-and-so.'

Thus:

<u>Formal Non-past Tentative</u>

To⌐modati desyo˥o. 'He's probably a friend.'

To⌐modati kara desyo˥o. 'It's probably from a friend.'

Ho⌐ñtoo desyo˥o. 'It's probably true.'

<u>Formal Past Tentative</u>

To⌐modati da˥tta desyoo. 'He was probably a friend.'

To⌐modati kara da˥tta desyoo. 'It was probably from a friend.'

Ho⌐ñtoo de˥sita desyoo? 'It was true, wasn't it?'

5. <u>mo˥o</u> + Affirmative; <u>ma˥da</u> + Negative

<u>Mo˥o</u> plus an affirmative means 'already' or 'yet,' or 'now already,' 'now—after a change has taken place,' 'soon now.'

<u>Ma˥da</u> plus a negative means 'not yet.' The non-past negative indicates that something has not happened up to the present moment (cf. Lesson 1, Grammatical Note 1).

<u>Ma˥da</u> occurs in the <u>iie</u> answer to a <u>mo˥o</u> question, and <u>mo˥o</u> occurs in the <u>iie</u> answer to a <u>ma˥da</u> question:

Tanaka-sañ wa ⌐mo˥o ki⌐ma˥sita ka⌐ 'Has Mr. Tanaka come already?'
    Ha˥i, mo˥o ki⌐ma˥sita. 'Yes, he's come already.'
    Iie, ⌐ma˥da ki⌐mase˥ñ. 'No, he hasn't come yet.'

Tanaka-sañ wa ⌐ma˥da ki⌐mase˥ñ ka⌐ 'Hasn't Mr. Tanaka come yet?'
    Ha˥i, ⌐ma˥da ki⌐mase˥ñ. 'That's right. He hasn't come yet.'
    Iie, ⌐mo˥o ki⌐ma˥sita. 'That's not right. He's already come.'

---

[1] A formal inflected form may also occur before <u>kara</u> in formal speech, as a more formal alternant. Many examples have already occurred.

Ma⌐da desu, meaning literally 'It is yet [to happen],' is the closest Japanese equivalent of English 'It hasn't happened yet'; 'Not yet.'

WARNING: Do not confuse the mo⌐o described above with moo (unaccented) occurring with immediately following numbers and indefinite quantity words, meaning 'more.' Compare the following examples:

Mo⌐o su⌐ko⌐si ta⌐bema⌐sita. 'I've eaten a little, already.'

Mo⌐o suko⌐si ta⌐bema⌐sita. 'I ate a little more.'

6. Goal Patterns with √suru

A nominal X + particle ni of goal + √suru[1] means 'make [something] into X,' 'make it X,' 'decide on X.' Compare the following pairs:

A⌐sita simasyo⌐o. 'Let's do [it] tomorrow.'
(Tells when we should do something)

A⌐sita⌐ ni si⌐masyo⌐o. 'Let's make [it] tomorrow.' or
'Let's decide on tomorrow.'
(Tells what day we should decide on)

So⌐o sima⌐sita. 'We did [it] that way.'
So⌐re ni sima⌐sita. 'We decided on that one.'

Hi⌐to⌐-tu si⌐masyo⌐o. 'Let's do one.'

Hi⌐to⌐-tu ni si⌐masyo⌐o. 'Let's make [it] into one' (for example, several sentences into one lesson, or several small packages into one bundle, or all the dough into one cake, etc.)

Similarly, a waitress asks Na⌐ñ ni (i⌐ta)simasyo⌐o ka '(Into) what shall I make [your order]?'

Now reread Lesson 10, Grammatical Note 4.

If √na⌐ru, preceded by nominal + ni, or the -ku form of an adjectival, is replaced by the corresponding form of √suru, the English equivalent changes from 'become X' to 'make [it] X.' Study the following pairs:[2]

---

[1] Or, of course, a more polite alternative.

[2] The subjects and objects of the English equivalents will vary, as always, depending on the context.

{ O⌐nazi ni narima⌐sita.   'They have become the same.'
{ O⌐nazi ni sima⌐sita.   'I made them the same.'

{ Na⌐niiro ni narima⌐sita ka↲   'What color did it become?'
{ Na⌐niiro ni sima⌐sita ka↲   'What color did you make it?'

{ O⌐okiku na⌐rima⌐sita.   'It has become big.'
{ O⌐okiku si⌐ma⌐sita.   'I made it big.'

{ A⌐tuku narimasu.   'It will become hot.'
{ A⌐tuku simasu.   'I will make it hot.'

7.   Counter -hai

Glassfuls and cupfuls are counted with the counter -hai, which combines with numerals of Series I. Numbers from one to ten are:

i⌐p-pai   '1 glassful or cupful'
ni⌐-hai   '2 glassfuls or cupfuls'
sa⌐ñ-bai   '3 glassfuls or cupfuls'
yo⌐ñ-hai   '4 glassfuls or cupfuls'
go-hai   '5 glassfuls or cupfuls'
ro⌐p-pai   '6 glassfuls or cupfuls'
na⌐na⌐-hai or si⌐ti⌐-hai   '7 glassfuls or cupfuls'
ha⌐p-pai or ha⌐ti⌐-hai   '8 glassfuls or cupfuls'
kyu⌐u-hai   '9 glassfuls or cupfuls'
zi⌐p-pai or zyu⌐p-pai   '10 glassfuls or cupfuls'

na⌐ñ-bai 'how many glassfuls or cupfuls?'

DRILLS

A.   Substitution Drill

1. Shall we decide on tem-pura?[1]	Te⌐ñpura ni simasyo⌐o ka.
2. Shall we decide on suki-yaki?	Su⌐kiyaki ni simasyo⌐o ka.
3. Shall we decide on sushi?	O⌐su⌐si ni si⌐masyo⌐o ka.
4. Shall we decide on noodles?	O⌐so⌐ba ni si⌐masyo⌐o ka.
5. Shall we decide on rice wine?	Sa⌐ke ni simasyo⌐o ka.

---

[1] Or 'Shall we (or I) make it tempura?'

6. Shall we decide on sa-
   shimi?

Sa⌐simi⌐ ni si⌐masyo⌐o ka.

7. Shall we decide on beer?

Bi⌐iru ni si⌐masyo⌐o ka.

8. Shall we decide on coffee?

Ko⌐ohi⌐i ni si⌐masyo⌐o ka.

9. Shall we decide on chick-
   en?

To⌐ri ni simasyo⌐o ka.

10. Shall we decide on fish?

Sa⌐kana ni simasyo⌐o ka.

B. Substitution Drill

1. Shall I make [it] hot?

A⌐tuku si⌐masyo⌐o ka.

2. It got hot.

A⌐tuku na⌐rima⌐sita.

3. It got cold.

Tu⌐metaku narima⌐sita.

4. I'll make [it] cold.

Tu⌐metaku sima⌐su yo⌐

5. I'm going to make [it] into
   a school.

Ga⌐kkoo ni sima⌐su yo⌐

6. It has become a school.

Ga⌐kkoo ni narima⌐sita.

7. It has become a company.

Ka⌐isya ni narima⌐sita.

8. He'll probably make [it]
   into a company.

Ka⌐isya ni suru desyo⌐o.

9. He'll probably make [it]
   cheap.

Ya⌐suku su⌐ru desyo⌐o.

10. It will probably get cheap.

Ya⌐suku ⌐na⌐ru desyoo.

C. Substitution Drill

1. I've been eating here for
   about two years now (already).

Mo⌐o ni-⌐neñ-ḡu⌐rai ko̅ko de ⌐ta⌐bete
(i)masu yo⌐

2. I've been eating here for
   about six months now.

Mo⌐o ro⌐k-kaḡetu-ḡu⌐rai ko̅ko de
⌐ta⌐bete (i)masu yo⌐

3. I've been buying here for
   about six months now.

Mo⌐o ro⌐k-kaḡetu-ḡu⌐rai ko̅ko de
ka⌐tte (i)ma⌐su yo⌐

4. I've been buying here for
   about two weeks now.

Mo⌐o ni-⌐syuukañ-ḡu⌐rai ko̅ko de ka-
⌐tte (i)ma⌐su yo⌐

5. I've been studying here
   for about two weeks now.

Mo⌐o ni-⌐syuukañ-ḡu⌐rai ko̅ko de be-
⌐ñkyoo-site (i)ma⌐su yo⌐

6. I've been studying here for
   about four hours now.

Mo⌐o yo-⌐zikañ-ḡu⌐rai ko̅ko de be⌐ñ-
kyoo-site (i)ma⌐su yo⌐

7. I've been reading here for
   about four hours now.

Mo⌐o yo-⌐zikañ-ḡu⌐rai ko̅ko de ⌐yo⌐-
ñde (i)masu yo⌐

8. I've been reading here for
   about twenty minutes now.

Mo⌐o ni⌐zip-puñ-ḡu⌐rai ko̅ko de ⌐yo⌐-
ñde (i)masu yo⌐

9. I've been waiting here for
   about twenty minutes now.

Mo⌐o ni⌐zip-puñ-ḡu⌐rai ko̅ko de ⌐ma⌐-
tte (i)masu yo⌐

D. Substitution Drill

1. I (compared with others)
   ate [it].

Wa⌐takusi wa tabema⌐sita.

2. The sashimi (compared with other things) [I] ate.	Sa⌈simi⌉ wa ta⊢bema⊣sita.
3. [I] ate sashimi.	Sa⌈simi⌉ o ta⊢bema⊣sita.
4. I ate [it].	Wa⌈takusi ga tabema⌉sita.
5. I ate [it], too.	Wa⌈takusi mo tabema⌉sita.
6. [I] ate sashimi, too.	Sa⌈simi⌉ mo ta⊢bema⊣sita.
7. [I] ate with chopsticks.	O⌈ha⌉si de ta⊢bema⊣sita.
8. [I] ate at home.	U⌈ti de tabema⌉sita.
9. [I] ate at eight.	Ha⌈ti⌉-zi ni ta⊢bema⊣sita.
10. [I] ate starting at eight.	Ha⌈ti⌉-zi kara ta⊢bema⊣sita.

E. Substitution Drill

1. It's delicious, isn't it—this beer.	O⌈isi⌉i desu ⌈ne⌉e—ko⊢no bi⊣iru wa.
2. It's hot, isn't it—this tea.	A⌈tu⌉i desu ⌈ne⌉e—kono otya wa.
3. It's cold, isn't it—this room.	Sa⌈mu⌉i desu ⌈ne⌉e—ko⊢no heya⊣ wa.
4. It's cold, isn't it—this milk.	Tu⌈meta⌉i desu ⌈ne⌉e—ko⊢no mi⊣ru-ku wa.
5. It's awful(-tasting), isn't it—this fish.	Ma⌈zu⌉i desu ⌈ne⌉e—kono sakana wa.
6. It's sour, isn't it—this fruit.	Su⌈ppa⌉i desu ⌈ne⌉e—ko⊢no kuda⊣mo-no wa.
7. It's bitter, isn't it—this coffee.	Ni⌈ga⌉i desu ⌈ne⌉e—ko⊢no koohi⊣i wa.
8. It's spicy, isn't it—this sushi.	Ka⌈ra⌉i desu ⌈ne⌉e—ko⊢no osu⊣si wa.
9. It's sweet, isn't it—this cake.	A⌈ma⌉i desu ⌈ne⌉e—ko⊢no oka⊣si wa.
10. It's strong, isn't it—this (black) tea.	Ko⌉i desu ⌈ne⌉e—kono kootya wa.

F. Substitution Drill

1. Please bring two bottles of sake.	Sake (o) ⌈ni⌉-hoñ mo⊢tte⊣ kite kudasai.
2. Please bring two glasses of beer.	Bi⌉iru (o) ⌈ni⌉-hai mo⊢tte⊣ kite kudasai.
3. Please bring three knives.	Na⌉ihu (o) ⌈sa⌉ñ-boñ mo⊢tte⊣ kite kudasai.
4. Please bring three pieces of toast.	To⌉osuto (o) ⌈sa⌉ñ-mai mo⊢tte⊣ kite kudasai.
5. Please bring three glasses of milk.	Mi⌉ruku (o) ⌈sa⌉ñ-bai mo⊢tte⊣ kite kudasai.
6. Please bring one fork.	Ho⌉oku (o) ⌈i⌉p-poñ mo⊢tte⊣ kite kudasai.
7. Please bring one glass of water.	Mizu (o) ⌈i⌉p-pai mo⊢tte⊣ kite kudasai.
8. Please bring a little more rice.	Go⌉hañ (o) mo⌈o suko⌉si mo⊢tte⊣ kite kudasai.

9. Please bring two cups. Tyawañ (o) hu⌐tatu motte⌐ kite kudasai.

10. Please bring two cups of Otya (o) ⌐ni⌐-hai mo⌐tte⌐ kite kuda-
    tea. sai.

G. Response Drill

(Reply in the negative.)

1. Ya⌐sai de⌐su ka↵	Iie, ya⌐sai zya arimase⌐ñ.
2. A⌐ma⌐i desu ka↵	Iie, a⌐maku arimase⌐ñ.
3. Ya⌐mema⌐sita ka↵	Iie, ya⌐memase⌐ñ desita.
4. Syo⌐kudoo de⌐su ka↵	Iie, syo⌐kudoo zya arimase⌐ñ.
5. O⌐sobaya kara de⌐su ka↵	Iie, o⌐sobaya kara zya arimase⌐ñ.
6. Ku⌐suri de⌐sita ka↵	Iie, ku⌐suri zya arimase⌐ñ desita.
7. Su⌐ppa⌐i desu ka↵	Iie, su⌐ppa⌐ku a⌐rimase⌐ñ.
8. Ko⌐i desu ka↵	Iie, ko⌐ku a⌐rimase⌐ñ.

H. Response Drill (based on Grammatical Note 5)

1. Mo⌐o ta⌐bema⌐sita ka↵ /iie/	Iie, ma⌐da ta⌐bemase⌐ñ.
2. Ma⌐da na⌐orimase⌐ñ ka↵ /iie/	Iie, mo⌐o na⌐orima⌐sita.
3. Mo⌐o ku⌐suri (o) nomima⌐si-ta ka↵ /e⌐e/	E⌐e, mo⌐o ku⌐suri (o) nomima⌐sita.
4. Ma⌐da ta⌐nomimase⌐ñ ka↵ /e⌐e/	E⌐e, ma⌐da ta⌐nomimase⌐ñ.
5. Mo⌐o de⌐kima⌐sita ka↵ /iie/	Iie, ma⌐da de⌐kimase⌐ñ.
6. Ma⌐da ka⌐erimase⌐ñ ka↵ /iie/	Iie, mo⌐o ka⌐erima⌐sita.
7. Mo⌐o ku⌐ruma (o) naosima⌐si-ta ka↵ /e⌐e/	E⌐e, mo⌐o ku⌐ruma (o) naosima⌐sita.
8. Ma⌐da a⌐imase⌐ñ ka↵ /e⌐e/	E⌐e, ma⌐da a⌐imase⌐ñ.
9. Mo⌐o wa⌐karima⌐sita ka↵ /iie/	Iie, ma⌐da wa⌐karimase⌐ñ.
10. Ma⌐da de⌐ñwa-simase⌐ñ ka↵ /iie/	Iie, mo⌐o de⌐ñwa-sima⌐sita.

I. Level Drill (based on Grammatical Notes 1 and 4)

Tutor: Mo⌐o i⌐kima⌐sita kara.
         (formal verbal)
                                        'Because I already went.'
Student: Mo⌐o i⌐tta⌐ kara.
         (informal verbal)

1. Sa⌐ke (o) yamema⌐sita kara.	Sa⌐ke (o) yameta⌐ kara.
2. Miti de to⌐modati ni aima⌐si-ta kara.	Miti de to⌐modati ni a⌐tta kara.
3. I⌐sogima⌐sita kara.	I⌐so⌐ida kara.
4. Mo⌐o i⌐ti-neñ-gu⌐rai ⌐ma⌐e ni yo⌐mima⌐sita kara.	Mo⌐o i⌐ti-neñ-gu⌐rai ⌐ma⌐e ni ⌐yo⌐ñ-da kara.

5. Ka꜒nai mo kŏdomo mo   Ka꜒nai mo kŏdomo mo byo꜖oki ni na꜒-
   byo꜖oki ni narima꜒sita   tta kara.
   kara.

6. Hu꜖ru꜒i sa꜖kana (o) tabe-   Hu꜖ru꜒i sa꜖kana (o) ta꜔beta kara.
   ma꜔sita kara.

7. Kinoo ꜖yo꜒ku be꜖ŋkyoo-   Kinoo ꜖yo꜒ku be꜖ŋkyoo-sita꜔ kara.
   sima꜔sita kara.

8. To꜖modati kara karima꜒-   To꜖modati kara karita꜒ kara.
   sita kara.

9. Ti꜒isa na ꜖ko꜔e de ha꜖na-   Ti꜒isa na ꜖ko꜔e de ha꜖na꜔sita kara.
   sima꜔sita kara.

10. Yuube ꜖bi꜒iru (o) ta꜖kusañ   Yuube ꜖bi꜒iru (o) ta꜖kusañ no꜒ñda
    nomima꜒sita kara.   kara.

J. Grammar Drill (based on Grammatical Notes 1, 2, 3, and 4)

         Tutor: I꜖ku desyo꜒o. 'He'll probably go.' (non-past)
         Student: I꜖tta desyo꜒o. 'He probably went.' (past)

1. Kyo꜒o de꜖ñwa (o) nao꜒su   Kyo꜒o de꜖ñwa (o) nao꜒sita desyoo.
   desyoo.

2. Ze꜒ñbu tu꜖taeru desyo꜔o.   Ze꜒ñbu tu꜖taeta desyo꜔o.

3. Koñna sara (wa) ta꜖ka꜒i   Koñna sara (wa) ꜖ta꜒kakatta desyoo.
   desyoo.

4. Byo꜖oki desyo꜒o.   Byo꜖oki da꜒tta desyoo.

5. Kyo꜒o to꜖temo isoḡasi꜒i   Kyo꜒o to꜖temo isoḡa꜒sikatta desyoo.
   desyoo.

6. Ha꜒yaku na꜖o꜔ru desyoo.   Ha꜒yaku na꜖o꜔tta desyoo.

7. Sono siḡoto (wa) tu꜖mara꜒-   Sono siḡoto (wa) tu꜖mara꜒nakatta de-
   nai desyoo.   syoo.

8. Ko꜖no koohi꜒i (wa) ma꜖zu꜒i   Ko꜖no koohi꜒i (wa) ꜖ma꜒zukatta de-
   desyoo.   syoo.

9. Sono tori (wa) o꜖isi꜒i de-   Sono tori (wa) o꜖isi꜒katta desyoo.
   syoo.

10. Ha꜖nasi-tyuu desyo꜒o.   Ha꜖nasi-tyuu da꜒tta desyoo.

K. Level Drill [1]

1. Ko꜖marima꜒sita ꜖ne꜔e.   Ko꜖ma꜒tta ꜖ne꜔e. (M)

2. So꜖re (wa) yo꜒katta desu.   So꜖re (wa) yo꜒katta.

3. So꜖no꜒ hito no ꜖ko꜔e (wa)   So꜖no꜒ hito no ꜖ko꜔e (wa) ꜖he꜒ñ datta
   ꜖he꜒ñ desita yo⌐.   yo⌐ (M)

---

[1]   In each case, the sentence on the right is the informal equivalent of the
sentence on the left. M = more typical of men's speech; W = more typical of
women's speech.

4. A⌐no kissa⌐teñ no oᴴka⁻si   A⌐no kissa⌐teñ no oᴴka⁻si (wa) o⌐isi⌐-
   (wa) o⌐isi⌐katta desu ᴴne⁻e.   katta ᴴne⁻e. (M)

5. Mo⌐o o⌐kaeri ni narima⌐si-   Mo⌐o o⌐kaeri ni na⌐tta? (W)
   ta ka↲

6. Sono miti (wa) da⌐izyo⌐obu   Sono miti (wa) da⌐izyo⌐obu datta?
   desita ka↲

7. So⌐no ho⌐ñ (wa) to⌐temo   So⌐no ho⌐ñ (wa) to⌐temo omosi⌐rokat-
   omosi⌐rokatta desu.   ta.

8. Na⌐ni (o) goᴴtyuumoñ-   Na⌐ni (o) goᴴtyuumoñ-nasa⁻tta? (W)
   nasaima⁻sita ka↲

9. Sono sakana (wa) da⌐me⌐   Sono sakana (wa) da⌐me⌐ datta.
   desita.

10. Mo⌐o zi⌐p-puñ-g̃u⌐rai ᴴma⁻e   Mo⌐o zi⌐p-puñ-g̃u⌐rai ᴴma⁻e ni de̊ka-
    ni de⌐kakema⌐sita yo↲   keta yo↲ (M)

L. Expansion Drill

1. They haven't brought it.   Mo⌐tte kimase⌐ñ yo↲
   They haven't brought it yet.   Ma⌐da mo⌐tte kimase⌐ñ yo↲
   I ordered but they haven't   Tyu⌐umoñ-sima⌐sita g̃a, ma⌐da mo-
   brought it yet.   ⌐tte kimase⌐ñ yo↲
   I ordered coffee but they   Ko⌐ohi⌐i (o) tyu⌐umoñ-sima⁻sita g̃a,
   haven't brought it yet.   ma⌐da mo⌐tte kimase⌐ñ yo↲
   I ordered coffee about fif-   Zyu⌐ugo-huñ-g̃u⌐rai ᴴma⁻e ni ko⌐o-
   teen minutes ago but they   hi⌐i (o) tyu⌐umoñ-sima⁻sita g̃a,
   haven't brought it yet.   ma⌐da mo⌐tte kimase⌐ñ yo↲
   I ordered coffee about fif-   Mo⌐o zyu⌐ugo-huñ-g̃u⌐rai ᴴma⁻e ni
   teen minutes ago but (al-   ko⌐ohi⌐i (o) tyu⌐umoñ-sima⁻sita
   ready) but they haven't   g̃a, ma⌐da mo⌐tte kimase⌐ñ yo↲
   brought it yet.

2. I got sick.   Byo⌐oki ni narima⌐sita yo.
   Because it was bad, I got   Da⌐me⌐ datta kara, byo⌐oki ni nari-
   sick.   ma⌐sita yo.
   Because that fish was bad,   Sono sakana wa da⌐me⌐ datta kara,
   I got sick.   byo⌐oki ni narima⌐sita yo.
   I ate fish. Because the fish   Sa⌐kana (o) tabema⌐sita g̃a; sono
   was bad, I got sick.   sakana wa da⌐me⌐ datta kara, byo-
                                       ⌐oki ni narima⌐sita yo.
   I ate fish at a cheap dining   Ya⌐su⌐i syokudoo de sa⌐kana (o) ta-
   room. Because the fish   bema⌐sita g̃a; sono sakana wa da-
   was bad, I got sick.   ⌐me⌐ datta kara, byo⌐oki ni nari-
                                       ma⌐sita yo.
   The day before yesterday   Ototoi ya⌐su⌐i syokudoo de sa⌐kana
   I ate fish at a cheap din-   (o) tabema⌐sita g̃a; sono s a k a n a
   ing room. Because the   wa da⌐me⌐ datta kara, byo⌐oki ni
   fish was bad, I got sick.   narima⌐sita yo.

3. [They] eat.   Ta⌐bema⌐su.
   [They] eat with chopsticks.   Ha⌐si de tabemasu.

Japanese eat with chop-   Ni⌐hoñzi⌐ñ wa ⌐ha⌐si de tabemasu.
sticks.
Americans eat with knives   A⌐merika⌐ziñ wa ⌐na⌐ihu to ⌐ho⌐oku
and forks, but Japanese   de ta⌐bema⌐su ḡa, ni⌐hoñzi⌐ñ wa
eat with chopsticks.   ⌐ha⌐si de tabemasu.

4. He has probably arrived. . . .   Tu⌐ita desyoo ḡa_
    He has probably arrived   O⌐taku ni tu⌐ita desyoo ḡa_
    home. . . .
    He has probably arrived   Mo⌐o o⌐taku ni tu⌐ita desyoo ḡa_
    home already. . . .
    He left about an hour ago   I⌐ti-zikañ-ḡu⌐rai ⌐ma⌐e ni ⌐de⌐ta ka-
    so he has probably ar-   ra, mo⌐o o⌐taku ni tu⌐ita desyoo
    rived home already. . . .   ḡa_
    He left the office about an   I⌐ti-zikañ-ḡu⌐rai ⌐ma⌐e ni zi⌐mu⌐syo
    hour ago so he has prob-   (o) ⌐de⌐ta kara, mo⌐o o⌐taku ni tu⌐-
    ably arrived home al-   ita desyoo ḡa_
    ready. . . .

5. Let's make it tomorrow.   A⌐sita⌐ ni si⌐masyo⌐o.
    I'm busy so let's make it   I⌐soḡasi⌐i kara, a⌐sita⌐ ni si⌐ma-
    tomorrow.   syo⌐o.
    I'm very busy so let's   To⌐ttemo isoḡasi⌐i kara, a⌐sita⌐ ni
    make it tomorrow.   si⌐masyo⌐o.
    Today I'm very busy so   Kyo⌐o wa to⌐ttemo isoḡasi⌐i kara,
    let's make it tomorrow.   a⌐sita⌐ ni si⌐masyo⌐o.

6. I telephoned.   De⌐ñwa-sima⌐sita.
    I telephoned his home.   O⌐taku e deñwa-sima⌐sita.
    I wanted to talk so I tele-   Ha⌐nasita⌐katta kara, o⌐taku e deñ-
    phoned his home.   wa-sima⌐sita.
    I didn't see him but I   A⌐imase⌐ñ desita ḡa; ha⌐nasita⌐katta
    wanted to talk to him so   kara, o⌐taku e deñwa-sima⌐sita.
    I telephoned his home.
    I didn't see him at the of-   Kaisya de a⌐imase⌐ñ desita ḡa; ha-
    fice but I wanted to talk   ⌐nasita⌐katta kara, o⌐taku e deñwa-
    to him so I telephoned   sima⌐sita.
    his home.

SUPPLEMENTARY CONVERSATION

(Two friends, Mr. Tanaka and Mr. Sato, sit down in a restaurant and are ap-
proached by a waitress)

Waitress: I⌐rassyaima⌐se. Na⌐ñ ni i⌐tasimasyo⌐o ka.
Tanaka: Mo⌐o hito⌐-ri ⌐ku⌐ru kara, tyo⌐tto ⌐ma⌐tte kudasai.
Waitress: Ha⌐a.
Tanaka: (to Sato)   Osoi ⌐ne⌐e—Yosida-kuñ wa.
Sato: So⌐o da ⌐ne⌐e. Na⌐ñ ni suru?
Tanaka: Tori wa?

Sato: Yosida-kuñ wa tŏri wa dame.
Tanaka: So˥o ˥so˦o. Teñpura wa do˥o? Teñpura wa ta˥beta ne? — boku no
           uti de.
Sato: So˥o datta ˥ne˦e.

           (Mr. Yoshida arrives)

Yoshida: O˥soku narima˥sita. Su˥mimase˥ñ.
Tanaka⎫
Sato ⎬: Iie.
          ⎭
Tanaka: Na˥ñ ni suru?
Sato: Teñpura do˥o?
Yoshida: A˥a, i˥i ˥ne˥e.
Sato: Zya˥a, teñpura tano˥mu yo. (To waitress) Tyo˥tto‿
Waitress: Ha˥a. Na˥ñ ni i˥tasimasyo˦o ka.
Sato: Teñpura mi-˥ttu onegai-sima˥su.
Waitress: Ha˥a, ka˥sikomarima˥sita.
Tanaka: (to Yoshida and Sato) Bi˥iru mo ˥no˦mu?
Yoshida: No˥mu yo‿ — tu˥meta˦i no o.
Sato: (to waitress) Zya˥a, bi˥iru mo. A˥rima˥su ka‿ — tu˥meta˦i no ḡa.
Waitress: Ha˥a gozaimasu. O˥bi˥iru [1] mo˥tte mairimasyo˥o ka.
Sato: O˥negai-sima˥su.

                  . . .

Waitress: O˥matase-itasima˥sita. Do˥ozo. Teñpura wa notihodo motte mai-
           rima˥su.
Tanaka: (to Yoshida and Sato) Tu˥metai bi˥iru wa ŏisii ˥ne˥e.

                  . . .

Yoshida: O˥isi˥katta ˥ne˥e — ko˥no bi˦iru wa.
Sato: Mo˥tto ta˥no˦mu?
Yoshida: Mo˥o takusañ. Zu˥ibuñ ˥no˦ñda yo‿
Tanaka: (to Sato) Mo˥o suko˥si ˥do˦o?
Sato: Boku mo ˥mo˥o ˥zu˥ibuñ ˥no˦ñda kara‿
Waitress: O˥matase-itasima˥sita. Do˥ozo. Go˥hañ mo mo˥tte mairimasyo˦o
           ka.
Tanaka: O˥negai-sima˥su.
Waitress: Ka˥sikomarima˥sita.

                  . . .

Yoshida: O˥tya onegai-sima˥su.
Waitress: Ha˥a ˥ha˦a.
Tanaka: (to Yoshida and Sato) O˥isi˥katta ˥ne˦e.

---

[1] The polite o˥bi˥iru˦ is regularly used by restaurant and hotel personnel.

Sato: Sa⌐kana ḡa atara⌐sikatta kara, o⌐isi⌐katta ⌐ne⌐e.
Yoshida: O⌐isii teñpura da⌐tta kara, ta⌐kusañ ta⌐beta yo⌐
Tanaka: (to waitress) Tyo⌐tto_ I⌐kura?
Waitress: A⌐ri⌐ḡatoo gozaimasu. Se⌐ñ happyaku ro⌐kuzyu⌐u-eñ de gozaimasu.
Yoshida: Kyo⌐o wa ⌐bo⌐ku ḡa_
Tanaka: Iie, boku ḡa_
Sato: Niseñ-eñ. Ha⌐i.

                    . . .

Waitress: Ma⌐ido ari⌐ḡatoo gozaimasu. Hyaku yo⌐ñzyu⌐u-eñ. Do⌐ozo. Ma⌐ta
             do⌐ozo.

Tanaka ⎫
Yoshida ⎬:   (to Sato) Do⌐o mo su⌐mimase⌐ñ. Gotisoosama.
Sato: Iie iie.

                         English Equivalent

Waitress: (Welcome.) What would you like?
Tanaka: One more is coming so just a minute.
Waitress: Certainly.
Tanaka: (to Sato) He's late, isn't he— Yoshida.
Sato: He is, isn't he. What are you going to have (lit. decide on)?
Tanaka: How about chicken?
Sato: Chicken is out for Yoshida.
Tanaka: That's right. How about tempura? Tempura he ate, didn't he— at
             my house?
Sato: He did, didn't he.
Yoshida: (joining his friends) I'm sorry I'm late.
Tanaka ⎫
Sato   ⎬:   Not at all.
Tanaka: What are you going to have?
Sato: How about tempura?
Yoshida: Oh, fine!
Sato: Then I'll order tempura. (Calling waitress) Miss!
Waitress: Yes. What would you like?
Sato: We'd like three [orders of] tempura.
Waitress: Yes, certainly.
Tanaka: (to Yoshida and Sato) Are you going to have beer, too?
Yoshida: I'll have some— some that's cold.
Sato: (to waitress) Well then, beer too. Do you have some— some that's
             cold?
Waitress: Yes, we have. Shall I bring beer?
Sato: Yes, please.

                    . . .

Waitress: I'm sorry to have kept you waiting. Here you are. The tempura
             I'll bring later.
Tanaka: (to Yoshida and Sato) Isn't cold beer good!

Yoshida:	Wasn't it good—this beer!
Sato:	Do you want more?
Yoshida:	No, thank you. I had an awful lot.
Tanaka:	(to Sato) How about a little more?
Sato:	I've had an awful lot already too so. . . .
Waitress:	(bringing the tempura) I'm sorry to have kept you waiting. Here you are. Shall I bring some rice too?
Tanaka:	Yes, please.
Waitress:	Certainly.

. . .

Yoshida:	We'd like some tea.
Waitress:	Certainly.
Tanaka:	(to Yoshida and Sato) Wasn't it good!
Sato:	The fish was fresh so it WAS good, wasn't it!
Yoshida:	It was delicious tempura so I ate a lot.
Tanaka:	(to waitress) Miss! How much?
Waitress:	(Thank you.) It's ¥1860.
Yoshida:	Today I [will pay the check].
Tanaka:	No, I [will pay].
Sato:	(paying) Here. ¥2000.
Waitress:	(Returning with change) Thank you. Here you are, ¥140. Please come again.
Tanaka } Yoshida }:	(to Sato) Thank you very much. It was delicious.
Sato:	Not at all.

EXERCISES

1. Tell the waitress:

        a. to bring 2 (portions of) sashimi.

        b. to bring some water.

        c. to bring more sake.

        d. that your tea is cold.

        e. that your coffee is weak.

        f . that the fish tastes bad.

        g. that you haven't ordered yet.

        h. that you want a little more rice.

        i . that you don't want any cake.

        j . that you enjoyed your meal.

2. Ask your guest: Your guest replies:

        a. what he will have to eat.   I'll have some sushi.

        b. if he will have some sake.   Yes, thank you.

        c. if he will have some more beer.   No, thank you.

　　　　d. if he will have some   Just half, please.
　　　　　　more coffee.
　　　　e. if he would like sugar.   Just a little, please.

3. Turn back to Level Drill I on pages 243–44.   Make up questions for which
    the sentences of this drill would be appropriate answers. For example,
    using the model sentence <u>Moo i⌐tta⌐ kara.</u>, an appropriate question would be:
    <u>Doo site g⌐iñkoo e ikimase⌐ñ ka↲</u> 'Why aren't you going to go to the bank?'
    Then drill on the questions together with their answers (informal alter-
    nants).

4. Practice the Basic Dialogues using appropriate variations.

Lesson 15. Eating and Drinking (cont.)

BASIC DIALOGUES: FOR MEMORIZATION

(a)

At the office

Smith

together	issyo
dining or a meal	syokuzi or osyokuzi [1]
dine or eat a meal	syokuzi o suru
dine together	issyo ni syokuzi o suru
1. Shall we have lunch [1] together?	I⌐ssyo ni syokuzi (o) simasyo⌐o ka.

Tanaka

2. Haven't you eaten yet?	Ma⌐da ta⌐bemase⌐ñ ka⌐
doesn't know (informal)	siranai
didn't know (informal)	si⌐rana⌐katta
with Mr. Saito	Saitoo-sañ to
together with Mr. Saito	Saitoo-sañ to issyo
eat together	i⌐ssyo ni tabe⌐ru
3. I didn't know so today I ate early (already) with Mr. Saito. . . .	Si⌐rana⌐katta kara, kyo⌐o wa ⌐mo⌐o Saitoo-sañ to issyo ni ⌐ha⌐yaku ta-⌐bema⌐sita ḡa⌐

Smith

other or another	hoka
day	hi⌐
another day	ho⌐ka no hi⌐
4. Well then, let's make it another day.	Zya⌐a, ho⌐ka no hi⌐ ni si⌐masyo⌐o.

Tanaka

whatever day of the week it is or any day of the week at all	na⌐ñyo⌐o(bi) de mo
5. Yes. Any day at all will be fine.	E⌐e. Na⌐ñyo⌐o de mo ⌐i⌐i desu yo⌐

---

[1] Or breakfast or dinner.

(b)

In a restaurant

Tanaka

which alternative	do⌐tira no ⌐ho⌐o
6. Which /alternative/ would be better, noodles or sushi?	So⌐ba to ⌐su⌐si to, do⌐tira /no ⌐ho⌐o/ ḡa ⌐i⌐i desyoo ka.

Smith

whichever of two it is <u>or</u> either one	do⌐tira de⌐ mo
7. Either one is fine, but let's make it sushi, shall we?	Do⌐tira de mo i⌐i desu ḡa, su⌐si ni si⌐masyo⌐o ne?

Tanaka (to waitress)

one portion	iti-niñmae
8. We'd like two portions of sushi.	Su⌐si (o) ni-⌐niñmae oneḡai-sima⌐su.

. . .

bill <u>or</u> accounting <u>or</u> check	kaikee <u>or</u> okaikee +
9. Check, please.	Ka⌐ikee (o) oneḡai-sima⌐su.
10. How much does it come to?	I⌐kura ni na⌐rima⌐su ka⌐

Waitress

11. It's ¥ 150 for one portion so it comes to ¥ 300. Thank you.	Iti-niñmae hya⌐ku gozyu⌐u-eñ de go-⌐zaima⌐su kara, sa⌐ñbyaku⌐-eñ ni narimasu. Ma⌐ido ari⌐ḡatoo gozai-masu.

(c)

Mrs. Smith (arriving home)

noon meal	hi⌐rugo⌐hañ <u>or</u> o⌐hirugo⌐hañ +
stomach	onaka
become empty	suku /-u/
12. I had lunch early so I'm hungry. (Lit. Lunch was early so my stomach has become empty.)	O⌐hirugo⌐hañ (ḡa) ⌐ha⌐yakatta kara, o⌐naka ḡa sukima⌐sita yo⌐
a meal	go⌐hañ
come into being <u>or</u> be(come) completed	de⌐ki⌐ru /-ru/
13. Is dinner ready?	Go⌐hañ (ḡa) de⌐kima⌐sita ka⌐

Maid

soon now <u>or</u> any minute now	mo⌐o su⌐ḡu

14. It will be ready any minute   Mo⌐o su⌐ḡu de⌐kima⌐su ḡa_
    now. . . .

(d)

Mr. Tanaka

    pleasing   su⌐ki⌐ /na/ or
                                               osuki⌐ /na/
15. Which /alternative/ do you   Sukiyaki to ⌐su⌐si to, do⌐tira /no
    prefer— sukiyaki or sushi?   ⌐ho⌐o/ ḡa o⌐suki de⌐su ka_

Mr. Smith

    the alternative of suki-   su⌐kiyaki no ho⌐o
    yaki
16. Me, I prefer sukiyaki.   Boku wa su⌐kiyaki /no ho⌐o/ ḡa su-
                                               ⌐ki⌐ desu yo. [1]

Mr. Tanaka

    more than sukiyaki   su⌐kiyaki yo⌐ri
    the alternative of sushi   su⌐si no ⌐ho⌐o
17. Oh? I like sushi more than   So⌐o desu ka. Boku wa su⌐kiyaki
    sukiyaki.   yo⌐ri ⌐su⌐si /no ⌐ho⌐o/ ḡa su⌐ki⌐
                                               desu.

    however or but   si⌐ka⌐si
    to the highest degree   i⌐ti⌐bañ
    the one that's most pleasing   i⌐tibañ suki⌐ na no
18. But what I like best is tempura.   Si⌐ka⌐si, i⌐tibañ suki⌐ na no wa te⌐ñ-
                                               pura de⌐su yo.

Mr. Smith

19. Oh, tempura?   A⌐a, te⌐ñpura de⌐su ka.

20. I like tempura best, too.   Bo⌐ku mo te⌐ñpura ḡa itibañ suki⌐
                                               desu yo.

    to the extent of tempura   te⌐ñpura hodo
    or as much as tem-
    pura
21. I like sukiyaki too, but not   Su⌐kiyaki mo suki⌐ desu ḡa, te⌐ñpura
    so much as tempura.   hodo zya arimase⌐ñ yo.

(e)

Tanaka

    for dining or for a   syokuzi ni
    meal

---

[1] Accent of short alternant: suki⌐.

	being fish and meat and fowl	sakana to ni⌐ku⌐ to tŏri de

being fish and meat and
fowl   sakana to ni⌐ku⌐ to tŏri de

[being] among fish and   sakana to ni⌐ku⌐ to tŏri no uti
   meat and fowl   [de]

22. Mr. Smith is coming to our   Su⌐misu - sañ (ḡa) u⌐ti e syokuzi ni
house for dinner. Which do   irassyaima⌐su ḡa; sakana to ni⌐ku⌐
you suppose he would like   to tŏri │de   │, do⌐re ḡa i⌐ti-
best, fish, meat, or fowl?   │no uti [de]│
                                                         bañ osuki desyo⌐o ka.

Jones

isn't meat (informal)   ni⌐ku⌐ zya ⌐na⌐i
it probably isn't meat   ni⌐ku⌐ zya ⌐na⌐i desyoo
wouldn't it be meat?   ni⌐ku⌐ zya ⌐na⌐i desyoo ka

23. Hmm. I'm not sure but would-   Sa⌐a, yo⌐ku wa⌐karimase⌐ñ ḡa; ni-
n't it be meat?   ⌐ku⌐ zya ⌐na⌐i desyoo ka.

Tanaka

24. I suppose so.   So⌐o desyoo ⌐ne⌐e.

Jones

whichever (of three or   do⌐re de mo
   more) it is or any
   one at all
most Americans   ta⌐itee no Amerika⌐ziñ

25. I guess any one (of the three   Ma⌐a, do⌐re de mo ⌐i⌐i desyoo ḡa;
alternatives) would be fine,   sa⌐simi⌐ wa ta⌐itee no Amerika⌐ziñ
but sashimi most Americans   wa a⌐ñmari suki⌐ zya a⌐rimase⌐ñ ḡa_
don't like very much. . . .

Tanaka

26. That's right, isn't it.   So⌐re wa so⌐o desu ⌐ne⌐e.

(f)

Mr. Tanaka

27. Which do you like better—   Bi⌐iru to sǎke to, do⌐tti [no ⌐ho⌐o]
beer or sake?   ḡa suki?

Mr. Yamamoto

the alternative of beer   bi⌐iru no ⌐ho⌐o
by far   zutto
a drink or beverage   no⌐mi⌐mono
displeasing   kirai /na/

28. I like beer much more—   Bi⌐iru [no ⌐ho⌐o] ḡa zu⌐tto suki⌐ da
since I hate hot drinks.   yo—a⌐tu⌐i no⌐mi⌐mono (wa) ki⌐rai
                                                     da⌐ kara.

Mr. Tanaka

29. Tea too?   Otya mo?

Mr. Yamamoto

of course <u>or</u> to be sure	mo⌐ti⌐ron
very pleasing	da⌐isuki /na/

30. Oh, tea is different. Of course
I like it a lot!

A⌐a, otya wa tiğau. Mo⌐ti⌐ron ⌐da⌐i-suki da yo.

(g)

Mr. Tanaka

throat	no⌐do
become dry	ka⌐wa⌐ku /-u/

31. I'm thirsty. (Lit. My throat
has become dry.)

No⌐do (ğa) ka⌐wa⌐ita.

Mr. Yamamoto

32. What do you want to drink?   Na⌐ni (ğa) nomitai?

Mr. Tanaka

no matter what it is	na⌐n de⌐ mo
<u>or</u> anything at all	

33. Anything will be fine.   Na⌐n de mo i⌐i yo.

(h)

At a restaurant

Tanaka

34. Is this coffee?   Kore ko⌐ohi⌐i?

Yamamoto

35. Yes, that's right.   E⌐e, so⌐o.

Tanaka

isn't strange (informal)	he⌐n zya ⌐na⌐i

36. Doesn't it taste funny? (Lit.
Isn't it strange?)

He⌐n zya nai?

Yamamoto (after tasting it)

isn't delicious	o⌐isiku na⌐i

37. It isn't good, is it!   O⌐isiku na⌐i ⌐ne⌐e.

NOTES ON THE BASIC DIALOGUES

3.   'but—if I had known, I would have waited for you.'

4.   Compare: <u>hoka no zassi</u> 'another magazine' or 'other magazines'; <u>zassi no hoka</u> 'other than magazines,' 'besides magazines.'

12. Hi⌐ru⌐ means 'noon' or 'daytime.'

Compare also <u>a⌐sago⌐han</u> 'breakfast' and <u>ba⌐ngo⌐han</u> 'dinner,' 'evening meal.'

Note also the following, all of which are in common use: o⌐naka ̄ga (or wa) sukimase⌐ñ 'I'm not hungry' (lit. 'my stomach hasn't become empty'); o⌐naka ̄ga suite (i)ma⌐su 'I'm hungry' (lit. 'my stomach is in a state of having become empty'); o⌐naka ̄ga (or wa) suite (i)mase⌐ñ 'I'm not hungry' (lit. 'my stomach is not in a state of having become empty').

14.   'but—will that be all right?'

15.   Both the thing which is pleasing and the person to whom it is pleasing are followed by particles ̄ga or wa (depending upon emphasis). Note that su⌐ki⌐ is a na-nominal: thus, su⌐ki⌐ na mono 'pleasing things,' 'things [I] like'; o⌐suki na mono⌐ 'things pleasing to someone else,' 'things [you] like.'

16.   Wa here is the wa of comparison: 'I, for my part.'

17.   See the immediately preceding note.

18.   Si⌐ka⌐si occurs at the beginning of sentences.

       No is the nominal no 'one,' referring here to a kind of food.

22.   Ni here is the ni of goal.

25.   'but—they like most other things.'

26.   Wa here is the wa of comparison.

28.   Zutto: note also zu⌐tto ma⌐e 'a long time before or ago,' zutto usiro 'way in back,' etc.

       No⌐mi⌐mono: compare ta⌐bemo⌐no 'food,' 'edibles.'

       Kirai is the opposite of su⌐ki⌐ and enters into the same kinds of patterns (except that it does not have a polite equivalent). Ki⌐rai de⌐su is a stronger, less tactful expression than su⌐ki⌐ zya a⌐rimase⌐ñ '[I] don't like [it],' '[I] don't care for [it].'

30.   Da⌐isuki is an informal word.

31.   Nōdo ̄ga ka⌐wa⌐ku occurs in the same kinds of patterns as onaka ̄ga suku. See the note on Sentence 12 above.

32.   Compare: Na⌐ni o ⌐no⌐mu? 'What are you going to drink?' but Na⌐ni ̄ga (or, less commonly, o) nomitai? 'What do you want to drink?' See Lesson 7, Grammatical Note 1.

28, 30, 33, and 37 contain informal non-past or past inflected words followed directly by yo or nee. Such combinations occur more commonly in men's speech.

GRAMMATICAL NOTES

1. Informal Negatives, Non-past and Past

The informal equivalent of a formal non-past negative ending in -mase⌐n is an ADJECTIVAL ending in -[a]nai.

To make the informal negative adjectival from the citation form of a verbal:

> -ru group: drop -ru and add -nai
>
>> Example: ta⌐be⌐ru 'eat' — ta⌐be⌐nai 'doesn't eat'
>
> -u group: drop -u and add -anai
>
>> Example: no⌐mu 'drink' — no⌐ma⌐nai 'doesn't drink'
>
>> but: for -u verbals ending in a vowel + -u, drop -u and add -wanai
>
>> Example: kau 'buy' — kawanai 'doesn't buy'
>
>> Note: The informal negative of a⌐ru 'be (inanimate),' 'have' is na⌐i.
>
> -aru group: change -aru to -aranai [1]
>
>> Example: ku⌐dasa⌐ru 'give me' — ku⌐dasara⌐nai 'doesn't give me'
>
>> Note: A corresponding informal negative does not exist for go⌐za⌐ru.
>
> Irregular group:
>
>> suru 'do' — sinai 'doesn't do'
>> ku⌐ru 'come' — ko⌐nai 'doesn't come'

An unaccented verbal has an unaccented informal negative equivalent; an accented verbal has an accented informal negative equivalent, with the accent occurring on the syllable immediately preceding the -nai ending.

The past informal negative ends in -nakatta; like all adjectival past informal forms, it is made by replacing the final -i of the non-past with -katta. It is accented on syllable na if derived from an unaccented non-past negative, and on the syllable immediate preceding -nakatta if derived from an accented non-past negative.

Examples:

---

[1] Or, worded differently: drop -u and add -anai.

AFFIRMATIVE	NEGATIVE	
Verbal Non-past Informal (Citation Form)	Non-past: Informal/Formal	Past: Informal/Formal
(-<u>ru</u> Group)		
deˈru 'go out'	deˈnai/deˈmaseˈ̄n	deˈnakatta/deˈmaseˈ̄n de- sita
miˈru 'see'	miˈnai/miˈmaseˈ̄n	miˈnakatta/miˈmaseˈ̄n de- sita
(-<u>u</u> Group)		
maˈtu 'wait'	maˈtaˈnai/maˈtima- seˈ̄n	maˈtaˈnakatta/maˈtima- seˈ̄n desita
kaˈeru 'return'	kaˈeraˈnai/kaˈeri- maseˈ̄n	kaˈeraˈnakatta/kaˈerima- seˈ̄n desita
iu 'say'	iwanai/iˈimaseˈ̄n	iˈwanaˈkatta/iˈimaseˈ̄n desita
haˈnaˈsu 'talk'	haˈnasaˈnai/haˈna- simaseˈ̄n	haˈnasaˈnakatta/haˈnasi- maseˈ̄n desita
kiku 'ask,' 'lis- ten,' 'hear'	kikanai/kiˈkima- seˈ̄n	kiˈkanaˈkatta/kiˈkima- seˈ̄n desita
iˈsoˈgu 'be in a hurry'	iˈsogaˈnai/iˈsogi- maseˈ̄n	iˈsogaˈnakatta/iˈsogima- seˈ̄n desita
yobu 'call'	yobanai/yoˈbima- seˈ̄n	yoˈbanaˈkatta/yoˈbima- seˈ̄n desita
yoˈmu 'read'	yoˈmaˈnai/yoˈmi- maseˈ̄n	yoˈmaˈnakatta/yoˈmima- seˈ̄n desita
(-<u>aru</u> Group)		
naˈsaˈru 'do'	naˈsaraˈnai/naˈsa- imaseˈ̄n	naˈsaraˈnakatta/naˈsai- maseˈ̄n desita
(Irregular Group)		
kuˈru 'come'	koˈnai/kiˈmaseˈ̄n	koˈnakatta/kiˈmaseˈ̄n de- sita
suru 'do,' 'make'	sinai/siˈmaseˈ̄n	siˈnaˈkatta/siˈmaseˈ̄n de- sita

The occurrences of non-negative adjectival forms like taˈkaˈi / taˈkakatta (i.e. informal non-past and past forms) parallel the occurrences of negative adjectivals.

Examples:

Informal sentences

     Siranai. 'I don't know.'
     Ikanai yo⌐ 'I'm not going!' (men's speech)

Ma¬da de⌐ki⁻nai ⌐ne¬e. 'It hasn't been finished yet, has it.' (men's speech)

Saitoo-sañ wa ⌐ma¬da ⌐ko⁻nai? 'Hasn't Mr. Saito come yet?'

Wa⌐kara¬nakatta. 'I didn't understand.'

Da⌐re mo de¬nakatta yo₋ 'Nobody answered (the telephone)!' (men's speech)

Pa¬ñ ka⌐wana¬katta? 'Didn't you buy any bread?'

Formal Sentences:

So⌐ñna hito¬ wa de⌐ki¬nai desyoo. 'That kind of person probably can't do it.'

Tanaka-sañ wa i⌐rassyara¬nai desyoo ka. 'Do you suppose Mr. Tanaka isn't in?'

So⌐o iwana¬katta desyoo. 'He probably didn't say that.'

Wa⌐kara¬nai kara, mo⌐o iti-do itte kudasa¬i. 'I don't understand so please say it again.'

I⌐kana¬katta kara, mi⌐mase¬ñ desita. 'I didn't go so I didn't see it.'

However, note this difference: a formal equivalent of a non-negative adjectival like ta⌐ka¬i/ta⌐kakatta is ta⌐ka¬i desu/ta⌐kakatta desu. While a corresponding formal negative pattern does exist—for example, na¬i desu / na¬katta desu are frequently occurring forms—the more usual formal negative pattern is the -mase¬ñ/-mase¬ñ desita pattern derived from the corresponding formal affirmative verbal.

Note, now, the following patterns:

Non-past Negative

	Formal	Informal
Verbal Pattern	-mase¬ñ form (or negative adjectival ending in -/a/nai + desu) (wa⌐karimase¬ñ or wa⌐kara¬nai desu)	Negative adjectival ending in -/a/nai (wa⌐kara¬nai)
Adjectival Pattern	Adjectival ending in -ku + a⌐rimase¬ñ or + na¬i desu (ta¬kaku a⌐rimase¬ñ or ta¬kaku ⌐na⁻i desu)	Adjectival ending in -ku + na¬i (ta¬kaku ⌐na⁻i)
Nominal Pattern	Nominal + zya a⌐rimase¬ñ or + zya ⌐na¬i desu (ho¬ñ zya a⌐rimase¬ñ or ho¬ñ zya ⌐na⁻i desu)	Nominal + zya ⌐na¬i (ho¬ñ zya ⌐na⁻i)

To form the corresponding past forms of the above:

(a) Add desita to -mase¬ñ forms.

(b) Change -nai to -nakatta and -nai desu to -nakatta desu.

An adjectival modifying a verbal o c c u r s in its -ku form (cf. Lesson 10, Grammatical Note 4).   For negative adjectivals, occurrence before naꞁru 'become' is the most common example of this pattern:

> deꞁkiꞁnaku ꜛnaˉru 'become unable'
> waꞁkaraꞁnaku ꜛnaˉru 'reach the point of not understanding'

The a c c e n t of a -naku form is the same as that of the corresponding -nai form.

2.   C o m p a r i s o n   o f   T w o   I t e m s ;   P a r t i c l e s   yori and hodo

X to Y to, doꞁtira —— asks: 'of X and Y, which is [more] ——?'[1] X and Y are both nominals (which may be preceded by descriptive words or phrases and/or followed by particles).   Following doꞁtira is an appropriate particle— u s u a l l y g̃a (if doꞁtira is the subject) or o (if doꞁtira is the object)—and an inflected expression.

Study the following examples:

> (a) Kore to sore to, doꞁtira g̃a ꜛkiˉree desu ka⌐
>   'Which is prettier—this or that?'
> (b) Oꞁokiꞁi no to tiꞁisaꞁi no to, doꞁtira g̃a ꜛiˉi desyoo ka.
>   'Which would be better—the big one or the small one?'
> (c) Tanaka-sañ no okosañ to oꞁtaku noꞁ to, doꞁtira g̃a oꞁokiˉi desu ka⌐
>   'Who is bigger—the Tanakas' child or yours?'
> (d) Koꞁno okaꞁsi to soꞁno okaꞁsi to, doꞁtti g̃a aꜛmaˉi desu ka⌐
>   'Which is sweeter—this cake or that cake?'
> (e) Tanaka-sañ to Yamamoto-sañ to, doꞁtira o ꜛyoˉku siꜛtte imaˉsu ka⌐
>   'Which one do you know better—Mr. Tanaka or Mr. Yamamoto?'

In examples of this kind, doꞁtira no ꜛhoˉo 'which alternative?' is interchangeable with doꞁtira 'which one?'

In the replies, the word or phrase which answers the question is followed b y the same particle that followed the interrogative word o r phrase in the question.   Hoꞁo 'alternative' may or may not be included in the answer.

Study the following answers to the questions above:

> (a) Koꞁre g̃a kiꞁree desu.   or   Koꞁno hoꞁo g̃a ꜛkiˉree desu.
>   'This is prettier.'
> (b) Oꞁokiꞁi no g̃a ꜛiˉi desu.   or   Oꞁokiꞁi ꜛhoˉo g̃a ꜛiˉi desu.
>   'The big one is better.'
> (c) Taꞁnaka-sañ no okosañ g̃a ookiꞁi desu.   or
>   Taꞁnaka-sañ no okosañ no hoꞁo g̃a oꞁokiˉi desu.
>   'The Tanakas' child is bigger.'

---

[1] For an alternate pattern, see Note 3 below.

(d) So⌐no okaˀsi ḡa aˠmaˀi desu.   or
     So⌐no okaˀsi no ˠhoˀo ḡa aˠmaˀi desu.
     'That cake is sweeter.'

(e) Yaˀmamoto-sañ o yoˀku sitte imasu.   or
     Yaˀmamoto-sañ no hoˀo o ˠyoˀku sitte imasu.
     'I know Mr. Yamamoto better.'

Yoˀri (yori after an accented word) 'more than' follows the nominal with
which another nominal is being compared. Again, the nominals may be preceded by descriptive words or phrases and/or followed by particles.

Study the following examples, noting the particles:

(a) So⌐re yoˀri ko⌐re ḡa kiˀree desu.   or   So⌐re yoˀri ko⌐no hoˀo ḡa
     ˠkiˀree desu.
     'THIS is prettier than that.' (Lit. 'More than that, THIS [or THIS
     ALTERNATIVE] is pretty.')

(b) Ti⌐isaˀi no yori o⌐okiˀi no ḡa ˠiˀi desu.   or   Ti⌐isaˀi no yori
     o⌐okiˀi ˠhoˀo ḡa ˠiˀi desu.
     'A BIG ONE is better than a small one.' (Lit. 'More than a small
     one, a BIG ONE [or ALTERNATIVE] is good.')

(c) Ta⌐naka-sañ yoˀri Yaˀmamoto-sañ o yoˀku sitte imasu.   or
     Ta⌐naka-sañ yoˀri Yaˀmamoto-sañ no hoˀo o ˠyoˀku sitte imasu.
     'I know MR. YAMAMOTO better than Mr. Tanaka.' (Lit. 'More
     than Mr. Tanaka I know MR. YAMAMOTO [or the alternative of
     MR. YAMAMOTO] well.')

In the above examples, the phrase ending with yori may occur after the ḡa
or o phrase without any difference in meaning other than a slight change in
emphasis.

Examples of the pattern X wa Y yori ——— also occur; here, X is already
under discussion or is being compared, and the emphasis is on what follows.

Hodo 'to the extent of' occurs in negative comparisons: X wa Y hodo /+
negative/ 'X is not as ——— as Y.'

Study the following examples:

(a) Sore wa kŏre hodo ⌐kiˀree zya aˠrimaseˀñ.
     'That is not as pretty as this.' (Lit. 'That is not pretty to the ex-
     tent of this.')

(b) Ti⌐isaˀi no wa o⌐okiˀi no hodo ⌐yoˀku aˠrimaseˀñ.
     'A small one is not as good as a big one.' (Lit. 'A small one is
     not good to the extent of a big one.')

(c) Tanaka-sañ wa Yămamoto-sañ hodo ⌐yoˀku siˠrimaseˀñ.
     'Mr. Tanaka I don't know as well as Mr. Yamamoto.' (Lit. 'Mr.
     Tanaka I don't know well to the extent of Mr. Yamamoto.')
          or
     'Mr. Tanaka doesn't know as well as Mr. Yamamoto.' (Lit. 'Mr.
     Tanaka doesn't know well to the extent of Mr. Yamamoto.')

3 .   C o m p a r i s o n   o f   T h r e e   o r   M o r e   I t e m s ;   i⌐ti⌐baṅ

I⌐ti⌐baṅ[1] 'to the greatest degree' occurs with verbals, adjectivals, nominals, and the copula:

> Ta⌐naka-saṅ ḡa itibaṅ dekima⌐su.   'Mr. Tanaka is the most capable.'
> I⌐tibaṅ taka⌐i no wa so⌐re de⌐su.   'The most expensive one is that one.'
> So⌐no sara ḡa itibaṅ ki⌐ree desyoo ne?   'I guess that plate is the prettiest, isn't it?'
> So⌐re mo i⌐i desu ḡa, ko⌐re ḡa iti⌐baṅ desu.   'That's good too, but this is the best.'

The two most common Japanese patterns f o r asking 'of X and Y and Z, which is most —— ?' are:

> X to Y to Z de, do⌐re + particle + i⌐ti⌐baṅ ——
> Lit. 'being X and Y and Z, which to the greatest extent —— ?'

and

> X to Y to Z no uti[2] [de], do⌐re + particle + i⌐ti⌐baṅ ——
> Lit. '[being] among X and Y and Z, which to the greatest extent ——
> ——?'

X, Y, and Z are nominals (which may be preceded by descriptive words or phrases and/or followed by particles); following do⌐re is an appropriate particle. These p a t t e r n s are used when three or more items are specifically m e n t i o n e d .   A cover phrase such as ko⌐no mi-ttu⌐ [no uti] [de] '[being] [among] these three things,' Nihoṅ no yasai [no uti] [de] '[being] [among] Japanese vegetables,' etc., may be used instead of naming the specific items. Also, question words other than do⌐re m a y be used when they are appropriate.

Statements involving the same kind of comparison have the same general pattern as questions.

Examples:

> Gaiziṅ wa, sukiyaki to teṅpura to ⌐su⌐si no uti de, taitee ⌐do⌐re o i⌐tibaṅ yo⌐ku ta⌐bema⌐su ka⌐ 'Which do Westerners usually eat most often— sukiyaki or tempura or sushi?'
> Ko⌐obe to Ōosaka to Yōkohama de, do⌐ko ḡa i⌐tibaṅ ooki⌐i desu ka⌐ 'Which is the biggest place—Kobe or Osaka or Yokohama?'
> So⌐no saṅ-ni⌐ṅ no uti de, da⌐re ḡa ni⌐hoṅḡo ḡa itibaṅ yo⌐ku wa⌐karima⌐su ka⌐ 'Of those 3 people, who understands Japanese best?'
> Ko⌐no yo-ttu⌐ no uti de, ko⌐re ḡa itibaṅ suki⌐ desu kara; ko⌐re ni sima⌐sita. 'Of these 4 I like this one best so I decided on this one.'

---

[1] I⌐ti⌐baṅ is regularly accented in isolation and immediately before √da.

[2] Uti (nominal) 'among'; other meanings will be introduced later.

Eeḡo to nihoñḡo to huḡañsuḡo de, i⌐tibañ hana⌐su no wa ni⌐hoñḡo de⌐su.
'Of English and Japanese and French, the one I speak most is Japanese.'

In comparing two alternatives, <u>X to Y de ⌐do⌐tira</u> ―― 'being <u>X</u> and <u>Y</u>, which one ――?' is sometimes used as an alternant of <u>X to Y to ⌐do tira ――</u>, the pattern introduced in Note 2 above.   Here too, a covering phrase may be used instead of mentioning specific items: <u>ko⌐no huta-tu⌐ de ⌐do⌐tira</u> ―― 'being these two things, which one ―― ?'

4.   Interrogative + <u>de⌐ mo</u>

An interrogative word or phrase (<u>na⌐ñ</u>, <u>do⌐re</u>, <u>do⌐tira</u>, <u>i⌐tu</u>, <u>do⌐ko</u>, <u>na⌐ñ-zi</u>, <u>do⌐no ⌐ho⌐ñ</u>, etc.) + <u>de</u> (the gerund of <u>da</u>) + particle <u>mo</u> 'even' means '――ever it is,' 'no matter ―― it is,' 'any ―― at all' (lit. 'even being ――').   Thus:[1]

da⌐re de⌐ mo 'whoever it is,' 'no matter who it is,' 'anyone at all'

do⌐ko de⌐ mo 'wherever it is,' 'no matter what place it is,' 'any place at all'

i⌐tu de⌐ mo 'whenever it is,' 'no matter when it is,' 'any time at all'

i⌐ku-tu de⌐ mo 'any number (of units) at all,' 'however many it is,' 'no matter how many it is'

na⌐ñ-niñ de⌐ mo 'any number of people at all,' 'however many people it is,' 'no matter how many people it is'

The interrogative may be followed by any of the particles which normally precede √<u>da</u>:

do⌐ko kara de⌐ mo 'wherever it is from,' 'no matter where it is from'

Examples:

Da⌐re de⌐ mo de⌐ki⌐ru desyoo. 'Anyone at all can probably do it.'
I⌐tu de⌐ mo ⌐i⌐i desu yo⌐ 'Any time at all will be all right.'
So⌐no⌐ hito wa na⌐ñ de⌐ mo tabemasu. 'He eats anything at all.'
Na⌐ñ-zi kara de⌐ mo ka⌐maimase⌐ñ. 'No matter what time it starts (lit. even being from what time), it makes no difference.'

――――――――――

[1] There is considerable variation in the accent of such combinations.   The original accent of the interrogative is sometimes retained, but is more often lost.

5.   Manner

To indicate how or in what manner something is done, the following patterns occur:

(a) a verbal gerund

Example: i⌐so⌐ide ⌐ka⌐ku 'write in a hurry'

(b) an adverbial adjectival (i.e. the -ku form)[1]

Example: o⌐mosi⌐roku ⌐ka⌐ku 'write interestingly'

(c) a nominal + particle ni of manner

Examples: i⌐ssyo ni ka⌐ku 'write together'
ki⌐ree ni ⌐ka⌐ku 'write beautifully'

(d) a nominal alone

Examples: so⌐o ka⌐ku 'write thus'
yu⌐kku⌐ri ⌐ka⌐ku 'write slowly'

Na-nominals are among those regularly followed by ni in patterns of manner. Otherwise, it is impossible to know which nominals are followed by ni and which may occur alone, except by observing the usage of native speakers.

6.   Particle to 'with'

To, the particle of accompaniment, following a nominal means 'with.' A phrase ending in to may modify an inflected word directly or it may be followed by other particles:

ni⌐hoñzi⌐ñ to kekkoñ-suru 'marry (with) a Japanese'
to⌐modati to hana⌐su 'talk with a friend'
to⌐modati to⌐ mo ha⌐na⌐su 'talk with a friend, too'

It may also modify certain nominals directly:

tomodati to issyo 'together with a friend'

But as a description of nominals, it is regularly followed by particle no:

a⌐merika⌐ziñ to no kekkoñ 'marriage with an American'
a⌐ni to no hanasi 'a talk with my (older) brother'

The particle to 'and' introduced in Lesson 4, Grammatical Note 1 (e), joins coordinate nominals. Compare:

---

[1] This is another example of an adjectival in its -ku form modifying an inflected word—a constantly recurring pattern.

Tanaka-sañ to Yamamoto-sañ wa haˉnasimaˉsita.   'Mr. Tanaka and Mr. Yamamoto talked. '

and :

Tanaka-sañ wa Yaˉmamoto-sañ to hanasimaˉsita.   'Mr. Tanaka talked with Mr. Yamamoto.'

WARNING :   To never means 'with' in the sense of 'the means by which an action is performed.'   Compare :

Toˉmodati to hanasimaˉsita.   'I talked with a friend.'

and :

Haˉsi de taˉbemaˉsita.   'I ate with chopsticks.'

For de 'by means of,' see Lesson 7, Grammatical Note 3 (d).

7. Counter -niñmae

The counter -niñmae combines with the numerals of Series I to count portions or servings— of a single item or of everything eaten by a single person:

iti-niñmae	' 1 portion'	roku-niñmae ' 6 portions'
ni-niñmae	' 2 portions'	siti-niñmae or nana-niñmae ' 7 portions'
sañ-niñmae	' 3 portions'	hati-niñmae ' 8 portions'
yo-niñmae	' 4 portions'	kyuu-niñmae or ku-niñmae ' 9 portions'
go-niñmae	' 5 portions'	zyuu-niñmae ' 10 portions'

nañ-niñmae 'how many portions? '

DRILLS

A. Substitution Drill (based on Grammatical Note 4)

1. Anything at all will be fine.
Naˉñ de mo iˉi desu yoⵧ

2. Either one will be fine.
Doˉtira de mo iˉi desu yoⵧ

3. Any one (of a group of 3 or more) at all will be fine.
Doˉre de mo iˉi desu yoⵧ

4. Any time at all will be fine.
Iˉtu de mo iˉi desu yoⵧ

5. Anybody at all will be fine.
Daˉre de mo iˉi desu yoⵧ

6. Any place at all will be fine.
Doˉko de mo iˉi desu yoⵧ

7. Any hour at all will be fine.
Naˉñ-zi de mo iˉi desu yoⵧ

8. Any number of people at all will be fine.
Naˉñ-niñ de mo iˉi desu yoⵧ

9. Any number of things (or any age) at all will be fine.
Iˉku-tu de mo iˉi desu yoⵧ

10. Any book at all will be
    fine.

Do⌐no hoñ de mo ῑi desu yo⌐

11. No matter whose it is,
    it will be fine.

Da⌐re no de mo i⌐i desu yo⌐

12. No matter what time it
    starts, it will be fine.

Na⌐ñ-zi kara de mo i⌐i desu yo⌐

B. Substitution Drill

1. How much is it for one
   portion?

Iti-niñmae ⌐i⌐kura desu ka⌐

2. How much is it for one
   glass (ful)?

I⌐p-pai ⌐i⌐kura desu ka⌐

3. How much is it for one
   bottle? [1]

I⌐p-poñ ⌐i⌐kura desu ka⌐

4. How much is it for one
   (thin, flat object)?

I⌐ti⌐-mai ⌐i⌐kura desu ka⌐

5. How much is it for one
   book?

Is-satu ⌐i⌐kura desu ka⌐

6. How much is it for one
   hour?

I⌐ti-zi⌐kañ ⌐i⌐kura desu ka⌐

7. How much is it for one
   day?

Iti-niti ⌐i⌐kura desu ka⌐

8. How much is it for one
   month?

I⌐k-ka⌐ḡetu ⌐i⌐kura desu ka⌐

9. How much is it for one
   person?

Hi⌐to⌐-ri ⌐i⌐kura desu ka⌐

10. How much is it for one
    (thing)?

Hi⌐to⌐-tu ⌐i⌐kura desu ka⌐

C. Substitution Drill (based on Grammatical Note 5)

1. They talked slowly.

Yu⌐kku⌐ri ha⌐nasima⌐sita.

2. They talked [in] simple
   [language].

Ya⌐sasiku hanasima⌐sita.

3. They talked together.

I⌐ssyo ni hanasima⌐sita.

4. They talked in a hurry.

I⌐so⌐ide ha⌐nasima⌐sita.

5. They talked that way.

So⌐o hanasima⌐sita.

6. They talked quickly.

Ha⌐yaku ha⌐nasima⌐sita.

7. They talked in the same
   way.

O⌐nazi ni hanasima⌐sita.

8. They talked [in] difficult
   [language].

Mu⌐zukasiku hanasima⌐sita.

---

[1] Or any long, cylindrical object.

D. Substitution Drill (based on Grammatical Note 6)

1. Last night I had dinner
    with a friend.
    Yuube to⌐modati to issyo ni syokuzi
    (o) sima⌐sita.

2. Last night I went [there]
    with my mother.
    Yuube ⌐ha⌐ha to issyo ni i⌐kima⌐si-
    ta.

3. Last night I went out with
    my father.
    Yuube ti⌐ti⌐ to issyo ni de⌐kakema⌐-
    sita.

4. Last night I studied with
    my cousin.
    Yuube i⌐to⌐ko to issyo ni be⌐ñkyoo-
    sima⌐sita.

5. Last night I came here with
    my parents.
    Yuube ⌐ryo⌐osiñ to issyo ni ki⌐ma⌐-
    sita.

6. Last night I returned home
    with my children.
    Yuube ko⌐domo to issyo ni kaerima⌐-
    sita.

7. Last night I saw [it] with
    my wife.
    Yuube ⌐ka⌐nai to issyo ni mi⌐ma⌐si-
    ta.

8. Last night I ate with my
    aunt.
    Yuube o⌐ba to issyo ni tabema⌐sita.

E. Substitution Drill (based on Grammatical Note 2)

1. Which do you like better,
    this one or that one?
    Kore to are to ⌐do⌐tira ʃno ⌐ho⌐oʃ ḡa
    o⌐suki de⌐su ka‿

2. Which is more expensive,
    this one or that one?
    Kore to are to ⌐do⌐tira ʃno ⌐ho⌐oʃ ḡa
    ta⌐ka⌐i desu ka‿

3. Which is bigger, this one
    or that one?
    Kore to are to ⌐do⌐tira ʃno ⌐ho⌐oʃ ḡa
    o⌐oki⌐i desu ka‿

4. Which tastes better, this
    one or that one?
    Kore to are to ⌐do⌐tira ʃno ⌐ho⌐oʃ ḡa
    o⌐isi⌐i desu ka‿

5. Which is better, this one
    or that one?
    Kore to are to ⌐do⌐tira ʃno ⌐ho⌐oʃ ḡa
    ⌐i⌐i desu ka‿

6. Which is easier, this one
    or that one?
    Kore to are to ⌐do⌐tira ʃno ⌐ho⌐oʃ ḡa
    ya⌐sasi⌐i desu ka‿

7. Which is newer, this one
    or that one?
    Kore to are to ⌐do⌐tira ʃno ⌐ho⌐oʃ ḡa
    a⌐tarasi⌐i desu ka‿

8. Which is more difficult,
    this one or that one?
    Kore to are to ⌐do⌐tira ʃno ⌐ho⌐oʃ ḡa
    mu⌐zukasi⌐i desu ka‿

9. Which is more interesting,
    this one or that one?
    Kore to are to ⌐do⌐tira ʃno ⌐ho⌐oʃ ḡa
    o⌐mosiro⌐i desu ka‿

F. Substitution Drill (based on Grammatical Note 3)

    (Insert na where required)

1. The one I like best is
    tempura.
    I⌐tibañ suki⌐ na no wa te⌐ñpura de⌐su
    yo.

2. The worst one is this pa-
    per.
    I⌐tibañ waru⌐i no wa ko⌐no siñbuñ de⌐-
    su yo.

3. The peppiest one is that
    child.
    I⌐tibañ ge⌐ñki na no wa a⌐no kodomo
    de⌐su yo.

4. The oldest one is our car.
    I⌐tibañ huru⌐i no wa u⌐ti no kuruma
    de⌐su yo.

5. The prettiest one is Miss Tanaka.

I⌐tibañ ki⌐ree na no wa Ta⌐naka-sañ no ozyo⌐osañ desu yo.

6. The slowest one is that bus.

I⌐tibañ oso⌐i no wa a⌐no ba⌐su desu yo.

7. The strangest one is that name.

I⌐tibañ he⌐ñ na no wa a⌐no namae de⌐su yo.

8. The busiest one is that company.

I⌐tibañ isoḡasi⌐i no wa a⌐no kaisya de⌐su yo.

9. The coldest one is the next room.

I⌐tibañ samu⌐i no wa to⌐nari no heya⌐ desu yo.

10. The most delicious (one) is the sushi at that place.

I⌐tibañ oisi⌐i no wa a⌐soko no osu⌐si desu yo.

G. Substitution Drill (based on Grammatical Note 3)

1. Which is most expensive— this one, that one, or the one over there?

Kore to sore to are de, do⌐re ḡa i⌐tibañ taka⌐i desu ka⌐

2. Which is most expensive— the blue one, the red one, or the black one?

A⌐o⌐i no to a⌐ka⌐i no to ku⌐ro⌐i no de, do⌐re ḡa i⌐tibañ taka⌐i desu ka⌐

3. Which is most expensive— this store, that store, or the store over there?

Ko⌐no mise⌐ to so⌐no mise⌐ to a⌐no mise⌐ de, do⌐re ḡa i⌐tibañ taka⌐i desu ka⌐

4. Which is most expensive— train, airplane, or ship?

Ki⌐sya⌐ to hi⌐ko⌐oki to ⌐hu⌐ne no uti de, do⌐re ḡa i⌐tibañ taka⌐i desu ka⌐

5. Which is most expensive of those three things?

A⌐no mittu⌐ no uti de, do⌐re ḡa i⌐tibañ taka⌐i desu ka⌐

6. Which is most expensive of these four (long, cylindrical objects)?

Ko⌐no yo⌐ñ-hoñ no uti de, do⌐re ḡa i⌐tibañ taka⌐i desu ka⌐

7. Which is most expensive— meat, fish, or fowl?

Ni⌐ku⌐ to sakana to to̅ri de, do⌐re ḡa i⌐tibañ taka⌐i desu ka⌐

8. Which is most expensive— tea, coffee, or milk?

Otya to ko⌐ohi⌐i to ⌐mi⌐ruku no uti, do⌐re ḡa i⌐tibañ taka⌐i desu ka⌐

H. Grammar Drill (based on Grammatical Note 2)

Tutor: Kore wa a̅re hodo ⌐yo⌐ku a⌐rimase⌐ñ. 'This one is not as good as that one.'

Student: Are wa ko⌐re yo⌐ri ⌐i⌐i desu. 'That one is better than this one.'

1. Ki⌐sya⌐ wa hi⌐ko⌐oki hodo ⌐ha⌐yaku a⌐rimase⌐ñ.

Hi⌐ko⌐oki wa ki⌐sya⌐ yori ha⌐ya⌐i desu.

2. Tookyoo wa Sa̅pporo hodo ⌐sa⌐muku a⌐rimase⌐ñ.

Sapporo wa To⌐okyoo yo⌐ri sa⌐mu⌐i desu.

3. Bi⌐iru wa sa̅ke hodo a⌐maku arimase⌐ñ.

Sake wa ⌐bi⌐iru yori a⌐ma⌐i desu.

4. Ro⌐ku-g̃atu⌐ wa ha⌐ti-g̃atu⌐   Ha⌐ti-g̃atu⌐ wa ro⌐ku-g̃atu⌐ yori a⌐tu⌐i
   hodo ⌐a⌐tuku a⌐rimase⌐ñ.   desu.
5. O⌐re⌐ñzi[1] wa re̅moñ[2] hodo   Remoñ wa o⌐re⌐ñzi yori su⌐ppa⌐i desu.
   su⌐ppa⌐ku a⌐rimase⌐ñ.
6. Ba⌐su wa ki⌐sya⌐ hodo ⌐ta⌐-   Ki⌐sya⌐ wa ⌐ba⌐su yori ta⌐ka⌐i desu.
   kaku a⌐rimase⌐ñ.
7. Nihoñg̃o wa e̅eg̃o hodo   Eeg̃o wa ni⌐hoñg̃o yo⌐ri ⌐yo⌐ku wa⌐ka-
   ⌐yo⌐ku wa⌐karimase⌐ñ.   rima⌐su.
8. Ko⌐ohi⌐i wa o̅tya hodo   Otya wa ko⌐ohi⌐i yori su⌐ki⌐ desu.
   su⌐ki⌐ zya a⌐rimase⌐ñ.

I. Grammar Drill (based on Grammatical Note 1)

> Tutor: A⌐ñmari wakarimase⌐ñ. 'He doesn't understand very much.'
> Student: A⌐ñmari wakara⌐nai desyoo? 'He doesn't understand very
> much, does he?'

1. Ma⌐da so⌐no ho⌐ñ (o) yo-   Ma⌐da so⌐no ho⌐ñ (o) yo⌐ma⌐nai de-
   ⌐mimase⌐ñ.   syoo?
2. Da⌐re mo kaimase⌐ñ desi-   Da⌐re mo kawana⌐katta desyoo?
   ta.
3. Be⌐tu ni oisiku arimase⌐ñ.   Be⌐tu ni oisiku na⌐i desyoo?
4. Ni⌐hoñg̃o de iimase⌐ñ de-   Ni⌐hoñg̃o de iwana⌐katta desyoo?
   sita.
5. Da⌐re mo demase⌐ñ desi-   Da⌐re mo de⌐nakatta desyoo?
   ta.
6. Ta⌐naka-sañ no o⌐kusañ   Ta⌐naka-sañ no o⌐kusañ (wa) ta⌐ba-
   (wa) ta⌐bako (o) suimase⌐ñ.   ko (o) suwana⌐i desyoo?
7. A⌐tarasi⌐i sakana zya a⌐ri-   A⌐tarasi⌐i sakana zya ⌐na⌐katta de-
   mase⌐ñ desita.   syoo?
8. Bi⌐iru to sa̅ke wa no⌐mi-   Bi⌐iru to sa̅ke wa no⌐ma⌐nai desyoo?
   mase⌐ñ.
9. E⌐eg̃o (o) beñkyoo-site (i)-   E⌐eg̃o o beñkyoo-site (i)na⌐i desyoo?
   mase⌐ñ.
10. Ta⌐isi⌐kañ ni tu⌐to⌐mete   Ta⌐isi⌐kañ ni tu⌐to⌐mete (i)⌐rassya-
    (i)⌐rassyaimase⌐ñ.   ra⌐nai desyoo?

J. Response Drill

> Tutor: Sore (wa) ⌐na⌐ñ desyoo ka. /hurosiki/ 'What do you suppose
>   that is?' /furoshiki/
> Student: Yo⌐ku wa⌐karimase⌐ñ g̃a, hu⌐rosiki zya na⌐i desyoo ka.   'I
>   can't tell for sure but isn't it a furoshiki?'

---

[1] 'Orange.'

[2] 'Lemon.'

1. Are (wa) ⌐na⌐n̄ desyoo
   ka.   /kusuri/

   Yo⌐ku wa⌐karimase⌐n̄ ḡa, ku⌐suri
   zya na⌐i desyoo ka.

2. Koko (wa) ⌐do⌐ko desyoo
   ka.   /Sin̄basi[1]/

   Yo⌐ku wa⌐karimase⌐n̄ ḡa, Si⌐n̄basi
   zya na⌐i desyoo ka.

3. I⌐ma ⌐na⌐n̄-zi desyoo ka.
   /sa⌐n̄-zi-ḡo⌐ro/

   Yo⌐ku wa⌐karimase⌐n̄ ḡa, sa⌐n̄-zi-
   ḡo⌐ro zya ⌐na⌐i desyoo ka.

4. A⌐no⌐ hito (wa) ⌐da⌐re desyoo ka.   /Ta⌐naka-san̄
   no oto⌐osan̄/

   Yo⌐ku wa⌐karimase⌐n̄ ḡa, Ta⌐naka-
   san̄ no oto⌐osan̄ zya ⌐na⌐i desyoo
   ka.

5. Sore (wa) na⌐n̄yo⌐obi desyoo ka.   /do⌐yo⌐obi/

   Yo⌐ku wa⌐karimase⌐n̄ ḡa, do⌐yo⌐obi
   zya ⌐na⌐i desyoo ka.

6. Sore (wa) ⌐i⌐kura desyoo
   ka.   /sa⌐n̄byaku⌐-en̄/

   Yo⌐ku wa⌐karimase⌐n̄ ḡa, sa⌐n̄bya-
   ku⌐-en̄ zya ⌐na⌐i desyoo ka.

7. Ta⌐naka-san̄ no ho⌐n̄ (wa)
   ⌐do⌐re desyoo ka.   /ku⌐ro⌐i
   no/

   Yo⌐ku wa⌐karimase⌐n̄ ḡa, ku⌐ro⌐i
   no zya ⌐na⌐i desyoo ka.

8. Are (wa) ⌐do⌐no da⌐iḡaku
   desyo⌐o ka.   /Toodai/

   Yo⌐ku wa⌐karimase⌐n̄ ḡa, To⌐odai
   zya na⌐i desyoo ka.

K. Response Drill (based on Grammatical Note 2)

> Tutor: Kore (wa) a⌐re yo⌐ri ⌐i⌐i desu ka﹈ 'Is this one better than
>   that one?'
> Student: Iie, a⌐re hodo yo⌐ku a⌐rimase⌐n̄ yo﹈ 'Why no, it isn't as
>   good as that one.'

1. Kono miti (wa) a⌐no miti
   yo⌐ri a⌐buna⌐i desu ka﹈

   Iie, a⌐no miti hodo abunaku arima-
   se⌐n̄ yo﹈

2. Kono kusuri (wa) a⌐no kusuri yo⌐ri ni⌐ḡa⌐i desu ka﹈

   Iie, a⌐no kusuri hodo ni⌐ḡaku a⌐ri-
   mase⌐n̄ yo﹈

3. Ko⌐no koohi⌐i (wa) a⌐no koo-
   hi⌐i yori ⌐ko⌐i desu ka﹈

   Iie, a⌐no koohi⌐i hodo ⌐ko⌐ku a⌐ri-
   mase⌐n̄ yo﹈

4. Ko⌐no ho⌐n̄ (wa) a⌐no ho⌐n̄
   yori ya⌐su⌐i desu ka﹈

   Iie, a⌐no ho⌐n̄ hodo ⌐ya⌐suku a⌐ri-
   mase⌐n̄ yo﹈

5. Kono tokee (wa) a⌐no tokee
   yo⌐ri ya⌐su⌐i desu ka﹈

   Iie, a⌐no tokee hodo ya⌐suku a⌐ri-
   mase⌐n̄ yo﹈

6. Kono uti (wa) a⌐no uti yo⌐ri
   ⌐ki⌐ree desu ka﹈

   Iie, a⌐no uti hodo ki⌐ree zya a⌐ri-
   mase⌐n̄ yo﹈

7. Ko⌐no oka⌐si (wa) a⌐no oka⌐si
   yori o⌐isi⌐i desu ka﹈

   Iie, a⌐no oka⌐si hodo o⌐isiku arima-
   se⌐n̄ yo﹈

8. Ko⌐no iro⌐ (wa) a⌐no iro⌐ yori u⌐su⌐i desu ka﹈

   Iie, a⌐no iro⌐ hodo u⌐suku arimase⌐n̄
   yo﹈

9. Kono o⌐su⌐si (wa) a⌐no osu⌐-
   si yori ka⌐ra⌐i desu ka﹈

   Iie, a⌐no osu⌐si hodo ⌐ka⌐raku a⌐ri-
   mase⌐n̄ yo﹈

10. Ko⌐no⌐ ko (wa) a⌐no⌐ ko
    yori ⌐ge⌐n̄ki desu ka﹈

    Iie, a⌐no⌐ ko hodo ⌐ge⌐n̄ki zya a⌐ri-
    mase⌐n̄ yo﹈

---

[1] Section of Tokyo.

L. Level Drill (based on Grammatical Note 1)

        Tutor: A⌐ñmari wakarimase⌐ñ kara. (Formal)
        Student: A⌐ñmari wakara⌐nai kara. (Informal)
          'Because I don't understand very much.'

1. So⌐re wa sirimase⌐ñ kara.

So⌐re wa sirana⌐i kara.

2. O⌐oki na ⌐ko⌐e de ha⌐nasi-
    mase⌐ñ desita kara.

O⌐oki na ⌐ko⌐e de ha⌐nasa⌐nakatta
kara.

3. Ko⌐ñna iro⌐ (wa) su⌐ki⌐ zya
    a⌐rimase⌐ñ kara.

Ko⌐ñna iro⌐ (wa) su⌐ki⌐ zya ⌐na⌐i
kara.

4. Ma⌐da ka⌐wakimase⌐ñ kara.

Ma⌐da ka⌐waka⌐nai kara.

5. Kinoo i⌐rassyaimase⌐ñ de-
    sita kara.

Kinoo i⌐rassyara⌐nakatta kara.

6. Ki⌐ree na uti zya a⌐rima-
    se⌐ñ desita kara.

Ki⌐ree na uti zya ⌐na⌐katta kara.

7. Ko⌐ñna ho⌐ñ (wa) o⌐mosi⌐-
    roku a⌐rimase⌐ñ kara.

Ko⌐ñna ho⌐ñ (wa) o⌐mosi⌐roku ⌐na⌐i
kara.

8. Kinoo da⌐re mo kimase⌐ñ
    desita kara.

Kinoo da⌐re mo ko⌐nakatta kara.

9. Kyo⌐o no si ̄goto (wa) mu⌐zu-
    kasiku arimase⌐ñ desita
    kara.

Kyo⌐o no si ̄goto wa mu⌐zukasiku na⌐-
katta kara.

10. Go⌐hañ (wa) ⌐ma⌐da de⌐ki-
    mase⌐ñ kara.

Go⌐hañ wa ⌐ma⌐da de⌐ki⌐nai kara.

M. Expansion Drill

1. Is it fast? (Indirect)

Ha⌐ya⌐i desyoo ka.

    Which is faster?

Do⌐tira no ⌐ho⌐o ga ha⌐ya⌐i desyoo
ka.

    Which is faster—bus or
    electric train?

Ba⌐su to de ̄ñsya to, do⌐tira no ⌐ho⌐o
ga ha⌐ya⌐i desyoo ka.

2. It isn't ready. . . .

De⌐kimase⌐ñ ḡa_

    It isn't ready yet. . . .

Ma⌐da de⌐kimase⌐ñ ḡa_

    The toast isn't ready yet. . . .

To⌐osuto wa ⌐ma⌐da de⌐kimase⌐ñ ḡa_

    The eggs are ready but the
    toast isn't ready yet. . . .

Ta⌐ma⌐ ̄go wa ⌐mo⌐o de⌐kima⌐sita
ḡa, to⌐osuto wa ⌐ma⌐da de⌐kimase⌐ñ
ḡa_

3. Please come.

I⌐ra⌐site kudasai.

    Please come to see us (lit.
    to our house).

U⌐ti e ira⌐site kudasai.

    Do please come to see us.

Do⌐ozo u⌐ti e ira⌐site kudasai.

    Any time will be fine but do
    please come to see us.

I⌐tu de mo ⌐i⌐i desu ḡa, do⌐ozo u⌐ti
e ira⌐site kudasai.

4. You know, it has grown
    empty.

Su⌐kima⌐sita yo.

    You know, I'm hungry.

O⌐naka ḡa sukima⌐sita yo.

You know, I'm hungry already.

Moˈo oˈnaka g̃a sukimaˈsita yo.

You know, I didn't eat so I'm hungry already.

Taˈbeˈnakatta kara, moˈo oˈnaka g̃a sukimaˈsita yo.

You know, I didn't eat breakfast so I'm hungry already.

Aˈsagoˈhañ o taˈbeˈnakatta kara, moˈo oˈnaka g̃a sukimaˈsita yo.

5. I went to the JTB. [1]

Koˈotuukoˈosya e iˈkimaˈsita.

We went to the JTB together.

Issyo ni koˈotuukoˈosya e iˈkimaˈsita.

I went to the JTB (together) with a friend.

Tomodati to issyo ni koˈotuukoˈosya e iˈkimaˈsita.

I went to the JTB (together) with a Japanese friend.

Niˈhoñziˈñ no tomodati to issyo ni koˈotuukoˈosya e iˈkimaˈsita.

I went to the JTB (together) with a Japanese friend this morning.

Keˈsa niˈhoñziˈñ no tomodati to issyo ni koˈotuukoˈosya e iˈkimaˈsita.

6. I don't like them.

Suˈkiˈ zya aˈrimaseˈñ.

I don't like them as much as ships.

Huˈne hodo suˈkiˈ zya aˈrimaseˈñ.

I like [them] but I don't like them as much as ships.

Suˈkiˈ desu g̃a, huˈne hodo suˈkiˈ zya aˈrimaseˈñ.

I like [them] more than airplanes, but I don't like them as much as ships.

Hiˈkoˈoki yori suˈkiˈ desu g̃a, huˈne hodo suˈkiˈ zya aˈrimaseˈñ.

Trains I like more than airplanes, but I don't like them as much as ships.

Kiˈsyaˈ wa hiˈkoˈoki yori suˈkiˈ desu g̃a, huˈne hodo suˈkiˈ zya aˈrimaseˈñ.

SHORT SUPPLEMENTARY DIALOGUES

(with questions)

1. Smith (host): Oˈnomiˈmono wa ˈnaˈni o meˈsiag̃arimaˈsu ka⌐
    Tanaka (guest): Oˈsake mo biˈiru mo iˈtadakimaseˈñ kara, zyuˈusu[2] o
          oneg̃ai-itasimasu.

    a. Tanaka-sañ wa ˈdoˈñna noˈmiˈmono o taˈnomimaˈsu ka⌐
    b. Doˈo site soˈre o tanomimaˈsu ka⌐

---

[1] 'Japan Travel Bureau.'

[2] 'Juice.'

2. Tanaka: Kyo⌐o wa ki⌐no⌐o hodo ⌐a⌐tuku ⌐na⌐i ⌐ne⌐e.
   Yamamoto: Kyo⌐o wa tyo⌐odo i⌐i ⌐ne⌐e.

 a. Kyo⌐o to ki⌐no⌐o to, ⌐do⌐tira ḡa a⌐tu⌐i desu ka⌐
 b. Tanaka-sañ to Yamamoto-sañ wa o⌐toko⌐ desyoo ka, o⌐ñna⌐ desyoo
  ka⌐

3. Tanaka: Su⌐misu-sañ no nihoñḡo ⌐do⌐o?
   Yamamoto: A⌐no⌐ hito na⌐ñ de mo waka⌐ru yo⌐

 a. Su⌐misu-sañ wa ni⌐hoñḡo ḡa yo⌐ku wa⌐karima⌐su ka, a⌐ñmari waka-
  rimase⌐ñ ka.
 b. Da⌐re ḡa so⌐o iima⌐su ka⌐

4. Tanaka: Su⌐misu-sañ mo ko⌐otuuko⌐osya e i⌐rassyaima⌐sita ka⌐
   Yamamoto: I⌐rassyara⌐nakatta desyoo. Tyo⌐tto ⌐ma⌐e ni zi⌐mu⌐syo ni i⌐ra-
   ssya⌐tta kara.

 a. Su⌐misu-sañ wa ko⌐otuuko⌐osya e i⌐kima⌐sita ka⌐
 b. Yamamoto-sañ wa ⌐do⌐o site wa⌐karima⌐su ka⌐

5. Smith: De⌐ñwa-sima⌐sita ka⌐
   Tanaka: E⌐e, si⌐ma⌐sita ḡa; da⌐re mo de⌐nakatta kara, ma⌐ta a⌐to de kake-
   masu.

 a. Ta⌐naka-sañ wa deñwa-sima⌐sita ka⌐
 b. Do⌐o site ma⌐ta a⌐to de ka⌐kema⌐su ka⌐

SUPPLEMENTARY CONVERSATION

(Mr. Saito is telephoning a restaurant to arrange for a dinner party.)

Saito: Mo⌐simosi.
Restaurant Employee: Mo⌐simosi. Su⌐ehiro[1] de gozaima⌐su.
Saito: Kotira wa To⌐okyoo-gi⌐ñkoo no Sa⌐itoo de⌐su ḡa_
R. E.: Ma⌐ido ari⌐ḡatoo gozaimasu.
Saito: Ko⌐ñbañ ro⌐ku-zi-ḡo⌐ro i⌐ku⌐ kara, o⌐negai-sima⌐su.
R. E.: Ha⌐a, ka⌐sikomarima⌐sita. Ko⌐ñbañ wa ⌐na⌐ñ-niñ-sama[2] de go⌐zaima⌐-
   su ka⌐
Saito: Go-⌐ni⌐ñ desu yo.
R. E.: Ha⌐a. Kyo⌐o wa ⌐do⌐ñna mo⌐no⌐ ni i⌐tasimasyo⌐o ka.
Saito: Do⌐ñna mo⌐no⌐ ḡa ⌐i⌐i desyoo ka ⌐ne⌐e. Kyo⌐o wa ni⌐ku⌐ to sākana   to
   do⌐tti ḡa ii?

---

[1] A restaurant name.

[2] Polite equivalent of na̱ñ-niñ used commonly by restaurant and hotel personnel.

R. E.:   Sa⌐yoo de gozaima⌐su ˧ne˧e.   Kyo⌐o wa a˧tarasi⌐i o˧sakana g̃a gozaima˧su kara, osasimi wa i⌐ka⌐g̃a de gozaimasu ka⌣

Saito: A⌐a, i⌐i desyoo.

R. E.:   I⌐i to˧ri mo gozaima˧su kara, tori no sukiyaki mo i⌐ka⌐g̃a de gozaimasyoo ka.

Saito: A⌐a, ke⌐kkoo.   So⌐re go-niñmae oneg̃ai-sima⌐su.   Hoka ni yãsai to ku-⌐da⌐mono su⌐ko⌐si oneg̃ai-simasu.

R. E.:   Ha⌐a, ka⌐sikomarima⌐sita.   O⌐nomi⌐mono wa o⌐sake to obi⌐iru to ⌐do⌐tira g̃a yo˧rosi˧i desyoo ka.

Saito: Tu⌐metai bi⌐iru oneg̃ai-simasu.

R. E.:   Ha⌐a ˧ha˧a.

Saito: Iti-niñmae i⌐kura-g̃u⌐rai?

R. E.:   Sa⌐yoo de gozaima⌐su ˧ne˧e.   Iti-niñmae se⌐ñ-eñ-g̃u⌐rai de gozaimasu g̃a＿   O⌐bi⌐iru wa hya⌐ku rokuzyu⌐u-eñ de gozaimasu.

Saito: Ke⌐kkoo.   Zya⌐a oneg̃ai-simasu.

R. E.:   Ka⌐sikomarima⌐sita.   Ro⌐ku⌐-zi de gozaimasu ne?   A⌐ri⌐g̃atoo gozaimasu.

English Equivalent

Saito: Hello.

Restaurant Employee: Hello.   (This is the) Suehiro (Restaurant).

Saito: This is [Mr.] Saito at the Bank of Tokyo (but) . . .

R. E.:   (Thank you for coming here often.)

Saito: Tonight I'm coming (lit. going) at about 6 so will you take care of us?

R. E.:   Certainly.   How many people will it be tonight?

Saito: It will be 5.

R. E.:   Certainly.   What kind of things would you like today?

Saito: I w o n d e r what (kind of things) would be good. . . .   Which is better today—meat or fish?

R. E.:   Let me see.   We have fresh fish today so how about sashimi?

Saito: Oh, that would be fine.

R. E.:   I have some good chicken too, so how about chicken sukiyaki (too)?

Saito: Oh, fine.   I'd like 5 portions of that.   In addition, I'd like a few vegetables and some fruit.

R. E.:   Certainly.   For drinks, which would be better—sake or beer?

Saito: I'd like cold beer.

R. E.:   All right.

Saito: About how much [will it be] per person?

R. E.:   Let me see. . . .   It will be about ¥1000 per person but [will that be all right?]   The beer will be ¥160 [i.e. extra].

Saito: Fine.   Well then, please take good care of us!

R. E.:   Certainly.   Six o'clock, isn't it?   Thank you.

EXERCISES

1.   Using appropriate magazine pictures, photographs, or line drawings, practice comparisons: 'Which is more ——, X or Y?'; 'X is more —— than Y'; 'Y is not as —— as X.'

2. You have taken some Japanese friends to a restaurant for dinner as your guests. Find out what each one wants, place the orders, and make any complaints that are necessary (for example: 'I ordered beer but you brought sake,' 'I ordered rice but you haven't brought it,' etc.), and at the end, take care of the check.

3. Telephone the Suehiro Restaurant and order dinner. Include the following information:

    a. who you are
    b. how many will be in your party
    c. when you are coming
    d. what you would like to eat and drink
    e. the price per person

4. Turn back to Drill L on page 271. Make up questions for which the sentences of Drill L would be appropriate answers (cf. Lesson 14, Exercise 3), and then drill on the questions with their answers (informal alternants).

5. Practice the Basic Dialogues, using appropriate variations.

Lesson 16. At Home

BASIC DIALOGUES: FOR MEMORIZATION

(a)

Smith

teacher or doctor	se⌐nse⌐e
Teacher Wada or Dr. Wada	Wa⌐da-sense⌐e
next week	raisyuu
next Friday	ra⌐isyuu no kiñyo⌐obi

1. Dr. Wada, won't you come to our house for dinner (lit. a meal) next Friday? — Wa⌐da-sense⌐e. Ra⌐isyuu no kiñyo⌐obi ni ūti e syo⌐kuzi ni irassyaima-se⌐ñ ka⌐

Dr. Wada

take pleasure in	yo⌐roko⌐bu /-u/
gladly or with pleasure	yo⌐roko⌐ñde
visit or call on	ukağau ⌐ /-u/

2. Next Friday? I'll be glad to come. — Raisyuu no ki⌐ñyo⌐obi desu ka⌐ Yo-⌐roko⌐ñde ukağaimasu.

residence	su⌐mai or o⌐su⌐mai ⌐

3. Where do you live? (Lit. Where is your residence?) — O⌐su⌐mai (wa) ⌐do⌐tira desyoo ka.

Smith

(a section of Tokyo)	A⌐ka⌐saka
apartment house	a⌐pa⌐ato
Harris (Apartment) House	Ha⌐risu-apa⌐ato

4. I live in (lit. it is) Harris House in Akasaka. You probably know it, don't you? — A⌐ka⌐saka no Ha⌐risu-apa⌐ato desu ğa, go⌐zo⌐ñzi desyoo ne?

Dr. Wada

5. Yes, I do (know). — E⌐e, zo⌐ñzite orimasu.

what floor? or how many floors?	nañ-ğai

6. What floor is your apartment? — Otaku (wa) na⌐ñ-ğai desyo⌐o ka.

Smith

first floor or one floor	ik-kai
third floor or three floors	sañ-ğai

7. It's number 306 on the third
    floor.

    Sañ-g̃ai no ⌐sa⌐ñbyaku ro⌐ku⌐ - bañ
    desu.

                 Dr. Wada

8. I see.

    Wa⌐karima⌐sita.

9. What time shall I come?

    Na⌐ñ-zi ni u⌐kag̃aimasyo⌐o ka.

               Smith

    night or night-time
10. How would about 7:30 in
    the evening be?

        yo⌐ru
    Yo⌐ru no si⌐ti-zi-hañ-g̃o⌐ro i⌐ka⌐g̃a
    desyoo ka.

              Dr. Wada

11. That will be fine. I'll come
    at 7:30. Thank you very
    much.

    Ke⌐kkoo desu. Si⌐ti-zi-ha⌐ñ ni uka-
    g̃aimasu. Do⌐o mo a⌐ri⌐g̃atoo goza-
    imasu.

               (b)

             Tanaka

    gray
    blue or green
    a gray and blue car
12. Is that gray and blue car
    yours?

    haiiro
    a⌐o
    haiiro to ⌐a⌐o no kuruma
    Ano haiiro to ⌐a⌐o no kuruma (wa)
    o⌐taku no⌐ desu ka⌐

              Smith

13. No. That's the doctor's (or
    teacher's), isn't it?

    Iie. Are wa se⌐ñse⌐e no desyoo?

    brown
14. Ours is brown.

    tyairo
    U⌐ti no⌐ wa tya⌐iro de⌐su yo.

               (c)

           Mr. Tanaka

    door
    [something] closes or
      shuts
    be closed or be shut

    to
    si⌐ma⌐ru /-u/

    si⌐ma⌐tte (i)ru or
    si⌐ma⌐tte ⌐o⌐ru +

15. Is the door closed?

    To (g̃a) si⌐ma⌐tte (i)ru?

            Maid

    close or shut [some-
      thing]
16. Yes. I just closed it. . . .

    si⌐me⌐ru /-ru/

    E⌐e, i⌐ma si⌐mema⌐sita g̃a⌐

          Mr. Tanaka

    key
    [something] locks

    ka⌐g̃i⌐
    ka⌐g̃i⌐ g̃a ka⌐ka⌐ru /-u/

be locked	ka⌐gi¬ ḡa ka˩ka˧tte (i)ru or
	ka⌐gi¬ ḡa ka˩ka˧tte oru⁺
17. Is it locked too?	Ka⌐gi¬ mo ka˩ka˧tte (i)ru?

Maid

lock [something]	ka⌐gi¬ o ka˩ke˧ru /-ru/
18. No. Shall I lock it?	Iie. Ka⌐kemasyo¬o ka.

Mr. Tanaka

yes	a¬a¹
19. Yes. Lock it. will you?	A¬a. ka¬kete ne?

(d)

Mrs. Tanaka

window	ma¬do
[something] opens	aku /-u/
be open	aite (i)ru or
	a⌐ite o̅ru⁺
20. Are the windows open?	Ma¬do (ḡa) a̅ite (i)ru?

Maid

have been closed or	si¬mete ˩a˧ru
shut	
21. The ones over there are open.	Mu⌐koo no¬ wa a˩ite orima˧su ḡa,
but the ones here have been	ko⌐tira no¬ wa ⌐si¬mete arimasu.
shut. . . .	
open [something]	akeru /-ru/
22. Shall I open them?	A⌐kemasyo¬o ka.

Mrs. Tanaka

23. Yes. It's a little hot.	E¬e. Tyo¬tto a˩tu¬i wa⌣

(e)

Mr. Tanaka

heater	su⌐to¬obu
[something] becomes	tu¬ku /-u/
attached or turned	
on	
be attached or be	tu¬ite (i)ru or
turned on	tu¬ite ˩o˧ru⁺
24. Is the heater on?	Su⌐to¬obu (ḡa) ⌐tu¬ite (i)ru?

Maid

attach or turn on	tu⌐ke¬ru /-ru/
[something]	

---

¹ Informal, man's word.

25. It's not on. Shall I turn it   Tu⌐ite o⌐rimase⌐ñ. Tu⌐kemasyo⌐o ka.
    on?

Mr. Tanaka

    no   i⌐ya [1]
    being that condition   so⌐no mama⌐ de
    is warm   a⌐tataka⌐i /-ku/ or
                                            a⌐ttaka⌐i /-ku/
26. No, it's fine as it is. (Since)   I⌐ya, so⌐no mama⌐ de ⌐i⌐i yo. Mo⌐o
    it's warm already.   a⌐ttaka⌐i kara.

(f)

Tanaka

    television   te⌐rebi
    electricity or electric   de⌐ñki
      light
    turn off or extinguish   kesu /-u/
      or erase [something]
27. I'm going to watch television   Te⌐rebi (o) ⌐mi⌐ru kara, de⌐ñki (o)
    so turn off the light.   ke⌐site.

Maid

    have been turned off   ke⌐site a⌐ru   or
                                            ke⌐site gozaima⌐su+
28. The ones here have all been   Ko⌐ko no⌐ (wa) mi⌐ñna kesite gozai-
    turned off. . . .   ma⌐su ḡa_

Tanaka

    entry hall   ge⌐ñkañ
29. How about the one in the   Ge⌐ñkañ no wa?
    entry hall?

Maid

30. Oh, that one is on, isn't it.   A⌐a, a⌐re wa tu⌐ite orimasu ⌐ne⌐e.
    I'll turn it off [right] now.   I⌐ma ke⌐sima⌐su.

(g)

Maid

    radio   ra⌐zio
    make small or turn   ti⌐isaku suru or
      down   ti⌐isaku i⌐tasima⌐su+
31. Shall I turn down the radio a   Ra⌐zio (o) mo⌐o suko⌐si ti⌐isaku i⌐ta-
    little more?   simasyo⌐o ka.

_____

[1] Informal, man's word.

Mr. Tanaka

being big <u>or</u> loud, as
  it is
door (Western style)

o⌐oki⌐i ma⌐ma⌐ de

do⌐a

32. No, it doesn't matter if it's
loud but close that door,
will you? — because Taro
is studying in there.

I⌐ya, o⌐oki⌐i ma⌐ma⌐ de ka⌐mawa⌐nai
ḡa, sono ⌐do⌐a (o) ⌐si⌐mete ne? —
⌐Ta⌐roo (ḡa) mu⌐koo de beñkyoo-
site (i)ru⌐ kara.

(h)

Mrs. Tanaka

is dirty

ki⌐tana⌐i /-ku/

33. Hasn't this place gotten
dirty!

Koko (wa) ki⌐tana⌐ku ⌐na⌐tta wa
⌐ne⌐e.

clean (verb)
after cleaning
straighten up

soozi-suru
so⌐ozi-site⌐ kara
ka⌐tazuke⌐ru /-ru/

34. Clean it up, will you? Then
after you clean it, straighten
up the entry hall.

So⌐ozi-site⌐ ne? Sore kara, so⌐ozi-
site⌐ kara, ge⌐ñkañ (o) ka⌐tazu⌐ke-
te.

Maid

preparation

sitaku

35. What about getting dinner
ready? (Lit. As for meal
preparations?)

Osyokuzi no sitaku wa?

Mrs. Tanaka

after straightening up

ka⌐tazu⌐kete kara

36. Do it after you straighten
up, will you?

Ka⌐tazu⌐kete kara si⌐te⌐ ne?

NOTES ON THE BASIC DIALOGUES

1. Se⌐ñse⌐e means 'teacher,' and 'doctor' in both the medical and non-
medical sense. It is the regular term of address for such persons, always
implying respect and deference on the part of the speaker. As a term of
address, it may be affixed to the family name or used independently.

   <u>Raisyuu</u> 'next week': compare also <u>raineñ</u> 'next year' and <u>ra⌐iḡetu</u> 'next
month.'

2. Yo⌐roko⌐bu is not used in reference to the speaker except in its gerund
form, when describing the manner in which something is done (cf. Lesson
15, Grammatical Note 5).   In this latter pattern, it may be used in reference to any subject. Thus: yo⌐roko⌐bu desyoo '[someone other than the
speaker] will probably enjoy it <u>or</u> be glad'; but yo⌐roko⌐ñde simasu '[some-
one] will gladly do it.'

6. A⌐pa⌐ato is an apartment house.   An apartment within an apartment house

is one's household—<u>uti</u> or <u>otaku</u>.

12. <u>Otaku no</u> means 'your(s),' i.e. '(the one) belonging to your household.'

14. <u>Uti no</u> means 'our(s),' i.e. '(the one) belonging to our household.'

16. 'but— is that all right?'

17-18. Note: X ⌐no kaḡi⌐ ḡa ka⌐ka┤ru 'X locks';
        X ⌐no kaḡi⌐ o ka⌐ke┤ru 'lock X'

21. 'but— how do you want them?'

26. Lit. 'Being that condition, it's fine.' The nominal <u>ma⌐ma⌐</u> refers to an existing condition defined by the descriptive word or sequence which always precedes it.

A⌐tataka⌐i, and contracted a⌐ttaka⌐i, mean 'warm'— i.e. 'nice and warm.' Typical days of spring, and unseasonably w a r m days of winter, are a⌐tataka⌐i.

28. 'but— is there anything else I can do?'

32. Lit. 'Even being its loud condition, it doesn't matter.'

An informal inflected word before <u>ḡa</u> 'but' occurs in the informal speech of men.

<u>To</u> (Sentence 15 above) is the general term for door and can refer to doors of any style. <u>Do⌐a</u>, on the other hand refers only to Western - style doors.

35. Note: <u>sitaku o suru</u> 'make preparations,' 'prepare'; <u>X no sitaku o suru</u> 'make preparations for <u>X</u>,' 'prepare for <u>X</u>.'

GRAMMATICAL NOTES

1. Verbals: Transitive and Intransitive; Gerund + √⌐a⌐ru

A verbal which may be preceded by a direct object + particle <u>o</u> is said to be TRANSITIVE. A verbal which never so occurs is said to be INTRANSITIVE. Thus, <u>kau</u> 'buy' is transitive (<u>za⌐ssi o kaima⌐sita</u> 'I bought a magazine') but <u>wa⌐ka⌐ru</u> 'be comprehensible' is intransitive (<u>e⌐ḡo ḡa wakarima⌐su</u> 'I understand English').

Some other transitive verbals are: <u>ta⌐be⌐ru</u> 'eat,' <u>no⌐mu</u> 'drink,' <u>mi⌐ru</u> 'see,' <u>mi⌐se⌐ru</u> 'show,' <u>wasureru</u> 'forget'; some other intransitive verbals are: <u>iru</u> 'be needed,' <u>ka⌐ka⌐ru</u> 'be required,' <u>kikoeru</u> 'be audible,' <u>a⌐ru</u> 'be (inanimate,' 'have,' <u>iku</u> 'go.'

In Japanese, there are many pairs of verbals whose stems resemble each other phonetically, one member of which is transitive and the other intransitive. Several examples occur in this lesson:

Transitive	Intransitive
akeru 'open [something]'	aku '[something] opens'
(Do⌐a o a˥kema˥sita.	(Do⌐a ḡa a˥kima˥sita.
'I opened the door.')	'The door opened.')
si˥me⌐ru 'close [something]'	si⌐ma⌐ru '[something] closes'
(Do⌐a o si˥mema˥sita.	(Do⌐a ga si˥marima˥sita.
'I closed the door.')	'The door closed.')
tu˥ke⌐ru 'attach [something]'	tu⌐ku '[something] becomes attached'
(De⌐ñki o tu˥kema˥sita.	(De⌐ñki ḡa tu˥kima˥sita.
'I turned on the light.')	'The light went on.')

A pair introduced previously is:

na˥o⌐su 'make [something or someone] better'	na˥o⌐ru '[something or someone] gets better'

Note also the following pair:

kesu 'turn [something] off'	kieru /-ru/ '[something] goes out or becomes extinguished'

A verbal gerund + (i)ru means that an action is now going on, or that the result of a previous action now exists (cf. Lesson 10, Grammatical Note 2). Usually the g e r u n d of a transitive verbal + (i)ru has the former meaning, whereas the gerund of an intransitive + (i)ru has the latter meaning:

Transitive	Intransitive
Do⌐a o a˥kete (i)ma˥su.	Do⌐a ḡa a˥ite (i)ma˥su.
'I'm opening the door.'	'The door is open.'
Do⌐a o ˥si˥mete (i)masu.	Do⌐a ḡa si˥ma˥tte (i)masu.
'I'm closing the door.'	'The door is closed.'
De⌐ñki o tu˥ke˥te (i)masu.	De⌐ñki ḡa ˥tu˥ite (i)masu.
'I'm turning on the light.'	'The light is on.'

The subject of a gerund + √(i)ru pattern may be animate or inanimate. When the subject is inanimate, √(i)ru is replaced by √a⌐ru (formal: √o⌐rima⌐su) in polite speech, [1] but never by √i⌐rassya⌐ru, an honorific which refers only to people.

A new combination appears in this lesson: the gerund of a TRANSITIVE v e r b a l + √a⌐ru 'so-and-so has been done.' [2] Like an intransitive gerund + √(i)ru, it indicates the existing result of a previous action, and the combination is itself intransitive; however, a transitive gerund + √a⌐ru always implies the result of an action that HAS BEEN DONE BY SOMEONE. Thus:

---

[1] The combination is polite neutral (+), not humble (+).

[2] This pattern includes transitive verbals in general—not only those having an intransitive partner.

Do˥a ḡa a˥kete arima˥su.   'The door has been opened.'
Do˥a ḡa ˥si˥mete arimasu.   'The door has been closed.'
De˥ñki ḡa tu˥ke˥te arimasu.   'The light has been turned on.'
Ti˥zu ḡa ˥ka˥ite arimasu.   'The map has been drawn.'
Si˥ñbuñ ḡa katte arima˥su.   'The newspaper has been bought.'

Compare these examples with one like Do˥a ḡa a˥ite ima˥su, which means simply 'The door is open'; whether it was opened by someone or whether it opened by itself is not made clear by the pattern which uses the intransitive gerund.

The object of a transitive verbal becomes the subject of the corresponding gerund + √a˥ru:

Sa˥kana o tabema˥sita.   'I ate the fish.'
Sa˥kana ḡa ta˥bete arimasu.   'The fish has been eaten.'

The subject of a gerund + √a˥ru pattern is always inanimate.

In the informal negative, the contracted form of a transitive gerund + √iru may coincide with the transitive gerund + √a˥ru, namely in those environments where the accent of the two forms is the same:

ta˥bete iru '[I] am eating'
ta˥bete inai, contracted ta˥bete nai '[I] am not eating';
ta˥bete ˥na˥i kara 'because [I] am not eating'

ta˥bete ˥a˥ru '[it] has been eaten'
ta˥bete ˥na˥i '[it] has not been eaten'
ta˥bete ˥na˥i kara 'because [it] has not been eaten'

The coinciding forms are distinguished only by context.

2.   Verbal Gerund + <u>kara</u>

A verbal gerund (-<u>te</u>/-<u>de</u> form) + <u>kara</u> means 'after doing so-and-so' or 'since doing so-and-so.' A regularly unaccented gerund acquires an accent on its final syllable when it occurs before <u>kara</u>. Thus:

ta˥bete kara 'after eating'
ka˥ette kara 'after returning home'
mi˥te kara 'after seeing'
i˥tte˥ kara 'after going'   <u>or</u>   'after saying'

A gerund + <u>kara</u> combination regularly modifies an inflected expression without a following particle; but when it describes a nominal, it is followed by <u>no</u>.

Examples:

Ta˥bete kara, ka˥isya e kaerima˥sita.
    'After eating, I went back to the office.'
Yo˥sida-sañ to hana˥site kara, ma˥ta koko e kite˥ kudasai.
    'After talking with Mr. Yoshida, please come back here.'
Si˥ñbuñ o yo˥ñde kara, so˥no zassi o mima˥su.
    'After I read the paper, I'm going to look at that magazine.'
Hu˥ne ḡa ˥de˥te kara, To˥okyoo e kaerima˥sita.
    'After the ship left, I returned to Tokyo.'

Ko⌐ko e kite⌐ kara, mo⌐o ro⌐k-ka⌐ḡetu ni narimasu.
'It is almost 6 months since I came here.'
(Lit. 'Since coming here, it will become 6 months already.')
Sore wa zi⌐mu⌐syo o ⌐de⌐te kara no siḡoto desu.
'That is work [to be done] after leaving the office.'

WARNING: Be sure to distinguish between the gerund + kara and the informal past + kara, which are easily confused by a beginner. Thus:

si⌐te⌐ kara 'after doing'   but si⌐ta⌐ kara 'because [I] did'
ki⌐ite⌐ kara 'after asking'   but ki⌐ita⌐ kara 'because [I] asked'
si⌐mete kara 'after shutting'   but si⌐meta kara 'because [I] shut'

3.   Color Words

Akai, a⌐o⌐i, kiiroi, si⌐ro⌐i, and ku⌐ro⌐i are color words which are adjectivals. Thus:

a. a⌐kai ho⌐n 'a red book'
b. akai 'it's red' (informal)
c. a⌐ka⌐i desu 'it's red' (formal)
d. a⌐ka⌐katta 'it was red' (informal)
e. a⌐ka⌐katta desu (or a⌐ka⌐i desita) 'it was red' (formal)
f. a⌐kaku narima⌐sita 'it's become red' (formal)
g. a⌐kaku arimase⌐ñ 'it isn't red' (formal)
h. a⌐kaku na⌐i 'it isn't red' (informal)

Tyairo and haiiro are color words which are nominals. Thus:

a. tya⌐iro no ho⌐ñ 'a brown book'
b. tyairo da 'it's brown' (informal)
c. tya⌐iro de⌐su 'it's brown' (formal)
d. tya⌐iro da⌐tta 'it was brown' (informal)
e. tya⌐iro de⌐sita 'it was brown' (formal)
f. tya⌐iro ni narima⌐sita 'it's become brown' (formal)
g. tya⌐iro zya arimase⌐ñ 'it isn't brown' (formal)
h. tya⌐iro zya na⌐i 'it isn't brown' (informal)

Some other color words which are nominals are: mu⌐ra⌐saki 'purple,' momo-iro 'pink,' mi⌐dori 'green.'

A⌐ka, a⌐o, kiiro, si⌐ro, and ku⌐ro are nominal alternants of the adjectival color words listed above. While they are often used interchangeably with their adjectival counterparts, they also have various special uses which distinguish them from the adjectivals, including the following:

a. Only the nominals are used to NAME the colors. Thus:

A⌐o ḡa su⌐ki⌐ desu. 'I like blue (i.e. the color blue).'
     but:
A⌐o⌐i no ḡa su⌐ki⌐ desu. 'I like the blue one (i.e. an object that is blue).'

b. Only the nominals are used when one object is described by several colors. Thus:

aｏ˥i haᵝizaᶜra 'a blue ashtray'
and :
siᵝroᵓi haᵝizaᶜra 'a white ashtray'
but :
aᶦo to ᵝsiᵝro no haᵝizaᶜra 'a blue and white ashtray'

c. Only the nominals are themselves described by adjectivals. Thus :

aｏ˥i haᵝizaᶜra 'a blue ashtray'
but :
uᵝsui aᶦo no haᵝizaᶜra 'a light blue ashtray'

akai kuruma 'a red car'
but :
koᶦi ᵝaᶜka no kuruma 'a dark red car'

4. Sentence Particle <u>wa</u>

The sentence particle <u>wa</u>[1] occurs as a sentence final, or pre-final before <u>yo</u>, <u>nee</u>, and <u>ne</u>, IN THE SPEECH OF WOMEN. It regularly follows non-past and past inflected words in the informal style,[2] plain and polite. It is a particle which indicates friendliness and assertiveness—in a gentle way—and some familiarity. Whereas <u>Soᶦo da.</u> is abrupt and masculine, <u>Soᶦo da wa⌟</u> is friendly and feminine.[3]

Informal patterns consisting of an informal non-past or past directly followed by <u>yo</u>, <u>neᶦe</u>, and <u>ne</u> are more typical of men's speech (cf. Lesson 13, Grammatical Note 2). If sentence particle <u>wa</u> is inserted before <u>yo</u>, <u>neᶦe</u>, and <u>ne</u> in such sequences they become typical of women's speech. However, the most frequently occurring women's equivalents of sentences ending in <u>da yo</u>, <u>da ᵝneᶦe</u>, and <u>da ne</u> simply omit the <u>da</u>.

	<u>Men's Speech</u>	<u>Women's Speech</u>
'I understand.'	Waᵝkaᶦru yo⌟	Waᵝkaᶦru wa yo⌟
'I understood.'	Waᵝkaᶦtta yo⌟	Waᵝkaᶦtta wa yo⌟
'Isn't it expensive!'	Taᵝkaᶦi ᵝneᶜe.	Taᵝkaᶦi wa ᵝneᶜe.
'Wasn't it expensive!'	Taᶦkakatta ᵝneᶜe.	Taᶦkakatta wa ᵝneᶜe.
'That's right, isn't it?'	Soᶦo da ne?	Soᶦo ne?
'It was strange, wasn't it?'	Heᶦñ datta ne?	Heᶦñ datta wa ne?

---

[1] It is best to consider this <u>wa</u> and the particle <u>wa</u> introduced previously as different words.

[2] It also occurs with the formal style, but less frequently.

[3] In some dialects of Japanese, sentence particle <u>wa</u> occurs in men's speech, but in standard Tokyo Japanese, it is a feminine particle.

Comparisons of some informal patterns which have already been introduced are shown in the following chart:

	Men and Women	Men	Women
'I understand.'	Wa⌐ka˥ru.		Wa⌐ka˥ru wa↲
'It's expensive.'	Ta⌐ka˥i.		Ta⌐ka˥i wa↲
'That's right.'	So˥o.	So˥o da.	So˥o da wa↲
'That's right!'		So˥o da yo↲	So˥o yo↲
'That's right, isn't it!'		So˥o da ⌐ne˥e.	So˥o ⌐ne˥e.
'That's right, isn't it?'		So˥o da ne?	So˥o ne?

5.   Counter -kai 'floor'

The counter -kai combines with the numerals of Series I to count and to name the floors of a building. Numbers from one to ten are:

ik-kai	'1 floor'	or '1st floor'
ni-kai	'2 floors'	or '2d floor'
sañ-ḡai	'3 floors'	or '3d floor'
yoñ-kai	'4 floors'	or '4th floor'
go-kai	'5 floors'	or '5th floor'
rok-kai	'6 floors'	or '6th floor'
nana-kai	'7 floors'	or '7th floor'
hati-kai or hak-kai	'8 floors'	or '8th floor'
kyuu-kai	'9 floors'	or '9th floor'
zik-kai or zyuk-kai	'10 floors'	or '10th floor'
nañ-ḡai	'how many floors?'	or 'what floor?'

Nikai (polite, onikai[+]) occurs as the equivalent of 'upstairs' when 'upstairs' refers to the second floor of a two-story building. The equivalent of 'downstairs' is sita ('below,' 'under').

DRILLS

A. Substitution Drill

1. Shall I turn down the radio? Ra˥zio (o) ⌐ti˥isaku si⌐masyo˥o ka.

2. Shall I turn up the television? Te˥rebi (o) ⌐o˥okiku si⌐masyo˥o ka.

3. Shall I heat the tea? Otya (o) ⌐a˥tuku si⌐masyo˥o ka.

4. Shall I chill the beer? Bi˥iru (o) tu⌐metaku simasyo˥o ka.

5. Shall I warm this room? Ko⌐no heya˥ (o) a⌐ttaka⌐ku si⌐masyo˥o ka.

6. Shall I make the coffee strong? Ko⌐ohi˥i (o) ⌐ko˥ku si⌐masyo˥o ka.

7. Shall I make the (black) tea weak? Kootya (o) u⌐suku simasyo˥o ka.

B. Substitution Drill (based on Grammatical Note 3)

1.	It's a gray and blue car.	Haiiro to ⌐a⌐o no ku⌐ruma de⌐su.
2.	It's a black and white ashtray.	Ku⌐ro to ⌐si⌐ro no ha⌐iza⌐ra desu.
3.	It's a green and yellow electric train.	Mi⌐dori to ki⌐iro no deñsya de⌐su.
4.	It's a gray and black ship.	Haiiro to ⌐ku⌐ro no ⌐hu⌐ne desu.
5.	It's a red and blue plate.	A⌐ka to ⌐a⌐o no sa⌐ra de⌐su.
6.	It's a black and red tray.	Ku⌐ro to ⌐a⌐ka no o⌐boñ de⌐su.
7.	It's a pink and white cake.	Momoiro to ⌐si⌐ro no o⌐ka⌐si desu.
8.	It's dark blue paper.	Ko⌐i ⌐a⌐o no ka⌐mi⌐ desu.
9.	It's a light brown pen.	U⌐sui tyairo no pe⌐ñ desu.
10.	It's a dark purple fu-roshiki.	Ko⌐i mu⌐ra⌐saki no hu⌐rosiki de⌐su.

C. Substitution Drill (based on Grammatical Note 1)

Practice this drill in two ways: (1) Omit the particles in parentheses; (2) Include the particles in parentheses with the student supplying them on the basis of what verbals occur.

1.	Did you lock the door?	To ⌐no kagi⌐ (o) ka⌐kema⌐sita ka↲
2.	Is the door locked?	To ⌐no kagi⌐ (ḡa) ka⌐ka⌐tte (i)masu ka↲
3.	Is the window locked?	Ma⌐do no ka⌐ḡi⌐ (ḡa) ka⌐ka⌐tte (i)masu ka↲
4.	Shall I lock the window?	Ma⌐do no ka⌐ḡi⌐ (o) ka⌐kemasyo⌐o ka↲
5.	Shall I lock the car?	Ku⌐ruma no kagi⌐ (o) ka⌐kemasyo⌐o ka↲
6.	Please lock the car.	Ku⌐ruma no kagi⌐ (o) ⌐ka⌐kete kudasai.
7.	Please lock the entry hall.	Ge⌐ñkañ no ka⌐ḡi⌐ (o) ⌐ka⌐kete kudasai.
8.	Has the entry hall been locked?	Ge⌐ñkañ no ka⌐ḡi⌐ (ḡa) ⌐ka⌐kete arima-su ka↲

D. Grammar Drill

Tutor: Ki⌐tana⌐i desu yo↲ 'It's dirty!'
Student: Ki⌐tana⌐ku na⌐rima⌐sita yo↲ 'It's gotten dirty!'

1.	Ku⌐ro⌐i desu yo↲	Ku⌐roku na⌐rima⌐sita yo↲
2.	Ha⌐iiro de⌐su yo↲	Ha⌐iiro ni narima⌐sita yo↲
3.	A⌐ttaka⌐i desu yo↲	A⌐tta⌐kaku na⌐rima⌐sita yo↲
4.	Se⌐ñse⌐e desu yo↲	Se⌐ñse⌐e ni na⌐rima⌐sita yo↲
5.	A⌐o⌐i desu yo↲	A⌐oku na⌐rima⌐sita yo↲
6.	Ge⌐ñki desu yo↲	Ge⌐ñki ni na⌐rima⌐sita yo↲
7.	A⌐buna⌐i desu yo↲	A⌐bunaku narima⌐sita yo↲
8.	Mi⌐dori desu yo↲	Mi⌐dori ni na⌐rima⌐sita yo↲

E. Grammar Drill (based on Grammatical Note 1)

> Tutor: Ma˥do o aˤkema˧sita. 'I opened the window.'
> Student: Ma˥do ḡa aˤkima˧sita. 'The window opened.'

1. Deˀ̄nki o tuˤkema˧sita.   Deˀ̄nki ḡa tuˤkima˧sita.
2. To ˤo simema˥sita.   To ˤga simarima˥sita.
3. Soˤre o naosima˥sita.   Soˤre ḡa naorima˥sita.
4. Suˤto˥obu o keˤsima˧sita.   Suˤto˥obu ḡa kiˤema˧sita.
5. To ˤno kaḡi˥ o kaˤkema˧si-   To ˤno kaḡi˥ ḡa kaˤkarima˧sita.
   ta.

F. Grammar Drill (based on Grammatical Note 1)

> Tutor: Ma˥do o aˤkema˥sita ka↲ 'Did you open the window?'
> Student: Ma˥do ḡa aˤkete arima˥su ka↲ 'Has the window been
>   opened?'

1. Kuˤruma o naˤosima˥sita   Kuruma ḡa naˤo˥site aˤrima˧su ka↲
   ka↲
2. Tiˤzu o kaˤkima˥sita ka↲   Tiˤzu ḡa ˤkaˀite aˤrima˧su ka↲
3. Suˤto˥obu o keˤsima˥sita   Suˤto˥obu ḡa keˤsite arima˥sita ka↲
   ka↲
4. Aˤtarasiˀi ziˤbiki˧ o   Aˤtarasiˀi ziˤbiki˧ ḡa gaˤkkoo e mot-
   gaˤkkoo e motte ikima˥si-   te iˀtte aˤrima˧su ka↲
   ta ka↲
5. Doˀa o siˤmema˥sita ka↲   Doˀa ḡa ˤsiˤmete aˤrima˧su ka↲
6. Teˤrebi o tuˤkema˥sita   Teˤrebi ḡa tuˤke˥te aˤrima˧su ka↲
   ka↲
7. Kuˤruma no kaḡi˥ o kaˤke-   Kuˤruma no kaḡi˥ ḡa ˤkaˤkete aˤri-
   ma˥sita ka↲   ma˧su ka↲
8. Paˀ̄n o kaˤima˥sita ka↲   Paˀ̄n ḡa kaˤtte arima˥sita ka↲

G. Grammar Drill (based on Grammatical Note 2)

> Tutor: Taˤbema˥sita. Sore kara, kaˤerima˥sita.
>   'I ate. After that, I went home.'
> Student: Taˤbete kara, kaˤerima˥sita.
>   'After eating, I went home.'

1. To ˤ(o) simema˥sita. Sore   To ˤ(o) siˤmete kara, ma˥do mo miˤn̄-
   kara, ma˥do mo miˤn̄na si-   na simema˥sita.
   mema˥sita.
2. Deˀ̄nki (o) miˤn̄na kesima˥si-   Deˀ̄nki (o) miˤn̄na kesite˥ kara, teˤre-
   ta. Sore kara, teˤrebi (o)   bi (o) tuˤkema˧sita.
   tuˤkema˧sita.
3. Uˤti (o) katazukema˥sita.   Uˤti (o) katazuˤkete kara, deˤkakema˥-
   Sore kara, deˤkakema˥si-   sita.
   ta.
4. Soˤozi-sima˥sita. Sore   Soˤozi-site˥ kara, syoˤkuzi no sitaku
   kara, syoˤkuzi no sitaku   (o) sima˥sita.
   (o) sima˥sita.

5. Si⌐nbuñ (o) yomima⌐si-   Si⌐nbuñ (o) yo⌐nde kara, ka⌐isya ni i-
   ta. Sore kara, ka⌐isya   kima⌐sita.
   ni ikima⌐sita.

6. Ni⌐honzi⌐ñ to ke⌐kkoñ-   Ni⌐honzi⌐ñ to ke⌐kkoñ-site⌐ kara,
   sima⌐sita. Sore kara,   A⌐merika e kaerima⌐sita.
   A⌐merika e kaerima⌐si-
   ta.

7. So⌐o iima⌐sita. Sore   So⌐o itte⌐ kara, he⌐ya⌐ (o) de⌐ma⌐si-
   kara, he⌐ya⌐ (o) de⌐ma⌐-   ta.
   sita.

8. De⌐nwa (o) kirima⌐sita.   De⌐nwa (o) ki⌐tte kara, ma⌐ta su⌐ḡu
   Sore kara, ma⌐ta su⌐ḡu   ka⌐kema⌐sita.
   ka⌐kema⌐sita.

9. Byo⌐oki ni narima⌐sita.   Byo⌐oki ni na⌐tte kara, o⌐sake to ta-
   Sore kara, o⌐sake to   bako (o) yamema⌐sita.
   tabako (o) yamema⌐si-
   ta.

10. Zyu⌐nsa ni kikima⌐sita.   Zyu⌐nsa ni kiite⌐ kara, su⌐ḡu mi⌐ti
    Sore kara, su⌐ḡu mi⌐ti   ḡa wakarima⌐sita.
    ḡa wakarima⌐sita.

H. Response Drill

(Give the _iie_ answer, same politeness and formality level, for each of
the following.)

1. A⌐kima⌐su ka⌐   Iie, a⌐kimase⌐ñ.
2. A⌐ite (i)ma⌐su ka⌐   Iie, a⌐ite (i)mase⌐ñ.
3. Mi⌐dori?   Iie, mi⌐dori zya ⌐na⌐i.
4. Yo⌐ru desu ka⌐   Iie, yo⌐ru zya a⌐rimase⌐ñ.
5. Ki⌐ete orima⌐su ka⌐   Iie, ki⌐ete orimase⌐ñ.
6. Ki⌐tana⌐i?   Iie, ki⌐tana⌐ku ⌐na⌐i.
7. A⌐na⌐ta wa se⌐nse⌐e de   Iie, se⌐nse⌐e de wa go⌐zaimase⌐ñ.
   (i)⌐rassyaima⌐su ka⌐
8. A⌐tataka⌐i desu ka⌐   Iie, a⌐tata⌐kaku a⌐rimase⌐ñ.
9. Na⌐o⌐site (i)ru?   Iie, na⌐o⌐site (i)nai.
10. Na⌐o⌐site ⌐a⌐ru?   Iie, na⌐o⌐site ⌐na⌐i.
11. A⌐o⌐i desu ka⌐   Iie, a⌐oku a⌐rimase⌐ñ.
12. A⌐o desu ka⌐   Iie, a⌐o zya a⌐rimase⌐ñ.

I. Response Drill

Tutor: O⌐okiku si⌐masyo⌐o ka.   'Shall I make it loud?'

Student: Iie, ti⌐isa⌐i ma⌐ma⌐ de	⌐i⌐ desu yo⌐ yo⌐rosi⌐i desu yo⌐ ⌐ke⌐kkoo desu yo⌐ ka⌐maimase⌐ñ yo⌐	(Practice all 4 for each answer)

'No, it's all right soft, as it is.'

1. Ti⌐isaku si⌐masyo⌐o ka.   Iie, o⌐oki⌐i ma⌐ma⌐ de ⌐i⌐i desu yo⌐
2. A⌐tuku si⌐masyo⌐o ka.   Iie, tu⌐metai mama⌐ de ⌐i⌐i desu yo⌐

3. Ko˥ku si˕masyo˥o ka.

Iie, u˕sui mama˥ de ˕i˩i desu yo⌐

4. Ki˥ree ni si˕masyo˥o ka.

Iie, ki˥tana˥i ma˕ma˩ de ˕i˩i desu yo⌐

5. Ya˕sasiku simasyo˥o ka.

Iie, mu˕zukasii mama˥ de ˕i˩i desu yo⌐

6. U˕suku simasyo˥o ka.

Iie, ko˥i ma˕ma˩ de ˕i˩i desu yo⌐

7. Ka˥raku si˕masyo˥o ka.

Iie, a˕mai mama˥ de ˕i˩i desu yo⌐

J. Expansion Drill

1. Have [they] been turned
   off?

Ke˕site arima˥su ka⌐

Are [they] on, or have
they been turned off?

Tu˥ite (i)˕ma˩su ka, ke˕site arima˥-
su ka⌐

Are the lights on, or
have they been turned
off?

De˥ñki wa ˕tu˥ite (i)˕ma˩su ka, ke-
˕site arima˥su ka⌐

Are the upstairs lights
on, or have they been
turned off?

Ni˕kai no de˥ñki wa ˕tu˥ite (i)˕ma˩su
ka, ke˕site arima˥su ka ⌐

2. It's grown cold. . . .[1]

Sa˥muku na˕rima˩sita g̃a_

It's grown very cold. . . .

To˕ttemo sa˥muku na˕rima˩sita g̃a_

It's gone out so it's
grown very cold. . . .

Ki˕ete (i)ru˥ kara, to˕ttemo sa˥muku
na˕rima˩sita g̃a_

The heater is off so it's
grown very cold. . . .

Su˕to˥obu (g̃a) ki˕ete (i)ru˥ kara, to-
˕ttemo sa˥muku na˕rima˩sita g̃a_

3. Hasn't it grown warm!

A˕tta˥kaku na˕rima˩sita ˕ne˥e.

Hasn't the room grown
warm!

He˕ya˥ (g̃a) a˕tta˥kaku na˕rima˩sita
˕ne˥e.

Since turning [it] on,
hasn't the room grown
warm!

Tu˕ke˥te kara, he˕ya˥ (g̃a) a˕tta˥kaku
na˕rima˩sita ˕ne˥e.

Since turning on the heater,
hasn't the room grown
warm!

Su˕to˥obu (o) tu˕ke˩te kara, he˕ya˥
(g̃a) a˕tta˥kaku na˕rima˩sita
˕ne˥e.

Hasn't the room grown
warm since Haruko
turned on the heater!

Ha˥ruko-sañ (g̃a) su˕to˥obu (o) tu˕ke˩-
te kara, he˕ya˥ (g̃a) a˕tta˥kaku na˕ri-
ma˩sita ˕ne˥e.

4. Because I don't like it.

Su˕ki˥ zya a˕rimase˩ñ kara.

Because I don't like it very
much.

A˕ñmari suki˥ zya a˕rimase˩ñ kara.

---

[1] 'but— can anything be done about it? '

Because I don't like sweet
things very much.

That's fine— because I
don't like sweet things
very much.

It's fine sour—as it is—
because I don't like
sweet things very much.

A⌐mai mono⌐ (wa) a⌐ñmari suki⌐ zya
a⊦rimase⌐ñ kara.

Ke⌐kkoo desu yo—a⊦mai mono⌐(wa)
a⊦ñmari suki⌐ zya a⊦rimase⌐ñ kara.

Su⌐ppa⌐i ma⊦ma⌐ de ⌐ke⌐kkoo desu
yo — a⊦mai mono⌐ (wa) a⊦ñmari
suki⌐ zya a⊦rimase⌐ñ kara.

5. It's pretty, isn't it?

The furoshiki is pretty,
isn't it?

The purple furoshiki is
pretty, isn't it?

The yellow and purple
furoshiki is pretty,
isn't it?

That yellow and purple
furoshiki is pretty,
isn't it?

Ki⌐ree desyoo?

Hurosiki (wa) ⌐ki⌐ree desyoo?

Mu⌐ra⌐saki no hurosiki (wa) ⌐ki⌐ree
desyoo?

Kiiro to mu⌐ra⌐saki no hurosiki (wa)
⌐ki⌐ree desyoo?

Ano kiiro to mu⌐ra⌐saki no hurosiki
(wa) ⌐ki⌐ree desyoo?

6. I understood.

After seeing [it] I understood.

After seeing his name
card I understood.

I couldn't hear but after
seeing his name card
I understood.

I couldn't hear but his name
but after seeing his
name card I could tell
[what it was].

Wa⌐karima⌐sita.

Mi⌐te kara, wa⌐karima⌐sita.

Me⌐esi (o) mi⌐te kara, wa⌐karima⌐-
sita.

Ki⌐koemase⌐ñ desita ḡa; me⌐esi (o)
mi⌐te kara, wa⌐karima⌐sita.

Namae (wa) ki⌐koemase⌐ñ desita ḡa;
me⌐esi (o) mi⌐te kara, wa⌐karima⌐-
sita.

SUPPLEMENTARY SELECTIONS

(with questions)

1. Ke⌐sa to⌐temo sa⌐mukatta kara, su⌐to⌐obu o tu⊦kema⌐sita ḡa; su⌐ḡu ki⊦ema⌐sita. To⌐nari no heya⌐ kara ho⌐ka no⌐ o mo⊦tte⌐ kite tu⊦ke⌐te kara, he⌐ya⌐ ḡa a⌐tata⌐kaku na⊦rima⌐sita.

   a. I⌐tu su⊦to⌐obu o tu⊦kema⌐sita ka⌐

   b. Na⌐ze su⊦to⌐obu o tu⊦kema⌐sita ka⌐

   c. Su⌐to⌐obu o hu⊦ta-tu tukema⌐sita ḡa, do⌐tira mo ko⌐syoo de⌐sita ka⌐

   d. Na⌐ni o si⊦te⌐ kara he⌐ya⌐ ḡa a⊦tta⌐kaku na⊦rima⌐sita ka⌐

2. Kyo⌐o úti ḡa ⌐zu⌐ibuñ ki⊦tana⌐ku ⊦na⌐tte ita kara, go⌐ḡo no ⌐sa⌐ñ-zi made so⊦ozi-sima⌐sita. So⌐ozi o site⌐ kara ótya o ⌐i⌐p-pai ⊦no⌐ñde; sore kara,

sa⌐kanaya ni deñwa o ka⌐kete, o⌐sasimi n o sakana o tyuumoñ-sima⌐sita.
Go⌐-zi kara ro⌐ku⌐-zi made syo⌐kuzi no sitaku o sima⌐sita. Ro⌐ku-zi-ha⌐ñ
ni ⌐syu⌐ziñ g̃a kǎisya kara ⌐ka⌐ette kite;[1] sore kara, i⌐ssyo ni syokuzi o si-
ma⌐sita.

    a. Do⌐o site u⌐ti o soozi-sima⌐sita ka⌐

    b. Na⌐ñ-zi made so⌐ozi-sima⌐sita ka⌐

    c. So⌐ozi-site⌐ kara ⌐su⌐g̃u ⌐na⌐ni o si⌐ma⌐sita ka⌐

    d. Da⌐re ni de⌐ñwa o kakema⌐sita ka⌐

    e. Na⌐ni o tyu⌐umoñ-sima⌐sita ka⌐

    f . Go⌐-zi kara ro⌐ku⌐-zi made ⌐na⌐ni o si⌐ma⌐sita ka⌐

    g. Go⌐syu⌐ziñ wa ⌐na⌐ñ-zi ni kǎisya kara ⌐ka⌐ette ki⌐ma⌐sita ka⌐

3. Ke⌐kkoñ-site⌐ kara ⌐mo⌐o ⌐ni⌐-neñ ni narimasu. A⌐merika de kekkoñ-si-
ma⌐sita g̃a, ke⌐kkoñ-site⌐ kara ⌐su⌐g̃u Ni⌐ho⌐ñ e ki⌐ma⌐sita. Watakusi wa
A⌐merika-taisi⌐kañ ni tu⌐to⌐mete ite, ka⌐nai wa Ni⌐ho⌐ñ no gǎkkoo de e⌐eg̃o
o osiete ima⌐su. Mo⌐o su⌐g̃u ka⌐erima⌐su g̃a; Ni⌐ho⌐ñ g̃a to⌐temo suki⌐ desu
kara, ka⌐erita⌐ku a⌐rimase⌐ñ.

    a. I⌐ma ⌐do⌐ko ni i⌐ma⌐su ka⌐

    b. Na⌐ñ-neñ ni ke⌐kkoñ-sima⌐sita ka⌐

    c. Na⌐ñ-neñ ma⌐e ni ke⌐kkoñ-sima⌐sita ka⌐

    d. Do⌐ko de ke⌐kkoñ-sima⌐sita ka⌐

    e. Ke⌐kkoñ-site⌐ kara ⌐do⌐ko e i⌐kima⌐sita ka⌐

    f . Go⌐syu⌐ziñ wa ⌐do⌐ñna si⌐g̃oto o site ima⌐su ka⌐

    g. O⌐kusañ wa ⌐do⌐ñna si⌐g̃oto o site ima⌐su ka⌐

    h. I⌐tu ka⌐erima⌐su ka⌐

    i . Do⌐o site ka⌐erita⌐ku a⌐rimase⌐ñ ka⌐

SUPPLEMENTARY CONVERSATION

(In an office building)

Smith (to receptionist):   Go-⌐kai e ikita⌐i ñ desu g̃a⌐
Receptionist: Zya⌐a, asoko ni e⌐rebe⌐eta [2] g̃a gozaimasu.
Smith: Do⌐o mo.
Elevator operator: U⌐e e mairima⌐su. Na⌐na-kai ma⌐de mairimasu.
Smith: Go-⌐kai oneg̃ai-sima⌐su.
Other passenger: Sañ-g̃ai.
Elevator operator: Ka⌐sikomarima⌐sita. . . . Sa⌐ñ-g̃ai de gozaima⌐su.
Other passenger: Do⌐o mo.
Elevator operator: Tu⌐g̃i⌐ wa go-⌐kai de gozaima⌐su. . . . O⌐matase-itasima⌐si-
    ta. Go-⌐kai de gozaima⌐su.
Smith: A⌐ri⌐g̃atoo.

---

[1] ka⌐ette ⌐ku⌐ru 'come back.'

[2] 'Elevator.'

English Equivalent

Smith: I want to go to the fifth floor. . . .
Receptionist: (In that case) there's an elevator over there.
Smith: Thanks.
Elevator operator: Going up. [This car] goes to the seventh floor.
Smith: Five, please.
Other passenger: Three.
Elevator operator: Certainly. . . . Third floor.
Other passenger: Thanks.
Elevator operator: Fifth floor next. . . . (I'm sorry to have kept you waiting.)
    Fifth floor.
Smith: Thanks.

EXERCISES

1. You ask Mr. Tanaka where he lives. He answers:

    a. In Akasaka.
    b. Near Kamakura Station.
    c. Right near the American Embassy.
    d. In an apartment in Shibuya.

2. Ask the salesgirl to show you:

    a. that green pen.
    b. that yellow ashtray.
    c. those gray teacups.
    d. those brown and white dishes.
    e. those red chopsticks.
    f. that red and blue pencil.
    g. that red and black tray.
    h. that pink paper.
    i. that light purple furoshiki.
    j. that dark blue book.

3. Tell Haruko to:

    a. open the door.
    b. shut the window.
    c. turn on the light.
    d. turn off the heater.
    e. turn the radio down.
    f. make the television louder.
    g. clean this room.
    h. straighten up the next room.
    i. get dinner ready.
    j. lock the door in the entry hall.
    k. take this upstairs.
    l. turn off the upstairs heater.

4. Indicate whether each of the following is M (more typical of men's speech),
   W (more typical of women's speech), or MW (used by men and women). If
   you are a man, give an M or MW equivalent for all sentences marked W; if
   you are a woman, give a W or MW equivalent for all sentences marked M.

   a. O⌐su⌐mai ⌐do⌐tira?
   b. Yameta yo↲
   c. Hoñtoo ⌐ne⌐e.
   d. Ki⌐ree da.
   e. Si⌐rana⌐katta?
   f. Abunai.
   g. So⌐o yo.
   h. Ze⌐ñbu wa⌐ka⌐tta?
   i. De⌐kita wa↲
   j. O⌐naka ga suita⌐ wa yo↲
   k. He⌐ñ da ⌐ne⌐e.
   l. Ki⌐koena⌐katta yo↲

5. Practice the Basic Dialogues with appropriate variations.

Lesson 17. At Home (cont.)

(The Smiths have just moved into a new house. Masao-sañ and
Fumiko-sañ are helping them.)

(a)

Smith (to Masao)

help or lend a hand	te⌐tuda⌐u /-u/
1. Give me a hand, will you?	Te⌐tuda⌐tte ne?
things like books and magazines	ho⌐ñ ya zássi
study (i.e. a room)	syosai
desk	tukue
onto the desk	tukue ni
top of the desk	tu⌐kue no ue⌐
onto the top of the desk	tu⌐kue no ue⌐ ni
put or place	oku /-u/
2. Put these books and magazines and things on [top of] the desk in the study.	Kono ⌐ho⌐ñ ya zássi (o) syo⌐sai no tukue [no ue⌐] ni oite. [1]
bookshelf	ho⌐ñdana
onto the bookshelf	ho⌐ñdana ni
put away or store	simau /-u/
3. (Because) I'll put them (away) on the bookshelves later.	A⌐to de ⌐ho⌐ñdana ni si┗mau┐ kara.
is small or fine or detailed	ko⌐maka⌐i /-ku/
drawer	hikidasi
into the drawer	hikidasi ni
inside	na⌐ka
inside the drawer	hi⌐kidasi no na⌐ka
into the inside of the drawer	hi⌐kidasi no na⌐ka ni
insert or put in	ireru /-ru/

---

[1] Accent of short alternant: syósai.

4. Then put all those little   Sore kara, ano ko⌐maka⌐i mo⌐no⌐(o)
    things in[side] the desk   ⌐ze⌐ñbu tu⌐kue no hikidasi [no na⌐ka]
    drawer.   ni irete. [1]

. . .

Masao

    finish putting in   irete simau
    following or subsequent   a⌐to
5. I finished putting everything   Mi⌐ñna irete simaima⌐sita ḡa, a⌐to
    in.   What shall I do next?   ⌐na⌐ni (o) si⌐masyo⌐o ka.

Smith

    dog   i⌐nu⌐
    hindrance or bother   zyama /na/   or
                                        ozyama [+]
    become a bother   or   zya⌐ma ni na⌐ru
      get in the way
    outside   so⌐to
    to the outside   so⌐to ni
    put out or send out or   da⌐su /-u/
      take out
6. The dog gets in the way so   I⌐nu⌐ ḡa zya⌐ma ni na⌐ru kara, so⌐to
    put him outside.   ni dasite.

(calling after Masao)

    give   yaru /-u/
7. Say! Give him some water   Ano ne! Mi⌐zu mo yatte⌐ ne?
    too, will you?

(b)

Masao

8. What shall I do with these   Kono sara (wa) ⌐do⌐o simasyoo ka.
    dishes?

Smith

    soap   sekkeñ
    wash   arau /-u/
    receive or get   morau /-u/
    have Fumiko wash   Hu⌐miko-sañ ni āratte morau
9. Those—have Fumiko wash   Sore (wa) ⌐Hu⌐miko-sañ ni sêkkeñ
    with soap and hot water.   to oyu de āratte moratte.

---

[1] Accent of short alternant: tŭkue.

	cupboard (with shelves)	todana
	into the cupboard	todana ni
10.	(Because) I'll put them (away) in the dining-room closet later.	A⌐to de syo⌐kudoo no todana ni simau⌐ kara.

. . .

Smith

	on top of this	kono ue
	take up _or_ take away	to⌐ru /-u/
11.	Say, take away the things on top of this.	Tyo⌐tto, ko⌐no ue no mono⌐ (o) ⌐to⌐t-te.

	table	teeburu
	kitchen	daidokoro
	into the kitchen	daidokoro ni
12.	(Because) I'm going to take this table into the kitchen.	Kono teeburu (o) da⌐idokoro ni motte i⌐ku kara.

Masao

| 13. | Shall I help you? | O⌐te⌐tudai-simasyoo ka_ |

Smith

| | alone (lit. being one person) | hi⌐to⌐ri de |
| 14. | No, I can manage alone. | Iie, hi⌐to⌐ri de da⌐izyo⌐obu. |

(c)

Masao

| | throw away | suteru /-ru/ |
| 15. | These old newspapers— shall I throw them away? | Kono hu⌐ru⌐i siñbuñ (wa) su⌐temasyo⌐o ka. |

Smith

	corner (of a room)	su⌐mi
	into the corner	su⌐mi ni
	put for the time being	oit(e) oku
16.	No, I need them so put them in that corner for the time being.	Iie, i⌐ru⌐ kara, a⌐no su⌐mi ni o⌐it(e) o⌐ite.

. . .

	be careful	ki⌐otuke⌐ru /-ru/
	[something] spills	ko⌐bore⌐ru /-ru/
	be spilt	ko⌐bo⌐rete (i)ru
17.	Oh, be careful! (Because) something's spilt.	A, ki⌐otuke⌐te. Na⌐ni ka ko⌐bo⌐rete (i)ru kara.

| | wipe | huku /-u/ |
| | have Fumiko wipe | Hu⌐miko-sañ ni hu̅ite morau |

18. Have Fumiko wipe it up!   Hu˺miko-sañ ni hu˹ite moratte˺ yo.

                    Masao

19. What'll she wipe it up   Na˺ñ de hu˼kimasyo˺o ka.
     with?

                    Smith

     box   hako
     into the box   hako ni
     cleaning rag   zookiñ
     dishrag or dish cloth   hu˼ki˹ñ
        or cloth
     things like rags and   zo˹okiñ ya huki˺ñ
        cloths
     go in or enter   ha˺iru /-u/
     be in or be entered   ha˺itte (i)ru
20. Clean rags and cloths and   Ano hako ni ˹ki˹ree na zo˹okiñ ya hu-
     things are in that box   ki˺ñ (ḡa) ˼ha˺itte (i)ru kara—
     (so. . .)

                         . . .

     become tired   tu˼kare˺ru̅-/-ru/
     become tired out or   tu˼ka˺rete simau or
        exhausted   tu˼ka˺retyau /-u/
     rest   ya˺su˺mu /-u/
21. You're (lit. You've become)   Tu˼ka˺rete si˼matta˹ desyoo? Tyo˺-
     tired out, aren't you? Let's   tto ya˼sumimasyo˺o.
     rest for a minute.

                    (d)

     (Smith is talking to his friend Tanaka, who has
      dropped in to see how things are coming along)

                    Smith

     head   a˼tama˺
     is painful   i˼ta˺i /-ku/
22. You know, I have a terrible   To˹temo atama˺ (ḡa) i˼ta˺i ñ desu
     headache.   yo.

                    Tanaka

     give (you)   aḡeru /-ru/
23. I have medicine. Would you   Ku˼suri ḡa arima˺su ḡa, a˼ḡemasyo˺o
     like some? (Lit. Shall I   ka⌐
     give you some?)

                    Smith

     receive from Fumiko   Hu˺miko-sañ ni morau or
                                        Hu˺miko-sañ kara morau
     same as this   kore to onazi
     same medicine   onazi kusuri

24. I already got this from Fu-   Huˈmiko-sañ │ ni │ ˈmoˈo koˈre (o)
    miko. Is it the same medi-   │ kara │
    cine as this?   moraimaˈsita g̱a, kore to oˈnazi ku-
                                   suri deˈsu ka⌐

                    Tanaka

     be different from that   sore to tig̱au
25. No, it's different from that.   Iie, soˈre toˈ wa tiˈg̱aimaˈsu.

     is strong   tuˈyoˈi /-ku/
26. It's a much stronger kind   Soˈre yoˈri zuˈtto tuyoˈi no desu g̱a—
    (lit. one) than that. . . .

                    Smith

27. Then may I have some?   Zyaˈa oˈneg̱ai-simaˈsu.

                    Tanaka

28. Aren't you hungry?   Oˈnaka g̱a suitaˈ desyoo?

     order for you   tyuumoñ-site ag̱eru
29. Shall I order something for   Deñwa de ˈnaˈni ka tyuˈumoñ-site
    you by telephone?   ag̱emasyoˈo ka.

                    Smith

     give me   kureru /-ru/
     request or order for   taˈnoˈñde kureru
       me
30. Thank you but Fumiko al-   Aˈriˈg̱atoo gozaimasu g̱a, Huˈmiko-
    ready ordered for me   sañ g̱a ˈmoˈo taˈnoˈñde kuˈremaˈsi-
    (so . . .)   ta kara—

                    ADDITIONAL VOCABULARY

1. Where is the stairway in   Kono uti no kaidañ (wa) ˈdoˈko desyoo
   this house?   ka.

        washroom or lavatory   señmeñzyo
        bathroom   huˈrobaˈ or ohuroba⁺
        family room (Japanese   tyanoma
          style)

2. That I saw in the bedroom.   Sore (wa) siˈñsitu de mimaˈsita.

        living room   iˈmaˈ
        hall or corridor   rooka
        garden   niwa or oniwa⁺

3. Where did you buy that furni-   Soˈno kaˈg̱u (wa) ˈdoˈko de kaˈimaˈsi-
   ture?   ta ka⌐

        bed   beˈttoˈ¹ or siñdai
        chair   isu
        couch or sofa   nag̱aisu
        lamp   sutañdo

――――――――――――

¹ Obsolete.

4. Put that in the <u>refrigerator</u>, Sore (o) re⌐ezo⌐oko ni irete ne?
   will you?

   chest of drawers   tañsu
   closet (for clothing,   osiire
        quilts, etc.)

5. The <u>sink</u> is dirty!   Na⌐gasi⌐ (ḡa) ki⌐tana⌐i desu yo↲

   wash basin   se⌐ñme⌐ñki
   stove (for cooking)   re⌐ñzi
   shelf   tana

6. There's a <u>cat</u> over there!   Asuko ni ⌐ne⌐ko (ḡa) i⊦ma⊣su yo↲

   horse   u⌐ma⌐ or ñ⌐ma⌐
   bull <u>or</u> cow   usi
   goat   ya⌐ḡi
   rabbit   usaḡi
   pig   buta

7. What kind of <u>animals</u> are   Ni⌐ho⌐ñ ni ⌐do⌐ñna do⊦obutu ḡa ima⊣-
   there in Japan?   su ka↲

   bird   tori <u>or</u> kotori
   snake   he⌐bi

8. My <u>ear</u> hurts!   Mi⌐mi⌐ (ḡa) i⊦ta⊣i ñ desu yo.

   tooth   ha⌐
   nose   hana
   mouth   kuti
   eye   me⌐
   neck   kubi
   arm   u⌐de⌐
   hand   te⌐
   finger   yu⌐bi⌐
   leg <u>or</u> foot   a⌐si⌐
   chest   mu⌐ne⌐
   back   senaka
   lower back   kosi
   body   karada

NOTES ON THE BASIC DIALOGUES

2. Particle <u>ni</u> here, and in Basic Sentences 3, 4, 6, 10, 12, 16, and 20, is
   the <u>ni</u> of goal or destination (cf. Lesson 7, Grammatical Note 3; Lesson 10,
   Note 4; and Lesson 14, Note 6).

4. Ko⌐maka⌐i means 'occurring in small pieces.' For example, in reference
   to an explanation, it indicates a detailed one.

6. Note also <u>zyama-suru</u> 'bother.' O⌐zyama-sima⌐sita (or -itasima⌐sita) is a
   common apology: 'I'm sorry to have bothered you.'

   Da⌐su is the transitive partner of intransitive de⌐ru: X ḡa ⌐de⌐ru 'X goes out'; X o ⌈da⌉su 'make X go out,' 'put X out.' Da⌉su occurs as the opposite of both ireru 'put in' and simau 'put away.'

11. Kono ue: compare kono saki in Lesson 7, Basic Sentence 16. Other equivalents of to⌉ru: 'pick up,' 'remove,' 'hand [me],' 'pass [me].' To⌉ru occurs as the opposite of oku 'put,' 'place.'

13. O⌈te⌉tudai-suru (or -itasu) is the humble equivalent of te⌈tuda⌉u (cf. Lesson 13, Grammatical Note 4).

15. Note the use of particle wa. Primary interest is in what follows: 'about these old papers — shall I throw them away [or what shall I do with them]?'

17. The transitive partner of intransitive ko⌈bore⌉ru is ko⌈bo⌉su: X o ko⌈bo⌉su 'spill X'; X ḡa ko⌈bore⌉ru 'X spills.'

20. A zookiñ would be used to wipe up the floor, but a hu⌈ki⌉ñ to wipe a table or a dish.

Ha⌉iru is the intransitive partner of transitive ireru (Sentence 4 above): X ḡa ⌈ha⌉iru 'X goes in,' X o ireru 'put X in.' Ha⌉iru may refer to a person's entering a room or building in general; a hospital, as a patient; a school, as a student; a company, as an employee; etc.

22. Ñ is the nominal meaning something like 'matter' or 'case' (cf. Lesson 7, Grammatical Note 1).

24. The nominal onazi 'same' (onazi da 'it's the same'; o⌈nazi zya na⌉i 'it isn't the same'; o⌈nazi ni na⌉ru 'become the same') occurs directly before a nominal without particle no: onazi kusuri 'the same medicine.'

24, 25. Note the use of particle to 'with' with onazi and tiḡau: X to onazi 'same as X,' X to tiḡau 'different from X.'

25. Wa, here, is the wa of comparison: 'From that it is different.'

26. 'but — would you like to try some?'

Supplementary Vocabulary:

Hu⌈roba⌉ refers only to the place for bathing, in a Japanese house or inn. It is not to be confused with be⌈ñzyo⌉ or te⌈a⌉rai.

Pieces of furniture like beds, chairs, etc., though commonly found in Japan, are Western style — not native Japanese style.

GRAMMATICAL NOTES

1. Verbals of Giving and Receiving

The following four verbals all mean 'give,' with specific differences in usage:

Aḡeru means 'someone gives to an equal or a superior, or to anyone present to whom one is being polite.' It NEVER means 'give to the speaker,' i.e. 'give to me.'

<u>Yaru</u> means 'someone gives to an inferior or [in plain, informal speech] to
an equal.' It is regularly used for giving to animals or to things (as in
'give water to the flowers'). Like a͟ge̲ru, it NEVER means 'give to the
speaker,' i.e. 'give to me.'

Ku⌐dasa̲ru means 'someone gives to me.' [1] It implies either that the speaker's position is inferior to that of the giver, or that the speaker is
deferring to persons present for the sake of politeness.

<u>Kureru</u> means 'someone gives to me.' It implies that the giver is the
speaker's equal or inferior. Sometimes it means 'he, she, or they give
to you'— i.e. 'a third person gives to the person addressed,' if the giver
and recipient are more or less equal. [2]

Particles (with all four verbals above): If expressed, the giver is followed
by g̲a or <u>wa</u>, the thing given by particle o̲ or <u>wa</u>, and the recipient by particle
ni̲.

Examples:

(a) A⌐g̲emasyo⌐o ka. 'Shall I give it to you?'
(b) Se⌐nse⌐e ni a⌐g̲ema⌐sita ka↵ 'Did you give it to the teacher?'
(c) U⌐ti no Ta⌐roo wa se⌐nse⌐e ni ⌐ho⌐n̲ o a⌐g̲ema⌐sita. 'Our Taro
     gave the teacher a book.'
(d) Musuko ni ⌐pe⌐n̲ o ya⌐rima⌐sita. 'I gave my son a pen.'
(e) Ko⌐oka⌐ n̲syu ni a⌐tarasi⌐i de⌐n̲watyoo o yarima⌐sita ka↵ 'Did you
     give the operator a new phone book?'
(f) Se⌐nse⌐e wa ⌐ma⌐initi ko̲domo ni ku⌐da⌐mono o yarimasu. 'The
     teacher gives the children some fruit every day.'
(g) Kore wa ⌐o⌐kusan̲ g̲a ku⌐dasaima⌐sita. 'This your wife gave me.'
(h) Ta⌐bako o kudasa⌐i. 'Please give me a cigarette.'
(i) Kore wa to̲modati g̲a kurema⌐sita. 'This a friend gave me.'
(j) Da⌐re g̲a /a⌐na⌐ta ni/ kureta? 'Who gave it to you?'

Situations involving giving can also be described from the point of view of
receiving. The Japanese equivalent of 'receive' is <u>morau</u>. This verbal may
refer to receiving by or from the speaker, the person addressed, or a third
person. Its polite honorific equivalent is o⌐morai ni na̲⌐ru (†) and its humble
equivalent is <u>itadaku</u> (↓).

Particles: If expressed, the person who receives is followed by g̲a or <u>wa</u>,
the thing received by particle o̲ or <u>wa</u>, and the person from whom it is received by particle <u>kara</u> or <u>ni</u>.

---

[1] Or to person(s) closely associated with me— for example, a member of
my family.

[2] Be careful of this usage. To rate a third party (not present) the equal of
the person addressed would, in some circumstances, be insulting.

Examples:

(k) Tomodati kara o⌈ka⌉si o mo⊢raima⊣sita. 'I received some candy from a friend.'

(l) Kore wa ⌈da⌉re ni mo⊢raima⊣sita ka⌴ 'From whom did you get this?'

(m) Kore wa ⌈da⌉re ḡa mo⊢raima⊣sita ka⌴ 'Who received this?'

(n) Tanaka-sañ kara ⌈na⌉ni o o⊢morai ni narima⊣sita ka⌴ 'What did you receive from Mr. Tanaka?'

(o) O⌉kusama ni ⌈ki⌉ree na hu⊢rosiki o itadakima⊣sita. 'I received a beautiful furoshiki from your wife.'

A situation in which one person does something for another is indicated in Japanese by a verbal gerund followed immediately in the same phrase by the appropriate verbal of giving or receiving. For example:

ka⌉ite aḡeru and ka⌉ite yaru 'write for someone' (lit. 'give writing')
ka⌉ite ku⊢dasa⌉ru 'write for me' (lit. 'give me writing')
ka⌉ite kureru 'write for me [or you]' (lit. 'give me [or you] writing')
ka⌉ite morau 'have someone write' (lit. 'receive writing')

The differences in usage of the verbals of giving and receiving described above apply equally to the combination of one of these verbals preceded by a gerund. The particles are also the same, except that the person by whom someone has something done is followed by particle ni but not kara. Also, the gerund preceding the verbal of giving or receiving may have its own direct object, goal phrase, etc.[1] Study the following examples carefully, comparing them with the corresponding examples above:

(a) Yo⌉ñde a⊢ḡemasyo⊣o ka. 'Shall I read it for you?'

(b) Se⌈ñse⌉e ni ⌈ka⌉ite a⊢ḡema⊣sita ka⌴ 'Did you write it for the teacher?'

(c) U⌈ti no Ta⌉roo wa se⌈ñse⌉e ni ⌈ho⌉ñ o tyu⊢umoñ-site aḡema⊣sita. '(Our) Taro ordered a book for the teacher.'

(d) Musuko ni ⌈pe⌉ñ o ka⊢tte yarima⊣sita. 'I bought a pen for my son.'

(e) Ko⌈oka⌉ñsyu ni a⌈tarasi⌉i de⊢ñwatyoo o tano⊣ñde ya⊢rima⊣sita ka⌴ 'Did you ask for a new telephone book for the operator?'

(f) Se⌈ñse⌉e wa ⌈ma⌉initi kodomo ni ku⌈da⌉mono o ki⊢tte⊣ yarimasu. 'The teacher cuts the fruit for the children every day.'

---

[1] Without sufficient context, some examples are ambiguous. For example, Ta⌈naka-sañ ni kiite moraima⌉sita. may mean 'I had Mr. Tanaka ask [him]' or 'I had [him] ask Mr. Tanaka.' If both 'Mr. Tanaka' and 'him' are expressed, the order determines the difference:

Tanaka-sañ ni a⌈no⌉ hito ni ki⊢ite moraima⊣sita. 'I had Mr. Tanaka ask him.'

A⌈no⌉ hito ni Ta⌈naka-sañ ni kiite moraima⌉sita. 'I had him ask Mr. Tanaka.'

    (g) Kore wa ⌐o⌐kusañ ḡa a⌐kete (or o⌐ake ni na⌐tte¹) kudasaima⌐sita. 'This your wife opened for me.'

    (h) Ta⌐bako o motte⌐ kite kudasai. 'Please bring the cigarettes (for me).'

    (i) Kore wa to⌐modati ḡa nao⌐site ku⌐rema⌐sita. 'This my friend fixed for me.'

    (j) Da⌐re ḡa ʃa⌐na⌐ta niʃ site kureta? 'Who did it for you?'

    (k) Tomodati ni o⌐ka⌐si o mo⌐tte⌐ kite mo⌐raima⌐sita. 'I had my friend bring some candy.'

    (l) Kore wa ⌐da⌐re ni ⌐mi⌐sete mo⌐raima⌐sita ka↲   'Who showed you this?' (Lit. 'As for this, by whom did you receive showing?')

    (m) Kore wa ⌐da⌐re ḡa si⌐te moraima⌐sita ka↲ 'For whom was this done?' (Lit. 'As for this, who received the doing?')

    (n) Tanaka-sañ ni ⌐na⌐ni o ka⌐tte omorai ni narima⌐sita ka↲ 'What did Mr. Tanaka buy for you?' (Lit. 'You received the buying of what by Mr. Tanaka?')

    (o) O⌐kusama ni ⌐ki⌐ree na hu⌐rosiki o katte (or okai ni na⌐tte¹) itadakima⌐sita. 'Your wife bought a beautiful furoshiki for me.' (Lit. 'I received the buying of a beautiful furoshiki by your wife.')

A gerund + <u>moraitai</u> (or <u>itadakitai</u>) is an indirect request— 'I want to have something done by someone.' Compare this with a direct request— '(you) do something.' For example:

    Mi⌐te moraitai. 'I want to have it looked at.' But:
    Mi⌐te. 'Look at it!'

    A⌐ratte moraita⌐i ñ desu. 'I want to have it washed.' But:
    A⌐ratte kudasa⌐i. 'Please wash it.'

    A⌐kete itadakita⌐i ñ desu. 'I'd like to have it opened.' But:
    A⌐kete kudasaimase⌐ñ ka↲ 'Would you be kind enough to open it?'

A gerund + √<u>morau</u> sequence occurs as a request when someone is directly asked to have something done by someone.

    Mi⌐te moratte. 'Have it looked at.'
    A⌐ratte moratte kudasa⌐i. 'Please have it washed.'
    A⌐kete moratte kudasaimase⌐ñ ka↲ 'Would you be kind enough to have it opened?'

2.   Verbal Gerund + √<u>simau</u>

A verbal gerund + √<u>simau</u> means 'do so-and-so completely' or 'finish doing so-and-so' or 'end up by doing so-and-so.' Examples:

    Wa⌐surete simaima⌐sita. 'I've forgotten [it] completely.'
    Kodomo ḡa o⌐ka⌐si o ⌐ta⌐bete si⌐maima⌐sita. 'The children finished eating the candy.' <u>or</u> 'The children ate up the candy.'
    I⌐kitaku na⌐katta desyoo ḡa, i⌐tte simaima⌐sita. 'He probably didn't want to go but he ended up by going.'

In this pattern, √simau follows the verbal gerund immediately in the same phrase without pause. Compare:

> Saʳra o aratte simaimaˈsita. 'I finished washing the dishes.'
> Sara o aratte, siˈmaimaˈsita. 'I washed the dishes and put them away.'

In conversational Japanese, a gerund + √simau is very commonly contracted:

> ----te √simau > √----tyau
> ----de √simau > √----zyau

Examples:

Uncontracted	Contracted
taˈbete simau	taˈbetyau
noˈñde simatte	noˈñzyatte
wasurete simatta	wasuretyatta
aʳratte simaimaˈsu	aʳrattyaimaˈsu
iʳtte simaimaˈsita	iʳttyaimaˈsita

3. Verbal Gerund + √oku

A verbal gerund followed immediately in the same phrase without pause by √oku [1] means 'do so-and-so and put aside,' or 'do so-and-so in advance,' or 'do so-and-so for future use or benefit,' or 'do so-and-so for the time being.' Examples:

> Tomodati g̃a ʳsuˈg̃u ˠkuˀru kara, doˈa o aʳkete oˈite kudasai. 'A friend is coming very soon so please open the door (for future benefit).'
> Aʳsita iruˈ kara, kyoˈo kaʳtte okimaˈsita. 'I'll need it tomorrow so I bought it (in advance) today.'
> Sono zassi o ʳaˈto de ˠyoˀmu kara, tuʳkue no ueˈ ni oʰite oʰite kudasai. 'I'm going to read that magazine later so please put it on top of the desk for the time being.'

In conversational Japanese, the final -e of the gerund is dropped before those forms of √oku which begin oi-. Examples:

Uncontracted	Contracted
aʳkete oˈita	aʳketoˈita
oˈite oˈite	oˈitoˈite
yoˈñde oite	yoˈñdoite

---

[1] The past oita and gerund oite, among other forms, acquire a first-syllable accent when they follow an unaccented gerund.

4.   Particle ya

The particle ya occurs between nominals A and B meaning 'A and B and others of the same kind,' 'A and B and so on,' 'A and B among others,' 'things like A and B.' Thus:

> oᵗoᵗosañ to oᵏkaᵗasañ 'your father and mother'
> but:
> oᵗoᵗosañ ya oᵏkaᵗasañ 'your father and mother and others in your family'
>
> oᵗtya to koohiᵗi 'tea and coffee'
> but:
> oᵗtya ya koohiᵗi 'tea and coffee and other similar drinks'

There may be more than two nominals in the series:

> hoᵗñ ya zassi ya siñbuñ 'books and magazines and newspapers and the like'

A series of two or more nominals joined by ya occurs in the same kinds of patterns as a nominal alone.

Examples:

> Hoᵗñ ya zassi wa ᵗdoᵗo simasyoo ka. 'What shall I do with the books and magazines and such things?'
> Peᵗñ ya eᵏñpitu ḡa irimaᵗsu. 'I need things like pens and pencils.'
> Yaᵗsai ya kudaᵗmono o kaᵏimaᵗsita. 'I bought vegetables and fruit among other things.'

DRILLS

A.   Substitution Drill

1. I finished putting in the dishes. What shall I do next?

Saᵗra (o) irete simaimaᵗsita ḡa, aᵗto ᵗnaᵗni (o) siᵏmasyoᵗo ka.

2. I finished putting away the little things. What shall I do next?

Koᵗmakaᵗi moᵏnoᵗ (o) siᵏmatte simaimaᵗsita ḡa, aᵗto ᵗnaᵗni (o) siᵏmasyoᵗo ka.

3. I finished washing the glasses. What shall I do next?

Koᵗppu (o) aratte simaimaᵗsita ḡa, aᵗto ᵗnaᵗni (o) siᵏmasyoᵗo ka.

4. I finished cleaning the kitchen. What shall I do next?

Daᵗidokoro (o) soozi-site simaimaᵗsita ḡa, aᵗto ᵗnaᵗni (o) siᵏmasyoᵗo ka.

5. I finished straightening up the study. What shall I do next?

Syoᵗsai (o) katazuᵗkete siᵏmaimaᵗsita ḡa, aᵗto ᵗnaᵗni (o) siᵏmasyoᵗo ka.

6. I finished turning on all the heaters. What shall I do next?

Suᵗtoᵗobu (o) miᵗnna tukeᵗte siᵏmaimaᵗsita ḡa, aᵗto ᵗnaᵗni (o) siᵏmasyoᵗo ka.

7. I finished opening all the windows. What shall I do next?

Maꜝdo (o) miꜛnna akete simaimaꜝsita ḡa, aꜝto ꜛnaꜝni (o) siꜜmasyoꜞo ka.

8. I finished locking all the doors. What shall I do next?

Toꜛno kaḡiꜞ (o) miꜛnna kaꜝkete siꜜmaimaꜝsita ḡa, aꜝto ꜛnaꜝni (o) siꜜmasyoꜞo ka.

B. Substitution Drill

1. I'm putting away the little things.

Koꜛmakaꜝi moꜛnoꜞ o siꜛmatte imaꜝsu.

2. I finished putting away the little things.

Koꜛmakaꜝi moꜛnoꜞ (o) siꜛmatte simaimaꜝsita.

3. I put away the little things for the time being.

Koꜛmakaꜝi moꜛnoꜞ (o) siꜛmatte okimaꜝsita.

4. I had the little things put away.

Koꜛmakaꜝi moꜛnoꜞ (o) siꜛmatte moraimaꜝsita.

5. Shall I put away the little things for you?

Koꜛmakaꜝi moꜛnoꜞ (o) siꜛmatte aḡemasyoꜞo ka.

6. [He] put away the little things for me.

Koꜛmakaꜝi moꜛnoꜞ (o) siꜛmatte kuremaꜝsita.

7. Please put away the little things.

Koꜛmakaꜝi moꜛnoꜞ (o) siꜛmatte kudasaꜝi.

8. Please have the little things put away.

Koꜛmakaꜝi moꜛnoꜞ (o) siꜛmatte moratte kudasaꜝi.

9. I'd like to have the little things put away. . . .

Koꜛmakaꜝi moꜛnoꜞ (o) siꜛmatte moraitaꜝi ñ desu ḡa

10. The little things have been put away.

Koꜛmakaꜝi moꜛnoꜞ (ḡa) siꜛmatte arimaꜝsu.

C. Substitution Drill

1. [He] cut it fine.

Koꜛmakaꜝku kiꜜrimaꜝsita.

2. It isn't fine (i.e. in small pieces).

Koꜛmakaꜝku aꜜrimaseꜞñ.

3. It isn't strong.

Tuꜝyoku aꜜrimaseꜞñ.

4. [He] has become strong.

Tuꜝyoku naꜜrimaꜝsita.

5. It has become painful.

Iꜛtaꜝku naꜜrimaꜝsita.

6. It isn't painful.

Iꜛtaꜝku aꜜrimaseꜞñ.

7. It isn't fast.

Haꜝyaku aꜜrimaseꜞñ.

8. [He] talked fast.

Haꜝyaku haꜜnasimaꜝsita.

9. [He] talked well.

Yoꜝku haꜜnasimaꜝsita.

10. [He] listened carefully.

Yoꜝku kiꜜkimaꜝsita.

D. Substitution Drill[1]

1. Where did you put (i.e.   Do⌐ko ni o⌐kima⌐sita ka⌐
    place) it?
2. Where did you put it (away)?   Do⌐ko ni si⌐maima⌐sita ka⌐
3. Where (i.e. into what) did   Do⌐ko ni i⌐rema⌐sita ka⌐
    you put it?
4. Where did you set it out?   Do⌐ko ni da⌐sima⌐sita ka⌐
5. Where did you take it?   Do⌐ko ni mo⌐tte ikima⌐sita ka⌐
6. What place (for example,   Do⌐ko ni ha⌐irima⌐sita ka⌐
    what school) have you en-
    tered?
7. What place did you call (on   Do⌐ko ni de⌐ñwa o kakema⌐sita ka⌐
    the telephone)?
8. Where did you go?   Do⌐ko ni i⌐kima⌐sita ka⌐

E. Grammar Drill (based on Grammatical Note 3)

    Tutor: Si⌐ma⌐sita. 'I did it.'
    Student: Si⌐te okima⌐sita. 'I did it in advance, or for future reference,
              or for the time being, etc.'

1. Kore (wa) a⌐no hako ni   Kore (wa) a⌐no hako ni irete okima-
    iremasyo⌐o ka.   syo⌐o ka.
2. Osakana ya yasai (o) su-   Osakana ya yasai (o) su⌐ko⌐si ka⌐tte
    ⌐ko⌐si ka⌐ima⌐sita.   okima⌐sita.
3. Syo⌐kudoo no teeburu no ue⌐   Syo⌐kudoo no teeburu no ue⌐ ni o⌐ite
    ni o⌐kima⌐sita.   okima⌐sita.
4. Ka⌐mi⌐ ya eñpitu (o) ta⌐ku-   Ka⌐mi⌐ ya eñpitu (o) ta⌐kusañ da⌐site
    sañ dasima⌐sita.   o⌐kima⌐sita.
5. Ni⌐kai no tañsu no na⌐ka ni   Ni⌐kai no tañsu no na⌐ka ni si⌐matte
    si⌐maima⌐sita.   okima⌐sita.
6. Su⌐ko⌐si ya⌐sumimasyo⌐o.   Su⌐ko⌐si ya⌐su⌐ñde o⌐kimasyo⌐o.
7. Ko⌐otuuko⌐osya de ki⌐ki-   Ko⌐otuuko⌐osya de ki⌐ite okima⌐sita.
    ma⌐sita.
8. A⌐tarasi⌐i meesi (o) tyu⌐u-   A⌐tarasi⌐i meesi (o) tyu⌐umoñ-site
    moñ-simasyo⌐o ka.   okimasyo⌐o ka.

F. Grammar Drill (based on Grammatical Note 1)

    Tutor: Si⌐te kudasa⌐i. 'Please do it.'
    Student: Si⌐te moratte kudasa⌐i. 'Please have it done.' or 'Please
              have someone do it.'

----

[1]   In contrast with the variety of the English equivalents, the Japanese pattern here is identical throughout: a place word + particle ni of goal indicating
the place toward or into which motion occurred.

1. Oˈsara (o) aratte kudasaˈi.
2. Miˈti (o) osiete kudasaˈi.
3. Haˈyaku naˈoˈsite kudasai.
4. Seˈñseˈe (o) yoˈñde kudasaˈi.
5. Kuˈruma no kagiˈ (o)
   ˈkaˈkete kudasai.
6. Yoˈkohama eˈ no miti (o)
   kiˈite kudasaˈi.
7. Niˈhoñḡo de itte kudasaˈi.
8. Kiˈree ni ˈkaˈite kudasai.

Oˈsara (o) aratte moratte kudasaˈi.
Miˈti (o) osiete moratte kudasaˈi.
Haˈyaku naˈoˈsite moˈratte kudasaˈi.
Seˈñseˈe (o) yoˈñde moratte kuda-
saˈi.
Kuˈruma no kagiˈ (o) ˈkaˈkete mo-
ˈratte kudasaˈi.
Yoˈkohama eˈ no miti (o) kiˈite mo-
ratte kudasaˈi.
Niˈhoñḡo de itte moratte kudasaˈi.
Kiˈree ni ˈkaˈite moˈratte kudasaˈi.

G. Grammar Drill (based on Grammatical Note 1)

Tutor: Taˈnaka-sañ ḡa site kuremaˈsita.   'Mr. Tanaka did it for me.'
Student: Taˈnaka-sañ ni site moraimaˈsita.   'I had it done for me by
         Mr. Tanaka.'   or   'I had Mr. Tanaka do it for me.'

1. Toˈmodati ḡa maˈtte kuˈremaˈsita.
2. Aˈni ḡa siˈñbuñ (o) katte kuremaˈsita.
3. Huˈmiko-sañ ḡa haˈtiˈ-zi
   made iˈte kuremaˈsita.
4. Musuko ḡa siˈñbuñ (o) motteˈ
   kite kuˈremaˈsita.
5. Seˈñseˈe ḡa koˈre (o) yoˈñde
   kuˈdasaimaˈsita.
6. Koˈokaˈñsyu ḡa baˈñḡoˈo (o)
   iˈtte kuremaˈsita.
7. Muˈsumeˈ ḡa syoˈkuzi no
   sitaku (o) site kuremaˈsita.
8. Goˈsyuˈziñ ḡa miˈti (o) osiete kudasaimaˈsita.

Toˈmodati ni maˈtte moˈraimaˈsita.
Aˈni ni siˈñbuñ (o) katte moraimaˈsita.
Huˈmiko-sañ ni haˈtiˈ-zi made iˈte
moraimaˈsita.
Musuko ni siˈñbuñ (o) motteˈ kite mo-
ˈraimaˈsita.
Seˈñseˈe ni koˈre (o) yoˈñde iˈtada-
kimaˈsita.
Koˈokaˈñsyu ni baˈñḡoˈo (o) iˈtte moraimaˈsita.
Muˈsumeˈ ni syoˈkuzi no sitaku (o)
site moraimaˈsita.
Goˈsyuˈziñ ni miˈti (o) osiete itada-
kimaˈsita.

H. Response Drill (based on Grammatical Note 1)

Tutor: Siˈmaˈsita kaˌ /tomodati/ 'Did you do it? /friend/'
Student: Toˈmodati ni site moraimaˈsita. 'I had it done by a friend.'
         or 'I had a friend do it.'

1. Reˈezoˈoko (o) naˈosimaˈsi-
   ta kaˌ /tomodati/
2. Zyuˈñsa ni kikimaˈsita kaˌ
   /niˈhoñziˈñ/
3. Aˈtarasiˈi ˈkaˈḡu (o) mi-
   ˈmaˈsita kaˌ /kaˈnai/
4. Suˈmisu-sañ ni aˈimaˈsita
   kaˌ /Tanaka-sañ/
5. Kusuri (o) kaˈimaˈsita kaˌ
   /musuko/

Toˈmodati ni naoˈsite moˈraimaˈsita.
Niˈhoñziˈñ ni kiˈite moraimaˈsita.

Kaˈnai ni ˈmiˈte moˈraimaˈsita.

Taˈnaka-sañ ni aˈtte moˈraimaˈsita.

Muˈsuko ni katte moraimaˈsita.

6. To (o) si⌐mema⌐sita ka⌐   Hu⌐miko-tyañ ni ┌si⌐mete mo┌rai-
   /Hu⌐miko-tyañ/   ma⌐sita.
7. Ho⌐ndana ni zässi (o)   A┌no⌐ hito ni si┌matte moraima⌐si-
   si⌐maima⌐sita ka⌐   ta.
   /a┌no⌐ hito/
8. Ne⌐ko (o) ┌so⌐to e da-   Ko┌domo ni da⌐site mo┌raima⌐sita.
   ┌sima⌐sita ka⌐
   /kodomo/

I. Response Drill

       Tutor: To g̃a a┌ite ima⌐su yo⌐   'You know, the door's open.'
       Student: Da┌re g̃a a┌kema⌐sita ka⌐   'Who opened it?'

   1. Na⌐ni ka ko┌bo⌐rete (i)masu   Da⌐re g̃a ko┌bosima⌐sita ka⌐
      yo⌐
   2. I┌nu⌐ (g̃a) ┌de⌐te (i)masu yo⌐   Da⌐re g̃a da┌sima⌐sita ka⌐
   3. Ano hako ni ┌ki⌐ree na   Da⌐re g̃a i┌rema⌐sita ka⌐
      hu┌ki⌐ñ ya zo┌okiñ (g̃a)
      ha⌐itte (i)masu yo⌐
   4. Da┌idokoro no de⌐ñki (g̃a)   Da⌐re g̃a tu┌kema⌐sita ka⌐
      ┌tu⌐ite (i)masu yo⌐
   5. Ka┌g̃i⌐ (g̃a) ka┌ka⌐tte (i)ma-   Da⌐re g̃a ka┌kema⌐sita ka⌐
      su yo⌐
   6. Syo┌sai no ma⌐do (g̃a) si-   Da⌐re g̃a si┌mema⌐sita ka⌐
      ┌ma⌐tte (i)masu yo⌐

J. Level Drill[1]

   1. Kyo⌐o no siñbuñ (o) su┌te-   Kyo⌐o no siñbuñ (o) o┌sute ni nari-
      ma⌐sita ka⌐   ma⌐sita ka⌐
   2. A┌tarasi⌐i ┌ho⌐ñ (o) si┌ma-   A┌tarasi⌐i ┌ho⌐ñ (o) o┌simai ni na-
      ima⌐sita ka⌐   rima⌐sita ka⌐
   3. Tu┌kue no ue⌐ ni o┌kima⌐-   Tu┌kue no ue⌐ ni o┌oki ni narima⌐-
      sita ka⌐   sita ka⌐
   4. Hi┌kidasi no na⌐ka ni i┌re-   Hi┌kidasi no na⌐ka ni o┌ire ni nari-
      ma⌐sita ka⌐   ma⌐sita ka⌐
   5. I┌tu-g̃oro hairima⌐sita ka⌐   I┌tu-g̃oro ohairi ni narima⌐sita ka⌐
   6. Do⌐nata kara mo┌raima⌐sita   Do⌐nata kara o┌morai ni narima⌐si-
      ka⌐   ta ka⌐
   7. Ta⌐naka-sañ ni aima⌐sita   Ta⌐naka-sañ ni oai ni narima⌐sita
      ka⌐   ka⌐
   8. Se┌ñse⌐e (o) yo┌bima⌐sita   Se┌ñse⌐e (o) o┌yobi ni narima⌐sita
      ka⌐   ka⌐

_____

[1] Each sentence on the right is the honorific (†) equivalent of the corresponding sentence on the left.

K. Expansion Drill

1. Is [it] in?
    What is in [it]?
    What is inside [it]?

    What is inside that big
    box?

Haᒡitte (i)masu kaˬ
Naˈni (ḡa) ˉhaˈitte (i)masu kaˬ
Naˈka ni ˈnaˈni (ḡa) ˉhaˈitte (i)ma-
su kaˬ
Ano oˈokiˈi hako no ˉnaˈka ni ˈnaˈni
(ḡa) ˉhaˈitte (i)masu kaˬ

2. I received help.
    I had Mr. Tanaka help me.

    I was very busy so I had
    Mr. Tanaka help me.
    Yesterday morning I was
    very busy so I had Mr.
    Tanaka help me.

Teˈtudaˈtte moˈraimaˈsita.
Tanaka-sañ ni teˈtudaˈtte moˈraimaˈsita.
Toˈtemo isoḡaˈsikatta kara, Tanaka-
sañ ni teˈtudaˈtte moˈraimaˈsita.
Kiˈnoo no aˈsa toˈtemo isoḡaˈsikatta
kara, Tanaka-sañ ni teˈtudaˈtte
moˈraimaˈsita.

3. Have [it] fixed.
    Have this fixed.
    Have this fixed by someone
    else (lit. another person).
    [I] can't do it so have this
    fixed by someone else.
    I (comparatively speaking)
    can't do it so have this
    fixed by someone else.

Naˈoˈsite moratte.
Koˈre (o) naoˈsite moratte.
Hoˈka no hitoˈ ni koˈre (o) naoˈsite
moratte.
Deˈkiˈnai kara, hoˈka no hitoˈ ni
koˈre (o) naoˈsite moratte.
Boˈku wa dekiˈnai kara, hoˈka no hi-
toˈ ni koˈre (o) naoˈsite moratte.

4. Have [them] thrown out.
    Have [them] thrown out to-
    morrow.
    [They] get in the way so
    have [them] thrown out
    tomorrow.
    [They] always get in the
    way so have [them] thrown
    out tomorrow.
    These old papers and maga-
    zines and things always
    get in the way so have
    them thrown out tomor-
    row.

Sutete moratte.
Asita sūtete moratte.

Zyaˈma ni naˈru kara, asita sūtete
moratte.

Iˈtu mo zyaˈma ni naˈru kara, asita
sūtete moratte.

Kono huˈruˈi siñbuñ ya zassi (wa)
ˈiˈtu mo zyaˈma ni naˈru kara,
asita sūtete moratte.

5. Is it all right?
    I'd like to rest. Is it all
    right?
    I'd like to rest [this] after-
    noon. Is it all right?
    I'm tired so I'd like to rest
    [this] afternoon. Is it all
    right?

Kaˈmaimaseˈñ kaˬ
Yaˈsumitaˈi ñ desu ḡa, kaˈmaimaseˈñ
kaˬ
Goˈḡo yaˈsumitaˈi ñ desu ḡa, kaˈmaimaseˈñ kaˬ
Tuˈkaˈrete (i)ru kara, goˈḡo yaˈsumitaˈi ñ desu ḡa; kaˈmaimaseˈñ kaˬ

	I'm awfully tired so I'd like to rest [this] afternoon. Is it all right?	Zu⌉ibuñ tu⊢ka⌉rete (i)ru kara, go⌉ḡo ya⌈sumita⌉i ñ desu ḡa; ka⌈maimase⌉ñ ka⎵
6.	It's all right.	Da⌈izyo⌉obu desu yo.
	[She] wiped [it] up for me so it's all right.	Hu⌈ite kureta⌉ kara, da⌈izyo⌉obu desu yo.
	[She] wiped it up for me right away so it's all right.	Su⌉ḡu hu⊢ite kureta⊣ kara, da⌈izyo⌉obu desu yo.
	Fumiko wiped it up for me right away so it's all right.	Hu⌉miko-sañ (ḡa) ⌈su⌉ḡu hu⊢ite kureta⊣ kara, da⌈izyo⌉obu desu yo.
	I spilled [it] but Fumiko wiped it up for me right away so it's all right.	Ko⌈bosima⌉sita ḡa; Hu⌉miko-sañ ḡa ⌈su⌉ḡu hu⊢ite kureta⊣ kara, da⌈izyo⌉obu desu yo.
	I spilled sake but Fumiko wiped it up for me right away so it's all right.	Sa⌈ke (o) kobosima⌉sita ḡa; Hu⌉miko-sañ ḡa ⌈su⌉ḡu hu⊢ite kureta⊣ kara, da⌈izyo⌉obu desu yo.
	I spilled sake on top of the new table but Fumiko wiped it up for me right away so it's all right.	A⌈tarasi⌉i te⊢eburu no ue⊣ ni sa⌈ke (o) kobosima⌉sita ḡa; Hu⌉miko-sañ ḡa ⌈su⌉ḡu hu⊢ite kureta⊣ kara, da⌈izyo⌉obu desu yo.

SUPPLEMENTARY SELECTIONS

(with questions)

1. A⌈tarasi⌉i ⊢ho⊣ñ o ta⌈kusañ katta⌉ kara, a⌈tarasi⌉i ⊢ho⌉ñdana mo ka⊢ima⊣sita. Ke⌉sa u⌈ti e motte⌉ kite mo⊢raima⊣sita ḡa; to⌈ttemo isoḡa⌉sikatta kara, ho⌉ñ mo ⌈ho⌉ñdana mo syo⌈sai no su⌉mi ni o⊢ito⊣ite de⊢kakema⊣sita ḡa; boku no rusu ni ⌈ka⌉nai ḡa hi⌈to⌉ri de so⌈no ho⌉ñ o mi⌉ñna ho⌉ñdana ni si⊢matte kurema⊣sita.

   a. Do⌉o site a⊢tarasi⊣i ⊢ho⊣ñdana o ka⊢ima⊣sita ka⎵
   b. I⌉tu u⊢ti e motte⊣ kite mo⊢raima⊣sita ka⎵
   c. Sono ⌈ho⌉ñ to ⊢ho⊣ñdana wa ⌈do⌉ko ni o⊢ite okima⊣sita ka⎵ Do⌉o site?
   d. Da⌉re ḡa ⊢ho⊣ñ o si⊢matte kurema⊣sita ka⎵
   e. Da⌉re ni ⊢ho⊣ñ o si⊢matte moraima⊣sita ka⎵
   f. Da⌉re ḡa te⊢tudaima⊣sita ka⎵

2. Kyo⌉o wa ⌈a⌉sa kara to⌈ttemo isoḡa⌉sikatta kara, tu⌈ka⌉rete si⊢maima⊣sita. U⌈ti no Ta⌉roo ḡa e⌈ḡo no ho⌉ñ o wa⊢sureta⊣ kara, ga⌈kkoo ma⌉de mo⌈tte itte yarima⌉sita. Sore kara, u⌈ti e ka⌉ette; Hu⌉miko to issyo ni u⌈ti o katazukema⌉sita. Zyu⌈uni⌉-zi ni ma⌉ta dekakete, Gi⌈ñza no depa⌉ato e i⊢kima⊣sita. Soko no syokudoo de to⌈modati ni a⌉tte, issyo ni syo⌈kuzi o sima⌉sita. Sore kara, u⌈ti no syosai no suto⌉obu ḡa ⌈mo⌉o se⌈ñsyuu kara dame⌉ desu kara; a⌈tarasi⌉i no o ka⊢ima⊣sita. Tyo⌉tto ⌈o⌉okikatta kara, de⌈pa⌉ato no hi⊢to⊣ ni ⌈ta⌉kusii made mo⊢tte⊣ kite moratte; ta⌉kusii de ka⊢erima⊣sita. To⌈temo tuka⌉rete i⊢ta⊣ kara, Hu⌉miko ni hi⌈to⌉ri de ba⌈ñgo⌉hañ

no sitaku o site moratte; i⌐ti-zikañ-g̃u⌐rai ya⌐sumima⌐sita.

    a. Na⌐ni o ga⌐kkoo ma⌐de mo⌐tte ikima⌐sita ka⌐

    b. Da⌐re ni mo⌐tte itte yarima⌐sita ka⌐

    c. Do⌐o site mo⌐tte itte yarima⌐sita ka⌐

    d. A⌐sa u⌐ti e ka⌐ette kara, na⌐ni o si⌐ma⌐sita ka⌐

    e. Hi⌐to⌐ri de si⌐ma⌐sita ka⌐

    f. Da⌐re ni te⌐tuda⌐tte mo⌐raima⌐sita ka⌐

    g. Da⌐re g̃a te⌐tuda⌐tte ku⌐rema⌐sita ka⌐

    h. Na⌐ñ-zi ni ma⌐ta dekakema⌐sita ka⌐

    i. Do⌐ko e i⌐kima⌐sita ka⌐

    j. Do⌐ko de syo⌐kuzi o sima⌐sita ka⌐

    k. Hi⌐to⌐ri de ta⌐bema⌐sita ka⌐

    l. Ta⌐bete kara ⌐na⌐ni o ka⌐ima⌐sita ka⌐ Do⌐o site?

    m. Da⌐re g̃a sore o ⌐ta⌐kusii made mo⌐tte⌐ kite ku⌐rema⌐sita ka⌐

    n. Ka⌐ette kara ⌐na⌐ni o si⌐ma⌐sita ka⌐ Do⌐o site?

    o. Hu⌐miko-sañ ni ⌐na⌐ni o si⌐te moraima⌐sita ka⌐

SHORT SUPPLEMENTARY DIALOGUES

(In each case, decide whether the speaker is best identified as M, or W, or MW. Change M utterances to W, and W utterances to M.)

1. A: Tu⌐ka⌐retyatta wa⌐
   B: Bo⌐ku mo.

2. A: Eeg̃o o⌐wakari ni na⌐ru?
   B: Wa⌐suretyatta⌐ yo.

3. A: Kore ⌐do⌐ko ni o⌐kimasyo⌐o ka.
   B: A⌐suko ni oito⌐ite kudasai.

4. A: Are ⌐to⌐tte ne?
   B: Do⌐o site?
   A: Zya⌐ma ni na⌐ru kara.

5. A: Kono zibiki a̅re to tig̃au?
   B: N̄. A⌐re yo⌐ri a⌐tarasi⌐i yo⌐

6. A: Kinoo ko⌐no zassi katta⌐ wa⌐
   B: A⌐a, bo⌐ku mo o⌐nazi zassi katta⌐ yo.

EXERCISES

1. Draw a plan of your home, and describe in Japanese what each room is and the location of the doors, windows, and furniture.

2. Draw a simple house plan, including doors and windows. Using model furniture—or labeled blocks of wood or cardboard—practice giving and

following instructions on where to put each piece of furniture.   (This exercise may also be done at the blackboard.   After hearing what is requested,
draw the appropriate object in the appropriate location.)

3.   Speaking informally, tell someone to:

     a.   put these books away.
     b.   put these pens and pencils and such in the top desk drawer.
     c.   throw away all these old magazines.
     d.   put the beer in the refrigerator.
     e.   put this on Mr. Tanaka's desk.
     f .   give you a hand.
     g.   put all these little things in that box.
     h.   get out more paper.
     i.   give this to the dog.
     j.   give this to the teacher.
     k.   wash this with soap.
     l.   pass you the salt.
     m.   put this under the kitchen table for the time being.
     n.   be careful.
     o.   have Fumiko buy more of this kind of medicine.

4.   Practice the Basic Dialogues with appropriate variations.

Lesson 18. Visiting

BASIC DIALOGUES: FOR MEMORIZATION

(a)

Maid

guest <u>or</u> customer
 kyaku <u>or</u>
 okyaku⁺

put in an appearance <u>or</u>
 show up <u>or</u> come
 mi⌐e⌐ru /-ru/

1. Mr. Tanaka. (Lit. Master.)
Your American guest has
come.
 Dan̄nasama⌐ A⌐merika⌐zin̄ no o-
 ⌐kyakusa⌐ma ḡa o⌐mie ni narima⌐-
 sita.

Host (going to entry hall)

go up <u>or</u> come up <u>or</u>
 enter
 aḡaru /-u/

2. Mr. Smith! It was good of
you to come. Please come
in.
 Su⌐misu-san̄. Yo⌐ku i⌐rassyaima⌐-
 sita. Do⌐ozo o⌐aḡari-kudasa⌐i.

Smith

3. (Lit. I commit the rudeness
[of entering your home].)
 Si⌐tu⌐ree-simasu.

Host (showing Smith into the living room)

4. This way, please.
 Do⌐ozo kotira e.

Smith

the other day (formal)
 sen̄zitu

5. (Lit. I committed a rudeness
the other day.)
 Sen̄zitu wa si⌐tu⌐ree-simasita.

Host

6. (<u>I</u> was the one [who was
rude].)
 Ko⌐tira ko⌐so.

Smith

rain
 a⌐me
fall (of rain, snow, etc.)
 hu⌐ru /-u/
weather <u>or</u> good weather
 te⌐n̄ki <u>or</u>
 o⌐te⌐n̄ki⁺

7. It rained terribly [hard]
yesterday but isn't it a beau-
tiful day today!
 Kinoo ⌐zu⌐ibun̄ ⌐a⌐me ḡa hu⌐rima⌐-
 sita ḡa, kyo⌐o wa ⌐i⌐i o⌐te⌐n̄ki de-
 su ⌐ne⌐e.

Host

8. [It] certainly [is].   Hoñtoo ni.

        a walk   sañpo
        for a walk   sañpo ni
        is cool   su⌐zusi⌐i /-ku/
9. I went for a walk this   Ke⌐sa sañpo ni ikima⌐sita ḡa,* su-
    morning. Hasn't it grown   ⌐zu⌐siku na⌐rima⌐sita ⌐ne⌐e.
    cool!

                              Smith

        fall or autumn   a⌐ki
10. Yes. Fall has come already,   E⌐e. Mo⌐o ⌐a⌐ki ni na⌐rima⌐sita
     hasn't it. (Lit. It has be-   ⌐ne⌐e.
     come fall already, hasn't
     it.)

                    (Maid brings tea)
                              Host

11. Please [have] some tea.   O⌐tya o do⌐ozo.

                              Smith

12. Please don't bother. or   Do⌐ozo o⌐kamai na⌐ku.
     Please don't go to any
     trouble.

                    Host (serving tea)

13. It will get cold, so please   Tu⌐metaku narima⌐su kara, do⌐ozo.
     [go ahead].

                              Smith

14. (I'll drink it.)   I⌐tadakima⌐su.

                              (b)

        Hostess (leading guests to dining room)

15. Please go in.   Do⌐ozo o⌐hairi-kudasaima⌐se.

                              Smith

16. [Excuse me for going] ahead.   Osaki ni.

        rice-straw floor mat   tatami
        room with floor mats   ta⌐tami no heya⌐
        feeling or mood   kimoti
        is pleasant or agreeable   ki⌐moti ḡa i⌐i
17. Aren't tatami rooms pleas-   Ta⌐tami no heya⌐ (wa) ki⌐moti ḡa i⌐i
     ant!   desu ⌐ne⌐e.

                              . . .

                    Hostess

        nothing   nani mo /+ negative/   or
                                                     nañni mo

18. There's nothing [worth men-   Na⌈ni mo gozaimase⌉n̄ ḡa, do⌉ozo.
    tioning] but please [eat].

                        Smith

19. (I'll have some.)   I⌈tadakima⌉su.

             . . .

                    Hostess

    second helping <u>or</u>   kawari   <u>or</u>
      additional serving   o⌈ka⌉wari +
20. How about some more?   O⌈ka⌉wari wa?

                  Smith

21. No, thank you.   Mo⌉o ⌐ke⌐kkoo desu.

                  Hostess

    reserve <u>or</u> restraint   eñryo <u>or</u>
                     goeñryo ⌐
22. Please don't hold back. <u>or</u> Do⌉ozo go⌈eñryo na⌉ku.
    Please don't stand on cere-
    mony.

                  Smith

23. Thank you but I've already   A⌈ri⌉ḡatoo gozaimasu ḡa, mo⌉o ta-
    had a lot (so. . .)   ⌈kusañ itadakima⌉sita kara_

      mountain   ya⌈ma⌉
      sea <u>or</u> ocean   u⌉mi
      be visible <u>or</u> can see   mi⌈e⌉ru /-ru/
      place   to⌈ko(ro)⌉
24. How beautiful it is here, with Ya⌈ma⌉ mo ⌈u⌉mi mo ⌐mi⌐ete, to⌐t-
    a view of the mountains and temo ki⌉ree na to⌐koro⌐ desu ⌈ne⌉e.
    the sea! (Lit. Both the
    mountains and the sea being
    visible, it's a very pretty
    place, isn't it!)

                  Hostess

25. Thank you.   O⌈so⌉re i⌐rima⌐su.

                  Host

    skilled <u>or</u> skillful   zyo⌈ozu⌉ /na/   <u>or</u>
                     ozyoozu ⌐ /na/
26. Isn't your Japanese good,   Su⌉misu-sañ (wa) * nihoñḡo (ḡa) o-
    Mr. Smith!   ⌐zyoozu de⌉su ⌈ne⌉e.

    still <u>or</u> yet   ma⌉da   / + affirmative/
    learn <u>or</u> take lessons   na⌈ra⌉u /-u/
27. Are you still taking les-   Ma⌉da na⌈ra⌉tte (i)masu ka⌟
    sons?

Smith

no more   mo⌐o / + negative/
28. No, (I'm) not (taking les-   Iie, mo⌐o na⌐ra⌐tte (i)⌐mase⌐ñ.
    sons) any more.

not skilled or poor at   he⌐ta⌐ /na/
these days   kono ḡoro
have time   zi⌐kañ ḡa a⌐ru
29. I'm still poor at it, but I   Ma⌐da he⌐ta⌐ desu ḡa, kono ḡoro
    don't have any time these   zi⌐kañ ḡa arimase⌐ñ kara_
    days (so. . .)

(c)

Smith

by means of Japanese   nihoñḡo de
    or in Japanese
say or be named or   iu /-u/ or
    be called   mo⌐osu⌐ /-u/ or
                                           o⌐ssya⌐ru⌐ /-aru/
say quote what? or   na⌐ñ to iu or
    be named quote what? or   nañ te iu
    be called quote what?
30. What is this kind of door   Koñna to (wa) nihoñḡo de ⌐na⌐ñ te
    called in Japanese?   i⌐ima⌐su ka_

Tanaka

sliding door (trans-   syoozi
    lucent)
say quote shoji or   syoozi to iu or
    be called quote shoji   syoozi tte iu
31. It's called a " shoji."   Syo⌐ozi tte iima⌐su.

Smith

32. How about that kind (of   A⌐nna⌐ no wa?
    one)?

Tanaka

sliding door (opaque)   hu⌐suma⌐ [1]
say quote fusuma or   hu⌐suma⌐ to iu or
    be called quote fusuma   hu⌐suma⌐ tte iu
33. That one is called a " fusu-   Are wa hu⌐suma⌐ tte iimasu.
    ma."

---

[1] Has commonly occurring unaccented alternant.

Smith

34. The outside ones, too?   So⌐to no mo?

Tanaka

    sliding storm door   a⌐ma⌐do
    say quote amado <u>or</u>   a⌐ma⌐do to iu <u>or</u>
    be called quote amado   a⌐ma⌐do tte iu
35. No, no. Those are called   Iie iie. Are wa a⌐ma⌐do tte iimasu.
    "amado."

(d)

Tanaka

    fine <u>or</u> handsome <u>or</u>   rippa /na/
      magnificent <u>or</u> im-
      posing
    Japanese-style alcove   tokonoma
36. What a handsome tokonoma!   Ri⌐ppa na tokonoma de⌐su ⌐ne⌐e.

    flower <u>or</u> flower ar-   ha⌐na⌐ <u>or</u>
      rangement   ohana +
    flower called quote what?   na⌐ñ to iu hana <u>or</u>
                                         na⌐ñ te iu hana
37. What kind of flowers are   Kore (wa) ⌐na⌐ñ te iu ha⌐na⌐ desyoo
    these? (Lit. These are   ka.
    flowers called quote what?)

Smith

    not know how one says [it]   do⌐o iu ka siranai
      <u>or</u> not know how [it] is
      called
38. I don't know what they are   Ni⌐hoñgo de do⌐o iu ka si⌐rimase⌐ñ
    called in Japanese, but there   ga, niwa ni ta⌐kusañ arima⌐su yo⌐
    are a lot of them in the gar-
    den.

(e)

Maid

    during someone's absence   rusu-tyuu ni <u>or</u>
      from home   orusu-tyuu † ni
39. Someone (lit. a guest) came   Orusu-tyuu ni o⌐kyakusa⌐ñ (ga) o⌐mie
    while you were out. . . .   ni narima⌐sita ga⌐

Tanaka

40. Oh? Who?   So⌐o? Da⌐re?

Maid

    be named quote Ueda <u>or</u>   Ueda to iu <u>or</u>
    be called quote Ueda <u>or</u>   Ueda tte iu
    say quote Ueda
41. His name was Ueda. . . .   U⌐eda to ossyaima⌐sita ga⌐

Tanaka

say quote what? or
be called quote what?
  or be named quote
  what?
	na⌐ɹn to iu or
	na⌐ɹn te iu

42. What did he say?	Na⌐ɹn te itta?

Maid

say quote he'll come, go, or be	i⌐rassya⌐ɹru to o⌐ssya⌐ɹru or i⌐rassya⌐ɹru tte o⌐ssya⌐ɹru
43. He said he'd come again.	Ma⌐ta irassya⌐ɹru tte o⌐ssyaima⌐ɹsi- ta.

Tanaka

ask [quote] will [some- one] come	ku⌐ɹru ka [to] kiku
44. Did you ask when he's com- ing?	I⌐ɹtu ⌐ku⌐ɹru ka kiita?

Maid

clearly or distinctly
  or precisely
say quote he doesn't
  understand or can't
  tell
	ha⌐kki⌐ɹri
	
	o⌐wakari ni nara⌐ɹnai to
	  o⌐ssya⌐ɹru or
	  o⌐wakari ni nara⌐ɹnai tte o⌐s-
	  sya⌐ɹru

45. Yes. I inquired but he said he couldn't tell ex- actly.	Ha⌐ɹa. U⌐kaḡaima⌐ɹsita ḡa, ha⌐kki⌐ɹri o⌐wakari ni nara⌐ɹnai tte o⌐ssyaima⌐ɹ- sita.

NOTES ON THE BASIC DIALOGUES

1. Remember that -sama is a more polite variant of -sañ.

2. Aḡaru 'enter' is usually used in reference to entering a Japanese-style
building—a home, inn, restaurant, etc.—which one enters by stepping up.
Note also kaidañ o aḡaru 'go up the stairs.'

3. Si⌐tu⌐ɹree-simasu, lit. 'I commit a rudeness,' covers a multitude of situations in Japanese: it is an apology for entering someone's home or office
—and for leaving, for taking a seat, even for relaxing!

5. Señzitu wa si⌐tu⌐ɹree-simasita frequently occurs as the formal beginning of
a conversation between people who have had some recent contact with each
other. Under similar circumstances, an English speaker might say, 'It
was nice seeing you the other day.'

6. Ko⌐ɹso is a particle of strong emphasis. Ko⌐tira ko⌐ɹso means 'this side,
not your side, [committed the rudeness].' Compare:

    A: Go⌐ku⌐ɹroosama desita. 'It's been a great deal of trouble for you.'
    B: A⌐na⌐ɹta koso. 'YOU're the one who has been troubled.'

This exchange might occur for example when two people have been working on a project together.

7. The gerund of hu⌐ru occurs with alternate accents: ⌐hu⌐tte and hu⌐tte⌐.

    Te⌐ñki may be described by words meaning 'good' or 'bad,' but unmodified it means 'good weather.'

8. Hoñtoo ni 'truly': ni is the particle of manner (cf. Lesson 15, Grammatical Note 5).

9. Ni here is the ni of goal or purpose. Note also sañpo-suru 'take a walk.'

    Su⌐zusi⌐i means 'is cool'—i.e. 'is nice and cool.' Besides referring to typical days of autumn, it is used to describe pleasantly cool days of summer.

10. Note also: hu⌐yu⌐ 'winter'; ha⌐ru 'spring,' na⌐tu⌐ 'summer.'

11. Otya o is a fragment. A possible major sentence substitute would be: O⌐tya o mesiaḡatte kudasa⌐i.

12. Okamai is a derivative of the verbal √ka⌐ma⌐u /-u/ 'mind,' 'care,' 'bother about,' from which ka⌐mawa⌐nai (formal, ka⌐maimase⌐ñ) 'I don't care,' 'it doesn't matter' is also derived.

14, 19. Remember that i⌐tadakima⌐su is regularly said by a guest as he begins to eat or drink.

16. Osaki ni, depending on context, is either an apology for doing something ahead of someone else, or an invitation to someone else to go ahead. Thus: Osaki ni si⌐tu⌐ree-simasu. 'Excuse me for taking my leave ahead of you.' but Do⌐ozo osaki ni. 'Please go ahead.'

17. Ki⌐moti ḡa i⌐i 'is pleasant or agreeable' and its opposite ki⌐moti ḡa waru⌐i 'is unpleasant or disagreeable' are often used in reference to people, as equivalents of English 'feel well' and 'not feel well.' The person or thing to which these sequences refer is followed by particle wa or ḡa, depending upon emphasis.

22. Note also: eñryo-suru 'hold back,' 'be reserved,' 'show restraint,' 'hesitate.'

23. 'so—I don't care for any more.'

24. Toko is an informal alternant of to⌐koro⌐.

25. O⌐so⌐re i⌐rima⌐su, lit. 'I'm overwhelmed [with gratitude or shame],' is an extremely polite way of saying 'Thank you' or 'I'm sorry.' It is used more frequently by women. A commonly occurring alternate form of it is o⌐so⌐reirimasu.

27. Na⌐ra⌐u is used in reference to any sort of learning or instruction; beñkyoo-suru is usually used only for scholastic studies.

29. 'so—I've given up taking lessons.'

30. Mo⌐osu and o⌐ssya⌐ru are polite equivalents of iu. Mo⌐osu, a humble verbal, is used in reference to the speaker and persons closely connected with him. O⌐ssya⌐ru, an honorific, refers only to persons other than the speaker, in polite speech.

39. 'but— did you know he was coming?'

Rusu-tyuu: compare sigoto-tyuu 'in the middle of work' and hanasi-tyuu
'in the middle of talking.'

41. 'but— do you know him?'

GRAMMATICAL NOTES

1. Quotatives /t/ te ~ to

/T/ te[1] and its more formal equivalent to are QUOTATIVES. They follow a
quotation (or the gist of a quotation) consisting of any sequence whatsoever— a
word, a part of a word, a sentence, a speech, an utterance in a foreign language, etc.— or nañ 'what?' substituting for a quotation.

Compare:

Ha⌐yaku i┌ima┤sita. 'He said [it] quickly.'
Ha⌐yaku to (or tte) i┌ima┤sita. 'He said, "Quickly."'

/T/ te usually follows quotations of utterances, whereas to also follows
thoughts, written words, etc. Following utterances, /t/ te is more common
than to in rapid conversational Japanese, particularly in informal and plain
speech. Occurrences of to are usually heard in formal and honorific speech,
and/or in precise speech.

Some quotations repeat the exact words of the original speaker. Usually,
however, a Japanese quotation gives— in the informal style— the gist of what
was said, from the point of view of the person reporting the quotation. The
quotation does retain the tense of the original.

Thus:

Original statement: A⌐ge ma⌐su. 'I'll give it to you.'
Quoted: Ku⌐reru tte iima⌐sita.[2] 'He said he'd give it to me.'

Original statement: Ki⌐noo itasima⌐sita. 'I did it yesterday.' (Humble)
Quoted: Ki⌐noo nasa⌐tta to o⌐ssyaima┤sita. 'He said he did it yesterday.'

The person who says or asks something, if expressed, is followed by particle wa or ga, and the person told or asked, by particle ni. Thus:

Tanaka-sañ wa Yamamoto-sañ ni ta⌐bako o yameta tte iima⌐sita.
'Mr. Tanaka said to Mr. Yamamoto that he had quit smoking.'

---

[1] Te follows ñ; tte follows vowels.

[2] Alternate accent: Ku⌐reru⌐ tte i┌ima┤sita., with the accent before /t/ te ~
to the same as that before kara.

The order of the phrases is not fixed: the quotation+quotative is not always followed immediately by the inflected expression it modifies. Thus:

> Tabako o yameta tte, Ya⌐mamoto-sañ ni iima⌐sita.
> '[He] said to Mr. Yamamoto that he had quit smoking.'

Sometimes only context and/or intonation distinguish parts of the quotation from modifiers of the following inflected expression. Compare:

> Tanaka-sañ wa ⌐ku⌐ru tte i⌐ima⌐sita.
> 'Mr. Tanaka said that [he]¹ would come.'
> (Quotation = ku⌐ru)

and:

> Ta⌐naka-sañ wa ku⌐ru tte i⌐ima⌐sita.
> ' [He]¹ said that Mr. Tanaka would come.'
> (Quotation = Ta⌐naka-sañ wa ku⌐ru)

Compare also:

> Tanaka-sañ ni ⌐a⌐tta tte i⌐ima⌐sita.
> '[He]¹ said to Mr. Tanaka that [he]¹ had met him.'
> (Quotation = a⌐tta)

and:

> Ta⌐naka-sañ ni a⌐tta tte i⌐ima⌐sita.
> ' [He]¹ said that [he]¹ had met Mr. Tanaka.'
> (Quotation = Ta⌐naka-sañ ni a⌐tta)

The quotative is often omitted after a quoted question ending with ka; and before ka, the informal non-past copula da is regularly omitted. Accentuation before ka is like that before kara.

Additional examples:

> Ueda-sañ wa i⌐ku tte (i)tte² (i)ma⌐sita ḡa—
> 'Mr. Ueda was saying that he would go but. . . .' (Lit. 'Mr. Ueda was saying quote he'll go but. . . .')
> Mo⌐o ⌐mi⌐ta tte i⌐ima⌐sita. 'I said that I had seen it already.'
> (Lit. 'I said quote I have seen it already.')
> I⌐i to o⌐ssyaima⌐sita ka— 'Did you say that it's all right?'
> Ko⌐no deñwa kosyoo da⌐ tte i⌐ima⌐sita.
> 'He said that this phone is out of order.'
> A⌐sita ka⌐eru to ka⌐kima⌐sita.
> 'He wrote that he is coming home tomorrow.'

---

¹ Or anyone else—made clear by the context.

² Following quotative [t]te, forms of √iu beginning it- (for example, itte, itta, etc.) lose their initial i- in rapid, contracted speech.

I⌈tu de mo i⌉i to, se⌈ñse⌉e ni de⊢ñwa-sima⊣sita.
'He telephoned the teacher that any time will be all right.'
O⌈namae o ka⌉ite kudasai to i⊢ima⊣sita.
'He said, "Please write your name."'
I⌉tu i⊢ku⊣ ka ki⊢kima⊣sita.
'I asked when he was going.'
I⌈ssyo ni ikana⌉i ka tte Ta⌈naka-sañ ni kikimasyo⌉o.
'Let's ask Mr. Tanaka if he won't go with us.'
So⌈no ka⌉ta ⊢do⊣nata ka ki⌈ite kudasaimase⌉ñ ka⌣ [1]
'Would you be kind enough to ask who that is?'
So⌈re wa na⌉ñ desu ka to ki⊢kima⊣sita.
'I asked, "What is that?"'
So⌈no ho⌉ñ wa ⌈na⌉ñ te i⊢ima⊣su ka⌣
'What's the name of that book?' (Lit. 'That book is called quote what?')
Ma⌈tuda to moosima⌉su.
'My name is Matsuda.' (Lit. 'I am called quote Matsuda.')

A quotation + quotative may be followed by particle wa—particularly in negative sentences. Thus:

Ma⌈zu⌉i tte wa i⊢imase⊣ñ desita ḡa⎯
'He didn't say it tasted bad but . . .' (Lit. 'As for quote it tastes bad, he didn't say but . . .')

The combination X to (or [t] te) iu Y, in which X is a name or designation (belonging to any word class) and Y is a nominal, is the Japanese equivalent of 'a Y named X' or 'a Y called X.' Na⌉ñ to (or te) iu Y 'a Y named quote what?' is a question equivalent.

[T] te (but not to) frequently occurs in statements and questions in sentence-final position, or pre-final before ne⌉e, or ne, following the quotation of someone other than the speaker. Thus:

De⌉ñki ḡa ki⊢eta⊣ tte. 'He said the light went out.'
A⌈rimase⌉ñ te? 'Did you say there isn't any?'
I⌉i tte. 'He said it's all right.'
So⌉o desu tte ⊢ne⊣e. 'That's what they say, isn't it.'

This use of [t] te is informal.

---

1 Note the omission of da before ka.

2. Indirect Questions Containing Interrogative Words

Questions containing interrogative words (na⌐n, da⌐re, do⌐ko, i⌐tu, etc.) and ending with particle ka occur as indirect questions before expressions of knowing, understanding, forgetting, informing, etc. They are usually in the informal style. As mentioned in the preceding note, informal non-past da is regularly lost before ka. Accentuation before ka is like accentuation before kara.

Examples:

Direct question:	Do⌐ko e iˈkimaˈsu ka⌐ 'Where are you going?'
Indirect question:	Do⌐ko e iˈkuˈ ka siˈrimaseˈn. 'I don't know where you are going.'
Direct question:	Do⌐re ḡa iˈtibañ takaˈi desu ka⌐ 'Which one is most expensive?'
Indirect question:	Do⌐re ḡa iˈtibañ takaˈi ka waˈkarimaseˈn. 'I can't tell which one is most expensive.'
Direct question:	Da⌐re desu ka⌐ 'Who is he?'
Indirect question:	Da⌐re ka waˈsuremaˈsita. 'I forgot who he is.'

3. More Imperatives

A nominal consisting of the polite prefix o- + a verbal stem (i.e. the -ma⌐su form minus -ma⌐su)[1] compounded with kuˈdasaˈi or (formal) kuˈdasaimaˈse[2] is a polite imperative. Examples:

oˈmati-kudasaˈi 'please wait'
oˈyobi-kudasaˈi 'please call'
oˈkaki-kudasaˈi 'please write'

If the -kudasaˈi is dropped, the result is a more informal equivalent.

The following are all used to ask someone to wait, but they differ in their degree of formality and politeness:

(a)	(b)	(c)
(1) Ma⌐tte.	Ma⌐tte kudasai.	Ma⌐tte kuˈdasaimaˈse.
(2) Omati.	Oˈmati-kudasaˈi.	Oˈmati-kudasaimaˈse.
(3) Oˈmati ni na⌐tte.	Oˈmati ni na⌐tte kudasai.	Oˈmati ni na⌐tte kuˈdasaimaˈse.

Forms in Row (2) are more polite than those in Row (1), and those in Row (3) are most polite. Forms in Column (a) are less formal than those in

---

[1] The combination o- + stem is unaccented.

[2] Forms ending in -ma⌐se are more typical of women's speech.

Column (b). Those in Column (c) are formal women's forms. (3)(a) is also typical of women's speech.

A gerund + ku⌐dasaimase⌐n̄ ka (for example, ma⌐tte ku⌐dasaimase⌐n̄ ka 'would you be kind enough to wait?'), though not an imperative, is a formal polite form of request. It is softer and less direct than an imperative.

WARNING: Not all verbals have imperatives of the o⌐mati-kudasa⌐i pattern. Use only those which you have heard or checked with a native speaker.

4. ma⌐da + Affirmative; mo⌐o + Negative

Reread Lesson 14, Grammatical Note 5, carefully.

Ma⌐da + an affirmative (except for the special combination ma⌐da desu 'not yet') means 'still' or 'yet.'

Mo⌐o + a negative means '(not) any more.'

As explained in the note referred to above, mo⌐o occurs in the direct iie answer to a ma⌐da question, and ma⌐da occurs in the direct iie answer to a mo⌐o question. Thus:

> Ma⌐da e⌐ēḡo o beñkyoo-site ima⌐su ka⌐ 'Are you still studying English?'
> E⌐e, ma⌐da be⌐ñkyoo-site ima⌐su. 'Yes, I'm still studying.'
> Iie, mo⌐o be⌐ñkyoo-site imase⌐n̄. 'No, I'm not studying any more.'

> Mo⌐o e⌐ēḡo o beñkyoo-site imase⌐n̄ ka⌐ 'Aren't you studying English any more?'
> E⌐e, mo⌐o be⌐ñkyoo-site imase⌐n̄. 'No (i.e. that's right), I'm not studying any more.'
> Iie, ma⌐da beñkyoo-site ima⌐su. 'Yes (i.e. that's wrong), I'm still studying.'

> Ma⌐da o⌐oki⌐i desu ka⌐ 'Is it still [too] big?'
> E⌐e, ma⌐da o⌐oki⌐i desu. 'Yes, it's still [too] big.'
> Iie, mo⌐o ⌐o⌐okiku a⌐rimase⌐n̄. 'No, it's not big any more.'

5. na⌐ku in Sentence-Final Position

> O⌐kamai na⌐ku.
> Go⌐eñryo na⌐ku.

Na⌐ku is the -ku form of na⌐i (informal equivalent of a⌐rimase⌐n̄) 'there isn't [any].' The -ku form in final position in these sentences signifies a request. Thus: o⌐kamai na⌐ku 'let there be no bother'; go⌐eñryo na⌐ku 'let there be no reserve.'

Compare also: do⌐ozo yōrosiku (from yorosii 'is good' or 'is favorable') 'let all be well' or 'I request your favor.'

A combination ending with na⌐ku is not limited to sentence-final position:

for example, like other -ku forms, it may occur within a sentence as the modifier of an inflected expression. Compare:

> Ha⌐yaku o⌐ssya⌐tte kudasai. 'Please speak quickly.'

and:

> Go⌐eñryo na⌐ku o⌐ssya⌐tte kudasai. 'Please speak freely (lit. without reserve).'

WARNING: Don't make up any —— + na⌐ku combinations. Use only those you have heard from a native speaker.

6. mi⌐e⌐ru

Mi⌐e⌐ru, an intransitive verbal, occurs in this lesson with two different meanings:

(a) mi⌐e⌐ru 'put in an appearance,' 'appear,' 'come'

The person who puts in an appearance, if expressed, is followed by wa or ḡa, depending upon emphasis. The polite o⌐mie ni na⌐ru † is used to show respect to him. This is never used in reference to the speaker.

Examples:

> O⌐mie ni narima⌐su ka⌐ 'Are you going to put in an appearance?'
> Ta⌐naka-sañ ḡa omie ni narima⌐sita. 'Mr. Tanaka has appeared.'
> A⌐tarasi⌐i ko⌐oka⌐ñsyu ḡa mi⌐ema⌐sita. 'The new telephone operator has come.'

(b) mi⌐e⌐ru 'be visible,' 'can see'

The person who can see and the object which is visible, if expressed, are followed by wa or ḡa, depending upon emphasis. The polite o⌐mie ni na⌐ru † is used to show respect to the person who can see.

Examples:

> U⌐mi ḡa mi⌐ema⌐sita. 'I could see the ocean.'
> (i.e. telling what I could see)
> Wa⌐takusi ḡa omie ni narima⌐su ka⌐ 'Can you see me?'
> (i.e. am I visible as far as you are concerned?)
> Da⌐re ḡa mi⌐emase⌐ñ ka . . . Ta⌐naka-sañ ḡa miemase⌐ñ.
> 'Who can't see? . . . Mr. Tanaka can't see.' or (depending upon context) 'Whom can't you see? . . . I can't see Mr. Tanaka.'
> Ta⌐isi⌐kañ to ryo⌐ozi⌐kañ ḡa mi⌐ema⌐su ka⌐ . . . Ta⌐isi⌐kañ wa mi⌐ema⌐su ḡa, ryo⌐ozi⌐kañ wa mi⌐emase⌐ñ.
> 'Can you see the embassy and the consulate? . . . The embassy I can see, but the consulate I can't see.'

Zyo⌐ozu⌐ da 'be proficient,' su⌐ki⌐ da 'be pleasing,' wa⌐ka⌐ru 'be comprehensible,' and de⌐ki⌐ru 'be possible' are among the many other intransitive inflected words and phrases which are preceded by wa phrases and ḡa phrases but not o phrases.

DRILLS

A. Substitution Drill

1. I haven't anything. or There isn't anything. — Na⌐ni mo na˺i.
2. I can't see anything. — Na⌐ni mo <u>mie˺nai</u>.
3. I can't hear anything. — Nani mo <u>kikoenai</u>.
4. I don't understand anything. — Na⌐ni mo <u>wakara˺nai</u>.
5. I don't know anything. — Nani mo <u>siranai</u>.
6. I didn't give [him] anything. — Na⌐ni mo <u>yarana˺katta</u>.
7. He didn't give me anything. — Na⌐ni mo <u>kurena˺katta</u>.
8. I couldn't do anything. — Na⌐ni mo <u>deki˺nakatta</u>.
9. I didn't do anything. — Na⌐ni mo <u>sina˺katta</u>.
10. I didn't say anything. — Na⌐ni mo <u>iwana˺katta</u>.

B. Substitution Drill

1. Isn't that good Japanese! — * <u>Zyo⌐ozu˺</u> na ni⌐hoñgo de˺su ⌐ne˺e.
2. Isn't that poor Japanese! — * <u>He⌐ta˺</u> na ni⌐hoñgo de˺su ⌐ne˺e.
3. Isn't that beautiful Japanese! — * <u>Ki˺ree</u> na ni⌐hoñgo de˺su ⌐ne˺e.
4. Isn't that a beautiful cake! — * <u>Ki˺ree</u> na o⌐ka˺si desu ⌐ne˺e.
5. Isn't that a wonderful cake! — * <u>Ke˺kkoo</u> na o⌐ka˺si desu ⌐ne˺e.
6. Isn't that a strange cake! — * <u>He˺ñ</u> na o⌐ka˺si desu ⌐ne˺e.
7. Isn't he a strange person! — * <u>He˺ñ</u> na <u>hi⌐to˺</u> desu ⌐ne˺e.
8. Isn't he a fine person! — * <u>Rippa</u> na hi⌐to˺ desu ⌐ne˺e.
9. Isn't he a rude person! — * <u>Si⌐tu˺ree</u> na hi⌐to˺ desu ⌐ne˺e.

C. Substitution Drill

1. Fall has come (lit. it has become fall) already, hasn't it! — Mo˺o ⌐a˺ki ni na⌐rima⌐sita ⌐ne˺e.
2. Winter has come already, hasn't it! — Mo˺o <u>hu⌐yu˺</u> ni na⌐rima⌐sita ⌐ne˺e.
3. Summer has come already, hasn't it! — Mo˺o <u>na⌐tu˺</u> ni na⌐rima⌐sita ⌐ne˺e.
4. Spring has come already, hasn't it! — Mo˺o ⌐ha˺ru ni na⌐rima⌐sita ⌐ne˺e.
5. It has cleared up (lit. become good weather) already, hasn't it! — Mo˺o o⌐te˺ñki ni na⌐rima⌐sita ⌐ne˺e.
6. You've become good at it already, haven't you! — Mo˺o o⌐zyoozu ni narima˺sita ⌐ne˺e.

7. They've become the same already, haven't they!   Mo⌐o o⌐nazi ni narima⌐sita ⌐ne⌐e.

8. You've recovered already, haven't you!   Mo⌐o o⌐ge⌐ñki ni na⌐rima⌐sita ⌐ne⌐e.

D. Substitution Drill

1. What kind of flower is it? (Lit. It's a flower called what?)   Na⌐ñ te iu ha⌐na⌐ desu ka⌐

2. Is it a man named Tanaka?   Ta⌐naka tte iu hito⌐ desu ka⌐

3. Are they cigarettes called "Peace"?   Pi⌐isu tte iu ta⌐bako de⌐su ka⌐

4. Is it a department store called "Mitsukoshi"?   Mi⌐tuko⌐si tte iu de⌐pa⌐ato desu ka⌐

5. Is it an American named Smith?   Su⌐misu tte iu A⌐merika⌐ziñ desu ka⌐

6. Is it the magazine "King"?   Ki⌐ñg̱u tte iu za⌐ssi de⌐su ka⌐

7. Is it the newspaper "Mainichi"?   Ma⌐initi tte iu siñbuñ de⌐su ka⌐

8. Is it an inn called "Imaiso"?   I⌐mai⌐soo tte iu ryo⌐kañ de⌐su ka⌐

E. Substitution Drill

1. This kind of door is called a "shoji" in Japanese.   Koñna to (wa) ni̱hoñg̱o de syo⌐ozi tte iima⌐su.

2. This kind of color is called "aka (red)" in Japanese.   Ko⌐ñna iro⌐ (wa) ni̱hoñg̱o de ⌐a⌐ka tte iimasu.

3. This kind of store is called a "yaoya (vegetable store)" in Japanese.   Ko⌐ñna mise⌐ (wa) ni̱hoñg̱o de ya⌐oya tte iima⌐su.

4. This kind of place is called a "koen (park)" in Japanese.   Ko⌐ñna tokoro⌐ (wa) ni̱hoñg̱o de ko⌐oeñ tte iima⌐su.

5. This kind of building is called a "byoin (hospital)" in Japanese.   Ko⌐ñna tate⌐mono (wa) ni̱hoñg̱o de byo⌐oiñ tte iima⌐su.

6. This kind of school is called a "daigaku (university)" in Japanese.   Koñna gakkoo (wa) ni̱hoñg̱o de da⌐ig̱aku tte iima⌐su.

7. This kind of drink is called "kotya (black tea)" in Japanese.   Ko⌐ñna nomi⌐mono (wa) ni̱hoñg̱o de ko⌐otya tte iima⌐su.

8. This kind of place is called a "daidokoro (kitchen)" in Japanese.   Ko⌐ñna tokoro⌐ (wa) ni̱hoñg̱o de da⌐idokoro tte iima⌐su.

9. This kind of shelf is called a "hondana (bookshelf)" in Japanese.

Koñna <u>tana</u> (wa) nǐhoñgo de <u>ho¹ñ-dana</u> tte iimasu.

10. This kind of animal is called an "uma (horse)" in Japanese.

Koñna <u>doobutu</u> (wa) nǐhoñgo de u⌐ma⌐ tte iimasu.

F. Substitution Drill

1. Who can't see?[1]
2. Which one can't you see?
3. Which one can't you do?
4. Who can't do it?
5. Who is good at it?
6. Who doesn't understand?
7. Which one don't you understand?
8. Which one do you need?
9. Who needs it?
10. Who doesn't like it?

Da⌐re g̃a mi⌐emase⌐ñ ka⌐
<u>Do⌐re</u> g̃a mi⌐emase⌐ñ ka⌐
Do⌐re g̃a <u>de⌐kimase⌐ñ</u> ka⌐
<u>Da⌐re</u> g̃a de⌐kimase⌐ñ ka⌐
Da⌐re g̃a zyo⌐ozu⌐ desu ka⌐
Da⌐re g̃a <u>wa⌐karimase⌐ñ</u> ka⌐
<u>Do⌐re</u> g̃a wa⌐karimase⌐ñ ka⌐

Do⌐re g̃a i⌐rima⌐su ka⌐
<u>Da⌐re</u> g̃a i⌐rima⌐su ka⌐
Da⌐re g̃a su⌐ki⌐ zya a⌐rimase⌐ñ ka⌐

G. Substitution Drill

1. I don't know how they say it in Japanese.
2. I can't tell how they say it in Japanese.
3. I forgot how they say it in Japanese.
4. Please tell me how they say it in Japanese.
5. He told me how they say it in Japanese.
6. Let's ask how they say it in Japanese.
7. I had [him] ask how they say it in Japanese.
8. I inquired how they say it in Japanese.

Ni⌐hoñgo de do⌐o iu ka si⌐rimase⌐ñ.

Ni⌐hoñgo de do⌐o iu ka <u>wa⌐karima-se⌐ñ</u>.

Ni⌐hoñgo de do⌐o iu ka <u>wa⌐surema⌐-sita</u>.

Ni⌐hoñgo de do⌐o iu ka <u>o⌐siete kuda-sa⌐i</u>.

Ni⌐hoñgo de do⌐o iu ka <u>o⌐siete kure-ma⌐sita</u>.

Ni⌐hoñgo de do⌐o iu ka <u>ki⌐kimasyo⌐o</u>.

Ni⌐hoñgo de do⌐o iu ka <u>ki⌐ite morai-ma⌐sita</u>.

Ni⌐hoñgo de do⌐o iu ka <u>u⌐kag̃aima⌐-sita</u>.

---

[1] Or, depending on the context, 'Whom can't you see?' or 'Who isn't going to come?' etc.

H. Substitution Drill

1. I don't know how they say
    it in Japanese.

    Ni⌐hoñḡo de do⌐o iu ka si⌐rimase⌐ñ.

2. I don't know who said
    that.

    Da⌐re ḡa so⌐o itta⌐ ka si⌐rimase⌐ñ.

3. I don't know what [he]
    got.

    Na⌐ni (o) mo⌐ratta⌐ ka si⌐rimase⌐ñ.

4. I don't know when [he] en-
    tered Tokyo University.

    I⌐tu To⌐odai ni ha⌐itta ka si⌐rima-
    se⌐ñ.

5. I don't know what is
    wrong with him (lit. what
    place is bad).[1]

    Do⌐ko ḡa wa⌐ru⌐i ka si⌐rimase⌐ñ.

6. I don't know which one is
    stronger.

    Do⌐tira no ⌐ho⌐o ḡa tu⌐yo⌐i ka si⌐ri-
    mase⌐ñ.

7. I don't know which one was
    most difficult.

    Do⌐re ḡa i⌐tibañ muzukasi⌐katta ka
    si⌐rimase⌐ñ.

8. I don't know what floor it
    is.

    Nañ-ḡai ka si⌐rimase⌐ñ.

9. I don't know which car is
    his.

    Do⌐no kuruma ḡa a⌐no⌐ hito no ka
    si⌐rimase⌐ñ.

10. I don't know what day it
    was.

    Na⌐ñyo⌐obi datta ka si⌐rimase⌐ñ.

I. Level Drill (based on Grammatical Note 3)

    Tutor: So⌐ko de ma⌐tte kudasai. ⎫
    Student: So⌐ko de omati-kudasa⌐i. ⎬ 'Please wait there.'
                                         ⎭

1. Do⌐ozo a⌐ḡatte kudasa⌐i.

    Do⌐ozo o⌐aḡari-kudasa⌐i.

2. Ko⌐tira ni ha⌐itte kudasai.

    Ko⌐tira ni ohairi-kudasa⌐i.

3. Do⌐ozo ōsaki ni ⌐ka⌐ette
    kudasai.

    Do⌐ozo ōsaki ni o⌐kaeri-kudasa⌐i.

4. Koko ni o⌐namae (o) ka⌐ite
    kudasai.

    Koko ni o⌐namae (o) okaki-kudasa⌐i.

5. Si⌐o⌐ to ko⌐syo⌐o (o) ⌐to⌐tte
    kudasai.

    Si⌐o⌐ to ko⌐syo⌐o (o) o⌐tori-kudasa⌐i.

6. Kore (o) ⌐ze⌐ñbu tu⌐taete ku-
    dasa⌐i.

    Kore (o) ⌐ze⌐ñbu o⌐tutae-kudasa⌐i.

---

[1] Refers to someone who is ill.

J. Grammatical Drill (based on Grammatical Note 1)

> Tutor: A⌐sita kima⌐su. 'I'll come tomorrow.'
> Student: A⌐no⌐ hito wa a⌐sita ku⌐ru tte (i⊦ima⊣sita). [1] 'He said he'd
> come tomorrow.'

1. Raineñ To⌐odai ni hai-
    rima⌐su.

    A⌐no⌐ hito wa rāineñ To⌐odai ni ha⌐-
    iru tte (i⊦ima⊣sita).

2. Na⌐ñ-zi de mo kamaima-
    se⌐ñ.

    A⌐no⌐ hito wa na⌐ñ-zi de mo kama-
    wa⌐nai tte (i⊦ima⊣sita).

3. To⌐ttemo he⌐ñ desita.

    A⌐no⌐ hito wa to⌐ttemo he⌐ñ datta
    tte (i⊦ima⊣sita).

4. Se⌐ñse⌐e desu.

    A⌐no⌐ hito wa se⌐ñse⌐e da tte (i⊦i-
    ma⊣sita).

5. Te⌐tuda⌐tte a g̃emasu. [2]

    A⌐no⌐ hito wa te⌐tuda⌐tte ku⊦reru⊣ tte
    (i⊦ima⊣sita).

6. Tomodati ni te⌐tuda⌐tte
    mo⊦raima⊣sita.

    A⌐no⌐ hito wa tōmodati ni te⌐tuda⌐tte
    mo⊦ratta⊣ tte (i⊦ima⊣sita).

7. A⌐tama⌐ g̃a i⌐ta⌐i desu.

    A⌐no⌐ hito wa a⌐tama⌐ g̃a i⌐ta⌐i tte
    (i⊦ima⊣sita).

8. A⌐sita⌐ made i⊦ma⊣su.

    A⌐no⌐ hito wa a⌐sita⌐ made i⊦ru⊣ tte
    (i⊦ima⊣sita).

9. A⌐me g̃a hu⊦tte⊣ (i)ma-
    su.

    A⌐no⌐ hito wa ⌐a⌐me g̃a hu⊦tte⊣ (i)ru
    tte (i⊦ima⊣sita).

10. Kinoo de⌐kakemase⌐ñ de-
     sita.

    A⌐no⌐ hito wa kinoo de⌐kakena⌐katta
    tte (i⊦ima⊣sita).

K. Grammar Drill (based on Grammatical Note 1)

> Tutor: A⌐no⌐ hito (wa) ki⌐ma⌐su ka↲ 'Is he coming?'
> Student: A⌐no⌐ hito ni ⌐ku⌐ru ka /tte/ ki⌐kimasyo⌐o. [3] 'Let's ask him
> if he is coming.'

1. A⌐no⌐ hito (wa) ⌐na⌐ni g̃a
    i⊦rima⊣su ka↲

    A⌐no⌐ hito ni ⌐na⌐ni g̃a i⊦ru⊣ ka /tte/
    ki⌐kimasyo⌐o.

2. A⌐no⌐ hito (wa) ⌐i⌐tu made
    i⊦sog̃asi⊣i desu ka↲

    A⌐no⌐ hito ni ⌐i⌐tu made i⊦sog̃asi⊣i
    ka /tte/ ki⌐kimasyo⌐o.

3. A⌐no⌐ hito (wa) ⌐na⌐ñ-zi
    ni tu⊦kima⊣sita ka↲

    A⌐no⌐ hito ni ⌐na⌐ñ-zi ni ⊦tu⊣ita ka
    /tte/ ki⌐kimasyo⌐o.

---

[1] Practice both the formal (with i⌐ima⌐sita) and informal (without i⌐ima⌐sita)
alternants.

[2] Meaning 'I'll help YOU.'

[3] Practice both with and without tte.

4. Aˈnoˈ hito (wa) byoˈoki
    deˈsita kaᶜ

    Aˈnoˈ hito ni byoˈoki daˈtta ka /tte/
    kiˈkimasyoˈo.

5. Aˈnoˈ hito (wa) teˈtudaˈt-
    te kuˈremaseˈn kaᶜ

    Aˈnoˈ hito ni teˈtudaˈtte kuˈrenaˈi
    ka /tte/ kiˈkimasyoˈo.

6. Aˈnoˈ hito (wa) niˈhoñgo
    (ga) dekimaˈsu kaᶜ

    Aˈnoˈ hito ni niˈhoñgo (ga) dekiˈru
    ka /tte/ kiˈkimasyoˈo.

7. Aˈnoˈ hito (wa) hiˈma
    deˈsu kaᶜ

    Aˈnoˈ hito ni hiˈma ka /tte/ kiˈkima-
    syoˈo.

8. Aˈnoˈ hito (wa) kiˈmoti
    ga waruˈi desu kaᶜ

    Aˈnoˈ hito ni kiˈmoti ga waruˈi ka
    /tte/ kiˈkimasyoˈo.

9. Aˈnoˈ hito (wa) ˈdoˈo site
    kiˈmaseˈn desita kaᶜ

    Aˈnoˈ hito ni ˈdoˈo site ˈkoˈnakatta
    ka /tte/ kiˈkimasyoˈo.

10. Aˈnoˈ hito (wa) ˈdoˈo site
    yaˈsumitaˈku aˈrimaseˈn
    kaᶜ

    Aˈnoˈ hito ni ˈdoˈo site yaˈsumitaˈku
    ˈnaˈi ka /tte/ kiˈkimasyoˈo.

L. **Response Drill** (based on Grammatical Note 4)

1. Maˈda ˈaˈme ga huˈtteˈ
    (i)masu kaᶜ   /iie/

    Iie, moˈo huˈtteˈ (i)ˈmaseˈn.

2. Moˈo aˈno uti (o) karite
    (i)maseˈn kaᶜ   /eˈe/

    Eˈe, moˈo kaˈrite (i)maseˈn.

3. Maˈda saˈmuˈi desu kaᶜ
    /iie/

    Iie, moˈo ˈsaˈmuku aˈrimaseˈn.

4. Maˈda eˈego (o) naraˈtte
    (i)masu kaᶜ   /eˈe/

    Eˈe, maˈda naˈraˈtte (i)masu.

5. Maˈda ˈheˈñ desu kaᶜ
    /iie/

    Iie, moˈo ˈheˈñ zya aˈrimaseˈn.

6. Maˈda tuˈkaˈrete (i)masu
    kaᶜ   /iie/

    Iie, moˈo tuˈkaˈrete (i)ˈmaseˈn.

7. Moˈo kono heñ ni deˈñwa
    (wa) arimaseˈn kaᶜ
    /eˈe/

    Eˈe, moˈo aˈrimaseˈn.

8. Moˈo ziˈkañ (wa) arima-
    seˈñ kaᶜ   /iie/

    Iie, maˈda aˈrimaˈsu.

M. **Response Drill**

    (Give _iie_ answers.)

1. Moˈo oˈtomodati ga mie-
    maˈsita kaᶜ

    Iie, maˈda miˈemaseˈñ.

2. Maˈda oˈnazi kaisya ni
    imaˈsu kaᶜ

    Iie, moˈo iˈmaseˈñ.

3. Moˈo oˈnazi zya arima-
    seˈñ kaᶜ

    Iie, maˈda oˈnazi deˈsu.

4. Maˈda Niˈhoˈñ ni tuˈki-
    maseˈñ kaᶜ

    Iie, moˈo tuˈkimaˈsita.

5. Moˈo aˈtuˈi desu kaᶜ

    Iie, maˈda ˈaˈtuku aˈrimaseˈñ.

6. Maˈda kiˈtanaˈi desu kaᶜ

    Iie, moˈo kiˈtanaˈku aˈrimaseˈñ.

7. Moˈo oˈyasumi deˈsu
    kaᶜ

    Iie, maˈda yaˈsumiˈ zya aˈrima-
    seˈñ.

8. Ma˥da i˩ssyo de˥su ka⌐   Iie, mo˥o i˩ssyo zya arimase˥ñ.
9. Mo˥o ko̅no ka˥mi˥ ya eñ-   Iie, ma˥da i˩rima˥su.
   pitu wa i˩rimase˥ñ ka⌐
10. Ma˥da a˥no ho˥ñ o ˩yo˥ñde   Iie, mo˥o ˩yo˥ñde (i)˩mase˥ñ.
    (i)masu ka⌐

N. Level Drill

Tutor: Ma˩irima˥sita. 'I went (or came).' (humble)
Student: Se˩ñse˥e mo i˩rassyaima˥sita.   'The teacher went (or came)
         too.' (honorific)

1. Ta˩naka to moosima˥su.   Se˩ñse˥e mo Ta˩naka to ossyaima˥su.
2. Mo˥o o˩tya (o) itadaki-   Se˩ñse˥e mo ˩mo˥o o˩tya (o) mesia-
   ma˥sita.   ga̅rima˥sita.
3. Ha˩zi˥mete Ta˩naka-sañ   Se˩ñse˥e mo ha˩zi˥mete Ta˩naka-sañ
   no o˩kusañ ni o˩me ni   no o˩kusañ ni o˩ai ni narima˥sita.
   kakarima˥sita.
4. Mo˥o o˩tutae-sima˥sita.   Se˩ñse˥e mo ˩mo˥o o˩tutae ni nari-
                                        ma˥sita.
5. Zyu˥u-neñ ˩ma˩e ni   Se˩ñse˥e mo ˩zyu˥u-neñ ˩ma˩e ni
   To˩odai de beñkyoo-itasi-   To˩odai de beñkyoo-nasaima˥sita.
   ma˥sita.
6. Ki˥ree na hu˩rosiki (o)   Se˩ñse˥e mo ˩ki˩ree na hu˩rosiki
   itadakima˥sita.   (o) omorai ni narima˥sita.
7. A˩merika-taisi˥kañ ni   Se˩ñse˥e mo A˩merika-taisi˩kañ ni
   tu˩to˥mete orimasu.   tu˩to˥mete (i)rassyaimasu.
8. Señsyuu ha˩zi˥mete ko˩ti-   Se˩ñse˥e mo se˩ñsyuu hazi˩mete
   ra e mairima˥sita.   ko˩tira e irassyaima˥sita.

O. Expansion Drill

1. Can you see?   Mi˩ema˥su ka⌐
   Can you see mountains too?   Ya˩ma˥ mo mi˩ema˥su ka⌐
   Can you see ocean AND   U˥mi mo ya˩ma˥ mo mi˩ema˥su
   mountains?   ka⌐
   Can you see ocean AND   Otaku kara ˩u˥mi mo ya˩ma˥ mo
   mountains from your   mi˩ema˥su ka⌐
   house?

2. He ended up forgetting.   Wa˩surete simaima˥sita.
   He ended up forgetting   Ma˩ta wasurete simaima˥sita.
   again.
   He said it but he ended up   I˩ima˥sita ga, ma˩ta wasurete si-
   forgetting again.   maima˥sita.
   He said he wouldn't forget   Wa˩surena˩i tte i˩ima˥sita ga, ma-
   but he ended up forgetting   ˩ta wasurete simaima˥sita.
   again.
   He said he wouldn't forget   Mo˥o wa˩surena˩i tte i˩ima˥sita ga̅,
   any more but he ended up   ma˩ta wasurete simaima˥sita.
   forgetting again.

3. I'm studying. — Beⁿkyoo-site (i)maˈsu.

Beˈnkyoo-site (i)maˈsu.

I'm still studying. — Maˈda beᵗñkyoo-site (i)maˈsu.

Japanese I'm still study-
ing. — Niᵗhoñḡo wa maˈda beᵗñkyoo-site
(i)maˈsu.

I gave up Spanish, but
Japanese I'm still
studying. — Suᵗpeiñḡo o yamemaˈsita ḡa, niᵗhoñḡo wa maˈda beᵗñkyoo-site
(i)maˈsu.

I gave up Spanish be-
cause I have no time
but Japanese I'm still
studying. — Ziᵗkañ ḡa naˈi kara, Suᵗpeiñḡo o
yamemaˈsita ḡa; niᵗhoñḡo wa maˈ-
da beᵗñkyoo-site (i)maˈsu.

4. It's Mr. Ito. — Iᵗtoo-sañ deˈsu.

Zyoᵗozuˈ na no wa Iᵗtoo-sañ deˈsu.

The one who's good at it
is Mr. Ito.

The one who is best at it
is Mr. Ito. — Iᵗtibañ zyoozuˈ na no wa Iᵗtoo-sañ
deˈsu.

Mr. Yamamoto is good
too, but the one who is
best at it is Mr. Ito. — Yaᵗmamoto-sañ mo zyoozuˈ desu ḡa,
iᵗtibañ zyoozuˈ na no wa Iᵗtoo-sañ
deˈsu.

Both Mr. Tanaka and Mr.
Yamamoto are good but
the one who is best at
it is Mr. Ito. — Taᵗnaka-sañ mo Yamamoto-sañ mo
zyoozuˈ desu ḡa, iᵗtibañ zyoozuˈ
na no wa Iᵗtoo-sañ deˈsu.

Both Mr. Tanaka and Mr.
Yamamoto are good at
English, but the one
who is best at it is Mr.
Ito. — Eeḡo wa Taᵗnaka-sañ mo Yamamoto-
sañ mo zyoozuˈ desu ḡa, iᵗtibañ
zyoozuˈ na no wa Iᵗtoo-sañ deˈsu.

5. [He] didn't let me know. — Oᵗsiete kuremaseˈñ desita.

[He] couldn't tell so he
didn't let me know. — Waᵗkaraˈnakatta kara, oᵗsiete kuremaseˈñ desita.

[He] couldn't tell for sure
so he didn't let me know. — Haᵗkkiˈri waᵗkaraˈnakatta kara,
oᵗsiete kuremaseˈñ desita.

He couldn't tell for sure
so he didn't let me know — Aᵗnoˈ hito (wa) haᵗkkiˈri waᵗkaraˈ-
nakatta kara, oᵗsiete kuremaseˈñ
desita.

I asked but he couldn't
tell for sure so he did-
n't let me know. — Kiᵗkimaˈsita ḡa; aᵗnoˈ hito (wa) haᵗkkiˈri waᵗkaraˈnakatta kara, oᵗsi-
ete kuremaseˈñ desita.

I asked if he would re-
turn home but he could-
n't tell for sure so he
didn't let me know. — Kaˈeru ka [tte] kiᵗkimaˈsita ḡa; aᵗnoˈ
hito (wa) haᵗkkiˈri waᵗkaraˈnakat-
ta kara, oᵗsiete kuremaseˈñ desita.

I asked by what time he
would return home but
he couldn't tell for
sure so he didn't let
me know. — Naˈñ-zi made ni ᵗkaˈeru ka [tte]
kiᵗkimaˈsita ḡa; aᵗnoˈ hito (wa)
haᵗkkiˈri waᵗkaraˈnakatta kara,
oᵗsiete kuremaseˈñ desita.

I asked Mr. Tanaka by what time he would return home but he couldn't tell for sure so he didn't let me know.	Tanaka-sañ ni ⌐naˈñ-zi made ni ˧ka⌐eru ka ⌐tte⌏ ki⌐kimaˈsita ḡa; aˈno⌐ hito (wa) ha⌐kkiˈri wa˧kara⌐-nakatta kara, o⌐siete kuremaseˈñ desita.

6. What shall I do?
  [She] said it. What shall I do?

Fumiko said [it]. What shall I do?

Fumiko said [he]'s waiting. What shall I do?

Fumiko said [he]'s still waiting. What shall I do?

Fumiko said [he]'s still waiting in the study. What shall I do?

Fumiko said [he] came and is still waiting in the study. What shall I do?

Fumiko said that a man named Hamada came and is still waiting in the study. What shall I do?

Fumiko said that a man named Hamada came while you were out and is still waiting in the study. What shall I do?

Do⌐o simasyoo ka.
Iˈimaˈsita ḡa, do⌐o simasyoo ka.

Hu⌐miko-sañ ḡa i˧imaˈsita ḡa, do⌐o simasyoo ka.

Maˈtte (i)ru tte, ⌐Hu⌐miko-sañ ḡa i˧imaˈsita ḡa; do⌐o simasyoo ka.

Maˈda ⌐maˈtte (i)ru tte, ⌐Hu⌐miko-sañ ḡa i˧imaˈsita ḡa; do⌐o sima-syoo ka.

Syosai de ⌐maˈda ⌐maˈtte (i)ru tte, ⌐Hu⌐miko-sañ ḡa i˧imaˈsita ḡa; do⌐o simasyoo ka.

Mi⌐ete, syosai de ⌐maˈda ⌐maˈtte (i)ru tte, ⌐Hu⌐miko-sañ ḡa i˧i-maˈsita ḡa; do⌐o simasyoo ka.

⌐Haˈmada tte iu hi˧to˧ ḡa ˧mi⌐ete, syosai de ⌐maˈda ⌐maˈtte (i)ru tte, ⌐Hu⌐miko-sañ ḡa i˧imaˈsita ḡa; do⌐o simasyoo ka.

Orusu-tyuu ni ⌐Haˈmada tte iu hi-˧to˧ ḡa ˧mi⌐ete, syosai de ⌐maˈda ⌐maˈtte (i)ru tte, ⌐Hu⌐miko-sañ ḡa i˧imaˈsita ḡa; do⌐o simasyoo ka.

GREETINGS, FAREWELLS, AND ASSORTED SMALL TALK

1. Hostess: Yo⌐ku i˧rassyaimaˈsita. Do⌐ozo o⌐aḡari-kudasaimaˈse.
  Mrs. Tanaka: A⌐riˈḡatoo gozaimasu. Si⌐tuˈree-itasimasu.

2. Host: Do⌐ozo o⌐aḡari-kudasaˈi.
  Caller: A⌐riˈḡatoo gozaimasu ḡa, kyo⌐o wa ⌐tyo⌐tto i˧soḡimaˈsu kara_

3. Tanaka: Ma⌐tuda-señseˈe, o⌐hayoo gozaimaˈsu.
  Matsuda: O⌐hayoo gozaimaˈsu.
  Tanaka: Señzitu wa si⌐tuˈree-simasita.
  Matsuda: Ko⌐tira koˈso.

4. Host: Tanaka-sañ, ⌐yo⌐ku i˧rassyaimaˈsita. Do⌐ozo kotira e.
  Mr. Tanaka: A⌐riˈḡatoo gozaimasu.
  Host: Osyokuzi wa?

Mr. Tanaka: Mo˺o si˻ma˺sita.
Host: Zya˺a, o˻tya wa ika˺ga desu ka.
Mr. Tanaka: Do˺ozo o˻kamai na˺ku.

5. Host: Do˺ozo go˻eñryo na˺ku me˻siagatte kudasa˺i. Do˺ozo ˻do˺ozo.
   Mr. Tanaka: E˺e, i˻tadaite ma˺su. Eñryo wa simase˺ñ kara_

6. A: Tyo˺tto o˻negai-sita˺i ñ desu ga_
   B: Na˺ñ desyoo ka. Do˺ozo go˻eñryo na˺ku i˻tte kudasa˺i.

7. Guest: Tyo˺tto de˻ñwa o kaketa˺i ñ desu ga_
   Hostess: Do˺ozo go˻eñryo na˺ku. A˻tira ni gozaima˺su kara, do˺ozo.

8. Smith: Watakusi wa ˻ma˺da Ni˻ho˺ñ wa na˻ñni mo sirimase˺ñ kara, o˻u-
   kagai-sita˺i ñ desu ga_
   Tanaka: Do˺ozo go˻eñryo na˺ku.

9. A: Osaki ni.
   B: Do˺ozo.

10. A: Osaki ni.   Sayonara.
    B: Sayonara.

11. A: Osaki ni si˻tu˺ree-simasu.   Sayoonara.
    B: Sayoonara.   Mata asita.

12. A: O˻saki ni itadakima˺su.
    B: Do˺ozo ˻do˺ozo.

13. Hostess: Tu˻metaku narima˺su kara, do˺ozo ˻su˺gu me˻siagatte kudasai-
    ma˻se.
    Guest: Zya˺a, o˻saki ni itadakima˺su.

14. Tanaka: Tyo˺tto ki˻moti ga waru˺i kara, i˻ma ka˻erita˺i ñ desu ga_
    Smith: Do˺o simasita ka_ Da˻izyo˺obu desu ka_
    Tanaka: O˻naka ga tyo˺tto_
    Smith: Wa˻ru˺i mo˻no˺ o ta˻bemase˺ñ desita ka_
    Tanaka: Sa˺a.
    Smith: Odaizi ni.
    Tanaka: Do˺o mo.

15. Host: Ko˻no isu no ho˺o ga ki˻moti ga i˺i kara, ko˻tira e do˺ozo.
    Mrs. Tanaka: O˻so˺re i˻rima˻su.

16. Hostess: Na˻ni mo gozaimase˺ñ ga, do˺ozo.
    Guest: I˻tadakima˺su.

17. Host: Na˻ni mo arimase˺ñ ga, i˻ssyo ni ta˺bete kudasai.
    Mrs. Tanaka: Do˺o mo o˻so˺re i˻rima˻su.

18. Mrs. Tanaka: Go⌐tisoosama de gozaima⌐sita.
     Hostess: Na⌐ni mo go⌐zaimase⌐ñ de_

19. Mrs. Tanaka: O⌐so⌐re i⌐rima⌐su g̃a, asita mo⌐o iti-do ira⌐site ku⌐dasai-
     mase⌐ñ ka⌐
     Mrs. Yamamoto: Ha⌐a, ka⌐sikomarima⌐sita.

20. Hostess: Yo⌐ku i⌐rassyaima⌐sita. Do⌐ozo o⌐ag̃ari ni na⌐tte ku⌐dasaima⌐-
     se.
     Mrs. Tanaka: Ha⌐a. O⌐so⌐reirimasu. Si⌐tu⌐ree-itasimasu.

21. Mrs. Tanaka: Nihoñg̃o g̃a o⌐zyoozu de irassyaima⌐su ⌐ne⌐e.
     Mrs. Smith: O⌐so⌐reirimasu.

22. Mrs. Tanaka: O⌐taku no ozyo⌐osañ wa o⌐tya[1] o nasaima⌐su ka⌐
     Mrs. Yamamoto: Ha⌐a, to⌐kidoki itasima⌐su. I⌐ma na⌐ra⌐tte orimasu
     kara_

23. Smith: Ko⌐nna heya⌐ wa nĩhoñg̃o de syo⌐kudoo tte iima⌐su ka⌐
     Tanaka: Iie, so⌐o iimase⌐ñ. Tya⌐noma tte iima⌐su. Ta⌐tami no heya⌐
     desu kara.[2]

24. Mrs. Tanaka: A⌐no amerika⌐ziñ wa ⌐i⌐tu mo watakusi ni ãno ne! ãno ne!
     tte i⌐ima⌐su g̃a_
     Mrs. Yamamoto: Si⌐tu⌐ree desu ⌐ne⌐e.

25. A: Na⌐ñ-zi ni i⌐kimasyo⌐o ka.
     B: Matuda-sañ wa ⌐na⌐ñ-zi de mo ka⌐mawa⌐nai to i⌐tta⌐ kara, ha⌐yaku
     i⌐kimasyo⌐o.

26. Mrs. Tanaka: Yosida-sañ wa ⌐ku⌐-zi made ni i⌐rassya⌐ru to o⌐ssyaima⌐-
     sita ka⌐
     Mrs. Yamamoto: Ha⌐a. Syo⌐kuzi o site⌐ kara ⌐su⌐g̃u i⌐rassya⌐ru to o⌐s-
     syaima⌐sita.

27. A: Ko⌐ma⌐ru tte?
     B: Iie, ka⌐mawa⌐nai tte.

28. A: Su⌐misu-sañ sa⌐simi tabe⌐ru tte?
     B: E⌐e. Da⌐isuki da tte.

---

[1] Otya here refers to the tea ceremony.

[2] Syokudoo is usually a Western-style room.

29. A: Tanaka-sañ wa ⌈ke⌉sa deⁿsya de kima⌉sita ḡa, kuruma wa ko⌈syoo
        de⌉su ka↲
     B: Ko⌈syoo da⌉ to wa iʰimaseⁿ desita ḡa, ko⌈syoo desyo⌉o ⌈neᵈe.

30. A: Kono zibiki ⌈Zi⌉roo-sañ no desu ka↲
     B: So⌉o desyoo? Tanaka ⌈Zi⌉roo to ⌈kaᵈite ᵗaᵈru kara_

31. Maid: Go-⌈zi-ḡo⌉ro Ūeda-sañ kara oᵈdeⁿwa ḡa goᵗzaima⌉sita.
     Employer: A⌉a ⌈so⌉o. Na⌉ñ te?
     Maid: O⌈hima na toki⌉ ni oᵈdeⁿwa o kuᵗdasaᵈi to oᵗssyaima⌉sita.
     Employer: Sore dake?
     Maid: Ha⌉a, so⌈re dake⌉ de gozaimasita.

32. Smith: Maᵗtuda-sañ no oto⌉osañ wa ⌈na⌉ñ to oᵗssyaima⌉su ka↲
     Matsuda: Matuda ⌈Zi⌉roo to moosimasu.

33. Mrs. Tanaka: O⌈taku no ozyo⌉osañ wa ⌈Ha⌉ruko-sañ to oᵗssyaima⌉su
        ka↲
     Mrs. Yamamoto: Iie, Ha⌈rue to moosima⌉su.

English Equivalents

1. Hostess: I'm so glad you came. Please come in.
    Mrs. Tanaka: Thank you. (Excuse me [for coming into your home].)

2. Host: Please come in.
    Caller: Thank you but today I'm in a bit of a hurry so [I'm afraid I
        can't].

3. Tanaka: Good morning, Dr. Matsuda.
    Matsuda: Good morning.
    Tanaka: It was nice seeing you the other day. (Lit. I was rude the other
        day.)
    Matsuda: (I was the one [who was rude].)

4. Host: I'm glad you came, Mr. Tanaka. This way, please.
    Mr. Tanaka: Thank you.
    Host: What about lunch?
    Mr. Tanaka: I've had it already.
    Host: Then how about some tea?
    Mr. Tanaka: Please don't bother.

5. Host: Do please help yourself (lit. eat without reserve).
    Mr. Tanaka: Yes, I'm doing very well (lit. I'm eating). I won't hold back
        so [don't give it another thought].

6. A: I'd like to ask you a favor. . . .
    B: What is it? Please speak freely.

7. Guest: I'd like to use the telephone. . . .
    Hostess: Please go right ahead. It's over there so please help yourself.

8. Smith: I don't know anything about Japan yet so I'd like to ask you. . . .
    Tanaka: Please, go right ahead.

9. A: [Excuse me for going] ahead.
    B: Go right ahead.

10. A: [Excuse me for leaving] ahead [of you].   Goodbye.
    B: Goodbye.

11. A: Excuse me for leaving ahead of you. Goodbye.
    B: Goodbye. [See you] again tomorrow.

12. A: Excuse me for eating before you.
    B: Please go ahead.

13. Hostess: Things will get cold so please eat right away.
    Guest: Well then, I'll start (lit. eat) before you.

14. Tanaka: I don't feel well so I'd like to go home now. . . .
    Smith: What happened? Are you all right?
    Tanaka: My stomach is a bit . . .
    Smith: You didn't eat something bad?
    Tanaka: I wonder.
    Smith: Take care of yourself.
    Tanaka: Thanks.

15. Host: This chair is more pleasant so please [sit] here.
    Mrs. Tanaka: Thank you.

16. Hostess: There's nothing here [to speak of] but please [have some].
    Guest: Thank you. (Lit. I'll have some.)

17. Host: We don't have anything [special] but do eat with us.
    Mrs. Tanaka: Thank you very much.

18. Mrs. Tanaka: It was delicious.
    Hostess: There was (lit. being) nothing [to speak of]. . .

19. Mrs. Tanaka: I'm sorry but would you be kind enough to come once more
        tomorrow?
    Mrs. Yamamoto: Yes, certainly.

20. Hostess: I'm so glad you came. Please come in.
    Mrs. Tanaka: Thank you. (Excuse me for entering your home.)

21. Mrs. Tanaka: You are very good in Japanese, aren't you.
    Mrs. Smith: Thank you.

22. Mrs. Tanaka: Does your daughter do the tea ceremony?
    Mrs. Yamamoto: Yes, she does sometimes. She's taking lessons now
    so . . .

23. Smith: Is this kind of room called a " shokudo" (dining room) in Japa-
    nese?
    Tanaka: No, we don't call it that. It's called a "chanoma" (Japanese-
    style family room where meals are eaten)— since it's a tatami room
    [and a " shokudo" is usually a Western-style dining room].

24. Mrs. Tanaka: That American always says, "Hey, hey!" to me but
    [what can I do?]
    Mrs. Yamamoto: Isn't it rude!

25. A: What time shall we go?
    B: Mr. Matsuda said that any time at all would be all right so let's go
    early.

26. Mrs. Tanaka: Did Mr. Yoshida say that he would come by 9 o'clock?
    Mrs. Yamamoto: Yes. He said that he would come right after he ate.

27. A: Did he say it's inconvenient?
    B: No, he said it doesn't matter.

28. A: Did Mr. Smith say he eats sashimi?
    B: Yes. He said he likes it very much.

29. A: Mr. Tanaka came by (electric) train this morning. Is his car out of
    order?
    B: He didn't say that it was out of order but it probably is (out of order),
    isn't it.

30. A: Is this dictionary Jiro's?
    B: It probably is, don't you think so?— since " Jiro Tanaka" is written
    [on it].

31. Maid: There was a call from Mr. Ueda at about 5 o'clock.
    Employer: Oh? What did he say?
    Maid: He said that you should call (lit. please call) when you are free.
    Employer: [Was] that all?
    Maid: Yes, that was all.

32. Smith: What is your father's name, Mr. Matsuda?
    Matsuda: His name is Jiro Matsuda.

33. Mrs. Tanaka: Is your daughter's name Haruko?
    Mrs. Yamamoto: No, her name is Harue.

EXERCISES

1. Using pictures, models, or actual objects, review vocabulary by taking turns asking and answering the question "What is this called in Japanese?"

2. As a host (or hostess):

   a. welcome Mr. Yamamoto to your home.
   b. invite him to come in.
   c. tell him to come this way.
   d. offer to let him precede you.
   e. comment on the weather.
   f. ask him if he smokes.
   g. offer him some tea.
   h. compliment him on his English.
   i. offer him a second helping.

3. As a guest:

   a. excuse yourself for going ahead.
   b. excuse yourself for your rudeness the other day. [1]
   c. refuse a cigarette.
   d. tell your host not to go to any trouble.
   e. refuse a second helping.
   f. remark on how pretty the garden is.
   g. remark on how handsome the alcove is.
   h. remark on how well you can see the mountains.
   i. remark on how pleasant this kind of room is.

_____

[1] See Basic Sentence 5 and note.

Lesson 19. Transportation

BASIC DIALOGUES: FOR MEMORIZATION

(a)

(At the station information booth)

Smith

first class	it-too
second class	ni-too
ticket	kippu

1. Where do you buy second-class tickets?   Do˥ko de ni-ᴸtoo no kippu (o) kaima˩su ka⌐

Clerk

ticket window	ma⌐do˥g̃uti
ticket window number seven	na⌐na˥-bañ no ma⌐do˩g̃uti

2. It's window number seven.   Na⌐na˥-bañ no ma⌐do˩g̃uti desu yo⌐

(At the ticket window)

Smith

(city near Yokohama)	Yokosuka

3. Two second-class tickets for Yokosuka.   Yokosuka, ni-too ⌐ni˥-mai.

Ticket seller

round trip	oohuku

4. Round trip?   O⌐ohuku de˥su ka⌐

Smith

one way	katamiti

5. No, one way, please.   Iie, ka⌐tamiti (o) oneg̃ai-sima˥su.

(At the information booth again)

Smith

Yokosuka-bound	Yokosuka-iki or Yokosuka-yuki
track number what?	nañ-bañ-señ

6. On what tracks are the Yokosuka trains? (Lit. The Yokosuka-bound are track number what?)   Yokosuka-iki (wa) na⌐ñ-bañ-señ de˥su ka⌐

Clerk

track number seven	nana-bañ-señ
track number eight	hati-bañ-señ

343

7. (They are) track number   Nana-bañ-señ to ha⌐ti-bañ-señ de⌐-
    seven and track number   su.
    eight.

Smith

    pass through or go   to⌐oru /-u/
        through or pass in
        front of
8. Do they go through Yoko-   Yo⌐kohama (o) toorima⌐su ka⌐
    hama?

Clerk

    come to a halt   tomaru /-u/
9. Yes, they stop at Yoko-   E⌐e, Yo⌐kohama⌐-eki ni to⌐marima⌐-
    hama Station.   su yo⌐

(On the platform)

Smith

    second-class car   ni⌐to⌐osya
    the second-class car   ni⌐to⌐osya ḡa tomaru
        stops
    the place where the   ni⌐to⌐osya ḡa tõmaru tokoro
        second-class car   or
        stops   ni⌐to⌐osya no tõmaru tokoro
    what part? or what   dono heñ
        section?
10. Which part [of the platform]   Ni⌐to⌐osya no to⌐maru tokoro⌐ (wa)
    is the place where the sec-   do⌐no heñ de⌐su ka⌐
    ond-class cars stop?

Stranger

    frontmost or furthest   i⌐tibañ ma⌐e
        forward
11. The second-class cars are   Ni⌐to⌐osya wa i⌐tibañ ma⌐e desu
    furthest forward so it's   kara, a⌐no heñ de⌐su yo⌐
    that part [of the platform].

(b)

(At the Japan Travel Bureau)

Smith

    get on (a vehicle) or   noru /-u/
        take (a vehicle) or
        ride
    I want to get on or ride   watakusi ḡa noritai
    the one I want to get on   wa⌐takusi ḡa norita⌐i no
        or ride   or
                                   wa⌐takusi no norita⌐i no
    night   bañ
    depart or leave for a   ta⌐tu /-u/
        trip

depart late at night	bañ o⌐soku ta⌐tu
express	kyuukoo
express that departs late at night	bañ o⌐soku ta⌐tu kyuukoo

12. I'd like to go to Kyoto. The train (lit. one) I want to take is an express that leaves late at night (but . . .)

Kyo⌐oto e i⌐kita⌐i ñ desu ḡa, wa-⌐takusi ḡa norita⌐i no (wa) bañ o-⌐soku ta⌐tu kyu⌐ukoo de⌐su ḡa—

Clerk

leave at 11 o'clock special express	zyu⌐u-iti⌐-zi ni ⌐de⌐ru to⌐kubetukyu⌐ukoo <u>or</u> tokkyuu
special express that leaves at 11 o'clock	zyu⌐uiti⌐-zi ni ⌐de⌐ru to̅kkyuu

13. There's a special express that leaves at 11 o'clock (but . . .)

Zyu⌐uiti⌐-zi ni ⌐de⌐ru to⌐kkyuu (ḡa) arima⌐su ḡa—

Smith

transfer (from one ve-hicle to another)	norikae

14. That's just fine! Of course there's no changing trains, is there?

Tyo⌐odo i⌐i desu ⌐ne⌐e. Mo⌐ti⌐roñ no⌐rikae wa na⌐i desyoo?

Clerk

15. No (lit. that's right), there isn't.

E⌐e a⌐rimase⌐ñ.

(c)

(At the station)

Smith

leaving at 11 o'clock Kyoto-bound	zyu⌐uiti⌐-zi hatu Kyooto-iki <u>or</u> Kyooto-yuki

16. What track [is the train] (bound) for Kyoto leaving at 11 o'clock?

Zyu⌐uiti⌐-zi hatu Kyo̅oto-iki (wa) nañ-bañ-señ?

Porter

(name of a train)	Ha⌐to

17. Do you mean the Hato? It's track number two.

Ha⌐to desu ka— Ni-⌐bañ-señ de⌐-su.

what car number?	na⌐ñ-ḡo⌐o-sya

18. What is your car number and seat number? (Lit. Your seat is what number in what number car?)

Oseki (wa) na⌐ñ-ḡo⌐o-sya no ⌐na⌐ñ-bañ desu ka—

Smith

car number three	saⁿ-g̃o¹o-sya

19. Number 17 in car number 3. Saⁿ-g̃o¹o-sya no zyuᶜunana¹-bañ.

(d)

Smith

(name of a train)	Tubame
(section of Tokyo)	Siⁿbasi

20. Does the Tsubame stop at Shimbashi? Tubame (wa) ⌐Siⁿbasi ni to⌐marima¹su ka⌐

Tanaka

down-train (i.e. going away from Tokyo)	kudari
up-train (i.e. going toward Tokyo)	nobori

21. The down-train does (stop) but the up-train doesn't (stop), isn't that right? Kuᶜdari wa tomarima¹su g̃a, nobori wa tŏmaranai desyoo?

Yamamoto

opposite	hañtai

22. Isn't it the opposite? Haⁿntai zya arimase¹ñ ka⌐

Tanaka

get on the train	kiᶜsya¹ ni nŏru
at the time [someone] gets on the train	kiᶜsya¹ ni noᵗru toᵗki /ni/
conductor	syasyoo
try asking or ask and see	kiᶜite mi¹ru

23. Oh? Well then, when we get on the train let's ask the conductor and find out. So¹o? Zya¹a, kiᶜsya¹ ni noᵗru toᵗki /ni/ syaᶜsyoo ni kiite mimasyo¹o.

(e)

(Smith and Tanaka are meeting a train)

Smith

on time	ziᶜkañ-do¹ori

24. Do you suppose it will arrive on time? Ziᶜkañ-do¹ori /ni/ ᵗtuᵗku desyoo ka.

Tanaka

information booth	aᶜññaizyo¹ [1]

25. I wonder. Let's ask at the information booth and find out. Sa¹a. Añnaizyŏ de kiᶜite mimasyo¹o.

---

[1] Has unaccented alternant.

(At the information booth)

Tanaka

leaving Kobe or coming from Kobe	Ko⌐obe hatu
arriving at one o'clock	i⌐ti⌐-zi tyaku
26. Will [the train] from Kobe due at one o'clock arrive on time?	Ko⌐obe hatu i⌐ti⌐-zi tyaku (wa) zi-⌐kañ-do⌐ori /ni/ tu⌐kima⌐su ka⌐

Clerk

fall behind or become late	okureru /-ru/
be late	okurete (i)ru
27. No, today it's about ten minutes late.	Iie, kyo⌐o wa zi⌐ppuñ-gu⌐rai o⌐kurete (i)ma⌐su.

ADDITIONAL VOCABULARY

1. Is there a first-class car on this train?	Ko⌐no kisya⌐ ni i⌐tto⌐osya (ḡa) a⌐rima⌐su ka⌐
third-class car[1]	sa⌐ñto⌐osya
sleeping car	si⌐ñda⌐isya
dining car	syo⌐kudo⌐osya
2. You need a berth ticket too, you know!	Si⌐ñdaikeñ mo irima⌐su yo⌐
express ticket	kyuukookeñ
special express ticket	tokkyuukeñ
passenger ticket	zyoosyakeñ

NOTES OF THE BASIC DIALOGUES

1. The former three-class system on Japanese trains has been replaced by a two-class system. First-class cars are referred to as gu⌐ri⌐iñsya or gu⌐riiñka⌐a because of their green color. The new high-speed lines are called si⌐ñka⌐ñseñ.

3. Note the use of counter -mai to count tickets.

6. -iki is derived from the verbal iku 'go,' and -yuki from yuku, an alternate form of iku which has the same meaning. Yuku is a slightly more formal form. The place which precedes -iki (or -yuki) is the final destination— the last stop.

8. The area through which (or— in some combinations— in front of which) one passes is followed by particle o. Note the following: ko⌐oeñ o to⌐oru 'pass through the park'; ko⌐oeñ no so⌐ba o ⌐to⌐oru 'pass near the park'; gi⌐ñkoo no ma⌐e o ⌐to⌐oru 'pass in front of the bank,' 'pass the bank.' The last has the shorter alternant gi⌐ñkoo o to⌐oru.

---

[1] Obsolete.

9. Tomaru 'stop'—i.e. 'come to a halt'—is the intransitive partner of the transitive tomeru 'stop'—i.e. 'bring to a halt.' Compare: Ku⌐ruma g̃a tomarima⌐sita. 'The c a r s t o p p e d.' and: Ku⌐ruma o tomema⌐sita. 'I stopped the car.' Tomaru also occurs as the equivalent of English 'stop at a place'—i.e. stay overnight or lodge.

12. 'but—is there such a train?'

Noru is the intransitive partner of transitive noseru /-ru/ 'give [someone] a ride' or 'carry' or 'take on board.'

Bañ 'night': compare ko⌐ñbañ 'tonight,' ma⌐ibañ 'every night,' ba⌐ñgo⌐hañ 'dinner'—i.e. evening meal.

Note the following particles occurring before ta⌐tu: To⌐okyoo o ta⌐tu 'leave Tokyo'; To⌐okyoo kara ta⌐tu 'leave from Tokyo'; To⌐okyoo e (or ni) ta⌐tu 'leave for Tokyo.' The same particles occur with de⌐ru. De⌐ru is a word of more general use than ta⌐tu: if Mr. Tanaka leaves Tokyo for a trip to America, either de⌐ru or ta⌐tu may be used; if he leaves the office to go to lunch, de⌐ru is used.

13. 'but—would that be all right?'

Tokubetu occurs as an independent nominal meaning 'special.' It may be followed by particle ni of manner, meaning 'specially,' 'especially,' 'extraordinarily.'

14. Norikae is a nominal derived from the verbal no⌐rikae⌐ru /-ru/ 'change vehicles' or 'transfer.'

16. Hatu and tyaku (Basic Sentence 26) are nominals which follow time and/or place words directly without intervening particles. Note (Basic Sentence 26) that phrases ending with hatu and tyaku may also follow each other directly. Hatu and tyaku expressions are commonly used in reference to trains, ships, airplanes, etc.

22. Hañtai is a nominal: hañtai da 'it's the opposite'; ha⌐ñtai zya na⌐i 'it's not the opposite.' Note also: hañtai-suru 'oppose.'

24, 26. Ni here is the ni of manner.

27. Note: X ni okureru 'be(come) late for X.'

GRAMMATICAL NOTES

1. S e n t e n c e   M o d i f i e r s

It has already been explained (a) that a non-past adjectival[1] is an independent sentence in the informal style (example: Ta⌐ka⌐i. 'It's expensive.') and

---

[1] With sentence intonation, of course.

(b) that non-past adjectivals directly describe following nominals (example: ta⌐ka⌐i ⌐ho⌐ñ 'an expensive book').

Examples in this lesson show that a sentence modifying a nominal does not necessarily consist of a non-past adjectival.   Actually, any kind of informal Japanese sentence, consisting of or ending with a non-past or past form, may directly describe a following nominal— subject to the two special points noted below.

Examples:

Nominal:	modified by the sentence:	equals:
hi⌐to⌐ 'man'	Ta⌐bete iru. 'He's eating.'	ta⌐bete iru hito 'the ' man who's eating'
hi⌐to⌐ 'man'	Tanaka to iu. 'He is named Tanaka.'	Ta⌐naka to iu hito⌐ 'a man who is named Tanaka'
zi⌐biki⌐ 'dictionary'	Kinoo katta. 'I bought [it] yesterday.'	ki⌐noo katta zibiki⌐ 'the dictionary I bought yesterday'
he⌐ya⌐ 'room'	Na⌐kanaka i⌐i. 'It's quite nice.'	na⌐kanaka i⌐i heya 'a room that's quite nice'
ho⌐ñ 'book'	Ma⌐e ni wa mu⌐zukasi⌐katta. 'It was difficult before.'	ma⌐e ni wa mu⌐zuka-si⌐katta ⌐ho⌐ñ 'a book that was difficult before'
to⌐koro⌐ 'place'	Asita ikitai. 'I want to go tomorrow.'	a⌐sita ikitai tokoro⌐ 'the place where I want to go tomorrow'
zassi 'magazine'	Da⌐re mo yo⌐ñde inai. 'No one is reading [it].'	da⌐re mo yo⌐ñde inai zassi 'a magazine no one is reading'
bi⌐ru 'building'	Ta⌐isi⌐kañ datta. 'It was the embassy.'	ta⌐isi⌐kañ datta ⌐bi⌐ru 'the building that was the embassy'

Note that there is no connecting particle between a modifying sentence and the modified nominal.

There are only two differences between an independent sentence and a sentence occurring as the modifier of a nominal, aside from the fact that the latter is almost invariably in the informal style:

(a) The informal non-past da at the end of an independent sentence has the form no or na when the same sentence modifies a nominal. The na alternant regularly occurs (1) if the following nominal is no 'one' or 'ones,' or (2) if the immediately preceding nominal belongs to the special group we designate as na words (cf. Lesson 12, Grammatical

Note (4). Otherwise, the <u>no</u> alternant regularly occurs.

In other words, <u>no</u> and <u>na</u> are special alternants of <u>da</u> which occur only at the end of a sentence which describes a nominal.

Examples:

Nominal:	modifed by the sentence:	equals:
he⌐ya⌐ 'room'	Rippa[1] da. 'It is magnif-icent.'	ri⌐ppa na heya⌐ 'a room which is magnificent,' 'a magnificent r o o m'
tomodati 'friend'	Su⌐ki⌐[1] da. 'I like [him].'	su⌐ki⌐ na tomodati 'a friend I like'
kodomo 'child'	Ge⌐ñki[1] da. 'He is healthy.'	ge⌐ñki na kodomo 'a child who is h e a l t h y,' 'a healthy child'
kodomo 'child'	Byooki da. 'He is sick.'	byooki no kodomo 'a child who is sick,' 'a sick child'
no 'one'	Byooki da. 'He is sick.'	byo⌐oki na⌐ no 'one who is sick'
musuko 'son'	Syasyoo da. 'He's a conductor.'	syasyoo no musuko 'my s o n who is a conduc-tor'[2]
Ta⌐roo 'Ta-ro'	Musuko da. 'He's my son.'	mu⌐suko no Ta⌐roo 'Taro who is my son,' 'my son Taro'
Siñtomi 'Shintomi'	Su⌐si⌐ya da. 'It's a sushi shop.'	su⌐si⌐ya no Siñtomi 'Shin-tomi which is a sushi shop,' 'the sushi shop "Shintomi"'

(b) The subject of a sentence occurring as a modifier of a nominal is fol-lowed by <u>ga</u> or <u>no</u>. <u>No</u> never follows the subject of an independent sen-tence.

---

[1] A <u>na</u>-nominal.

[2] This can also mean 'the conductor's son,' depending on context.

Examples:

Nominal:	modified by the sentence:	equals:
zi⌐do⌐osya 'car'	Tomodati ḡa katta. 'A friend bought [it].'	to⌐modati ḡa katta zido⌐o-sya or to⌐modati no katta zido⌐o-sya 'the car a friend bought'
kaisya 'com-pany'	Bo⌐ku ḡa tu⌐to⌐mete iru. 'I am employed.'	bo⌐ku ḡa tu⌐to⌐mete iru kaisya or bo⌐ku no tu⌐to⌐mete iru kaisya 'the company where I am employed'
ki⌐ssa⌐teñ 'tearoom'	Ko⌐ohi⌐i ḡa oisii. 'The cof-fee is good.'	ko⌐ohi⌐i ḡa o⌐isii kissa⌐-teñ or ko⌐ohi⌐i no o⌐isii kissa⌐-teñ 'a tearoom where the coffee is good,' 'a tea-room with good coffee'
hi⌐to⌐ 'man'	Mi⌐mi⌐ ḡa i⌐ta⌐i. '[His] ear hurts.'	mi⌐mi⌐ ḡa i⌐ta⌐i hito or mi⌐mi⌐ no i⌐ta⌐i hito 'the man whose ear hurts,' 'the man with an earache'

NOTE: Four different no's have now been introduced:

(a) the nominal meaning 'one,' 'ones'

   Example: a⌐ka⌐i no 'red one(s)'

(b) the copula—i.e. a special alternant of da

   Example: syasyoo no musuko 'my son who is a conductor'

(c) the particle meaning 'of,' 'pertaining to,' 'belonging to'

   Example: bo⌐ku no zassi 'my magazine'

(d) the particle which follows the subject of a sentence modifier

   Example: bo⌐ku no katta zassi 'the magazine I bought'

A nominal may be described by more than one modifier, any or all of which are sentence modifiers. (Modifiers of nominals which are not sentence modi-fiers are demonstratives—kono, sono, etc.—or phrases ending in particle no 'of,' 'pertaining to.') For example, in the following sequences, each modi-fier (underlined by an unbroken line) modifies the nominal at the end. In such sequences, the beginning of a new modifier is also the beginning of a new ac-cent phrase.

tu⌐kue no ue⌐ ni ⌐a⌐ru ku⌐ro⌐i ⌐ho⌐ñ 'the black book which is on top
of the desk'

watakusi g̱a karita Ta⌐naka-sañ no zibiki⌐ 'Mr. Tanaka's dictionary
which I borrowed'

kinoo katta so⌐no ho⌐ñ 'that book which I bought yesterday'

ke⌐sa ⌐mi⌐ta Si⌐buya ni a⌐ru o⌐oki⌐i uti 'the large house which is in
Shibuya, which I saw this morning'

Or, a nominal may be described by a modifier containing or consisting of a
word which is itself modified. For example, in the following sequences, the
first modifier modifies all or part of the second modifier, which, in turn,
modifies the nominal at the end of the sequence:

ta⌐isi⌐kañ ni tu⌐to⌐mete iru tomodati no ⌐ho⌐ñ

'a book belonging to a friend who works for the embassy'

ke⌐sa itta giñkoo ni tu⌐to⌐mete iru tomodati

'a friend who works for the bank where I went this morning'

ki⌐noo ki⌐ta tomodati no uti

'the home of the friend who came yesterday'

si⌐ñbuñ o yo⌐ñde iru hi⌐to⌐ g̱a ⌐no⌐ñde iru tabako

'the cigarette which the man who is reading the newspaper is smoking'

Note that while there are Japanese equivalents f o r English sequences like
'the man who ——,' 'the thing which ——,' 'the place where ——,' 'the time
when——,' etc., there are no Japanese equivalents for the words 'who,' 'which,'
'where,' 'when' in these sequences.

2.   to⌐ki⌐

To⌐ki⌐ [1] 'time,' 'occasion,' 'when' is a nominal and the patterns in which it
occurs are typical nominal patterns.

---

[1] Also occurs with a first-syllable accent and with no accent.

Sentence modifier + Nominal	Literally:	Normal equivalent:

Compare:

kinoo suteta zassi 'threw-away-yesterday magazine' 'the magazine I threw away yesterday'

with:

ki⌐noo suteta to⌐ki 'threw-away-yesterday time' 'when I threw [it] away yesterday'

Also:

Kyo⌐oto e iku tomodati 'go-to-Kyoto friend' 'a friend who's going to Kyoto'

with:

Kyo⌐oto e i⌐ku to⌐ki 'go-to-Kyoto time' 'when I go to Kyoto'

To⌐ki⌐ is one of the time words which occur both with and without following particle ni, indicating the time when something happens: cf. Lesson 8, Grammatical Note 4(b). Followed by particles ni + wa, it refers to repeated action— 'at times when——.' Thus:

> Ko⌐obe e i⌐tta toki⌐ [ni] to⌐modati no uti ni tomarima⌐sita.
> 'When I went to Kobe, I stopped at a friend's house.'
> Ko⌐obe e i⌐ku toki⌐ ni wa to⌐modati no uti ni tomarima⌐su.
> 'At times when I go to Kobe, I stop at a friend's house.'

Examples with other particles:

> Bo⌐ku ḡa i⌐tta toki⌐ wa ku̇ruma de go-⌐zikañ-ha⌐ñ ka⌐karima⌐sita ḡa—
> 'When I went (comparatively speaking), it took five and a half hours by car but [I don't know how long it takes now.]'
> Yamada Yu̇kio-sañ wa wa⌐takusi ḡa gakkoo e itte ita toki⌐ no to⌐modati de⌐su yo—
> 'You know, Yukio Yamada was a friend when (lit. is a friend of the time when) I was going to school.'
> Ko⌐domo no toki⌐ kara ⌐mi⌐ruku ḡa su⌐ki⌐ desu.
> 'I've liked milk since I was a child (lit. from child time).'
> Ga⌐kkoo o de⌐ta toki kara o⌐nazi kaisya ni tuto⌐mete imasu.
> 'I've been working for the same company from the time I left school.'

3.   Verbal Gerund + √mi⌐ru

A verbal gerund followed directly in the same accent phrase by √mi⌐ru means 'do so-and-so and see,' 'do so-and-so and find out,' 'try doing so-and-so.'

Examples:

Yuube sa⌐simi˥ o ⌐ta˥bete mi┌ma˥sita.
'I tried eating sashimi last night.'
Na˥ni ḡa ┌ha˥itte iru ka wa⌐kara˥nai kara, a⌐kete mimasyo˥o.
'I can't tell what's in it so let's open it and find out.'
Si⌐rana˥i kara, ki⌐ite mima˥su.
'I don't know so I'll ask and see.'

4. Counters : -<u>too</u>, -<u>ḡoo-sya</u>, -<u>bañ-señ</u>

-<u>Too</u> occurs with numerals of Series I to name classes as applied to train
and boat travel, theater seats, etc.

-<u>Ḡoo-sya</u> combines with the same series of numerals to name the passenger
cars of a train.

-<u>Bañ-señ</u> combines with the same series of numerals to name the tracks in
a station.

Study the following lists:

it-too	'1st class'	iti-bañ-señ	'track # 1'	i⌐ti-ḡo˥o-sya	'car # 1'
ni-too	' 2d class'	ni-bañ-señ	'track # 2'	ni-⌐ḡo˥o-sya	'car # 2'
sañ-too	'3d class'	sañ-bañ-señ	'track # 3'	sañ-ḡo˥o-sya	'car # 3'
[higher numbers		yoñ-bañ-señ	'track # 4'	yoñ-ḡo˥o-sya	'car # 4'
rare with this		go-bañ-señ	'track # 5'	go-⌐ḡo˥o-sya	'car # 5'
meaning]		roku-bañ-señ	'track # 6'	ro⌐ku-ḡo˥o-sya	'car # 6'
				si⌐ti-ḡo˥o-sya	
		nana-bañ-señ	'track # 7'	<u>or</u>	
				na⌐na-ḡo˥o-sya	'car # 7'
		hati-bañ-señ	'track # 8'	ha⌐ti-ḡo˥o-sya	'car # 8'
		kyuu-bañ-señ	'track # 9'	kyu⌐u-ḡo˥o-sya	'car # 9'
		zyuu-bañ-señ	'track # 10'	zyu⌐u-ḡo˥o-sya	'car # 10'
nañ-too		nañ-bañ-señ		na⌐ñ-ḡo˥o-sya	
'what class?'		'what track number?'		'car number what?'	

DRILLS

A. Substitution Drill

1. What track is [the train]   Kyooto-iki (wa) na⌐ñ-bañ-señ de˥su
    for Kyoto?   ka⌐

2. What track is [the train]   Yo˥-zi tyaku (wa) na⌐ñ-bañ-señ de˥-
    arriving at 4 o'clock?   su ka⌐

3. What track is [the train]   Yo˥-zi hatu (wa) na⌐ñ-bañ-señ de˥-
    leaving at 4 o'clock?   su ka⌐

4. What track is [the train]   Ko˥obe hatu (wa) na⌐ñ-bañ-señ de˥-
    from Kobe?   su ka⌐

5. What track is [the train] for Kobe?

Koobe-yuki (wa) na⌐n̄-bañ-señ de⌐su ka⌐

6. What track is the 7 o'clock up-train?

Si⌐ti⌐-zi no nōbori (wa) na⌐n̄-bañ-señ de⌐su ka⌐

7. What track is the 7 o'clock down-train?

Si⌐ti⌐-zi no kūdari (wa) na⌐n̄-bañ-señ de⌐su ka⌐

B. Substitution Drill

1. The special express Hato[1] will arrive late tonight.

To⌐kkyuu no Ha⌐to (wa) ⌐ko⌐n̄bañ o⌐soku tukima⌐su.

2. My son Taro will arrive late tonight.

Mu⌐suko no Ta⌐roo (wa) ⌐ko⌐n̄bañ o⌐soku tukima⌐su.

3. My (older) brother Yukio will arrive late tonight.

A⌐ni no Yukio (wa) ⌐ko⌐n̄bañ o⌐soku tukima⌐su.

4. My (younger) sister Haruko will arrive late tonight.

I⌐mooto no Ha⌐ruko (wa) ⌐ko⌐n̄bañ o⌐soku tukima⌐su.

5. My daughter Akiko will arrive late tonight.

Mu⌐sume no A⌐kiko (wa) ⌐ko⌐n̄bañ o⌐soku tukima⌐su.

6. My friend Mr. Tanaka will arrive late tonight.

Tomodati no Tanaka-sañ (wa) ⌐ko⌐n̄bañ o⌐soku tukima⌐su.

7. My Japanese friend will arrive late tonight.

Ni⌐hoñzi⌐n̄ no tomodati (wa) ⌐ko⌐n̄-bañ o⌐soku tukima⌐su.

8. My American teacher will arrive late tonight.

A⌐merika⌐ziñ no se⌐ñse⌐e (wa) ⌐ko⌐n̄bañ o⌐soku tukima⌐su.

C. Substitution Drill

1. Is the train that leaves at 11 o'clock an express?

Zyu⌐uiti⌐-zi ni ⌐de⌐ru ki⌐sya⌐ (wa) kyu⌐ukoo de⌐su ka⌐

2. Is the train that leaves late tonight an express?

Ko⌐n̄bañ o⌐soku ta⌐tu ki⌐sya⌐ (wa) kyu⌐ukoo de⌐su ka⌐

3. Is the train that stops at Shimbashi an express?

Si⌐ñbasi ni to⌐maru kisya⌐ (wa) kyu⌐ukoo de⌐su ka⌐

4. Is the train that you are going to take an express?

A⌐na⌐ta ḡa[2] no⌐ru kisya⌐ (wa) kyu-⌐ukoo de⌐su ka⌐

5. Is the train that you are waiting for an express?

A⌐na⌐ta ḡa[2] ⌐ma⌐tte (i)ru ki⌐sya⌐ (wa) kyu⌐ukoo de⌐su ka⌐

---

[1] I.e. 'the Hato which is a special express.'

[2] Or no.

6. Is the train that left at 9 o'clock an express?

Ku⌐-zi ni ⌐de⌐ta ki⌐sya⌐ (wa) kyu⌐u-koo de⌐su ka⌐

7. Is the train that is (arrived) on track #2 an express?

Ni-⌐bañ-señ ni tu⌐ite (i)ru ki⌐sya⌐ (wa) kyu⌐ukoo de⌐su ka⌐

8. Is the train that your friend is (riding) on an express?

O⌐tomodati ḡa¹ notte (i)ru kisya⌐ (wa) kyu⌐ukoo de⌐su ka⌐

9. Is the train that is (stopped) on track #4 an express?

Yo⌐ñ-bañ-señ ni tomatte (i)ru ki-sya⌐ (wa) kyu⌐ukoo de⌐su ka⌐

10. Is the train that your (older) brother just got on an express?

Ni⌐isañ ḡa¹ ⌐i⌐ma no⌐tta kisya⌐ (wa) kyu⌐ukoo de⌐su ka⌐

D. Substitution Drill

1. Is that (man) the man who wants to see Mr. Tanaka?

Ta⌐naka-sañ ni aita⌐i hito (wa) a⌐no⌐ hito desyoo ka.

2. Is that (man) the man whom Mr. Tanaka wants to see?

Ta⌐naka-sañ ḡa¹ aita⌐i hito (wa) a-⌐no⌐ hito desyoo ka.

3. Is that (man) the man whom the doctor wants to look at?

Se⌐ñse⌐e ḡa¹ mi⌐ta⌐i hito (wa) a⌐no⌐ hito desyoo ka.

4. Is that (man) the man who wants to have the doctor look at him?

Se⌐ñse⌐e ni ⌐mi⌐te moraitai hito (wa) a⌐no⌐ hito desyoo ka.

5. Is that (man) the man who wanted to go by taxi?

Ta⌐kusii de i⌐kita⌐katta hito (wa) a⌐no⌐ hito desyoo ka.

6. Is that (man) the man who doesn't want beer?

Bi⌐iru ḡa¹ i⌐ranai hito⌐ (wa) a⌐no⌐ hito desyoo ka.

7. Is that (man) the man who didn't say anything?

Na⌐ni mo iwana⌐katta hito (wa) a⌐no⌐ hito desyoo ka.

8. Is that (man) the man with the toothache?

Ha⌐ ḡa¹ i⌐ta⌐i hito (wa) a⌐no⌐ hito desyoo ka.

9. Is that (man) the man who isn't very good in Japanese?

Ni⌐hoñḡo ḡa¹ añmari zyoozu⌐ zya ⌐na⌐i hito (wa) a⌐no⌐ hito desyoo ka.

10. Is that (man) the man who doesn't have a car?

Ku⌐ruma ḡa¹ na⌐i hito (wa) a⌐no⌐ hito desyoo ka.

---

¹ Or no.

E. Substitution Drill

1. When I went to the bank this morning, I saw[1] Mr. Hamada.

Ke⌐sa gi⌐n̄koo e itta to⌐ki, Ha⌐mada-sañ ni a⌐ima⌐sita.

2. When I opened the door, I saw Mr. Hamada.

To ⌐(o) aketa to⌐ki, Ha⌐mada-sañ ni a⌐ima⌐sita.

3. When I bought a newspaper at the station, I saw Mr. Hamada.

E⌐ki de si⌐nbun (o) katta to⌐ki, Ha⌐mada-sañ ni a⌐ima⌐sita.

4. When I left the house, I saw Mr. Hamada.

U⌐ti (o) de⌐ta toki, Ha⌐mada-sañ ni a⌐ima⌐sita.

5. When I arrived at the station, I saw Mr. Hamada.

E⌐ki ni ⌐tu⌐ita toki, Ha⌐mada-sañ ni a⌐ima⌐sita.

6. When I went into the tearoom, I saw Mr. Hamada.

Ki⌐ssa⌐teñ ni ⌐ha⌐itta toki, Ha⌐mada-sañ ni a⌐ima⌐sita.

7. When I set out early this morning, I saw Mr. Hamada.

Ke⌐sa ⌐ha⌐yaku de⌐kaketa to⌐ki, Ha⌐mada-sañ ni a⌐ima⌐sita.

8. When I transferred at Shimbashi, I saw Mr. Hamada.

Si⌐n̄basi de no⌐rika⌐eta toki, Ha⌐mada-sañ ni a⌐ima⌐sita.

F. Grammar Drill (based on Grammatical Note 1)

Tutor: Ki⌐ree na hu⌐rosiki (o) kaima⌐sita. 'I bought a pretty furoshiki.'

Student: Ki⌐ree na no (o) ka⌐ima⌐sita. 'I bought a pretty one.'

1. Watakusi no i⌐tibañ suki⌐ na o̅sakana (wa) e⌐bi de⌐su.

Watakusi no i⌐tibañ suki⌐ na no (wa) e⌐bi de⌐su.

2. Byooki no kodomo (wa) ⌐Ta⌐roo desu.

Byo⌐oki na⌐ no (wa) ⌐Ta⌐roo desu.

3. Ta⌐naka-sañ no uti da⌐tta ta⌐te⌐mono (wa) ⌐i⌐ma ryo⌐kañ ni narima⌐sita.

Ta⌐naka-sañ no uti da⌐tta no (wa) ⌐i⌐ma ryo⌐kañ ni narima⌐sita.

4. Itibañ rippa na niwa (wa) ⌐Kyo⌐oto ni ⌐a⌐ru desyoo?

I⌐tibañ rippa na⌐ no (wa) ⌐Kyo⌐oto ni ⌐a⌐ru desyoo?

5. Nihoñg̅o g̅a i⌐tibañ zyoozu⌐ na hi⌐to⌐ (wa) ⌐Su⌐misu-sañ desyoo?

Nihoñg̅o g̅a i⌐tibañ zyoozu⌐ na no (wa) ⌐Su⌐misu-sañ desyoo?

---

[1] I.e. 'met up with.'

G. Grammar Drill (based on Grammatical Note 1)

> Tutor: Ke⌐sa ki⌐mase⌐n̄ desita. '[He] didn't come this morning.'
> Student: Ke⌐sa ⌐ko⌐nakatta hito (wa) ⌐da⌐re desu ka⌐ 'Who is the person who didn't come this morning?'

1. A⌐na⌐ta ḡa si⌐tte (i)ma⌐su.

A⌐na⌐ta no[1] si⌐tte (i)ru hito⌐ (wa) ⌐da⌐re desu ka⌐

2. A⌐na⌐ta o si⌐tte (i)ma⌐su.

A⌐na⌐ta o si⌐tte (i)ru hito⌐ (wa) ⌐da⌐re desu ka⌐

3. A⌐na⌐ta ni ki⌐ppu o aḡe-ma⌐sita.

A⌐na⌐ta ni ki⌐ppu o aḡeta hito⌐ (wa) ⌐da⌐re desu ka⌐

4. A⌐na⌐ta ni ki⌐ppu o morai-ma⌐sita.

A⌐na⌐ta ni ki⌐ppu o moratta hito⌐ (wa) ⌐da⌐re desu ka⌐

5. A⌐na⌐ta ḡa ⌐ma⌐tte (i)ma-su.

A⌐na⌐ta no[1] ⌐ma⌐tte (i)ru hi⌐to⌐ (wa) ⌐da⌐re desu ka⌐

6. A⌐na⌐ta ḡa a⌐ita⌐i desu.

A⌐na⌐ta no[1] a⌐ita⌐i hi⌐to⌐ (wa) ⌐da⌐re desu ka⌐

7. A⌐tama⌐ ḡa i⌐ta⌐i desu.

A⌐tama no[1] ita⌐i hi⌐to⌐ (wa) ⌐da⌐re desu ka⌐

8. Ko⌐domo ḡa arimase⌐n̄.

Ko⌐domo no[1] na⌐i hi⌐to⌐ (wa) ⌐da⌐re desu ka⌐

9. Byo⌐oki de⌐su.

Byo⌐oki no hito⌐ (wa) ⌐da⌐re desu ka⌐

10. O⌐sake ḡa kirai de⌐su.

O⌐sake no[1] kirai na hito⌐ (wa) ⌐da⌐re desu ka⌐

H. Grammar Drill (based on Grammatical Note 1)

> Tutor: A⌐no señse⌐e (wa) ni⌐hoñḡo o osiema⌐su. 'That teacher teaches Japanese.'
> Student: Ni⌐hoñḡo o osieru señse⌐e desu. 'He's a teacher who teaches Japanese.'

1. A⌐no kisya⌐ (wa) Yo⌐koha-ma o toorima⌐su.

Yo⌐kohama o to⌐oru ki⌐sya⌐ desu.

2. A⌐no ba⌐su (wa) Yo⌐koha-ma ni tomarima⌐su.

Yo⌐kohama ni tomaru ba⌐su desu.

3. A⌐no yama⌐ (wa) ko⌐ko kara miema⌐su.

Ko⌐ko kara mie⌐ru ya⌐ma⌐ desu.

4. A⌐no señse⌐e (wa) I⌐too to ossyaima⌐su.

I⌐too to ossya⌐ru se⌐ñse⌐e desu.

5. Ano kodomo (wa) ⌐mi⌐ruku o ko⌐bosima⌐sita.

Mi⌐ruku o ko⌐bo⌐sita ko⌐domo de⌐su.

6. Ano tomodati (wa) e⌐eḡo ḡa wakarimase⌐n̄.

E⌐eḡo no[1] wakara⌐nai to⌐modati de⌐su.

---

[1] Or ḡa.

7. Aˤno musume˥ (wa) byo-   Byoˤoki no musume˥ desu.
   ˤoki de˥su.

8. Ano Tanaka-sañ (wa)   Oˤhana no[1] zyoozu˥ na Taˤnaka-sañ
   oˤhana ḡa zyoozu˥ desu.   de˩su.

9. Ano kodomo (wa) miˤmi˥   Miˤmi no[1] ita˥i koˤdomo de˩su.
   ḡa iˤta˩i desu.

10. Aˤno˥ hito (wa) aˤtarasi˥i   Aˤtarasi˥i kuruma no[1] kaˤitai hito˩
   kuruma ḡa kaˤita˥i desu.   desu.

I. Grammar Drill (based on Grammatical Note 3)

      Tutor: Kiˤkimasyo˥o. 'Let's ask.'
      Student: Kiˤite mimasyo˥o. 'Let's try asking.' or 'Let's ask and
          see.' or 'Let's ask and find out.'

1. Niˤhoñḡo de iima˥sita.   Niˤhoñḡo de itte mima˥sita.

2. Aˤsita no a˥sa siˤmasyo˩o.   Aˤsita no a˥sa siˤte mimasyo˥o.

3. Haˤzi˥mete oˤsasimi (o) ta-   Haˤzi˥mete o̎sasimi (o) ˤta˥bete mi-
   bema˥sita.   ˤma˩sita.

4. Do˥ñna ˤho˩ñ ka waˤkari-   Do˥ñna ˤho˩ñ ka waˤkarimase˥ñ ḡa,
   mase˥ñ ḡa, yoˤmita˩i   yo˥ñde miˤta˩i desu.
   deṣu.

5. Daˤme˥ desu kara, miˤma-   Daˤme˥ desu kara, miˤte miˤma-
   syo˥o.   syo˩o.

6. Asita a̅no aˤtarasi˥i ha-   Asita a̅no aˤtarasi˥i haˤna˩ya e iˤtte
   ˤna˩ya e iˤkimasyo˥o.   mimasyo˥o.

7. Amerika no tabako (o)   Amerika no tabako (o) iˤti-do no˥ñ-
   iˤti-do nomita˥i ñ desu   de miˤta˩i ñ desu ḡa_
   ḡa_

8. Na˥ni ḡa ˤha˩itte iru ka   Na˥ni ḡa ˤha˩itte iru ka waˤkara˥-
   waˤkara˥nai kara, aˤke-   nai kara, aˤkete mimasyo˥o.
   masyo˥o.

J. Expansion Drill

1. Does it pass through?   Toˤorima˥su ka↲
   Does it pass in front?   Maˤe o toˤorima˩su ka↲
   Does it pass in front of   Taˤisi˥kañ no ˤma˩e o toˤorima˩su
    the embassy?   ka↲
   Which bus passes in front   Do˥no ˤba˩su ḡa taˤisi˥kañ no ˤma˩e
    of the embassy?   o toˤorima˩su ka↲

2. It's a number.   Baˤñḡo˥o desu.
   It's the seat number.   Seˤki no baˤñḡo˩o desu.

The thing (lit. one) which is written is the seat number.   Ka⌐ite ⌐a⌐ru no wa ⌐se⌐ki no ba⌐ñ-ḡo⌐o desu.

The thing which is written here is the seat number.   Ko⌐ko ni ka⌐ite ⌐a⌐ru no wa ⌐se⌐ki no ba⌐ñḡo⌐o desu.

3. How was it?   Do⌐o desita ka﹃

How was the inn?   Ryokañ wa ⌐do⌐o desita ka﹃

How was the inn in Kyoto?   Kyo⌐oto no ryokañ wa ⌐do⌐o desita ka﹃

How was the inn in Kyoto where you stopped?   A⌐na⌐ta ḡa tomatta ⌐Kyo⌐oto no ryokañ wa ⌐do⌐o desita ka﹃

4. He's a friend.   To⌐modati de⌐su.

He's a friend who is employed.   Tu⌐to⌐mete (i)ru to⌐modati de⌐su.

He's a friend who is working for a bank.   Gi⌐ñkoo ni tuto⌐mete (i)ru to⌐modati de⌐su.

He's a friend who is working for the bank [I] went to this morning.   Ke⌐sa itta giñkoo ni tu⌐to⌐mete (i)ru to⌐modati de⌐su.

He's a friend who is working for the bank I went to this morning.   Watakusi ḡa ⌐ke⌐sa itta giñkoo ni tu⌐to⌐mete (i)ru to⌐modati de⌐su.

5. It's new, isn't it?   A⌐tarasi⌐i desyoo?

It's newer than the one [you]'re reading, isn't it?   Yo⌐ñde (i)⌐ru⌐ no yori a⌐tarasi⌐i desyoo?

It's newer than the one you're reading, isn't it?   A⌐na⌐ta ḡa ⌐yo⌐ñde (i)⌐ru⌐ no yori a⌐tarasi⌐i desyoo?

The magazine on the table is newer than the one you're reading, isn't it?   Te⌐eburu ni a⌐ru zassi wa a⌐na⌐ta ḡa ⌐yo⌐ñde (i)⌐ru⌐ no yori a⌐tarasi⌐i desyoo?

The magazine on the dining room table is newer than the one you're reading, isn't it?   Syo⌐kudoo no teeburu ni a⌐ru zassi wa a⌐na⌐ta ḡa ⌐yo⌐ñde (i)⌐ru⌐ no yori a⌐tarasi⌐i desyoo?

6. I arrived.   Tu⌐kima⌐sita.

I arrived on time.   Zi⌐kañ-do⌐ori [ni] tu⌐kima⌐sita.

[He] gave me a ride so I arrived on time.   No⌐sete kurema⌐sita kara, zi⌐kañ-do⌐ori [ni] tu⌐kima⌐sita.

[He] gave me a ride in his car so I arrived on time.   Zi⌐do⌐osya ni no⌐sete kurema⌐sita kara, zi⌐kañ-do⌐ori [ni] tu⌐kima⌐sita.

A friend gave me a ride
in his car so I arrived
on time.

Tomodati ḡa zi⌐do⌐osya ni no⌐sete
kurema⌐sita kara, zi⌐kañ-do⌐ori
[ni] tu⌐kima⌐sita.

I was late for the bus, but
a friend gave me a ride
in his car so I arrived
on time.

Ba⌐su ni o⌐kurema⌐sita ḡa; tomodati ḡa zi⌐do⌐osya ni no⌐sete ku-
rema⌐sita kara, zi⌐kañ-do⌐ori
[ni] tu⌐kima⌐sita.

I was late for the 8
o'clock bus but a friend
gave me a ride in his
car so I arrived on
time.

Ha⌐ti⌐-zi no ⌐ba⌐su ni o⌐kurema⌐-
sita ḡa; tomodati ḡa zi⌐do⌐osya
ni no⌐sete kurema⌐sita kara, zi-
⌐kañ-do⌐ori [ni] tu⌐kima⌐sita.

7. It's Haruo.
    It's Haruo Yamamoto.
    [My] friend is Haruo Ya-
      mamoto.

Ha⌐ruo-sañ de⌐su.
Yamamoto Ha⌐ruo-sañ de⌐su.
Tomodati wa Yāmamoto Ha⌐ruo-
sañ de⌐su.

    My friend is Haruo Ya-
      mamoto.

Boku no tomodati wa Yāmamoto
Ha⌐ruo-sañ de⌐su.

    There are two people,
      but my friend is Haruo
      Yamamoto.

Hu⌐tari ima⌐su ḡa, boku no tomodati wa Yāmamoto Ha⌐ruo-sañ
de⌐su.

    There are two people
      named Yamamoto, but
      my friend is Haruo Ya-
      mamoto.

Ya⌐mamoto to iu hito⌐ ḡa hu⌐tari
ima⌐su ḡa, boku no tomodati wa
Yāmamoto Ha⌐ruo-sañ de⌐su.

    In this company there are
      two people named Yama-
      moto, but my friend is
      Haruo Yamamoto.

Ko⌐no kaisya ni⌐ wa Ya⌐mamoto to
iu hito⌐ ḡa hu⌐tari ima⌐su ḡa, boku no tomodati wa Yāmamoto
Ha⌐ruo-sañ de⌐su.

8. I've forgotten.
    The name I've forgotten.
    I stopped [there] but I've
      forgotten the name.

Wa⌐surema⌐sita.
Na⌐mae wa wasurema⌐sita.
To⌐marima⌐sita ḡa, na⌐mae wa wa-
surema⌐sita.

    I stopped at an inn but
      I've forgotten the name.

Ryo⌐kañ ni tomarima⌐sita ḡa, na-
⌐mae wa wasurema⌐sita.

    I stopped at a pleasant inn
      but I've forgotten the
      name.

Ki⌐moti no i⌐i ryo⌐kañ ni tomari-
ma⌐sita ḡa, na⌐mae wa wasure-
ma⌐sita.

    I stopped at a pretty, pleas-
      ant inn, but I've forgotten
      the name.

Ki⌐ree na ki⌐moti no i⌐i ryo⌐kañ ni
tomarima⌐sita ḡa, na⌐mae wa wa-
surema⌐sita.

    When I went [there], I
      stopped at a pretty, pleas-
      ant inn, but I've forgotten
      the name.

I⌐tta to⌐ki [ni], ki⌐ree na ki⌐moti no
i⌐i ryo⌐kañ ni tomarima⌐sita ḡa;
na⌐mae wa wasurema⌐sita.

    When I went to Kyoto, I
      stopped at a pretty, pleas-
      ant inn, but I've forgotten
      the name.

Kyo⌐oto e i⌐tta to⌐ki [ni], ki⌐ree na
ki⌐moti no i⌐i ryo⌐kañ ni tomari-
ma⌐sita ḡa; na⌐mae wa wasurema⌐-
sita.

QUESTION SUPPLEMENT

1. A⌐sa ta⌐be¬ru ⌐go¬hañ wa ⌐na¬ñ to i⌐ima¬su ka⌐
2. Kyuukoo no kippu wa ⌐na¬ñ to i⌐ima¬su ka⌐
3. Ho⌐ñ o oku tana wa ⌐na¬ñ to i⌐ima¬su ka⌐
4. To⌐okyoo no ho¬o e i⌐ku kisya¬ wa miñna ⌐na¬ñ to i⌐ima¬su ka⌐
5. To⌐kubetu ni haya¬i kyuukoo wa ⌐na¬ñ to i⌐ima¬su ka⌐
6. Nobori no hañtai wa ⌐na¬ñ desu ka⌐
7. Byo⌐oki no hito¬ ḡa ta⌐kusañ ha¬itte iru ta⌐te¬mono wa ⌐na¬ñ to i⌐ima¬su
    ka⌐
8. Ta⌐tami no na¬i ta⌐be¬ru he⌐ya¬ wa ⌐na¬ñ to i⌐ima¬su ka⌐
9. Te¬ ḡa ki⌐tana¬ku ⌐na¬tta to⌐ki¬ ni wa ⌐na¬ñ de a⌐raima¬su ka⌐
10. Zi⌐do¬osya ḡa ko⌐syoo-sita toki¬ ni wa ⌐do¬o simasu ka⌐
11. De⌐ñwaba¬ñḡoo o si⌐ranai toki¬ ni wa ⌐na¬ni o mi⌐ma¬su ka⌐
12. Zi⌐kañ ḡa wakara¬nai to⌐ki¬ ni wa ⌐na¬ni o mi⌐ma¬su ka⌐
13. I⌐tibañ taka¬i kippu wa na⌐ñ-too no¬ desu ka⌐
14. Ue no hañtai wa ⌐na¬ñ desu ka⌐
15. Ho¬ñ ḡa ka⌐itai toki¬ ni wa ⌐do¬ñna mi⌐se¬ e i⌐kima¬su ka⌐

EXERCISES

1. Making any changes necessary, use each of the following sentences within
    a longer sentence, as a modifier of a nominal, and translate the completed
    sentence into English.

    (Example: A⌐soko ni arima¬su. 'It's over there.'
     Answer: A⌐soko ni a¬ru zi⌐biki¬ wa wa⌐takusi no¬ desu.
                'The dictionary that's over there is mine.')

    a. Mi¬ruku o ko⌐bosima¬sita.
    b. Ni⌐hoñḡo ḡa zyoozu¬ desu.
    c. Gi⌐ñkoo ni tuto¬mete (i)rassyaimasu.
    d. Ha¬ ḡa i⌐ta¬i desu.
    e. To⌐modati de¬su.
    f. Wa⌐karimase¬ñ desita.
    g. Wa⌐takusi ḡa kakima¬sita.
    h. Ryo⌐ozi¬kañ desita.
    i. Si⌐rimase¬ñ.
    j. Si⌐ñbuñ o yo¬ñde (i)masu.
    k. A⌐soko ni simatte arima¬su.
    l. Zu⌐ibuñ ta⌐ka¬i desu.
    m. E¬ki no ⌐ma¬e o to⌐orima¬su.
    n. Ko⌐ohi¬i ḡa no⌐mita¬i desu.
    o. Si⌐ta no musume¬ desu.
    p. Kyo¬oto e i⌐kima¬sita.
    q. I⌐ro¬ ḡa ⌐ki¬ree desu.

2. Express the following in Japanese.

    a. Buy the following tickets:

        (1) One second-class for Kyoto.
        (2) Two first-class for Yokohama, round trip.
        (3) One first-class for Osaka.
        (4) One second-class round trip for Nikko.

    b. Ask at the information booth:

        (1) when the next train for Yokohama leaves.
        (2) if you need an express ticket.
        (3) if the 8 o'clock train for Nagoya has already left.
        (4) if the 5 o'clock train from Nikko has arrived yet.
        (5) what track the Yokohama trains leave from.
        (6) if the Hato will be on time.

    c. Ask the conductor:

        (1) if the train stops at Shimbashi.
        (2) whether the train has a diner.
        (3) what time you arrive at Tokyo Station.
        (4) where the sleeping cars are.
        (5) where car # 3 is.
        (6) where seat # 4 is.

    d. Tell Mr. Tanaka that:

        (1) you went from Tokyo to Osaka by train and returned by plane.
        (2) you went from Tokyo to Numazu by electric train and from there to Mito by boat.
        (3) you came from New York to San Francisco by train and from San Francisco to Japan by plane.
        (4) you came from Yokohama to Shimbashi by electric car and from there to the office by taxi.

3. Using a local timetable, take turns asking and answering the following kinds of questions in Japanese:

    a. What time does the train that leaves (place) at (time) arrive at (place)?
    b. What time does the train that arrives at (place) at (time) leave (place)?
    c. Does the train for (place) that leaves (place) at (time) stop at (place)?
    d. How long does it take from (place) to (place) on the train that leaves (place) at (time)?

4. Practice the Basic Dialogues with appropriate variations.

Lesson 20. Transportation (cont.)

BASIC DIALOGUES: FOR MEMORIZATION

(a)

(At the station)

Smith

baggage <u>or</u> things to
carry
is heavy

1. This baggage is terribly
heavy, isn't it!

ni⌐motu <u>or</u>
o⌐ni⌐motu ˥
omoi /-ku/
Ko⌐no ni⌐motu (wa) ⌐zu⌐ibuñ o⌐mo⌐i
desu ⌐ne⌐e.

Tanaka

porter <u>or</u> redcap
engage
come having engaged
<u>or</u> go and engage

2. Shall I go and get a porter?

akaboo
ta⌐no⌐mu /-u/
ta⌐no⌐ñde ⌐ku⌐ru
A⌐kaboo (o) tano⌐ñde ki⌐masyo⌐o ka.

Smith

3. Yes, please (go and engage).

E⌐e ta⌐no⌐ñde ki⌐te⌐ kudasai.

(b)

(At the information booth)

Smith

put into someone else's
keeping temporarily
<u>or</u> check
place where one checks

4. I'd like to check my baggage.
Where is the checking place?

a⌐zuke⌐ru /-ru/

a⌐zuke⌐ru toko(ro)
Ni⌐motu (o) a⌐zuketa⌐i ñ desu ḡa,
a⌐zuke⌐ru to⌐ko(ro)⌐ (wa) ⌐do⌐ko
desu ka⌐

Clerk

waiting room

5. It's to the right of the waiting
room.

ma⌐tia⌐isitu
Ma⌐tia⌐isitu no mi⌐ḡi no ho⌐o desu.

(c)

(Smith and Tanaka are on the platform after getting off a train)

Smith

subway

6. Shall we take the subway?

tikatetu
Ti⌐katetu ni norimasyo⌐o ka.

364

Tanaka

even though it is fast (or early) or it is fast (or early) but	ha⌐ya⌐i keredo
become crowded	ko⌐mu /-u/
be crowded	ko⌐ñde (i)ru

7. The subway is fast but it's always crowded so let's go by taxi.

Ti⌐katetu wa haya⌐i keredo; i⌐tu mo ⌐ko⌐ñde (i)ru kara, ta⌐kusii de i⌐ki-masyo⌐o.

Smith

is near	ti⌐ka⌐i /-ku/
place for boarding vehicles	noriba

8. [Where is] the nearest stand? (Lit. As for the nearest boarding place?)

I⌐tibañ tika⌐i noriba wa?

Tanaka

exit	de⌐ḡuti
one unit of wheeled vehicles	i⌐ti⌐-dai
two or three units of vehicles	ni-sañ-dai
[something] lines up	narabu /-u/
even though they are lined up or they are lined up but	na⌐rañde (i)ma⌐su keredo

9. Usually two or three [taxis] are lined up at the exit (but . . .)

Taitee ⌐de⌐ḡuti ni ni-⌐sañ-dai na-rañde (i)ma⌐su keredo_

Smith

10. Well, let's go and see.

Zya⌐a, i⌐tte mimasyo⌐o.

(d)

(At home)

Husband

intention or plan	tumori
intention of going or a plan to go	iku tumori

11. How do you plan to go? (Lit. A plan of going by what?)

Na⌐ñ de iku tumori?

Wife

(section of Tokyo)	Sibuya
go by riding or ride	notte (i)ku
to a place go by transferring	no⌐rika⌐ete (i)ku

             even though it is the plan   no⌐rika⌐ete (i)┗ku tumori da┑
               to go by transferring   kedo
             <u>or</u> it is the plan to go
               by transferring but
12. I plan to ride as far as Shi-   Si⌐buya ma⌐de ⌐ba⌐su ni notte (i)t-
     buya on the bus and transfer   te, [1] asuko de ti⌐katetu ni norika⌐-
     (lit. go by transferring) to   ete (i)┗ku tumori da┑ kedo⌣
     the subway there (but. . .)

                              Husband

             go down <u>or</u> descend   o⌐ri⌐ru /-ru/
             <u>or</u> get off (a vehicle)
13. Where will you get off? (Lit.   O⌐ri⌐ru toko wa?
     As for the place where you
     get off?)

                               Wife

             (section of Tokyo)   Toranomoñ
14. Toranomon.   Toranomoñ yo⌣

                              Husband

15. And from there?   So⌐ko kara⌐ wa?

                               Wife

             walk   a⌐ru⌐ku /-u/
             go by walking <u>or</u>   a⌐ru⌐ite (i)ku
             walk to a place
16. I'll walk—since it's   A⌐ru⌐ite (i)ku wa⌣ — ti┗ka┑i kara.
     close.

                              Husband

             come having gone <u>or</u>   i⌐tte ku⌐ru <u>or</u>
             go and come   i⌐tte ma⌐iru↑ <u>or</u>
                                                  i⌐tte (i)rassya⌐ru↑
17. Well, goodbye (lit. go and   Zya⌐a, i⌐tte (i)rassya⌐i.
     come)!

                               Wife

18. Goodbye. (Lit. I'll go and   I⌐tte mairima⌐su.
     come.)
                                  . . .

                        Wife (returning)

19. Hello! <u>or</u> I'm back!   Tadaima.

----

[1] Accent of contracted alternant: no┗tte┑ tte.

Husband

20. Hello!   Oᒥkaeri(-nasaᒣi).

(e)

Smith

gasoline	gasoriñ
one liter	iᒥti-riᒣttoru
one or two liters	iᒥti-ni-riᒣttoru
be(come) left (over)	noᒥkoᒣru /-u/
or be(come) left behind	
even though they're left (over) or they're left (over) but	noᒥkoᒣtte (i)ru keredo
airport	hikoozyoo
it will be better to have put in (for future use) or [I]'d better put in (for future use)	iᒥret(e) oᒣita hoo ḡa ᒥiᒣi

21. Even though there are still
     one or two liters of gasoline
     left, since we're going as
     far as the airport, it would
     probably be better to put
     [some] in now (for future
     use), wouldn't it.

Gasoriñ (ḡa) ᒥmaᒣda iᒥti-ni-riᒣttoru
noᒥkoᒣtte (i)ru keredo; hiᒥkoozyoo
maᒣde iᒥkuᒣ kara, iᒣma iᒥret(e) oᒣ-
ita hoo ḡa ᒥiᒣi desyoo ᒥneᒣe.

Tanaka

bridge	haᒥsiᒣ
go over or go across	wataru /-u/
intersection	yotukado
gasoline station	gaᒥsoriñsutaᒣñdo

22. Yes. You go over that bridge,
     and there's a big gas station
     at the next intersection.

Eᒣe. Aᒥno hasiᒣ (o) watatte, tuᒥgiᒣ
no yōtukado ni oᒥokiᒣi gaᒥsoriñ-
sutaᒣñdo (ḡa) aᒥrimaᒣsu yo⌐

. . .

(At the gas station)

Attendant

how many liters?	naᒥñ-riᒣttoru

23. How many (liters)?   Naᒥñ-riᒣttoru desu ka⌐

Smith

full	ippai
fill [something] (lit. make full)	ippai ni suru

24. Fill it up.   Iᒥppai ni site kudasaᒣi.

oil	oᒣiru
tire	taiya

air   ku⌐uki
be sufficient   tariru /-ru/
enough   zyu⌐ubu⌐ñ /na/

25. Look at the oil, too, and   O⌐iru mo ⌐mi⌐te; sore kara, ma⌐e
     then there's too little air   no taiya no ⌐ku⌐uki (g̃a) ta⌐rina⌐i
     in the front tires so put in   kara, zyu⌐ubu⌐ñ /ni/ irete.
     the right amount (lit. air
     of the front tires is insuf-
     ficient so put it in suffi-
     ciently).

(f)

Tanaka

26. I'm sorry you were kept   O⌐matidoosama de⌐sita.
     waiting.

         become punctured   pañku-suru
         become completely flat   pañku-site simau or
                                                pañku-sityau
27. I'm late because I had a   Ta⌐iya (g̃a) pañku-sityatta⌐ kara,
     flat.   o⌐soku narima⌐sita.

Smith

         awful or dreadful or   taiheñ /-na/
             terrible or a nuisance
28. Don't mention it. What a nui-   Do⌐o itasimasite. Ta⌐iheñ da⌐tta
     sance it must have been!   desyoo?
     (Lit. It was a nuisance, was-
     n't it?)

         oneself   zibuñ or
                                                gozibuñ↑
         by oneself   zibuñ de
         exchange   torikaeru /-ru/
29. Did you change [it] your-   Go⌐zibuñ de torikaema⌐sita ka↵
     self?

Tanaka

         garage   ga⌐re⌐ezi
30. No, I had [it] changed at a   Iie, su⌐g̃u ⌐so⌐ba no ga⌐re⌐ezi de
     garage right nearby.   to⌐rikaete moraima⌐sita yo.

(g)

Smith

         even though there   na⌐i keredo
             isn't or there
             isn't but
         brakes   bu⌐re⌐eki
         condition   guai
         is funny   o⌐kasi⌐i /-ku/

> look into <u>or</u> check
> <u>or</u> investigate

si⌐rabe⌐ru /-ru/

> it will be better to have
> had [them] checked
> <u>or</u> [I] should have
> [them] checked

si⌐ra⌐bete mo⌐ratta ho⌐o ḡa ⌐i⌐i

31. Even though we don't have very much time, there's something funny about the brakes (lit. the condition of the brakes has become funny) so I guess I should have them checked right away, shouldn't I.

Zi⌐kañ (ḡa) añmari na⌐i keredo; bu⌐re⌐eki no guai (ḡa) o⌐ka⌐siku ⌐na⌐tta kara, ha⌐yaku si⌐ra⌐bete mo⌐ratta ho⌐o ḡa ⌐i⌐i desyoo ⌐ne⌐e.

Tanaka

> important

taisetu /na/

32. Yes. You'd better do it quickly (lit. the fast alternative is good)—because brakes are important.

E⌐e, ha⌐ya⌐i hoo ḡa ⌐i⌐i desu yo⌐ —bu⌐re⌐eki wa ta⌐isetu da⌐ kara.

(At the garage)

Attendant

> go around

mawaru /-u/

33. Brakes? I'm sorry but please go around toward the back. [That's] because this (place) is just [for] gas and oil and things like that.

Bu⌐re⌐eki desu ka⌐ Su⌐mimase⌐ñ ḡa, u⌐siro no ho⌐o e ma⌐watte kudasa⌐i. Kotira wa ga⌐soriñ ya o⌐i-ru da⌐ke⌐ desu kara.

NOTES ON THE BASIC DIALOGUES

1. The opposite of <u>omoi</u> is <u>karui</u> /-ku/ 'is light (i.e. not heavy).'

2. Note: hi⌐to⌐ o ta⌐no⌐mu 'engage a person,' 'retain a person'; mo⌐no⌐ o ta-⌐no⌐mu 'order or request a thing'; hi⌐to⌐ ni ta⌐no⌐mu 'order or request from a person.'

4. Note also: a⌐zuka⌐ru 'receive in custody,' 'take charge of,' 'keep.'

9. 'but—I don't know whether or not there are any there now.'

The opposite of de⌐ḡuti is <u>iriḡuti</u> 'entrance.'

<u>Narabu</u> is the intransitive partner of transitive <u>naraberu</u> /-ru/ 'line [things or people] up'

12. 'but—do you think that's all right?'

13. Note: <u>X o o⌐ri⌐ru</u> (or, less commonly, <u>X kara o⌐ri⌐ru</u>) 'go down from <u>X</u>'
     or 'get off <u>X</u>.' (For particle <u>o</u>, see Lesson 7, Grammatical Note 3.) <u>O⌐ri⌐-
     ru</u> is the intransitive partner of transitive <u>o⌐ro⌐su</u> /-<u>u</u>/ 'lower' or 'let
     down' or 'discharge (a passenger).'

17. I⌐tte irassya⌐i is the farewell regularly said by the person remaining be-
     hind, to someone leaving his own home (or, in some circumstances, his
     office, his town, city, or country, etc.).   <u>Sayonara</u> is not used in this
     situation.   I⌐rassya⌐i (formal women's form, i⌐rassyaima⌐se) is the im-
     perative of i⌐rassya⌐ru.

18. I⌐tte mairima⌐su, or a less polite equivalent, is the farewell regularly
     said by someone leaving his home, to the person remaining behind. It is
     the reply to Sentence 17, preceding. Men regularly use i⌐tte kima⌐su or
     i⌐tte ku⌐ru.

19. <u>T̲adaima</u>, lit. 'just now'—i.e. '[I've] just now [returned],' is the greeting
     regularly said by someone returning home.

20. O⌐kaeri(-nasa⌐i), an imperative of <u>ka⌐eru</u> 'return home,' is the greeting
     regularly said to someone who has just returned home.   It is the reply to
     Sentence 19, preceding. The formal women's form is o⌐kaeri-nasaima⌐se.

21. No⌐ko⌐ru is the intransitive partner of transitive <u>no⌐ko⌐su</u> /-<u>u</u>/ 'leave be-
     hind,' 'leave over (for another time).'

22. For particle <u>o</u>, see Lesson 7, Grammatical Note 3.

     <u>Wataru</u> is the intransitive partner of <u>watasu</u> /-<u>u</u>/ 'hand over.'

     <u>Y̲otukado</u> is an intersection of two streets forming four corners.

24. <u>Ippai</u> is a nominal: <u>ippai da</u> '[it] is full'; i⌐ppai zya na⌐i '[it] is not full';
     i⌐ppai ni na⌐ru 'become full'; <u>ippai ni suru</u> 'fill' (lit. 'make full'). It oc-
     curs without a following particle as an expression of manner: <u>ippai ireru</u>
     'fill up' (lit. 'insert fully').   The opposite of <u>ippai</u> is ka⌐ra⌐ 'empty,' also
     a nominal.

25. In expressions of manner, zyu⌐ubu⌐n̄ occurs both with and without particle
     <u>ni</u>.

26. O⌐matidoosama (de⌐sita) is used in the same kinds of situations as
     o⌐matase-itasima⌐sita, but the latter is more polite.

28. Some other English equivalents of <u>taihen̄ da</u> are: 'Good heavens!' 'Good
     night!' 'What a mess!' 'What a fix to be in!' <u>Taihen̄</u> also occurs without
     a following particle as an expression of manner, meaning 'awfully,'
     'very,' 'terribly.'

29. Compare: <u>zibun̄ de</u> 'by oneself—i.e. by one's own power or ability' and
     hi⌐to⌐-ri de 'by oneself—i.e. unaccompanied.' <u>Zibun̄</u> also occurs followed
     by particle <u>no</u>, meaning 'one's own.'

     Note: <u>X o Y to torikaeru</u> 'exchange <u>X</u> for (lit. with) <u>Y</u>.'

30. Ga⌐re⌐ezi usually refers to a garage where cars are repaired. Garages
     attached to homes for private cars are rare in Japan.

31. Many of the Japanese words for parts of a car are, like <u>bu⌐re⌐eki</u> and

taiya, loan-words from English. Thus: e⌐ñziñ 'engine,' ho⌐oñ 'horn,' ba⌐tterii 'battery,' kya⌐burettaa 'carburetor,' etc.

Note: gu⌐ai ḡa i⌐i 'be in good condition' or 'be fine' or 'be in good health'; gu⌐ai ḡa waru⌐i 'be in bad condition' or 'be out of order' or 'feel unwell' or 'be sick.'

O⌐kasi⌐i, like 'funny' in English, means either 'strange' or 'amusing.'

33. Mawaru is the intransitive partner of transitive mawasu /-u/ 'send around.'

GRAMMATICAL NOTES

1. Gerunds of Condition and Manner; Errands

(Reread Lesson 15, Grammatical Note 5.)

A verbal gerund, by itself or at the end of a sequence, may occur as the modifier of another verbal, an adjectival, or a phrase ending in √da. In one such pattern, the gerund (or sequence ending in the gerund) asks or answers the question 'how?' or 'in what condition?' For example, in ti⌐katetu ni notte kima⌐sita 'I rode here on the subway' (lit. 'I came by riding on the subway'), tikatetu ni notte describes ki⌐ma⌐sita and tells how I came.

In this pattern, the action or state represented by the gerund may precede or be simultaneous with that represented by the inflected expression it modifies.

The gerund does not always immediately precede the word or phrase it modifies.

Examples:

A⌐ru⌐ite i⌐kima⌐sita. 'I walked (to a specific place)'— lit. 'I went by walking.'

O⌐kurete tukima⌐sita. 'I arrived late.'

Ki⌐otuke⌐te o⌐sara o aratte kudasa⌐i. 'Please wash the dishes carefully.'

I⌐so⌐ide ikitai. 'I want to go in a hurry.' (informal style)

I⌐so⌐ide u⌐ti e kaerita⌐i ñ desu ḡa_ 'I'd like to go home in a hurry. . . .'

Na⌐ñ ni notte Yo⌐kosuka e ikima⌐sita ka_ 'How (lit. riding on what) did you go to Yokosuka?'

This pattern also covers errand situations in Japanese— situations involving going somewhere, doing something, and coming back. In such cases, √ku⌐ru (or a more polite equivalent) follows the appropriate gerund of doing, and the first step— the going— is usually not mentioned. (Compare English, which normally omits mentioning the last step— the coming back.) Thus, the Japanese equivalent of 'go and buy' is ka⌐tte ku⌐ru 'buy and come,' 'come having bought.'

Examples:

Si⌐ñbuñ o katte kima⌐su. 'I'll go and buy a paper.' (Lit. 'I'll come having bought a paper.')

Ki⌐ite kimasyo⌐o⌐ka. 'Shall I go and ask?' (Lit. 'Shall I come having asked?')

De⌐ñwatyoo o sira⌐bete mairimasu. 'I'll go and check the phone book.' (Lit. 'I'll come having checked the phone book.')

Actually, most uses of the gerund introduced thus far are covered by the statement at the beginning of this note. For example:

(a) a⌐ru⌐ku + ku⌐dasa⌐i > a⌐ru⌐ite kudasai 'please walk'
(b) a⌐ru⌐ku + iru > a⌐ru⌐ite iru '[I] am walking'
(c) a⌐ru⌐ku + ka⌐eru > a⌐ru⌐ite ⌐ka⌐eru '[I] will walk home'
(d) sañpo-suru + ka⌐eru > sañpo-site, ka⌐eru '[I] will take a walk, and then go home'

In patterns (a) and (b) only, the gerund is always immediately followed in the same accent phrase by the inflected word it modifies.

Patterns (c) and (d) are distinguished by intonation: in pattern (d),[1] the gerund usually ends with comma intonation and the word following the gerund starts a new accent phrase.

2. keredo 'even though'

Keredo 'even though' or 'although' is a particle which follows verbals, adjectivals, and √da, non-past, past, and tentative. When it occurs in the middle of a sentence, it regularly ends with comma intonation. If the final inflected form in the sentence is informal, only the informal occurs before medial keredo; otherwise it may be preceded by formal or informal forms. Before keredo, an unaccented verbal or copula expression regularly acquires an accent on its final syllable and an unaccented adjectival on its pre-final syllable.

Examples:

Mo⌐o wa⌐ka⌐tta (or wa⌐karima⌐sita) keredo, mo⌐o iti-do itte kudasaimase⌐ñ ka⌐ 'Even though I've already understood, would you please say it again?'

A⌐tu⌐i (desu) keredo, ma⌐do wa a⌐ketaku arimase⌐ñ. 'Even though it's hot, I don't want to open the window.'

Ki⌐ree da keredo, a⌐ñmari oisiku na⌐i. 'Even though it's pretty, it's not very tasty.'

Da⌐izyo⌐obu da⌐tta desyo⌐o keredo, ta⌐bemase⌐ñ desita. 'Even though it was probably safe, I didn't eat it.'

---

[1] Described in Lesson 7, Grammatical Note 5.

Like g̱a, keredo within a sentence implies contrast or is simply a clause connective (cf. Lesson 4, Note 1); but as an indication of contrast, medial ke-redo is a slightly stronger 'but.' Thus:

> Yo⌐mima⌐sita g̱a, mo⌐o wa⌐surema⌐sita. 'I read it but I've forgotten it already.'
>
> Yo⌐ñda keredo, mo⌐o wa⌐surema⌐sita. 'Even though I read it, I've forgotten it already.'

Kedo is a less formal, contracted equivalent of keredo; there is also a more formal equivalent, keredomo.

The use of keredo and kedo in sentence-final position closely resembles that of sentence-final g̱a. Thus:

> Ikitai ñ desu ḡa_ ⎫
> Ikitai ñ desu keredo_ ⎬ 'I'd like to go but. . . .'
> Ikitai ñ desu kedo_ ⎭

Note that whereas an informal inflected form before g̱a occurs only in men's informal speech, informal forms before keredo occur in formal and informal speech of men and women.

3. tumori 'intention'

Tumori (honorific, otumori †) 'intention' is a nominal which is always preceded by a modifier—usually a sentence modifier consisting of a non-past affirmative verbal or negative adjectival—and is followed by some form of √da (including no before another nominal). Tumori in statements usually refers to the speaker's own intentions, and in questions to those of the person addressed. Thus:

> I⌐ku tumori de⌐su. 'I intend to go,' 'I expect to go,' 'I plan to go,' etc.
>
> I⌐ku tumori de⌐su ka_ 'Do you intend to go?' 'Do you expect to go?' 'Do you plan to go?' etc.

A negative may precede or follow tumori. Compare:

> I⌐kanai tumori de⌐su. 'I intend not to go,' 'It is my intention not to go.'

and:

> I⌐ku tumori zya arimase⌐ñ. 'I don't intend to go,' 'It is not my intention to go.'

Additional examples:

> Ko⌐ñbañ ⌐na⌐ni o su⌐ru otumori de⌐su ka_ 'What do you intend to do this evening?'
>
> Ki⌐no⌐o wa de⌐kakenai tumori da⌐tta keredo, de⌐kakete simaima⌐sita. 'Yesterday I planned not to go out, but I ended up by going out.'
>
> Ka⌐u tumori zya na⌐katta keredo; a⌐ñmari ya⌐sukatta kara, ka⌐tte simaima⌐sita. 'Even though I didn't intend to buy it, it was so cheap that (lit. because it was so cheap) I ended up by buying it.'

Zyu⸢uni⸣-zi ni ta⸢be⸣ru tumori no mo⸢no⸣ o zyu⸢uiti⸣-zi ni ⸢ta⸣bete si⸢maima⸣sita. 'At 11 I ate up the things I planned to eat at 12.'
Do⸢ñna tumori de i⸢tta⸣ ka wa⸢karimase⸣ñ ǧa_ 'What sort of thing he had in mind when he said it I can't tell but . . .' (Lit. 'Being what kind of intention he said [it] I can't tell but . . .')

The immediately preceding sentence is an example of the pattern —— tumori de suru 'do with a —— intention,' 'do with —— in mind'; de is the gerund of da, and suru stands for any verbal.

4. Further Notes on Comparisons

Reread Lesson 15, Grammatical Note 2.

When comparing two courses of action, the nominal ho⸣o 'alternative' is preceded by a sentence modifier consisting of—or ending with—an affirmative verbal or a negative adjectival. A non-past before ho⸣o is more often used in general statements, whereas the past often refers to action on a specific occasion (lit. 'the alternative of having done will be ——').

Thus:

Ko⸢ñna ho⸣ñ no ⸢ho⸣o ǧa o⸢mosiro⸣i. 'This kind of book is more interesting.'

but:

Ko⸢ñna ho⸣ñ o ⸢yo⸣mu hoo ǧa o⸢mosiro⸣i. 'Reading this kind of book is more interesting.'

and:

Ko⸢ñna ho⸣ñ o ⸢yo⸣ñda hoo ǧa o⸢mosiro⸣i. 'It will be more interesting to read (lit. to have read) this kind of book.'

The combination si⸢ta ho⸣o ǧa ⸢i⸣i '[lit.] the alternative of having done [it] will be good' is often equivalent to English '[someone] had better do [it].' Sita may be replaced by other past verbals in this pattern.

Additional examples:

Hi⸢ko⸣oki de i⸢ku ho⸣o ǧa ha⸢ya⸣i. 'It's faster to go by plane.' (Lit. 'The alternative of going by plane is fast.')
Ni⸢hoñǧo o yo⸣mu hoo ǧa mu⸢zukasi⸣i desyoo? 'It's more difficult to read Japanese, isn't it?'
Ha⸣yaku na⸢o⸣sita hoo ǧa ⸢i⸣i desu yo_ 'You'd better fix it quickly.' (Lit. 'The alternative of having fixed it quickly will be good.')
Ko⸢ñbañ i⸢tta ho⸣o ǧa ⸢i⸣i desyoo ⸢ne⸣e. 'I guess I'd better go tonight!' (Lit. 'The alternative of having gone tonight will probably be good, won't it.')
Na⸢ni mo iwanai ho⸣o ǧa ⸢i⸣i desyoo? 'It's better to say nothing, isn't it?'

A sequence consisting of— or ending with— an informal non-past affirmative verbal or negative adjectival + yori 'more than' indicates the course of action with which another is being compared. Before yori, a normally unaccented inflected word regularly acquires an accent—a verbal on its final syllable, and an adjectival on its pre-final syllable.

Examples:

Ki⌐sya⌐ de i⌐ku⌐ yori hi⌐ko⌐oki de i⌐ku ho⌐o ḡa ha⌐ya⌐i. 'It's faster to go by plane than to go by train.' (Lit. 'More than going by train, the alternative of going by plane is fast.')

Ha⌐na⌐su yori nihoñḡo o ⌐yo⌐mu hoo ḡa mu⌐zukasi⌐i desyoo? 'It's more difficult to read Japanese than to speak, isn't it?'

Ra⌐isyuu ma⌐de ⌐ma⌐tu yori ⌐ha⌐yaku na⌐o⌐sita hoo ḡa ⌐i⌐i desu yo⌐ 'You'd better fix it quickly rather than wait until next week.'

A⌐sita iku⌐ yori ⌐ko⌐ñbañ i⌐tta ho⌐o ḡa ⌐i⌐i desyoo ⌐ne⌐e. 'I guess I'd better go tonight rather than go tomorrow.'

5.   Approximate Numbers

The combination of two consecutive numerals of Series I, from 1 to 9, plus a single counter, indicates approximation equivalent to English patterns like '1 or 2 hours,' '2 or 3 days,' '3 or 4 months,' etc.

The same pattern occurs in approximations of higher rank, like these:

ni-sañ-zeñ	'2 or 3 thousand'
si-ḡo-hyaku	'4 or 5 hundred'
ro⌐ku-siti-zyu⌐u	'60 or 70' (lit. '6 or 7 tens')

In this pattern, the consecutive numerals occurring in pairs are from 1 through 9 only. Kyu⌐uzyuu means '90'—not '9 or 10.'

Some combinations are irregular and must be memorized separately, but in general si⌐ '4' and si⌐ti⌐ '7' are the more common alternants of those numerals; and before ku⌐/kyu⌐u '9,' ha⌐ti⌐ occurs in its hak- alternant.

Examples:

iti-ni-mai	'1 or 2 thin, flat objects'
ni-⌐sañ-zi⌐kañ	'2 or 3 hours'
sañ-si-hoñ	'3 or 4 long, cylindrical objects'
si-⌐ḡo⌐-niti	'4 or 5 days'
go-⌐ro⌐p-puñ	'5 or 6 minutes'
ro⌐ku-siti-syu⌐ukañ	'6 or 7 weeks'
si⌐ti-hak-ka⌐ḡetu	'7 or 8 months'
hak-ku-neñ	'8 or 9 years'

6.   Counters: -dai, -rittoru

The counter -dai combines with numerals of Series I to count units of wheeled vehicles—cars, busses, carts, carriages, etc. The numbers from one to ten are:

i⌐ti⌐-dai	'1 wheeled vehicle'
ni⌐-dai	'2 wheeled vehicles'
sa⌐ñ-dai	'3 wheeled vehicles'
yo⌐ñ-dai or yo-dai	'4 wheeled vehicles'
go-dai	'5 wheeled vehicles'
ro⌐ku⌐-dai	'6 wheeled vehicles'
na⌐na⌐-dai or si⌐ti⌐-dai	'7 wheeled vehicles'
ha⌐ti⌐-dai	'8 wheeled vehicles'
kyu⌐u-dai	'9 wheeled vehicles'
zyu⌐u-dai	'10 wheeled vehicles'
na⌐ñ-dai	'how many wheeled vehicles?'

The counter -rittoru combines with numerals of Series I to count liters. [1]

The numbers from one to ten are:

i⌐ti-ri⌐ttoru	'1 liter'
ni-⌐ri⌐ttoru	'2 liters'
sa⌐ñ-ri⌐ttoru	'3 liters'
yo⌐ñ-ri⌐ttoru	'4 liters'
go-⌐ri⌐ttoru	'5 liters'
ro⌐ku-ri⌐ttoru	'6 liters'
na⌐na-ri⌐ttoru or si⌐ti-ri⌐ttoru	'7 liters'
ha⌐ti-ri⌐ttoru	'8 liters'
kyu⌐u-ri⌐ttoru	'9 liters'
zyu⌐u-ri⌐ttoru	'10 liters'
na⌐ñ-ri⌐ttoru	'how many liters?'

-Rittoru is one of a large number of counters borrowed from English metric system terms. Others are -meetoru 'meter,' -kiro(meetoru) 'kilometer,' -guramu 'gram,' -kiro(guramu) 'kilogram,' etc.

In the late 1950's Japan adopted the metric system as its official measurement system. Before that time, three systems were in use simultaneously: along with the metric system, there was a native Japanese system with its own terms, and the American system with another set of borrowed terms (-yaado 'yard,' -iñti 'inch,' -garoñ 'gallon,' -poñdo 'pound,' etc.). The various measures of the last two systems are being— or have already been— abandoned since the official adoption of the metric system.

---

[1] One liter = 1.06 quarts.

DRILLS

A. Substitution Drill

1.	Please get off now.	I⌐ma ⌐o⌐rite kudasai.
2.	Please let me off now.	I⌐ma o⌐ro⌐site kudasai.
3.	Please get on now.	I⌐ma no⌐tte kudasa⌐i.
4.	Please let me on now.	I⌐ma no⌐sete kudasa⌐i.
5.	Please line up now.	I⌐ma na⌐rañde kudasa⌐i.
6.	Please line [them] up now.	I⌐ma na⌐rabete kudasa⌐i.
7.	Please go across now.	I⌐ma wa⌐tatte kudasa⌐i.
8.	Please hand [it] over now.	I⌐ma wa⌐tasite kudasa⌐i.
9.	Please go around now.	I⌐ma ma⌐watte kudasa⌐i.
10.	Please send [it] around now.	I⌐ma ma⌐wasite kudasa⌐i.

B. Substitution Drill

1.	There are 1 or 2 taxis left. . . .	Ta⌐kusii (ḡa) i⌐ti-ni-dai noko⌐tte (i)masu ḡa_
2.	There are 2 or 3 portions of sashimi left. . . .	Osasimi (ḡa) ni-⌐sañ-niñ-mae noko⌐tte (i)masu ḡa_
3.	There are 3 or 4 pencils left. . . .	Eñpitu (ḡa) sa⌐ñ-si-hoñ noko⌐tte (i)masu ḡa_
4.	There are 4 or 5 glasses of beer left. . . .	Bi⌐iru (ḡa) si-⌐go-hai noko⌐tte (i)masu ḡa_
5.	There are 5 or 6 children left. . . .	Kodomo (ḡa) go-⌐roku-niñ noko⌐tte (i)masu ḡa_
6.	There are 6 or 7 liters of gasoline left. . . .	Gasoriñ (ḡa) ro⌐ku-siti-ri⌐ttoru no-⌐ko⌐tte (i)masu ḡa_
7.	There are 7 or 8 books left. . . .	Ho⌐ñ (ḡa) si⌐ti-has-satu noko⌐tte (i)masu ḡa_
8.	There are 8 or 9 sheets of paper left. . . .	Ka⌐mi⌐ (ḡa) ha⌐k-ku-mai noko⌐tte (i)masu ḡa_

C. Substitution Drill

1.	I went to the airport in a taxi.	Hikoozyoo e ⌐ta⌐kusii ni no⌐tte ikima⌐sita.
2.	I walked to the airport.	Hikoozyoo e a⌐ru⌐ite i⌐kima⌐sita.
3.	I went to the airport happily.	Hikoozyoo e yo⌐roko⌐ñde i⌐kima⌐sita.
4.	I went to the airport in a hurry.	Hikoozyoo e i⌐so⌐ide i⌐kima⌐sita.
5.	I went to the airport late.	Hikoozyoo e o⌐kurete ikima⌐sita.
6.	I went back to the airport.	Hikoozyoo e mo⌐do⌐tte i⌐kima⌐sita.
7.	I went to the airport, [after] transferring to a bus.	Hikoozyoo e ⌐ba⌐su ni no⌐rika⌐ete i⌐kima⌐sita.
8.	I went to the airport by way of (lit. passing through) the park.	Hikoozyoo e ko⌐oeñ (o) to⌐otte i-⌐kima⌐sita.

D. Substitution Drill

1. Shall I go and hire a por-   A⌐kaboo (o) tano⌐ńde ki⌐masyo⌐o ka.
   ter?
2. Shall I go and check the   Ni⌐motu (o) a⌐zu⌐kete ki⌐masyo⌐o
   baggage?   ka.
3. Shall I go and get (lit. put   Ga⌐soriń (o) irete kimasyo⌐o ka.
   in) some gas?
4. Shall I go and look up the   De⌐ńwaba⌐ńḡoo (o) si⌐ra⌐bete ki⌐ma-
   phone number?   syo⌐o ka.
5. Shall I go and buy a pa-   Si⌐ńbuń (o) katte kimasyo⌐o ka.
   per?
6. Shall I go and ask at the   A⌐ńnaizyo de kiite kimasyo⌐o ka.
   information booth?
7. Shall I go and call the   Se⌐ńse⌐e (o) yo⌐ńde kimasyo⌐o ka.
   doctor?
8. Shall I go and pick up the   Ni⌐motu (o) to⌐tte kimasyo⌐o ka.
   baggage?

E. Substitution Drill

1. Even though I didn't have   Zi⌐kań ḡa ańmari na⌐katta keredo,
   much time, I went.   i⌐kima⌐sita.
2. Even though I didn't feel   Gu⌐ai ḡa wa⌐rukatta keredo, i⌐kima⌐-
   well, I went.   sita.
3. Even though I was very   To⌐ttemo tuka⌐rete (i)⌐ta⌐ keredo,
   tired, I went.   i⌐kima⌐sita.
4. Even though I wanted to   Ya⌐sumita⌐katta keredo, i⌐kima⌐sita.
   rest, I went.
5. Even though it was raining,   A⌐me ḡa hu⌐tte⌐ (i)ta keredo, i⌐kima⌐-
   I went.   sita.
6. Even though I didn't want to   I⌐kitaku na⌐katta keredo, i⌐kima⌐sita.
   go, I went.
7. Even though it was winter,   Hu⌐yu⌐ datta keredo, i⌐kima⌐sita.
   I went.
8. Even though it was awfully   Zu⌐ibuń to⌐o⌐katta keredo, i⌐kima⌐-
   far, I went.   sita.
9. Even though it wasn't very   A⌐ńmari tika⌐ku ⌐na⌐katta keredo,
   near, I went.   i⌐kima⌐sita.
10. Even though I was very   Ta⌐iheń isoḡa⌐sikatta keredo, i⌐kima⌐-
    busy, I went.   sita.

F. Substitution Drill

1. I plan to go (riding) on the   Ba⌐su ni no⌐tte iku tumori da⌐
   bus (but . . .)[1]   kedo—

---

[1] 'but—I'm not sure I will'   or   'but—it isn't definite,' etc.

2. I plan to get off in front
   of the park (but. . .)
      Ko⌐oeñ no ma�len de o⌐ri⌐ru tu⌐mori
   da⌐ kedo—

3. I plan to deposit ¥ 5000 in
   the bank (but. . .)
      Giñkoo ni go⌐señ-eñ azuke⌐ru tu⌐mo-
   ri da⌐ kedo—

4. I plan to have the car
   checked (but. . .)
      Ku⌐ruma (o) sira⌐bete mo⌐rau tumo-
   ri da⌐ kedo—

5. I plan to leave early in the
   morning (but. . .)
      A⌐sa ⌐ha⌐yaku ⌐ta⌐tu tu⌐mori da⌐
   kedo—

6. I plan to stop at an inn in
   Kyoto (but. . .)
      Kyo⌐oto no ryo⌐kañ ni tomaru tu-
   mori da⌐ kedo—

7. I plan to check the baggage
   at the station (but. . .)
      E⌐ki de ⌐ni⌐motu (o) a⌐zuke⌐ru tu-
   ⌐mori da⌐ kedo—

8. I plan to return to America
   next week (but. . .)
      Raisyuu A⌐merika e ka⌐eru tu⌐mo-
   ri da⌐ kedo—

9. I plan to study English next
   year (but. . .)
      Raineñ e⌐ēgo (o) beñkyoo-suru tu-
   mori da⌐ kedo—

10. I plan to transfer to the
    bus at Yokohama (but. . .)
       Yokohama de ⌐ba⌐su ni no⌐rika⌐eru
    tu⌐mori da⌐ kedo—

G. Grammar Drill (based on Grammatical Note 3)

> Tutor: I⌐kimase⌐ñ. 'I'm not going to go.'
> Student: I⌐kanai tumori de⌐su. 'I plan not to go.'

1. Ko⌐ñbañ de⌐kakemase⌐ñ.
      Ko⌐ñbañ de⌐kakenai tumori de⌐su.

2. Asita ki⌐mase⌐ñ.
      Asita ⌐ko⌐nai tumori desu.

3. Koñna siḡoto wa ⌐mo⌐o
   si⌐mase⌐ñ.
      Koñna siḡoto wa ⌐mo⌐o si⌐nai tumo-
   ri de⌐su.

4. Ra⌐ineñ ma⌐de wa ka⌐eri-
   mase⌐ñ.
      Ra⌐ineñ ma⌐de wa ka⌐era⌐nai tumori
   desu.

5. Ze⌐ñbu wa si⌐mase⌐ñ.
      Ze⌐ñbu wa si⌐nai tumori de⌐su.

6. So⌐ñna hito⌐ ni wa na⌐ni
   mo yarimase⌐ñ.
      So⌐ñna hito⌐ ni wa na⌐ni mo yaranai
   tumori de⌐su.

H. Response Drill

> Tutor: Hu⌐ru⌐i desu ka— 'Is it old?'
> Student: Hu⌐ruku a⌐rimase⌐ñ. A⌐tarasi⌐i desu yo— 'It isn't old. It's
> new.'

1. O⌐mo⌐i desu ka—
      O⌐moku arimase⌐ñ. Ka⌐ru⌐i desu
   yo—

2. Ti⌐ka⌐i desu ka—
      Ti⌐ka⌐ku a⌐rimase⌐ñ. To⌐oi⌐ desu
   yo—

3. Zyo⌐ozu⌐ desu ka—
      Zyo⌐ozu⌐ zya a⌐rimase⌐ñ. He⌐ta⌐
   desu yo—

4. Tu⌐meta⌐i desu ka—
      Tu⌐metaku arimase⌐ñ. A⌐tu⌐i desu
   yo—

5. O⌐isi⌐i desu ka—
      O⌐isiku arimase⌐ñ. Ma⌐zu⌐i desu yo—

6. O⌐mosiro⌐i desu ka—
      O⌐mosi⌐roku a⌐rimase⌐ñ. Tu⌐mara⌐-
   nai desu yo—

7. A⌐kema⌐su ka⌐   A⌐kemase⌐ñ. Si⌐mema⌐su yo⌐
8. Ko⌐i desu ka⌐   Ko⌐ku a⌐rimase⌐ñ. U⌐su⌐i desu yo⌐
9. Ka⌐ra⌐ desu ka⌐   Ka⌐ra⌐ zya a⌐rimase⌐ñ. I⌐ppai de⌐-
                          su yo⌐
10. Su⌐ppa⌐i desu ka⌐   Su⌐ppa⌐ku a⌐rimase⌐ñ. A⌐ma⌐i desu
                          yo⌐

I. Response Drill (based on Grammatical Note 4)

> Tutor: I⌐kimasyo⌐o ka. 'Shall I go?'
> Student: E⌐e, i⌐tta ho⌐o ḡa ⌐i⌐i desyoo?   'Yes, you'd better go, don't
> you think so?'

1. Ha⌐yaku si⌐ra⌐bete mo-   E⌐e, si⌐ra⌐bete mo⌐ratta ho⌐o ḡa
   ⌐raimasyo⌐o ka.   ⌐i⌐i desyoo?
2. Gasoriñ (o) i⌐rete okima-   E⌐e, i⌐ret(e) o⌐ita hoo ḡa ⌐i⌐i de-
   syo⌐o ka.   syoo?
3. Akaboo (o) ta⌐nomimasyo⌐o   E⌐e, ta⌐no⌐ñda hoo ḡa ⌐i⌐i desyoo?
   ka.
4. Ha⌐si⌐ (o) wa⌐tarimasyo⌐o   E⌐e, wa⌐tatta ho⌐o ḡa ⌐i⌐i desyoo?
   ka.
5. Kono taiya (o) to⌐rikaema-   E⌐e, to⌐rikaeta ho⌐o ḡa ⌐i⌐i de-
   syo⌐o ka.   syoo?
6. Oohuku no kippu (o) ka⌐i-   E⌐e, ka⌐tta ho⌐o ḡa ⌐i⌐i desyoo?
   masyo⌐o ka.
7. Ka⌐ḡi⌐ (o) ka⌐kemasyo⌐o   E⌐e, ka⌐keta hoo ḡa ⌐i⌐i desyoo?
   ka.
8. A⌐ma⌐do (o) si⌐memasyo⌐o   E⌐e, si⌐meta hoo ḡa ⌐i⌐i desyoo?
   ka.
9. To⌐kkyuu ni norimasyo⌐o ka. E⌐e, no⌐tta ho⌐o ḡa ⌐i⌐i desyoo?
10. Sya⌐syoo ni kiite mimasyo⌐o E⌐e, ki⌐ite mi⌐ta hoo ḡa ⌐i⌐i de-
    ka.   syoo?

J. Level Drill

(Change all formal inflected forms except the final one to the informal.)

1. Zi⌐p-puñ ⌐ma⌐e ni ta⌐nomi-   Zi⌐p-puñ ⌐ma⌐e ni ta⌐no⌐ñda kere-
   ma⌐sita keredo, ma⌐da mo-   do, ma⌐da mo⌐tte kimase⌐ñ.
   ⌐tte kimase⌐ñ.
2. I⌐ti-do aima⌐sita keredo,   I⌐ti-do a⌐tta keredo, mo⌐o wa⌐su-
   mo⌐o wa⌐surete simaima⌐-   rete simaima⌐sita.
   sita.
3. I⌐ti-zikañ-ḡu⌐rai ⌐ma⌐e ni   I⌐ti-zikañ-ḡu⌐rai ⌐ma⌐e ni su⌐to⌐-
   su⌐to⌐obu (o) tu⌐kema⌐sita   obu (o) tu⌐ke⌐ta keredo, ma⌐da
   keredo, ma⌐da sa⌐mu⌐i   sa⌐mu⌐i desyoo?
   desyoo?
4. To⌐oi⌐ desu kara, zu⌐ibuñ   To⌐oi⌐ kara, zu⌐ibuñ zi⌐kañ ḡa ka-
   zi⌐kañ ḡa kakarima⌐su ke-   ka⌐ru keredo; i⌐kima⌐su yo⌐
   redo; i⌐kima⌐su yo⌐

5. A˹no˺ hito wa wa˹karima-
   se˺ñ keredo, i˺tu mo wa˹ka˺-
   ru tte i˞tte (i)ma˞su ˹ne˺e.

A˹no˺ hito wa wa˹kara˺nai keredo,
i˞tu mo wa˹ka˺ru tte i˞tte (i)ma˞-
su ˹ne˺e.

6. Mo˞o ni-˹sañ-do mima˞sita
   keredo; a˹ñmari omosiro˺i
   desu kara, ma˹ta mita˺i
   desu yo.

Mo˞o ni-˹sañ-do mi˞ta keredo; a˹ñ-
mari omosiro˺i kara, ma˹ta mi-
ta˺i desu yo.

7. Se˹ñse˺e g̃a so˹o ossyaima˺-
   sita keredo, ho˹ñtoo zya
   arimase˺ñ yo⌟

Se˹ñse˺e g̃a so˹o ossya˞tta keredo,
ho˹ñtoo zya arimase˺ñ yo⌟

8. Ki˹koemase˺ñ desita keredo, yo˹ku mi˹ema˺sita.

Ki˹koena˺katta keredo, yo˹ku mi˹e-
ma˞sita.

9. I˹ku tumori de˺su keredo,
   ma˞da si˹taku wa sima-
   se˺ñ.

I˹ku tumori da˺ keredo, ma˞da si-
˹taku wa simase˺ñ.

10. De˹kakenai tumori de˺sita
    keredo, de˹kakete simai-
    ma˞sita.

De˹kakenai tumori da˞tta keredo,
de˹kakete simaima˞sita.

K. Expansion Drill

1. [He] didn't see me.

A˹imase˺ñ desita.

   [He] was waiting at the exit
   so he didn't see [me].

De˹g̃uti de ˞ma˞tte (i)˞ta˞ kara, a˹i-
mase˺ñ desita.

   My friend was waiting at
   the exit so he didn't see
   me.

To˹modati wa de˹g̃uti de ˞ma˞tte (i)-
˞ta˞. kara, a˹imase˺ñ desita.

   I was waiting in the waiting room but my friend
   was waiting at the exit so
   he didn't see me.

Ma˹tia˞isitu de ˞ma˞tte (i)˞ta˞ keredo; to˹modati wa de˹g̃uti de ˞ma˞tte
(i)˞ta˞ kara, a˹imase˺ñ desita.

   I was waiting in the waiting
   room for about a half
   hour but my friend was
   waiting at the exit so he
   didn't see me.

Sa˹ñ-zip-puñ-g̃u˺rai ma˹tia˞isitu de
˞ma˞tte (i)˞ta˞ keredo; to˹modati wa
de˹g̃uti de ˞ma˞tte (i)˞ta˞ kara, a-
˹imase˺ñ desita.

2. I ended up by going.

I˞tte simaima˞sita.

   I ended up by going (riding)
   in the car.

Ku˹ruma ni notte itte simaima˞si-
ta.

   There wasn't enough time
   so I ended up by going
   (riding) in the car.

Zi˹kañ g̃a tarina˞katta kara, ku˹ru-
ma ni notte itte simaima˞sita.

   Even though I planned to
   walk (lit. go walking),
   there wasn't enough time
   so I ended up by going
   (riding) in the car.

A˹ru˺ite i˞ku tumori da˞tta keredo;
zi˹kañ g̃a tarina˞katta kara, ku˹ru-
ma ni notte itte simaima˞sita.

   Even though I planned to
   walk to the station, there
   wasn't enough time so I

E˹ki e a˹ru˺ite i˞ku tumori da˞tta
keredo; zi˹kañ g̃a tarina˞katta
kara, ku˹ruma ni notte itte

ended up by going (riding) in the car.

Even though I planned to walk to the station this morning, there wasn't enough time so I ended up by going (riding) in the car.

simaima⌐sita.

Ke⌐sa ⌐e⌐ki e a⌐ru⌐ite i⌐ku tumori da⌐tta keredo; zi⌐kañ ḡa tarina⌐-katta kara, ku⌐ruma ni notte itte simaima⌐sita.

3. I ended up by going. (M)[1]

I ended up by going (riding) on the bus.

I arrived late so I ended up by going (riding) on the bus.

I arrived at the station late, so I ended up by going (riding) on the bus.

I intended to take the train but I arrived at the station late, so I ended up by going (riding) on the bus.

I intended to take a train that stops at Numazu but I arrived late, so I ended up by going (riding) on the bus.

I⌐ttyatta⌐ yo.

Ba⌐su ni no⌐tte (i)ttyatta⌐[2] yo.

O⌐kurete tu⌐ita kara, ba⌐su ni no⌐tte (i)ttyatta⌐ yo.

E⌐ki ni o⌐kurete tu⌐ita kara, ba⌐su ni no⌐tte (i)ttyatta⌐ yo.

Ki⌐sya⌐ ni no⌐ru tumori da⌐tta ke-do; e⌐ki ni o⌐kurete tu⌐ita kara, ba⌐su ni no⌐tte (i)ttyatta⌐ yo.

Nu⌐mazu ni tomaru ki⌐sya⌐ ni no-⌐ru tumori da⌐tta kedo, e⌐ki ni o⌐kurete tu⌐ita kara, ba⌐su ni no⌐tte (i)ttyatta⌐ yo.

4. [He] didn't say.

[He] didn't say anything.

Nobody said anything.

I ended up by going in but nobody said anything.

I ended up by going in through (lit. from) the exit but nobody said anything.

I couldn't tell so I ended up by going in through the exit, but nobody said anything.

I⌐imase⌐ñ desita yo↲

Na⌐ni mo iimase⌐ñ desita yo↲

Da⌐re mo nani mo iimase⌐n desita yo↲

Ha⌐itte si⌐matta⌐ kedo, da⌐re mo nani mo iimase⌐ñ desita yo↲

De⌐ḡuti kara ⌐ha⌐itte si⌐matta⌐ ke-do, da⌐re mo nani mo iimase⌐ñ desita yo↲

Wa⌐kara⌐nakatta kara, de⌐ḡuti kara ⌐ha⌐itte si⌐matta⌐ kedo; da⌐re mo nani mo iimase⌐ñ desita yo↲

---

1 M = more typical of men's speech.

2 Notte itte is regularly contracted to notte tte in informal speech.

I couldn't tell which was the
entrance so I ended up by
going in through the exit, but
nobody said anything.

Do˥tira ḡa i˥riḡuti ka wa˥kara˥naka-
tta kara, de˥ḡuti kara ˥ha˥itte si-
˥matta˧ kedo; da˥re mo nani mo
iimase˥n̄ desita yo⌐

5. There isn't enough. (Lit.
   It has become insuffi-
   cient.)

Ta˥rinaku narima˥sita.

   Again there isn't enough.

Ma˥ta tarinaku narima˥sita.

   Even though I had [some]
   put in, again there isn't
   enough.

I˥rete moratta˥ keredo, ma˥ta tarinaku narima˥sita.

   Even though I had enough
   put in, again there is-
   n't enough.

Zyu˥ubu˥n̄ i˥rete moratta˧ kedo, ma-
˥ta tarinaku narima˥sita.

   There wasn't enough (lit.
   it had become insuffi-
   cient) so I had the right
   amount put in, but again
   there isn't enough.

Ta˥rinaku na˥tte (i)˥ta˧ kara, zyu˥u-
bu˥n̄ i˥rete moratta˧ kedo; ma˥ta
tarinaku narima˥sita.

• There wasn't enough air
   so I had the right amount
   put in, but again there is-
   n't enough.

Ku˥uki ḡa ta˥rinaku na˥tte (i)˥ta˧
kara, zyu˥ubu˥n̄ i˥rete moratta˧
kedo; ma˥ta tarinaku narima˥si-
ta.

   There wasn't enough air in
   the tires so I had the right
   amount put in, but again
   there isn't enough.

Ta˥iya no ku˥uki ḡa ta˥rinaku na˥tte
(i)˥ta˧ kara, zyu˥ubu˥n̄ i˥rete mo-
ratta˧ keredo; ma˥ta tarinaku na-
rima˥sita.

   There wasn't enough air in
   the tires this morning so
   I had the right amount
   put in, but again there is-
   n't enough.

Ke˥sa ta˥iya no ku˥uki ḡa ta˥rinaku
na˥tte (i)˥ta˧ kara, zyu˥ubu˥n̄ i˥re-
te moratta˧ keredo; ma˥ta tarinaku
narima˥sita.

6. Let's go (and come).

I˥tte kimasyo˥o.

   Let's go to the J. T. B.

Ko˥otuuko˥osya e i˥tte kimasyo˧o.

   Let's go to the J. T. B. right
   nearby.

Su˥ḡu ˥so˧ba no ko˥otuuko˥osya e
i˥tte kimasyo˧o.

   [They] are waiting so let's
   go to the J. T. B. right
   nearby.

Ma˥tte (i)ru kara, su˥ḡu ˥so˧ba no
ko˥otuuko˥osya e i˥tte kimasyo˧o.

   [They] are waiting in line
   so let's go to the J. T. B.
   right nearby.

Na˥rande ma˥tte (i)ru kara, su˥ḡu
˥so˧ba no ko˥otuuko˥osya e i˥tte
kimasyo˧o.

   Lots of people are waiting
   in line so let's go to the
   J. T. B. right nearby.

Hi˥to˥ ḡa ta˥kusan narande ma˥tte
(i)ru kara, su˥ḡu ˥so˧ba no ko˥o-
tuuko˥osya e i˥tte kimasyo˧o.

   Lots of people are always
   waiting in line so let's go
   to the J. T. B. right nearby.

I˥tu mo hi˥to˥ ḡa ta˥kusan narande
ma˥tte (i)ru kara, su˥ḡu ˥so˧ba
no ko˥otuuko˥osya e i˥tte kima-
syo˧o.

Lots of people are always waiting in line at the ticket windows so let's go to the J. T. B. right nearby.

Ma⌐do¬guti ni wa ⌐i¬tu mo hi⌐to¬ ḡa ta⌐kusañ narañde ma¬tte (i)ru kara, su¬ḡu ⌐so⌐ba no ko⌐otuuko¬-osya e i⌐tte kimasyo¬o.

Lots of people are always waiting in line at the ticket windows in this station so let's go to the J. T. B. right nearby.

Ko⌐no e⌐ki no ma⌐do¬guti ni wa ⌐i¬-tu mo hi⌐to¬ ḡa ta⌐kusañ narañde ma¬tte (i)ru kara, su¬ḡu ⌐so⌐ba no ko⌐otuuko¬osya e i⌐tte kima-syo¬o.

QUESTION SUPPLEMENT

(The following questions are based on the Basic Dialogues of this lesson.)

(a) 1. Su¬misu-sañ to Tānaka-sañ wa ⌐do⌐ko de ha⌐na¬site imasu ka⌐

2. Tanaka-sañ wa ⌐do¬o site a⌐kaboo o tano⌐ñde ki⌐ma¬su ka⌐

(b) 3. Su¬misu-sañ wa ⌐na¬ni o a⌐zuketa¬i ñ desu ka⌐

4. A⌐zuke¬ru to⌐koro¬ wa ⌐do¬ko desu ka⌐

5. Su¬misu-sañ wa ⌐do¬ko de o⌐siete moraima¬sita ka⌐

6. E⌐ki no hi⌐to o ma⌐tu he⌐ya¬ wa ⌐na¬ñ to i⌐ima¬su ka⌐

(c) 7. Tanaka-sañ wa ⌐do¬o site ti⌐katetu ni noritaku arimase¬ñ ka⌐

8. Tanaka-sañ wa ⌐na¬ñ ni no⌐rita¬i ñ desu ka⌐

9. Ta⌐kusii no i⌐tibañ tika¬i noriba wa ⌐do¬ko desu ka⌐

10. Taitee ⌐e⌐ki no ⌐de¬ḡuti ni ⌐na¬ni ḡa na⌐rañde ima¬su ka⌐

(d) 11. O⌐kusañ wa ⌐na¬ñ to ⌐na¬ñ ni no⌐tte iku tumori de¬su ka⌐

12. O⌐kusañ wa ⌐do¬ko made ⌐ba¬su ni no⌐tte iku tumori de¬su ka⌐

13. O⌐kusañ wa Sibuya de ⌐na¬ni o su⌐ru tumori de¬su ka⌐

14. O⌐kusañ wa ⌐do¬ko de ti⌐katetu o ori¬ru desyoo ka.

15. O⌐kusañ wa To⌐ranomoñ de o¬rite kara ⌐do¬o simasu ka⌐

16. Go⌐syu¬ziñ mo i⌐kima¬su ka⌐

17. Ni⌐hoñzi¬ñ wa zi⌐buñ no uti o de⌐ru to⌐ki¬ ni wa ⌐na¬ñ to i⌐ima¬su ka⌐

18. Ni⌐hoñzi¬ñ wa zi⌐buñ no uti ni ka¬etta to⌐ki¬ ni wa ⌐na¬ñ to i⌐ima¬-su ka⌐

19. U⌐ti ni iru hito¬ wa de⌐kakeru hito¬ ni ⌐na¬ñ to i⌐ima¬su ka⌐

20. U⌐ti ni iru hito¬ wa u⌐ti ni ka¬ette ⌐ki⌐ta hi⌐to¬ ni ⌐na¬ñ to i⌐ima¬su ka⌐

(e) 21. Su¬misu-sañ no zi⌐do¬osya ni ḡasoriñ ḡa na⌐ñ-rittoru-ḡu¬rai no-⌐ko¬tte imasu ka⌐

22. Do¬o site ⌐i¬ma ḡasoriñ o ⌐mo¬tto i⌐rete o¬ita hoo ḡa ⌐i¬i desyoo ka.

23. Ta⌐naka-sañ no sitte iru gasoriñsuta¬ñdo wa ⌐do¬ko desyoo ka.

24. Su¬misu-sañ wa ga⌐re¬ezi de ⌐na¬ni o si⌐te moraima¬su ka⌐

(f) 25. Tanaka-sañ wa ⌐do⌐o site o⌐soku narima⌐sita ka⌐

 26. Tanaka-sañ wa zi⌐buñ de pañku-sita taiya o torikaema⌐sita ka⌐

(g) 27. Su⌐misu-sañ wa ⌐do⌐o site ga⌐re⌐ezi e i⌐kima⌐sita ka⌐

 28. Su⌐misu-sañ wa zi⌐buñ de bure⌐eki o si⌐rabema⌐sita ka, ga⌐re⌐ezi
      no hi⌐to⌐ ni si⌐ra⌐bete mo⌐rau tumori de⌐su ka⌐

SUPPLEMENTARY CONVERSATION

Smith: Ga⌐soriñ o ireta⌐i ñ desu ḡa, kono heñ ni ga⌐soriñsuta⌐ñdo wa
⌐na⌐i desyoo ⌐ne⌐e.

Tanaka: Sa⌐a. . . . A, asuko ni zyu⌐ñsa ḡa iru⌐ kara, ki⌐ite mima-
syo⌐o.

(To policeman) Tyo⌐tto u⌐kaḡaima⌐su ḡa, kono heñ ni ga⌐soriñ-
suta⌐ñdo wa a⌐rimase⌐ñ ka⌐

Policeman: Ga⌐soriñsuta⌐ñdo desu ka⌐ Kono miti o mo⌐o suko⌐si itte, hasi
no temae o mi̅ḡi e maḡatte; sore kara, ni-⌐sañ-byaku-meetoru-
ḡu⌐rai saki ni o⌐oki⌐i ga⌐re⌐ezi mo ga⌐soriñsuta⌐ñdo mo arimasu.

Tanaka: Wa⌐karima⌐sita. Do⌐o mo a⌐ri⌐ḡatoo gozaimasita.

 . . .

Smith: A, mi⌐ema⌐su yo⌐ — ha⌐si⌐ ḡa.

Tanaka: Mi̅ḡi no ho⌐o desu ne?

Smith: E⌐e.

(At the gas station)

Smith: O⌐neḡai-sima⌐su.

Attendant: O⌐matase-sima⌐sita.

Smith: Ga⌐soriñ oneḡai-sima⌐su.

Attendant: I⌐ppai ni simasyo⌐o ka.

Smith: E⌐e. . . . O⌐iru mo mi̅zu mo ⌐mi⌐te ne?

Attendant: Ha⌐a, ka⌐sikomarima⌐sita.

Tanaka: Ta⌐iya wa daizyo⌐obu desu ka⌐

Smith: E⌐e, da⌐izyo⌐obu desyoo. Señsyuu si⌐ra⌐bete mo⌐ratta⌐ kara.

Tanaka: Mi⌐ti ḡa waru⌐i kara, taiya ḡa ⌐su⌐ḡu ⌐wa⌐ruku narimasu ⌐ne⌐e.

Smith: Ho⌐ñtoo de⌐su ⌐ne⌐e. Ki⌐no⌐o mo ⌐ma⌐e no ta⌐iya ḡa pañku-sima⌐-
sita yo.

Tanaka: Kono kuruma ⌐na⌐ñ-neñ no desu ka⌐

Smith: Yo-⌐neñ ma⌐e no desu ḡa, e⌐ñziñ no guai ḡa ⌐ma⌐da to⌐temo i⌐i
desu kara⌐

Tanaka: So⌐re wa i⌐i desu ⌐ne⌐e.

Attendant: Omatidoosama. Gasoriñ wa sa⌐ñzyuu-ri⌐ttoru i⌐rema⌐sita. O⌐iru
mo mi̅zu mo ⌐ma⌐da da⌐izyo⌐obu desu kara⌐

Smith: A⌐a ⌐so⌐o. Do⌐o mo go⌐ku⌐roosama.

Attendant: Maido a⌐ri⌐ḡatoo gozaimasu.

English Equivalent

Smith: I'd like to get (lit. put in) some gas, but there probably isn't a gas
station around here, is there.

Tanaka: I wonder. . . .   Oh, there's a policeman over there so let's
              ask him and find out.
              (To policeman) Excuse me but is(n't) there a gas station around
              here?
Policeman: A gas station? You go a little further along this street, turn right
              this side of the bridge, and then about two or three hundred me-
              ters ahead there's a big garage and gas station.
Tanaka: I understand. Thank you very much.

                     . . .

Smith: Oh, I see it— the bridge.
Tanaka: It's to the right, isn't it?
Smith: Yes.

              (At the gas station)

Smith: Will you wait on me?
Attendant: I'm sorry to have kept you waiting.
Smith: Let me have some gas.
Attendant: Shall I fill it up?
Smith: Yes. . . .   look at (both) the oil and water, will you?
Attendant: Yes, certainly.
Tanaka: Are the tires all right?
Smith: Yes, I think they're all right.   (Because) I had them checked last
              week.
Tanaka: The roads are bad so the tires go bad right away, don't they.
Smith: They certainly do.   Why, I had a flat in the front tire yesterday
              again (lit. too).
Tanaka: What year is this car? (Lit. This car is one of what year?)
Smith: It's four years old but the engine is still in very good condition
              so. . . (Lit. It's one of four years ago but the condition of the en-
              gine is still very good so . . .)
Tanaka: Isn't that fine!
Attendant: I'm sorry to have kept you waiting.   I put in 30 liters of gas.
              (Both) the oil and water are still all right (so. . . .)
Smith: Oh. Thanks very much for your trouble.
Attendant: Thank you (again and again).

EXERCISES

1. Make up questions based on the immediately preceding conversation, and
    then practice the questions and answers.

2. Tell the porter:

    a. that you want to check your luggage.
    b. to take your luggage to the waiting room.
    c. to take only the heavy luggage.
    d. that you will take the light things.

3. Ask a stranger:

    a. where the waiting room is.

    b. which way the airport is.
    c. where you get the subway.
    d. if the next station is Shibuya.
    e. if there's a gas station around here.

4. Tell the garage attendant:

    a. that you want 20 liters of gasoline.
    b. to fill the tank.
    c. that there isn't enough air in the tires.
    d. that there's something wrong with the engine.
    e. that you have a flat.
    f. that your brakes are out of order.
    g. to check the oil and water.

5. Tell Mr. Tanaka:

    a. that you walked here.
    b. that you came here on the subway.
    c. that you got on at Shimbashi.
    d. that you got off at Shibuya.
    e. that you came here by transferring at Shibuya.
    f. that you are going to go and buy a newspaper.
    g. that he'd better check his luggage.
    h. that he'd better get (lit. engage) a porter.
    i. that it will be faster to go by taxi.
    j. that you plan to try walking to the office tomorrow.
    k. that you plan to walk to Mr. Tanaka's house and ride back.
    l. that you plan to have the engine of your car checked tomorrow.

Japanese–English Glossary

Except for proper names, the following list contains all the vocabulary introduced in this text — words occurring in the Notes and as additional vocabulary as well as those appearing in the Basic Dialogues. Numbers following the entries refer to lessons: a number alone means that the entry first occurs in the Basic Dialogues of that lesson; a number followed by '-A' refers to the Additional Vocabulary of that lesson; a number followed by '-N' indicates that the item first occurs in the Notes of that lesson. CI and Int. refer to Classroom Instructions [1] and Introductory Lesson respectively. An asterisk (*) means that the item is included in the Index to the Grammatical Notes, with a reference to the location of the appropriate note(s).

Except in special cases, verbals and adjectivals are listed in their citation form only. Every verbal is identified as transitive /tr/ or intransitive /intr/ [2] and is assigned to the appropriate subclass; [3] its gerund is also given. For example, akeru /tr: -ru: akete/ identifies akeru as a transitive verbal belonging to the -ru subclass (i.e. the subclass to which ta⌐be¬ru 'eat' and mi¬ru 'see' belong), with gerund akete.

Every adjectival is identified by '/-ku/' [4] after the citation form. Thus, the adjectival meaning 'is big' appears as: o⌐oki¬i /-ku/.

All forms of the copula which occur in the text are listed and identified.

Nominals occur with no special designation, except that the members of the subclass of na-nominals [5] are identified by a following '/na/.'

Particles and quotatives are so identified. All are marked with asterisks, since all are included in the index.

Pre-nominals are identified by the designation '/+ nom/.'

Counters are so identified and are listed with a preceding hyphen.

'/M/' and '/W/' follow entries typical of men's or women's speech respectively.

---

[1] Words designated as CI are those which occur only in the Classroom Instructions.

[2] For a description of transitive and intransitive verbals, see Lesson 16, Grammatical Note 1.

[3] For a description of verbal subclasses, see Lesson 11, Grammatical Note 1.

[4] See Lesson 2, Grammatical Note 1.

[5] See Lesson 12, Grammatical Note 4.

Except in a few special cases, words having a polite alternant that differs from the plain alternant only in the addition of the polite prefix o- or go- are listed only in the plain alternant.

For purposes of alphabetizing, hyphens and the macron of ḡ are ignored. Syllabic ñ is assigned to the position immediately following nonsyllabic n.

In most cases, combinations occurring as indented sublistings match the first occurrence in the lessons; but a simpler, more generally occurring example of the pattern is cited in cases where the combination which occurs first in the lessons seems less desirable as the model for a pattern of wide general use.

A

a   oh!   4
aˡa   oh!   Int.
(aˡa /M/   yes   16)
abunai /-ku/   is dangerous   7
aḡaru /intr:-u:aḡatte/   go up, come up,
    enter   18
aḡeru /tr:-ru:aḡete/   give (to someone
    other than the speaker)   17
    site aḡeru   do for someone   17
aida   interval, space between   7
    Tookyoo to Yokohama no aida   be-
    tween Tokyo and Yokohama   7
akaboo   porter, redcap   20
akai /-ku/   is red   4
akeru /tr:-ru:akete/   open [it]   16
aˡki   autumn, fall   18
aku /intr:-u:aite/   [it] opens   16
aˡmaˡdo   sliding storm door   18
amai /-ku/   is sweet or sugary or
    insufficiently salted   14-A
aˡme   rain   18
    aˡme ḡa ˡhuˡru   it rains   18
aˡmerikaˡziñ   an American   10
aˡnaˡta   you   Int.
ane   older sister   11-A
aˡni   older brother   11-A
ano* /+ nom/   that —— over there   3
Ano ne!   Say!   Hey there!   13
añmari /+ negative/   not very much,
    not so much, not too much   3
    /+ affirmative/   so much, too much
    14
añna*   that kind, that kind of   5
añnaizyo, aˡñnaizyoˡ   information booth   19
aˡo   blue, green   16
aˡoˡi /-ku/   is blue or green   4; is
    pale   14
aˡpaˡato   apartment house   16
arau /tr:-u:aratte/   wash   17
are*   that thing over there   2

Aˡriˡḡatoo (gozaimasita).+   Thank you
    (for what you did).   Int.
Aˡriˡḡatoo (gozaimasu).+   Thank you.
    Int.
aˡru* /intr:-u:aˡtte; neg:naˡi/   be lo-
    cated (of inanimate objects), have   2
    siˡmete ˡaˡru   have been closed   16
aˡruˡku /intr:-u:aˡruˡite/   walk   20
aˡsa   morning   9
aˡsagoˡhañ   breakfast   15-N
aˡsiˡ   leg, foot   17-A
aˡsitaˡ   tomorrow   1
asoko   that place over there, over there
    6
asuko /see asoko/   6
aˡtamaˡ   head   17
    aˡtamaˡ ḡa iˡtaˡi   have a headache
    17
aˡtarasiˡi /-ku/   is new or fresh   2
aˡt(a)takaˡi /-ku/   is warm   16
atira   that one (of two); that way, there-
    abouts, over there   6
aˡto   later, afterward   4
    aˡto de   later, at a later time   4
    Aˡto ˡnaˡni o simasyoo ka.   What
    shall I do next?   17
aˡttiˡ /see atira/   6
aˡtuˡi /-kuˡ/   is hot   14
aˡu /intr:-u:aˡtte/   meet, see (and talk
    to) a person   11
    Yaˡmada-sañ ni aˡu   meet or see Mr.
    Yamada   11
aˡzukaˡru /tr:-u:aˡzukaˡtte/   receive
    in custody, take charge of, keep
    20-N
aˡzukeˡru /tr:-ru:aˡzuˡkete/   put into
    someone else's keeping tempo-
    rarily, check, deposit   20

B

bañ   night   19
-bañ /counter for naming numbers in
    a series/   12
baˡñgoˡhañ   evening meal, dinner   15-N
baˡñgoˡo   number   12
-bañ-señ /counter for naming track
    numbers/   19
baˡsu   bus   8
baˡta   butter   14-A
baˡtterii   battery   20-N
beˡekokuˡziñ   an American   10-A

beñkyoo-suru /tr:irreg:beñkyoo-site/
    study   11
beˡñzyoˡ /M/   toilet   6-A
beˡtto   bed   17-A
betu ni /+ negative/   not especially
    13
biˡiru   beer   14
biˡru   building (Western style)   6
boˡku, boku /M/   I, me   5
boˡttyañ†   son   11-A
buˡreˡeki   brakes   20

buta   pig   17-A
byooiñ   hospital   7

byooki   sickness, sick   11

D

da* /copula: informal non-past/
-dai /counter for vehicles/   20
daidokoro   kitchen   17
daiḡaku   university   13
daⁿisuki /na/   very pleasing   15
daⁱizi⁷ /na/   important, valuable   11-N
   Odaizi ni.   Take care of yourself!
   11
daⁱizyo⁷obu /na/   safe, all right   7
daᵣke⁷* just, only   4
   soᵣre dake⁷ just that, that's all   4
   mi-ᵣttu⁷ dake   just three (units)   5
daᵣme⁷ /na/   no good, bad, broken   2
daᵣññasa⁷ma ˥ master   12
da⁷re   who?   10
   dare mo /+ negative/   nobody   10
da⁷su /tr:-u:da⁷site/   put out, send out,
   take out   17
da⁷tta* /copula: informal past/
de* /copula: gerund/
de* /particle/   by means of   7;
   at, in   7
de⁷ḡuti   exit   20
dekakeru /intr:-ru:dekakete/   set out,
   go out   13
deᵣki⁷ru /intr:-ru:de⁷kite/   be possible,
   can do   9; come into being, be-
   (come) completed   15
   niᵣhoñḡo ḡa deki⁷ru   can [speak] Japanese   9
de⁷ñki   electricity, electric light   16
de⁷ñsya, deñsya   electric train, street
   car   8
deñwa   telephone   6
   de⁷ñwa o kake⁷ru   telephone (verb)
   12
de⁷ñwaba⁷ñḡoo   telephone number   12
deñwa-suru /intr:irreg:deñwa-site/
   make a telephone call   12
deñwatyoo   telephone book   12
deᵣpa⁷ato   department store   6
de⁷ru /intr:-ru:de⁷te/   go out, leave   9

de⁷sita* /copula: formal past/
de⁷su* /copula: formal non-past/
de⁷syo⁷o* /copula: formal non-past
   tentative/
-do /counter for number of times/   1
do⁷a   door (Western style)   16
doituḡo   German language   11-A
doᵣitu⁷ziñ   a German   10-A
do⁷ko   what place?   where?   6
do⁷nata ˥   who?   10
do⁷no* /+ nom/   which— ?   3
dono-ḡurai   about how long?   about how
   much?   8
do⁷ñna*   what kind?   what kind of?   5
do⁷o   how?   what way?   2
   Do⁷o itasimasite. ˥   Don't mention it.
   You're welcome.   Int.
   do⁷o mo   in every way   Int.
   Do⁷o mo.   [Thanks] very much.   Int.
   do⁷o sita   what happened?   14
   do⁷o site   why?   how?   11
   do⁷o suru   do what?   act how?   13
doobutu   animal   17-A
-doori /see to⁷ori⁷/   avenue, street
   7-N
-doori   in accordance with   19
   ziᵣkañ-do⁷ori   on time   19
do⁷ozo   please   Int.
do⁷re*   which thing (of three or more)?
   2
   do⁷re de⁷ mo   whichever (of three or
   more) it is, any one at all   15
do⁷tira   which one (of two)?; which
   way?   whereabouts?   where?
   6
   do⁷tira de⁷ mo   either one   15
   do⁷tira no ᵣho⁷o   which alternative?
   15
   dotira mo   both   10
do⁷tirasama ˥   who?   12
do⁷tti /see do⁷tira/   6
doᵣyo⁷o(bi), doyoo   Saturday   8

E

e* /particle/   to, into, onto   7
ebi   shrimp, prawn   14
e⁷e   yes; that's right   Int.

eᵣeḡa⁷kañ   movie theater   7
eeḡo   English language   11-A
eᵣekoku⁷ziñ   Englishman   10-A

eˈki station 6
-eñ /counter for yen/ 3
eñpitu pencil 2
eñryo reserve, restraint 18

eñryo (cont.)
　　Goˈeñryo naˈku.   Don't hold back.
　　　Don't stand on ceremony. 18
eˈñziñ engine 20-N

G

ḡa* /particle/ 4
　　Haˈizaˈra ḡa arimasu.   There's an
　　　ashtray. 4
　　Kiˈree desu ḡa＿   It's pretty but. . .
　　　4
gaikoku foreign country 11-N
gaikokuḡo foreign language 11
gaˈikokuˈziñ foreigner 11-N
gaˈimuˈsyoo Foreign Office 11
-ḡaisya /see kaisya/　　company
　　12-N
gaiziñ foreigner, Westerner, Ameri-
　　can 11-N
gakkoo school 6-A
gaˈñneñ the year 1, first year of an
　　emperor's reign 8-N
gaˈreˈezi garage (commercial) 20
gasoriñ gasoline 20
gaˈsoriñsutaˈñdo gas station 20
gaˈsuḡaˈisya gas company 12-N
-ḡatu /counter for naming the months
　　of the year/ 8
gekizyoo theater 6-A
geˈñkañ entry hall 16
geˈñki /na/ health, pep, good spirits
　　Int.
　　(O)ˈgeˈñki desu ka＿   Are you well?
　　　How are you? Int.
geˈtuyoˈo(bi), getuyoo Monday 8
giñkoo bank 6
goˈ five 3
goˈḡo afternoon, p.m. 9

goˈhañ   cooked rice, food 14-A; meal
　　15
Goˈkuˈroosama (desita).   Thanks for your
　　trouble. 1
Goˈmeñ-kudasaˈi(maˈse).   Excuse me
　　(for breaking away or interrupt-
　　ing). 12
-ḡoo-sya /counter for naming train
　　car numbers/ 19
-ḡoˈro* approximate point of time,
　　about 8
　　haˈti-ḡatu-ḡoˈro about August 8
gotisoo a feast, delicious food and/or
　　drink 14-N
　　Goˈtisoosama (deˈsita).   It was a
　　　feast. Thank you for the delicious
　　　refreshments. 14
goˈzaˈru⁺* /intr:-aru/ be located (of
　　inanimate objects), have Int.
goˈzeñ a.m. 9-N
goˈzoˈñzi da ⁺ know 13
guai condition 20
　　guˈai ḡa iˈi be in good condition, be
　　　fine, be in good health 20-N
　　guˈai ḡa waruˈi be in bad condition,
　　　be out of order, feel unwell, feel
　　　sick 20
guˈriiñkaˈa 'green car' (i.e. first-
　　class car) 19-N
guˈriˈinsya 'green car' (i.e. first-
　　class car) 19-N
-ḡuˈrai* approximate extent, about 8
　　dono-ḡurai about how much? 8
　　ni-ˈsyuukañ-ḡuˈrai about two weeks
　　　8
gyuunyuu cow's milk 14-A

H

haˈ tooth 17-A
haˈa⁺ yes; that's right 4
haˈha mother 11-A
haˈi yes; that's right Int.; here you
　　are 3
-hai /counter for glassfuls and cup-
　　fuls/ 14
haiiro gray 16
haˈiru /intr:-u:haˈitte/ enter, go in
　　17
　　haˈitte (i)ru be inside 17

haˈizaˈra ashtray 3
haˈkkiˈri clearly, distinctly, precisely
　　18
hako box 17
hana nose 17-A
haˈnaˈ flower 6-A; flower arrange-
　　ment 18
haˈnasiˈ talking, a talk, a story 13
hanasi-tyuu in the middle of talking;
　　the line is busy 13
haˈnaˈsu /tr:-u:haˈnaˈsite/ speak, talk 13

haˈnaˈya   flower shop, florist   6-A
-hañ   half   8
    saˈñ-zikañ-haˈñ   three hours and a
      half   8
    go-ˈzi-haˈñ   5:30   9
haˈñbuˈñ   half, half part   14
hañtai   opposite   19
hañtai-suru   /intr:irreg:hañtai-site/
    oppose   19-N
haˈru   spring (season)   18-N
haˈsi   chopsticks   14-A
haˈsiˈ   bridge   20
haˈtati   20 years of age   10-N
haˈtiˈ   eight   3
hatu   leaving   19
    zyuˈuitiˈ-zi hatu   leaving at 11 o'-
      clock   19
    Koˈobe hatu   leaving Kobe, coming
      from Kobe   19
hatu-ka   20 days; twentieth day of the
    month   8
haˈyaˈi   /-ku/   is fast or early   9
Haˈzimemaˈsite.   How do you do?   11
haˈziˈmete   the first time   11
    Haˈziˈmete ome ni kakarimasu. ↓
      How do you do?   11
heˈbi   snake   17-A
heñ   area, section, part   6
    kono heñ   this area, around here   6
    doˈno heñ   what part? what section?
      19
heˈñ   /na/   strange   13
heˈtaˈ   /na/   unskilled, poor at   18
heˈyaˈ   room   13
hi   day   15
hidari   left   6
    hiˈdari no hoˈo   left side; toward the
      left   6
hikidasi   drawer   17
hiˈkoˈoki   airplane   8
hikoozyoo   airport   20
hima   /na/   free time, leisure   12
    hiˈma na tokiˈ   time when [someone]
      is free   12
hiˈruˈ   noon, daytime   15-N
hiˈrugoˈhañ   noon meal, lunch   15
hito, hiˈtoˈ   person   10
    oˈnnaˈ no hito   woman   10
    oˈtokoˈ no hito   man   10
hiˈtoˈ-ri   one person; single (person)
    10
    hiˈtoˈ-ri de   alone, by oneself   17

hiˈtoˈ-tu   one unit   5
hodo*   approximate extent   15
    teñpura hodo suˈkiˈ zya ˈnaˈi   [I]
      don't like [it] as much as tempu-
      ra   15
hoka   other, another, other than   4
    hoka ni   in addition   4
    Tanaka-sañ no hoka ni   in addition
      to Mr. Tanaka, other than Mr.
      Tanaka   15-N
    hoka no hi   another day   15
hoˈñ   book   2
-hoñ   /counter for long, cylindrical
    units/   5
hoˈñdana   bookshelf   17
hoñtoo   truth, true   3
hoˈñya   bookstore, book dealer   6-A
hoˈo   side; direction; alternative   6
    hiˈdari no hoˈo   left side, toward
      the left   6
    koˈtira no hoˈo   this side, this di-
      rection   6
    miˈgi no hoˈo   right side, toward
      the right   6
    siˈta hoˈo ga ˈiˈi   it will be better
      to have done [it], [you]'d better
      do [it]   20
hoˈoku   fork   14-A
hoˈoñ   horn   20-N
hoˈteru   hotel   6
huˈkiˈñ   dishrag, dish cloth, cloth   17
huku   /tr:-u:huite/   wipe   17
huˈne   ship, boat   8
-huñ   /counter for naming and counting
    minutes/   8
hurañsuˈgo   French language   11-A
huˈrañsuˈziñ   Frenchman   10-A
huˈrobaˈ   bathroom (not toilet)   17-A
hurosiki   furoshiki (cloth square for
    wrapping)   4
huˈru   /intr:-u:huˈtte, huˈtteˈ/   fall (of
    rain, snow, etc.)   18
    aˈme ga ˈhuˈru   it rains   18
huˈruˈi   /-ku/   is old (i.e. not new) or
    stale   2-A
huˈsumaˈ, husuma   sliding door (opaque)
    18
huˈta-tuˈ   two units   5
huˈyuˈ   winter   18-N
hyaˈkuˈ   one hundred   3
-hyaku   /counter for hundreds/   3

I

iˉgirisuˈziñ   Englishman   10-A
iˈi   /yoˈku/   is good <u>or</u> fine <u>or</u> all
    right; never mind   2
iie   no; that's not right   Int.
iˈkaˈga   how?   4
    Iˈkaˈga desu ka﹍   How are you?
    How are things?   How about it
    (offering something)?   4
Iˈkemaseˈñ ˈneˈe.   That's too bad.
    11
ikenai   /-ku/   it won't do, that's too bad
    11
-iki   -bound   19
    Kyooto-iki   bound for Kyoto   19
iku*   /intr:-u:itte/   go   1
iˈkura   how much?   3
iˈkutu   how many units?   5; how old (of
    people)?   10
iˈma   now   7
iˈmaˈ   living room   17-A
iˈmoˈoto   younger sister   11-A
iˈnuˈ   dog   17
iˈñdoˈziñ   an Indian (from India)   10-A
ippai   full   20
    iˈppai ni naˈru   become full   20-N
    ippai ni suru   fill [something]   20
iˈrassyaˈru ⊺ *   /intr:-aru:iˈrassyaˈtte ∼
    iˈraˈsite/   be   6; go   7; come
    8
    Iˈrassyaˈi(maˈse).   Welcome!   4
    Doˈnata de (i)rassyaimasu ka﹍ ⊺
    Who is it? Who are you?   10
ireru   /tr:-ru:irete/   put in, insert
    17
iriguti   entrance   20-N
iˈroˈ   color   5
    doˈñna iro   what (kind of) color?   5
iru*   /intr:-ru:ite/   be located (of ani-
    mate beings)   6
    beñkyoo-site (i)ru   be studying   11

iru (cont.)
    huˈtte (i)ru   be raining   18
    kekkoñ-site (i)ru   be married   10
iru   /intr:-u:itte/   be necessary, need,
    want   4
iˈsoˈgasiˈi   /-ku/   is busy   13
iˈsoˈgu   /intr:-u:iˈsoˈide/   be in a hur-
    ry   7
issyo   together   15
    Saˈitoo-sañ to issyo   together with
    Mr. Saito   15
isu   chair   17-A
itadaku ⊺   /tr:-u:itadaite/   eat, drink
    14; receive, accept   17
iˈtaˈi   /-ku/   is painful   17
iˈtaˈmu   /intr:-u:iˈtaˈñde/   be(come)
    hurt <u>or</u> spoiled   14
    iˈtaˈñda ebi   spoiled shrimp   14
itasu ⊺   /tr:-u:itasite/   make, do   13
    Doˈo itasimasite. ⊺   Don't mention it.
    You're welcome.   Int.
iˈtiˈ   one (numeral)   3
itibañ, iˈtiˈbañ*   to the highest degree
    15
    iˈtibañ takaˈi   is most expensive   15
iˈtoˈko   cousin   11-A
Iˈtte irassyaˈi.   Goodbye. (Lit. Go and
    come.)   20
Iˈtte kimaˈsu.   Goodbye. (Lit. I'll go
    and come.)   20-N
Iˈtte mairimaˈsu. ⊺   Goodbye. (Lit. I'll
    go and come.)   20
iˈttoˈosya   first-class car   19-A
iˈtu   when?   8
    iˈtu mo   always   9
iˈtuˈ-tu   five units   5
iu   /tr:-u:itte/   say, be named, be
    called   1
iˈya   /M/   no; that's not right   16

K

ka*   /sentence particle/   (question)   Int.
    Oˈgeˈñki desu ka﹍ ⊺   Are you well?
    Int.
-ka ∼ -niti   /counter for naming and
    counting days/   8
kaˈdo   street corner   7

kaˈeru   /intr:-u:kaˈette/   return (home)
    9
-kagetu   /counter for number of months/
    8
kaˈgiˈ   key   16
    kaˈgiˈ ga kaˈkaˈru   [something] locks   16

ka⌐gi˥ (cont.)
    ka⌐gi˥ o ka┌ke˥ru lock [something]
    16
ka˥gu furniture 17-A
-kai /counter for naming and counting
    floors/ 16
kaidañ stairway 17-A
kaikee bill, accounting, check 15
kaisya business company, company
    office 12
ka┌ka˥ru /intr:-u:ka┌ka˥tte/ be re-
    quired, take 8; be suspended
    11
    ka⌐gi˥ ga ka┌ka˥ru [something]
      locks 16
    o⌐me ni kaka˥ru ꜛ see (a person),
      meet 11
    Ha⌐zi˥mete ome ni kakarimasu. ꜛ
      How do you do. 11
    zi┌kañ ga kaka˥ru take time
      8
ka┌ke˥ru /tr:-ru:ka┌kete/ hang [some-
    thing] 12
    de┌ñwa o kake˥ru telephone (verb)
      12
    ka⌐gi˥ o ka┌ke˥ru lock [something]
    16
ka˥ku /tr:-u:ka˥ite/ write, draw 7
ka┌ma˥u /intr:-u:ka┌ma˥tte/ mind, care
    about 18-N
    ka┌mawa˥nai doesn't matter, makes
      no difference, is all right 9
ka┌mi˥ paper 5
ka˥nai wife (one's own) 11
ka┌ñkoku˥ziñ a South Korean 10-A
kao face; expression 14
    a˥o˥i kao o suru be pale 14
kara* /particle/ from 8; because
    11; after 16
    sore kara from that point, after
      that, and then, and 4
karada body 17-A
ka┌ra˥i /-ku/ is spicy or salty 14
kariru /tr:-ru:karite/ borrow, rent
    [from someone] 13
karui /-ku/ is light (i.e. not heavy)
    20-N
Ka┌sikomarima˥sita. ꜛ Certainly. I'll
    do as you have asked. 4
ka┌ta˥ ꜛ person 10
    o┌ñna no kata˥ ꜛ woman 10
    o┌toko no kata˥ ꜛ man 10
katamiti one-way 19
ka┌tazuke˥ru /tr:-ru:ka┌tazu˥kete/
    straighten up 16

kau /tr:-u:katte/ buy 4
ka┌wa˥ku /intr:-u:ka┌wa˥ite/ become
    dry 15
kawari a change; a second helping 18
ka┌yo˥o(bi), kayoo Tuesday 8
ka˥zoku family 11-A
kedo /see keredo/ 20
kekkoñ-suru /intr:irreg:kekkoñ-site/
    marry 10
    kekkoñ-site (i)ru be married 10
ke˥kkoo /na/ fine, all right 9
    Mo˥o ˥ke˥kkoo desu. I'm fine as I
    am. I've had enough already. 14
ke(re)do* /particle/ although 20
ke˥sa this morning 9
kesu /tr:-u:kesite/ turn off, extin-
    guish, erase 16
kieru /intr:-ru:kiete/ become extin-
    guished, go out 16-N
kiiroi /-ku/ is yellow 4
kikoeru /intr:-ru:kikoete/ be audi-
    ble, can hear 13
kiku /tr:-u:kiite/ ask a question, lis-
    ten, hear 12
kimoti feeling, mood 18
    ki┌moti ga i˥i˙ is pleasant or agree-
    able 18
ki┌no˥o, kinoo yesterday 1
ki┌ñyo˥o(bi), kiñyoo Friday 8
ki┌otuke˥ru /intr:-ru:ki┌otuke˥te/ be
    careful 17
kippu ticket 19
kirai /na/ displeasing 15
ki┌ree /na/ pretty, clean 3
ki˥ru /tr:-u:ki˥tte, ki┌tte˥/ cut, cut
    off, hang up (the telephone) 13
ki┌ssa˥teñ, kissateñ tearoom 14-A
ki┌sya˥ (steam) train 8
ki┌tana˥i /-ku/ is dirty 16
ko child 10
    o┌ñna˥ no ko little girl 10
    o┌toko˥ no ko little boy 10
ko┌bore˥ru /intr:-ru:ko┌bo˥rete/ [some-
    thing] spills 17
    ko┌bo˥rete (i)ru be spilled 17
ko┌bo˥su /tr:-u:ko┌bo˥site/ spill
    [something] 17-N
kodomo child 10
ko˥e voice 13
    o˥oki˥i ┌ko˥e de or o˥oki na ┌ko˥e
    de with a loud voice 13
ko˥i /-ku/ is strong or thick (of li-
    quids); is dark (of colors) 14-A
koko this place, here 6
ko┌ko˥no-tu nine units 5

ko⌐maka¬i /-ku/ is small or fine or
    detailed 17
ko⌐ma¬ru /intr:-u:ko⌐ma¬tte/ be(come)
    distressing or troublesome or
    annoying or inconvenient or per-
    plexing 9
ko⌐me¬ uncooked rice 14-A
ko̚mu /intr:-u:ko̚nde/ be(come) crowded 20
    ko¬nde (i)ru be crowded 20
kono* /+ nom/ this — 3
kono-ḡoro these days, nowadays 18
ko¬ñbañ this evening, tonight 13
    Koñbañ wa. Good evening. Int.
koñḡetu this month 10
koñna* this kind, this kind of 5
    Koñniti wa. Good afternoon. Int.
koobañ police box 7
kooeñ park 6-A
ko⌐ohi¬i coffee 14
ko⌐ohiizya¬wañ cup (with handles) 14-A
ko⌐oka¬ñsyu telephone operator 12
koori ice 14-A
ko⌐otuuko¬osya Japan Travel Bureau
    12
kootya black tea 14-A
koppu glass for drinking 14-A
kore* this thing 2
ko⌐si¬ lower part of the back 17-A
ko⌐syo¬o pepper 14-A
kosyoo out of order 13
kosyoo-suru /intr:irreg:kosyoo-site/
    break down 13-N
ko⌐tae¬ru, ko⌐ta¬eru /intr:-ru:ko⌐ta¬ete/
    answer CI
kotira this one (of two); this way,
    hereabouts, here 6; this per-
    son 11; the person speaking 12
    ko⌐tira no ho¬o this side, this di-
    rection 6
kotori bird 17-A
kotosi this year 8
kotozuke message; the giving of a mes-
    sage 13

ko⌐tti¬ /see kotira/ 6
ku¬ nine 3
kubi neck 17-A
ku⌐da¬mono fruit 14-A
kudari down-train (i.e. going away
    from Tokyo) 19
ku⌐dasa¬i* /imperative of ku⌐dasa¬ru/
    give me 1
    Ko⌐re o kudasa¬i. Please give me
    this one. 4
    Ma¬tte kudasai. Please wait. 1
    I⌐soḡa¬nai de kudasai. Please don't
    hurry. 7
ku⌐dasa¬ru ꜛ * /tr:-aru:ku⌐dasa¬tte ∼
    ku⌐dasu¬tte/ give me 4
    ka¬ite ku⌐dasaimase¬ñ ka˩ ꜛ
    would (lit. won't) you be kind
    enough to write (or draw) for me?
    7
-kuñ /M/ /suffix attached to men's
    and boys' names; familiar/ 13
kureru /tr:-ru:kurete/ give me 17
    ta⌐no¬ñde kureru request (or order)
    for me 17
ku⌐ro¬i /-ku/ is black 4
ku¬ru /intr:irreg:ki⌐te¬/ come 5
    ta⌐no¬ñde kuru come having engaged,
    go and engage 20
kuruma car, cart 7
kusuri medicine 6-N
kusuriya drugstore, druggist 6-A
kuti mouth 17-A
ku¬uki air 20
kya¬burettaa carburetor 20-N
kyaku guest, customer 18
kyo¬neñ last year 10-A
kyo¬o today 1
kyo¬odai brothers and/or sisters
    11-A
kyu¬u nine 3
kyuukoo express 19
kyu⌐uko¬okeñ express ticket 19-A

M

ma¬a oh well; I guess 4
ma¬da* /+ affirmative/ still, yet
    18; /+ negative/ not yet 14
    ma¬da da it is yet to happen; not
    yet 14
made* /particle/ as far as; up to and
    including 7

made (cont.)
    To⌐okyo¬o-eki made as far as Tokyo
    Station 7
    na¬ñ-zi made until what time? 9
    zyu⌐u-ḡatu¬ made ni by October 9
ma¬do window 16
ma⌐do¬ḡuti ticket window 19

ma⌐e front 6; before 8
  e⌐ki no ⌐ma⌐e front of the station 6
  zi⌐p-pu⌐ñ mae ten minutes before the hour 8
  zi⌐p-puñ ma⌐e, zi⌐p-puñ ⌐ma⌐e ten minutes ago 8
maḡaru /intr:-u:maḡatte/ make a turn 7
  ka⌐do o maḡaru turn at the corner, turn the corner 7
ma⌐ḡo⌐ grandchild 11-A
-mai /counter for thin, flat units/ 5
ma⌐iasa every morning 9-N
ma⌐ibañ every night 19-N
maido every time 4
  Ma⌐ido ari⌐ḡatoo gozaimasu.⁺ Thank you again and again. 4
maiḡetu every month 9-N
maineñ every year 9-N
ma⌐initi every day 9
ma⌐iru↓* /intr:-u:ma⌐itte/ go 7; come 8
maisyuu every week 9-N
maitosi every year 9-N
maituki every month 9-N
ma⌐kita⌐bako cigarette 3-N
ma⌐ma⌐ condition 16
  so⌐no mama⌐ de being that condition as it is 16
-mañ /counter for ten thousands/ 3
ma⌐ssu⌐ḡu straight 7
mata again 4
  Ma⌐ta do⌐ozo. Please [come] again. 4
ma⌐tia⌐isitu waiting room 20
ma⌐tti match 3
ma⌐tu /tr:-u:ma⌐tte/ wait, await, wait for 1
mawaru /intr:-u:mawatte/ go around 20
mawasu /tr:-u:mawasite/ send around 20
ma⌐zu⌐i /-ku/ is bad-tasting 14
me⌐ eye 17-A
me⌐e niece 11-A
me⌐eḡosañ↑ niece 11-A
meesi name card, calling card 13
me⌐ezi Meiji Era (1868-1912) 8
mesiaḡaru↑ /tr:-u:mesiaḡatte/ eat; drink; smoke 14
mi⌐dori green 16-N
mi⌐e⌐ru* /intr:-ru:mi⌐ete/ be visible, can see; put in an appearance, show up, come 18

miḡi right (i.e. not left) 6
  mi⌐ḡi no ho⌐o right side, toward the right 6
mi⌐mi⌐ ear 17-A
mi⌐na⌐sañ↑ everyone 11
mi⌐nna⌐ everyone; everything 11
mi⌐ru* /tr:-ru:mi⌐te/ look at, see 12
  si⌐te mi⌐ru try doing, do and see 19
mi⌐ruku milk 14
mi⌐se⌐ store, shop 6-A
mi⌐se⌐ru /tr:-ru:mi⌐sete/ show, let [someone] see 4
miti street, road, way 7
mi-⌐ttu three units 5
mizu cold water 14
mo* /particle/ also, too 4
  a⌐o⌐i no mo blue one(s) too 4
  de⌐pa⌐ato ni mo in the department store too 6
  o⌐oki⌐i no mo ti⌐isa⌐i no mo both big ones and small ones 5
  do⌐o mo in every way Int.
  i⌐tu mo always 9
  dotira mo both 10
  dare mo /+ negative/ nobody 13
mo⌐do⌐ru /intr:-u:mo⌐do⌐tte/ go back, back up 7
mo⌐kuyo⌐o(bi), mokuyoo Thursday 8
momoiro pink 16-N
mo⌐no⌐ thing (tangible) 14
moo* /+ quantity expression/ more, additional 1
  moo iti-do one time more 1
  mo⌐o suko⌐si a little more, a few more 4
mo⌐o* /+ affirmative/ already, yet, now already, soon now 14
  /+ negative/ no more 18
  mo⌐o su⌐ḡu soon now, any minute now 15
mo⌐osu↓ /tr:-u:mo⌐osite/ say, be named, be called 18
morau /tr:-u:moratte/ receive, get 17
  site morau have [someone] do [it], have [something] done 17
mo⌐simosi hello (on the telephone); say there! 12
mo⌐ti⌐roñ of course 15
motte iku take [something somewhere] 14-N

mo'tte ku'ru bring [something] 14
mo'tto* more 5
mukoo beyond, over there; the far
   side 6
  bi'ru no mukoo beyond the building 6
  mu'koo no bi'ru the building over
   there 6

na* /pre-nominal alternant of da/
   12
  hi'ma na toki' time when [someone]
   is free 12
nagaisu couch, sofa 17-A
na'gasi' sink 17-A
na'ihu knife 14-A
naiseñ telephone extension 12
na'ka inside 17
  hi'kidasi no na'ka inside the drawer 17
nakanaka considerably; more than expected 11
namae name 10
na'na seven 3
na'na'-tu seven units 5
na'ni what? 2
  na'ni ka something, anything 4
  nani mo /+ negative/ nothing
   18
naniiro what color? 5-N
naniziñ what nationality? 10-A
na'ñ what? 2
  na'ñ de' mo no matter what it is,
   anything at all 15
nañni mo /see nani mo/ 18
na'o'ru /intr:-u:na'o'tte/ get well,
   recover 14
na'o'su /tr:-u:na'o'site/ fix, repair
   13
na'pukiñ napkin 14-A
naraberu /tr:-ru:narabete/ line
   [something or someone] up
   20-N
narabu /intr:-u:narañde/ [something
   or someone] lines up 20
na'ra'u /tr:-u:na'ra'tte/ learn, take
   lessons 18
na'ru* /intr:-u:na'tte/ become, get
   to be 10
  o'okiku 'na'ru get big 10
  ya-'ttu' ni 'na'ru get to be eight
   years old 10

N

na'ru (cont.)
  o'kaeri ni na'ru ' /honorific equivalent of ka'eru/ 9
na'sa'ru ' /tr:-aru:na'sa'tte ~ na'su'-
   tte/ do, make 13
na'tu' summer 18-N
na'ze why? 11
ne?* /sentence particle/ isn't it
   true? do you agree? 13
ne'e* /sentence particle/ isn't it true!
   don't you agree! 1
  Do'ko desyoo ka 'ne'e. Where
   WOULD it be! I wonder where it
   is! 11
ne'esañ ' older sister 11-A
ne'ga'u ' /tr:-u:ne'ga'tte/ request
   Int.
  O'negai-sima'su. ' I'd like it.
   Please let me have it. Please do
   so. I have a request to make of
   you. Int.
ne'ko cat 17-A
-neñ /counter for naming and counting
   years/ 8
ni' two 3
ni* /particle/ in, on, at 6; into,
   onto, to 7; by 17
  hoka ni in addition 4
  To'okyoo ni a'ru be in Tokyo 6
  sa'ñ-zi ni iku go at 3 o'clock 8
  koko ni oku put here 17
  tomodati ni iu say to a friend 18
  to'modati ni tuku'tte morau have a
   friend make [it] 17
ni'ga'i /-ku/ is bitter 14-A
nihoñgo Japanese language 11
ni'hoñzi'ñ a Japanese 10
ni'isañ ' older brother 11-A
ni'ku' meat 6-N
ni'ku'ya meat market, butcher 6-A
ni'motu baggage, things to carry 20
-niñ /counter for people/ 10
-niñmae /counter for portions/ 15

nippoñḡo   Japanese language   11
ni⌐ppoñzi˥ñ   a Japanese   10-A
-niti   /counter for naming and counting
   days/   10
ni⌐tiyo˥o(bi), nitiyoo   Sunday   8
ni⌐to˥osya   second-class car   19
niwa   garden   17-A
no*   one, ones   4
   a⌐ka˥i no   red one(s)   4
   kyo˥o no wa   as for today's (one)   5
no*   /particle/
   To⌐okyoo no ti˥zu   map of Tokyo   5
   kyo˥o no siñbuñ   today's newspaper
   5
   watakusi no siñbuñ   my newspaper   5
   ni⌐to˥osya no tomaru tokoro   the place
     where the second-class cars stop   19
no*   /pre-nominal alternant of da/
   19-N
   byooki no kodomo   sick child   19-N
nobori   up-train (i.e. going toward Tokyo)   19

o*   /particle/
   Hu⌐rosiki o mi˥sete kudasai.   Please
   show me a furoshiki.   4
   Kono miti o ma⌐ssu˥ḡu i⌐tte kuda-
   sa˥i.   Please go straight along
   this street.   7
oba   aunt   11-A
o⌐ba˥asañ ⁺   grandmother; old lady
   11-A
obasañ ⁺   aunt; woman   11-A
oboñ⁺   tray   14-A
Odaizi ni. ⁺   Take care /of yourself/!
   11
O⌐hayoo (gozaima˥su). ⁺   Good morning.
   Int.
oi   nephew   11-A
o⌐ide ni na˥ru ⁺   be, come, go   9-N
oiḡosañ ⁺   nephew   11-A
oimotosañ ⁺   younger sister   11-A
o⌐iru   oil (for automobiles)   20
oisii /-ku/   is delicious   14
o⌐ka˥asañ ⁺   mother   11-A
O⌐kaeri-nasa˥i.   Welcome home.
   Hello.   20
okaḡesama de ⁺   thanks to you; thanks
   for asking   Int.
O⌐kamai na˥ku. ⁺   Don't bother.   Don't
   go to any trouble.   18
o⌐ka˥si ⁺   cake, sweets   14-A

no˥do   throat   15
   no˥do ḡa ka⁺wa⁺ku   become thirsty
   15
no⌐ko˥ru   /intr:-u:no⌐ko˥tte/   be(come)
   left over or left behind   20
no⌐ko˥su   /tr:-u:no⌐ko˥site/   leave behind, leave over (for another
   time)   20-N
no⌐mi˥mono   a drink, beverage   15
no˥mu   /tr:-u:no˥ñde/   drink   14
noriba   place for boarding vehicles   20
norikae   a transfer (from one vehicle
   to another)   19
no⌐rikae˥ru, no⌐rika˥eru   /intr:-ru:no-
   ⌐rika˥ete/   change vehicles, transfer   19-N
noru   /intr:-u:notte/   get on (a vehicle),
   take (a vehicle), ride   19
noseru   /tr:-ru:nosete/   give [someone]
   a ride, carry, take on board   19-N
notihodo   later   12
ñ /M/   yeah   16
ñ⌐ma˥   horse   17-A

O

o⌐kasi˥i /-ku/   is funny (strange or
   amusing)   20
okosañ ⁺   child   10
oku* /tr:-u:oite/   put, place   17
   site oku   do in advance, do now for
   later reference   17
okureru   /intr:-ru:okurete/   fall behind, become late   19
   okurete (i)ru   be late   19
o˥kusañ ⁺   wife; madam; mistress   11
O⌐matase-(ita)sima˥sita. ⁺   I'm sorry
   to have kept you waiting.   4
O⌐matidoosama de˥sita.   I'm sorry you
   were kept waiting.   20
o⌐me ni kaka˥ru ⁺   see (a person), meet
   11
   Ha⌐zi˥mete ome ni kakarimasu. ⁺
   How do you do?   11
omoi /-ku/   is heavy   20
o⌐mosiro˥i /-ku/   is interesting, is unusual, is fun   2
onaka   stomach   15
   onaka ḡa suku   become hungry   15
onazi   same   2
   onazi kusuri   same medicine   17
   kore to onazi   same as this   17
O⌐neḡai-sima˥su. ⁺   Please (speaker
   requesting something; lit. I make
   a request).   Int.

oˈnnaˈ female 10
  oˈnnaˈ no hito woman 10
  oˈnna no kataˈ⁺ woman 10
  oˈnnaˈ no ko little girl 10
oohuku round trip 19
oˈoki* /na/ big 13
  oˈoki na ˈkoˈe loud voice 13
oˈokiˈi /-ku/ is big 2
oˈriˈru /intr:-ru:oˈrite/ go down, descend, get off (a vehicle) 20
oˈroˈsu /tr:-u:oˈroˈsite/ lower, let down, discharge (from a vehicle) 20-N
oˈru⁺* /intr:-u:oˈtte/ be located (of animate beings) 6
  keˈkkon-site oˈru⁺ be married 10
  beˈnkyoo-site oˈru⁺ be studying 11
  huˈtte ˈoˈru⁺ be raining 18
Osaki ni.⁺ [Excuse me for going] ahead. 18
  Doˈozo, osaki ni.⁺ Please [go] ahead. 18-N
osieru /tr:-ru:osiete/ teach, inform 7
osiire closet (for clothing, quilts, etc.) 17-A

osoi /-ku/ is late or slow 11
Oˈsoˈreirimasu. Thank you. I'm sorry. 18
oˈssyaˈru⁺ /tr:-aru:oˈssyaˈtte/ say, be named, be called 13
otaku⁺ home, household 9
  otaku no pertaining or belonging to your household 10
oˈtokoˈ male 10
  oˈtokoˈ no hito man 10
  oˈtoko no kataˈ⁺ man 10
  oˈtokoˈ no ko little boy 10
oˈtoˈosañ⁺ father 11
oˈtootoˈ younger brother 11-A
oˈtotoˈi, ototoi day before yesterday 8
otya⁺ tea 14
oya parent 11-A
oyaḡosañ⁺ parent 11-A
Oˈyasumi-nasaˈi. Good night. Int.
oyu⁺ hot water 14-A
ozi uncle 11-A
oˈziˈisañ⁺ grandfather; old man 11-A
ozisañ⁺ uncle; man 11-A
oˈzyoˈosañ⁺ daughter; young girl; little girl 11-A

P

paˈñ bread 14-A
pañku-suru /intr:irreg:pañku-site/ become punctured 20

pañku-suru (cont.)
  taiya ḡa pañku-suru have a flat tire 20
peˈñ pen 2

R

raˈiḡetu next month 16-N
raineñ next year 16-N
raisyuu next week 16
raˈitaa lighter 4
raˈzio radio 16
reˈe zero 12
reˈezoˈoko refrigerator 17-A
reˈñzi stove (for cooking) 17-A
reˈsutorañ restaurant 14-A
-ri ~ -niñ /counter for people/ 10
rippa /na/ fine, handsome, magnificent, imposing 18

-rittoru /counter for liters/ 20
roˈkuˈ six 3
rooka hall, corridor 17-A
rosiaḡo Russian language 11-A
roˈsiaˈziñ a Russian 10-A
ruˈsu away from home 12
  rusu-tyuu ni during [someone's] absence from home 18
ryokañ inn (Japanese style) 6-A
ryoˈoriˈya restaurant (Japanese style) 14-A
ryoˈosiñ both parents 11-A
ryoˈoziˈkañ consulate 6

S

sa⌐a   hmm . . .   6
sakana   fish   6-N
sakanaya   fish market, fish man   6-A
sake   rice wine   14
saki   ahead   6
   kono saki   up ahead from here   7
-sama **'**   (more polite alternant of -sañ)
   12
sa⌐mu⌐i   /-ku/   is cold (of weather or
   atmosphere)   14
sañ   three   3
-sañ **'**   Mr., Mrs., Miss   Int.
sañpo   a walk   18
sañpo-suru   /intr: irreg: sañpo-site/
   take a walk   18-N
sa⌐ñto⌐osya   third-class car   19-A
sara   plate, dish   14-A
sa⌐simi⌐   sashimi (raw fish)   14-A
sa⌐to⌐o   sugar   14-A
-satu   /counter for books, magazines,
   etc./   5
Sayonara.   Goodbye.   Int.
sayoo   that way, thus, so   12
Sayoonara.   Goodbye.   Int.
seereki   Western calendar, Christian
   Era   8-N
se⌐ki, seki   seat, assigned place   12
sekkeñ   soap   17
senaka   back (part of the body)   17-A
se⌐ñ   thousand   3
-señ   /counter for thousands/   3
se⌐ñgetu   last month   14
se⌐ñme⌐ñki   wash basin   17-A
señmeñzyo   washroom, lavatory   17-A
se⌐ñse⌐e   teacher, doctor   16
señzitu   the other day   18
si⌐   four   3
si⌐ba⌐raku   a while (short or long)   11
   Si⌐ba⌐raku desita.   It's been a long
     time [since I last saw you].   11
sigoto   work   10
   sigoto-tyuu   in the middle of work
     12
si⌐ka⌐si   however, but   15
si⌐ma⌐ru   /intr: -u: si⌐ma⌐tte/   [some-
   thing] closes or shuts   16
simau* /tr: -u: simatte/   put away, store
   17

simau   (cont.)
   irete simau   finish putting in, put in
     for good, end up by putting in   17
si⌐me⌐ru   /tr: -ru: si⌐mete/   close or
   shut [something]   16
siñbuñ   newspaper   2
siñdai   bed   17-A
si⌐ñda⌐ikeñ   berth ticket   19-A
si⌐ñda⌐isya   sleeping car   19-A
si⌐ñka⌐ñseñ   new trunk-line   19-N
siñsitu   bedroom   17-A
si⌐o⌐   salt   14-A
si⌐rabe⌐ru   /tr: -ru: si⌐ra⌐bete/   look into, check, investigate   20
si⌐ro⌐i   /-ku/   is white   4
siru   /tr: -u: sitte/   come to know   10
   sitte (i)ru   know   10
sita   under, below, bottom, youngest
   10
   si⌐ta no ho⌐ñ   bottom book   10-N
   ho⌐ñ no sita   under the book   10-N
sitaku   preparation   16
   sitaku o suru   prepare   16
si⌐ti⌐   seven   3
si⌐tu⌐ree   /na/   rudeness, rude   10
   Si⌐tu⌐ree desu ḡa_   Excuse me
     but . . .   10
   Si⌐tu⌐ree(-simasu).   Excuse me (on
     leaving).   Int.
   Si⌐tu⌐ree(-simasita).   Excuse me
     (for what I did).   Int.
so⌐ba   vicinity   6
   e⌐ki no ⌐so⌐ba   near the station   6
   so⌐ba no ⌐e⌐ki   a nearby station   6
   su⌐ḡu ⌐so⌐ba   immediate vicinity   6
so⌐ba   noodles   14-A
so⌐ba⌐ya   noodle shop   14-A
so⌐bo   grandmother   11-A
so⌐hu   grandfather   11-A
soko   that place, there   6
sono*   / + nom/   that —   3
soñna*   that kind, that kind of   5
so⌐o   that way, thus, so   2
   So⌐o desu.   That's right.   2
   So⌐o desu ka.   Is that right?   Oh?
     2
   So⌐o desu ⌐ne⌐e.   That's right, isn't
     it.   2; Let me see . . . Hmm . . .
     4

Japanese-English Glossary

403

soozi-suru /tr: irreg: soozi-site/   clean
  16
sore*   that thing 2
  sore kara   after that, and then, and
    4
sotira   that one (of two); that way,
    thereabouts, there 6; that per-
    son 11; the person addressed
    12
so⌐to   outside 17
so⌐tti⌐ /see sotira/ 6
su⌐gi⌐   past, after 8
  ni-⌐hu⌐n sugi   two minutes after
    8
su⌐gu   soon, any minute, right away
    5
  su⌐gu ⌐so⌐ba   immediate vicinity
    6
su⌐iyo⌐o(bi), suiyoo   Wednesday 8
su⌐ki⌐ /na/   pleasing; like [something]
    15
sukiyaki   sukiyaki (stew of vegetables
    with meat or chicken or fish) 14-A
su⌐ko⌐si   a little, a few 4
  mo⌐o suko⌐si   a little more, a few
    more 4
suku /intr: -u: suite/   become empty
    15
  onaka ḡa suku   become hungry 15
su⌐mai   residence 16
su⌐mi   corner (of a room) 17
Su⌐(m)imase⌐ñ.   I'm sorry. Thank you
    for your trouble. Int.

Su⌐(m)imase⌐ñ desita.   I'm sorry (for
    what I did).   Thank you (for
    the trouble you took).
    Int.
supeiñḡo   Spanish language 11-A
su⌐ppa⌐i /-ku/   is acid or sour 14-A
su⌐pu⌐uñ   spoon 14-A
suru* /tr: irreg: site/   do, perform,
    make 1
su⌐si   sushi (rice with fish, seaweed,
    egg, etc.) 14-A
su⌐si⌐ya   sushi shop 14-A
sutañdo   lamp 17-A
suteru /tr: -ru: sutete/   throw away
    17
su⌐to⌐obu   heater 16
suu /tr: -u: sutte/   smoke (cigarettes,
    cigars, etc.) 14
su⌐zusi⌐i /-ku/   is cool 18
syasyoo   train conductor 19
syokudoo   dining room 14-A
syo⌐kudo⌐oosya   dining car 19-A
syokuzi   dining, a meal 15
  syokuzi o suru   dine, eat a meal
    15
syo⌐osyoo   a little 4
syoowa   Showa Era (1926–   ) 8
syooyu   soy sauce 14-A
syoozi   sliding door (translucent) 18
syosai   study (i.e. a room) 17
-syuukañ /counter for number of
    weeks/ 8
syu⌐ziñ   husband 11-A

T

tabako   cigarette, tobacco 3
tabakoya   cigar store 6-A
ta⌐bemo⌐no, ta⌐bemono⌐   food, edibles
    15-N
ta⌐be⌐ru /tr: -ru: ta⌐bete/   eat 14
Tadaima.   Hello, I'm back. 20
taiheñ /na/   awful, dreadful, terrible,
    a nuisance; very 20
taisetu /na/   important 20
ta⌐isi⌐kañ   embassy 6
taisyoo   Taisho Era (1912–1926) 8
taitee   usual, usually 9
  ta⌐itee no Amerika⌐ziñ   most Amer-
    icans 15
taiya   tire 20
ta⌐ka⌐i /-ku/   is expensive 3
ta⌐kusa⌐ñ, takusañ   much, many 5

ta⌐kusii   taxi 7
ta⌐ma⌐ḡo   egg 14-A
tana   shelf 17-A
ta⌐no⌐mu /tr: -u: ta⌐no⌐ñde/   make a re-
    quest, place an order 14; en-
    gage, hire 20
tañsu   chest of drawers 17-A
tariru /intr: -ru: tarite/   be sufficient
    20
tatami   rice-straw floor mat 18
  ta⌐tami no heya⌐   room with tatami
    18
ta⌐temo⌐no, ta⌐te⌐mono   building 6
ta⌐tu /intr: -u: ta⌐tte/   depart, leave for
    a trip 19
te⌐   hand 17-A
te⌐a⌐rai   toilet 6-A

teeburu   table   17
temae   this side   6
  byooiñ no temae   this side of the
    hospital   6
te˞ñki   weather; good weather   18
teñpura   tempura (batter-fried fish or
    vegetables)   14
teñpuraya   tempura shop   14-A
te˞rebi   television   16
te˞tuda˞u   /tr:-u:te˞tuda˞tte/   help,
    lend a hand   17
tigau   /intr:-u:tigatte/   be wrong; be
    different   2
  sore to tigau   be different from that
    17
  Ti˞gaima˞su.   Wrong number (on the
    telephone).   13
ti˞isa   /na/   small   13-N
  ti˞isa na ˞ko˞e   a low voice   13-N
ti˞isa˞i   /-ku/   is small   2
ti˞ka˞i   /-ku/   is near   20
tikatetu   subway   20
ti˞ti˞   father   11
ti˞zu   map   5
to*   /particle/   and   4; with   15
  ho˞ñ to zassi   book and magazine
    4
  Sa˞itoo-sañ to issyo   together with
    Mr. Saito   15
to*   /quotative/   18
  na˞ñ to iu   say what?   be named or
    called what?   18
to   door   16
todana   cupboard (with shelves)   17
to˞ire(tto)   toilet   6-A
tokee   clock, watch   8
to˞ki*   time, occasion   12
  no˞ru toki˞   /ni/   when [someone]
    rides   19
to˞kidoki˞   sometimes   9
tokkyuu   special express   19
to˞kkyu˞ukeñ   special-express ticket   19-A
tokonoma   Japanese-style alcove   18
to˞ko(ro)˞   place   18
tokubetu   special   19-N
to˞kubetukyu˞ukoo   special express   19
tomaru   /intr:-u:tomatte/   come to a
    halt; stop at, lodge   19
tomeru   /tr:-ru:tomete/   bring to a
    halt   7

tomodati   friend   10
tonari   next door, adjoining   6
  e˞ki no tonari   next door to the sta-
    tion   6
To˞ñde mo na˞i.   Heavens no!   8
to˞o   ten units   5
-too   /counter for naming classes/   19
Toodai   Tokyo University   13
tooi   /-ku/   is far   13
  deñwa ḡa tooi   have trouble hear-
    ing (on the telephone)   13
to˞ori˞   avenue, wide street   7
to˞oru   /intr:-u:to˞otte/   pass through,
    go through, pass in front of   19
to˞osuto   toast   14-A
tori   bird   17-A; chicken, fowl   14-A
torikaeru   /tr:-ru:torikaete/   exchange
    20
to˞ru   /tr:-u:to˞tte/   take up, take away,
    remove, take off, pass [to someone]
    17
totemo   exceedingly, very   8
tottemo   exceedingly, very   8
to˞zi˞ru   /tr:-ru:to˞zite/   close [some-
    thing]   CI
[t]te*   /quotative/   18
  na˞ñ te iu   say what?   be named
    or called what?   18
-[t]tu   /counter for number of units/
    5; /counter for years of people's
    age/   10
tu˞gi˞   next   7
  tu˞gi˞ no ˞ka˞do   next corner   7
tu˞itati˞   first day of the month   8
tu˞kare˞ru   /intr:-ru:tu˞ka˞rete/   be-
    come tired   17
tu˞ke˞ru   /tr:-ru:tu˞ke˞te/   attach,
    turn [something] on   16
tukiatari   end of a street or corridor
    7
tu˞ku   /intr:-u:tu˞ite/   arrive   9;
    [something] becomes attached or
    turned on   16
tukue   desk   17
tu˞mara˞nai   /-ku/   is dull or boring;
    is trifling   2
tumetai   /-ku/   is cold   14
tumori*   intention, plan   20
  iku tumori da   [I] intend to go, [I]
    plan to go   20
tutaeru   /tr:-ru:tutaete/   report,
    communicate, convey a message
    13

tu⌐tome⌐ru /intr:-ru:to⌐to⌐mete/ become employed 10
tu⌐to⌐mete (i)ru be employed 10
tu⌐yo⌐i /-ku/ is strong 17
tyairo brown 16
tyaku arriving 19
i⌐ti⌐-zi tyaku arriving at 1 o'-
clock 19
tyanoma family room (Japanese
style) 17-A
-tyañ ⌐ /suffix added to children's
given names/ 10
tyawañ cup or small bowl (Japanese
style) 14-A
tyoodo exactly 8
-tyoome /counter for naming
chomes/ 7

tyooseñg̃o Korean language
11-A
tyo⌐oseñzi⌐ñ a Korean 10-A
tyo⌐tto a bit, a little 1; just
5
Tyo⌐tto. Say there! 4
tyo⌐tto_ I'm afraid it won't
do . . . 4
-tyuu in the middle of —, now busy
with — 12
sig̃oto-tyuu in the middle of work
12
tyuug̃okug̃o Chinese language 11-A
tyu⌐ug̃oku⌐ziñ a Chinese 10-A
tyuumoñ-suru /tr:irreg:tyuumoñ-site/
place an order 14

U

u⌐de⌐ arm 17-A
u⌐e⌐, ue over, above, top, topmost,
oldest 10
u⌐e no ho⌐ñ top book 10-N
ho⌐ñ no ue top of the book
10-N
ukag̃au ⌐ /tr:-u:ukag̃atte/ inquire 6
tyo⌐tto u⌐kag̃aima⌐su g̃a excuse
me but ; I'm just going to ask
[you something] but 6
ukag̃au ⌐ /intr:-u:ukag̃atte/ visit 16
u⌐ma⌐ horse 17-A
u⌐mi sea, ocean 18
usag̃i rabbit 17-A
usi bull, cow 17-A

usiro back, rear 7
ta⌐isi⌐kañ no usiro back of the embassy 7
usui /-ku/ is weak or thin (of
liquids); is light (of colors)
14
u⌐ti⌐, uti home, house, household
9
uti no our household's, our
10
uti among 15
A to B to C no uti /de/ /being/
among A and B and C
15

W

wa* /sentence particle/ /W/ 16
wa* /particle/ as for, comparatively speaking Int.
A⌐na⌐ta wa? How about you? Int.
Sore wa ⌐na⌐ñ desu ka_ What is
that? (Lit. As for that, what is
it?) 2
Si⌐ñbuñ wa kaimase⌐ñ desita. A
newspaper I didn't buy. 4
Ko⌐ko ni⌐ wa a⌐rimase⌐ñ. Here
there isn't one. 6

wa⌐ka⌐ru /intr:-u:wa⌐ka⌐tte/ be comprehensible, understand, can tell 1
wañ bowl 14-A
wa⌐ru⌐i /-ku/ is bad 2-A
wasureru /tr:-ru:wasurete/ forget 4
watakusi I, me 5
watakusi no my, mine 5
wataru /intr:-u:watatte/ go over, go
across 20
watasu /tr:-u:watasite/ hand over
20-N

Y

ya* /particle/ and 17
  hoⁿ ya zassi   books and maga-
     zines and the like 17
ya⌐g̃i   goat 17-A
ya⌐ma¬   mountain 18
yameru /tr:-ru:yamete/ quit, give up 14
yaoya   vegetable store   6-A
yaru /tr:-u:yatte/ give (to someone
  other than the speaker) 17
yasai   vegetable   14-A
yasasii /-ku/ is easy 11
ya⌐su¬i /-ku/ is cheap 3
ya⌐sumi¬   vacation, holiday, time off 8
ya⌐su¬mu /tr:-u:ya⌐su¬nde/ rest, re-
  lax, take time off 17
ya-⌐ttu¬   eight units 5
yo* /sentence particle/ 2
  Pe¬ⁿ desu yo.   It's a pen (I tell
  you). 2
yobu /tr:-u:yoñde/   call, summon
  13
yo¬i /-ku/ is good 2-N
yoko   side 6
  de⌐pa¬ato no yoko   the side of the
  department store 6
yo⌐ku /adverbial of i¬i∼ yo¬i/ well,
  a good deal, often 1

yo¬mu /tr:-u:yoñde/ read 13
yo¬ñ   four 3
yori* /particle/ more than 15
  ko⌐re yo⌐ri ⌐¬i¬i is better than
     this 15
yo⌐roko¬bu /intr:-u:yo⌐roko¬ñde/ take
  pleasure in 16
yo⌐roko¬ñde /gerund of yo⌐roko¬bu/
  gladly, with pleasure 16
yorosii /-ku/ is good or fine or
  all right; never mind 5
  Do¬ozo yorosiku. (Lit. Please
  [treat me] favorably.)
  11
  Mi⌐na¬sañ ni yorosiku. Give my regards to everyone. 11
yo¬ru   night, night-time 16
yo-⌐ttu¬   four units 5
yotukado   intersection 20
yu⌐bi¬   finger 17-A
-yuki -bound 19
  Yokosuka-yuki   Yokosuka-bound
  19
yu⌐kku¬ri   slowly 13
yuku /alternant of iku/ 19-N
yu⌐ube¬   last night 11
yu⌐ubi¬ñkyoku   post office 6

Z

zassi   magazine 2
ze¬ñbu   all, the whole thing 1
ze¬ro   zero 12
-zi /counter for naming o'clocks/
  8
zi⌐biki¬   dictionary 2
zibuñ   oneself 20
  zibuñ de   by oneself 20
  zibuñ no   one's own 20
zi⌐do¬osya   automobile 7
zikañ   time 18
  zi⌐kañ g̃a a¬ru   have time
     18
  zi⌐kañ-do¬ori   on time 19
-zikañ /counter for hours/ 8
zi⌐mu¬syo   office 9
zi⌐syo   dictionary 2
zo¬ñzi¬nai ⌐ /-ku/ don't know 13
zo¬ñzite ⌐o¬ru ⌐ know 13

zookiñ   cleaning rag 17
zu¬ibuñ   extremely, to a considerable
  degree 3
zutto   by far 15
  zu⌐tto ma¬e kara   since a long time
     ago 15
zya /contraction of de¬ wa/ 2
  e⌐ñpitu zya na¬i   it isn't a pencil
  2
zya¬ [a]   then, well then, in that case
  2
zyama /na/ hindrance, bother 17
  zya⌐ma ni na¬ru   become a bother,
  get in the way 17
zyo⌐osya¬keñ   passenger ticket 19-A
zyo⌐ozu¬ /na/ skilled, skillful 18
zyu¬ñsa, zyuñsa   policeman 7
zyu¬u   ten 3
zyu⌐ubu¬ñ /na/ enough 20

Index to the Grammatical Notes

References are to Lesson and Grammatical Note; for example, 6.4 refers to Lesson 6. Grammatical Note 4.